Handbook of Optical Fibers and Cables

OPTICAL ENGINEERING

Series Editor

Brian J. Thompson
Provost
University of Rochester
Rochester, New York

Laser Engineering Editor:
Peter K. Cheo
United Technologies Research Center
Hartford, Connecticut

Laser Advances Editor:
Leon J. Radziemski
Head, Department of Physics
New Mexico State University
Las Cruces, New Mexico

Optical Materials Editor:
Solomon Musikant
Paoli, Pennsylvania

1. Electron and Ion Microscopy and Microanalysis: Principles and Applications, *by Lawrence E. Murr*
2. Acousto-Optic Signal Processing: Theory and Implementation, *edited by Norman J. Berg and John N. Lee*
3. Electro-Optic and Acousto-Optic Scanning and Deflection, *by Milton Gottlieb, Clive L. M. Ireland, and John Martin Ley*
4. Single-Mode Fiber Optics: Principles and Applications, *by Luc B. Jeunhomme*
5. Pulse Code Formats for Fiber Optical Data Communication: Basic Principles and Applications, *by David J. Morris*
6. Optical Materials: An Introduction to Selection and Application, *by Solomon Musikant*
7. Infrared Methods for Gaseous Measurements: Theory and Practice, *edited by Joda Wormhoudt*
8. Laser Beam Scanning: Opto-Mechanical Devices, Systems, and Data Storage Optics, *edited by Gerald F. Marshall*
9. Opto-Mechanical Systems Design, *by Paul R. Yoder, Jr.*

10. Optical Fiber Splices and Connectors: Theory and Methods, *by Calvin M. Miller with Stephen C. Mettler and Ian A. White*
11. Laser Spectroscopy and Its Applications, *edited by Leon J. Radziemski, Richard W. Solarz, and Jeffrey A. Paisner*
12. Infrared Optoelectronics: Devices and Applications, *by William Nunley and J. Scott Bechtel*
13. Integrated Optical Circuits and Components: Design and Applications, *edited by Lynn D. Hutcheson*
14. Handbook of Molecular Lasers, *edited by Peter K. Cheo*
15. Handbook of Optical Fibers and Cables, *by Hiroshi Murata*

LASER HANDBOOKS—*Edited by Peter K. Cheo*

Handbook of Molecular Lasers

Other Volumes in Preparation

Handbook of
Optical Fibers and Cables

Hiroshi Murata

Optics System Development Division
The Furukawa Electric Co., Ltd.
Tokyo, Japan

MARCEL DEKKER, INC.   New York and Basel

Library of Congress Cataloging-in-Publication Data

Murata, Hiroshi
　　Handbook of optical fibers and cables.

　　(Optical engineering ; v. 15)
　　Includes bibliographies and index.
　　1. Optical fibers--Handbooks, manuals, etc. I. Title.
II. Series: Optical engineering (Marcel Dekker, Inc.) ;
v. 15.
TA1800.M87　　1987　　621.36'92　　87-27158
ISBN 0-8247-7694-1

Copyright © 1988 by MARCEL DEKKER, INC. All Rights Reserved

Neither this book nor any part may be reproduced or transmitted in any form or by any means, electronic or mechanical, including photocopying, microfilming, and recording, or by any information storage and retrieval system, without permission in writing from the publisher.

MARCEL DEKKER, INC.
270 Madison Avenue, New York, New York 10016

Current printing (last digit):
10 9 8 7 6 5 4 3 2 1

PRINTED IN THE UNITED STATES OF AMERICA

Preface

Startling progress has been made during the past few years in the development and implementation of optical fiber transmission systems. While many books on optics and optical transmission systems have been published, not many of them deal with the fiber cables that form an important part of the systems. This book is intended to provide information exclusively on this subject. In writing it I focused on "practicability." Therefore, where the book presents formulas, used for instance for cable design and splicing, I give only the results of the calculations.

This book is intended to help fiber optics engineers in the practical design, manufacture, and splicing of fiber cables. Chapter 1 presents a history of optical communications. Chapter 2 concerns optical fibers. I discuss chiefly the design and manufacture of the fibers. Chapter 3 gives the basic concepts of fiber cable design and shows cable designs of all fiber-cable-producing countries, with comparisons among them. Chapters 4, 5, and 6 describe the processes involved in splicing and joining optical cables, and the different connectors used for splicing and joining. Chapter 7 is concerned with measuring fibers and cables, and Chapter 8 describes the installation of fiber cables.

I must offer my warmest thanks to Dr. Etsuji Kusakabe, President, and Mr. Masao Matsumoto, Senior Managing Director, of the Furukawa Electric Co., who supported me in the preparation of my book; Mr. Shigeo Sugiura of the Furukawa Electric Co., who helped me with the English translation; Dr. Yoshikazu Matsuda, who wrote

Chapter 7 in the book; Ms. Akiko Kurita and Ms. Yumiko Bando of Japan Foreign Rights Centre; Dr. Eileen Gardiner of Marcel Dekker, Inc., who always encouraged me to keep writing; and my young colleagues in the Furukawa Electric Co., who discussed with me various subjects contained in the book.

Hiroshi Murata

Contents

Preface   iii

1. **INTRODUCTION**   1

   1.1 History of Optical Communications   1
   1.2 History of Optical Fibers   2
   1.3 History of Optical Fiber Cables   6
   1.4 Features of Optical Fiber and Comparison with Other Transmission Media   8
   References   14

2. **OPTICAL FIBERS**   15

   2.1 Introduction   15
   2.2 Optical Fiber Materials   19
   2.3 Transmission Bandwidth of the Fiber   37
   2.4 Mechanical Properties of the Fiber   59
   2.5 Reliability of Fibers   67
   2.6 Manufacturing of Optical Fiber   88
   2.7 Single-Mode Fibers   139
   2.8 1.55 μm Zero Dispersion SM Fibers   151
   References   169

3. OPTICAL FIBER CABLE — 179

3.1 Introduction — 179
3.2 Basic Conditions of Optical Fiber Cable Design — 181
3.3 Design, Construction, and Properties of Optical Fiber Cable — 237
References — 315

4. SPLICING OF FIBERS — 321

4.1 Introduction — 321
4.2 General Concepts — 322
4.3 Fiber Splicing Loss — 323
4.4 Fiber Splicing — 337
4.5 Examples of Fusion Splicing Machines — 361
4.6 Fiber Splicing Accessories — 268
References — 372

5. CONNECTORS — 375

5.1 Single-Fiber Connectors — 377
5.2 Precision Ferrule Connectors — 377
5.3 Lens Connector — 382
5.4 Biconic Connector — 383
5.5 Ball Connector — 385
5.6 Multifiber Connector — 386
5.7 V-Groove Round Connector — 386
5.8 Fiber Ribbon Connector — 388
5.9 Plastic Connectors (Single and Multifiber Connectors) — 394
References — 394

6. JOINING OF OPTICAL FIBER CABLES — 397

6.1 General Concepts — 397
6.2 Basic Conditions — 397
6.3 Optical Fiber Cable Joining — 398
6.4 Test Conditions for the Cable Joint — 406
References — 406

7. MEASUREMENT OF OPTICAL FIBER — 407

    7.1   Measurement of Structural Parameters of the Fiber — 408
    7.2   Measurement of Transmission Characteristics — 428
    7.3   Profile Measurement of the Preform — 441
    References — 444

8. INSTALLATION OF OPTICAL FIBER CABLE — 447

    References — 459

Index — 461

1
Introduction

In this chapter I relate the history of optical communications, including the history of optical fibers.

1.1 HISTORY OF OPTICAL COMMUNICATIONS

1.1.1 Early Optical Communications

The flare has been a means of communication from the days of ancient Egypt to relatively modern times. Romans are said to have built flaring towers, changed the color of the flaring smoke, and sent information of more than two bits with smoking and smokeless flares. Later, people used telescopes in addition to such flares, and in the seventeenth century, the distance of effective communication covered by flare signaling reached a few kilometers.

1.1.2 Optical Communications at a Standstill [1]

In 1791, the semaphore signaling system was invented by Chappe of France. It was used in all regions of Europe and spread even to North Africa. Its golden age came around 1844, when it was capable of a total coverage of 5000 km.

In 1845 Morse invented telegraphy, and as this invention was put to practical use, the semaphore signal was gradually phased out of service. The invention of wireless telegraphy by Marconi of Italy in 1896 directed radio engineering to the development of high frequencies, that is, short wavelengths. Progress in this

1

somewhat slowed, however, after the development of millimeter wave communications in 1940.

After the invention of laser in 1960, which led to the development of the 1 = 0.5 μm wavelength band, and the announcement of a low-loss optical fiber in 1970, the center of development in telecommunications jumped from the 1 mm wavelength to the 1/1000 mm wavelength.

1.2 HISTORY OF OPTICAL FIBERS

Table 1.1 gives a chronology or research into optical fibers. Because of its coherent characteristics, the laser, when first developed was expected to be a light source for future information transmission, but more than a decade has passed without its practical application in telecommunications. During that period, the solid-state laser was devoloped into the semiconductor laser, which permits easy modulation. The semiconductor laser, however, had a short life at room temperature and had very little chance of practical application.

In 1966, Kao and Hockham [2] published their report of a new concept for a transmission medium. This was the first report of optical communications, in which they pointed out the possibility of information transmission by optical fibers.

In 1970, the Corning Glass Works in the United States announced its development of fiber with a loss of 20 dB/km [3, 4]. According to our experience, when the loss of a transmission medium is not more than 20 dB/km and when the transmission device has a lifetime of more than 1500 hr, its potential for transmission is worth study.

The Corning announcement gave impetus to the study of the semiconductor laser, which in turn accelerated research on optical fibers. An outstanding invention or development usually has an impact on technological progress. In the case of optical fiber communications, two important developments, the semiconductor laser and the optical fiber, proceeded in parallel, with each alternately playing a leading role. (Such a course of development is very rare, and those concerned with optical communications were lucky to see it.)

It is no exaggeration to say that after the 10 dB/km fiber was announced by the Corning Glass Works in 1970, research has focused on how to reduce loss. Figure 1.1 shows the yearly reductions made in loss of optical fibers. Loss has been reduced by two digits in 10 years: 20 dB/km (0.85 μm) in 1970, 0.5 dB/km (1.2 μm) in 1976 [5], 0.157 dB/km (1.55 μm) in 1984 [6], and 0.154 dB/km (1.55 μm) in 1986 [7], when it approached its theoretical minimum. It can be said that these figures represent the smallest losses of transmission media so far obtained.

Table 1.1 Chronology or Research and Development of Optical Transmission

Year	Light source	Transmission medium
1879		Theoretical study of waveguide (Rayleigh)
1910		Theoretical study of dielectric waveguide (Hondros and Debye)
1920		Experimental study of dielectric waveguide (Schriever)
1951		Development of glass fiber for medical use
1960	Invention of ruby laser (Maiman, Javan)	
1961	He-Ne laser oscillation (Bell Laboratories)	Mode theory of dielectric waveguide (Snitzer)
1962	GaAs semiconductor laser (General Electric, IBM, MIT)	Study of lens array waveguide (Goubou et al.)
1964		Experiments of the above (Bell Labs)
		Study of gas lens (Bell Labs)
		Suggestion of graded index fiber (Nishizawa and Sasaki, Tohoku University)

Table 1.1 (Continued)

Year	Light source	Transmission medium
1965	CO_2 laser oscillation (Bell Labs)	Study of thin-film optical waveguide (Karbowiak)
1966		Dielectric fiber surface waveguides for optical frequencies (Kao and Hockharm)
1969		Trially made graded index fiber—Selfoc (Uchida and Kitano) Graded index rod (Bell Labs)
1970	GaAlAs laser continuous oscillation (Bell Labs, USSR, NEC)	Development of low-loss silica fiber (20 dB/km) (Corning Glass Works) Concept of weakly guiding fiber (Gloge)

Optical Fibers

1972	GaAlAsSb laser oscillation (NTT)	Development of 4 dB/km fiber (Corning Glass Works)
1973		Development of the MCVD process (Bell Labs)
1974		Installation and splicing of optical fiber cable on site (Furukawa)
1976	GaInAsP laser continuous oscillation (MIT, KDD, NTT, Tokyo Institute of Technology)	Development of 0.5 dB/km fiber (1.2 μm) (NTT, Fujikura)
1977	Estimated life of GaAlAs, 1,000,000 hr.	Invention of the VAD process (NTT)
1978		Development of ultra-low-loss fiber (0.2 dB/km; 1.55 μm) (NTT)

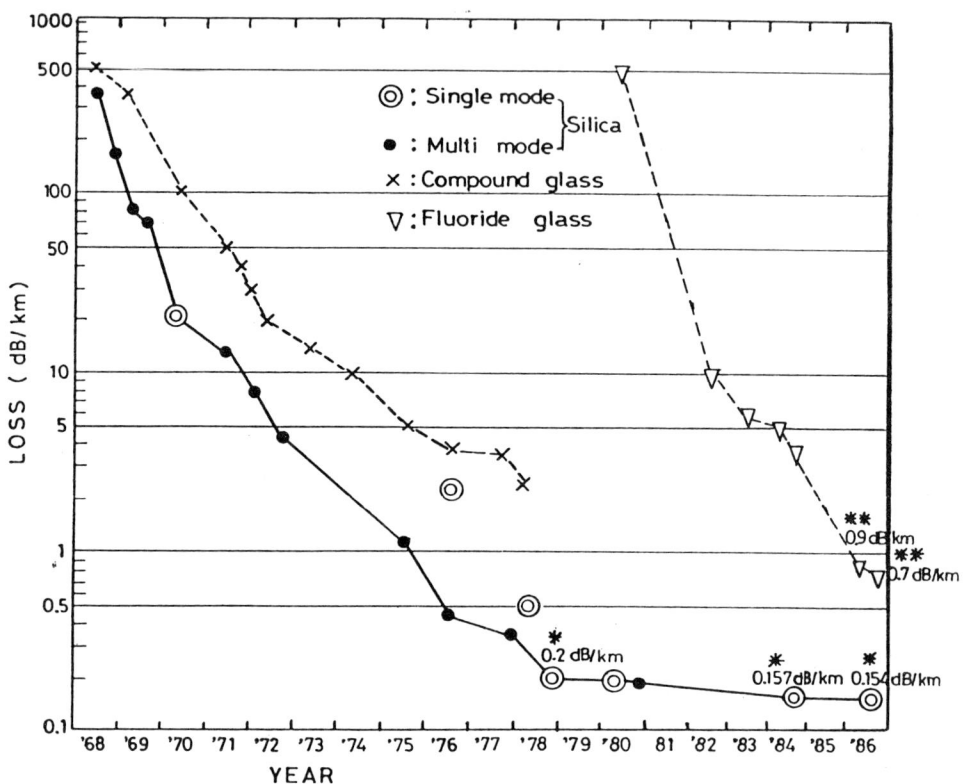

Figure 1.1 Progress of transmission loss of optical fibers: at 1.55 μm (*) and at 2.55 μm (**).

1.3 HISTORY OF OPTICAL FIBER CABLES

The history of wire transmission technology dates back about 100 years, beginning with telegraphy using copper conductors. The subsequent development of this technology followed a step-by-step pattern. A deadlock in bare-wire technology gave birth to the balanced type of communication cable, and the limit to the transmission property of the balanced communication cable brought forth the coaxial cable and then the circular waveguide. Telecommunications has developed through the repeated encountering of such problems and their subsequent resolution. The greatest leap in wire transmission technology, which holds the greatest potential for future telecommunications, is the development of the optical fiber and semiconductor laser.

Optical Fiber Cables

Figure 1.2 Installation of optical fiber in the Furukawa Electric compound. The optical fiber cable was installed in 1974. Details of construction are as follows: aerial, 200 m; spliced on site, four fiber; loose stranding; loss, 5.5 dB/km (0.85 µm).

Fiber was first made into a cable and laid experimentally in the field in 1974 [8]. Figure 1.2 shows this optical fiber cable installation at the Furukawa Electric Company compound. From 1976 on, experimental field installation tests of optical fiber cables were made in many parts of the world. In parallel with these trials, the installation of optical fiber cables for commercial use was begun on a small scale. Large-scale commercial installations began in 1981.

1.4 FEATURES OF OPTICAL FIBER AND COMPARISON WITH OTHER TRANSMISSION MEDIA

Since the Corning Glass Works invented a low-loss fiber in 1970, the world's fiber optics researchers embarked upon the development of fibers that surpass Corning's, with the distinctive features listed below, which are not found in other transmission media. It is expected that these fibers will provide a wonderful means of transmitting information.

1. Small size: The outer diameter of an optical fiber is generally small—0.125 mm (125 μm). The outer diameter remains about 1 mm even if the fiber is coated with plastic. In comparison, the outer diameter of an ordinary communications cable pair or the conductor of a coaxial cable is 1 = 10 mm.
2. Light weight: The specific gravity of silica is 2.2 and that of copper is 8.9. Further, as the dimensions of the fibers are small, the weight of an optical fiber cable is one-third to one-tenth that of conventional cables with the same transmission capacity.
3. Good flexibility: In general, below 3 mm in diameter, an optical fiber does not break even if it is bent. Therefore, optical fiber cables with almost the same flexibility as that of conventional communications cables can be produced and installed utilizing almost the same installation techniques as those of conventional communication cables.
4. Free from rust: Glass materials, such as silica, are stable chemically, and optical fibers are entirely impervious to rust which is not the case with metals. Therefore, optical fibers endure well in adverse environments, such as the ocean floor.
5. Low loss: It is easy to obtain a transmission loss below 0.5 dB/km (1.3 μm) with optical fibers, and the loss value is generally 0.35 to 0.45 dB/km (1.3 μm). Compared with a coaxial cable, with a loss of 19 dB/km (60 MHz), and a broadband city cable, with a loss of 20 dB/km (4 MHz), the transmission loss of optical fibers is small.
6. Broad bandwidth: The bandwidth characteristics of a fiber differ according to its construction and the method by which

6. Broad bandwidth: The bandwidth characteristics of a fiber differ according to its construction and the method by which it is made. A graded index fiber can easily be given a very broad bandwidth, ranging from 1 to 10 GHz·km. The single-mode fiber also has a very broad bandwidth of more than several tenfold GHz·km. Therefore it is easy to form a transmission system of 400 Mb/sec to 1.6 Gb/sec. It is also easy to increase the amount of transmitted information by several to ten times as much by the wavelength division multiplex (WDM) method in which different carrier wavelengths are used for the transmission of information. In the transmission system using coaxial cable, 400 Mb is considered the broadest possible band from a practical viewpoint, and the WDM method cannot be used.
7. Very large information-transmitting capacity per unit cross-sectional area of the fiber cable: The small size of the fiber, broad bandwidth of transmission, and very large capacity of transmitting information produce an extremely high density of information transmission per unit cross-sectional area of the cable. The transmitting information capacity of optical fiber per unit cross-sectional area is about 100 times that of pair cables and about 10 times that of coaxial cables.
8. Free from electromagnetic induction and lightning damage: Glass is generally a good dielectric and is immune to electromagnetic induction and lightning.
9. Very little cross talk: Leaking of light from optical fibers is extremely minor, and almost no external light enters the fibers to propagate. This means that there is extremely little cross talk between fibers. This characteristic, coupled with the non-induction characteristics already mentioned, cannot be obtained with copper cables.
10. Resistance to high temperature: The melting point of silica is about 1900°C, far above that of copper or plastics. Therefore, cables made with silica are resistant to high temperature.
11. Fibers do not generate sparks: No discharge occurs at spliced points of fibers. Optical fibers can be used in potentially inflammable or explosive environments.
12. Cannot be branched easily: Optical fibers are thin, and it is difficult to branch them directly. Where branching is required, branching is done after converting that particular section into an electrical system.
13. The optical fiber is glass: The optical fiber is nothing other than silica or compound glass. It is generally brittle and has an elongation of only 5% or so. When the fiber is used, this brittle characteristic must be fully taken into account.
14. Material for optical fiber is not copper: Copper resources are limited. Optical fibers are primarily made of silica, which is abundant.

Table 1.2 Comparison of Properties of Transmission Media[a]

	Pair or quadruple cable	Coaxial cable	Circular waveguide	Optical fiber cable
Diameter (mm)*	1–4	10	50	0.1–0.2
Bending diameter (cm)	>0.1	>90	>6000	>0.3
Weight ratio of cable (same transmission capacity)*	1	1	1	0.1
Cable length (m)*	100–500	100–500	3–10	1000–2000
Loss (dB/km)*	20 (4 MHz)	19 (60 MHz)	2	0.2–4

Comparison of Optical Fibers and Other Media

	6 MHz	400 MHz	40–120 GHz	1–10 GHz·km
Bandwidth*				
Installation	Conventional	Conventional	Special	Almost same as conventional
Splicing and jointing*	Conventional	Conventional	Special	Special
Repeater*	Conventional	Conventional	Conventional	Conventional + laser + photodiode
Repeater span (km)*	1–2	1.5	10	10–60
Transmission capacity (same diameter)*	0.1	1	1	10

[a]Entries marked with an asterisk (*) indicate those characteristics that are notably different in optical fiber cables.
[b]Plastic covered.

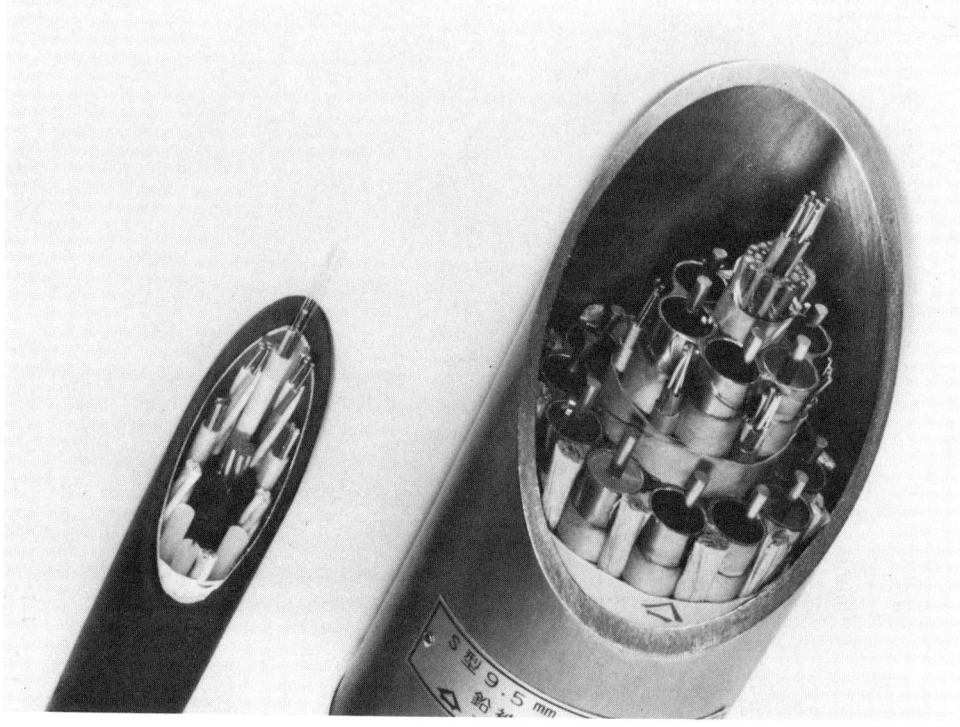

Figure 1.3 Cables: an 18-fiber cable (left) and an 18-tube coaxial cable (right).

The optical fiber has many distinctive characteristics, as explained above, and a cable using optical fibers has a number of outstanding features compared with the conventional copper conductor communication cable. Table 1.2 shows how they differ, with notable differences indicated by an asterisk (*). Note particularly that the information transmission density of an optical fiber cable is 10 to 100 times higher than that of conventional copper conductor communications cable. The use of optical fiber cable is conceivable, for instance, when cable ducts in urban areas are all filled and additional cable installation is needed. Replacement of conventional communication cables in the ducts with optical fiber cables would increase the information-transmitting capacity more than 10 times without the installation of additional ducts.

Figure 1.3 shows a fiber cable (left, 18 fibers) and a coaxial cable (right, 18 tubes). The transmission capacity of both cables is about same. The outer diameter of the fiber cable is about one-third that of the coaxial cable.

Table 1.3 Applications of Optical Fiber Cables

Characteristics	Applications
Low loss and wide bandwidth	Ordinary telecommunication cables: long-haul toll trunk cable, short-haul toll cable, city trunk cable, city distribution cable, city subscriber cable, submarine cable, switchboard cable
	Video transmission cable, CATV cables, etc.
High density of information transmission	Ordinary communication cables, particularly in densely populated cities and inside buildings
Light weight and small size	Military applications (aircraft, ships, missiles, etc.), computers, inside-premise transmission
No electromagnetic induction	Military applications (withstand electromagnetic pulse triggered by nuclear explosion), railways, areas exposed to lightning, installation with power cables, monitoring and control of power apparatus
High heat resistance	Fire-retardant and heat-resisting wires
No sparking	Explosion-proof application (oil fields, oil factory, mines, etc.)
Difficulty to branch	Communication of classified information

The possible applications of optical fiber cables that can be expected in consideration of the foregoing characteristics of the optical fiber and cable are listed in Table 1.3.

Table 1.3 shows chiefly how optical fibers and cables can be used in information transmission. The following applications are also possible:

1. Utilization of light itself
   Image transmission: Measurements, supervision, observation, monitoring
   Light transmission: light source, measurement, monitoring, supervision
2. Transmission of optical energy
   When optical energy is transmitted, because of the light source

the wavelength is about 4 to 11 μm, which is far longer than the wavelength for information transmission (0.8 to 1.6 μm). In a fiber consisting mainly of silica, loss becomes very high owing to the infrared absorption of silica (several hundreds to several thousands of decibels per kilometer). Therefore research is being made on fibers using such materials as fluoride or TlBr, which are presumed to have a low transmission loss at the 4 to 11 μm band.

REFERENCES

1. T. Ohkoshi, Fundamental of optical fiber, *OHM*, 1–17 (1977).
2. C. K. Kao and G. A. Hockham, Dielectric-fiber surface waveguides for optical frequencies, *Proc. IEE (Lond.)*, *133*: 1151–1158 (July 1966).
3. F. P Kapron, D. B. Keck, and R. D. Maurer, Radiation losses in glass optical waveguides, *Trunk Telecom. Guided Waves, IEE*, 148–153 (September 1970).
4. F. P. Kapron, D. B. Keck, and R. D. Maurer, Radiation losses in glass optical waveguide, *Appl. Phys. Lett.* *17*: 423–425 (Novermber 1970).
5. M. Horiguchi and H. Osanai, Spectral losses of low-OH-content optical fibers, *Electron Lett.*, *12*: 310–312 (June 1976).
6. R. Csencsits, P. J. Lemaire, W. A. Reed, D. S. Shenk, and K. L. Walker, Fabrication of low-loss single-mode fibers, OFC '84, TU13, January 1984, pp. 54–55.
7. H. Yokota, H. Kanamori, Y. Ishiguro, G. Tanaka, S. Tanaka, H. Takada, M. Watanabe, S. Suzuki, K. Yano, M. Hoshikawa, and H. Shimba, Ultra-low-loss pure-silica-core single-mode fiber and transmission experiment, OFC '86, PD3-1, February 1986, pp. 11–18.
8. H. Murata, S. Inao, and Y. Matsuda, Step index type optical fiber cable 1st ECOC, September 1975, pp. 70–72.

2
Optical Fibers

2.1 INTRODUCTION

As mentioned in Chap. 1, since a low-loss optical fiber, 20 dB/km (0.85 μm), made mainly of silica was developed in 1970, fiber loss has surprisingly been reduced year after year—as low as 0.2 dB/km (1.55 μm) in 1976 [1], 0.157 dB/km (1.55 μm) in 1984 [2], and 0.154 dB/km (1.55 μm) in 1986 [3]—by the effort of worldwide optical fiber research. It is nearly equal to the theoretical minimum of 0.13 dB/km (1.55 μm). Over a period of about 10 years, the loss was reduced to 1/100. For a broad-band transmission medium, this 0.16 dB/km signifies a strikingly low loss.

The following are goals of optical fiber development:

1. Low loss
2. Broad bandwidth according to the application for which the fiber is used (fiber has a well-controlled refractive index as required)
3. Strong enough to meet a specific condition of use (fiber is free of flaws, cracks, bubbles, and other discontinuities)
4. Low cost

The fibers used now are roughly classified into three types, the step index (SI), the graded index (GI), and the single-mode (SM) type, which are illustrated in Fig. 2.1.

Section 2.2 covers the kinds and transmission properties of fibers, which are listed briefly in the table on the next page.

Section 2.3 cover the bandwidths of spliced fibers (see especially Sec. 2.3.3.6.), where the equations are for the SM fiber

Kinds of Fibers and Their Transmission Properties

Fiber	SM (single mode)	GI (graded index)	SI (step index)
Size of (conventional) core (od, μm)	8.5 (125)	50 (125)	50 (125)
$\Delta = (n_1 - n_2)/n_1$ (%)	0.3	1	1
Mode	Single	Multiple	Multiple
Loss, μm (dB/km, mainly $\propto A/\lambda^4$)			
0.85		2.6	2.6
1.3	0.35	0.4	0.4
1.55	0.2	0.25	
Bandwidth, μm (GHz·km)			
0.85		1 ($\alpha = 2.1$)	40 MHz·km
1.3	>10	1 ($\alpha = 1.85$)	

Introduction

Type	Construction	Bandwidth
Step index (SI)	The refractive index of core is constant 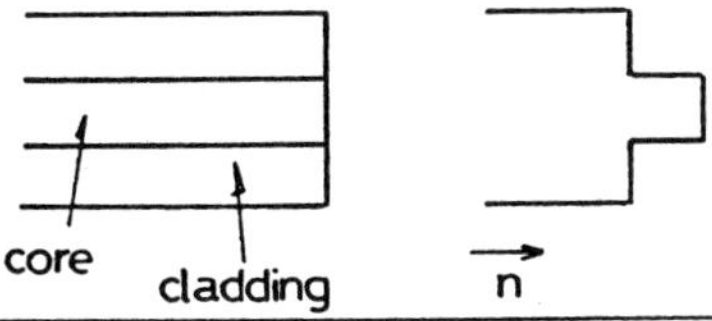 core cladding n	≑50MHz·km
Graded Index (GI)	The refractive index of core is changing 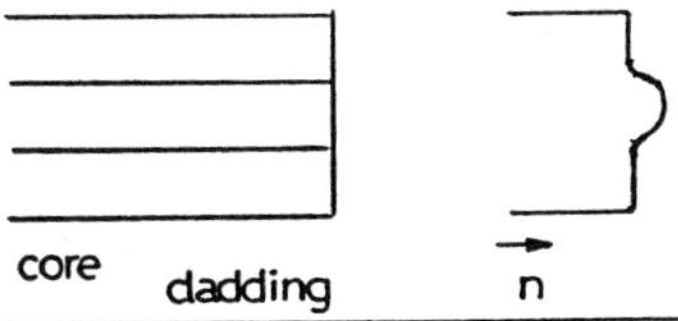 core cladding n	≑0.5~3 GHz·km
Single mode (SM)	The core dia is very small (5~10 μm), and the refractive index of the core is slightly larger than that of the cladding (by 0.2~0.8‰) 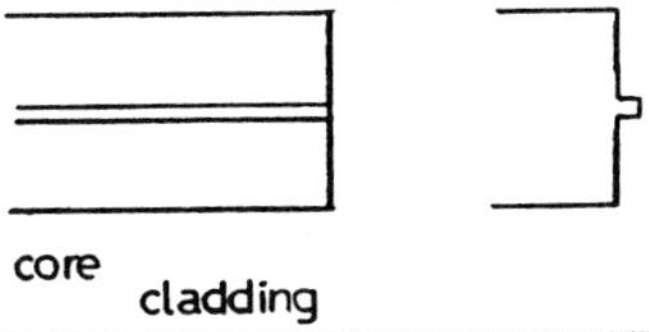 core cladding	>10 GHz·km

Figure 2.1 Types of fiber.

$$f_n = \frac{f_0}{L}$$

and for the GI fiber

$$f_n - 1/\gamma_2 = \sum_i f_i - 1/\gamma_2$$

and

$$\gamma_2 \doteqdot 0.85$$

The dispersion of SM fiber is also covered in Section 2.3: for a conventional 1.3 μm SM fiber, dispersion is 0 to 2 psec/nm·km and for the 1.55 μm fiber, 15 psec/nm·km. The relation between dispersion and bandwidth is

$$f_i = \frac{0.44}{\sigma_t} \Delta \lambda$$

The mechanical properties of fibers are reviewed in Sec. 2.4, including

> Breakage strength averages about 5 to 6 kg per fiber, with a minimum of about 1 kg per fiber.
> Elongation averages about 5 to 6%, with about 1% minimum.
> The screen (or proof test for land cable gives 0.5 to 0.7% and for submarine cable, 2.2%.

The reliability of fibers, both mechanical and chemical, is covered in Sec. 2.5. Section 2.6 discusses the manufacturing of fibers (see especially Sec. 2.6.1 and Table 2.14). Some of the methods of manufacturing fibers are

> Modified chemical vapor deposition (MCVD): profile control is easy; applied in many countries
> Plasma-enhanced CVD (PMCVD): high deposition rate; suitable for SM fiber; under development at AT&T
> Plasma CVD (PCVD): high-precision profile control; used at Philips (Holland)
> Outside vapor deposition (OVD): high deposition rate; used at Corning Glass Works
> Vapor-phase axial deposition (VAD): continuous production; suitable for SM fiber; used in Japan

Recommended combinations of dopants are as follows:

Core	Cladding
$SiO_2 \cdot GeO_2$	SiO_2 or $SiO_2 \cdot F$ or $SiO_2 \cdot F \cdot P_2O_5$ (P_2O_5: the smaller, the better)
SiO_2	$SiO_2 \cdot F$

Sections 2.7 and 2.8 present recent topics for discussion, including the whole-synthesis VAD SM fiber, with the properties of

a low loss of 0.35 dB/km (1.3 μm) (in manufacturing), 0.2 dB/km (1.55 μm), and high strength—2.2% proof test (in manufacturing, 50% yield; 50 km), and the 1.55 μm zero dispersion fiber, with loss for the multiple-step type of 0.17 dB/km (1.55 μm) and of 0.20 dB/km (1.55 μm) for the step type.

Countermeasures against the loss increase by hydrogen include the following.

1. P_2O_5 should not be used as a dopant, or should be minimum in amount if it is used.
2. Fluorine should be used as a dopant.
3. A synthetic cladding layer should be used.
4. Materials that do not generate hydrogen must be selected for the cable core.

2.2 OPTICAL FIBER MATERIALS

2.2.1 Optical Fiber Materials and Dopants for Silica Fiber

The first consideration in the selection of fiber materials is that they have a low optical loss; that is, they must have a high degree of transparency. It is also desirable that they be highly processible, excel in mechanical strength, have a refractive index suitable for transmission, retain a high reliability, and that these properties are minimally affected over a long period.

Table 2.1 shows an example of transmission loss of light energy measured on some glass materials. The table indicates that the light energy loss in the bulk silica glass is smaller than that in other materials. The optical fiber consists essentially of this silica glass (SiO_2) doped with a small amount of GeO_2 or P_2O_5, for example, which have a larger refractive index than SiO_2, to increase the refractive index, or with B_2O_3 or F, for example, to reduce the refractive index.

Ordinary compound glass and plastics are also available as fiber materials, but they have a high transmission loss. Therefore, silica fiber with a low optical transmission loss is chiefly discussed here.

The optical fiber consists essentially of this silica (SiO_2). Silica has a refractive index of 1.458. It is one of light-passing materials with the lowest refractive index. When used for fiber, SiO_2 must be given a material that changes its refractive index. Such a material is called "dopant." The dopant needs to have the following characteristics (this is further discussed in Sec. 2.6).

1. It is of high purity and easily available.
2. It is easy to liquify.
3. It differs from the transition metal in vapor pressure.

Table 2.1 Scattering Loss (dB/km) for Several Representative Glass Materials[a]

Scattering loss (dB/km)	633 nm	800 nm	1060 nm
Corning Code 7940 (Fused silica)	4.8	1.9	0.6
Corning Code 8361 (soda-lime type)	8.5	3.3	1.1
Bausch and Lomb 517-645 (borosilicate crown)	7.7	3.0	1.0
Schott F-2 (lead silicate)	47.5	18.6	6.0

[a]These measurements on bulk glass represent only the intrinsic material loss to which must be added any other scattering losses. *Source*: From Ref. 4.

4. It is easy to vitrify with silica and gives a proper refractive index.
5. After being vitrified, its coefficient of thermal expansion is nearly equal to that of SiO_2.
6. When vitrified, it has stable properties.

Figure 2.2 shows some example of materials that can be used as dopants [5, 6].

The following dopants are mainly used to increase or reduce the refractive index of silica: to increase refractive index, GeO_2, P_2O_5, TiO_2, and Al_2O_3; to reduce refractive index, B_2O_3 and F.

Low-loss fibers are now chiefly in use at 1.3 to 1.6 µm. They must naturally be made of a material with low OH absorption loss and H_2-induced loss (described later). Table 2.2 shows general characteristics of the above-mentioned dopants. The wavelengths at which low-loss fibers are now used are generally 1.3 to 1.6 µm. The dopants mainly used now for low-loss, high-reliability fibers are GeO_2 and F.

2.2.2 Transmission Loss of Fiber

As shown in Table 2.1 it is evident that silica is a promising raw material of fiber. At first the loss of a fiber made of this material was extremely high, 100 to 1000 dB/km. As a result of studies, impurities contained in silica—transition metal ions (e.g., Cu, Fe, and Co) and OH^- ion—were found to be the main causes of the high loss. It was learned that the content of the former must be held below 0.1 ppb (10^{-10}) and that of the latter below 10 ppb. A special process was

Materials

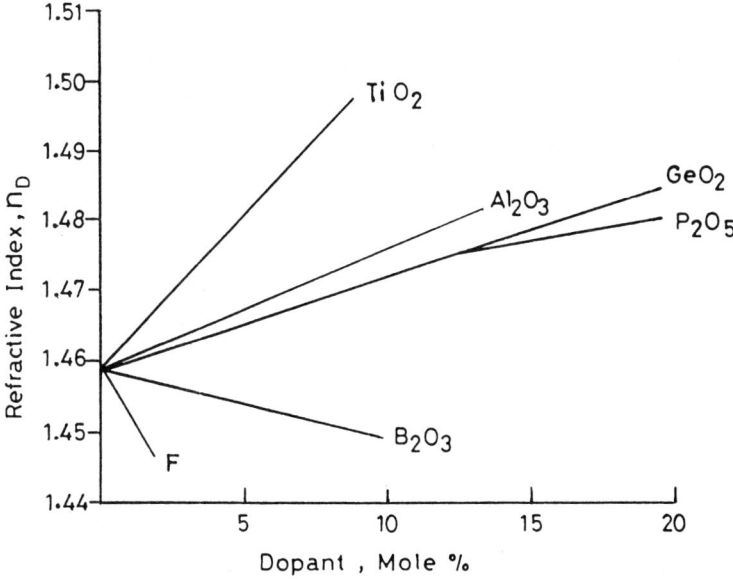

Figure 2.2 Refractive index of common dopants for silica. (From Refs. 5 and 6.)

Table 2.2 Properties of Dopants

Dopant	Wavelength at which IR absorption loss generated (μm)	Loss increase by OH⁻	Loss increase by H_2
GeO_2	1.6	Small	Small
P_2O_5	1.4	Small	Large
TiO_2		Large	Large
Al_2O_3	Easy crystallization		
B_2O_3	1.2		
F			

Table 2.3 Main Loss Causes of Fiber[a]

Loss	Intrinsic	Extrinsic
Scattering	Rayleigh*	Waveguide imperfection*
	Brillouin	
	Raman	
Absorption	Ultraviolet	Metal
	Infrared*	OH ion,* H_2

[a]Losses marked with an asterisk may be particularly large.

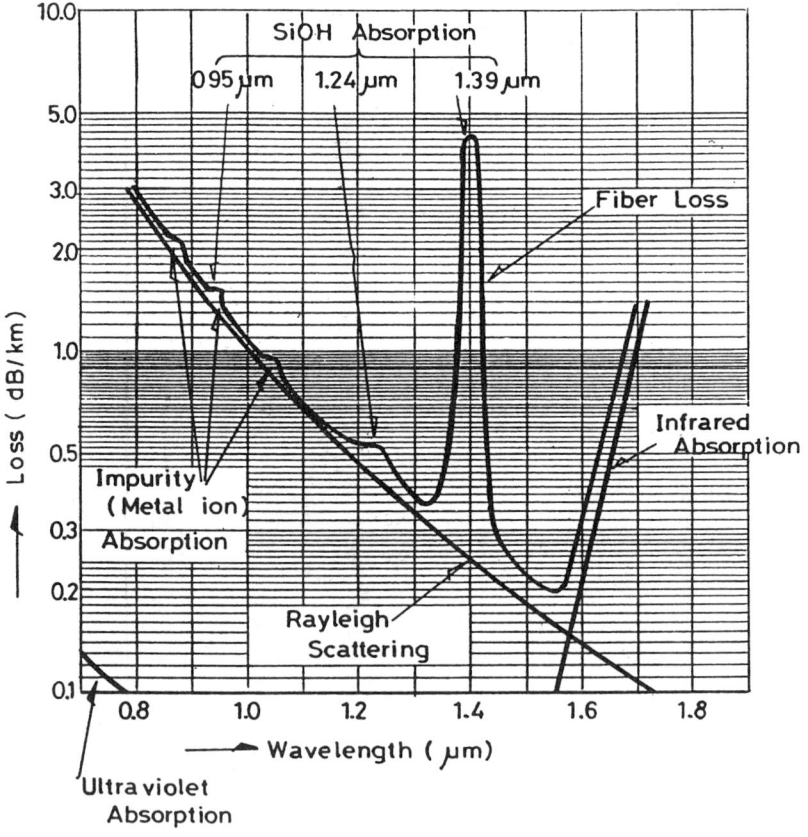

Figure 2.3 Transmission loss of fiber.

Materials

Table 2.4 Loss due to Representative Impurities in Glass

Ion	Absorption peak (nm)	Concentration of 20 dB/km	
		Absorption at the peak (ppb)	Absorption at 800 nm (ppb)
Cu^{2+}	800	9	9
Fe^{2+}	1100	8	15
Ni^{2+}	650	4	26
V^{3+}	475	18	36
Cr^{3+}	675	8	83
Mn^{3+}	500	18	1800

Source: From Ref. 4.

needed to make such a high-purity material, as introduced in Sec. 2. Absorption loss due to impurities in now almost nil and so is the peak of loss caused by OH^- ion at 0.89 and 1.24 μm.

As shown in Table 2.3, the transmission loss of the fiber is roughly divided into scattering loss and absorption loss. In the table, the losses marked by an asterisk are especially important and sometimes show large values. Such losses of silica fiber are approximately in the following order.

Rayleigh scattering: 2.3 to 0.15 dB/km (0.85 to 1.55 μm)
OH ion absorption: 0.01 to 5 dB/km (1.39 μm)
Infrared (IR) absorption: Sharply increases at wavelengths longer than 1.6 μm
Waveguide imperfection: 0 to 0.1 dB/km

Figure 2.3 shows one example of the wavelength characteristics of fiber loss.

2.2.3 Loss of Optical Fiber Caused by Extrinsic Factors

2.2.3.1 Metal Impurities [4]

Table 2.4 shows the attenuation due to representative metal impurities in soda-lime glasses [4]. According to this table, the concentration of transition metal ions must be about 0.1 ppb or less when absorption

Table 2.5 OH Ion Absorption Loss[a]

Wavelength (μm)	Frequency[b]	Loss (dB/km) per 1 ppm OH
2.72	γ_3^1	6000
2.22	$\gamma_1 + \gamma_3^1$	160
1.90	$2\gamma_1 + \gamma_3^1$	6.2
1.38	$2\gamma_3^1$	39
1.24	$\gamma_1 + 2\gamma_3^1$	1.72
1.13	$2\gamma_1 + 2\gamma_3^1$	0.07
0.945	$3\gamma_3^1$	0.62
0.88	$\gamma_1 + 3\gamma_3^1$	0.055
0.82	$2\gamma_1 + 3\gamma_3^1$	0.002
0.72	$4\gamma_3^1$	0.039
0.68	$\gamma_1 + 4\gamma_3^1$	0.002
0.64	$2\gamma_1 + 4\gamma_3^1$	0.001
0.60	$5\gamma_3^1$	0.004

[a] OH overtones and combinational vibration in silica glass and their peak absorption.
[b] γ_3^1: Si—O—H vibration; γ_1: SiO_4 tetrahedral vibration.
Source: From Refs. 5 and 7.

Materials

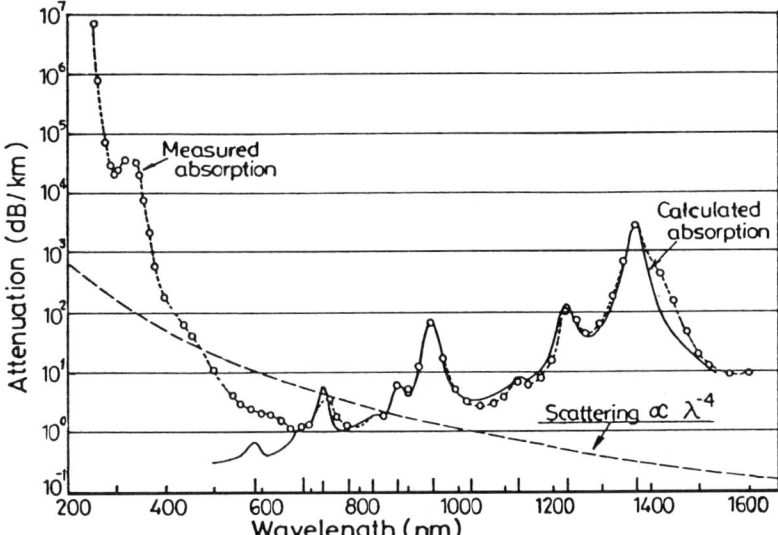

Figure 2.4 Measured and calculated absorptive and scattering attenuations as a function of wavelength. The observed total attenuation for the waveguide is obtained by adding absorptive and scattering attenuations. (From Ref. 7.)

loss due to transition metal ions must be held at 0.1 dB/km or under. The chemical vapor deposition (CVD) method was developed to make such a high-purity material in optical fiber production. In Sec. 2.6 I discuss this impurity problem in detail.

2.2.3.2 Loss Due to OH Ion [5, 7]

The loss increase by OH^- ion is the absorption loss by vibrations of Si and OH coupling (Si—OH), dopant material and OH coupling (e.g., Ge—OH), and combinational vibrations. Of all impurities, the OH^- ion causes the largest loss increase and is the most difficult to remove. Therefore, utmost care must be used to select a material containing no OH ion and to prevent the OH ion from entering the fiber during production. The absorption loss due to the OH ion has a very large peak value at 2.72 μm wavelength.

Coupling of this absorption with Si—OH, Ge—OH, and P—OH and their higher harmonics produces great loss peaks from the visual region to the near infrared region. Table 2.5 indicates the OH absorption wavelength of silica glass and the magnitude of its loss. Especially important are the losses at 0.945, 1.24, 138, 190, 2.22, and 2.72 μm in the practical range of wavelengths.

Table 2.6 Absorption Peaks of H_2 in Silica Fiber

Wavelength (μm)	Increased loss relative	Frequency[a]
36.4	–	γ_1
21.0	–	γ_2
12.5	–	γ_3
9.1	–	γ_4
2.42	2220	γ_H
2.24	830	$\gamma_1 + \gamma_H$
2.14	800	$\gamma_2 + \gamma_H$
2.04	440	$\gamma_3 + \gamma_H$
1.88	410	$\gamma_4 + \gamma_H$
1.78	40	$\gamma_1 + \gamma_4 + \gamma_H$
1.70	30	$\gamma_2 + \gamma_4 + \gamma_H$
1.63	12	or $^2\gamma_3 + \gamma_H$
	–	$\gamma_3 + \gamma_4 + \gamma_H$
1.59	6	$^2\gamma_4 + \gamma_H$
1.24	22	$^2\gamma_H$
1.20	7	$\gamma_1 + {}^2\gamma_H$
1.17	9	$\gamma_2 + {}^2\gamma_H$
1.13	5	$\gamma_3 + \gamma_H$
1.08	6	$\gamma_4 + {}^2\gamma_H$
1.55	–	P-OH
1.41	–	Ge-OH
1.39	–	Si-OH

[a] γ_H: H_2 fundamental vibration; γ_1, γ_2, and γ_4: SiO_4 tetrahedral vibration.
Source: From Ref. 8.

Materials

An example of measurement taken on the silica fiber is shown in Table 2.5 [5, 7] and Fig. 2.4 [7]. This clearly illustrates how the absorption loss of the OH ion is at the above-mentioned wavelengths. Loss peak of fiber with a concentration of 1 ppm is about 39 dB/km at 1.38 μm.

The OH ion content is 100–200 ppm in natural silica generally on the market and 1–10 ppm in synthetic silica glass. These materials, as they are, cannot be made into low-loss silica fiber. We may be able to say that the history of low-loss fiber development has centered on how to remove the OH ion. Now it has become relatively easy to make a fiber with an OH ion content of less that 10 ppb.

2.2.3.3 Loss Due to H_2 [8]

When H_2 diffuses in the fiber, it is trapped by the network of SiO_2 glass and its vibration causes an absorption loss. The trapped H_2 undergoes a chemical reaction (for instance, in a high-temperature atmosphere) within the network of SiO_2 and makes a coupling of Si–OH, Ge–OH, and so on, the vibration of which results in the absorption loss. This increase is very great at wavelengths longer than 1 μm. It is shown in Table 2.6 and is further discussed in Sec. 2.5 [8].

2.2.3.4 Loss Due to Waveguide Imperfection

The principal causes of loss of an optical fiber lie in the material of which it is made and in the impurities contained in it. The loss is also increased by an irregular cross-sectional or uneven longitudinal construction of the fiber, such as the following.

1. Imperfect fiber core/cladding interface
2. Longitudinal deviation at the core/cladding interface
3. Change in fiber core diameter; deformation of the core
4. Bubbles, reaming (irregularity of material), foreign matter, minute crystals, and other imperfections in the glass

In these cases, the loss is about 0–0.2 dB/km, not depending on the wavelength. In 1.3–1.6 μm bands, the total loss of the fiber has been reduced to 0.4–0.16 dB/km. Therefore, the loss due to waveguide imperfection has to be small (0–0.02 dB/km).

2.2.4 Intrinsic Loss in Material [5, 9]

2.2.4.1 Ultraviolet Absorption [5, 9]

SiO_2 has an absorption by the electron transition at the ultraviolet region. Its center wavelength is 0.122 μm. The ultraviolet absorption of a fiber doped with n% by weight of GeO_2 is generally expressed by the following formula.

$$\alpha_{UV}(\lambda) = \alpha_0' \times n \times 10^9 \, e^{4.63/\lambda}$$

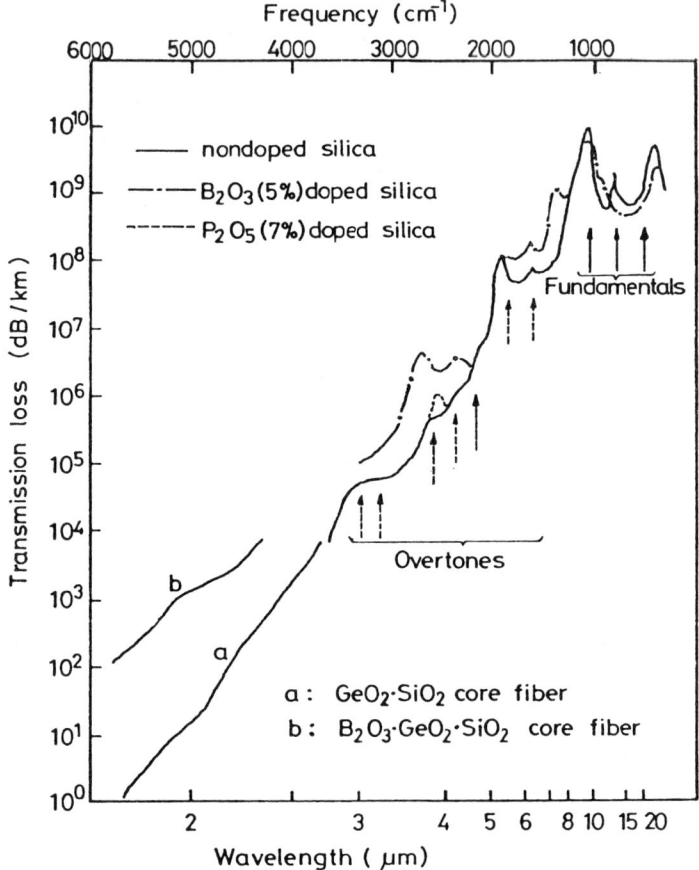

Figure 2.5 Infrared absoption spectra of nondoped silica glass, doped silicas, and fibers. (From Refs. 10 and 11.)

where

$\alpha_{UV}(\lambda)$ = ultraviolet absorption at wavelength λ

n = % by weight of doped GeO_2

α_0' = constant obtained experimentally

   = 1.474×10^{-11} dB/km per ppb GeO_2

Materials

The value of α_{UV} is about 1 dB/km (0.6 μm) and 10^{-2} dB (1.3 μm) and has little practical effect on the total loss of the fiber.

2.2.4.2 Infrared Absorption [5, 9-12]

Absorption by the molecular vibration of SiO_2 in the infrared region takes place at 9.1, 12.5 and 21 μm. Its value reaches 10^{10} dB/km at 9.1 μm and 10^5 dB/km at 3.5 μm, with an overtone of 9.1 μm. Figure 2.5 shows some measured properties of silica glass and doped silica glass, from which it is learned that the wavelength at which the loss is 1 dB/km is 1.85 μm or under.

The value of infrared absorption loss shown in Fig. 2.5 is expressed approximately by the following empirical formula.

$$\alpha_{IR}(E) = \alpha_0 e^{-E/E_0}$$

where

$\alpha_{IR}(E)$ = infrared absorption loss at photon energy E

α_0, E_0 = constants obtained empirically

In the case of a fiber so doped with GeO_2 as to make the relative refractive index difference $\Delta = 0.3\%$,

$$\alpha_{IR}(E) = 4.2 \times 10^{11} \text{ dB/km} \qquad E_0 = 0.0256 \text{ eV}$$

In that case [12],

$$\alpha_{IR}(E) \doteq 4.2 \times 10^{11} e^{-47.5/\lambda} \text{ dB/km}$$

The location of the peak of this infrared absorption differs according to the kind of dopant used. Let the basic oscillation frequencies corresponding to the locations of atomic absorption in the converted mass of μ_R and μ_R' be ν_R and ν_R', respectively. Then the following formula holds [5]:

$$\frac{\nu_R'}{\nu_R} = \sqrt{\frac{\mu_R}{\mu_R'}}$$

Therefore, infrared absorption by a heavy atom shows itself on the side of a longer wavelength.

Let us study GeO_2, P_2O_5, and B_2O_3, which are used ordinarily as dopants for SiO_2. Atomic weights go down in the order of Ge, P, and B. The wavelength at which infrared absorption takes place becomes shorter in the same order. It is at a wavelength of about 1.6 μm that infrared absorption begins in GeO_2-doped SiO_2. In the case of P_2O_5-doped SiO_2, there are peaks of absorption at 7.6 and 3.8 μm owing to the molecular vibration of P=O. Also, P_2O_5 has vibrations about P—O—P, P—P=O, O—P—O, and other bonds. From the viewpoint of fiber transmission loss, it may be said that the wavelength at which infrared absorption begins in the P_2O_5-doped SiO_2 glass is practically in the neighborhood of 1.4 μm.

The basic and higher harmonic vibrations of B—O coupling occur at 3.7, 7.9, 13.9 μm, and so on. The values of these absorptions are very large. The B_2O_3 dopant has a substantial effect on the fiber transmission loss at 0.8–1.5 μm. When B_2O_3 is used as a dopant, loss by its infrared absorption begins around 1.2 μm and becomes greater in the long-wavelength band beyond 1.2 μm. Therefore the B_2O_3 dopant is not desirable for a fiber for use at a 1.3–1.6 μm band.

2.2.4.3 Scattering Loss [5, 9, 12, 13]

There are four types of scattering loss for optical fibers:

1. Rayleigh scattering
2. Mie scattering
3. Brillouin scattering
4. Raman scattering

Loss due to scatterings 2-4 is small, less than 1/100 of the Rayleigh scattering loss mentioned later. Rayleigh scattering in glass is determined as a scattering caused by a local fluctuation of density, which is very small compared with the wavelength of light that propagates in glass.

The Rayleigh scattering loss α_R in SiO_2 glass is given by the following formula:

$$\alpha_R = \frac{8\pi^3}{3\pi^4} n^8 C_p^2 k_B \beta T_F = \frac{A}{\lambda^4}$$

where:

n = refractive index

C_p = constant of optical elasticity

k_B = Boltzmann's constant (1.381×10^{-3} J/K)

Materials

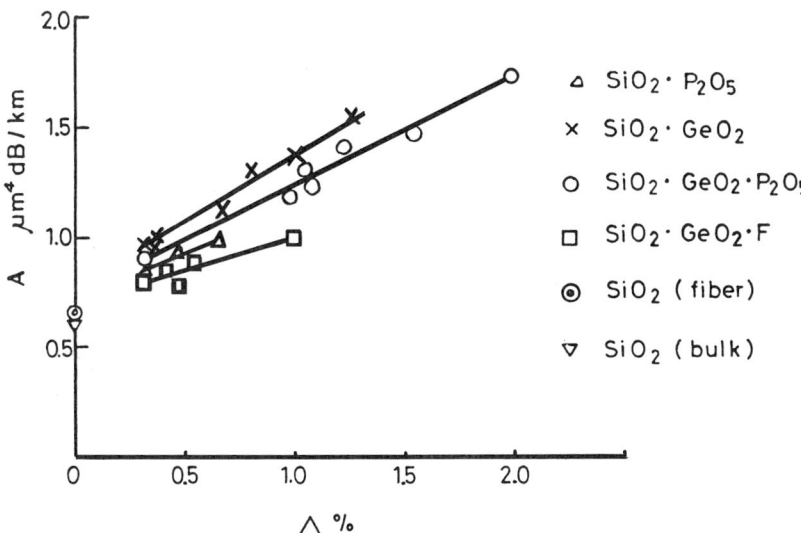

Figure 2.6 Coefficient of Rayleigh scattering loss A. Rayleigh scattering loss $\alpha_R = A/\lambda^4$. (From Refs. 12-16.)

T_F = solidifying temperature (absolute temperature)
β = isothermal compressibility
A = coefficient of Rayleigh scattering loss

Of these factors, β can be determined by experiment. When T_F = 1400 K, Cp = 0.286, and $\beta = 6.9 \times 10^{-12}$ cm^2/dyn (these are the values for pure SiO$_2$), the Rayleigh scattering loss of SiO$_2$ is λ = 0.85, 1.3, and 1.55 µm and α_R = approximately 1.3, 0.3, and 0.1 dB/km. These α_R are the scattering losses of pure SiO$_2$ (no dopant).

The Rayleigh scattering loss can be expressed by $\alpha_R = A/\lambda^4$ dB/km. Needless to say, the smaller the value of A, the smaller is the value of the Rayleigh scattering loss α_R. For the silica fiber, the value of A is related to (1) the kind of dopant and (2) the amount of dopant (or difference in refractive index between the core and the cladding, $\Delta\%$), as is evident from the scattering formula.

$$\Delta\% = \frac{n_1 - n_2}{n_1}$$

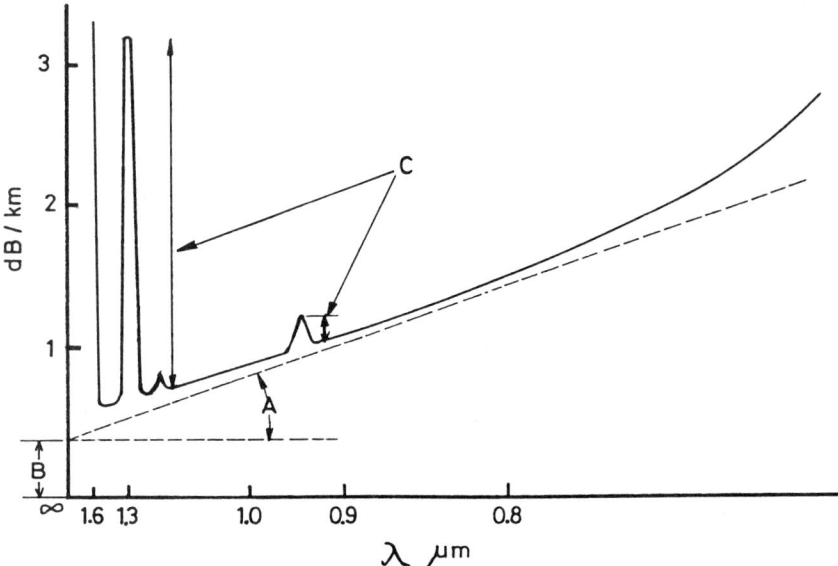

Figure 2.7   Fiber loss and wavelength (scale of abscissa: $1/\lambda^4$). (From Ref. 17.)

where:

Δ = relative refractive index difference

n_1 = maximum refractive index of core

n_2 = refractive index of cladding

Figure 2.6 shows the value of A thus obtained [12–16]. From this figure A = 0.65 db μm^4/km in the case of Δ = 0, that is, in the pure silica core of fiber (A = 0.63 dB μm^4/km in the bulk pure silica).

The value of A of $SiO_2 \cdot F \cdot GeO_2$ and $SiO_2 \cdot P_2O_5$ is smallest when $\Delta \leq 1\%$. However, P_2O_5 is not used as a dopant in the core because of the problem of loss increase due to H_2, discussed later. P_2O_5 is used as a dopant with the combination of $P_2O_5 \cdot F \cdot SiO_2$ in the cladding of MCVD fiber. (In this case, the mol% of P_2O_5 is small.)

In the case of $1\% \leq \Delta \leq 2\%$, the value of A of $SiO_2 \cdot GeO_2$ is small. Many dopants in various combinations have been used in the core and cladding of low-loss fiber for telecommunications. They have been reduced to only three (core, GeO_2; cladding, F; and P_2O_5, no use or very little) for reasons of low loss and long-term stability of

Materials

properties. (For nontelecommunications fibers, many other dopants are used.)

2.2.5 Graphs Convenient for Expressing Fiber Loss [17]

The loss of fiber is expressed as follows.

$$\alpha = \frac{A}{\lambda^4} + B + C(\lambda) + \alpha_{IR}(\lambda) + \alpha_{UV}(\lambda) \tag{2.1}$$

where:

A = coefficient of Rayleigh scattering loss

B = loss due to waveguide imperfection

$C(\lambda)$ = loss caused by impurities

α_{IR} = loss due to infrared absorption

α_{UV} = loss due to ultraviolet absorption

α = total loss of fiber

The loss of fiber is plotted on a graph scaled in $1/\lambda^4$ on the abscissa and in decibels per kilometer dB/km on the ordinate (Fig. 2.7) [17].

The loss curve of a fiber is nearly linear, but its slope is A. Deviations from this straight line are $C(\lambda)$, $\alpha_{IR}(\lambda)$, and $\alpha_{UV}(\lambda)$. At $\lambda \rightarrow \infty$, that is, the point where the loss curve crosses the ordinate axis, indicates the value of B. The smaller the slope of A and B, the lower is the loss of fiber.

2.2.6 Ultimate Low Loss of Silica Fiber [12, 18–20]

From Fig. 2.6 and Eq. (2.1), the fiber loss of core (pure SiO_2) and cladding ($SiO_2 \cdot F$) is the ultimate low loss. The minimum value of A for SiO_2 bulk glass is about 0.63 (Fig. 2.6). The A for SiO_2 fiber is estimated as about 0.65. The minimum value of α will be [12]

$$\alpha \doteq \frac{0.65}{\lambda^4} + 4.2 \times 10^{11} e^{-47.5/\lambda}$$

A minimum loss of 0.13 dB/km at 1.55 μm can be obtained from this equation. The minimum loss values obtained to date are 0.157 dB/km (in 1984) [18] and 0.154 dB/km (in 1986) [20].

Ideal ultimate low-loss curves of fibers are shown in Fig. 2.8 [19]. In the figure, the Δ value for the fiber core ($GeO_2 \cdot SiO_2$) and

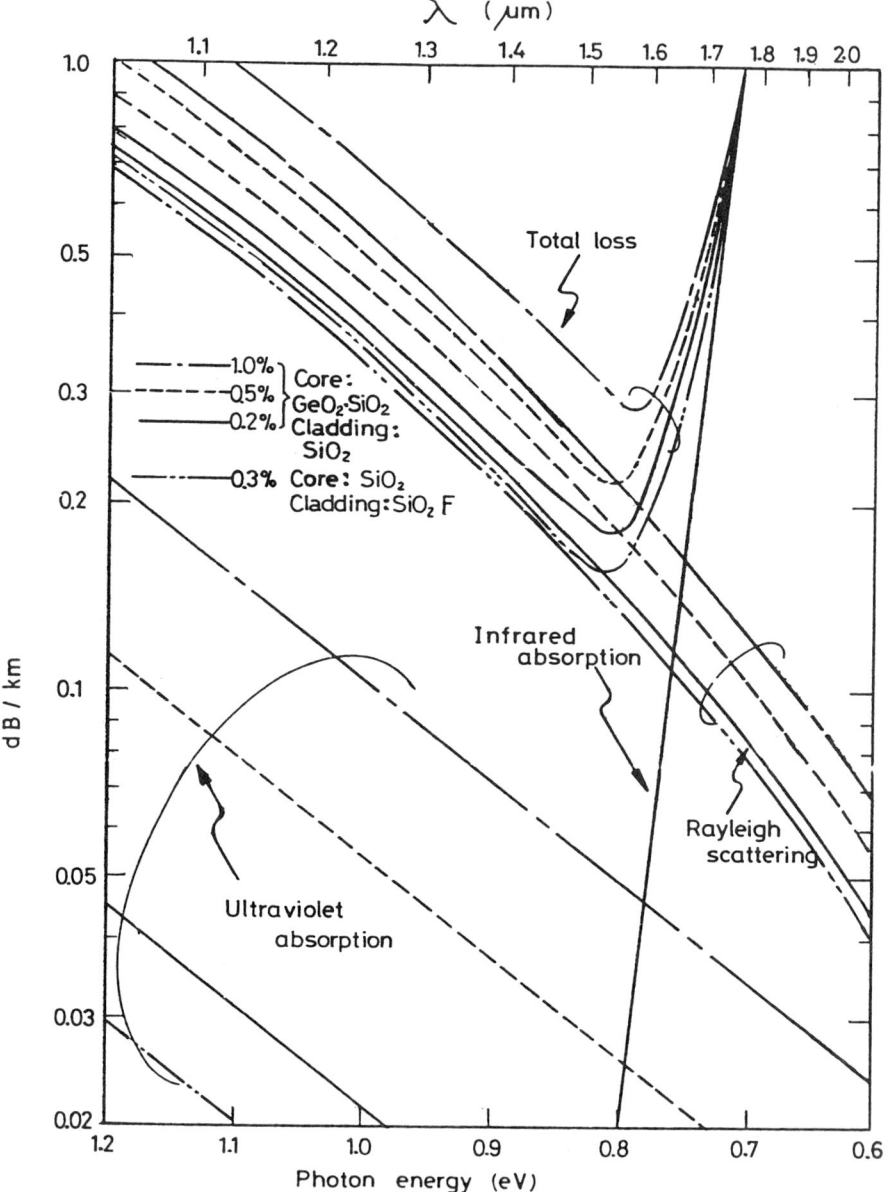

Figure 2.8 Ultimate loss limit of silica fiber. (From Ref. 19.)

cladding (SiO_2) = 0.2–1% versus Δ = 0.3% for SiO_2 core and $SiO_2 \cdot F$ cladding.
These values are derived from

$$\Delta = \frac{n_1 - n_2}{n_1}$$

where:

Δ = relative refractive index difference

n_1 = refractive index of core

n_2 = refractive index of cladding

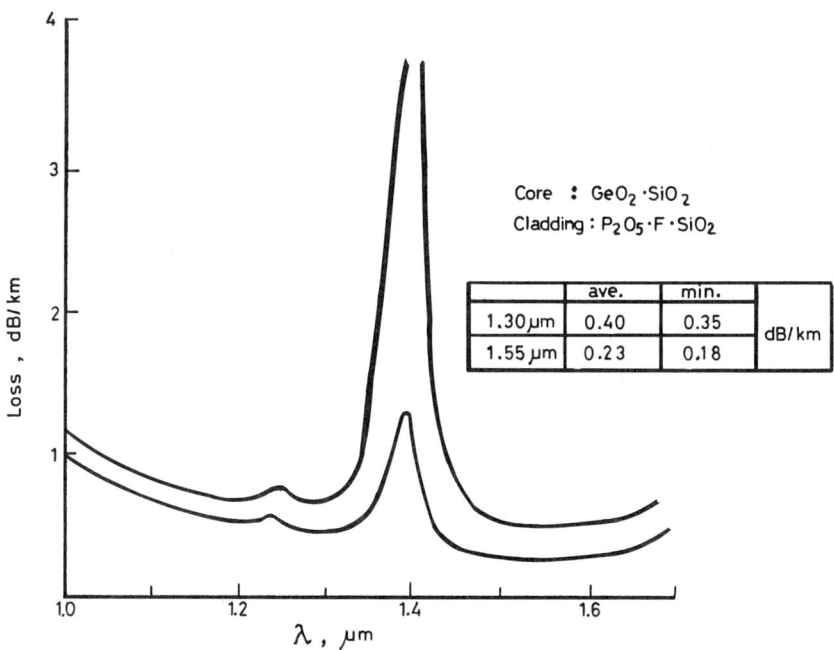

(a)

Figure 2.9 Loss distribution curves for MCVD and VAD fibers. (a) MCVD single-mode fiber 9/125, Δ = 0.3%. (b) MCVD graded index fiber 50/125, Δ = 1%. (c) VAD single-mode fiber 9/125, Δ = 0.3%. (d) VAD graded index fiber 50/125, Δ = 1%.

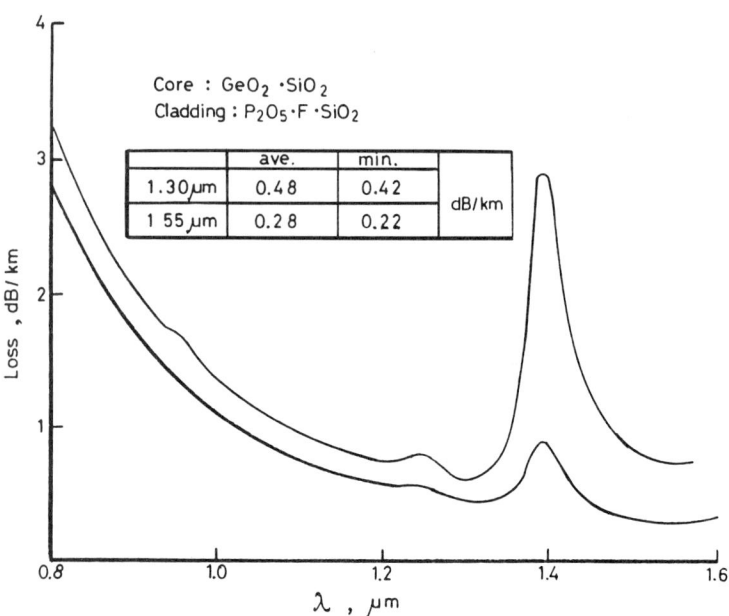

(b)

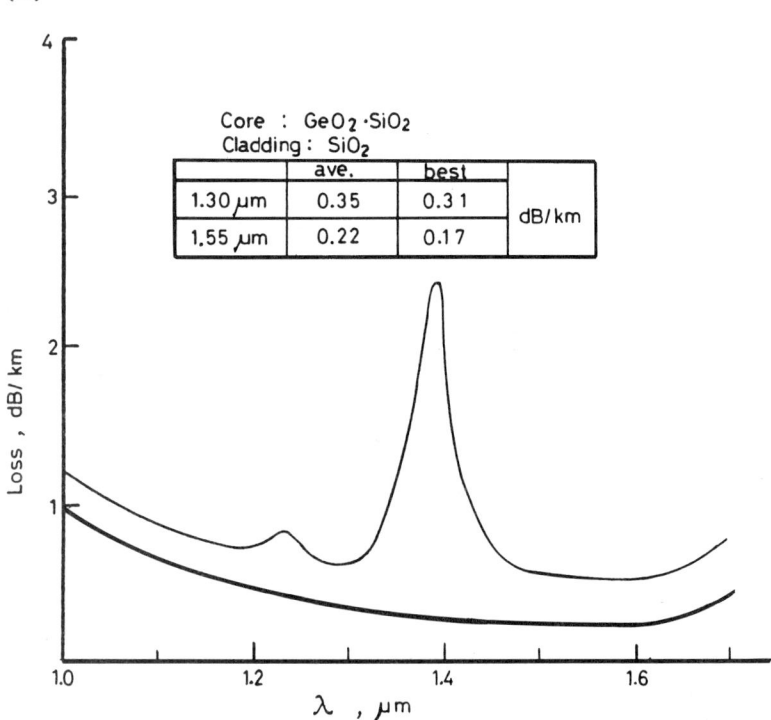

(c)

Figure 2.9 (Continued)

Transmission Bandwidth

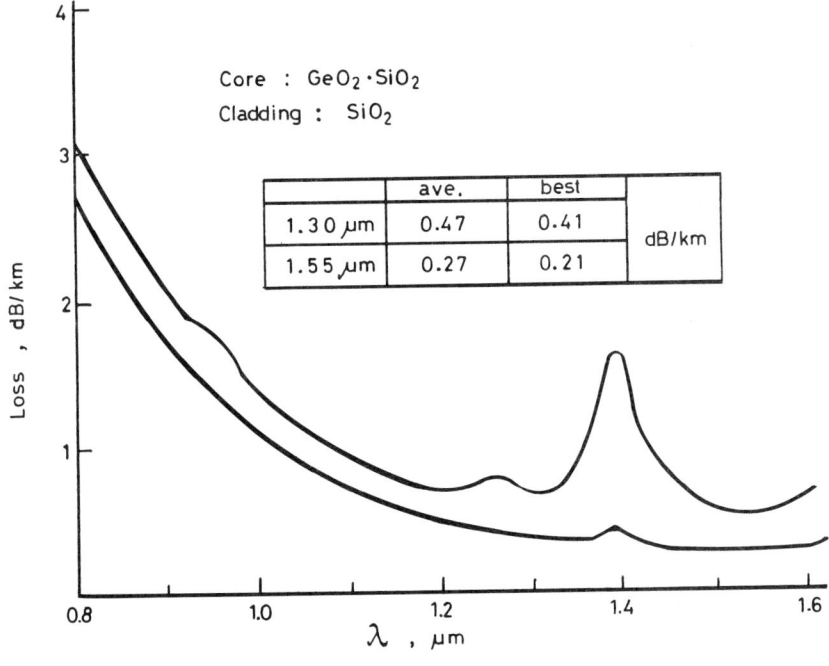

(d)

Figure 2.9 (Continued)

2.2.7 Change in the Loss of Silica Fiber

Figure 2.9 shows examples of loss distribution curves of fibers that are currently mass produced.

2.3 TRANSMISSION BANDWIDTH OF THE FIBER

2.3.1 General

Of the transmission properties of the fiber, transmission loss is determined mainly by the purity and properties of the fiber material, as mentioned in the preceding section. This section relates the relation between the transmission bandwidth and the construction of the fiber, with emphasis on the formulas and figures widely in use.

2.3.2 Types and Transmission Bandwidth of the Fiber

As is well known, fibers are roughly classified into three types, the step index, the graded index, and the single-mode, shown in Fig. 2.1.

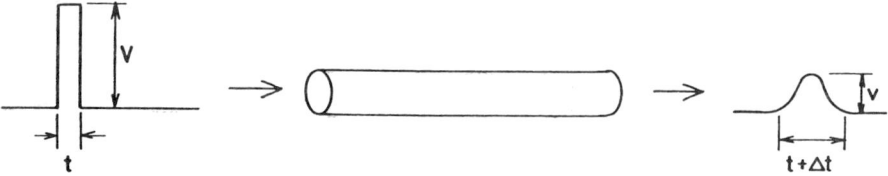

Figure 2.10   Pulse broadening in the fiber.

2.3.3   Transmission Bandwidth of Graded Index Fiber

The transmission bandwidth of the fiber can be measured by the pulse broadening, the extent to which the pulse launched at the input end of the fiber broadens at its output (Fig. 2.10). This broadening of the pulse is expressed in two ways, in terms of time and in terms of frequency.

Figure 2.11a shows how the output pulse broadens when the fiber length changes from 1 to 5 km. The pulse broadening of the output impulse, converted into frequency, is shown in Fig. 2.11b. A curve drawn with the baseband frequency on abscissa and the output on the ordinate is called the "base band frequency characteristic." Generally, a frequency that shows an output lower by 6 dB than that undergoing no modulation is defined as the bandwidth of fiber.

Broadening of the pulse width is generally termed "dispersion," which is classified into the following three types:

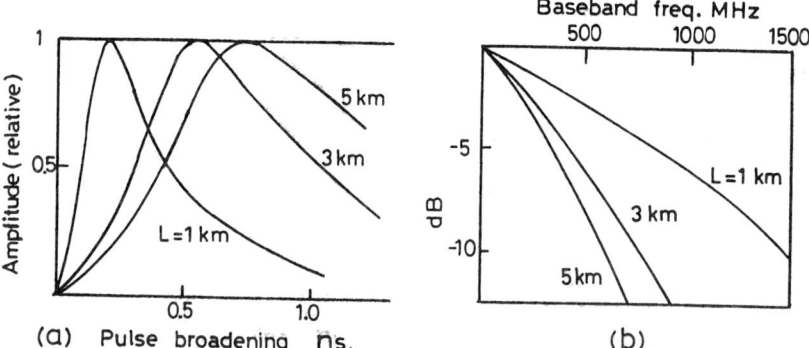

Figure 2.11   Impulse response and baseband frequency characteristics of GI fiber.

Transmission Bandwidth

1. Mode dispersion σ_{inter} (rms pulse width)
2. Material dispersion σ_m (rms pulse width)
3. Waveguide dispersion σ_w (rms pulse width)

The mode dispersion σ_{inter} is the broadening of pulse width caused by a difference in propagation speed between each mode. If the propagation speeds of all modes are equal, then no mode dispersion results; that is, $\sigma_{inter} = 0$.

2.3.3.1 Mode Dispersion σ_{inter} of Graded Index Fiber

The refractive index of the core of the graded index type fiber is as follows:

$$n^2(r) = n_1^2 \left(1 - 2\Delta\right)\left(\frac{r}{a}\right)^\alpha \qquad 0 \leq r \leq a: \text{ core}$$

$$n(r) = n_2 \qquad a < r: \text{ cladding}$$

where:

$n(r)$ = refractive index of the core

n_1 = refractive index of the core center ($r = 0$)

n_2 = refractive index of the cladding

$\Delta = n_1 - n_2/n_1$, relative refractive index difference

a = core radius

r = radius

α = profile (distribution) coefficient of refractive index

The mode dispersion σ_{inter} is explained briefly as follows (Fig. 2.12). The speed of light traveling in a medium is inversely proportional to its refractive index. In the graded index fiber, the refractive index n_1 at the center of the core is largest and decreases toward the outside in inverse proportion to nearly the square of its radius. When light is launched in the core of the fiber, the light path bends according to the refractive index distribution of the core, as shown in Figure 2.12. Light propagating on the center part of core is slowest where the refractive index is largest and fastest at the boundary of the core and cladding where the refractive index is smallest.

The optical paths of light propagating in the core are assumed to be as shown in a, b, and c in the figure.

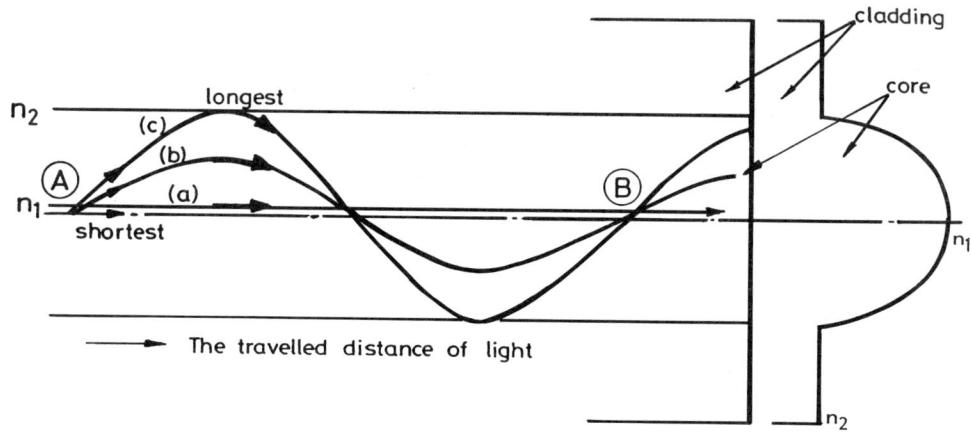

Figure 2.12 Mode dispersion of GI fiber.

1. In a, light proceeds from the center of the core in parallel with the optical axis, in which case the propagation speed in lowest and the length of optical path is shortest.
2. In c, the optical paths of light intersect, forming a largest angle with the fiber axis, in which case light propagates faster than a at the outside of the core and the length of the optical path is longer than in a.

If the refractive index of the core is properly distributed, light incident at point A at various angles to the axis can be made to pass through optical paths, such as a, b, and c and arrive simultaneously at point B. That is, irrespective of the launching angle of light, the time to reach the exit from the point of incidence can be made equal; in other words, the speed along the fiber axis of all modes of light that propagate in the core can all be made equal. This means that the fiber has a wide band. In this case, the refractive index of the core shows a nearly square distribution against its radius (i.e., $\alpha = 2$).

2.3.3.2 Material Dispersion σ_m [21]

The speed of light propagating in the fiber is inversely proportional to the refractive index of the fiber material, which generally changes with wavelength. Figure 2.13 shows, by way of example, the refractive index-wavelength characteristic of SiO_2 doped with GeO_2 or B_2O_3 [21].

The value of this refractive index can be formulated by Sellmeier's dispersion equation, as follows [21].

Transmission Bandwidth

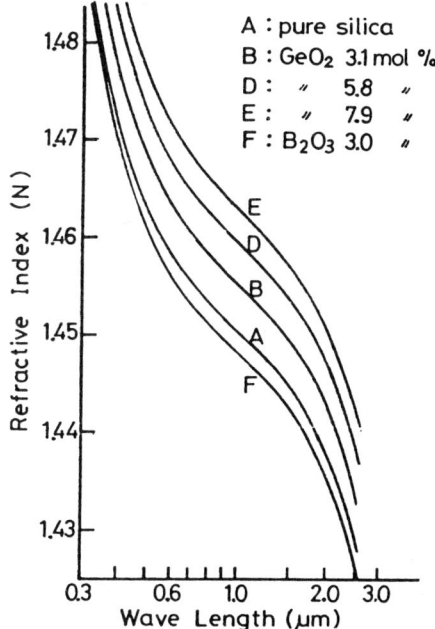

Figure 2.13 Refractive index of doped fused silica and pure fused silica. (From Ref. 21.)

$$n^2 - 1 = \frac{a_1 \lambda^2}{\lambda^2 - b_1} + \frac{a_2 \lambda^2}{\lambda^2 - b_2} + \frac{a_3 \lambda^3}{\lambda^2 - b_3} \qquad (2.2)$$

The values of a and b can be obtained experimentally from Fig. 2.13 and are shown in Table 2.7. Light-emitting diode or laser is used as a light source. The former generally has a spectrum width of 10-50 nm and the latter, 1-0.01 nm.

Let us suppose that the pulse light source has a spectrum width of λ_1 (= $\lambda_0 + \frac{1}{2}\Delta\lambda$) to λ_2 (= $\lambda_0 - \frac{1}{2}\Delta\lambda$) (Fig. 2.14a). When, in Fig. 2.14b, the refractive indices corresponding to λ_1 and λ_2 are denoted by n_1 and n_2, respectively, n_1 is smaller than n_2. If a mode that propagates in the fiber is assumed to be dispersed only by the material dispersion, the speed of optical powers of wavelengths λ_1 and λ_2 that propagate in the fiber are C/n_1 and C/n_2, respectively, and the optical power of λ_1 reaches the point of exist sooner than that of λ_2. As shown in Fig. 2.14c, therefore, the pulse width is broadened by material dispersion.

Table 2.7 Parameters of Sellmeier Dispersion Equation

Sample dopant	A, None	B, GeO_2 3.1 mol%	C, GeO_2 3.5 mol%	D, GeO_2 5.8 mol%	E, GeO_2 7.9 mol%	F, B_2O_3 3.0 mol%
a_1	0.6961663	0.7028554	0.7042038	0.7088896	0.7136824	0.6938408
a_2	0.4079426	0.4146307	0.4160032	0.4206803	0.4254807	0.4052977
a_3	0.8974994	0.8974540	0.9074049	0.8956551	0.8964226	0.9111432
b_1	0.004679148	0.00529581	0.00264623	0.00370945	0.003803952	0.005141195
b_2	0.01351206	0.01306644	0.0166823	0.01573806	0.01614969	0.01578530
b_3	97.934002	97.93400	97.93390	97.93402	97.93401	97.93387

Source: From Ref. 21.

Transmission Bandwidth

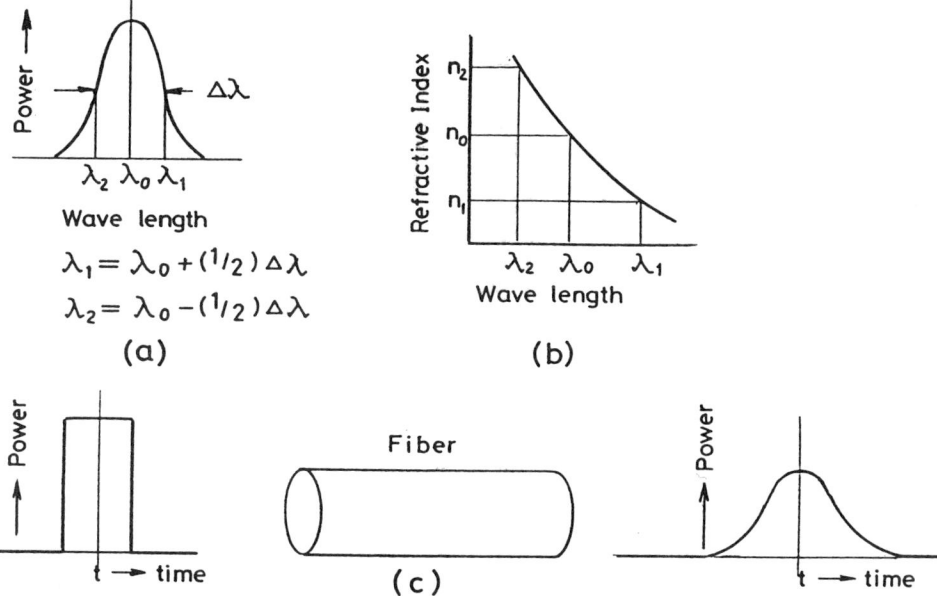

Figure 2.14 Material dispersion of fiber.

2.3.3.3 Waveguide Dispersion σ_w

It is not easy to explain physically waveguide dispersion. As mentioned in the preceding section, the group speeds of the modes that propagate in the fiber differ according to the refractive index of the fiber material. They also vary with the spectrum wavelength width of the light source and fiber construction, that is, Δ, profile, and so on. The pulse broadening caused by both the spectrum of light source and fiber construction is called the waveguide dispersion σ_w.

2.3.3.4 Calculation of Dispersion [22-28]

The propagating pulse in the fiber broadens according to the distance of propagation. This pulse broadening is caused by a difference in delay time between each propagation mode. The delay time $\tau(m)$ per unit length of the mode specified by the mode number $\tau(m)$ is defined by the formula

$$\tau(m) = \frac{1}{Vg} = \frac{1}{C} \frac{d\beta(m)}{dk} \qquad (2.3)$$

where:

>Vg = group velocity
>C = velocity of light (3×10^8 n/sec)
>k = $2\pi/\lambda$, wave number in free space
>β(m) = propagation constant

The refractive index distribution of the fiber is defined by the formula

$$n^2(r) = n_1^2 \left[1 - 2\Delta \left(\frac{r}{a}\right)^\alpha \right] \qquad (2.4)$$

where

$0 \leq r \leq a$.

$$\Delta = \frac{n1^2 - n2^2}{2n_1^2} \doteqdot \frac{n1 - n2}{n1}$$

The propagation constant β(m) is expressed by the following formula.

$$\beta(m) = kn_1 \left[1 - 2\Delta \left(\frac{m}{M}\right)^{2\alpha/(\alpha+2)} \right]^{1/2} \qquad (2.5)$$

where:

>m = mode number
>M = number of all modes

The delay time τ(m) of a fiber having the refractive index distribution of Eq. (2.4) is

$$\tau(m) = \frac{N_1}{C} \left[1 + \Delta \frac{\alpha - 2 - \varepsilon}{\alpha + 2} \left(\frac{m}{M}\right)^{2\alpha/(\alpha + 2)} \right.$$
$$\left. + \Delta^2 \frac{3\alpha - 2 - 2\varepsilon}{2(\alpha + 2)} \left(\frac{m}{M}\right)^{4\alpha/(\alpha + 2)} \right] + 0(\Delta^3)$$

where:

$$N_1 = n_1 - \frac{\lambda dn_1}{d\lambda}$$

Transmission Bandwidth

N_1 is called the "group index."
Also,

$$\varepsilon = -\frac{2n_1}{N_1}\frac{\lambda}{\Delta}\frac{d\Delta}{d\lambda} \tag{2.6}$$

When the value of Δ is small,

$$\tau(m) \doteqdot \frac{N_1}{C}\left[1 + \Delta\,\frac{\alpha - 2 - \varepsilon}{\alpha + 2}\,\frac{m}{M}\,2\alpha/(\alpha + 2)\right] \tag{2.7}$$

When $\alpha = 2 + \varepsilon$ in Eq. (2.7), the second term of Eq. (2.7) becomes zero and $\tau(m)$ is nearly constant; that is, the difference in delay time between modes is zero.

The terms σ_{inter}, σ_m, and σ_w in uniform excitation of the fiber are expressed by the following formulas.

$$\sigma_{inter} = \frac{LN_1\,\Delta}{2C}\,\frac{\alpha}{\alpha+1}\left(\frac{\alpha+2}{3\alpha+2}\right)^{1/2}\left[C_1^2 + \frac{4C_1C_2\Delta(\alpha+1)}{2\alpha+1}\right.$$

$$\left.+\,\frac{4\Delta^2\,C_2^2(2\alpha+2)}{(5\alpha+2)(3\alpha+2)}\right]^{1/2} \tag{2.8}$$

$$\sqrt{\sigma_m^2 + \sigma_w^2} = \sigma_{intra} = \frac{L}{C}\frac{\sigma_s}{\lambda}\left[\left(-\lambda^2\,\frac{d^2n_1}{d\lambda^2}\right)^2\right.$$

$$\left.-2\lambda^2\,\frac{d^2n_1}{d\lambda^2}N_1\,\Delta C_1\,\frac{\alpha}{\alpha+1} + (N_1\Delta)^2 C_1^2\,\frac{2\alpha}{3\alpha+2}\right]^{1/2} \tag{2.9}$$

The total dispersion σ_t is

$$\sigma_t = \sqrt{\sigma_{inter}^2 + \sigma_{intra}^2} = \sqrt{\sigma_{inter}^2 + \sigma_m^2 + \sigma_w^2} \tag{2.10}$$

$$C_1 = \frac{\alpha - 2 - \varepsilon}{\alpha + 2} \qquad C_2 = \frac{3\alpha - 2 - 2\varepsilon}{2(\alpha + 2)} \tag{2.11}$$

In Eq. (2.9), σ_s is the term that indicates the spectrum width of the light source and is expressed as shown below. $S(\lambda)$ represents the distribution of the light source spectrum and is also defined as follows.

$$S_0 = \int_0^\infty S(\lambda) \, d\lambda \qquad \text{total output of light source} \qquad (2.12)$$

$$\lambda_0 = \frac{1}{S_0} \int_0^\infty \lambda S(\lambda) \, d\lambda \qquad \text{average wavelength of light source} \qquad (2.13)$$

$$\sigma_s = \frac{1}{S_0} \left[\int_0^\infty (\lambda - \lambda_0)^2 S(\lambda) \, d\lambda \right]^{1/2} \qquad \text{rms spectrum width} \qquad (2.14)$$

The term α_{opt}, which is the minimum value of σ_{inter}, is

$$\alpha_{opt} = 2 + \varepsilon - \Delta \frac{(4 + \varepsilon)(3 + \varepsilon)}{5 + 2\varepsilon} \qquad (2.15)$$

$$\alpha_{opt} \doteq 2 - \Delta \frac{12}{5} \qquad (2.16)$$

When $\alpha = \alpha_{opt}$,

$$\sigma_{inter} \doteq 0$$

$$\sigma_{intra} \doteq \sigma_m \doteq \frac{\sigma_s}{\lambda} \left(-\lambda^2 \frac{d^2 n_1}{d\lambda^2} \right)^2 \doteq -\frac{L}{C} \frac{2\sigma_s}{\lambda} \left(\frac{d^2 n_1}{d\lambda^2} \right)^2 \qquad (2.17)$$

When an impulse is launched to a graded index fiber, Eq. (2.18) holds between the bandwidth (6 dB down) f_i and the total dispersion σ_t of the fiber. The impulse response of the GI fiber is assumed to be a Gaussian function [29].

$$f_i = \frac{1}{\pi} \sqrt{\frac{\ln^2 2}{2}} \frac{1}{\sigma_t} = \frac{0.188}{\sigma_t} \qquad (2.18)$$

Equation (2.19) is also established between the $\Delta\lambda$ (half-value) of the light source and its rms spectrum width σ_s.

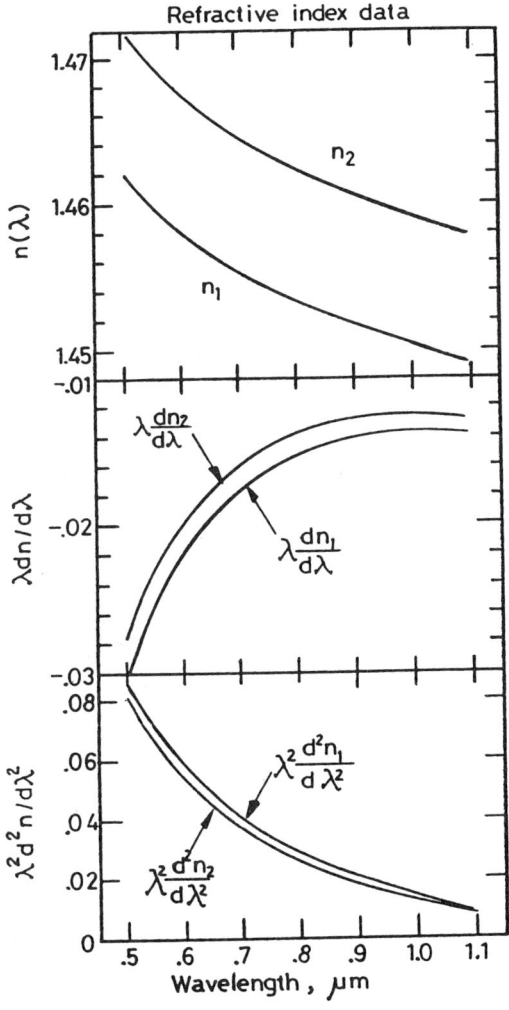

(a)

Figure 2.15 (a) Refractive index data for 3.4 wt% TiO_2-doped silica (n_2) and fused silica (n_1) are shown for Sellmeier fit to the refractive index (top), $\lambda \, dn/d\lambda$ (center), and $\lambda^2 \, d^2n/d\lambda^2$ (bottom). (b) The index difference Δ determined from the data of (a). (From Ref. 24.)

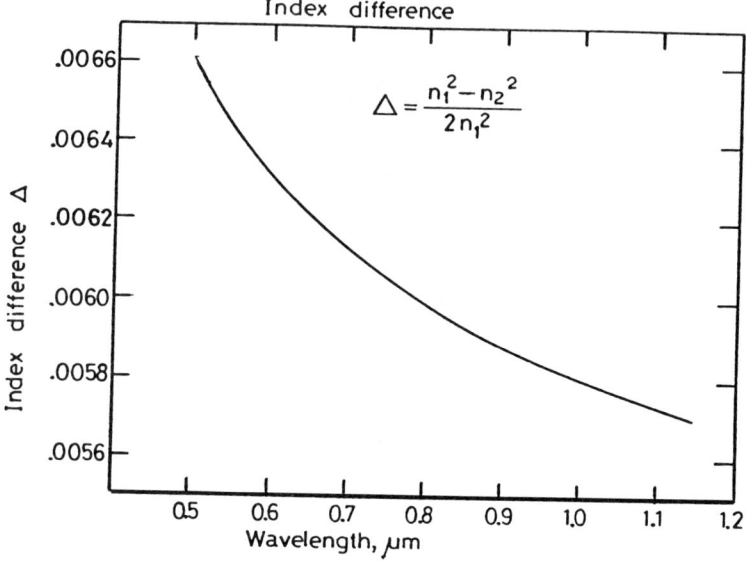

(b)

Figure 2.15 (Continued)

$$\Delta\lambda = 2(2\ln 2)^{1/2} \sigma_s = 2.36\sigma_s \qquad (2.19)$$

When $\alpha \doteq \alpha_{opt}$,

$$f_i = 0.188 \times 2.36 \times \frac{1}{\sigma_t} \times \frac{1}{\Delta\lambda} = \frac{0.44}{\sigma_t}\Delta\lambda \qquad (2.20)$$

2.3.3.5 Basic Data and Examples of Dispersion

Basic data for the calculation of dispersion examples concerning dispersion are shown on p. 49.

2.3.3.6 Bandwidths for 0.85 and 1.3 μm GI Fiber

We have studied α, which determines the maximum bandwidth of a GI fiber. In this case, the wavelength is fixed. For example, the bandwidth of a GI fiber is largest when α is 1.85 at a wavelength of 1.3 μm. The bandwidth of this fiber is small at 0.85 μm, as shown in Fig. 2.21, which gives the wavelength characteristics of the fiber at α = 2.1 and 1.85 [32]. Ordinary GI fiber has a broad bandwidth at a single wavelength.

Figure	Data	Material
2.15 [24]	Δ, n, $\dfrac{dn}{d\lambda}$, $\lambda^2 \dfrac{d^2n}{d\lambda^2}$	3.4 wt% TiO_2, SiO_2
2.16 [30]	n, $\dfrac{dn}{d\lambda}$, $\lambda \dfrac{d^2n}{d\lambda^2}$	Fused silica
2.17 [29]	Optimum α (α_{opt}) for doped silica GI fibers; note: α_{opt} of GI fibers = 0.85 μm, α_{opt} ÷ 2.1; 1.3 μm, α_{opt} = 1.85	$GeO_2 \cdot SiO_2 + GeO_2$, 11 mol% $P_2O_5 \cdot SiO_2 + P_2O_5$, 10 mol% $B_2O_3 \cdot SiO_2 + B_2O_3$, 10 mol% + GeO_2, 10 mol% $GeO_2 \cdot P_2O_5 \cdot SiO_2 + GeO_2$, 10 mol% $GeO_2 \cdot P_2O_5 \cdot SiO_2 + P_2O_5$, 0.9 mol%
2.18 [31, 32]	Relationship between α and bandwidth of GI fiber λ = 1.3 μm	Core, $GeO_2 \cdot P_2O_5 \cdot SiO_2$; cladding: SiO_2
2.19 [28]	Relation between bandwidth and light source of GI fiber α = 1.95	
2.20 [33, 34]	Dispersion of SM fiber	

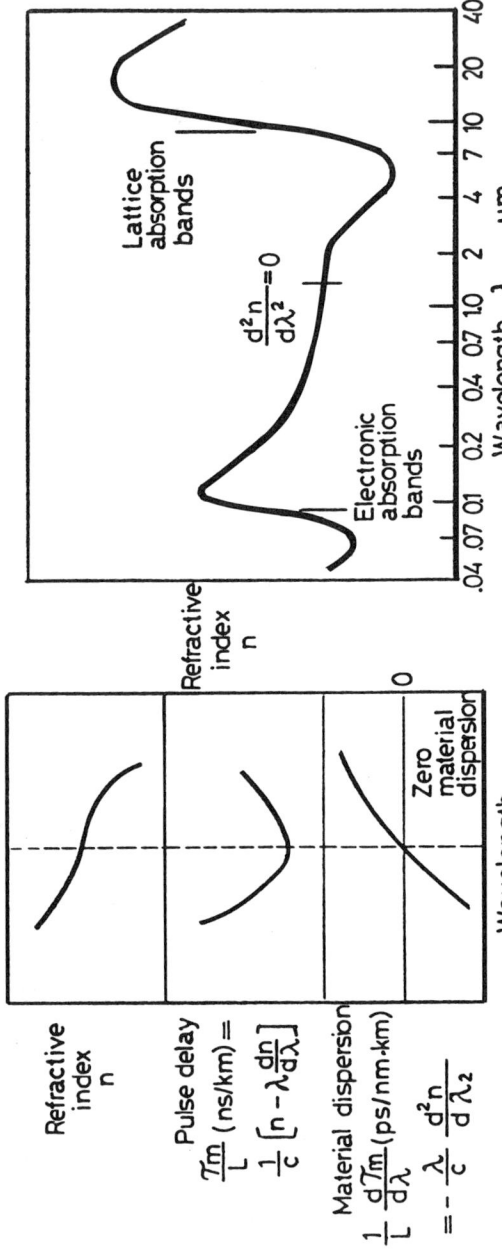

Figure 2.16 Origin of material dispersion (left) and refractive index variation of fused silica. (From Ref. 30.)

Transmission Bandwidth 51

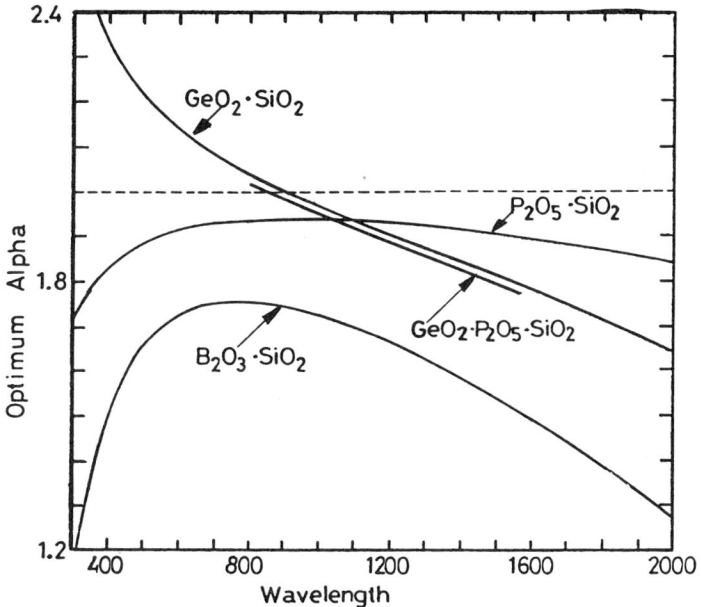

Figure 2.17   Optimum profile for doped silica fiber. (From Ref. 29.)

There are cases in which a broad band characteristic is required at two wavelengths, e.g., 0.85 and 1.3 μm. In order to meet this requirement, called multiple α, enlargement of bandwidth at 0.85 and 1.3 μm by changing the value of α in the radial direction of the fiber was studied. However, because of the difficulty of manufacturing the required profiles, this has no practical use.

Figure 2.22 [35] shows the results of a calculation made on the bandwidth (6 dB down) of a fiber with a single α at 0.85 and 1.3 μm. The figure indicates that the allowable range of α for obtaining a band of 2 GH_2 · km and over at 0.85 and 1.3 μm is extremely limited, 1.91–1.97 [35].

Figure 2.23 shows examples of the bandwidths of MCVD and VAD fibers.

2.3.3.7 Bandwidth of Spliced Fibers

The relation between the bandwidth and the spliced fibers is discussed below. Only one mode is transmitted in the single-mode fiber. Therefore, the bandwidth of the single-mode fiber is considered inversely proportional to the length of the cable.

When multimode fibers are spliced, the value of α slightly differs from fiber to fiber. The different values of α and their compensation

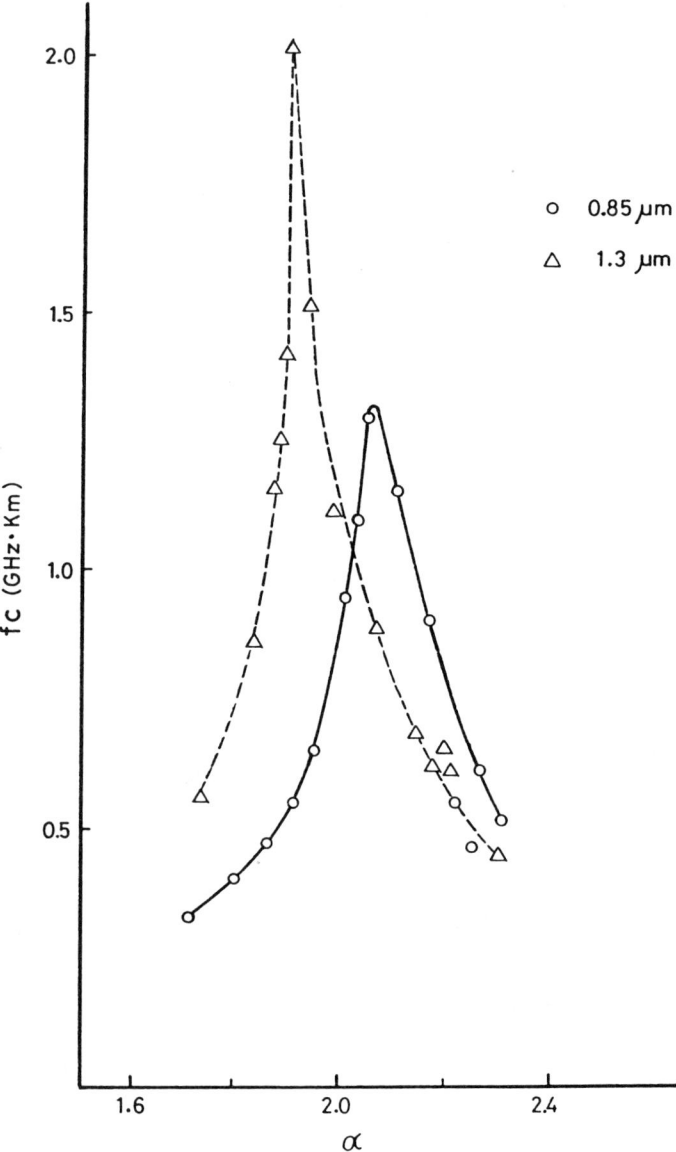

Figure 2.18 Relation between α and bandwidth of different GI fibers. (From Refs. 31 and 32.)

Transmission Bandwidth

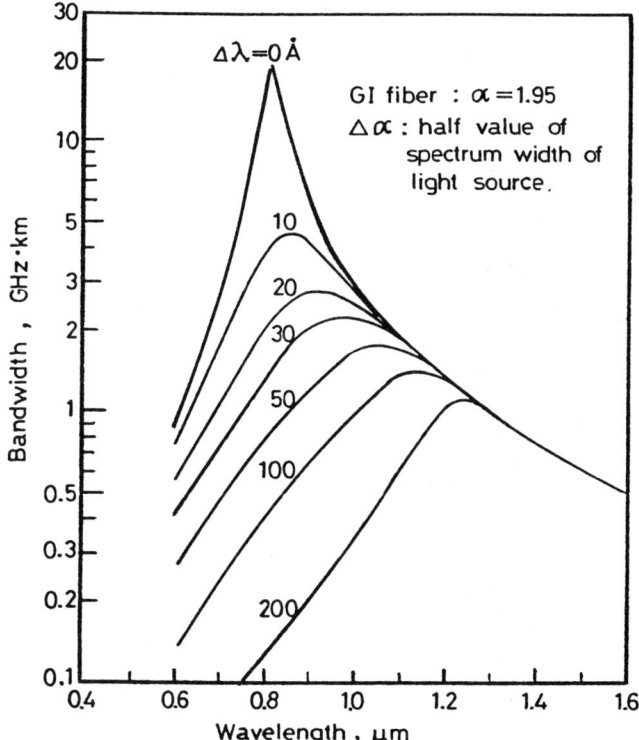

Figure 2.19 Relation between bandwidth and light source.

effects change the bandwidths of the spliced GI fibers as expressed by the equations

$$f_i = f_0 L^{-\gamma_1}$$

$$f_n - 1/\gamma_2 = \sum_i f_i - 1/\gamma_2$$

where:

f_0 = bandwidth of a continuous fiber (unit length)

f_i = bandwidth of a continuous fiber (length L)

f_n = bandwidth of the spliced fibers

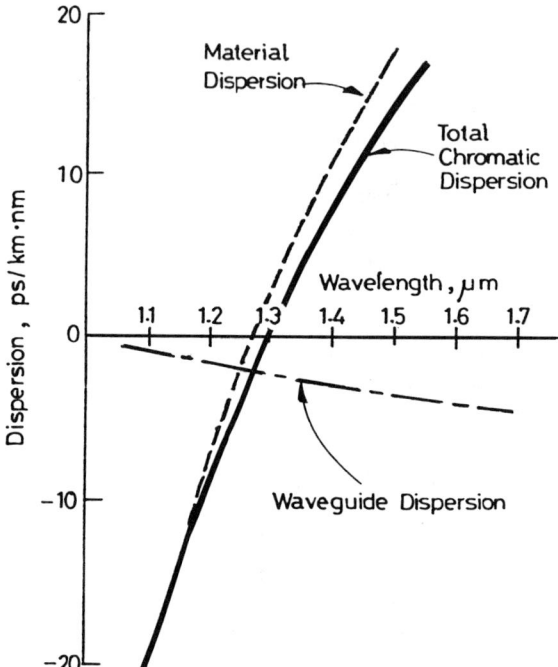

Figure 2.20 Dispersion of SM fiber. (From Refs. 33 and 34.)

From experiment, γ_1 is 0.85–0.95. γ_2 idffers according to the properties of the fiber. It is 0.6–0.7 when there are many variations in fiber production and 0.8–0.95 when such variations are few. At present, ordinarily the value of γ_2 is about 0.85.

2.3.3.8 Technical Terms Used in SM Fiber Design: Cutoff Wavelength and Mode Field Diameter or Spot Size

The following is a brief explanation of technical terms used frequently in the design of SM fiber.

Cutoff Wavelength λ_c

In fiber transmission, the single mode alone is transmitted under the following conditions.

$$\frac{2\pi a}{\lambda} \sqrt{n_1^2 - n_2^2} < 2.405$$

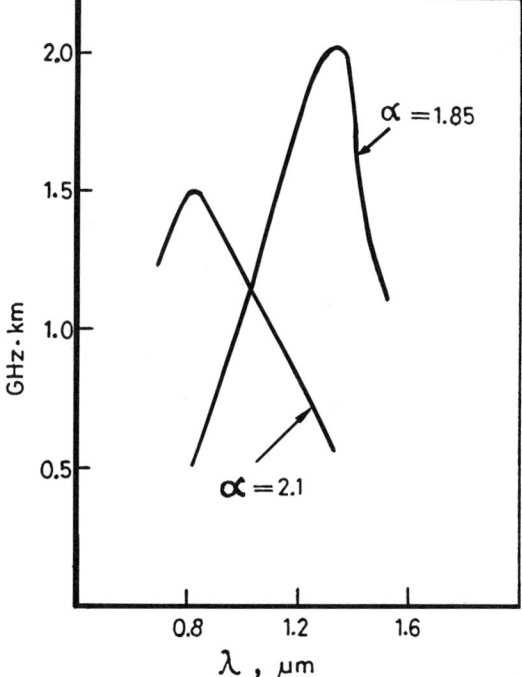

Figure 2.21 Relation between bandwidth and wavelength. (From Ref. 32.)

where:

a = core radius

λ = wavelength

n_1, n_2 = refractive index of core and cladding, respectively

At wavelengths shorter than those (λ_c) that meet the above condition, a multimode is generated in the fiber, which causes multimode transmission.

$$\lambda_c = \frac{2\pi a}{2.405} \sqrt{n_1^2 - n_2^2}$$

The value of this λ_c is called the (theoretical) cutoff wavelength. The actual cutoff wavelength is somewhat shorter than the

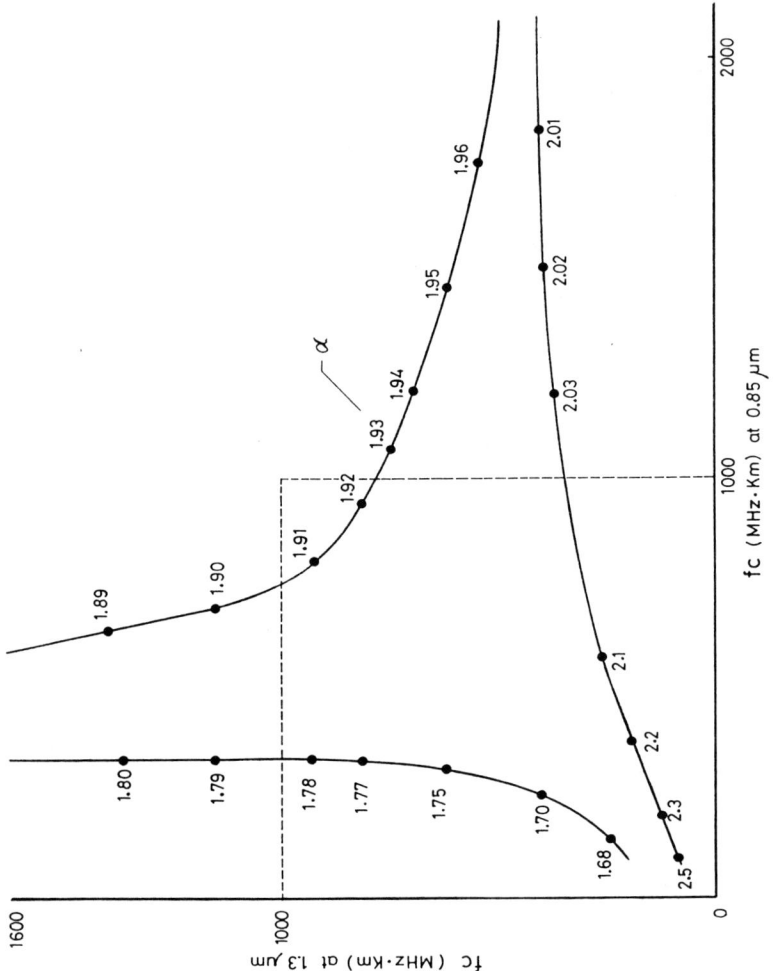

Figure 2.22 Relation between α and bandwidth (6 dB down) of 0.85 and 1.3 μm in the same fiber (parameter α). (From Ref. 35.)

Transmission Bandwidth

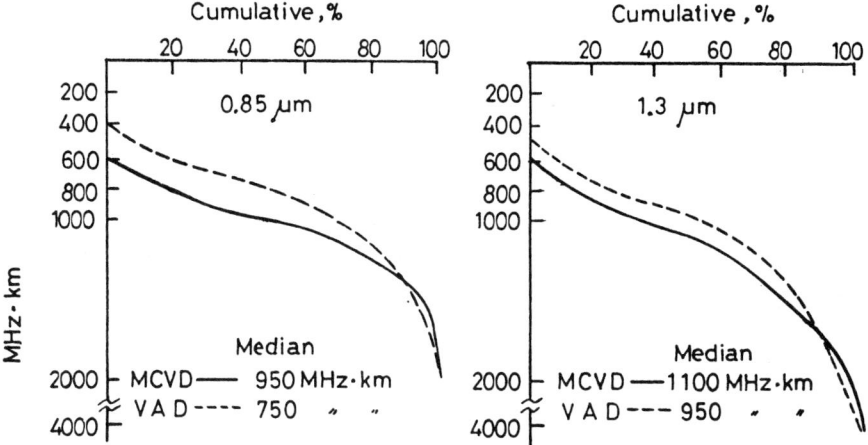

Figure 2.23 Fiber bandwidth (-6 dB electrical).

theoretical cutoff length. The actual cutoff wavelength also becomes shorter when the fiber length is increased. This is because if a secondary higher mode is generated, the loss of the cladding of this secondary mode is high and the secondary mode is relatively attenuated over the short length of fiber. For this reason, the actual cutoff wavelength becomes slightly shorter than the theoretical cutoff wavelength.

Mode Field Diameter or Spot Size

When electromagnetic energy is expressed as a Gaussian function, the diameter at which this energy becomes 1/e is called the "mode field diameter" = two times the spot size. This value is a parameter that indicates the degree of concentration of the electromagnetic energy of a single-mode fiber, which is used for various calculations in fiber splicing, bending, and so on.

The mode field diameter ω is defined as

$$\omega = 2W_0$$

where:

ω = mode field diameter

W_0 = spot size

$$W_0 = \left[\frac{2 \int_0^\infty f^2(r) r^3 \, dr}{\int_0^\infty f^2(r) r \, dr} \right]^{1/2}$$

that is, definition by the second moment of the electrical power, where:

  Wo = spot size

  f(r) = near field

  r = radial direction of fiber

$$\eta = \frac{\left[\int_0^\infty f(r) g(r) r \, dr \right]^2}{\left[\int_0^\infty f^2(r) r \, dr \right] \left[\int_0^\infty g^2(r) r \, dr \right]}$$

where:

  $g(r) = A \, e^{-r^2/W_0^2}$

W_0 is determined to maximize the value of η, and η is the coupling coefficient between the transmitted fiber mode and the Gaussian mode.

$$W_0 = \left[\frac{2 \int_0^\infty f^2(r) r \, dr}{\int_0^\infty [\partial/\partial r f(r)]^2 r \, dr} \right]^{1/2}$$

If the transmitted electromagnetic field is expressed as a Gaussian function, the mode field diameter becomes the diameter of $(1/e) \times$ the transmitted electromagnetic energy of the fiber.

2.4 MECHANICAL PROPERTIES OF THE FIBER

2.4.1 General

The optical fiber is silica glass itself. It is smaller in elongation and larger in Young's modulus than copper, aluminum, or other wire materials used for communication cables. Table 2.8 shows the mechanical properties of the materials that are generally used for such applications.

The theoretical breaking stress of flawless silica glass is expressed by [36].

$$\sigma_0 = \sqrt{\frac{E\gamma}{a}} \qquad (2.21)$$

where:

E = Young's modulus

γ = surface energy of material

a = atomic spacing of bond length

σ_0 = theoretical breakage of silica

In the case of silica glass, when $E = 7000$ kg/mm^2, $\gamma = 7 \times 10^{-5}$ kg/mm, and $a = 2$ Å $= 2 \times 10^{-7}$ mm, $\sigma_0 = 1.6 \times 10^4$ N/mm^2 = 1.6 $\times 10^3$ kg/mm^2

The theoretical value obtained from Eq. (2.21) is for the breaking stress of silica glass material that is flawless on the surface and inside.

This value of breaking stress is far larger than is actually obtained. Table 2.9 compares the theoretical value σ_0 and actual value of breaking stress for several materials.

Consider a material with a flaw on the surface. Tensile stress applied to this material concentrates on the flaw and makes it larger, thereby reducing the cross-sectional area of that particular part. This in turn increases the stress, which works on the reduced cross-sectional area and further enlarges the flaw. This is thought to be the way that breakage occurs.

The breaking stress of a material with a surface flaw is calculated by Griffith [36]. Supposing, as in Fig. 24, the material has a flaw with a depth L and a radius (at the tip) r; its breaking stress σ_t is

$$\sigma_t = \sqrt{\frac{2E\gamma}{\pi L}} \qquad (2.22)$$

The stress σ_m that works on the tip is

Table 2.8 Physical Properties of Materials

Property	Silica glass	Copper	Aluminum	Steel
Chemical sign	SiO_2	Cu	Aℓ	Fe
Specific gravity, g/cm^3	2.20	8.9	2.70	7.9
Tensile strength, kg/mm^2	500	25	10	120
Young's modulus, kg/mm^2	7200	12,000	6300	20,000
Elongation, %	2–8	20–30	7–20	5–15
Coefficient of thermal expansion	5×10^{-7}	1.7×10^{-6}	2.3×10^{-5}	1×10^{-5}
Specific heat, cal/°C·g	0.20	0.09	0.5	0.1

Mechanical Properties

Table 2.9 Theoretical Breaking Stress and Actual Breaking Stress

Material	Breaking stress (kg/mm^2)	
	Theoretical	Actual
Silica glass	1,600	50–600
Graphite	140	2
Diamond	20,000	200
Steel	4,000	100–200
Wolfram	9,000	100–300

$$\sigma_m = \sigma \left[1 + 2\left(\frac{L}{r}\right)^{1/2}\right] \doteqdot 3\sigma \qquad (2.23)$$

where $L \doteqdot r$.

From Eqs. (2.21) and (2.22),

$$\sigma_t \doteqdot \frac{1}{3} \sigma_0 \sqrt{\frac{2a}{\pi L}}$$

$$\doteqdot 3.8 \times 10^{-3} \frac{\sigma_0}{\sqrt{L(\mu m)}}$$

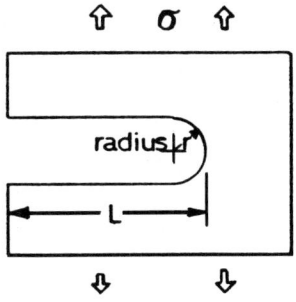

Figure 2.24 Material with surface flaw.

$$\doteqdot \frac{6.1}{\sqrt{L(\mu m)}} \quad kg/mm^2 \tag{2.24}$$

When the depth of the flaw is $L = 10^{-3}$ mm $= 1$ μm, σ_0/σ_t is nearly equal to 100 when r is 2 Å $= 2 \times 10^{-7}$ mm. That is, when a material has a flaw, about 1 μm deep, its breaking stress becomes 1/100 of the theoretical breaking stress. (It will be difficult to detect a flaw of such a small depth.) Figure 2.25 shows the breakage stress of silica glass with a flaw. From these studies, we learn that a flaw on the material is the main reason that its actual breaking stress is 1/10 to 1/100 of the theoretical value.

2.4.2 Breaking of Silica Fiber

As mentioned, the tensile strength of the silica fiber is four times that of iron and more than ten times that of copper and aluminum. When tension is applied to the fiber, a stress concentrates on the flaw and the fiber breaks when the stress exceeds the allowable level.

Flaws on the fiber spread at random in its longitudinal direction, and the deepest flaw determines the breaking strength of the fiber. The breaking probability of a fiber is expressed by the Weibull distribution function.

When the probability $R_0(\sigma)$ that a fiber of unit length L_0 will not be broken by an external stress of σ has a Weibull distribution, $R_0(\sigma)$ is expressed by

$$R_0(\sigma) = e^{-(\sigma/\sigma_0)^m} \tag{2.26}$$

where σ_0 is a constant.

When the length of the fiber is L, from Eq. (2.25),

$$R(\sigma) = R_0(\sigma) \frac{L}{L_0} = e^{-(\sigma/\sigma_0)^m (L/L_0)} \tag{2.26}$$

$R(\sigma)$ is the probability that a fiber of length L will not be broken by an external stress σ.

Let $F(\sigma)$ be the breaking probability; then

$$1 - F(\sigma) = e^{-(\sigma/\sigma_0)^m (L/L_0)}$$

$$\ln \ln \frac{1}{1 - F(\sigma)} = m \ln \frac{\sigma}{\sigma_0} + \ln \frac{L}{L_0} \tag{2.27}$$

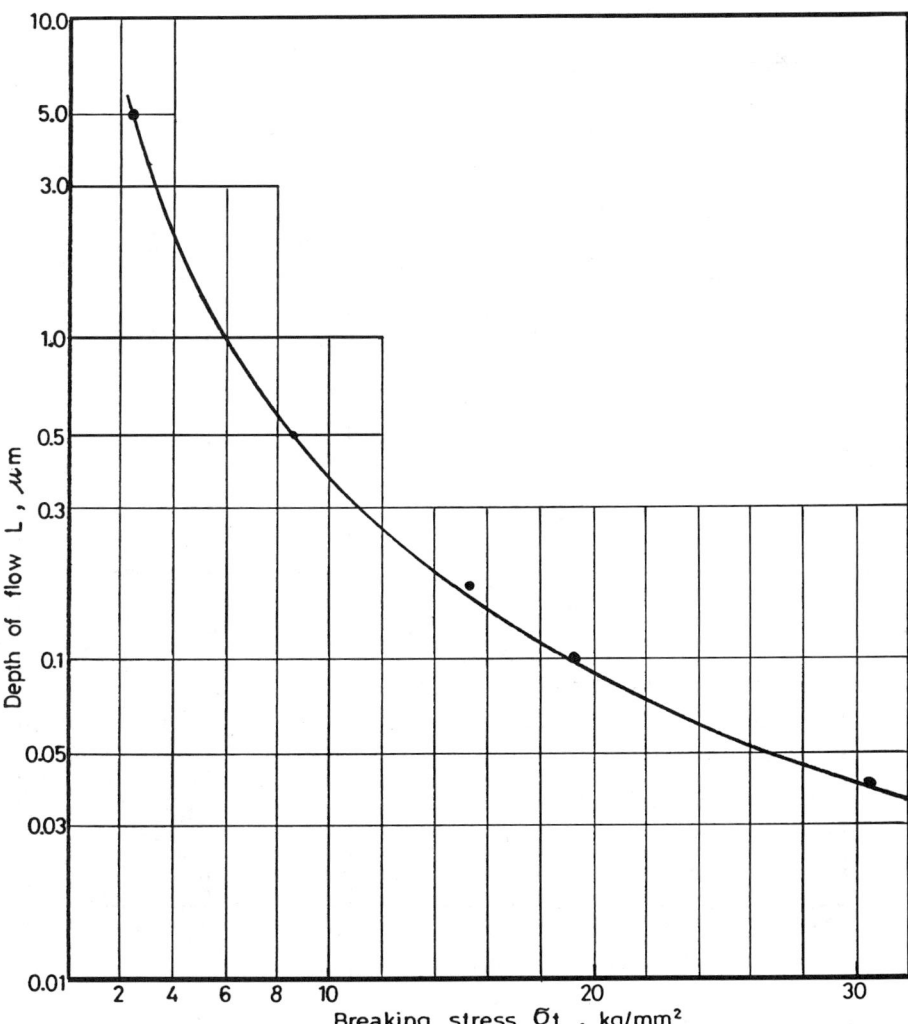

Figure 2.25 Relation between flaw depth and breaking stress of silica glass.

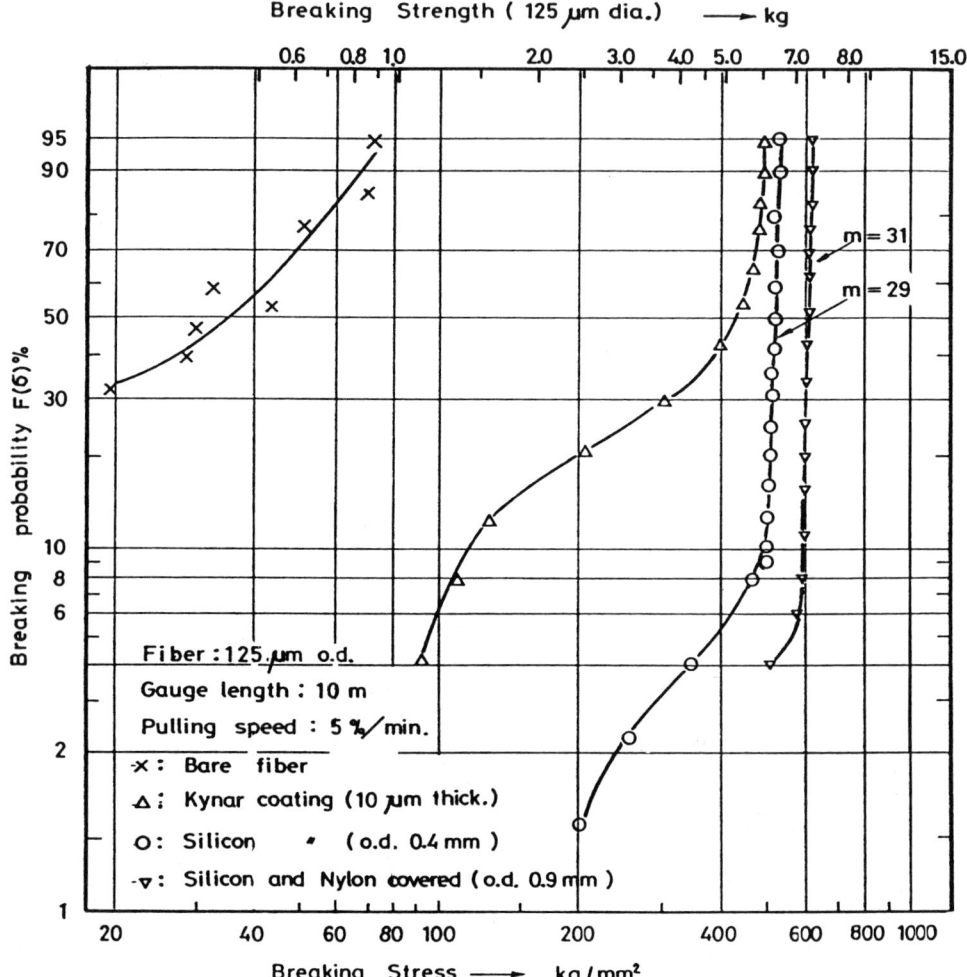

Figure 2.26   Breaking strength of fibers.

Mechanical Properties

where:

$F(\sigma)$ = breaking probability under stress

L = length of fiber

L_0 = unit length of fiber

σ = stress given

σ_0 = constant

m = constant dependent upon ambient condition

The principal causes of fiber are as follows:

1. The fiber material itself (preform rod) has flaws.
2. Adhesion of dust, water, or other contaminants to the fiber surface during drawing.
3. Contact of the fiber with the drawing machine or other object during drawing.

Therefore, the fiber is normally drawn in a clean atmosphere and immediately thereafter covered with plastics, with care used to keep it from contact with other objects.

Figure 2.26 shows examples of the breaking strength of fibers coated with different types of plastics. Examples of the tensile strength of a bare fiber without plastic coating are marked with "X" in Fig. 2.26. Those of plastic-covered fibers are shown by the symbols Δ, 0, and ∇. The length of the sample is 10 m. The gradient of the tensile strength curve is m from Eq. (2.27). According to the figure, the tensile strength of the uncoated fiber is less than 1/10 that of the coated fiber. The value of m of the plastic-covered fiber is about 25 to 35. This curve, however, sometimes forms a gentle gradient at the lower part, which indicates that, with a certain probability, a larger flaw than ordinary exists in the fiber.

The average breaking strength of a plastic-coated fiber (outer diameter, 125 µm) is about 6 to 7 kg and the minimum breaking strength is about 1 to 3 kg.

Equation (2.27) is used to determine the breaking stress of a fiber having a length of L when the Weibull distribution of the breaking stress of a fiber of length L_0 is known (that is, when m, ln σ_0, and L_0 are known.) The breaking strength of 1 km long fibers which is converted from the breaking strength of 1, 10, and 30 m long fibers [37], is shown in Fig. 2.27.

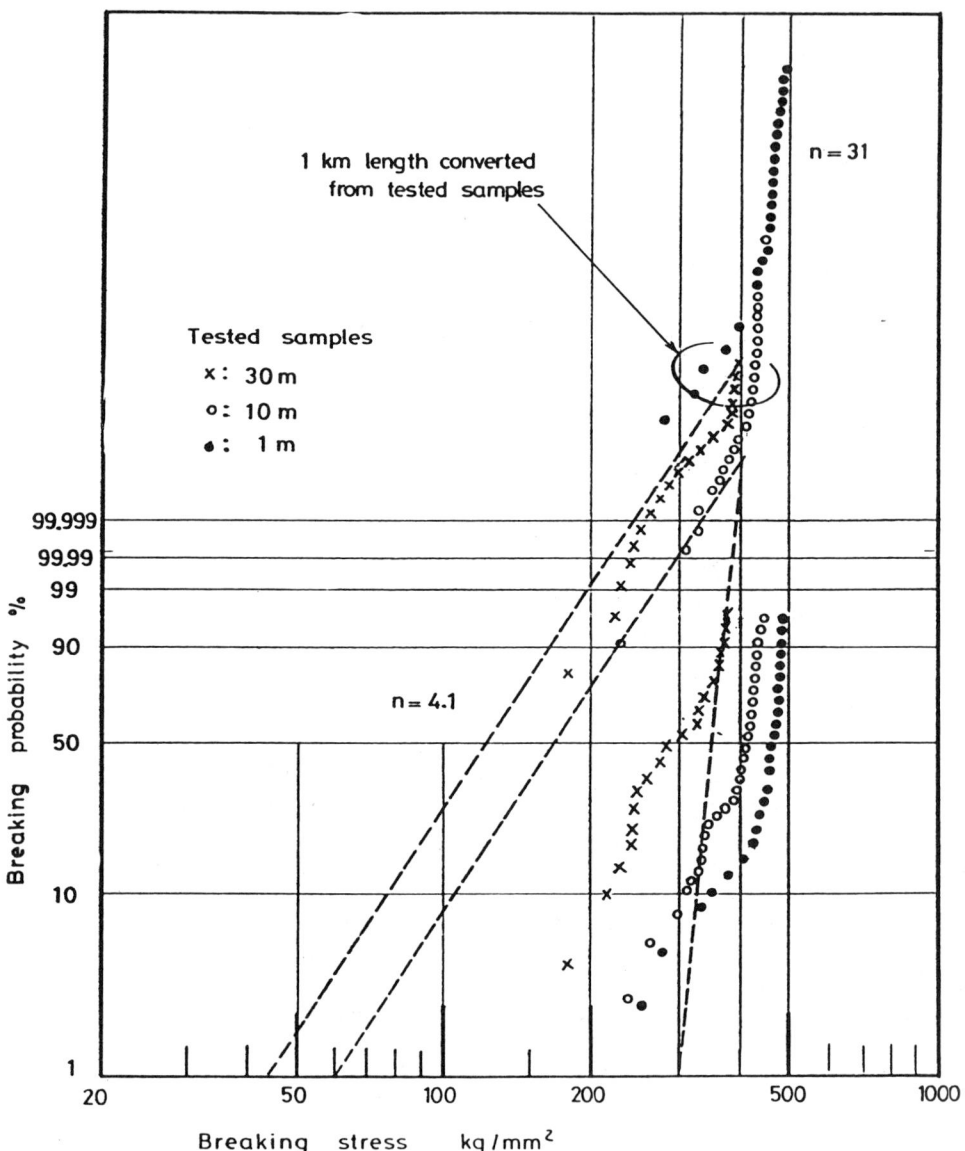

Figure 2.27 Relation between breaking stress of fiber and fiber length. (From Ref. 37.)

Reliability 67

2.5 RELIABILITY OF FIBERS

Mechanical reliability and chemical reliability are considered in this section.

2.5.1 Mechanical Reliability of Fiber

The following three items are most important for the mechanical reliability of a fiber.

Static fatigue. The fiber is given a static stress (e.g., static load), and the time to breakage of the fiber is measured. This measurement usually takes a long time. The sample used is short. This is a destructive test.
Dynamic fatigue. The fiber is pulled at a fixed speed, and the stress at breakage and stressing rate are measured. Only a short time is required for measurement. The sample used is short. This is a destructive test.
Screen test. A long fiber is given a smaller stress than its rupture stress, and the stress, time of stress application, and number of ruptures in the unit length of the fiber are measured. The fiber is broken in the screen test if it has a flaw that makes it incapable of withstanding the stress of the screen test. The fiber so broken is reduced in continuous length. With the flaw removed, however, it does not break under the same stress as is given in the first screen test.

2.5.1.1 Static Fatigue of Fiber [38-40]

The following equation holds empirically when the fiber is given static stress σ_S and breads after the lapse of time t_S.

$$\log t_s = -n \log \sigma_s + \log k_s \qquad (2.28)$$

where:

σ_s = static fatigue stress
t_s = time to failure by static fatigue
k_s = constant

For a fiber with a plastic primary coating, n = 25-35 in air and 15-25 in water.
Figure 2.28 shows an example of the static fatigue test performed on a silica fiber with a plastic primary coating.

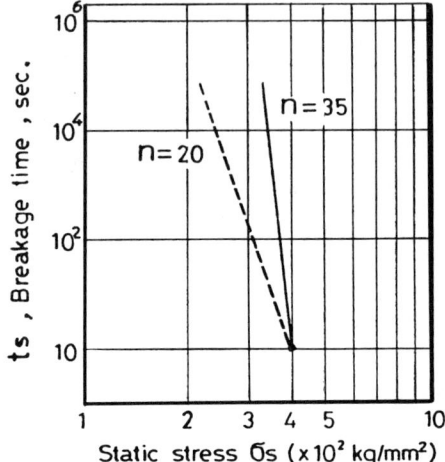

Figure 2.28 Static fatigue test; gage length = 1 m.

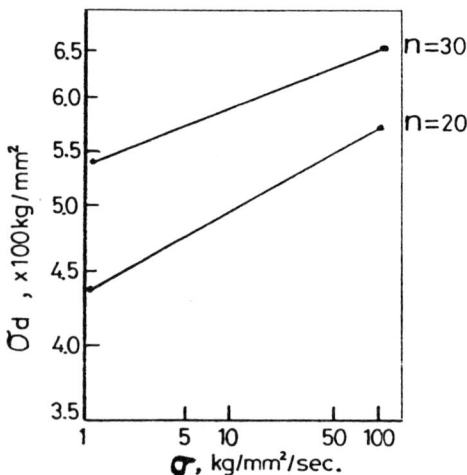

Figure 2.29 Dynamic fatigue test; gage length = 1 m.

Reliability

2.5.1.2 Dynamic Fatigue of Fiber [38-40]

The fiber is pulled at a fixed speed, and the stress at breakage and stressing rate are measured. The following equation holds empirically.

$$\log \sigma_d = \frac{1}{n+1} \log \dot{\sigma} + \frac{1}{n+1} \log k_d \qquad (2.29)$$

$$\log t_d = -n \log \sigma_d + \log k_d \qquad (2.30)$$

where:

σ_d = dynamic fatigue stress

$\dot{\sigma}$ = stressing rate

n = 25-35 in air, 15-25 in water

t_d = time to failure by dynamic fatigue

The relation between constants of the dynamic and static fatigue is as follows.

$$\log k_d = \log k_s + \log (n+1) \qquad (2.31)$$

An example of the dynamic fatigue test is shown in Fig. 2.29.

2.5.1.3 Screen (or Proof) Test of Fiber [41, 42]

A smaller stress than its rupture stress is applied to the fiber. Generally, a tension W is applied to the fiber while it is taken up, as shown in the Fig. 2.30. This is called the screen or proof test. It is very effective in proving the strength of the fiber.

If the fiber has a flaw and is broken under the tension of the screen test, the breakage removes the damaged section. However, if the fiber is not so broken, the damage will be enlarged, making the fiber vulnerable.

The rupture rate of a fiber of length L after receiving a tension σ_p for t_p seconds and then σ_s for t_s seconds is as follows, provided that the breakdown strength of the fiber is assumed to follow a Weibull distribution. (σ_p and t_p represent, for example, the values in the screen test in fiber production. σ_s and t_s denote the tension that works on the fiber for a long time after cable installation and the time up to the breakage of the fiber after installation, respectively.)

$$F_s \doteqdot 1 - \exp \left\{ -N_p L \left[\left(1 + \frac{\sigma_s^n t_s}{\sigma_p^n t_p} \right)^{m/n-2} - 1 \right] \right\} \qquad (2.32)$$

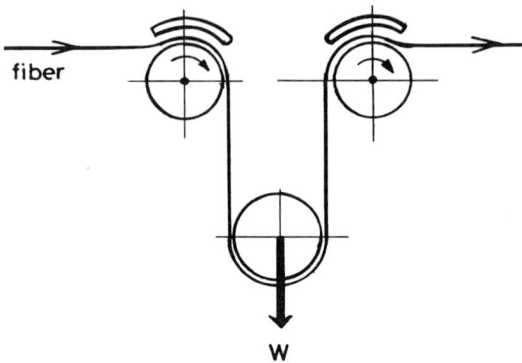

Figure 2.30 Screen (or proof) test.

$$\frac{\sigma_s}{\sigma_p} \doteq \left\{ \left[\left(1 - \frac{\ln(1-Fs)}{N_p L}\right)^{(n-2)/m} - 1 \right] \frac{t}{t_s} \right\}^{1/n}$$

$$\lambda = -\frac{\ln(1-Fs)}{L}$$

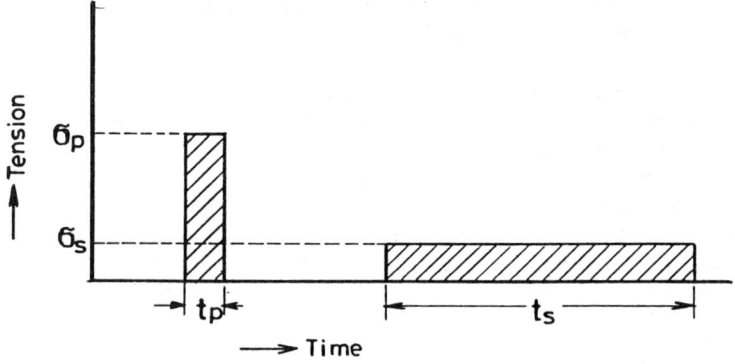

Figure 2.31 Screen test of fibers. (From Refs. 41 and 42.)

Reliability

where:

Fs = rate of fiber rupture after application of a screen test with a tension σ_p for t_p and then σ_s for t_s (Fig. 2.31)

N_p = $N_p(\sigma_p)$ = number of ruptures in the unit length of fiber given a tension of σ_p for t_p seconds

L = length of fiber

σ_p, t_p = tension given to the fiber and time of its application in the first screen test

σ_s, t_s = stress given to the fiber and time of its application in the second screen test (or after the installation of cable)

m = index of Weibull distribution

$$N(\sigma_1) = \left(\frac{\sigma_1}{\sigma_0}\right)^m$$

The breakdown strength of the fiber is assumed to follow a Weibull distribution, where n is a constant (25 to 35 in air, 15 to 25 in water) and λ is the failure ratio per unit length.

The time of the first screen test (generally, after fiber drawing) is assumed to be 1 sec. Also, the value of m is assumed to be 10. This is the minimum for an actual fiber. Fs and n are assumed as follows: Fs = 0.01 → λ = 0.01 km^{-1} and n = 25 (in dry air). When NL = 1 to 100, the relation between σ_s/σ_r and t_s is obtained. When it is assumed that a tension σ_s works on the fiber in an installed cable, t_s represents the allowable stressing time. This relationship is shown in Fig. 2.32.

When NL = 1 to 100, that is, L = 1000 km and N = 0.001 to 0.1 times km^{-1}, σ_s/σ_p is 0.4 to 0.3 when the life of the fiber is assumed to be 25 years. When the stress remaining in the fiber after cable installation is assumed to be 0.2%, the value in the screen test (1 sec) after fiber drawing is σ_p = 0.5 to 0.7%.

2.5.2 Chemical Reliability of Fiber (Hydrogen Problems)

2.5.2.1 General

Approximately 10 years after the low-loss silica fiber was announced in 1970, the development of this optical fiber was advancing smoothly and optical fiber cable systems were about to be used widely throughout the world. In 1982, the transmission losses of optical fiber cables installed in 1980 greatly increased, a nearly simultaneous

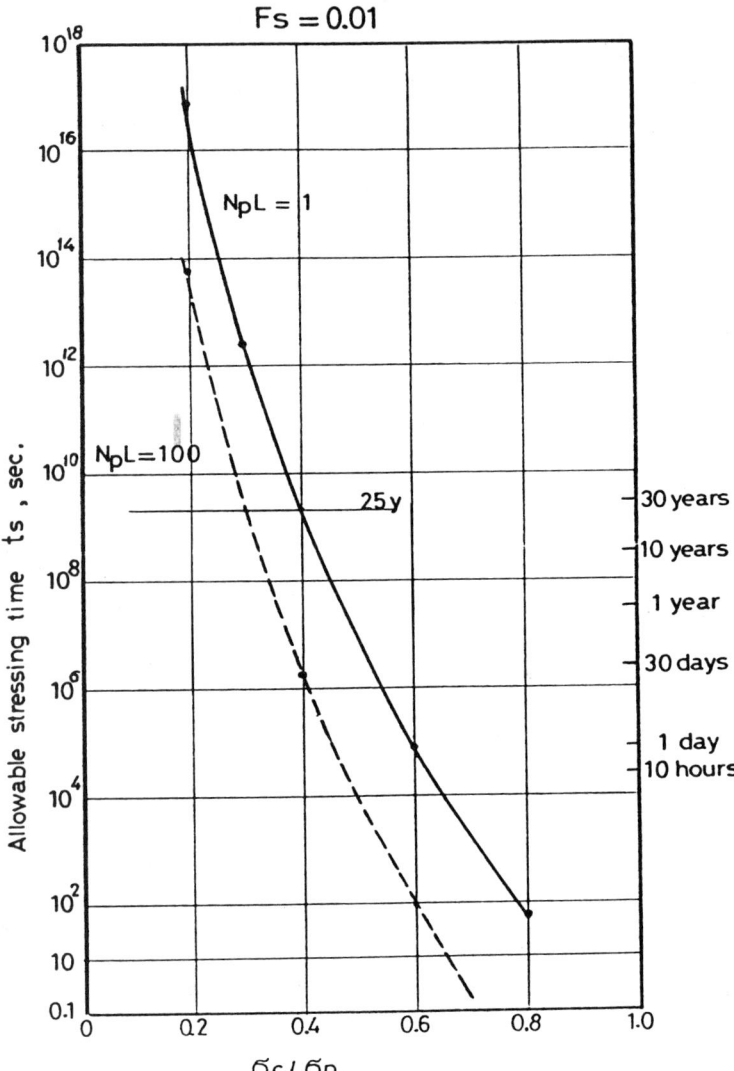

Figure 2.32 Relation between the ratio of allowable stress σ_s to proof stress σ_p and allowable stressing time t_s. (From Refs. 41 and 42.)

Reliability 73

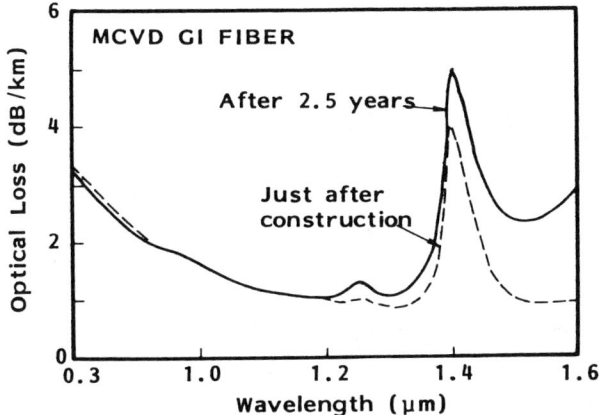

Figure 2.33   Loss change of the fiber in the installed cable.   (From Ref. 43.)

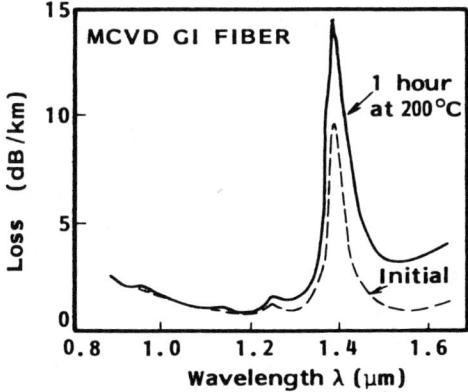

Figure 2.34   Loss increase of plastic-covered fiber.   (From Refs. 43 and 45.)

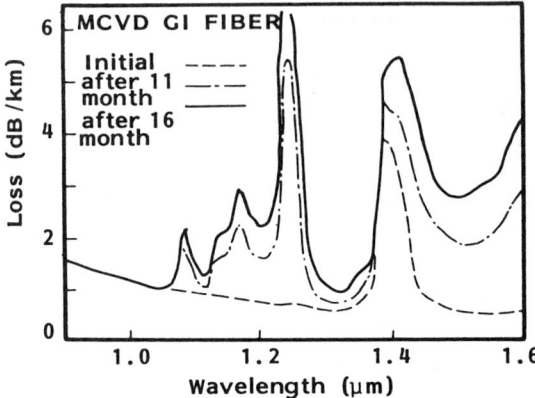

Figure 2.35 Loss increase of fiber in water-filled cable. (From Refs. 43 and 46.)

phenomenon in Japan and England [43, 44]. The loss increases were large in the wavelength regions of 1.0 to 1.6 µm and were 10% to several times the fiber losses (see Fig. 2.33).

The fibers were doped with GeO_2 and P_2O_5 and were covered with silicone and nylon. In such a case, cable engineers would normally perform high-temperature heating and cable water-immersion tests. Plastic-covered GI optical fibers ($GeO_2 \cdot P_2O_5$ doped) were heated for 1 hr at 200°C. The fiber loss increased at 1.2 to 1.6 µm, and the loss-peak value at 1.39 µm also sharply increased (Fig. 2.34) [43, 45]. (The small loss peak at 1.39 µm was noticed from the beginning.)

Optical fiber cables were immersed in water at room temperature, and fiber loss increases were measured. Several months later, the fiber losses increased. However, the loss increase behavior differed from that in the high-temperature tests, and the loss sharply increased near 1.24 µm in a peak form. The loss-peak value at 1.39 µm also increased [43, 47]. Although the loss peak at 1.39 µm existed from the beginning that at 1.24 µm did not exist before the test (Fig. 2.35).

An electric current was applied to the water-filled cable. A loss peak showed in the 1.24 µm band. There was no loss peak in this wavelength region before the test. In this test, the water was electrolyzed, and H_2 and O_2 were generated (Fig. 2.36) [43, 48]. Figure 2.37 shows the results of similar tests made with other samples [43]. Measurement was made up to the long wavelength region of 2.4 µm. The loss-peak values in these tests coincided with the H_2 and Si—OH vibration wavelengths presented in Table 2.10.

Reliability

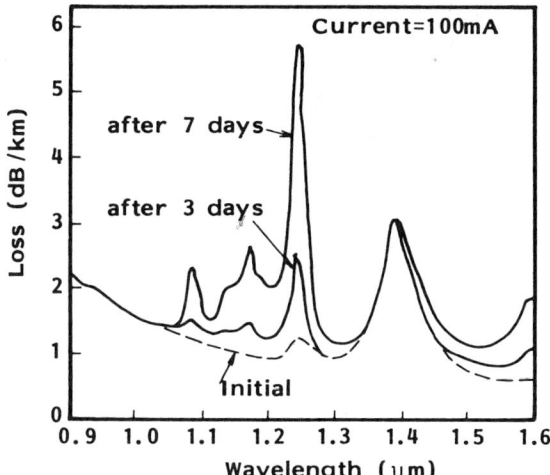

Figure 2.36 Loss increase of the fiber by the flow of electric current in the water-filled cable. (From Refs. 43 and 47.)

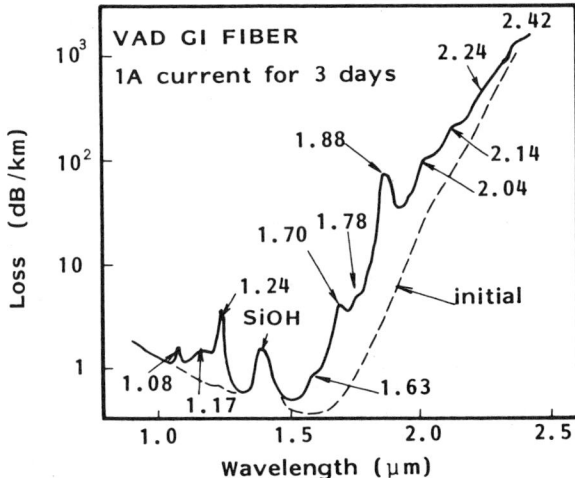

Figure 2.37 Loss spectrum for fiber diffused by H_2 gas. (From Ref. 43.)

Table 2.10 H_2 Fundamental Vibration and Combinational Vibrations with SiO_4 Tetrahedral Vibrations

Wavelength (μm)	Frequency[a]	Increased loss (relative)
~36.4	ν_1	
~21.0	ν_2	
~12.5	ν_3	
~9.1	ν_4	
2.42	ν_H	2220
2.24	$\nu_1 + \nu_H$	830
2.14	$\nu_2 + \nu_H$	800
2.04	$\nu_3 + \nu_H$	440
1.88	$\nu_4 + \nu_H$	410
1.78	$\nu_1 + \nu_4 + \nu_H$	40
1.70	$\nu_2 + \nu_4 + \nu_H$ or $2\nu_3 + \nu_H$	30
1.63	$\nu_3 + \nu_4 + \nu_H$	12
1.59	$2\nu_4 + \nu_H$	6
1.55	P−OH	
1.41	Ge−OH	
1.39	Si−OH	
1.24	$2\nu_H$	22
1.2	$\nu_1 + 2\nu_H$	7
1.17	$\nu_2 + 2\nu_H$	9
1.13	$\nu_3 + 2\nu_H$	5
1.08	$\nu_4 + 2\nu_H$	6

[a] ν_1, ν_2, ν_3, and ν_4 are SiO_4 tetrahedral vibrations.

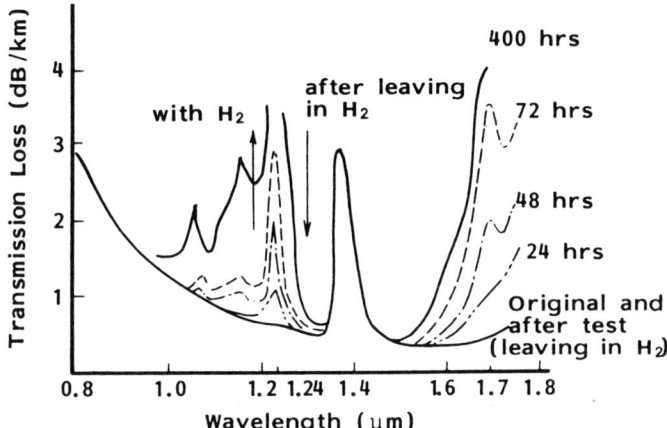

Figure 2.38 Transmission loss of germanium-doped silica fiber after placing in hydrogen atmosphere at 20°C. (From Ref. 48.)

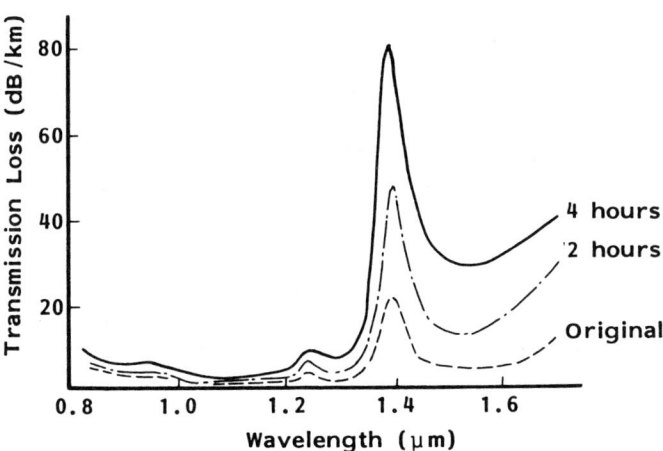

Figure 2.39 Transmission loss of germanium-doped silica fiber after heating in hydrogen atmosphere (1 atm) at 200°C. (From Ref. 48.)

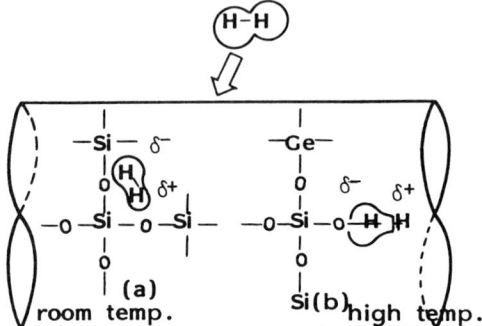

Figure 2.40 (a) Hydrogen molecule trapped in silica network. (b) Hydrogen molecule chemically bonded with silica. (From Ref. 49.)

It may be hypothesized based on these tests that the optical fiber loss increases were mainly caused by H_2.

2.5.2.2 Optical Fiber Loss Increase by Hydrogen

First, $GeO_2 \cdot P_2O_5$-doped GI optical fibers covered with silicone and nylon were placed in a hydrogen atmosphere to increase losses. Optical fiber loss increases at a room temperature of 20°C and in a H_2 (1 atm) atmosphere are shown in Fig. 2.38 [48]. A prominent loss increase peak was generated at 1.24 μm, but the losses did not change at 1.39 μm. (The loss peak at 1.39 μm existed from the beginning. However, this peak value did not change in a H_2 atmosphere or at room temperature.) When the optical fibers were moved from the H_2 atmosphere to the ordinary air atmosphere, the increased loss-peak value at 1.24 μm returned to the previous value. The loss increase at 1.24 μm is reversible at room temperature.

Figure 2.39 shows the optical fiber loss increases in a H_2 atmosphere at high temperature of (200°C) [48]. The principal differences from those at room temperature are as follows.

The loss peak value at 1.39 μm greatly increased. This increased loss did not change even if the optical fibers were moved from the H_2 atmosphere to the ordinary air atmosphere. The loss was not reversible.
The loss increase at 1.24 μm was not large, as expected.

These data can be explained as follows (Fig. 2.40) [49]. The H_2 molecules diffused in the SiO_2 glass network are trapped by the SiO_2 network at room temperature. A dipole moment occurs in the

H_2 molecules owing to a local electric field, and absorption takes place at 1.24 μm owing to the vibration of this H_2. This trapping force is weaker compared with ordinary intermolecular bonding. For this reason, H_2 escapes the SiO_2 network if the H_2 atmosphere is removed. Therefore, the loss increase at 1.24 μm reverses.

However, at a high temperature of 200°C, the H_2 trapped by the SiO_2 network is bonded chemically to the defective part of the SiO_2 network ($GeO_2 \cdot P_2O_5$ doped) by a chemical reaction bonding Si—OH, Ge—OH, and P—OH. The defects of the silica network arise chiefly from three causes: insufficient oxygen, nonbridging oxygen, and excessive oxygen.

Defects due to insufficient oxygen:

```
     O       O
     |       |
   - R - O - R - ( )←  Defect
     |       |         E' center
     O       O
```

This is what is called the E' center, defined by the presence of dangling bond of R (Si, P, Ge, and so on). This defect is more liable to develop when R is Ge than when it is Si because the electron bond energy of Ge is smaller than that of Si.

Defect due to nonbridging oxygen:

```
     O       O
     |       |
   - R - O - R - O - ( )←  Defect
     |       |
     O       O
```

This defect is defined as a dangling bond of nonbridging oxygen.

Defect due to excessive oxygen:

```
     O       O
     |       |
   - R - O - R - (O - O) - R
     |       |
     O       O
```

This defect is caused by oxygen-oxygen bridging. The bridging force is weak and easy to break.

Absorption losses are caused by these vibrations. The loss peak value at 1.39 μm increases. This chemical bonding force is large. The bonding remains even if the H_2 atmosphere is removed, but the absorption loss value does not change.

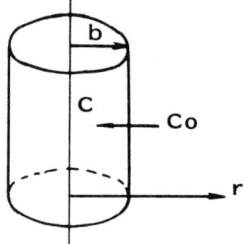

Figure 2.41 Diffusion of material.

2.5.2.3 Hydrogen Diffusion Constant in Silica

If a material diffuses from the outside of a cylinder to the inside, the concentration of this material inside the cylinder can be expressed by the following equation (Fig. 2.41):

$$\frac{C(r,t)}{C_0} = 1 - \sum_{i=1}^{\infty} \frac{2J_0(\lambda_i r/b)}{bJ_1(\lambda_i)} e^{-\lambda_i^2 D(T)t/b^2}$$

where:

$C(r, t)$ = material (hydrogen) concentration
C_0 = initial concentration of material (hydrogen)
J_1 = Bessel function of order 1
λ_i = ith zero of $J_0(\lambda)$
$D(T)$ = diffusion constant of material (hydrogen) at T (°K), cm^2/sec per K
t = time
T = temperature (K)
b = radius of cylinder

The absorption loss increase at 1.24 μm $\Delta\alpha_{1.24}$ caused by hydrogen diffusion can be calculated as follows [50]:

$$\Delta\alpha_{1.24} = 2\pi \int_0^{\infty} c(r,t) e^{-2r^2/w^2} r \, dr$$

Reliability

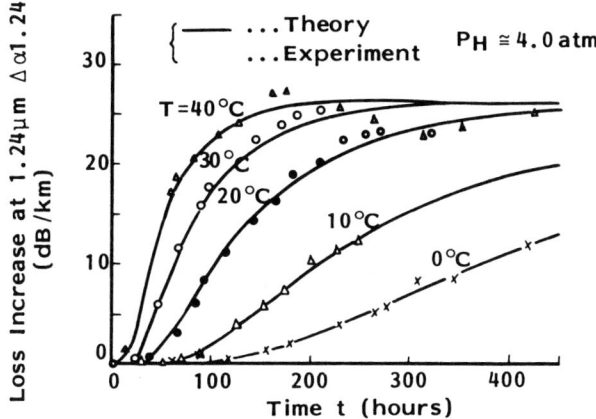

Figure 2.42 Time dependence of loss increase at 1.24 µm under 4.0 atm hydrogen pressure at different temperatures. (From Ref. 50.)

$$\dot{=} \Delta\alpha_0 \left(1 - \sum_{i=1}^{\infty} \frac{2}{bJ_1(\lambda_i)} e^{-\lambda^2 D(T)t/b^2}\right)$$

where:

$\Delta\alpha_0$ = absorption loss in a saturated condition = $C_0 (\pi w^2/2)$
$\dot{=} AP_H = 8P_H$ dB/km per atm.

A = absorption loss at 1 atm hydrogen = 8 dB/km

P_H = partial pressure of hydrogen

w = modal field radius

Figure 2.42 [50] shows the loss increase (at 1.24 µm) of the fiber in H_2 atmosphere (4 atms). From Fig. 2.42, the following equation can be obtained (Fig. 2.43) [50].

$$D(T) = D_0 T e^{-E/RT} \quad cm^2/sec$$

where:

D_0 = constant 2.03×10^{-7}, cm^2/sec

D(T) = diffusion constant of hydrogen in silica, cm^2 K/sec.

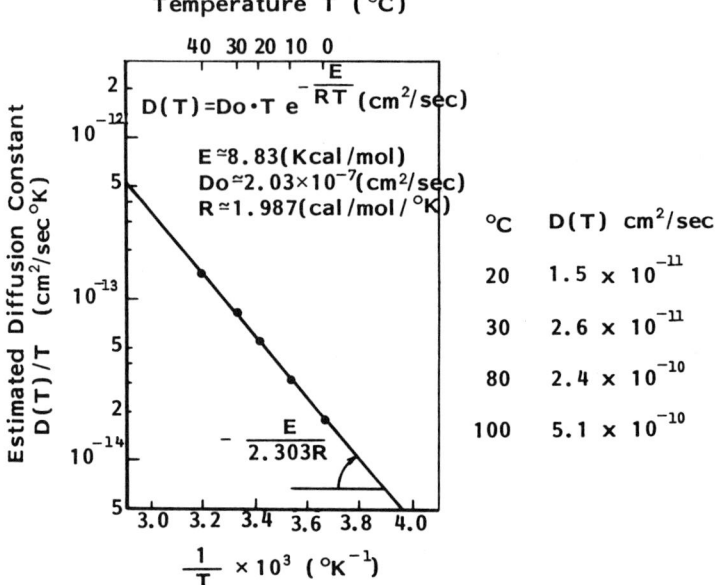

Figure 2.43 Estimated diffusion constant $D(T)/T$ in GeO_2-doped silica-based optical fibers as a function of $1/T$. (From Ref. 50.)

T = temperature, K

E = active energy = 8.83 cal/mol

R = gas constant = 1.987 cal/mol K

Figure 2.44 [50] shows the time for hydrogen to saturate in an optical fiber (125 µm in diameter) using this diffusion constant. The point labeled 100% shows the time in which hydrogen is perfectly saturated ($\Delta\alpha_{1.24}$ = 8 dB/km) and 90 and 80%, the time for $\Delta\alpha_{1.24}$ = 7.2 and 6.4 dB/km. This figure shows that the time to 80-90% saturation at 20°C is about 30 hr, or approximately 13 days. This is a very short time.

2.5.2.4 Countermeasures of Loss Increase
         by Hydrogen Effect

The following four methods are effective in preventing the loss increase by hydrogen.

1. P_2O_5 should not be used as a dopant, or should be minimum in amount if it is used.

Reliability

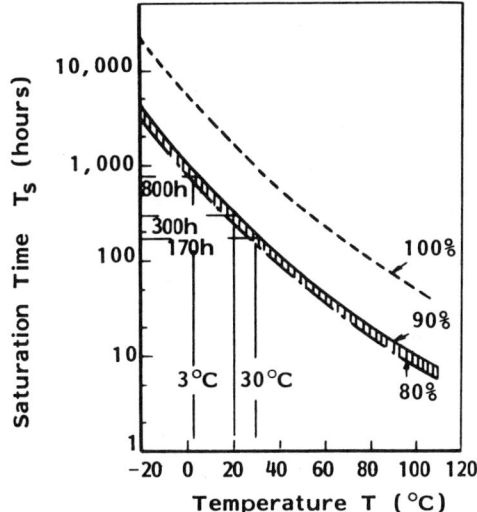

Figure 2.44 Saturation trial T_s of Δ α 1.24 and temperature T. (From Ref. 50.)

2. Fluorine should be used as a dopant.
3. A synthetic cladding layer should be used.
4. Materials to be used in optical fibers and cables should be carefully selected.

Loss Increase by Hydrogen of Optical Fibers Containing P_2O_5 as Dopant [51]

Figure 2.45 shows loss increases by hydrogen of optical fibers containing P_2O_5 as a dopant [51]. As test conditions, plastic-covered optical fibers were placed in an atmosphere of H_2 (1 atm) at 200°C for 4 hr. Figure 2.45 shows that P_2O_5 should not be used at all, or should be less than 0.1 mol% in amount if it is used.

If only pure SiO_2 is deposited as a dopant in the cladding in the MCVD process, instead of depositing $P_2O_5 \cdot SiO_2$, a high deposition temperature is required. Care should be exercised to prevent silica tube deformation by suitably controlling this high temperature.

Only pure SiO_2 can be easily deposited as cladding in the VAD process.

Loss Increase by Hydrogen of Fiber Containing Fluorine as Dopant

Fluorine was found useful for minimizing the hydrogen effect by occupying the dangling bond that would be coupled by hydrogen.

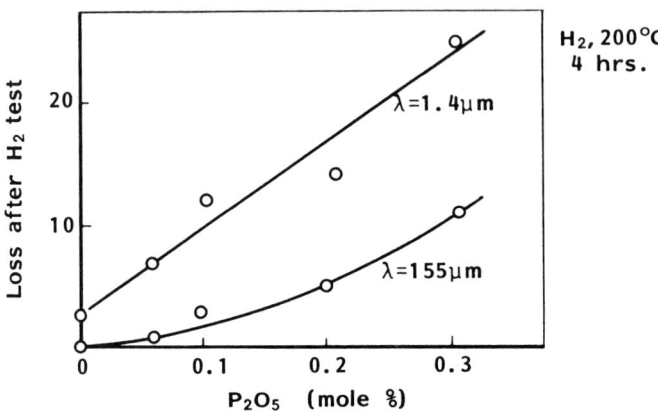

Figure 2.45 Loss increase of silicone-coated MCVD GI fiber; $\Delta = 1\%$. Core $P_2O_5 \cdot GeO_2 \cdot SiO_2$. Cladding: $P_2O_5 \cdot F \cdot SiO_2$. (From Ref. 51.)

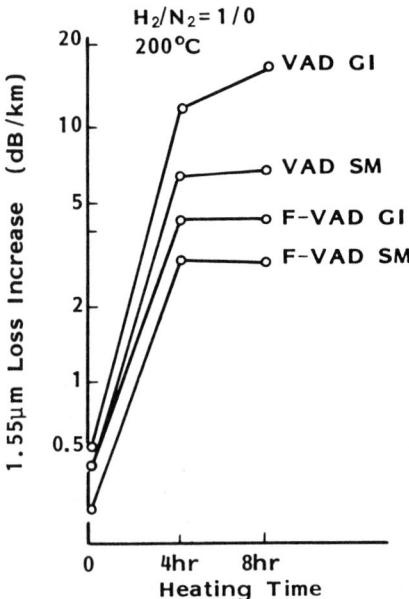

Figure 2.46 Hydrogen effect with F-doped SM fiber. (From Ref. 52.)

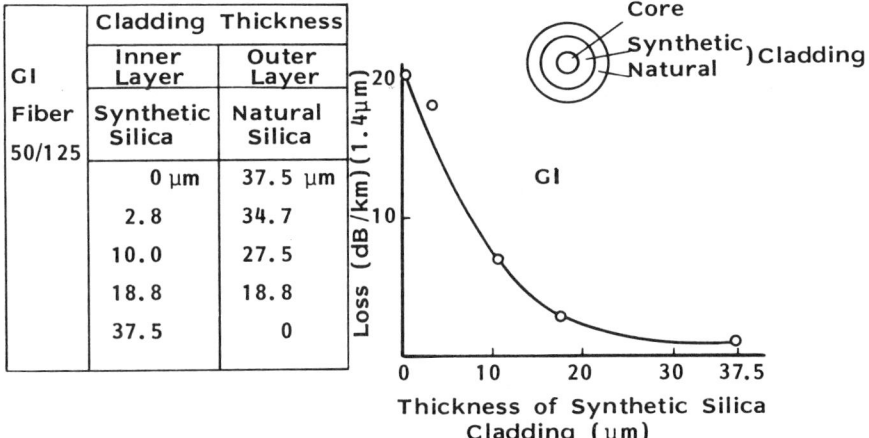

Figure 2.47 Loss increase by hydrogen effect; 1 atm H_2, 200°C, 4 hr. (From Ref. 53.)

Figure 2.46 shows the test results of a loss increase by hydrogen of fiber doped with fluorine [52].

Loss Increase by Hydrogen of Fiber Using Synthetic Silica Tube

Figure 2.47 shows the loss increase by hydrogen of fiber that has a synthetic cladding (inner) and a natural silica tube (outer) [53]. The total cladding thickness is constant, 37.5 µm. There is no difference between the hydrogen diffusion constants of natural and synthetic silica. The hydrogen loss increase was small with the fibers that had a synthetic silica cladding. In the VAD process, the all-synthetic cladding process (no use of a silica tube) is easy to apply.

Plastic Materials Coated on Optical Fibers and Hydrogen Effect

Materials that do not generate hydrogen must be selected as materials that form the cable core. Some of the materials used to cover optical fibers and the amounts of hydrogen generated by such materials are presented in the table on the next page [54]. The test conditions are a H_2 atmosphere, 1 atm, 200°C, and 4 hr.

Covering material		Hydrogen evolution (ml/g)	Loss increase at 1.55 μm (dB/km)
Inner OD, 0.4 mm	Outer OD, 0.9 mm		
Silicone	Nylon	0.5	4.0
Improved silicone	Nylon	0.002	0.1
UV-curable resin	Nylon	0.001	0.05

Generally, UV-curable resins generate less hydrogen than does silicone. Therefore, the recommended covering materials for optical fibers are a UV-curable resin only or a combination of a UV-curable resin and nylon.

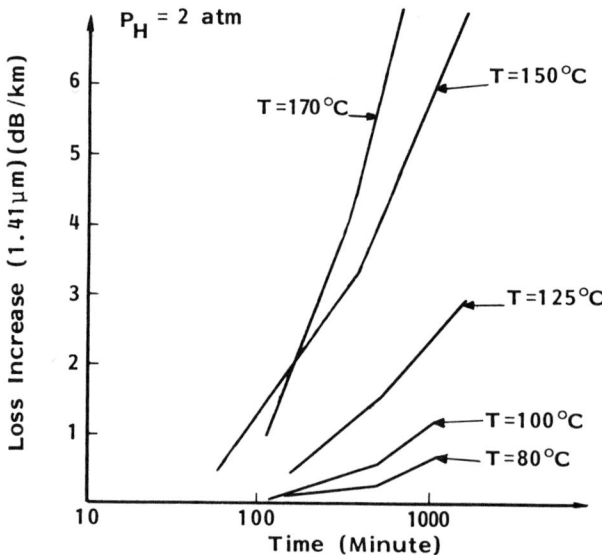

Figure 2.48 Loss increase of GeO_2-doped GI fiber. (From Ref. 49.)

Reliability

The gas maintenance or jelly-filled cable constructions are suitable to prevent the diffusion of hydrogen or water. In this case a jelly material that does not generate hydrogen has to be selected.

2.5.2.5 Long-term Reliability of Plastic–Covered Fiber [49]

Figure 2.48 shows the loss increase at 1.41 μm of a GeO_2-doped fiber in an environment of hydrogen at 4 atm [49]. The loss increase at 1.41 μm can be expressed by the formula

$$L(1.41) = A \log t - B \quad \text{dB/km}$$

where:

$L(1.41)$ = loss increase, dB/km at 1.41 μm

t = time, minutes

The 1.41 μm loss increase is due to OH absorption and is considered to depend on a chemical reaction speed. Based on Fig. 2.48, A and B can be expressed as

$$\log A = -\frac{1.54 \times 10^3}{T} + 4.30$$

$$\log B = -\frac{1.34 \times 10^3}{T} + 4.17$$

At 20°C, H_2(1 atm), and 25 years,

$$L(1.41) = 0.27 \sqrt{P_H}$$

The loss increase L of 1.30 and 1.55 at wavelengths 1.3 and 1.55 μm, respectively, can be expressed as

$$L(1.30) = 0.015 L(1.41) = 0.004 \sqrt{P_H} \quad \text{dB/km}$$

$$L(1.55) = 0.014 L(1.41) = 0.004 \sqrt{P_H} \quad \text{dB/km}$$

These formulas show that the loss increase after 25 years would be 0.004 dB/km at the 1.3 and 1.55 μm wavelengths even in an environment of hydrogen at 1 atm, for example.

2.6 MANUFACTURING OF OPTICAL FIBER

2.6.1 General

Empirically speaking, a transmission system deserves study if the loss of its transmission medium is 20 dB/km or less. An optical fiber can be widely used in practical information transmission if its loss is 5 dB/km or less. As discussed in the previous section, the content of a metal ion in the fiber should be 1 ppb (ppb = 10^{-9}) or less and that of OH ion 10 ppb or less. It is relatively easy to obtain a high-purity material with a metal ion content of about 10^{-6} (= 1 ppm). It is not so easy, however, to make a superhigh-purity material with a metal ion content of about 10^{-9} by ordinary methods. The chemical vapor deposition (CVD) method is a possible means of making such a high-purity material. Developed to meet the demand of the semiconductor industry, it is suitable for the production of high-purity materials. In CVD, a material is made to react in a vapor phase and is then deposited. Since vapor pressure differs from substance to substance, when a liquid material is vaporized at a nearly fixed temperature, impurities in the liquid are left unvaporized and only the desired substance can be vaporized. Therefore, the purity of the material becomes much higher in the vapor phase than in the liquid phase—sufficiently high to make it usable for fiber making. If a material is properly chosen, the vaporizing temperature need not be kept so strictly constant and vaporization can be controlled relatively easily.

As mentioned in the foregoing, a highly pure silica SiO_2 is used as the principal material of the optical fiber. It has a refractive index of about 1458. A material must be mixed into the silica to change this refractive index to a proper level. This is called the "dopant." To be used as a dopant, a material must meet the following requirements.

1. It is of high purity and easily available.
2. It is easy to liquefy.
3. It differs from the transition metal in vapor pressure.
4. It is easy to vitrify with silica and gives a proper refractive index.
5. After being vitrified, its coefficient of thermal expansion is nearly equal to that of SiO_2.
6. When vitrified, it has stable properties.

Figures 2.49 and 2.50 shows some examples of material that can be used as dopants [55, 56]. In practice, GeO_2 and P_2O_5 are used to increase and F to decrease the refractive index of SiO_2.

Table 2.11 shows the relative refractive index difference $\Delta = (n1 - n2)/n_1$ (n_1 and n_2 are the refractive indices of core and cladding, respectively) that could be given to SiO_2 containing a

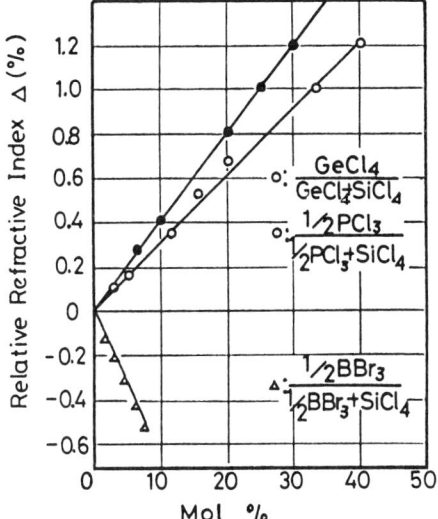

Figure 2.49 Mol% versus relative refractive index for dopant materials. (From Ref. 55.)

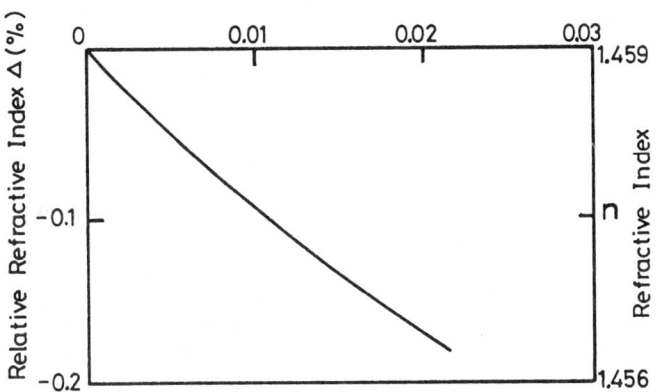

Figure 2.50 Refractive index for SF_6 ($SF_6/SiCl_4$). (From Ref. 56.)

Table 2.11 Δ of Material with Dopant

Material	Approximate maximum value of Δ (%)
$GeO_2 \cdot SiO_2$	3.5
$P_2O_5 \cdot SiO_2$	1.2
$B_2O_3 \cdot SiO_2$	−0.5
$F \cdot SiO_2$	−0.7[a]

[a]MCVD and VAD method; see Secs. 2.6.2 and 2.6.6.

dopant, where Δ is the maximum value actually obtained. Any attempt to obtain a larger value would result in a failure to vitrify the dopant with SiO_2 and would cause cracks in the glass when it is made into fiber, owing to the difference in the coefficient of thermal expansion between the two materials.

The raw starting materials mainly used for optical fibers are $SiCl_4$, $GeCl_4$, $POCl_3$, SF_6, SiF_4, and others. These materials exhibit outstanding optical properties (loss, refractive index, and dispersion) when vitrified and made into fibers. Figure 2.51 compares the vapor pressure of these materials with that of other materials [57]. These materials differ greatly in vapor pressure from the transition element impurities, such as $FeCl_3$ and VCl_4. Such transition element impurities are easy to remove by the CVD method. It is difficult, however, to remove $POCl_3$, CrO_2, and other impurities by the CVD method because their vapor pressure is close to that of the raw starting material for the fiber.

An example of how the purity of materials is improved by the MCVD method is shown in Table 2.12. $SiCl_4$, $GeCl_4$, and $POCl_3$ are used as raw materials in the semiconductor industry and are easily available, with a impurity content of less then 10^{-6}. These materials are liquid at relatively moderate temperatures of less then 50°C. In the presence of O_2, their reaction rate k at a temperature of T°C is as shown in Fig. 2.52 [57]. As is learned from Fig. 2.52, when the temperature is 1300°C (1573°K) or higher, the reaction rate k is 1 or more. The reaction takes place homogeneously, producing fine particles of glass, which are called "soot." According to Fig. 2.52, 99% of the reaction of $SiCl_4 + O_2 \rightarrow SiO_2 + 2Cl_2$ is completed in 0.58 sec at a temperature of 1300°C and in 0.09 sec at 1400°C [57]. This soot is extremely pure and consists of very fine

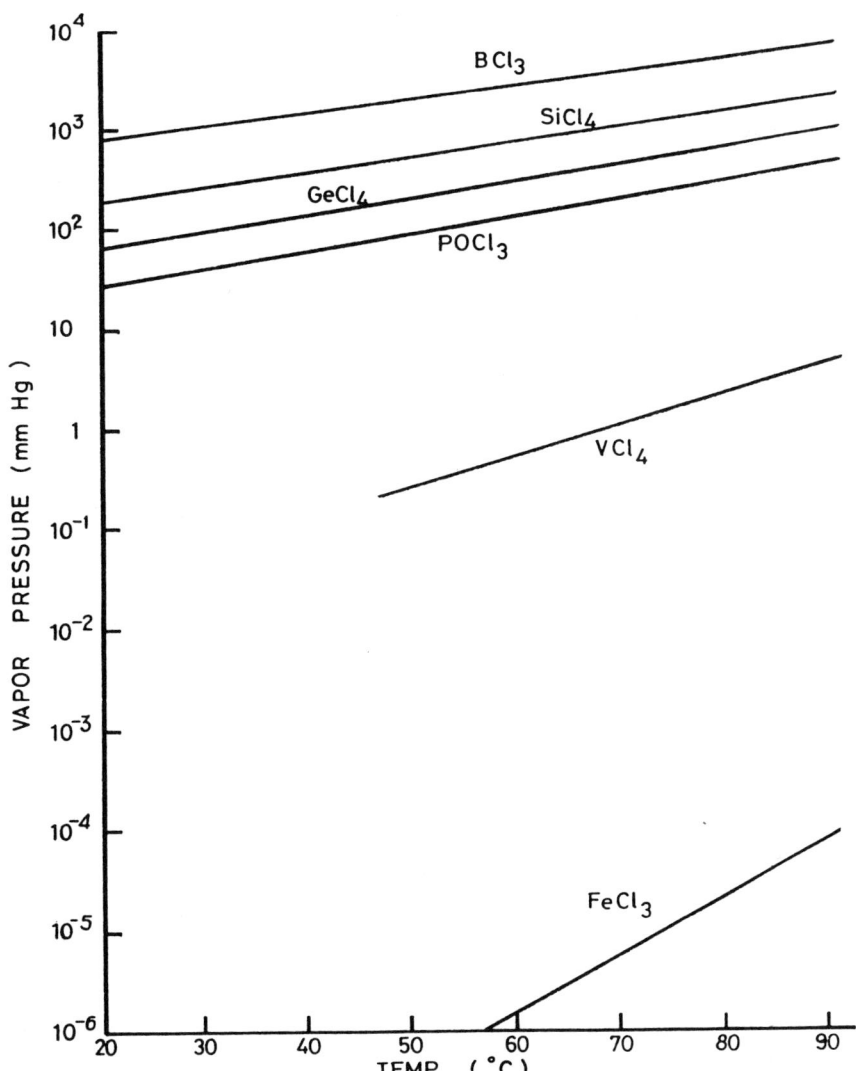

Figure 2.51 Relation of vapor pressures for metal halide additives and potential impurities. (From Ref. 57.)

Table 2.12 Analytic Results of Raw Materials

Material	Impurities (ppb)					
	Cu	Fe	Ni	Cr	Mg	Co
$SiCl_4$ in the ampoule	9	10	4	2	0.5	<0.8
$SiCl_4$ in the bubbler	8	11	4	2	0.5	<0.8
$SiCl_4$ passed through CVD machine	2	<0.8	1	2	<0.2	<0.8

particles. SiO_2, for instance, has a surface area of about 20 m^2/g. Such particles are therefore easily vitrified. After this CVD process, such impurities as Fe and Cu are less than 10^{-9} (ppb). A fiber material is made in this manner using the vapor-phase reaction and is drawn into a fiber.

The methods of optical fiber production are roughly classified as follows.

1. MCVD method (modified CVD)
2. PCVD method (plasma CVD)
3. PMCVD method (plasma-enhanced CVD)
4. OVD method (outside vapor deposition)
5. VAD method (vapor-phase axial deposition)

These methods are for the production of silica fibers. In addition there are the double-crucible method, (for compound glass), drawing-covering method (for silica core and plastic cladding), extruding method (for plastic fiber), sol-gel method, and others.

2.6.2 MCVD Method (Modified CVD) [55, 58-62]

As shown in Fig. 2.53, a gas (e.g., $SiCl_4$, $GeCl_4$, or $POCl_3$) for chemical vapor deposition is made to flow with a carrier gas of O_2 into a rotating silica tube and heated with oxyhydrogen flames applied form outside the tube. An oxidizing reaction takes place in the tube, and glass soots of $GeO_2 \cdot SiO_2$, $P_2O_5 \cdot SiO_2$, and so on deposit and vitrify on the inner wall of the tube. This is,

$$GeCl_4 + O_2 \rightarrow GeO_2 + 2Cl_2$$

$$SiCl_4 + O_2 \rightarrow SiO_2 + 2Cl_2$$

$$4POCl_3 + 3O_2 \rightarrow 2P_2O_5 + 6Cl_2$$

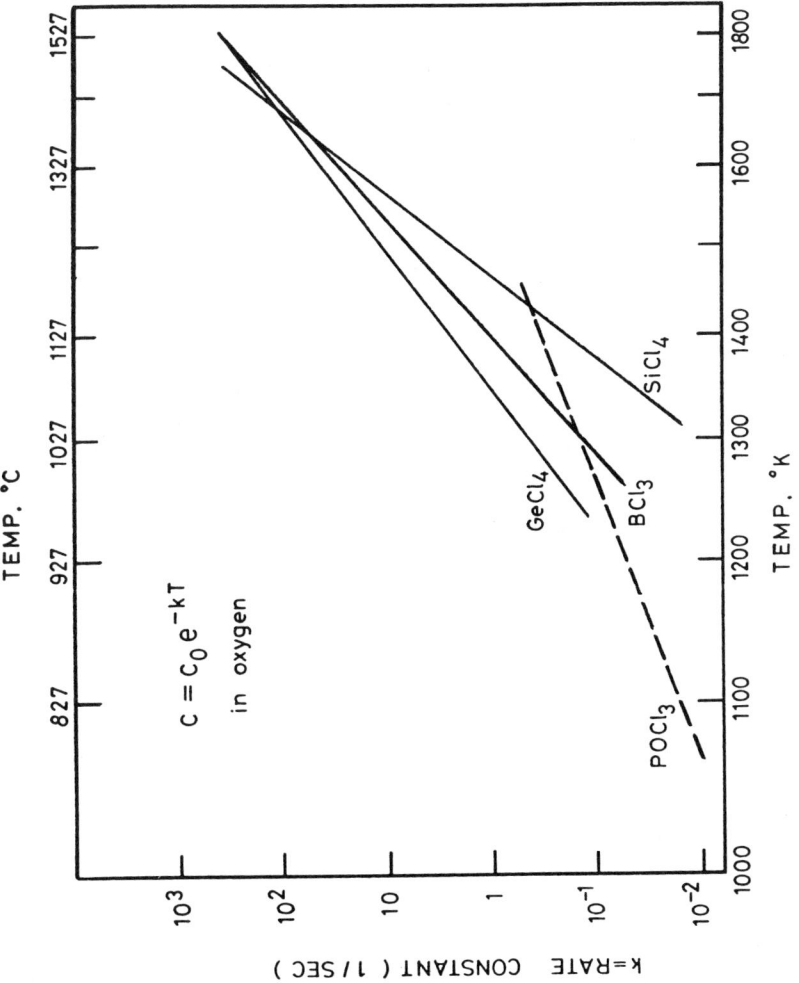

Figure 2.52 Reaction kinetics for selected metal halides in oxygen. (From Ref. 57.)

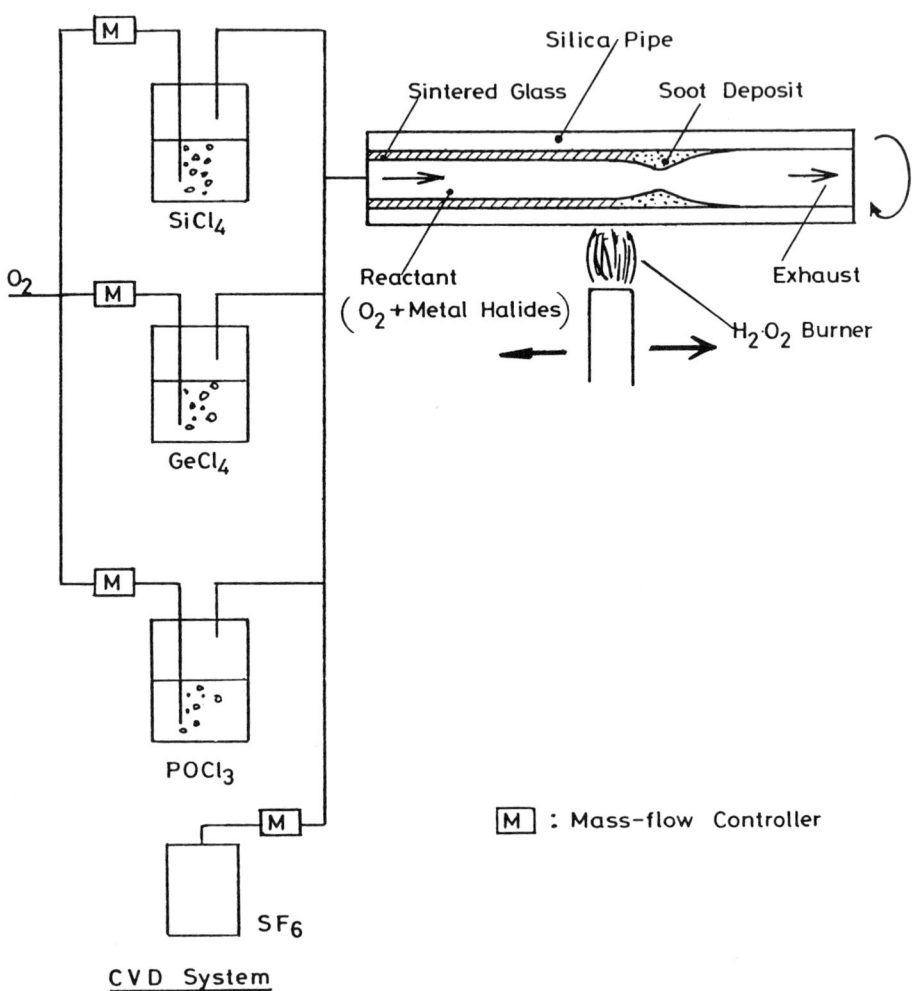

Figure 2.53   MCVD method; M = mass-flow controller. (From Ref. 57.)

Manufacturing

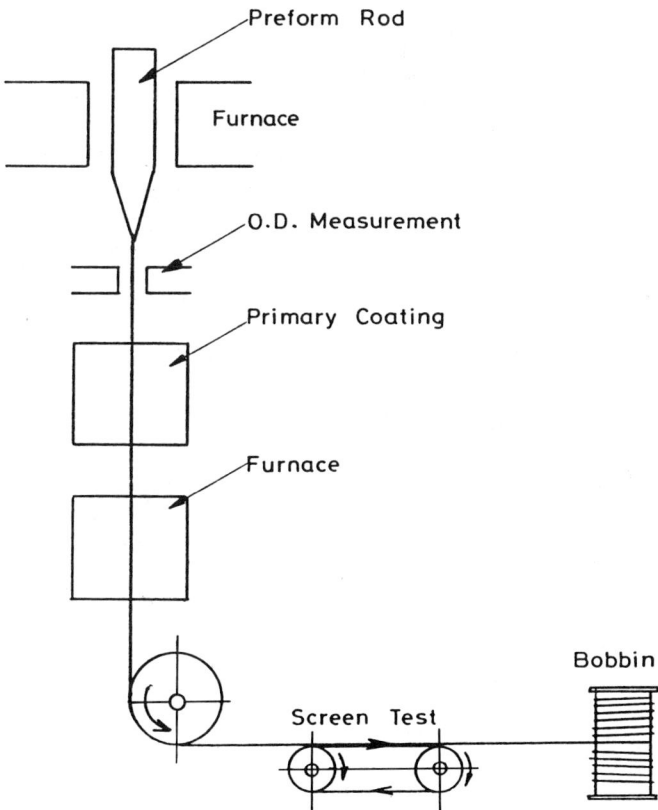

Figure 2.54 Fiber drawing.

This deposited glass becomes a part of the fiber core and cladding. The tube is heated and collapsed into a rod with a round, solid cross section (called a "preform rod"). This preform rod is heated in a furnace and drawn into a fiber (Fig. 2.54). The fiber must be coated with plastic or other material to prevent flaws and cracks from developing on its surface during drawing. Figure 2.55 shows a silica tube and the torch of the MCVD machine during the deposition process.

The following are the merits and disadvantages of the MCVD method. Merits:

1. A closed space is kept throughout fiber production, making it difficult for impurities to enter. A low-loss fiber can therefore be made easily.

Figure 2.55 The silica tube and the torch of the MCVD machine.

2. It is easy to control the refractive index of the fiber.
3. A single-mode fiber is made easily.
4. The equipment used is relatively simple in construction and easy to control.

Disadvantages:

1. The size of the preform rod is limited by the size of the glass lathe and the silica tube. Therefore, the rod cannot be made very large or long. The fiber cannot be made very long, generally 3 to 5 km, with a maximum or 20 to 40 km.
2. A silica tube must be used. It is difficult to prevent the diffusion of OH ion and H_2 from the tube to the fiber core.
3. There is a possibility of depression in the refractive index at the center of the core.
4. Since soot making and vitrification are done by indirect heating from outside the tube, the deposition rate is not as large as expected from the large consumption of heating fuel gas. The deposition rate is about 0.5 to 2 g/min.

Manufacturing

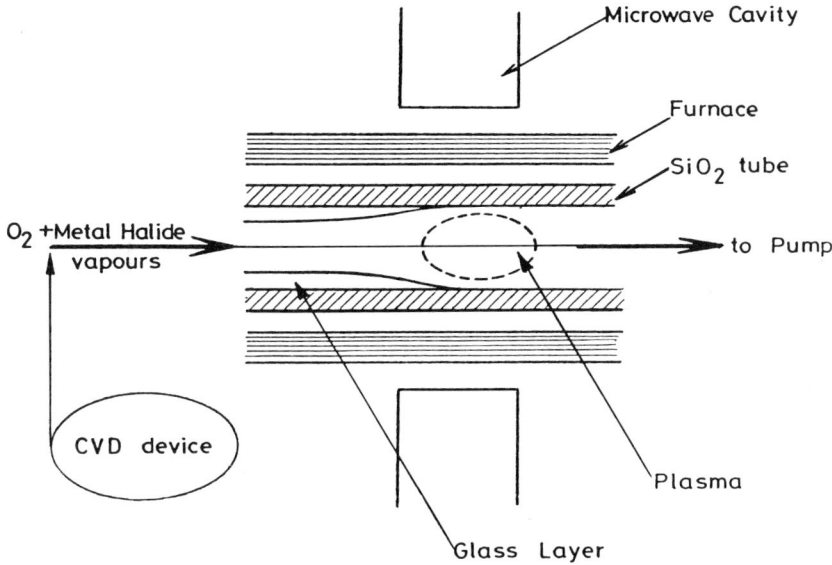

Figure 2.56 PCVD method. (From Refs. 63-65.)

The MCVD method is easily controlled and requires equipment of relatively simple construction. It is therefore in use in many countries.

2.6.3 PCVD Method (Plasma CVD) [63-65]

This is a method developed chiefly by Philips (Netherlands). It is basically the same as the MCVD method except that plasma flames are used in place of oxyhydrogen flames. The heat source by plasma flame is generated in the inner side of the silica tube, and an oxidizing reaction is caused by its heat (Fig. 2.56).

The inner pressure of the SiO_2 tube (not rotated) is reduced to 10-30 torr, and the material gas is introduced to generate a nonisothermal plasma (the electrical source, 200 W; 2.45 GHz) using a cavity oscillator. The inner gas turns into a glass layer deposited on the inner wall of the silica tube. (It does not become soot.) The plasma has a high temperature, and therefore the cavity oscillator moves fast, about 5 m/min. The thickness of the deposition layer is appproximately 1/10 to 1/50 that of the layer made according to the MCVD method. About 2000 layers are required to form a fiber.

Since the plasma has a high temperature, the SiO_2 tube must be preheated to about 1100°C, usually by placing it in a furnace.

The plasma CVD method is characterized by the following merits and disadvantages. Merits:

1. The plasma heat source inside the tube is easily controlled compared with that in other methods. It is therefore easier to control the profile of fiber core.
2. The deposition efficiency is close to 100%. The deposition rate is about 0.5 to 1 g/min with a maximum of 2.5 g/min [65].

Disadvantages:

1. The whole tube must be preheated.
2. The size of the preform rod is limited by the size of the silica tube. The length of the fiber is generally 2 to 5 km, with a maximum of 20 to 40 km.
3. A larger apparatus is required than in other methods.
4. The entire system must be used at an inner pressure of 10 to 30 torr. Maintenance of system is slightly difficult.

2.6.4 PMCVD (Plasma-Enhanced MCVD) [66, 67]

The PMCVD process was developed to increase the deposition rate of fiber material in the MCVD process. Plasma produced inside the silica tube under normal pressure is used as the heat source in the oxidation of the fiber material. A power source (1–10 MHz, 10–20 kW) is used for the plasma. Since the temperature of this plasma is high, it must be kept from contact with the inner wall of the tube. Therefore it is important to produce stable plasma of a suitable size in the center of the tube.

Figure 2.57 is a schematic view of a plasma-making machine. The plasma is generated by an ac coil and cooled with water on both sides. Water cooling keeps the temperature inside the pipe at a suitable level and reduces the temperature of the oxidized gas passing through the pipe to turn it into soot and accumulate it on the inner surface of the pipe. The deposition rate in this process is 6 g/min or over (target, 20 g/min).

The following are the merits of the PMCVD process:

1. High deposition rate and high deposition efficiency.
2. Since a large silica tube (outer diameter, 50 to 60 mm) is used, the fiber can be made in a long continuous length (approximately 50 km).
3. MCVD equipment can be applied.

The disadvantage of the PMCVD process is as follows. Since one layer of deposition is thick, the profile is liable to have an uneven surface. The process is therefore suitable for the production of SM fiber, although it is difficult to use for GI fiber production.

Manufacturing

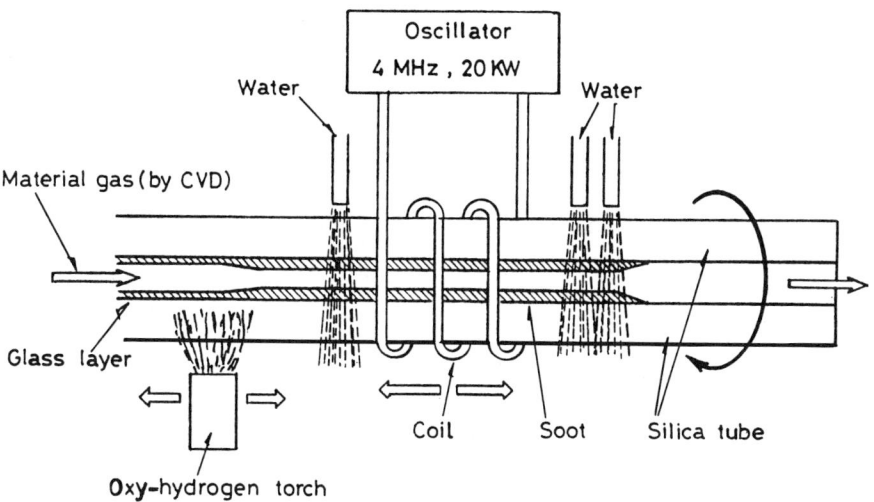

Figure 2.57 PMCVD method. (From Refs. 66 and 67.)

2.6.5 OVD Method (Outside Vapor Deposition) [57]

This is a method developed chiefly by the Corning Glass Works for the production of optical fibers. As shown in Figure 2.58, $SiCl_4$ or $GeCl_4$, for examples and the carrier gas O_2 are made to blow, with a fuel gas H_2, onto a rotating starting rod (generally ceramic) using the same CVD apparatus. A cylindrical layer of soot containing $SiO_2 \cdot GeO_2$, produced by hydrolysis, forms on the starting rod. That is,

$$GeCl_4 + O_2 + 2H_2 \rightarrow GeO_2 + 4HCl$$

$$SiCl_4 + O_2 + 2H_2 \rightarrow SiO_2 + 4HCl$$

The average pore size is about 0.3 μm and the overall porosity is about 75%. The starting rod is then pulled off and dehydrated and vitrified in a heating furnace (1400° to 1600°C) to form a preform rod. The rod is drawn into a fiber. The following are the merits and disadvantages of this method. Merits:

1. There is no limit to the size of preform rod. The fiber can therefore be made in a long continuous length, for example, 50-100 km.

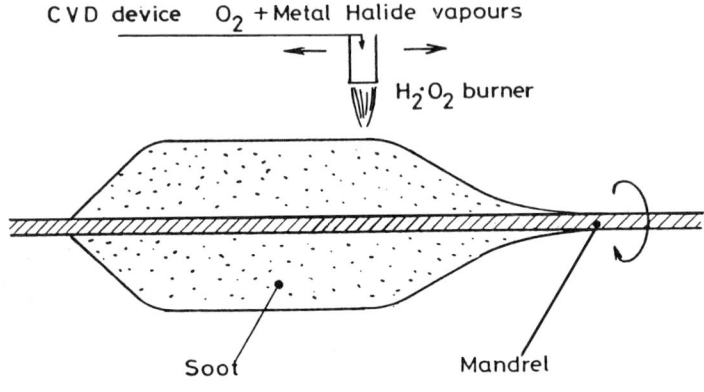

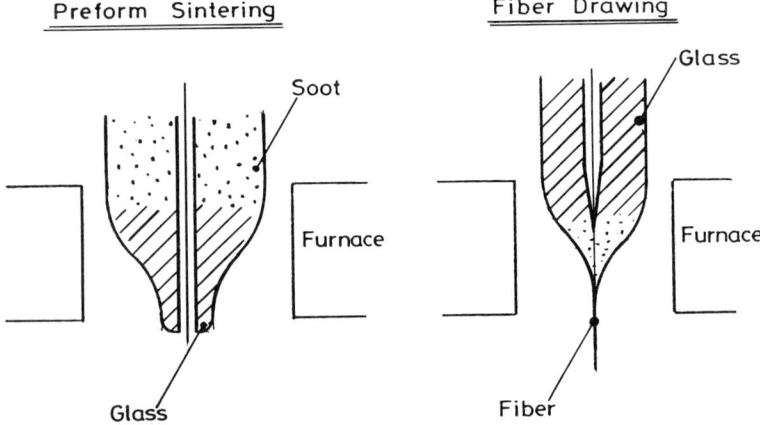

Figure 2.58   OVD method. (From Ref. 57.)

2. The sooting, dehydrating, and sintering processes are separated from each other. Since hydrolysis is effected by direct heating with the fuel gas, the soot material is made fast. The deposition rate is about 5 g/min or over.
3. No substrate tube is required. All synthetic fibers can be manufactured.

Disadvantages:

1. Although in the MCVD method chemical reactions are all effected in a closed space, the OVD method carries out all chemical reactions in an open space, making it easier for impurities to enter.

Manufacturing

To prevent this, a clean space must be made by covering the reaction space or the equipment.
2. Pulling off of the starting material is liable to cause a structural irregularity at the center of the core.
3. When a cylindrical preform rod is made by pulling off the starting material, a tensile stress concentrates on the inner wall of the cylinder, causing damage to the preform rod. Such damage sometimes occurs when the coefficients of thermal expansion of the core and cladding materials differ. For this reason, it is somewhat difficult to make a fiber with a high NA.

Solutions to these problems have recently been approached. For instance, with respect to tensile stress, a fiber with NA = 0.3 can be made by reducing as much as possible the difference in the coefficients of thermal expansion of the core and cladding materials.

2.6.6 VAD Method (Vapor-Phase Axial Deposition) [68-71]

The VAD method is now the only method that permits continuous production of endless silica fiber. It was developed by the Ibaraki Electrical Communication Laboratory, NTT. The VAD apparatus is shown in Figure 2.59. The VAD method proceeds as follows.

1. Materials, such as $SiCl_4$ and $GeCl_4$, are blown with O_2 and H_2 gas onto the lower end of a rotating silica boule. The flame causes hydrolysis.
2. A porous soot rod of $SiO_2 \cdot GeO_2$ is thus made.
3. The soot rod is pulled up while being rotated.
4. The porous soot rod is dehydrated and consolidated in the furnace.

Figure 2.60 shows the deposited soot rod and the torch of the VAD machine.

The refractive index distribution of the preform rod in step 1 is determined by the following conditions

1. Temperature distribution on the lower surface of the preform soot rod.
2. Construction and location of the torches; angles at which flames are blown against the soot-rod
3. Number of torches
4. Change in the rate of flow of $SiCl_4$ and $GeCl_4$
5. Distribution of gas materials in flames
6. Other factors

The following are the merits and disadvantages of the VAD method. Merits:

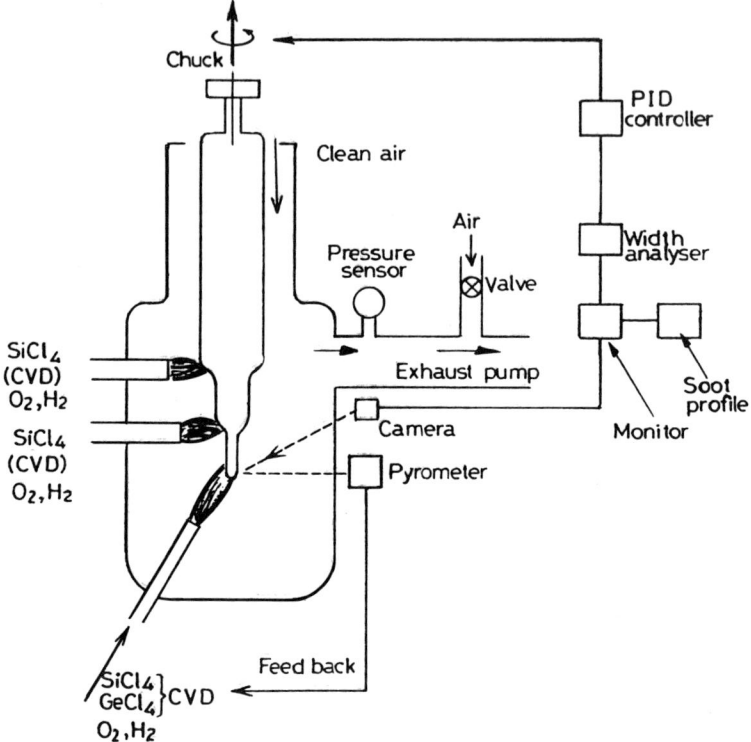

Figure 2.59 VAD machine. (From Refs. 68–71.)

1. The preform rod can be made continuously in an endless length.
2. The torch does not move, and the rate of the gases flowing from it is always constant.
3. The deposition rate is about 1 to 3 g/min, with a maximum of about 6 g/min.
4. A low-loss fiber is easily obtained using the dehydration process.
5. SM fiber is easily manufactured by the VAD process.

Disadvantages:

1. Flame control to make a satisfactory profile is somewhat difficult.
2. It is also more or less difficult to make a fiber with a broad bandwidth.

Manufacturing

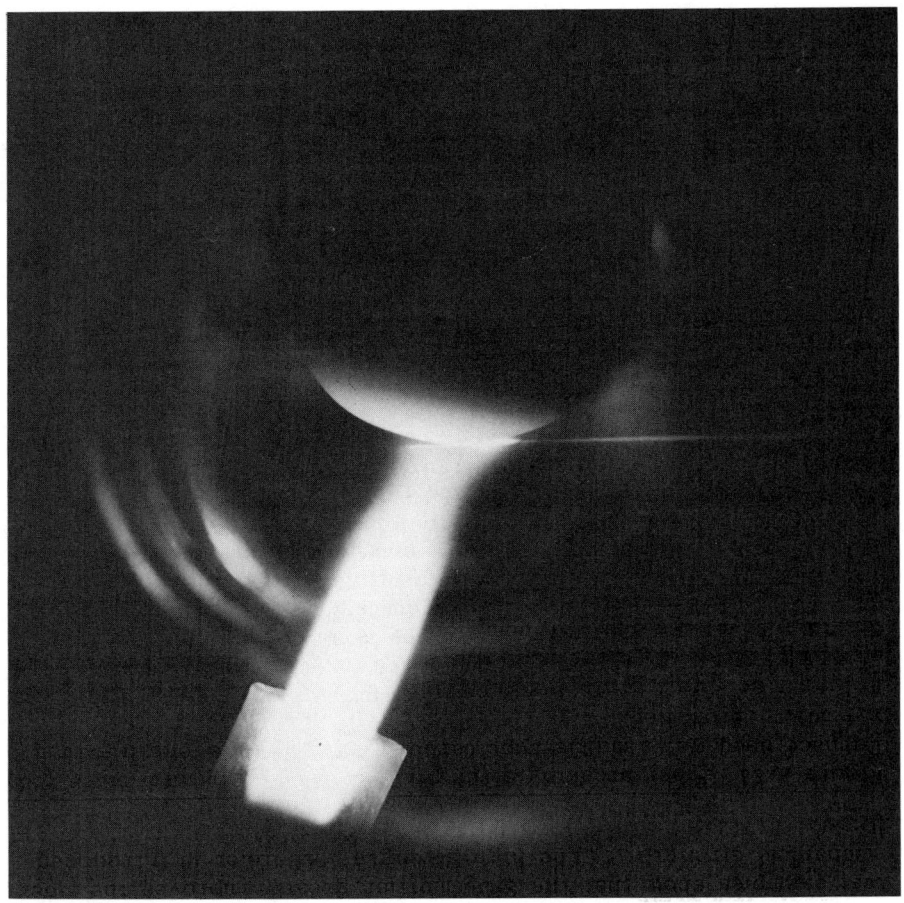

Figure 2.60 Deposited soot rod and torch of the VAD machine.

2.6.7 Fiber Drawing

The fiber diameter must be uniform. The drawn fiber must have a sufficient mechanical strength to withstand practical use. The preform is heated in the furnace and is drawn into the fiber (OD, 125 to 140 µm). Normally, the preform is 10 to 50 mm in diameter and is drawn into the fiber. The melting temperature of silica is approximately 1900°C. Fiber drawing is performed at approximately 2000 to 2100°C. The narrower the high-temperature zone is for melting of the preform, the better.

The fiber outside diameter is measured by a noncontact measuring device of fiber diameter that uses a LED. The measured outside diameter value is fed back to the take-up capstan, and the rotation speed of the take-up capstan is automatically changed to maintain a constant fiber outside diameter.

The surface temperatures of the preform and fiber are high during drawing. Surface cracks and other flaws are easily caused if the surface conditions of the preform or fiber change in this condition, as when dust and moisture adhere to them and foreign matter comes in contact with them. Therefore, a plastic layer should be coated on the fiber surface immediately after drawing. For this reason, the primary coating applicator is located immediately below the heating furnace. A soft plastic resin, such as a soft UV-curable plastic, is used for the primary coating to prevent the microbending loss increase. The outside diameter of the primary coating is 0.25–0.4 mm for a fiber of OD 125 µm.

The furnace used for fiber drawing must have the following characteristics:

1. The atmosphere can be controlled.
2. The furnace does not generate dusts, particles, or other contaminants.
3. The furnace should be able to withstand a high temperature (2200°C).
4. Furnace temperature control is easy.
5. Furnace maintenance is easy.
6. The furnace operates with high reliability, having a long, stable life.

The following are the heating sources for silica preform:

1. Oxyhydrogen torch
2. Electric resistance furnace (graphite)
3. Induction heating furnace (graphite)
4. Zirconia furnace
5. CO_2 laser

The graphite resistance and zirconia furnaces that are ordinarily used at present are described below.

Manufacturing

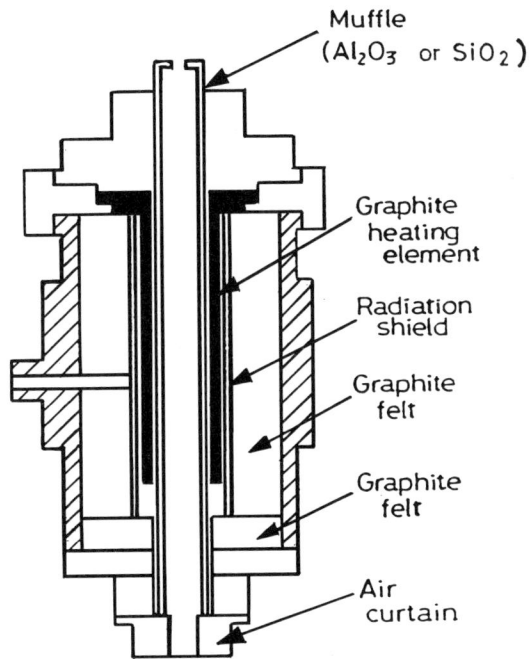

Figure 2.61 Graphite resistance furnace.

Figure 2.61 shows an example of the construction of the graphite furnace. The graphite furnace is heated by dc or ac power at 50 or 60 Hz. High-purity argon-flashed graphite is used for heating elements to prevent dust from begin generated from it. A muffle is additionally provided on the innermost side of the furnace to prevent dust from heating elements from adhering to the preform surface.

Typical dimensions of the graphite furnace are 200 to 300 mm height, 300 to 500 mm outside diameter, 20 to 50 mm inside diameter, and 10 to 25 mm hot zone. The maximum furnace temperature is approximately 2600°C.

For the muffle material, SiO_2 or Al_2O_3, for example is used [72]. Normally, argon is made to flow inside the furnace to prevent the oxidation of graphite [73].

Examples of the effects of the muffle and preform surface treatment are shown below.

Figure 2.62 shows the relation between preform surface treatment and fiber mechanical strength. Under test conditions,

1. The furnace is an ordinary graphite furnace that does not use a muffle.

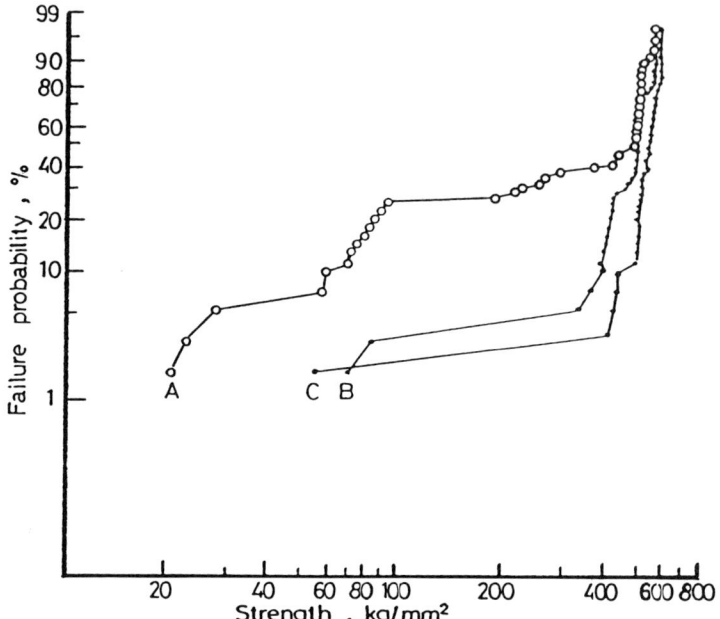

Figure 2.62 Fiber breaking strength (a) 125 μm: A, no treatment; B, flame polishing; C, treatment with hydrofluoric acid and flame polishing. Furnace used was a common carbon furnace (gage length = 10 m; n = 50). (From Ref. 72.)

2. The preform is a natural silica rod.
3. The outside diameter of the fiber after drawing is 125 μm, and the plastic primary coating outside diameter is 0.4 mm.

Figure 2.62 demonstrates that flame polishing after surface etching using fluoric acid is the most effective surface treatment in improving fiber mechanical strength.

Figure 2.63 shows the mechanical strength of the fiber after drawing. Figure 2.64 shows the mechanical strength of wholly synthesized VAD preforms tested under the same conditions. These test examples show that the SiO_2 muffler greatly improves the fiber mechanical strength. (The high-strength VAD fiber is introduced in Sec. 2.7.2.)

Figure 2.63 Fiber breaking strength, 125 μm with natural silica rod. Furnace used was a muffle-type carbon furnace (gage length = 10 m; n = 50). (From Ref. 72.)

Figure 2.64 VAD preform rod, wholly synthesized. Core, $GeO_2 \cdot SiO_2$; cladding, SiO_2. Furnace used was a muffle-typed carbon furnace (gage length = 10 m; n = 300). (From Ref. 72.)

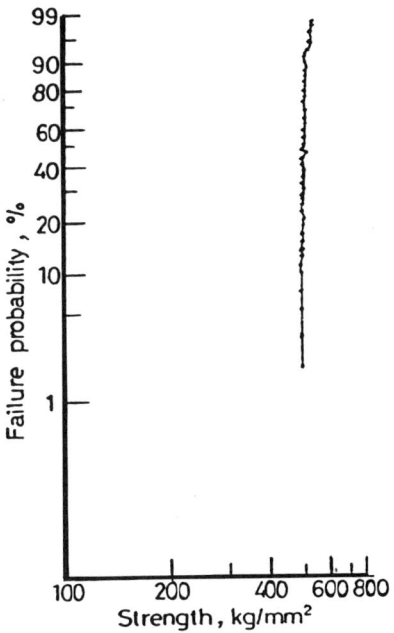

Figure 2.63

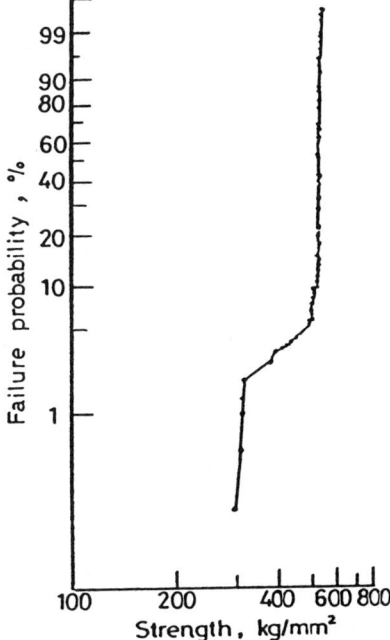

Figure 2.64

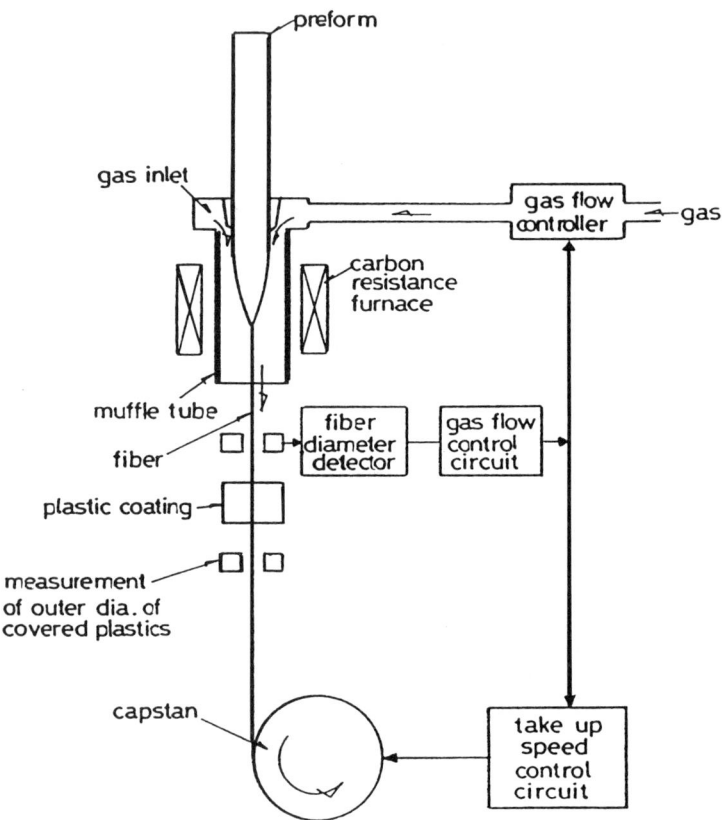

Figure 2.65 Fiber drawing machine using gas flow rate control. (From Ref. 73.)

To avoid the oxidation of graphite in the graphite furnace, the furnace is filled with argon. The outside diameter of the fiber sometimes changes in accordance with the argon flow.

The argon flow rate was changed in accordance with the measured values of the outside diameter of the fiber, as shown in Fig. 2.65 [73]. Fluctuations of the outside diameter of the fiber could easily be maintained at less than 1 μm.

At a normal temperature, zirconia is an insulator. However, at approximately 1500°C, zirconia becomes a conductor. Its oxidation temperature is approximately 2500°C. The zirconia furnace utilizes these physical properties of zirconia. Figure 2.66 shows the construction of a zirconia furnace [74]. Representative zirconia furnace dimensions are 250 mm height and 250 mm outside diameter. The

Manufacturing

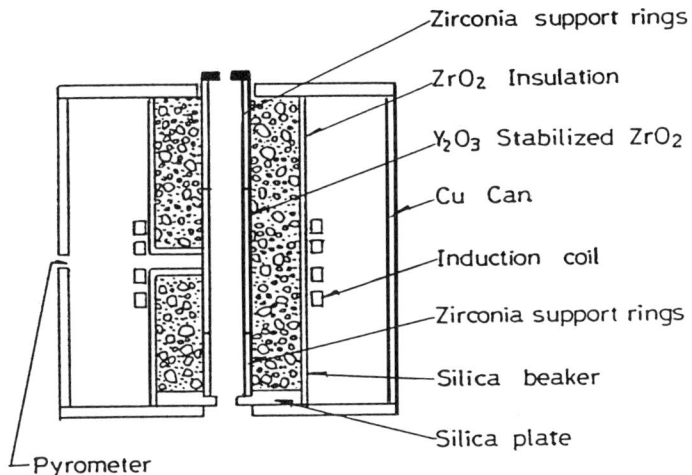

Figure 2.66 ZrO_2 susceptor induction furnace.

outside diameter of the zirconia tube is 45 mm, and the tube wall thickness is 3 mm. A water-cooled RF coil is wound in the middle of the furnace. A graphite plug sealed in the silica tube is inserted into the furnace and is heated by the RF coil. The graphite plug is removed when the zirconia tube temperature reaches higher than 1500°C. The zirconia tube becomes a conductor at 1500°C or higher. The temperature of the tube is increased to 2000 to 2200°C by the RF coil and the fiber is drawn.

Zirconia does not oxidize at temperatures in this range, and the furnace does not have to be filled with argon as in the graphite furnace. Clean air is used in the furnace.

The output power of the RF generator for the coil is approximately 15 to 20 kW.

Figure 2.67 [75] outlines the CO_2 laser beam fiber drawing machine. As shown in Fig. 2.67, a mirror that has its surface tilted toward the CO_2 laser beam is rotated. The laser beam is rotated to irradiate the tip of the preform in a ring shape to provide a sharp thermal gradient and fast thermal response to melt the preform in order to draw the fiber.

The heat is by a CO_2 laser beam and is very clean, offering possibilities of producing fibers with a high mechanical strength. However, the radiation heat loss from the preform tip is large, and this method can be used only with small preforms. The equipment cost may be high, and the equipment itself may be bulky. For these reasons, the CO_2 laser beam drawing machine is used in experimental setups.

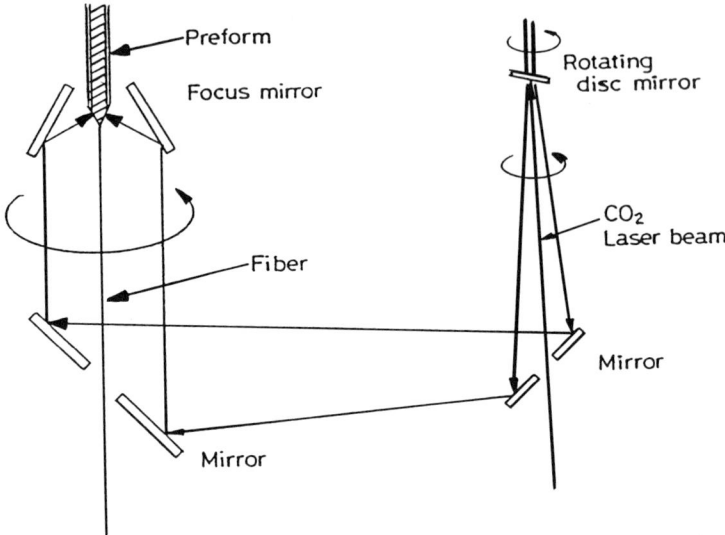

Figure 2.67   A laser drawing method.

The furnaces are roughly compared in Table 2.13.

The preform is heated and drawn in the furnace. Normally, a plastic resin is coated on the fiber immediately after drawing to prevent degradation of the fiber surface (from surface cracks, for example). This plastic coating is generally called a primary coating. The primary coating is 0.25 to 0.4 mm on the outside diameter. A soft plastic material is normally selected as the plastic for primary coating to prevent a microbending loss increase. In many cases, a hard plastic is additionally coated on the soft plastic by the same process.

A thermosetting plastic, such as silicone, was initially used. However, the fiber drawing speed was limited owing to the fiber drawing speed increase, which lowered the coated plastic viscosity, and the coated plastic temperature increase, which changed the coated plastic characteristics and shortened the plastic pot life. Compared with silicone, by using an ultraviolet-curable plastic for coating, the plastic temperature is increased to lower the plastic viscosity. As a result, the fiber drawing speed can be increased.

Many thermosetting plastics generate hydrogen, but some of the UV-curable plastics do not generate hydrogen. Therefore, coating using a UV-curable plastic has recently been generally performed.

The coating material has to be applied on the fiber at a high speed if the fiber drawing speed is high. Bubbles should not be pulled

Table 2.13 Comparison of Furnaces for Fiber Drawing

Furnace	Temperature (°C)	Thermal inertia	Atmosphere	Cleanliness	Maintenance
Graphite resistance	2500	High	Ar	Poor	Good
Graphite resistance with muffler	2200	High	Ar	Good	Good
Zirconia	2200	Middle	Air	Good	Good
CO_2 laser	2400	Low	Air	Very good	Good

into the fiber surface. This is accomplished by the following measures [76].

1. The coating material temperature is increased to lower its viscosity.
2. The coating applicator should be of an enclosed type and should be pressurized.

In pressurized coating, the shear rate of the coating material to the fiber surface should be minimized. In this case, the following equation establishes [76]

$$\frac{\Delta P}{L} = \frac{4\eta V_t}{a^2 - R^2 - 2a^2 \ln a/R}$$

where:

ΔP = pressure

L = effective die length

η = viscosity

V_t = fiber speed

2a, 2R = diameters of fiber and die

The drawing tension (sum of fiber and coating tensions) should be minimized. The fiber tension can be expressed by $\Delta P\ 2\pi rA$. A is a proportional constant and relates to the die profile. Figure 2.68 shows the relation among the drawing speed, drawing tension, and pressure. In the figure, the fiber outside diameter is 125 μm, the coating diameter is 250 μm, and a UV-curable resin is used for the coating material. To reduce ΔP, η is reduced. A drawing tension of 120 g and a pressure of 7 kg/cm^2 can be obtained from Fig. 2.68 at a drawing speed of 1200 m/min. These studies show that fibers can be drawn at a maximum speed of 1200 m/min.

At present, fibers are normally drawn at 100 to 600 m/min, taking into consideration the preform size, coating material viscosity, and fiber cooling.

2.6.8 Comparison of Manufacturing Processes of Fiber

A comparison of the manufacturing processes of fiber is shown in Table 2.14.

Manufacturing

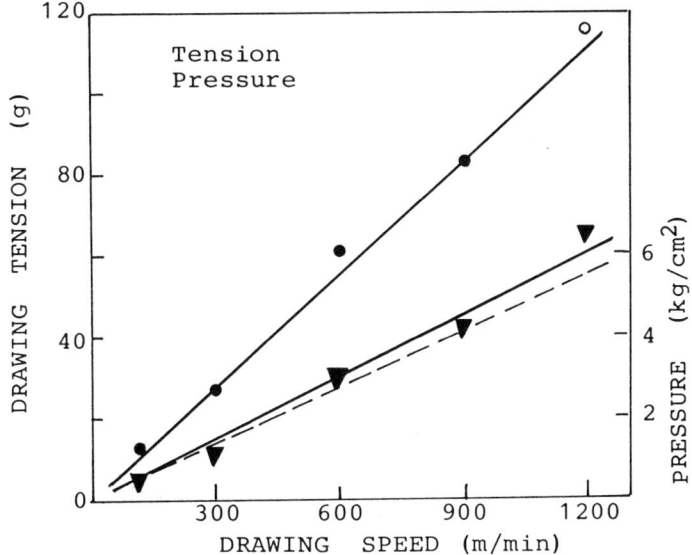

Figure 2.68 Drawing tension and pressure versus drawing speed. The broken line represents the bare fiber tension.

2.6.9 MCVD Process Data

2.6.9.1 Dopant and Refractive Index

The MCVD process is the basis of fiber production. The data necessary for this process are described below.

Figure 2.69 shows the MCVD facility [77].

The relation between the amount of dopant and the refractive index is expressed by the following equation [78].

$$\Delta n = \beta \frac{P_2 FC2/(760 - P_2)}{P_1 FC1/(760 - P_1) + P_2 FC2/(760 - P_2)}$$

where:

β = constant

P_1 = vapor pressure of $SiCl_4$ in raw material container

P_2 = vapor pressure of dopant gas in raw material container

F_{C1} = flow of $SiCl_4$

F_{C2} = flow of dopant gas

Table 2.14 Comparison of MCVD, PMCVD, PCVD, OVD, and VAD processes

	MCVD	PMCVD	PCVD	OVD	VAD
Chemical reaction	Oxidation	Oxidation	Oxidation	Hydrolysis	Hydrolysis
Heat source	Oxyhydrogen torch	Plasma (1 atm) Oxyhydrogen torch	Microplasma (10 torr)	Oxyhydrogen torch	Oxyhydrogen torch
Deposition rate, g/min	0.5–2	3–6	0.5–2.5	5	3–6
Deposition efficiency, %	50–60	70–90	$SiCl_4 \cong 100$ $GeCl_4 \cong 85$	50–70	50–70
Size of preform rod (fiber km)	5–10	20–50	5–10	>50	50–100
Profile control	Very easy	Easy	Very easy	Easy	For SM fiber, easy For GI fiber, required some techniques
Application	AT&T and in many countries	AT&T (under development)	Philips	Corning	Japan

Manufacturing

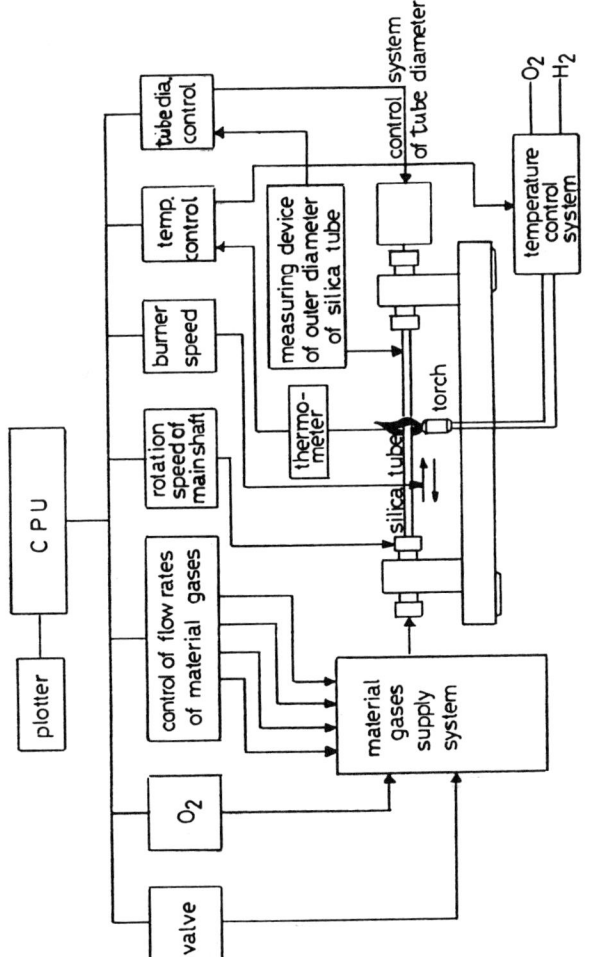

Figure 2.69 CPU-controlled MCVD facility. (From Ref. 77.)

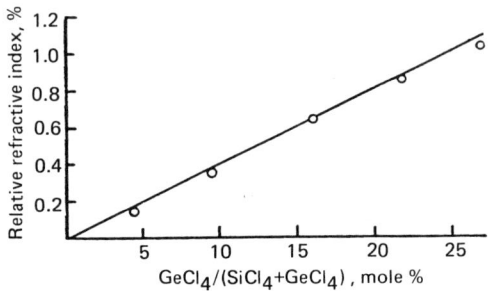

(a)

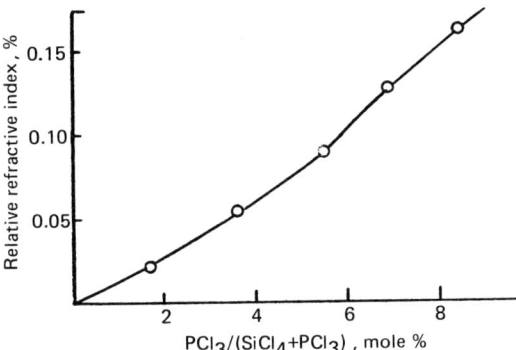

(b)

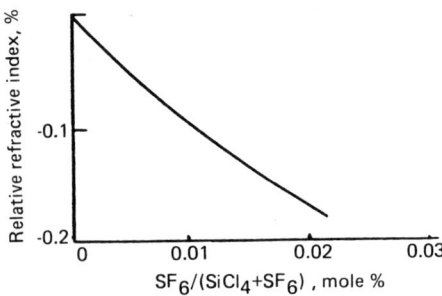

(c)

Figure 2.70 Flow rate of dopant gas versus relative refractive index; (a) $GeCl_4$, (b) PCl_3, (c) SF_6. Data are normalized to a $SiCl_4$ flow rate of 45 cm^3/min. (Parts a and b from Ref. 78 and part c from Ref. 79.)

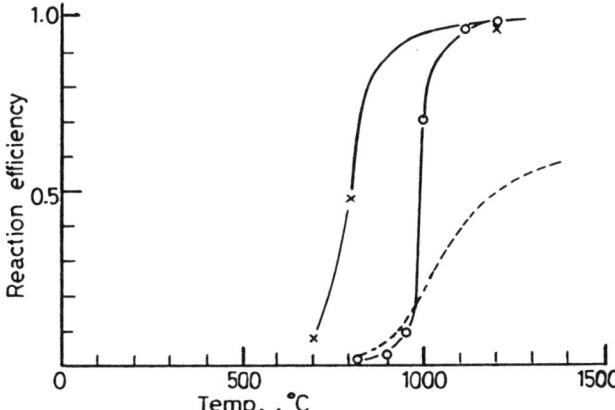

Figure 2.71 Reaction efficiency of raw material gases: ○ $SiCl_4 + O_2 \rightarrow SiO_2 + 2Cl_2$; × $POCl_3 + 3/4 O_2 \rightarrow 1/2 P_2O_5 + 3/2 Cl_2$; – – – $GeCl_4 + O_2 \rightarrow GeO_2 + 2Cl_2$. (From Ref. 80.)

Figure 2.70 [78, 79] shows the relation between the relative refractive index difference and the flow rates of dopant gases. The relation between the reaction efficiency and the temperature is shown in Fig. 2.71 [80]. The temperature of the inner surface of the silica tube (21 mm ID × 24 mm OD) is about 1200°C, when that of its outer surface is 1500°C. From Fig. 2.71, therefore, it is learned that the outer surface temperature of the tube must be in the neighborhood of 1500°C.

Figure 2.72 [77] shows the relation between the deposition temperature of the outer surface of the silica tube and the difference in relative refractive index. This figure indicates that the refractive index difference of the fiber is most stable when its deposition temperature is near 1400°C.

The relation between the profile and the gas flow is derived as follows [77, 78].

$$n(r) = n_1 \left[1 - 2\Delta \frac{r}{a}^\alpha \right]^{1/2}$$

where:

r = distance from the center of the fiber

a = core diameter of the fiber

$\Delta = (n_1 - n_2)/n_1$

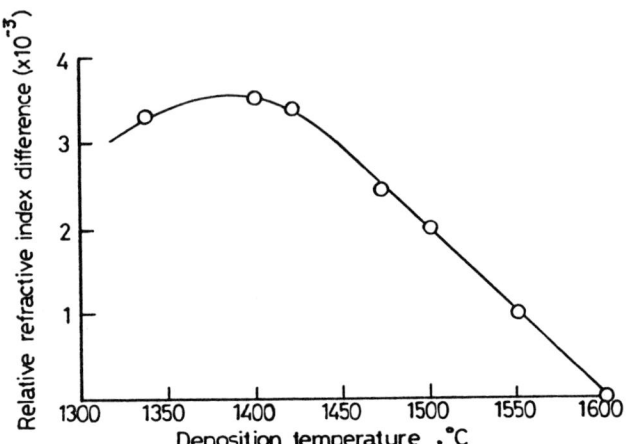

Figure 2.72 Deposition temperature versus relative refractive index difference for fabricated preform rods. Silica tube dimensions, 20 × 17 mm; torch velocity, 150 mm/min; carrier gas flow rates, $SiCl_4$, 75 cm^3/min at 20°C; $GeCl_4$, 220 cm^3/min at 4°C; and $POCl_3$. 22 cm^3/min at 5°C. (From Ref. 77.)

n_1, n_2 = refractive indices of the core and the cladding

α = profile parameter

$n(r)$ = refractive index distribution

When the amount of material deposited during each complete pass of the oxyhydrogen torch is assumed to be uniform, the molar fraction X of the dopant for $n(r)$ is determined by the formula [78].

$$X = X_0 \left[1 - \left(\frac{N - i}{N} \right)^{\alpha/2} \right]$$

where:

X_0 = mol% of the dopant in the center of core

N = total number of deposited layers

i = number of the deposited layer at radius r (outermost layer taken as the first layer, i = 1)

The mol% of the dopant is proportional to the flow rate of carrier gas,

Manufacturing

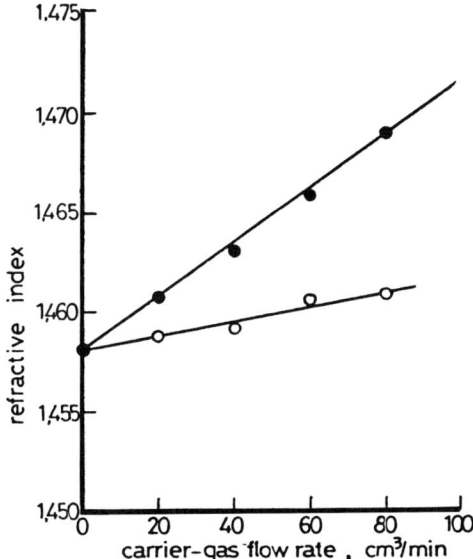

Figure 2.73 GeCl$_4$ carrier gas flow rate versus refractive index. SiCl$_4$ flow rate, 40 cm^3/min at 10°C; ○ GeCl$_4$ at -10°C; ● GeCl$_4$ at 0°C. (From Ref. 77.)

$$G = G_0 \left[1 - \left(\frac{N - i}{N} \right)^{\alpha/2} \right]$$

where:

G = carrier gas flow rate

G_0 = carrier gas flow rate in the center of the core

Figure 2.73 [77] shows the relation between the refractive index and the carrier gas (GeCl$_4$) flow rate. Figure 2.74 [77] shows the relation between the carrier gas (GeCl$_4$) flow rate α and deposition number.

The refractive index is changed by changing the quantity of GeCl$_4$ carrier gas. In that case, the total quantity of gas flowing in the silica tube naturally changes, and this in turn changes the deposition condition of the glass material. It is therefore possible that the fiber profile deviates from the value determined theoretically.

An improved process is now used in which an additional quantity of Ar gas corresponding to the change in the quantity of GeCl$_4$

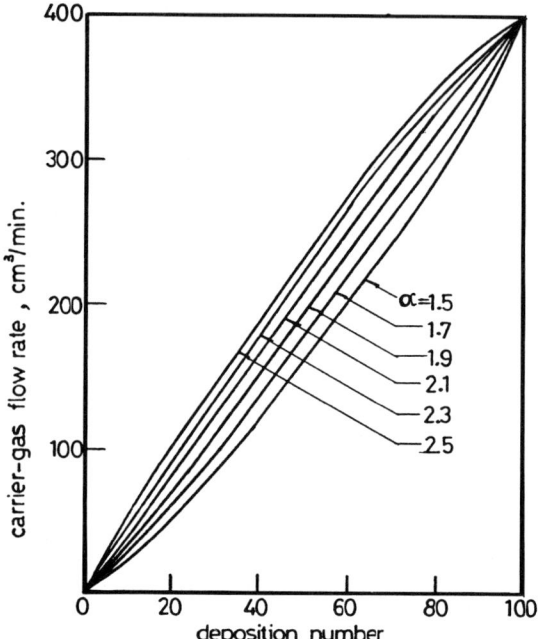

Figure 2.74 Deposition number versus carrier gas flow rate. $GeCl_4$ flow rate, 0–400 cm^3/min. (From Ref. 77.)

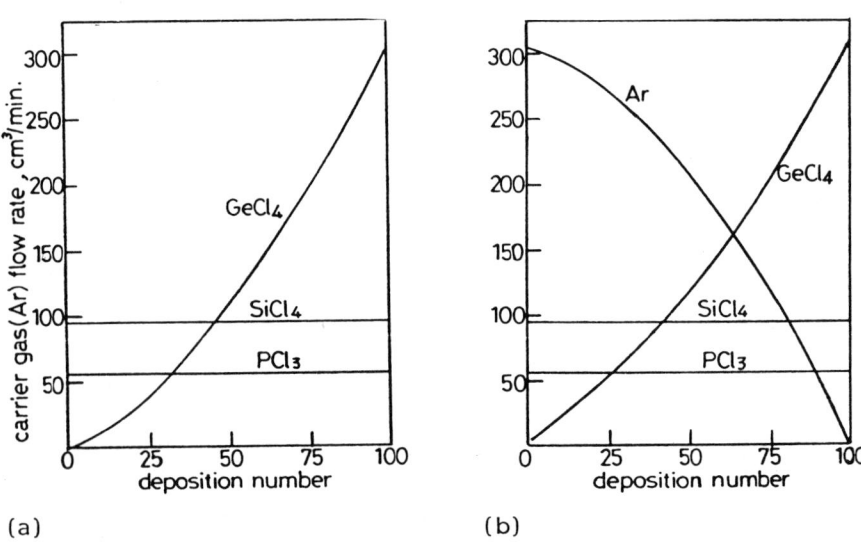

Figure 2.75 Deposition number versus carrier gas flow rate. (a) conventional; (b) improved. (From Ref. 81.)

Manufacturing

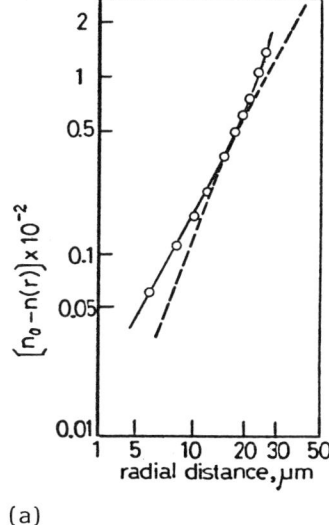
(a)

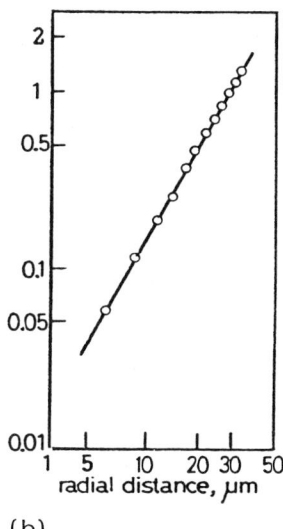
(b)

Figure 2.76 Refractive index distribution in the core: (a) conventional, $\alpha = 1.95$, $\Delta = 0.93\%$; (b) improved, $\alpha = 1.93$, $\Delta = 0.97\%$. (From Ref. 82.)

carrier gas is made to flow through the furnace to keep the total flow constant.

Figure 2.75a shows the conventional gas flow rate and Fig. 2.75b the gas flow rate in the improved method with additional Ar gas flow [81]. The profile of a fiber made with this gas flow rate is shown in Fig. 2.76 [82]. In Fig. 2.76a for a fiber made by the conventional method, the profile is in two straight lines, deviating from its theoretical value. By contrast, the profile of the fiber made by the improved method is very close to its theoretical value.

2.6.9.2 Dimension of the Tube

In the deposition process, the silica tube is heated to about 1500°C over a long time. Therefore the tube is sometimes deformed. Such deformation can be prevented by giving a slight inside pressure to the tube [82].

The force of contraction P_s caused by the surface tension is expressed as

$$P_s = 2\gamma \left(\frac{1}{a} + \frac{1}{b} \right)$$

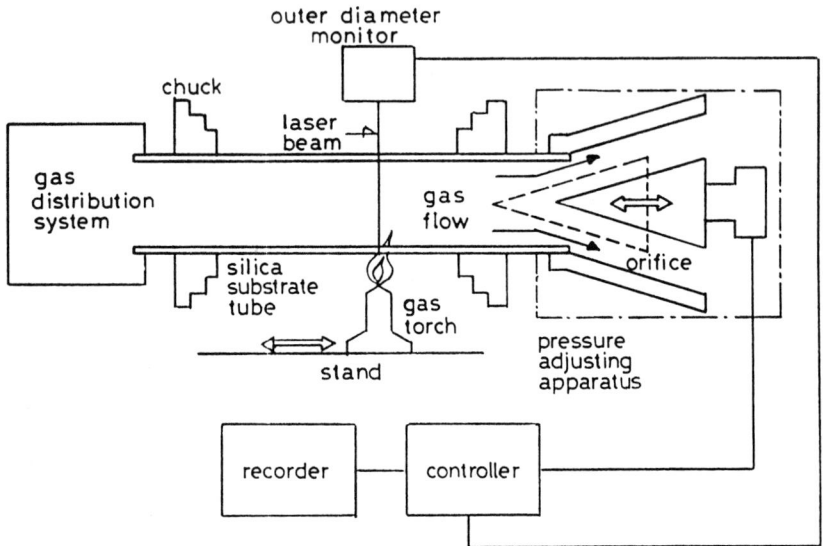

Figure 2.77 Schematic diagram of the improved CVD system with control of the internal pressure of the substrate tube. (From Ref. 82.)

where:

    γ = surface tension of silica $\doteqdot$ 300 dyn/cm (at 1600°C)

    a = inner diameter of tube (cm)

    b = outer diameter of tube (cm)

When a = 2.1 cm and b = 2.5 cm, P_s is 510 dyn/cm² = 5 mm H_2O.

Figure 2.77 [82] shows an apparatus that is used to control the internal pressure of the tube. The outer diameter of the tube is measured by laser beam, and the internal pressure is controlled according to the measured value. The result is shown in Figs 2.78 and 2.79 [82]. When the internal pressure is controlled, the variation of the outer diameter of the tube is ±0.05 mm or less and its ellipticity 0.5% or less.

Eccentricity of the fiber is caused mainly by a change in the wall thickness of the silica tube used. The eccentricity d' of a preform rod is expressed by the following equation [78].

$$\Delta d' = \sqrt{R_1^2 - R_3^2} - \sqrt{(R_1 - \Delta d)^2 - R_3^2}$$

Manufacturing

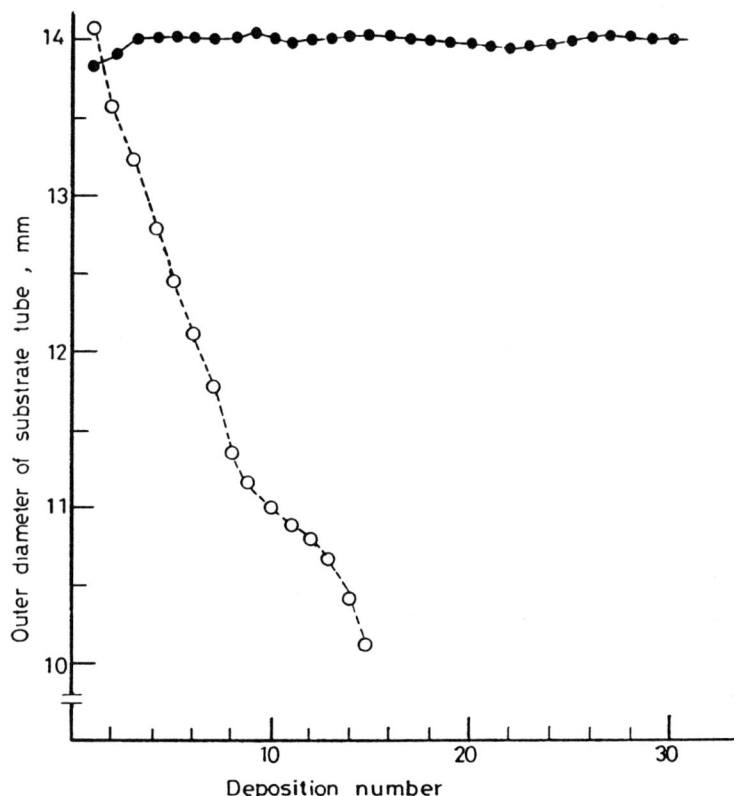

Figure 2.78 Examples of the outer diameter variation of the silica tube during deposition. Silica tube dimensions, 14 × 11 mm; temperature, 1600 ± 5°C; deposition material, $SiCl_4$; ● with control; ○ without control. (From Ref. 82.)

where:

Δd = eccentricity of inner diameter of silica tube

R_1 = outer diameter of silica tube

R_3 = inner diameter of the silica tube after deposition of the glass layers

When R_1 = 25 mm and R_3 = 21 mm, $\Delta d'$ is as in Figure 2.80.

If a fiber core is required to have an eccentricity of no more than 1 μm, Δd must be 0.07 mm or less.

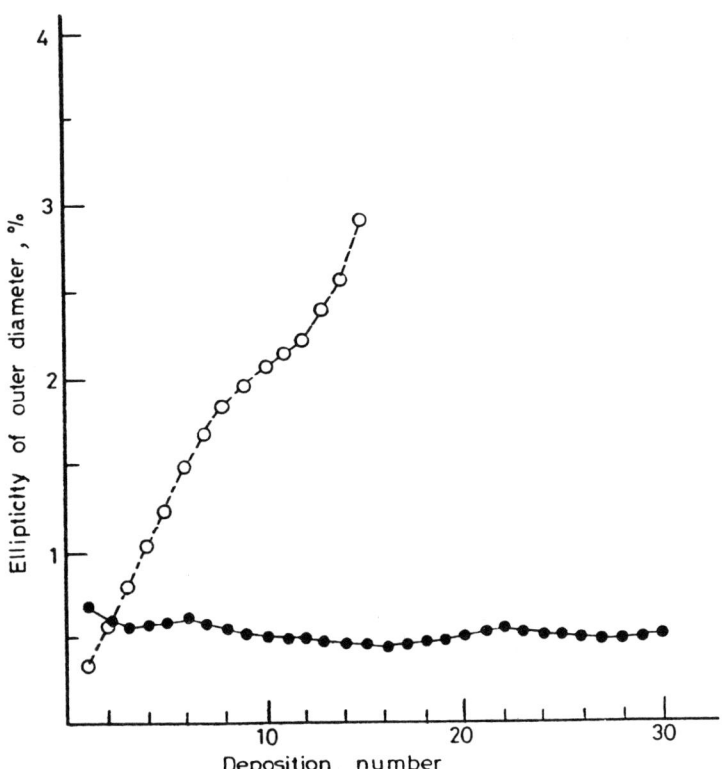

Figure 2.79 Examples of the ellipticity variation of the outer diameter of substrate tubes. Silica tube dimensions, 14 × 11 mm; temperature, 1600 ± 5°C; deposition material, $SiCl_4$; ● with control; ○ without control. (From Ref. 82.)

2.6.9.3 Diffusion of OH^- Ion

The natural silica tube used in MCVD contains about 100 to 200 ppm OH^- ion. The synthetic silica tube contains about 1 ppm OH^- ion.

In the deposition and collapsing processes, the silica tube is heated at about 1500°C for a long time (normally 4 to 8 hr). This possibly causes OH ions in the tube to diffuse into the deposition layer.

Let us consider an example in which C_0 diffuses from an object A to another object B. The material concentration in B after a lapse of t seconds is expressed by the following equation.

Manufacturing

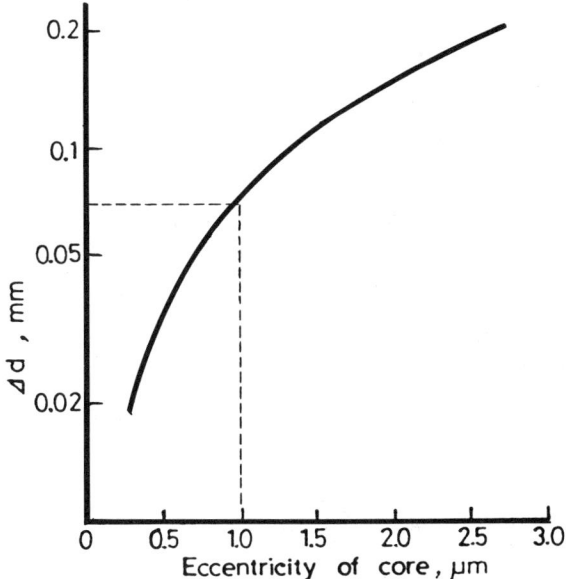

Figure 2.80 Eccentricity of fiber core and thickness deviation of silica tube.

$$C(x) = \frac{1}{2} C_0 \text{ erf } \frac{x}{\sqrt{4Dt}} = \frac{1}{2} C_0 \text{ erf } \frac{x}{L}$$

where:

C_0 = material concentration at $x = 0$, $t = 0$
$C(x)$ = material concentration at length = x
D = diffusion constant
$L = \sqrt{4Dt}$ defined as diffusion length

The OH ion concentration in the fiber after collapsing by the MCVD method is [83].

$$\frac{C(r)}{C_0} = \frac{1}{2}\left(1 - \text{erf } \frac{r_0^2 - r^2}{2R_0\sqrt{4Dt}}\right)$$

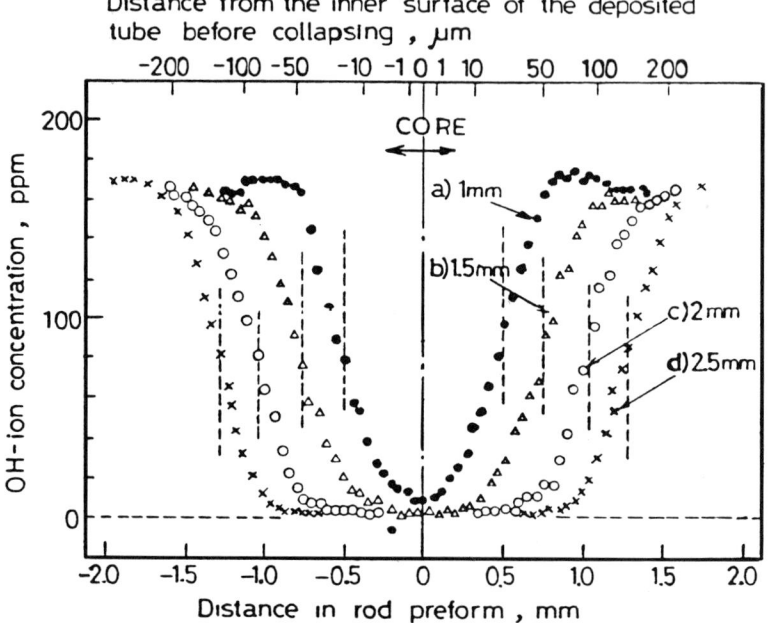

Figure 2.81 OH ion distribution for various diameters of deposited silica. (From Ref. 83.)

where:

C_0 = OH ion concentration of the silica tube

$C(x)$ = OH ion concentration at radius r after collapse

R_0 = deposited radius before collapse

r_0 = deposited radius after collapse

r = location in the radial direction after collapse

D = diffusion constant (cm^2/sec)

t = diffusion time (sec)

L = diffusion length (cm)

SiO_2 is deposited on the inner surface of a 14 × 17 mm natural silica tube by the MCVD method, and the tube is collapsed. The tube is heated to 1600°C and collapsed at 1800 to 1900°C. Figure 2.81 shows the OH ion distribution in preform rods differing in the thickness

Manufacturing 127

of deposited silica glass [84]. The diameters of silica glass deposited on preform rods are (a) 1 mm, (b) 1.5 mm, (c) 2 mm, and (d) 2.5 mm.

Figure 2.82 shows the diffusion constant of OH ion in silica glass [83].

2.6.10 VAD Process Data

Among VAD optical fibers, the recent advances of single-mode optical fibers are particularly prominent.

2.6.10.1 Profile Control

The profile by the VAD process is mainly determined by the surface temperature of the soot preform rod. Figure 2.83 [85] shows the relation between the GeO_2 content in the $SiO_2 \cdot G_2O_2$ soot particle and the surface temperature of the soot rod. At a surface temperature of 500°C or more, $GeO_2 \cdot SiO_2$ is noncrystalline and the GeO_2 concentration increases linearly until about 700°C. At even higher temperatures, GeO_2 evaporates and becomes nonexistent in the SiO_2 glass network.

Figure 2.84 [86] shows the relation between the GeO_2 concentration and the surface temperature of the soot preform.

Figure 2.85 [85] shows the profile obtained when the porous soot preform rod was made by changing the H_2 flow and, therefore, the flame temperature of the oxyhydrogen torch.

Figure 2.86 [87] shows the relation between the highest temperature at the bottom surface of the soot preform and the value of α.

Figure 2.87 shows the flow ratio and profile.

$$\text{Flow ratio } R = \frac{SiCl_4 \text{ flow from nozzle II}}{SiCl_4 \cdot GeCl_4 \cdot POCl_3 \text{ from nozzle I}}$$

Using these data, a GI fiber with a wide bandwidth of 4 GHz · km (at 1.3 μm) was experimentally manufactured [88].

2.6.10.2 Manufacture of Single-mode Optical Fiber by VAD

Manufacture of Core

The core diameter of the single-mode optical fiber is small. The VAD soot preform rod diameter is ordinarily 50–200 mm. Compared with this, the required SM core soot diameter is approximately 5 to 15 mm.

Figure 2.60 demonstrates one way of fabricating VAD preform rods. Of the three torches used, the lowest torch is used for the

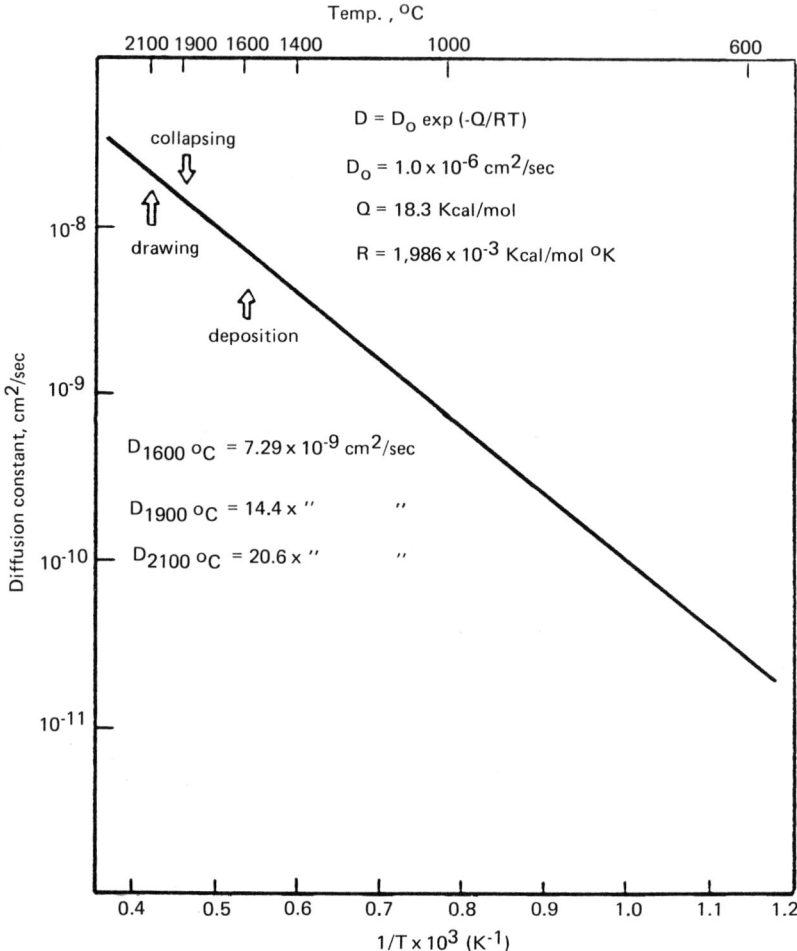

Figure 2.82 Hydroxyl ion diffusion constants in silica glass. (From Ref. 84.)

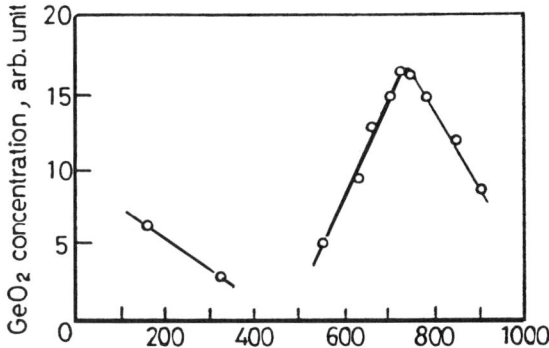

Figure 2.83 Surface temperature of soot rod and GeO_2 concentration. (From Ref. 85.)

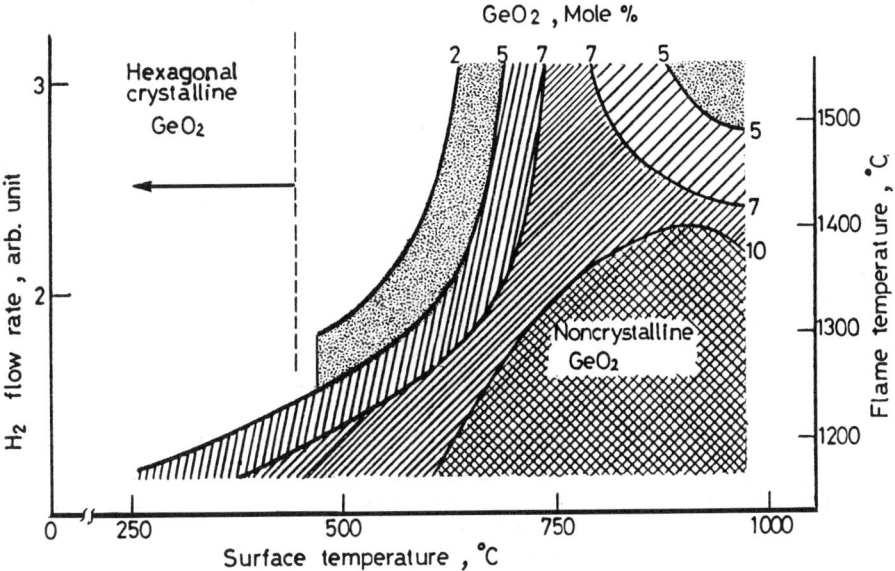

Figure 2.84 Surface temperature dependence of GeO_2 concentration in SiO_2 for porous soot preforms. (From Ref. 86.)

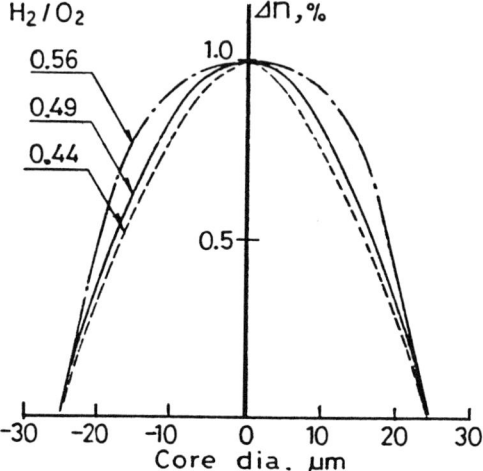

Figure 2.85 Relation between flame composition and refractive index profile. (From Ref. 85.)

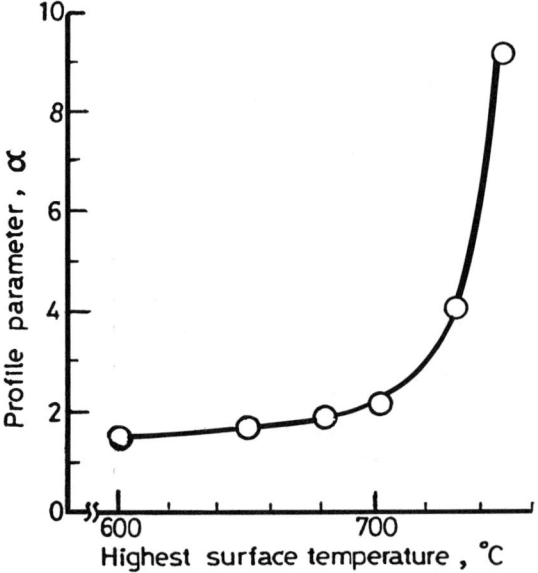

Figure 2.86 Relation between α and the highest surface temperature at the soot preform. (From Ref. 87.)

Manufacturing

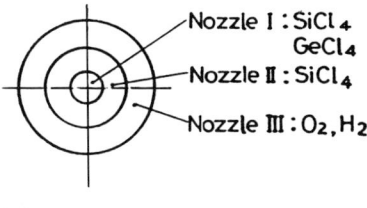

(a)

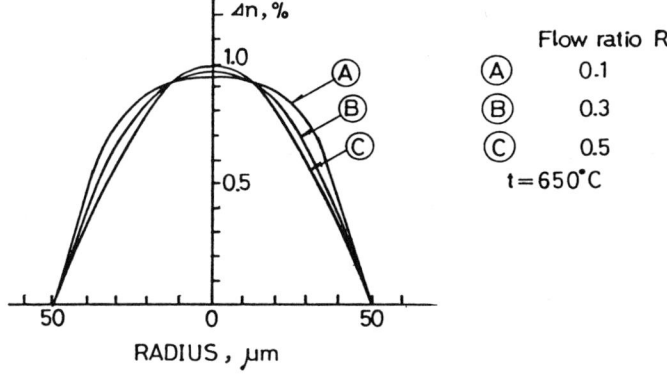

(b)

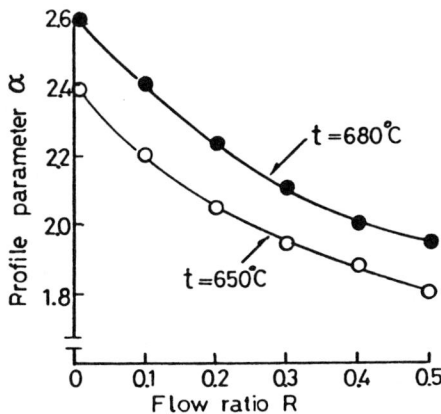

(c)

Figure 2.87 Flow ratio and profile. (From Ref. 67.)

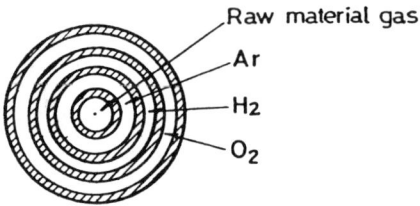

(a) The coaxial torch

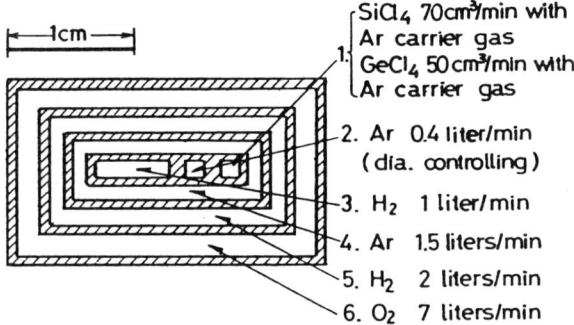

(b) The rectangular torch

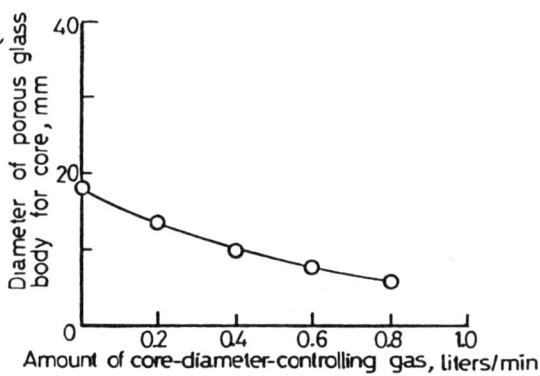

(c) Effect of diameter-controlling gas on core diameter.

Figure 2.88 VAD torch for the core of a single-mode fiber. (From Refs. 89 and 90.)

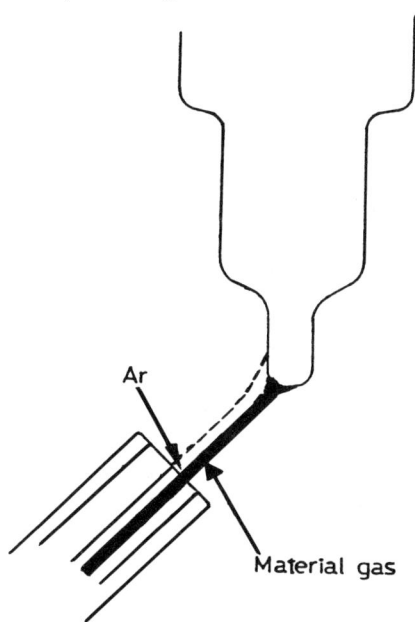

Figure 2.89 Torch for the core of a single-mode fiber. (From Refs. 89 and 90.)

core and the remaining two torches are used for cladding material deposition.

If a circular torch, as shown in Fig. 2.88a [89, 90], is used, the material gas unavoidably spreads when it reaches the surface of the lower part of the boule. It is difficult to keep the soot rod outside diameter less than 30 mm even if the torch diameter is reduced. Compared with this circular torch, a square torch, as shown in Fig. 2.88b [89, 90], is used to fabricate soot preforms less than 10 mm in diameter. The characteristic of this torch is that the material gas nozzle is positioned approximately 5 mm off center. When mounted on the VAD machine, this nozzle is positioned downward. An Ar nozzle to control the spreading of the material gas is positioned next to the material gas nozzle. When mounted on the VAD machine, the Ar nozzle is mounted above the nozzle for material gases and controls the spread of the material gas. Figure 2.88c shows the relation of the Ar gas flow for controlling the soot core and the diameter of the soot core. Figure 2.89 shows the construction of the VAD machine installed with this torch. This allows a soot core 10 mm in diameter to be manufactured at 40 mm/hr. A tapered shroud [91] is mounted on the outermost layer of the circular torch, and the air is made to flow to the outermost layer of the torch for air shielding of the flame. The flame expansion can be reduced in this case, and soot cores 16 to 17 mm in size can be manufactured.

Total Synthesis VAD Fiber [92-94]

In fiber manufacture, a silica tube is often jacketed on the preform rod and fiber is fabricated using this preform rod. The manufacturing speed of this process is high. Nevertheless, silica tube adversely affects optical fiber loss increases, mechanical characteristics, and so on. To improve this situation, the so-called total sythesis process technology for fabricating only the cladding by a deposition process has been developed. This process mainly consists of the following two procedures.

1. The cladding is deposited on the core using more than two torches. Preform rods are fabricated by dehydration and sintering.
2. The cladding layer, whose thickness is not very great, is deposited on the core using one or two torches. A glass rod is fabricated by dehydrating and sintering it. A glass rod is drawn, after which soot for the cladding is deposited on it. The rod is then dehydrated, sintered, and drawn again. This process is repeated several times to fabricate an SM preform rod that has the required core-cladding ratio.

As mentioned again later (Sec. 2.7.2), optical fibers manufactured by this whole-synthesis VAD process have excellent characteristics, such as a low loss, high mechanical strength, and stability of characteristics to H_2.

2.6.10.3 Increase of Deposition Rate [95-97]

The deposition rate with the VAD process is generally approximately 1 to 2 g/min. The deposition efficiency is lowered if the material gas-blowing velocity to the boule is increased in order to increase the deposition rate. The deposition rate can be increased by studying the materials to be used and studying the VAD flame deposition mechanism.

Study of Materials

$SiHCl_3$, which has good reaction properties, is used instead of $SiCl_4$. Table 2.15 shows the characteristics of $SiHCl_3$ and $SiCl_4$. GI optical fibers were test manufactured using $SiHCl_3$ instead of $SiCl_4$. The depositon rate increased approximately 1.5 times and the deposition efficiency, approximately 15%. A deposition rate of 6.5 g/min could be obtained in the test.

Table 2.15 Characteristics of $SiHCl_3$ and $SiCl_4$

Characteristic	$SiHCl_3$	$SiCl_4$
Molecular weight	135.43	169.90
Heat of reaction, kcal/mol	−116.7	−156.7
Reaction heat, kcal/mol	−118	−24
Boiling temperature, °C	31.8	57.57
Liquid condition	Colorless, fuming	Colorless, fuming

Source: From Ref. 97.

Study of Torch Construction (Application of Multiflame Torch) [95–99]

A flame is burned outside a conventional torch to increase the diameters of the glass particles by its heat in order to increase the deposition rate. Figures 2.90 [98, 99] and 2.91 [91, 98, 99] show its construction. The glass particle diameters increase from 0.1 to 0.4 or 0.5 μm when a double-flame torch is used. Figure 2.92 [100] compares the depositoin efficiencies and rates for the double- and triple-flame torches. A deposition rate of 7 g/min and deposition efficiency of 70% were obtained with a triple-flame torch.

2.6.10.4 Fluorine Doping [101–106]

Fluorine doping in the VAD process was studied. Several processes were studied, and the following two processes are generally used at present:

1. CF_4, SF_6, or CCl_2F_2, for example, are mixed in $SiCl_4$ for spouting by the cladding torch [101, 102]. In this case, fluorine hardly enters the SiO_2 network, and the value of Δ^- [$= (n_1 - n_2)/n_1$, n_1, n_2: refractive indexes of SiO_2 and $SiO_2 \cdot F$, respectively] is approximately 0.2% [101, 102].
2. An optical fiber core is manufactured by the VAD process and is sintered after dehydrating [103–106]. SiO_2 soot is deposited on the outside, and the preform is dehydrated in a furnace for heating to approximately 1200°C in an atmosphere of SF_6, CF_4, or C_2F_6, for example. The following chemical equation is established, and F, for example, enters the silica network [107].

$$SiO_2 + SF_6 \rightarrow SiF_4 + SO_2F_2$$

$$3SiO_2 + SiF_4 \rightleftharpoons 4SiO_{1.5}F$$

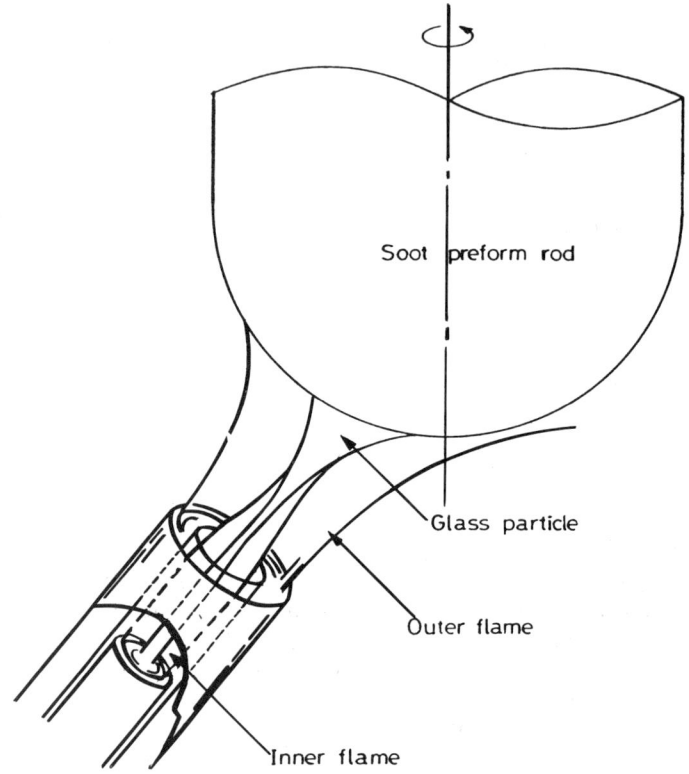

Figure 2.90   Multiflame torch (double flame).   (From Refs. 98 and 99.)

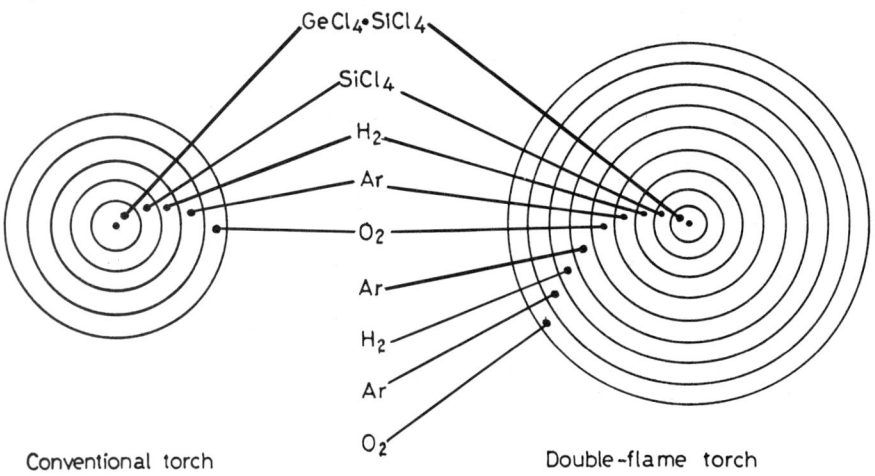

Figure 2.91   Examples of torches.   (From Refs. 98 and 99.)

Manufacturing

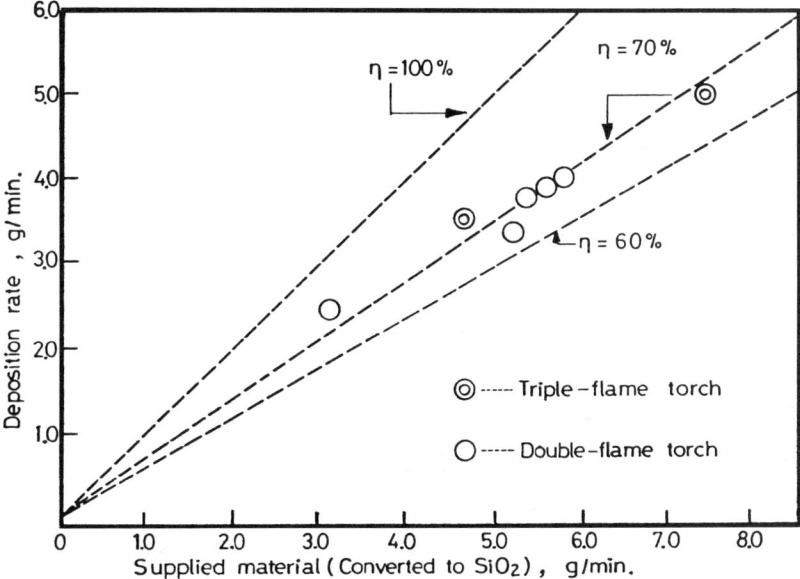

Figure 2.92   Deposition rate and efficiency and torch style. (From Ref. 100.)

Δ^- (%) varies in proportion to the one-quarter power of the partial pressure of SiF_4 [107]. The Δ^- value is considered to be a maximum of 0.75% and to be approximately 0.6% in practice.

2.6.10.5   Dehydration of VAD Soot Preform

Soot preforms are fabricated in the VAD process by a hydrolysis reaction and contain a large amount of OH^- ions. A process is necessary to sinter them to fabricate glass preform rods after dehydrating them. $SOCl_2$ or Cl_2 gas is effective in dehydration. $SOCl_2$ gas is nearly harmless. However, its ability to dehydrate is lower than that of Cl_2 gas. At present, Cl_2 gas is mainly used.

Figure 2.93 [108] shows the OH^- content when VAD soot preform rods are dehydrated in a $SOCl_2 + O_2$ atmosphere for about 5 hr ($SOCl_2$ is in a saturated condition). The temperature increased slowly from 200 to 1450°C. The minimum OH^- content value was 30 ppb.

Figure 2.94 [109] shows soot preform dehydration by Cl_2 gas. The soot preform (core, $SiO_2 \cdot GeO_2 \cdot P_2O_5$; cladding, SiO_2) was inserted in a furnace at 1200°C at a speed of 200 mm/hr. The soot preform was treated for 2 hr. A mixture of Cl_2 and He gases was

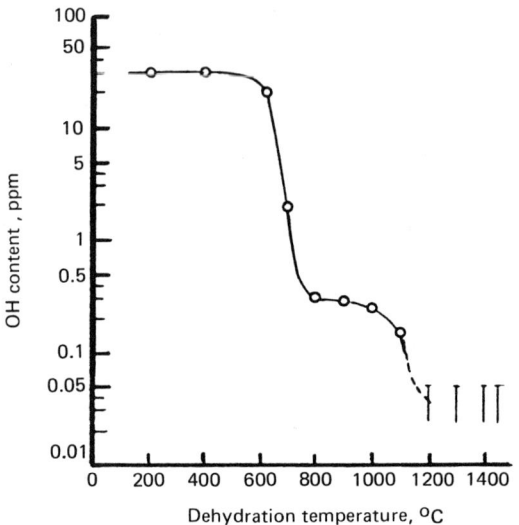

Figure 2.93   OH content versus dehydration temperature.   (From Ref. 108.)

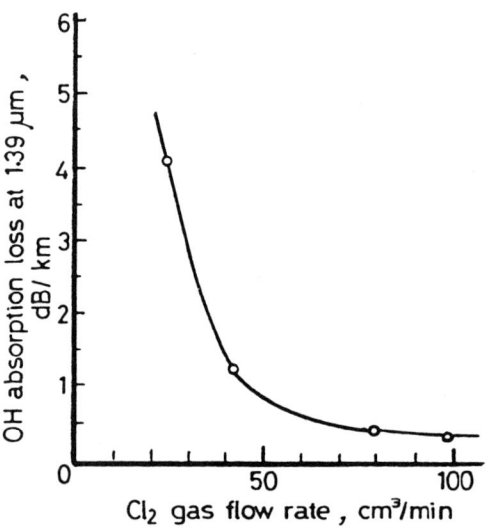

Figure 2.94   Relation between Cl_2 gas flow rate and OH absorption loss at 1.39 μm.   (From Ref. 109.)

Single-Mode Fibers 139

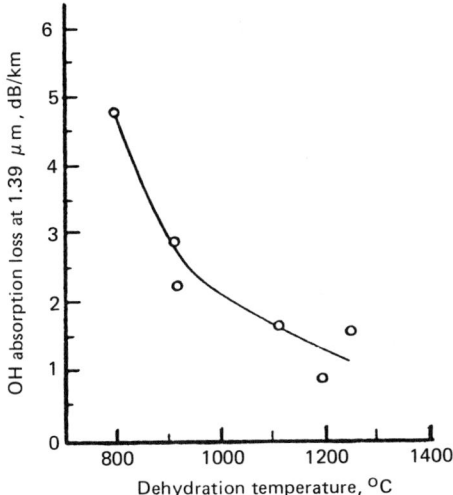

Figure 2.95 Relation between dehydration temperature and OH absorption loss at 1.39 μm. (From Ref. 109.)

made to flow inside the furnace. Figure 2.94 [86] shows the relation between the Cl_2 gas flow rate and OH absorption loss at 1.39 μm.

Figure 2.95 shows the relation between the dehydration temperature and OH absorption loss at 1.39 μm. The Cl_2 gas flow was constant at 40 cm^2/min, and the preform soot had begun to be sintered when the temperature exceeded 1200°C.

Optical fibers were test manufactured using these data. A loss increase of 0.04 dB/km was obtained at 1.39 μm. When converted into an OH content, this value is <1 ppb (refer to Sec. 2.2.3.2).

2.7 SINGLE-MODE FIBERS

The research into and experimental manufacture of GI fibers were mainly conducted in the early development stage of optical fibers. The core dimensions of SM fibers were less than 10 μm, and there was anxiety about whether cores with such small diameters could be manufactured continuously.

However, the technological and developmental advances have allowed easy manufacture of SM fibers. Compared with SM fibers, the profile control of GI fibers was unexpectedly difficult, and it became clear that a considerably high level of technology would be required to stably manufacture broad-band GI fibers. Furthermore, it was somewhat difficult to forecast how the band characteristics of GI optical fibers would vary with the cable length.

Compared with this situation for GI fibers, the manufacture of SM fibers has progressed satisfactorily, and optical fibers used at present are mainly SM fibers. This can be attributed to the following advantages of SM optical fibers: (1) much wider bandwidths of SM fibers compared with those of GI fibers; (2) the bandwidth simply varies in inverse proportion to the distance so that SM fibers can be used conveniently in systems; (3) the simple construction of SM fibers and a small amount of the dopant allow optical fibers with low transmission losses that can be manufactured easily; and (4) SM fiber splicing has been automated, and connectors for SM fibers have been developed and manufactured.

It was wholly unconceivable 10 years age, that mainly SM fibers would be used, amply demonstrating the speed of their development.

The characteristics of SM fibers used at present for transmission at 1.3 μm are roughly as follows: core diameter, 8–9 μm; optical fiber outside diameter, 125 μm; $\Delta = 0.3\%$ (1.3 μm zero dispersion).

Wavelength (μm)	Loss (dB/km)	Dispersion (ps/nm · km)
1.3	0.35	2
1.55	0.20	15

The loss of a 1.55 μm zero dispersion SM fiber is 0.25 dB/km (at 1.55 μm).

2.7.1 SM Fiber Design

Minimizing the transmission loss is the most important task in designing an SM fiber.

Next, a study of dispersion should be made. In normal design, the dispersion of silica optical fibers becomes nearly zero at 1.3 μm. However, the optical fiber loss is smaller at 1.55 μm, and studies of dispersion in the 1.55 μm region become necessary.

2.7.1.1 SM Fiber Construction and Transmission Loss

As is well known, the following equation expresses the conditions necessary for modes propagated in optical fibers to become a single mode:

Single-Mode Fibers

$$V = \frac{2\pi a \sqrt{n_1^2 - n_2^2}}{\lambda} \leqslant 2.405 \tag{2.33}$$

where:

  a = core radius of fiber
  n_1 = refractive index of core
  n_2 = refractive index of cladding

In this case, roughly the following values are used as practical values:

  $\lambda = 1.3$ μm

  $\Delta = \dfrac{n_1 - n_2}{n_1} = 0.3\%$

  $2a = 8.5$ μm

The electromagnetic field and energy distribution of SM transmission can be expressed approximately by the following equation and by Fig. 2.96:

$$E(r) = A \frac{J_0(ur/a)}{J_0(u)} \qquad 0 \leqslant r \leqslant a$$

$$= A \frac{K_0(wr/a)}{K_0(u)} \qquad r \geqslant 0 \tag{2.34}$$

where:

  $u = a(k^2 n_1^2 - \beta^2)^{1/2}$
  $w = a(\beta^2 - k^2 n_2^2)^{1/2}$
  $v^2 = u^2 + w^2 = a^2 k^2 (n_1^2 - n_2^2)$
  $k = \dfrac{2\pi}{\lambda}$

  $\beta = k \left[n_2^2 + (n_1^2 - n_2^2)\left(1 - \dfrac{u^2}{v^2}\right) \right]^{1/2}$

  $A = \dfrac{1}{\sqrt{\pi} a} \dfrac{1}{\sqrt{J_1^2(u)/J_0^2(u) + K_1^2(w)/K_0^2(w)}}$

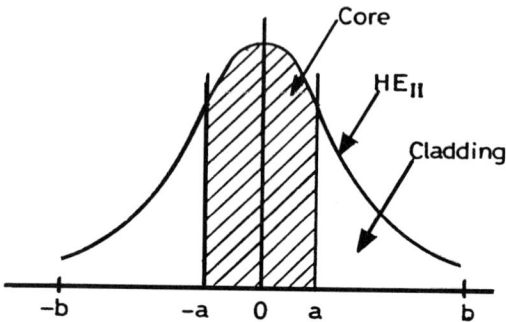

Figure 2.96 Electrical field of a single-mode fiber.

The power distribution can be expressed by the equation

$$P \propto \int 2\pi r E^2(r) \, dr \tag{2.35}$$

Based on Eq. (2.35) the power distribution of the SM fiber can be shown by Fig. 2.97. These data demonstrate that a considerably large portion of the SM energy transmits through the cladding. Therefore, the transmission loss of the cladding layer should also be studied carefully, in addition to that of the core.

In fabricating the cladding, the following two items should be prevented as much as possible:

1. Impurities included in the raw materials
2. Diffusion of hydrogen and OH^- ions in the cladding layer

Item 1 can be prevented by increasing the thickness of the cladding layer to be deposited by the CVD process. For item 2, the diffusion of hydrogen or OH^- ions from the silica tube should be minimized if a silica tube is to be used in fabricating preform rods of optical fibers. This can be prevented by not using a silica tube (for example, the cladding layer can be fabricated using the whole synthesis with the VAD or OVD process) or by increasing the wall thickness of the cladding layer to be deposited, as mentioned earlier.

As mentioned before, OH^- ions in the silica tube diffuse into the optical fiber cladding layer and core if a silica tube is used in manufacturing fibers. For this reason, the loss increases owing to the presence of OH^- ions. Figures 2.98 and 2.99 show the relation between the ratio of the deposited cladding diameter to the core diameter and the OH absorption loss by the MCVD process. Based on these data, the following equations are obtained for the MCVD process [110, 111].

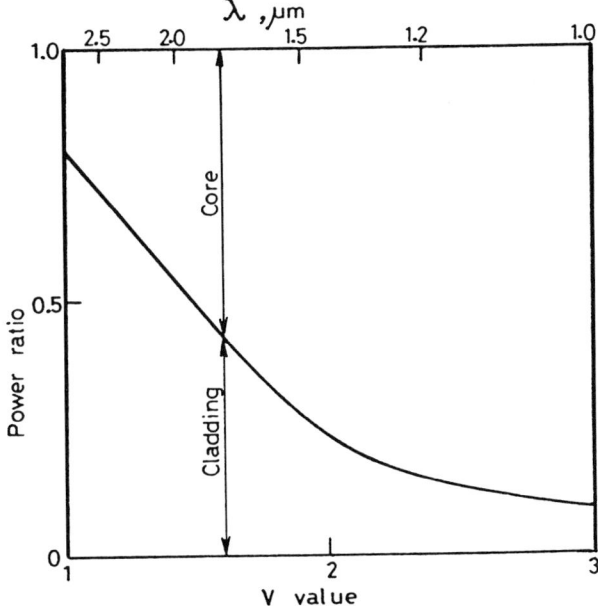

Figure 2.97 Energy distribution of a single-mode fiber. (From Ref. 111.)

$$\frac{\text{Deposited cladding diameter}}{\text{Core diameter}} = \frac{b}{a} > 6$$

$$2.4 \geqslant V > 1.8$$

The core and cladding layer can be easily manufactured by the VAD process wholly by synthesis without using a silica tube.

2.7.1.2 Dopant

In the initial development period, B_2O_3, P_2O_5, GeO_2, F, and others were used individually or in combination as dopants of optical fibers. As mentioned earlier, these dopants have the following properties:

B_2O_3: infrared absorption loss occurs near 1.2 m.
P_2O_5: infrared absorption loss occurs near 1.4 m. This dopant easily bonds with H_2 molecules to increase the loss.
GeO_2: infrared absorption loss occurs near 1.6 m.

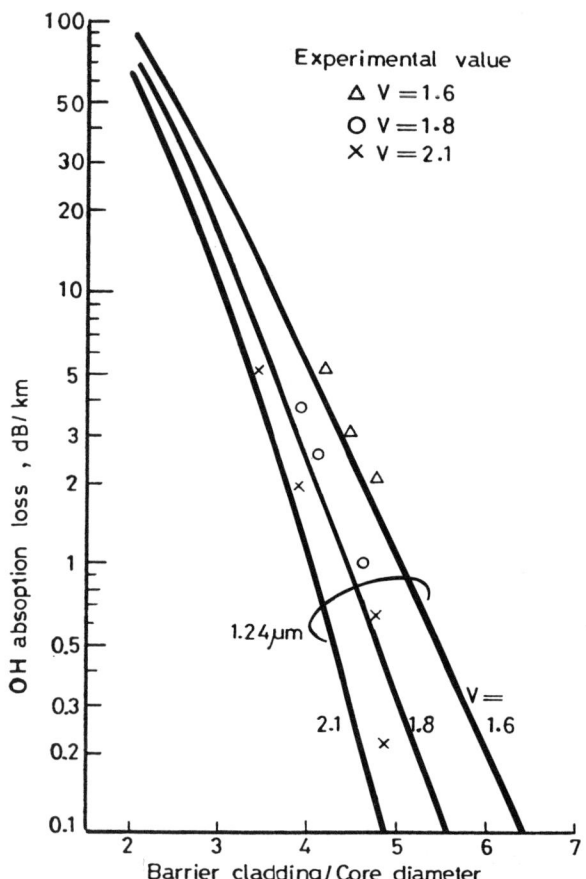

Figure 2.98 Ratio of barrier cladding to core diameter. (From Refs. 111 and 112.)

Single-Mode Fibers 145

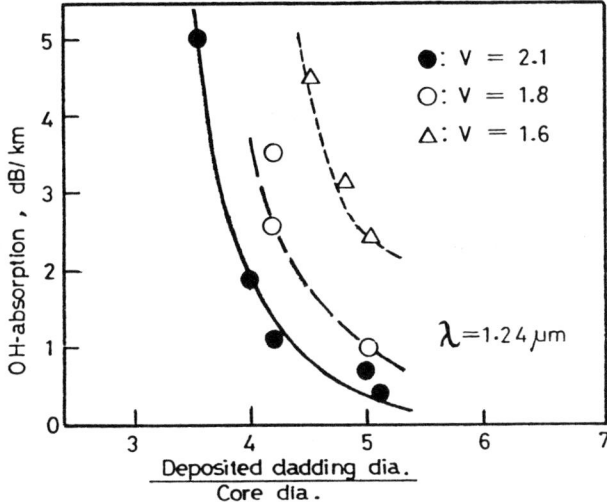

Figure 2.99 OH absorption versus cladding-core ratio. (From Refs. 111 and 112.)

The SM fiber is used in the wavelength band of 1.3 to 1.6 μm, and the following combinations are in practical use at present.

	1	2	3
Core	SiO_2	$SiO_2 \cdot GeO_2$	$SiO_2 \cdot GeO_2 \cdot F$
Cladding	$SiO_2 \cdot F$	$SiO_2 (F)(P_2O_5)$	$SiO_2 \cdot F(P_2O_5)$

Combinations 1 and 2 are mainly used. In 1, the scattering loss may become minimal. Based on Fig. 2.6, the A values are as follows.

Δ (%)	A (dB/km · μm^4)	
	$SiO_2 \cdot GeO_2$	$SiO_2 \cdot GeO_2 \cdot F$
1	1.35	—
0.5	1.1	0.95
0.3	0.95	0.8
0 (pure SiO_2)	0.65	

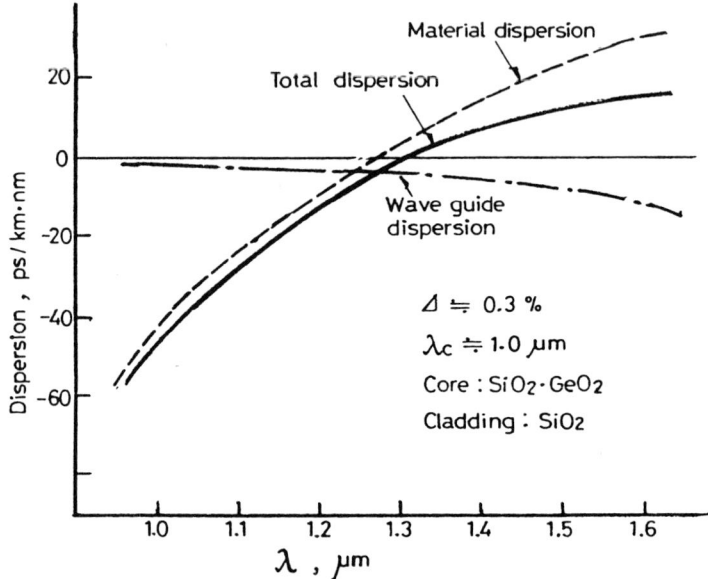

Figure 2.100 Dispersion of single-mode fiber. (From Ref. 111.)

The optical fiber loss values that are practically obtained at present are as follows: at 1.3 μm, 0.35 dB/km; at 1.55 μm, 0.20 dB/km (the minimum value obtained so far is 0.154 dB/km). The minimum loss value is estimated to be 0.13 dB/km at 1.55 μm.

2.7.1.3 Dispersion

Figure 2.100 shows the dispersion properties of SM fiber. In the figure, dopants of the core and the cladding are $SiO_2 \cdot GeO_2$ and SiO_2, respectively. Material dispersion is greater in $SiO_2 \cdot GeO_2$ than in pure SiO_2, and the zero dispersion wavelength shifts to a slightly longer wavelength side.

Waveguide dispersion is small in the 0.85 μm band—2 to 5% of material dispersion. At the 1.30 μm band, it becomes equal to material dispersion. At a longer wavelength, the signs of material and waveguide dispersion are reversed.

The dispersions of SM fiber with Δ = 0.3% and λ_c = 1.0 μm are as follows: 1.30 μm, approximately 2 psec/nm/km; 1.55 μm, approximately 15 psec/nm/km.

2.7.1.4 Depressed Cladding

The single-mode fiber has been studied on the basis of a constant cladding refractive index. This cladding construction is called a

Single-Mode Fibers

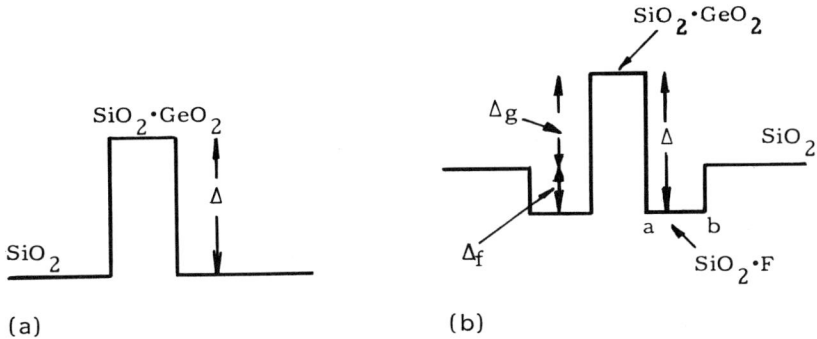

Figure 2.101 Single-mode fibers: (a) matched cladding SM fiber; (b) depressed cladding SM fiber. (From Ref. 112.)

matched cladding (Fig. 2.101). It is most preferable in design to achieve Δ = approximately 0.3% for the cladding construction. If pure silica is used to fabricate the cladding, the dopant amount to Δ = 0.3% is determined, and the minimum loss value is also determined relative to the dopant amount. It is difficult to control the zero dispersion wavelength.

To avoid these problems, by doping the cladding layer with fluorine as shown in Fig. 2.102b [112], the dopant amount of the core part of Δ_g becomes smaller than the dopant amount of the core part of Δ in Fig. 2.101a.

Therefore, the fiber loss of b becomes smaller than that of a. The zero dispersion wavelength can be controlled to some extent by the refractive index part of Δ_f ($\overline{ab}$ part), which has become smaller than that of silica by fluorine doping. The minimum loss value is possible when the core is fabricated with pure SiO_2 (Δ_g = 0) and a cladding layer of $SiO_2 \cdot F$. In this construction, the refractive index of the outside of the cladding becomes relatively larger than that of the cladding. For this reason, the bending loss of the SM fiber (Fig. 2.101b) is larger than that in Fig. 2.101a. The SM fiber of construction b is called a depressed-cladding single-mode fiber [112]. Figure 2.102 [112] shows calculation examples of Δ and the minimum dispersion wavelength of this depressed-cladding SM fiber.

2.7.2 Precautions in Manufacturing SM Fibers for 1.3 μm Wavelength

The zero dispersion wavelength of SM fibers manufactured in a regular process is near 1.3 μm. The fiber loss decreases in inverse proportion to λ^4 and decreases to approximately 0.15 dB/km near 1.55 μm (0.13 dB/km is considered an ideal minimum value).

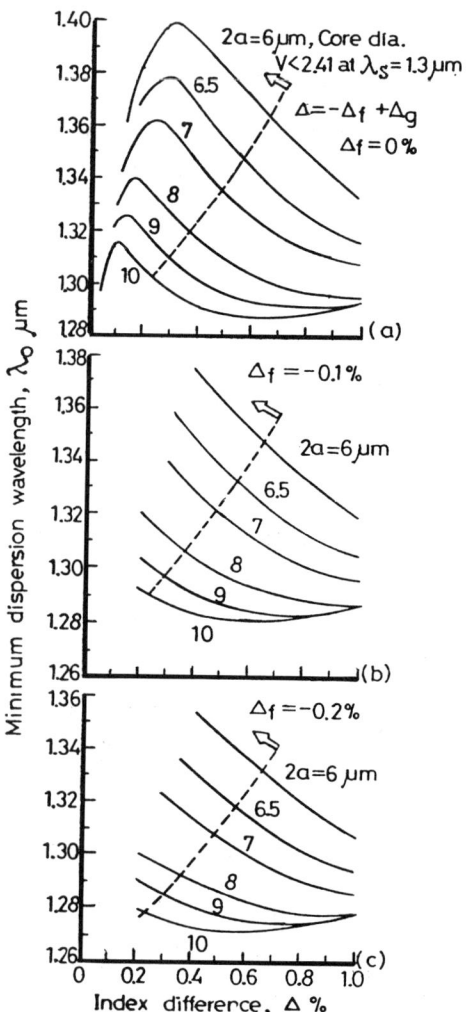

Figure 2.102 Minimum dispersion wavelength versus index difference. (From Ref. 112.)

Single-Mode Fibers

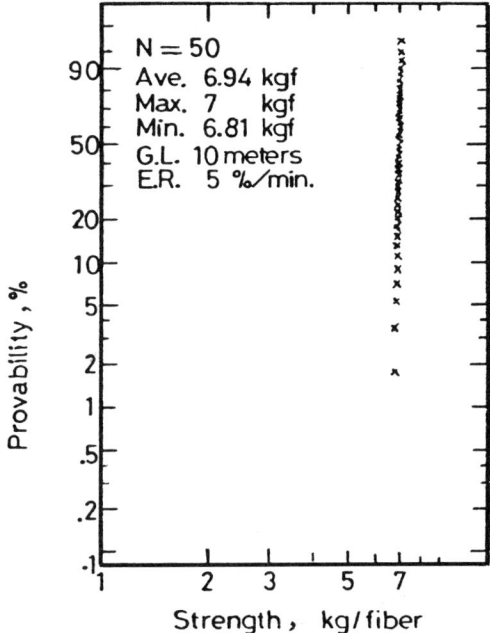

Figure 2.103 Weibull distribution of fiber breakage strength. (From Ref. 113.)

First, the transmission loss should be small. At present, the following methods are used to meet these requirements.

For the MCVD process, the cladding layer mainly consists of SiO_2. Therefore, the deposition temperature becomes high. In the case of SiO_2 cladding, the deposition temperature is approximately 200°C higher than that in $SiO_2 \cdot P_2O_5$ deposition and reaches approximately 1600°C. An inner pressure of approximately 5 mm H_2O is normally applied to prevent deformation of the SiO_2 tube used in the MCVD process, as mentioned in the preceding section.

As mentioned earlier, using the whole-synthesis SM fiber by the VAD process, losses of SM fibers may increase owing to the diffusion of OH ions and H_2 from the silica tube, if a silica tube is used in manufacturing the SM fibers. The wall thickness variations of the silica tube cause optical fiber core eccentricity, and these wall thickness variations should be minimized.

To solve these problems, efforts are made to manufacture fibers by wholly synthesizing the cladding layer by the VAD process without using a silica tube. VAD fibers manufactured by this process have yielded good results with a small eccentricity of core (average value,

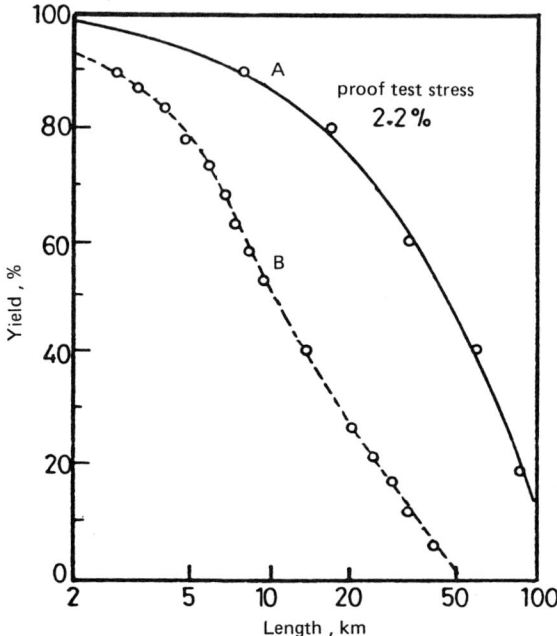

Figure 2.104 Yield of survival length at 2.2% proof test: A, wholly synthesized; B, jacketed by synthetic tube. (From Ref. 113.)

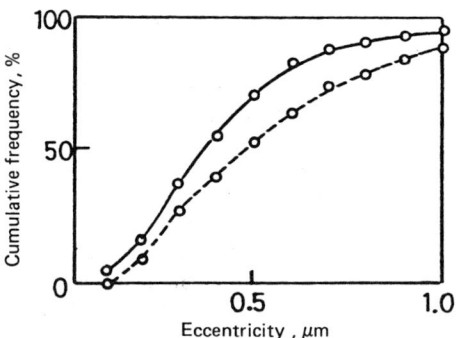

Figure 2.105 Eccentricity: ○—○ wholly synthesized; ○---○ jacketed by synthetic tube. (From Ref. 113.)

Zero Dispersion Fibers

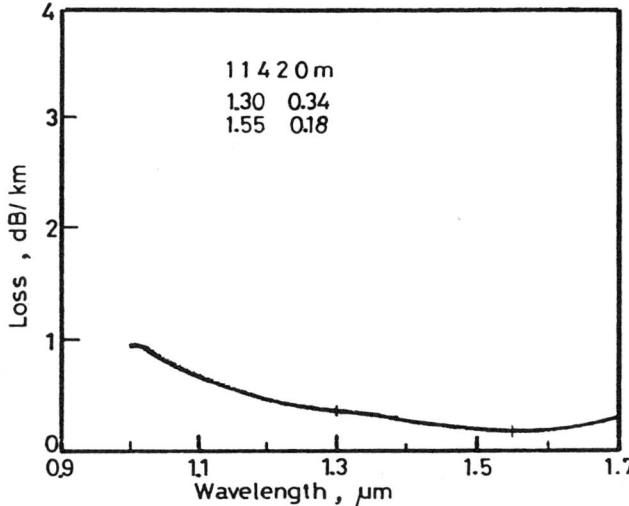

Figure 2.106 Transmission loss spectrum of low-loss SM fiber. (From Ref. 113.)

0.4 μm) and large strength (2.2% proof test, 50% yield, 50 km), in addition to the low-loss characteristic (0.35 dB/km average at 1.3 μm; 0.20 dB/km average at 1.55 μm). Figures 2.103 through 2.106 show examples of these characteristics [113].

2.8 1.55 μm ZERO DISPERSION SM FIBERS

As mentioned earlier, ordinary SM fibers have zero dispersion near 1.3 μm, allowing broad-band transmission. However, the transmission loss of the fiber becomes minimal near 1.55 μm, and the loss value at this wavelength is approximately one half that at 1.3 μm. One naturally believes that large-capacity transmission with long repeater spans must be possible using this small transmission loss at 1.55 μm. However, the dispersion at 1.55 μm is approximately 15 ps/nm · km and blocks broad-band transmission.

Figures 2.107 and 2.108, as well as Table 2.16 show the relation between the repeater span and bit rate in transmissions at 1.3 and 1.55 μm [114]. These data show that transmission of only a low bit rate is possible owing to the dispersion if conventional SM fibers (zero dispersion at 1.3 μm) are used in transmission at 1.55 μm with a conventional laser (spectrum width 2 nm) as a light source.

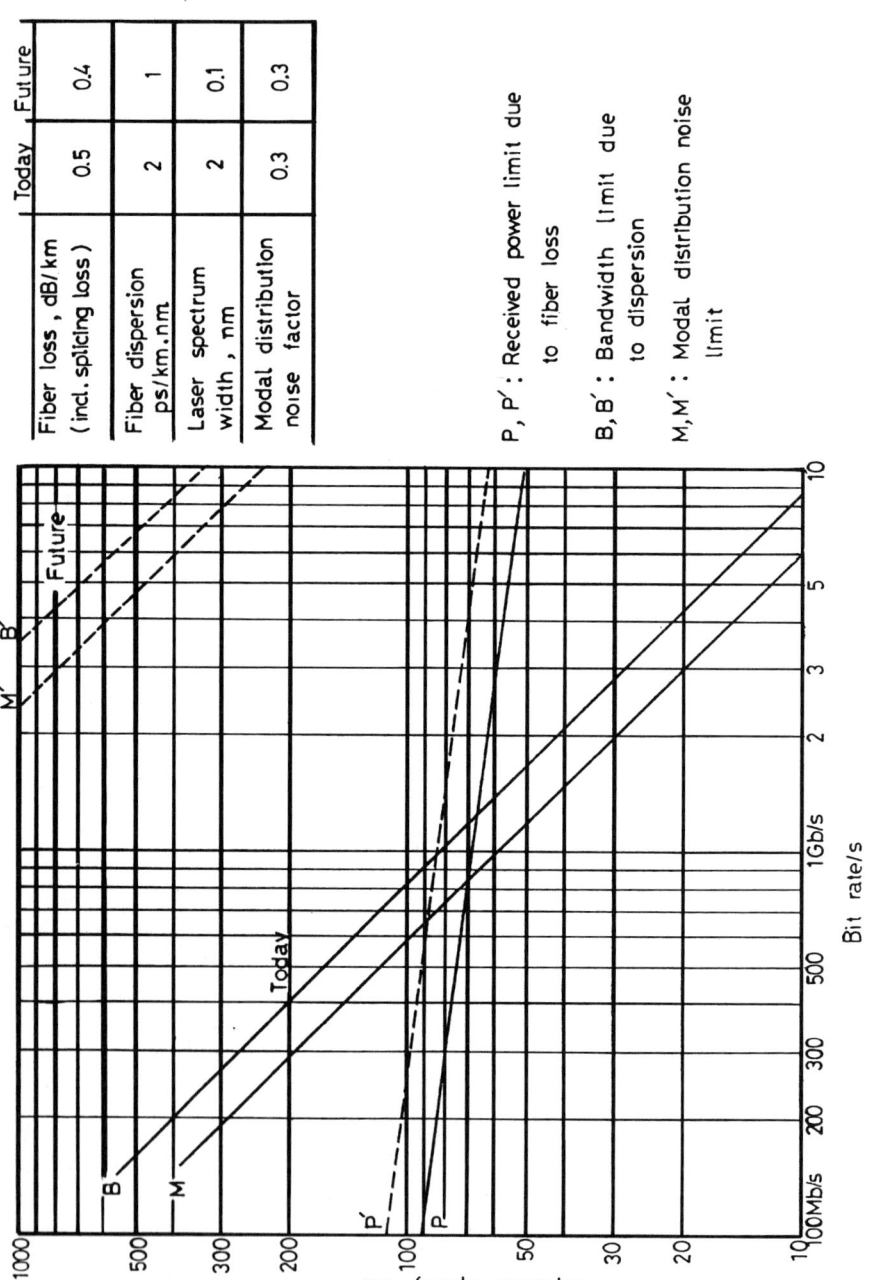

Figure 2.107 Transmission at 1.3 μm. (From Ref. 114.)

Zero Dispersion Fibers

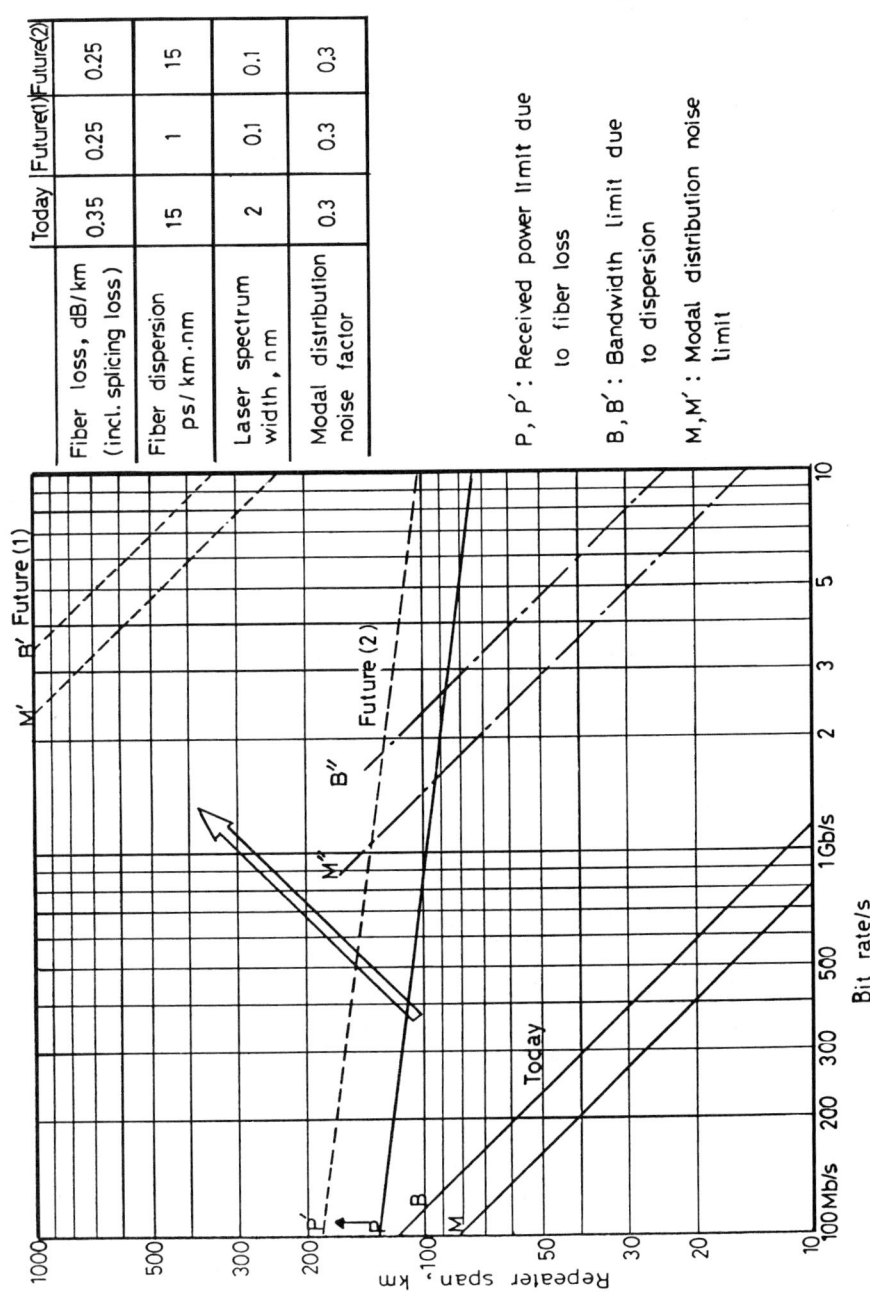

Figure 2.108 Transmission at 1.55 μm. (From Ref. 114.)

Table 2.16 Fibers, Lasers, Repeater Spans, and Bandwidths

Fiber	Laser specified width (nm)	Repeater span (km)	Bit rate (Gb/sec)
1.3 μm zero dispersion	2	50	2
1.3 μm transmission	0.1	50	10
1.3 μm zero dispersion	2	50	0.2
1.55 μm transmission	0.1	100	2
1.55 μm zero dispersion	2	100	2
1.55 μm transmission	0.1	100	10
		150	2

A DFB laser (spectrum width 0.1 nm) is needed in broad-band and long repeater span transmission using these fibers.

The 1.55 μm transmission using a 1.55 μm zero dispersion SM fiber and the conventional laser has nearly the same performance as 1.55 μm transmission using a 1.3 μm conventional SM fiber (1.3 μm zero dispersion) and the DFB laser.

In transmission at 1.55 μm, combining the 1.55 μm zero dispersion fiber and DFB laser, transmission with repeater spans of 100 to 150 km and at a bit rate of 2 to 10 Gb/sec are possible.

Based on these considerations, studies of a 1.55 μm zero dispersion fiber were made.

2.8.1 Dispersion of SM Fibers [115, 116]

The dispersion S of SM fibers is

$$S = -\frac{\lambda}{C}\left[H(v)\frac{d^2 n_1}{d\lambda^2} + (1-H(v))\frac{d^2 n_2}{d\lambda^2}\right] - \frac{n_1 \Delta}{\lambda C}G(v) \qquad (2.36)$$

= material dispersion + waveguide dispersion

where:

$$H(v) = \frac{d(vb)/dv + vb}{2}$$

$$G(v) = v\frac{d^2(vb)}{dv^2}$$

Zero Dispersion Fibers

$$b = \frac{{}^2\!/_{\!k^2} - n_2^2}{n_1^2 - n_2^2} \qquad \text{normalized propagation constant}$$

$$v = ka(n_1^2 - n_2^2)^{1/2} \qquad \text{normalized frequency}$$

$$k = \frac{2\pi}{\lambda}$$

$$\Delta = \frac{n_1^2 - n_2^2}{2n_1^2} \doteq \frac{n_1 - n_2}{n_1} \qquad \text{relative refractive index difference}$$

The first term in Eq. (2.36) represents the material dispersion. When the materials are determined, the values of material dispersion are fixed for fixed wavelengths.

The second term is called waveguide dispersion and is a produce of Δ and v $(d^2(vb)/dv^2)$.

In the wavelength region near 1.5 μm with SM silica fibers, the material dispersion values have a plus sign and the waveguide dispersion values, a minus sign.

To shift the zero dispersion wavelength to the longer wavelength, increase in the absolute value of the waveguide dispersion is necessary. To accomplish this, either one or both of the following are used: $\Delta \to$ large or $v(d^2(vb)/dv^2)$ is large. In order to increase $v(d^2(vb)/dv^2)$, the value of b is changed (i.e., the profile of fiber is changed) or v is changed from approximately 1 to 1.5 [the value of $v(d^2(vb)/dv^2)$ is approximately 1 to 2 at $v = 1.2$].

2.8.2 1.55 μm Zero Dispersion Fiber 1 with Large Δ [115]

Figure 2.109 [115] shows curves of the material dispersion and waveguide dispersion (sign is reversed) of an SM fiber at 1.5 μm. (The abscissa shows the core radius.) The point of intersection of these two curves is the zero dispersion point at 1.5 μm.

With conventional SM fibers with $\Delta = 0.3\%$, the two curves do not intersect. The two curves intersect when $\Delta \geq 0.4\%$, and the point of intersection of these two curves gives the zero dispersion condition (the value of core radius and Δ) at 1.5 μm. Two core radii are obtained in this case, and the larger value is used in practice.

Figure 2.110 shows the relation between the core radius and Δ with zero dispersion in case of constant wavelength. The dotted line shows the cutoff condition of the second higher mode. Points a and b in Figure 2.110 show conditions that achieve a loss increase 0.1

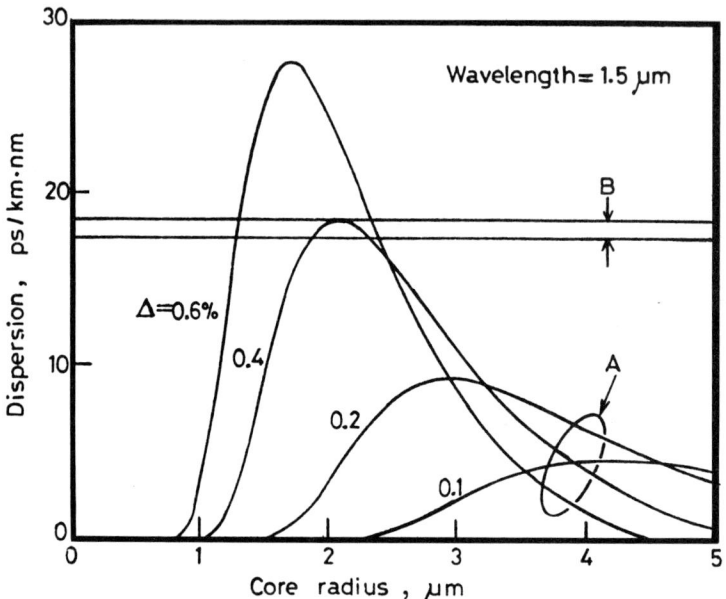

Figure 2.109 Waveguide dispersion (negative), A; and material dispersion, B. (From Ref. 115.)

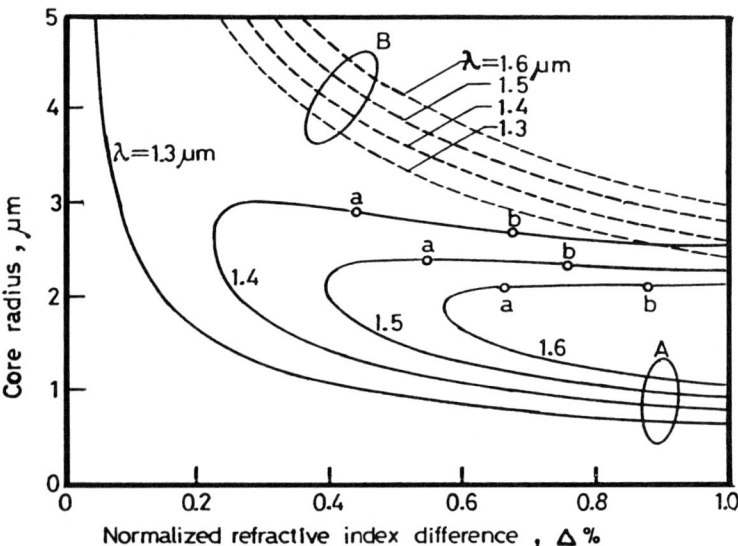

Figure 2.110 The core radius and Δ for zero dispersion: A, zero dispersion; B, cutoff condition, second higher mode. (From Ref. 115.)

Zero Dispersion Fibers

dB/km with a bending radius of 50 mm [117] and a splice loss of 0.1 dB in fiber splicing with an 0.5 μm offset [118], respectively, as optimal conditions in cabling optical fibers.

Therefore, $\overline{ab}$ in this curve becomes the optimal fiber construction in cabling. This construction uses the following formulas in calculating bending and splicing losses:

$$\alpha_c = \frac{4.34}{\sqrt{\pi a R w}} \left(\frac{u}{v}\right)^2 \exp\left(\frac{4}{3} \frac{w^3}{v^2} \Delta \frac{R}{a}\right)$$

$$\alpha_s = \frac{1}{2}\left(\frac{w J_1(u)}{J_0(u)}\right)^2 \left(\frac{x}{a}\right)^2$$

where:

$$u^2 = a(k^2 n_1^2 - \beta 2)$$

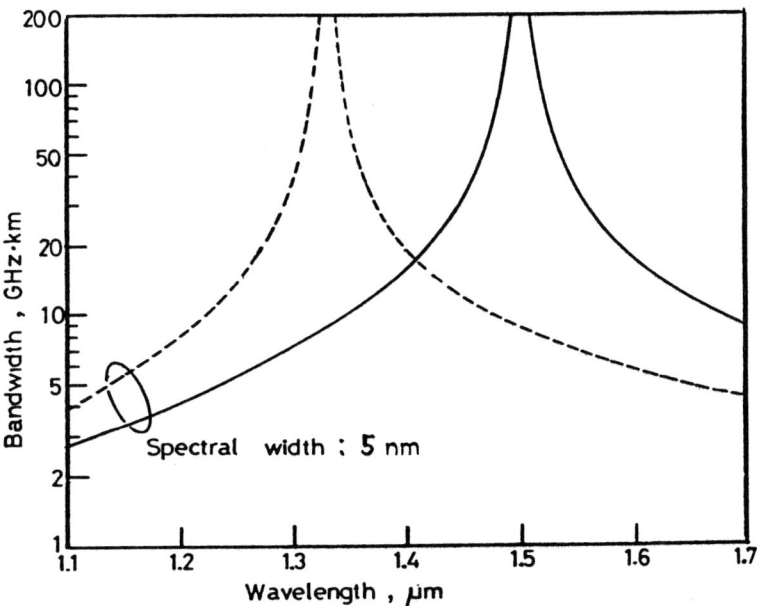

Figure 2.111 Bandwidth of single-mode fiber: solid line, 1.5 μm zero dispersion shift; dashed line, conventional 1.3 μm zero dispersion. (From Ref. 115.)

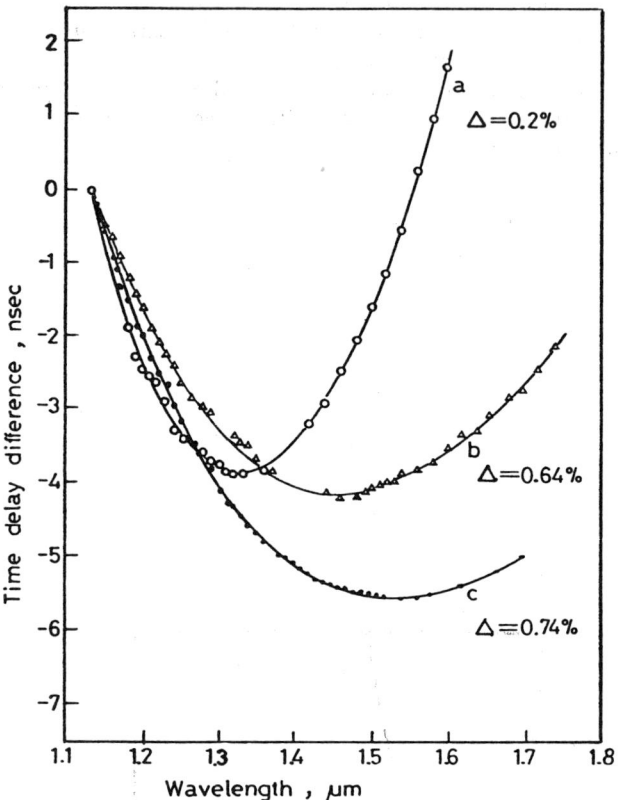

Figure 2.112 Time delay. (From Refs. 119 and 120.)

$$v^2 = ak(n_1^2 - n_2^2)$$
$$w^2 = a^2(\beta^2 - k^2 n_2^2)$$

Figure 2.111 [115] shows a calculation example of SM optical fiber bandwidths. The laser spectral width is assumed to be 5 nm at 1.5 μm.

Examples of step index SM fibers with different Δ values are shown next. Figures 2.112, 2.113, and 2.114 show measured values of time delay differences, dispersions, and zero dispersion wavelengths of experimentally manufactured SI single-mode fibers at Δ = 0.2, 0.64, and 0.74% [119, 120]. The fiber profiles are of the step index type. The core is made of $GeO_2 \cdot SiO_2$ and the cladding of

Zero Dispersion Fibers

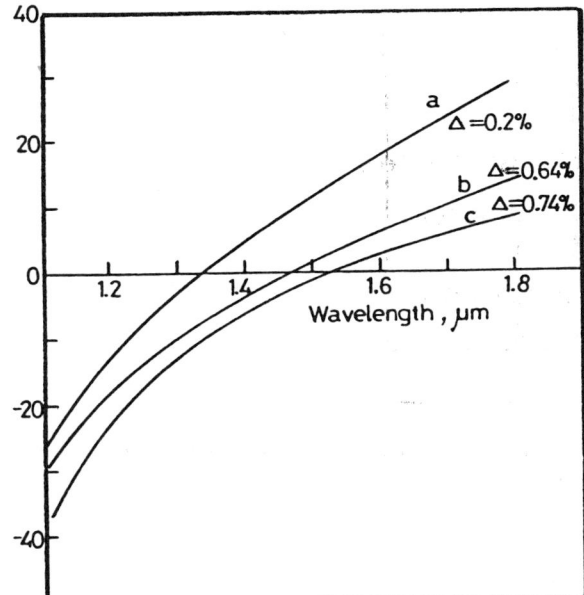

Figure 2.113 Dispersion of single-mode fiber. (From Refs. 119 and 120.)

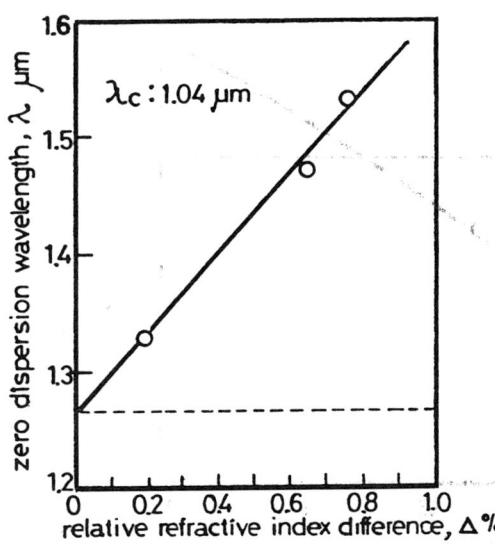

Figure 2.114 Zero dispersion wavelength of single-mode fiber. (From Refs. 119 and 120.)

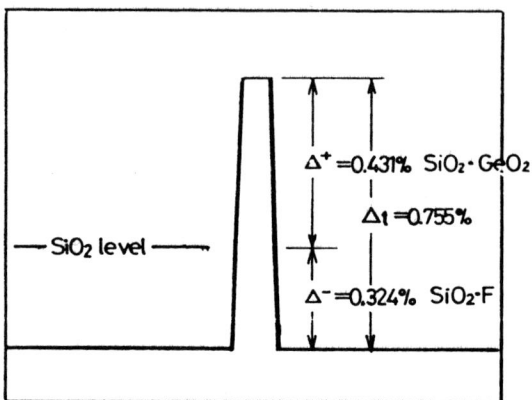

Figure 2.115 Profile of 1.55 μm zero dispersion fiber. (From Ref. 121.)

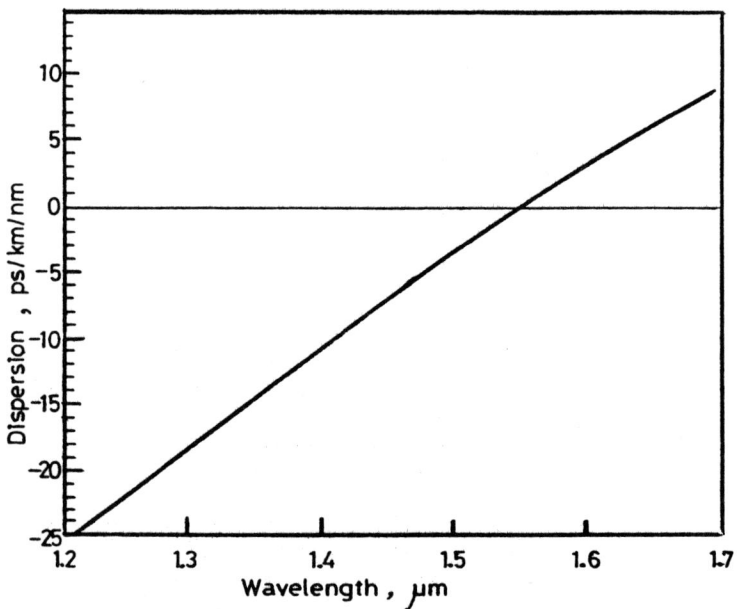

Figure 2.116 Dispersion of dispersion-shifted fiber. (From Ref. 121.)

Zero Dispersion Fibers

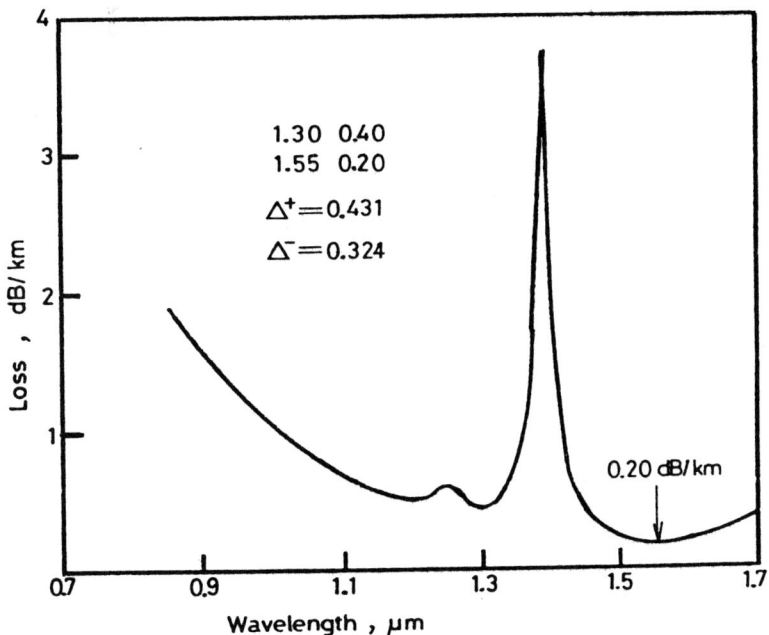

Figure 2.117 Loss spectrum of dispersion-shifted fiber. (From Ref. 121.)

SiO_2. In this case, the optimal design of zero dispersion at 1.55 µm would be

$\Delta = 0.80 \pm 0.1\%$

$a = 2.2$ to 2.5 µm

An example of a low-loss SM fiber of a 1.55 µm zero dispersion step index profile is described next. Figure 2.115 shows the profile of an SM fiber manufactured by the wholly synthesized VAD process [121]. Figures 2.116 and 2.117 show the dispersion and loss data of this fiber. The loss at 1.55 µm is less than 0.20 dB/km [121].

2.8.3 1.55 µm Zero Dispersion Fiber 2: Modification of Relatively Simple Profile

The zero dispersion shift fiber with a step index profile was described in the preceding section. The fiber has a large Δ, and the

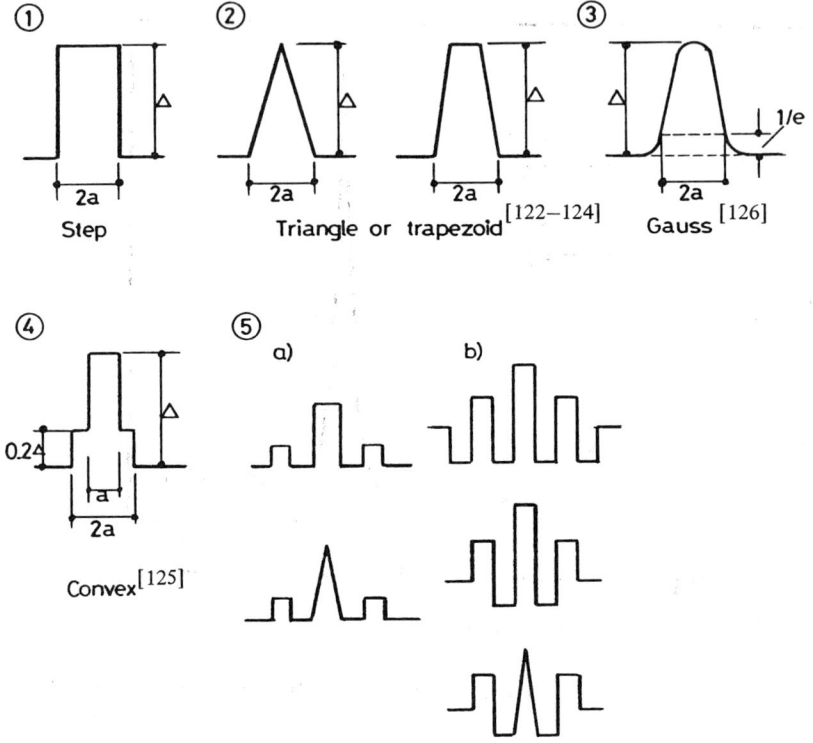

Figure 2.118 Profiles of 1.5 μm zero dispersion fibers.

glass components and characteristics greatly change in the boundary between the core and the cladding of the fiber. For this reason, low-loss fibers cannot be manufactured easily.

To solve this problem, a fiber is studied by modifying the profile from the step type to one that is relatively simple, as shown in Fig. 2.118 [122-126]. First, a comparative study is made of triangular, Gaussian, and convex fibers experimentally manufactured using the VAD process shown in Fig. 2.118. A profile with a small variation in the zero dispersion wavelength and small variations in the value of dispersion to variations of the core diameter, Δ, and so on, is desired in terms of engineering and manufacturing. Table 2.17 presents dispersion variations to the core diameter of fibers $\Delta\sigma/\Delta a$ of the four types of profile [125]. Figures 2.119 through 121 show the relation between the core radius, Δ, and dispersion. The data indicate that the triangular profile has the most stable characteristics, followed by the convex and Gaussian profiles. Figure

Zero Dispersion Fibers

Table 2.17 Variation of Dispersion $\Delta\sigma$ to Variation of Core Diameter Δa, $\Delta\sigma/\Delta a$[a]

$\Delta\%$	0.7	0.9	1.0
Step	19	24	26
Triangle	4	8	9
Gaussian	11	12	13
Convex	7	8	9

[a]Unit: ps/km · nm · μm.

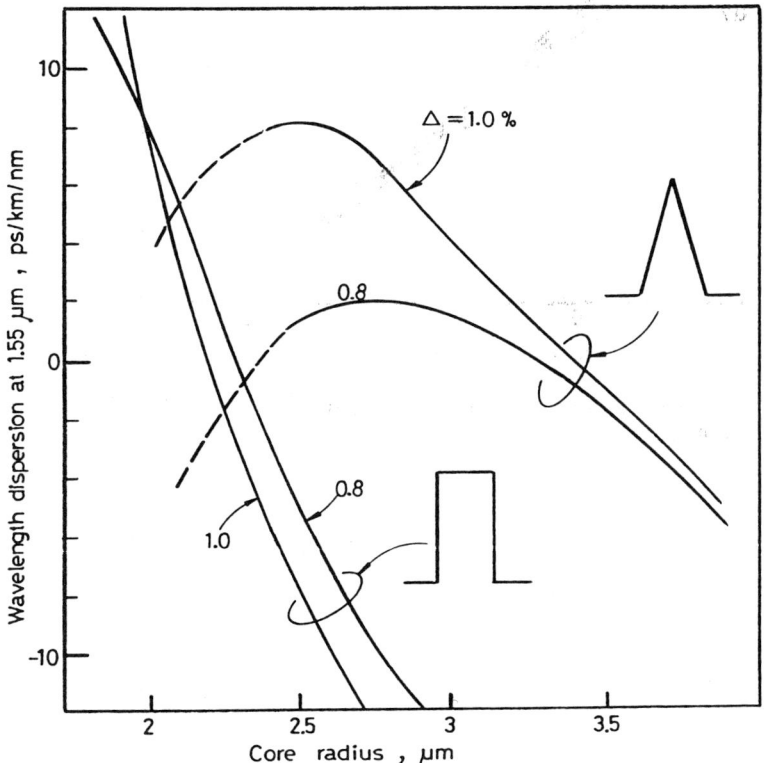

Figure 2.119 Wavelength dispersion of fiber. (From Ref. 126.)

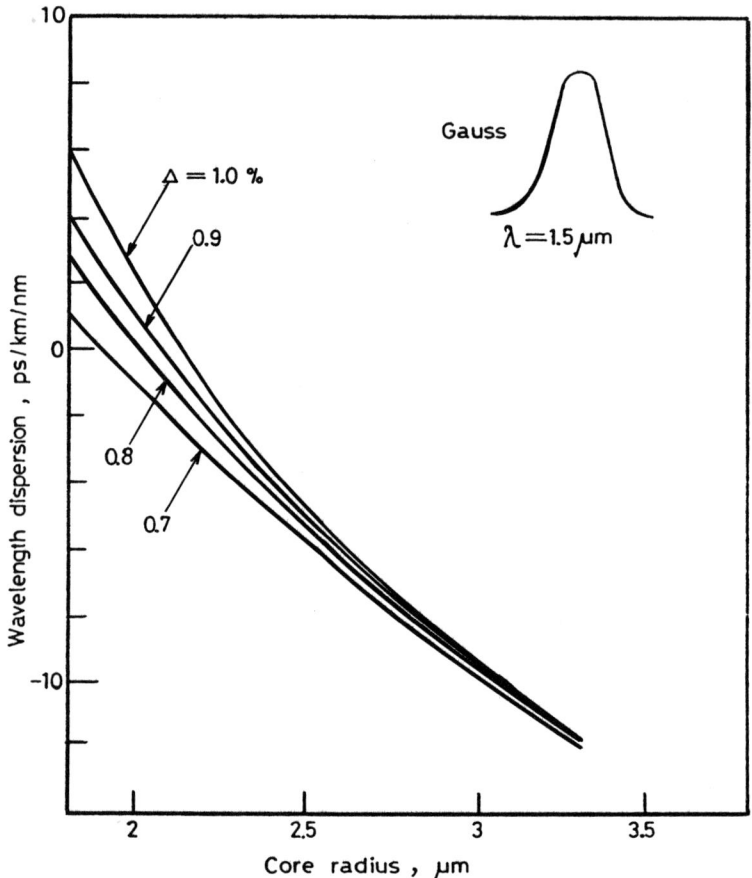

Figure 2.120 Wavelength dispersion of Gaussian-type fiber. (From Ref. 126.)

Zero Dispersion Fibers

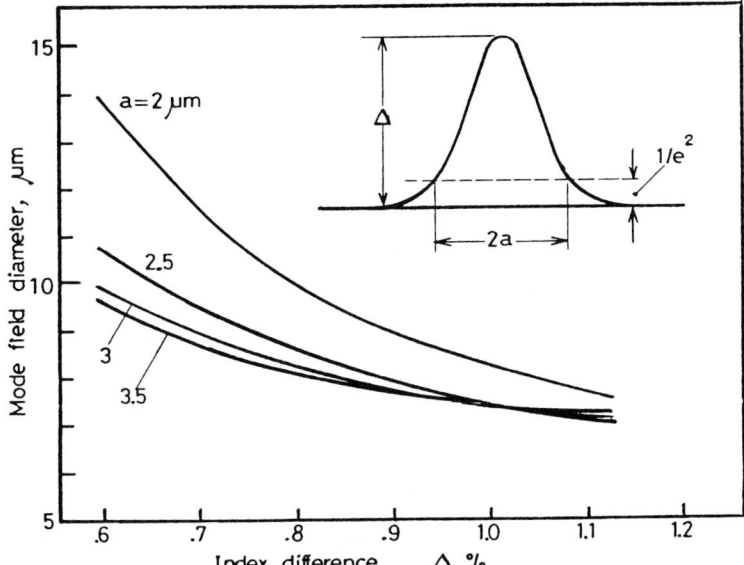

Figure 2.121 Mode field diameter of Gaussian-type fibers (calculated). (From Ref. 126.)

2.122 [125] shows the bending characteristics of fibers with these profiles. The bending characteristics of these profiles do not differ greatly. Figures 2.123 [126] and 2.124 [126] show examples of the loss and dispersion of fibers of the Gaussian type.

At present, fibers of 1.55 µm zero dispersion (with modification of relatively simple profile) with a loss of approximately 0.2 to 0.25 dB/km are produced.

2.8.4 1.55 µm Zero Dispersion Fiber 3: Slightly Complex Profile

One fiber construction has a step index peak outside the optical fiber core, as shown in Fig. 2.118 [118, 123, 127–130]. The profiles shown in Fig. 2.118a have zero dispersion that becomes small, such as ≤2 psec/km · nm in the wavelength range of 1.3–1.55 µm, provided the profile is optimal.

The conceptual curves of the delay and dispersion of these optical fibers are shown in Fig. 2.125.

Figures 2.126 and 2.127 [127] show profile and loss data of the fiber, which has the minimum loss value of the data already provided. A minimum loss value at 1.55 µm of 0.17 dB/km is obtained [127].

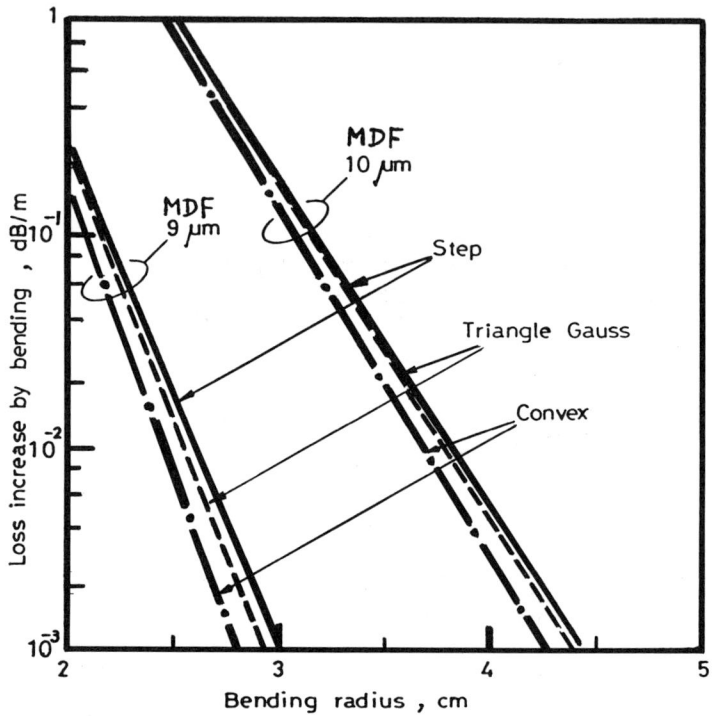

Figure 2.122 Loss and bending radius. (From Ref. 125.)

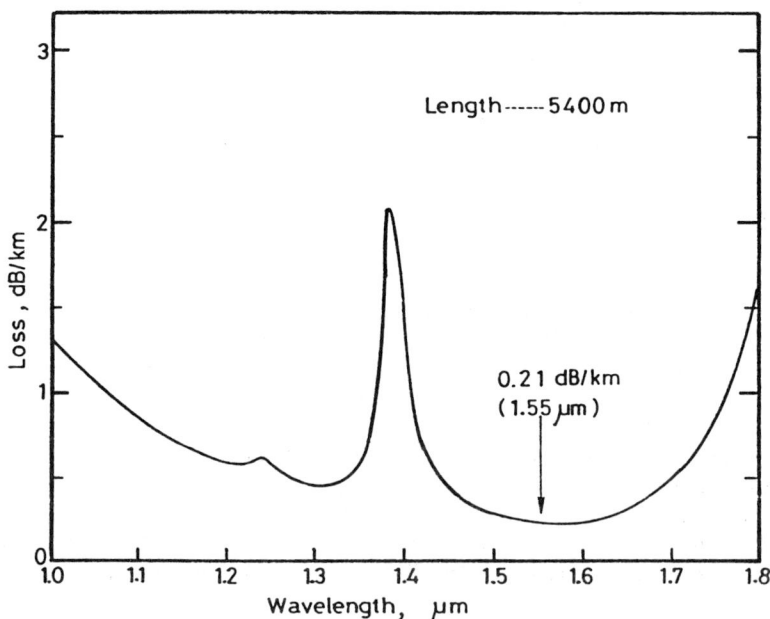

Figure 2.123 Spectral loss of Gaussian-type fiber. (From Ref. 126.)

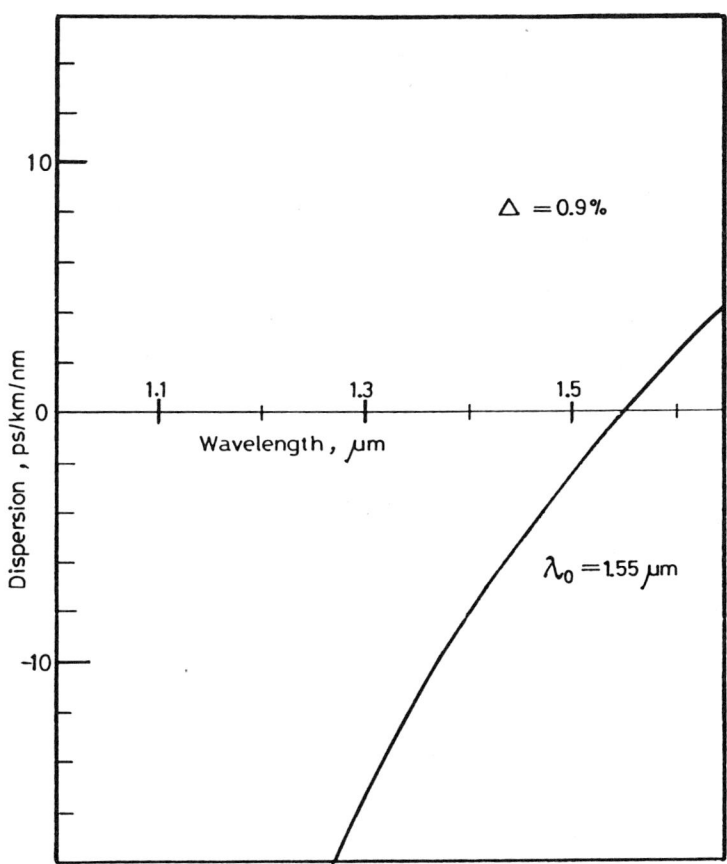

Figure 2.124 Wavelength dispersion of Gaussian-type fiber. (From Ref. 126.)

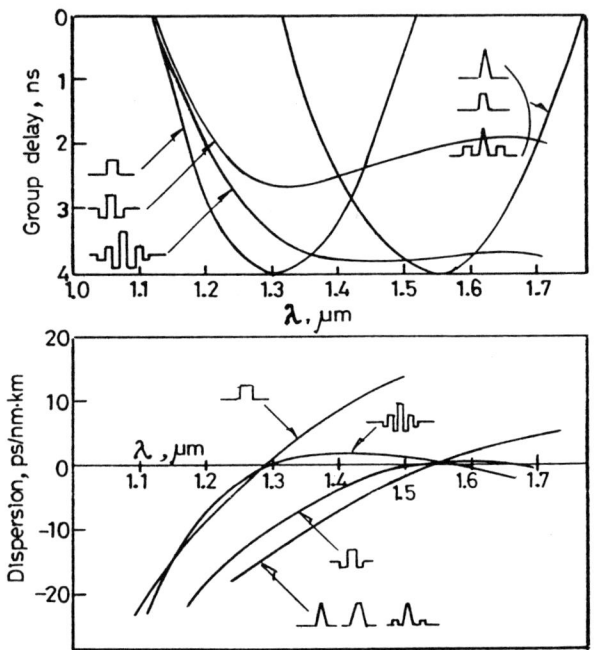

Figure 2.125 Single-mode fiber profile and dispersion. (From Refs. 122 and 129.)

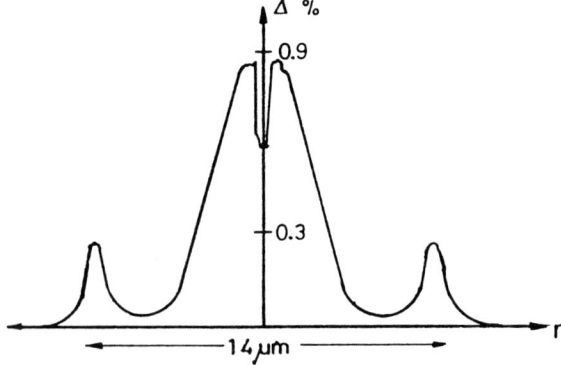

Figure 2.126 Refractive index profile of dispersion-shifted fiber. (From Ref. 127.)

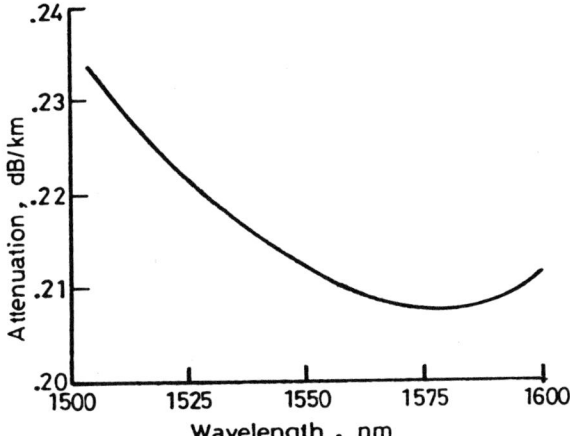

Figure 2.127 Spectral attenuation of dispersion-shifted fiber. (From Ref. 127.)

Studies are being made at present throughout the world of fibers of construction other than those presented here. Generally, the loss values of these fibers obtained on a test basis are approximately 0.2 to 0.25 dB/km.

REFERENCES

1. F. P. Kapron, D. B. Keck, and R. D. Maurer, Radiation losses in glass optical waveguides; *Trunk Telecom. Guid. Waves, IEE*, 148–153, September 1970.
2. R. Csencsits, P. J. Lemaire, W. A. Reed, D. S. Shenk, and K. L. Walker, Fabrication of low-loss single-mode fibers, OFC '84, TU13 (January 1984), pp. 54–55.
3. H. Yokota, H. Kanamori, Y. Ishiguro, G. Tanaka, S. Tanaka, H. Takada, M. Watanabe, S. Suzuki, K. Yano, M. Hoshikawa, and H. Shimba, Ultra-low-loss pure-silica-core single-mode fiber and transmission experiment, OFC '86, PD3-1 (February 1986), pp. 11–18.
4. R. D. Maurer, Glass fibers for optical communications, *Proc. IEEE*, 61(4): 452–462 (April 1973).
5. M. Nakahara, T. Edahiro, and N. Inagaki, Loss reduction in optical fibers, *Appl. Phys.*, 50(10): 1006–1020 (October 1981).
6. R. D. Maurer and C. C. Schultz, U. S. Pat. Ser. No. 72325 (September 15, 1970) (abandoned January 3, 1972).

7. D. B. Keck, R. D. Maurer, and D. C. Schultz, On the ultimate lower limit of attenuation in glass optical waveguide, *Appl. Phys. Lett.*, 22: 307–309 (1973).

8. N. Uchida, N. Uesugi, Y. Murakami, M. Nakahara, T. Tanifuji, and N. Inagaki, Infrared loss increase in silica optical fiber due to chemical reaction of hydrogen, 9th ECOC, PDP (October 1983).

9. H. Takata, Loss properties of optical fiber glass, *Appl. Phys.*, 47(5): 462–467 (May 1978).

10. N. Shibata, S. Shibata, S. Horiguchi, T. Izawa, and H. Osanai, Infrared absorption properties of silica glass, Nat'l Conv. IECE J., 820: 4–124 (March 1977).

11. T. Izawa, N. Shibata, and H. Takata, Optical attenuation in pure doped fused silica in the IR wavelength region, *Appl. Phys. Lett.*, 31(1): 33 (January 1977).

12. H. Yokota, G. Tanaka, H. Kanamori, F. Mizutani, H. Suganuma, and T. Kanzuka, Loss characteristics of pure-silica core single-mode optical fiber, Nat'l Conv. IECE J., 1127: 4–251 (March 1985).

13. H. Murata, S. Iano, Y. Matsuda, and T. Kuroha, Optimum design for optical fiber used in optical cable system, 4ECOC (September 1978), pp. 242–248.

14. M. I. Schwartz and M. J. Buckler, The choice of refractive index difference for multimode fibers operated at 1.3 μm, ICC '81, 27.1: 1–4 (June 1981).

15. M. Ogai, S. Yano, A. Iino, M. Higashimoto, K. Kokura, and K. Matsubara, Loss loss dispersion shifted fiber with fluorine doped cladding and step like index profile, OFC '86, P.D.P.4 (February 1986), pp. 19–22.

16. J. Schroeder, R. Mohr, P. B. Marcedo, and C. J. Montrose, Rayleigh and Brillouin scattering in K_2O-SiO_2 glasses, *J. Amer. Ceram. Soc.*, 56: 510–514 (1973).

17. K. Inada, A new graphical method relating optical fiber attenuation, *Opt. Comm.*, 19(3): 437–439 (December 1976).

18. R. Csencsite, P. J. Lemaire, W. A. Reed, D. S. Shenk, and K. L. Walker, Fabrication of low-loss single-mode fibers, OFC '84, TUI-3 (January 1984), pp. 54–55.

19. T. Miyahita, T. Miya, and M. Nakahara, An ultimate low loss single mode fiber at 1.55 μm, Top. Meet. Opt. Fiber Comm. P.D.1 (March 1979), pp. 1–5.

20. H. Yokota, H. Kanamori, Y. Ishiguro, G. Tanaka, S. Tanaka, H. Takata, M. Watanabe, S. Suzuki, K. Yano, M. Hoshikawa, and H. Shimba, Ultra-low-loss pure-silica-core single-mode fiber and transmission experiment, OFC '86, P.D.3–1 (February 1986), pp. 11–18.

References

21. S. Kabayashi, S. Shibata, N. Shibata, and T. Izawa, Refractive-index dispersion of doped fused silica, IOCC '77 (June 1977), pp. 309–312.

22. D. Gloge, and E. Z. J. Marcatili, Multimode theory of graded-core fibers, B.S.T.J., 52(9): 1563–1978 (November 1973).

23. D. Gloge, Weakly guiding fibers, Appl. Opt., 10(10): 2252–2258 (October 1971).

24. R. Olshansky and D. B. Keck, Pulse broadening in graded-index optical fibers, Appl. Opt., 15(2): 483–491 (February 1976).

25. T. Ohkoshi, Fundamental of optical fiber, Ohm, 83–130 (July 1977).

26. S. Ohhara and T. Kimura, Optical communication, Corona, 40–53 (November 1981).

27. Y. Matsuda, Transmission properties of multimode fiber, Furukawa Elec. Rev., 17–30 (March 1980).

28. M. Horiguchi, Y. Ohmori, K. Jinguji, and K. Okamoto, Evaluation of dispersive effects on transmission bandwidths in optical fiber waveguides, ECL Tech. Jr., 29(10): 1759–1770 (October 1980).

29. N. Shibata and T. Edahiro, Refractive-index despersion for GeO_2-, P_2O_5- and B_2O_3-doped silica glasses in optical fibers, Trans. IECE J., E65(3): 166–172 (March 1982).

30. S. R. Nagel, Fiber fabrication, OFC '85 Minitutorial, TUR1 (February 1985).

31. Y. Ohmori, H. Okazaki, M. Horiguchi, and I. Hatakeyama, Long wavelength graded index optical fiber, Nat'l. Conv. IECE J., S3–8: 4.241–4.242 (March 1979).

32. S. Sentsui, Y. Furui, T. Kamiya, K. Yoshida, and S. Horiguchi, A study on the optimum α of GI fiber for long-wavelength region, Nat'l Conv. IECE J., 885: 4–145 (March 1980).

33. T. Miyashita, T. Miya, Y. Terunuma, and A. Kowana, Low loss, Low dispersion single mode fiber, Nat'l Conv. Opt. Elec. Wave, S3–1 (September 1978).

34. T. Miyahita, Research for low loss single mode fiber, Ph.D. dissertation (June 1979).

35. K. Iwasaki, H. Yokota, S. Horiguchi, and K. Kitayama, Characteristics of graded index type fiber in the short and long wavelength regions, Nat'l Conv. IECE J., 882: 4–142 (March 1980).

36. A. A. Griffith, The phenomena of rupture and flaw in solid, Phys. Trans. Roy. Soc. (Lond.), 221: 163–198 (1920).

37. K. Noda, Optical fiber transmission, IECE J., Ohm, 142–147 (1978).

38. R. J. Charles, Static fatigue of glass I and II, J. Appl. Phys., 29(11): 1549–1560 (November 1958).

39. R. J. Charles, Dynamic fatigue of glass, *Appl. Phys.*, 29(11): 1657-1662 (December 1958).

40. D. Kalish and B. K. Tariyal, Static and dynamic fatigue of a polymer-coated fused silica optical fiber, *J. Amer. Ceram. Soc.*, 61(11-12): 518-523 (December 1978).

41. Y. Misunaga, Y. Katsuyama, and Y. Ishida, Reliability assurance for long-length optical fiber based on proof testing, *Electron Lett.*, 17(16): 567-568 (August 1981).

42. Y. Mitsunaga, Y. Katsuyama, H. Kobayashi, and Y. Ishida, Failure prediction for long length optical fiber based on proof testing, *J. Appl. Phys.*, 53(7): 4847-4853 (July 1982).

43. N. Uchida, N. Uesugi, Y. Murakami, M. Nakahara, T. Tanifuji, and N. Inagaki, Infrared loss increase in silica optical fiber due to chemical reaction of hydrogen, ECOC '83, P.D.P. (October 1983).

44. K. J. Beales, D. M. Copper, J. D. Rush, M. Fox, D. W. Plessner, and S. I. Stannard-Powell, Increased attenuation of optical fibers caused by diffusion of hydrogen, ECOC '83, P.D.P. (October 1983).

45. N. Uesugi, T. Kuwabara, Y. Koyamada, Y. Ishida, and N. Uchida, Optical loss increase of phosphor-doped silica fiber at high temperature in the long wavelength region, *Appl. Phys. Lett.*, 43(4): 327-328 (August 1983).

46. N. Uesugi, Y. Murakami, C. Tanaka, Y. Ishida, Y. Mitsunaga, Y. Negishi, and N. Uchida, Infrared optical loss increase for silica fiber in cable filled with water, *Electron Lett.*, 19(19): 762-764 (September 1983).

47. Y. Murakami, N. Uesugi, K. Noguchi, and Y. Mitsunaga, Optical fiber loss increase in the infrared wavelength region induced by electric current, *Appl. Phys. Lett.*, 43(10): 896-987 (November 1983)

48. M. Ogai, K. Orimo, K. Kokura, T. Kamiya, M. Takahina, and M. Azuma, Infrared loss increase of silica fiber in hydrogen atmosphere, OFC '84, P.D.P., WI 2-1-2-4 (January 1984).

49. M. Kawazuru, Y. Namihira, K. Mochizuki, and M. Nunokawa, A study on the long-term stability of optical submarine cables, Tech. Res. Report, *IECE J.*, CS84-47: 35-42 (July 1984).

50. Y. Namihira, M. Kawazuru, K. Mochizuki, and Y. Iwamoto, Hydrogen problems in optical fibers, Tech. Res. Report, *IECE J.*, CS84-46: 27-34 (July 1984).

51. T. Kamiya, N. Uchiyama, Y. Shibayama, M. Ogai, and M. Takanashi, Infrared loss stability of MCVD graded-index fibers with various glass composition, 10th ECOC, P.9 (September 1984), pp. 86-87.

52. M. Ogai, Effects of hydrogen on long-term reliability of optical fiber cable, OFC '85, TUKI (February 1985), pp. 46-47.

References

53. A. Iino, K. Kokura, M. Ogai, K. Orimo, and M. Azuma, Reduction of hydrogen effect on SiO_2—GeO_2 fiber by synthetic silica cladding, 10th ECOC, 15A6 (Deptember 1984), pp. 316–318.
54. H. Murata, S. Inao, and M. Ogai, Hydrogen problems and long term reliability of fiber cables, SPIE, 2nd Internt'l Tech. Symp. Opt. Electro-Opt. Appl. Sci. Eng. Optical Fiber Char. Standard (November 1985).
55. Y. Ohmori, H. Okazaki, M. Moriguchi, and I. Hatakeyama, Fabrication techniques of graded index optical fibers optimized for 1.3 μm wave length region, *ECL Tech. J.*, 29(2): 233–246 (Feb. 1980).
56. Y. Furui, T. Kamiya, A. Yeki, and S. Sentsui, Fabrication study of single-mode optical fibers with P/F-doped cladding, IOOC '81, WD5 (April 1981), pp. 100–101.
57. P. C. Schultz, Vapor phase materials and process for glass optical waveguides, a lecture at short course on recent advances in fiber optics, Univ. Rhode Island, (June 1978), pp. 1–40.
58. J. B. MacChesney, P. B. O'Connor, F. V. DiMarcello, J. R. Simpson, and P. D. Lazay, Preparation of low loss optical fibers using simulaneous vapor phase deposition and fusion, 10th Internl. Cong. Glass Cer. Soc. J. (July 1974), pp. 6–40-6–45.
59. T. Edahiro, K. Chida, Y. Omori, and H. Okazaki, Fabrication techniques for graded index optical fibers, *ECL Tech. J.*, 27(11): 2355–2382 (November 1978).
60. K. Chida, M. Okada, Y. Terunuma, and T. Edahiro, A machine aided fiber optic MCVD system, *ECL Tech. J.*, 27(11): 2369–2382 (November 1978).
61. H. Murata, Manufacturing of optical fibers in Japan, in *Optical Fiber Communications*, Vol. 1, edited by T. Li (January 1985), pp. 297–352.
62. M. Okada, M. Kawachi, and A. Kawana, Improved chemical vapor deposition method for long-length optical fibre, *Electron Lett.*, 14(4): 89–90 (February 1978).
63. D. Küppers and J. Koenings, Preform fabrication by deposition of thousands of layers with the aid of plasma activated CVD, 2nd ECOC, II.2 (September 1976), pp. 49–54.
64. D. Küppers, H. Lydtin, and F. Meijer, Preparation for optical fibers applied in Philips Research, IOOC '77 (June 1977), pp. 319–322.
65. P. K. Bachmann, P. Geittner, and H. Lydtin, Progress in the PCVD process, OFC '86, WA1 (February 1986), pp. 76–78.
66. S. R. Nagel, K. L. Walker, and J. B. MaChesney, Current status of MCVD: Process and performance, OFC '82, TUCC2 (April 1982), pp. 8–9.

67. J. W. Fleming, Status and prognosis for plasma MCVD, OFC '83, WG1 (February 1983), pp. 88–89.
68. T. Izawa, S. Kobayashi, S. Sudo, and F. Hanawa, Continuous fabrication of high silica fiber preform, IOOC '77, C1–1 (June 1977), pp. 375–378.
69. N. Niizeki, Recent progress in glass fibers for optical communication, *Jpn. J. Appl. Phys.*, 20(8): 1347–1360 (August 1981).
70. T. Izawa and N. Inagaki, Materials and processes for fiber preform fabrication, vapor-phase axial deposition, *Proc. IEEE*, 68(10): 1184–1187 (October 1980).
71. N. Inagaki, T. Edahiro, and M. Nakahara, Recent progress in VAD fiber fabrication process, *JPS. J. Appl. Phys.*, 20 (Suppl. 20–1): 175–180 (1981).
72. S. Sakaguchi, F. Hanawa, Y. Tajima, and M. Nakahara, High strength fiber drawing by carbon furnace, Natl. Conv. Semicond. Mater., 370: 371 (October 1981).
73. K. Imoto, S. Aoki, and M. Sumi, High speed fiber drawing by gas-flow controlling system, Natl. Conv. *IECE J.*, 925: 4–182 (March 1978)
74. R. B. Runk, A zirconia induction furnace for drawing precision silica waveguides, Top. Meet. Opt. Fiber Trans. (February 1977), pp. TuB5–1–5–4.
75. R. E. Jaeger, *Amer. Ceramic Soc. Bull.*, 55: 270–273 (1976).
76. S. Sakaguchi and T. Kimura, A 1200 m/min speed drawing of optical fibers with pressurized coating, OFC '85, MG-2 (February 1985), pp. 18–19.
77. K. Chida, M. Okada, Y. Terunuma, and T. Edahiro, A machine aided fiber optic MCVD system, *ECL Tech. J.*, 27(11): 2369–2382 (October 1978).
78. T. Edahiro, K. Chida, Y. Omori, and H. Okazaki, Fabrication techniques for graded index optical fibers, *ECL Tech. J.*, 27(11): 2355–2368 (October 1978).
79. Y. Furui, T. Kamiya, A. Ueki, and S. Sentsui, Fabrication study of single-mode optical fibers with P/F-doped cladding, IOOC '81 (April 1981), pp. 100–101.
80. G. Tanaka, M. Yoshida, N. Yoshioka, and Y. Masuda, A study on the reaction speed of MCVD process, Natl. Conv. 908, *IECE J.*, 4–165 (March 1978).
81. Y. Omori, H. Okazaki, M. Horiguchi, and I. Hatakeyama, Fabrication techniques of graded index optical fibers optimized for 1.3 μm wave length region, *ECL Tech. J.* 29(2): 233–246 (February 1980).

References

82. M. Okada, M. Kawachi, and A. Kawana, Improved chemical vapour deposition method for long-length optical fibre, *Electron Lett.*, *14*(4): 89–90 (February 1978).

83. T. Miyashita, Research for low loss single mode fiber, PhD. dissertion (June 1979).

84. M. Kawachi, M. Horiguchi, A. Kawana, and T. Miyashita, OH-ion distribution profiles in rod preforms of high-silica optical waveguide, *Electron Lett.*, *13*: 247–248 (April 1977).

85. M. Nakahara, S. Sudo, F. Hanawa, K. Chida, and K. Okamoto, Fabrication of optical fibers for long wavelength region by vapor-phase axial deposition method, Tech. Res. Report, OQE 79–79, *IECE J.*, 89–92 (September 1979).

86. K. Chida, S. Sudo, M. Nakahar, and N. Inagaki, On-line monitoring technique for refractive-index-profile in VAD process, 7th ECOC (September 1981), pp. 6.3.1–6.3.4.

87. S. Sudo, H. Suda, F. Hanawa, K. Chida, and M. Nakahara, Refractive-index profile control tehcniques in the vapor-phase axial deposition method, Tech. Res. Report, OQE 80–151, *IECE J.*, 67–74 (March 1981).

88. K. Yoshida, S. Shibuya, K. Kokura, S. Sentsui, T. Kuroha, M. Nakahara, and N. Inagaki, Ultrawide bandwidth optical fibers fabricated by VAD method, 6th ECOC (September 1980), pp. 6–9.

89. A. Tomaru, A. Sudao, M. Kawachi, and T. Edahiro, Japanese patent, Tokukai-Sho 56–52420 (1979).

90. M. Kawachi, S. Tomaru, T. Edahiro, and S. Sudo, U.S. patent 4,345 928 (1980).

91. M. J. Yuen and R. Fanucci, Fabricating small diameter soot forms as cores for single mode preforms: A technique, OFC '86, MF3 (February 1985), pp. 14–16.

92. F. Hanawa, M. Nakahara, K. Ogura, and T. Shioda, Manufacturing of all synthesized fiber, Natl. Conv. *IECE J.*, *941*: 4–138 (March 1982).

93. T. Shioda, Y. Ichikawa, T. Moriyama, K. Sanada, O. Fukuda, K. Chida, and T. Miya, All synthesized SM fiber by VAD, Natl. Conv. *IECE J.*, *942*: 4–139 (March 1982).

94. A. Sarker and T. M. Merritt, Design and performance of a hybrid process, OFC '85, MF1 (February 1985), pp. 14–15.

95. H. Suda, S. Shibata, and M. Nakahara, High-rate fabrication of wholly synthesized fibre preforms by the multi-frame VAD method using $SiHCl_3$ raw materials, *Electron Lett.*, *21*(24): 1123–1124 (November 1985).

96. H. Suda, S. Shibata, and M. Nakahra, High-rate fabrication of wholly synthesized fiber preforms by the multi-flame VAD method with SiHCl$_3$ raw materials, IOOC-ECOC '85 (October 1985), pp. 65–68.

97. T. Kanzuka, H. Yokota, I. Tsuchiya, and H. Takimoto, Investigation of SiHCl$_3$ on high speed deposition of VAD Natl. Conv. Opt. Wave, *IECE J.*, 416: 2–160 (October 1984).

98. H. Suda, S. Shibata, and M. Nakahara, Double-flame VAD process for high-rate optical preform fabrication, *Electron Lett.*, 21(1): 29–30 (January 1985).

100. T. Danzuka, H. Yokota, and I. Tsuchiya, High-speed deposition of grade-index fiber by the multi-flame vapor axial deposition method, OFC '85, MF5 (February 1985), pp. 16–17.

101. M. Miyamoto, M. Akiyama, T. Shiota, and K. Sanada, Fabrication and transmission characteristics of VAD fluorine doped single mode fibers, 9th ECOC (October 1983), pp. 9–12.

102. H. Kanamori, N. Yoshioka, M. Kyoto, M. Watanabe, and G. Tanaka, Fluorine doping in the VAD method and its application to optical fiber fabrication, 9th ECOC (October 1983), pp. 13–16.

103. K. Kokura, K. Yoshida, A. Iino, and K. Orimo, Fluorine doping in the consolidation process of VAD soot preform for single-mode fibers, OFC '84, MG6 (January 1984), pp. 22–23.

104. T. Abiru, M. Miyamoto, T. Ohashi, K. Kosaka, and O. Fukuda, Dehydration and fluorine doping in VAD sintering process, Natl. Conv. *IECE J.*, 1148: 4–202 (March 1984).

105. T. Ohashi, A. Wada, M. Miyamoto, R. Yamauchi, and O. Fukuda, Fabrication of fluorine doped graded index optical fibers by VAD method, Natl. Conv. Opt. Wave *IECE J.*, 442: 2–186 (October 1984).

106. S. Yano, K. Kokura, A. Iino, M. Koguchi, and K. Orimo, Characteristics of synthesized F-doped single-mode fiber, Natl. Conv. *IECE J.*, 1142: 4–226 (March 1985).

107. M. Kyoto, H. Kanamori, G. Tanaka, N. Yoshioka, and H. Goto, Refractive index control by using fluoride gas in the VAD sintering process, Natl. Conv. *IECE J.*, 1143: 4–197 (March 1984).

108. T. Edahiro, M. Kawachi, S. Sudo, and H. Takata, OH$^-$ ion reduction in VAD optical fibres, *Electron Lett.*, 15(16): 482–483 (August 1980).

109. T. Moriyama, O. Fukuda, K. Sanada, and K. Inada, Ultimately low OH content VAD optical fibres, *Electron Lett.*, 16(18): 698–699 (August 1980).

110. M. Kawachi, A. Kawana, and T. Miyashita, Low-loss single mode fiber at the material-dispersion-free wavelength of 1.27 μm, *Electron Lett.*, *13*: 442–443 (July 1977).

111. T. Miyashita, Research for low loss single mode fiber, Ph.D. dissertation (June 1979).

112. L. G. Cohen, D. Marcuse, and W. L. Mammel, Controlling leaky-mode loss and dispersion in single-mode lightguides with depressed-index cladding, OFC '82, THCC1 (April 1982), pp. 52–53.

113. Y. Kamikura, M. Mikami, Y. Mizota, and K. Okubo, Low loss, high strength SM fiber wholly synthesized by VAD process, Natl. Conv. 1093, *IECE J.*, 4–264 (March 1986).

114. K. Ogawa, Considerations for single-mode fiber systems, *BSTJ*, *61*(8): 1919–1931 (October 1982).

115. H. Tsuchiya and N. Imoto, Single-mode fiber delay equalization and baseband response, Tech. Res. Report, OQE 79-22, *IECE J.*, 31–38 (May 1979).

116. N. Imoto, A. Sugimura, K. Daikoku, and T. Miya, Dispersion characteristics of single-mode optical fibers, *ECL Tech. J.* *28*(6): 963–979 (June 1979).

117. A. W. Snyder, I. White, and D. T. Michell, Radiation from bent optical waveguide, *Electron Lett.*, *11*(15): 332–333 (1975).

118. Y. Murakami, I. Hatakeyama, and H. Tsuchiya, Normalized frequency dependence of splices in single-mode optical fibers, *Electron Lett.*, *14.9*: 277 (1978).

119. S. Terunuma, T. Miya, Y. Omori, M. Horiguchi, and A. Kawana, Manufacture of 1.5 μm band zero-dispersion single-mode fiber, Natl. Conv. *IECE J.*, *921*: 4–181 (March 1980).

120. N. Imoto, H. Tsuchiya, and A. Kawana, Properties of 1.5 μm zero-dispersion fiber, Natl. Conv. *IECE J.*, *922*: 4–182 (March 1980).

121. M. Ogai, S. Yano, A. Iino, M. Higashimoto, K. Kokura, and K. Matsubara, Low loss dispersion shifted fiber with fluroine doped cladding and step like index profile, OFC '86, P.D.P.4 (February 1986), pp. 19–22.

122. M. A. Saifi, S. J. Tang, L. G. Cohen, and J. Stone, Triangular-profile single-mode fiber, *Opt. Lett.*, *7*(1): 43–45 (January 1982).

123. A. D. Peason, L. G. Cohen, W. A. Reed, J. T. Krause, E. A. Sigety, and F. V. Dimarcello, Transmission, splicing, cabling performance of dispersion-shifted single-mode fiber, OFC '84, TUI 5 (January 1984), pp. 56–57.

124. T. J. Miller and D. H. Smithgall, Fabrication of trapezoidal-index profile single-mode fiber, OFC '84, TUI 4 (January 1984), pp. 54–55.

125. N. Kuwaki, M. Ohashi, C. Tanaka, and N. Uesugi, Characteristics of zero-chromatic dispersion fibers at 1.5 μm wave-length region, Natl. Conv. Semi-Cond. Mater. *IECE J.*, *412*: 1–227 (November 1985).

126. M. Miyamoto, T. Abiru, T. Ohashi, R. Yamauchi, and O. Fukuda, Gaussian profile dispersion shifted fibers made by VAD method, IOOC-ECOC '85 (October 1985), pp. 193–196.

127. T. D. Craft and J. E. Ritter, Low-loss dispersion shifted single-mode fiber manufactured by the OVD process, WD2, OFC '85 (February 1985), pp. 94–95.

128. D. M. Cooper, S. P. Craig, C. R. Day, and B. J. Ainslie, Multiple-index structure for dispersion shifted single-mode fibers, WD4, OFC '85 (February 1985), pp. 96–97.

129. L. G. Cohen, W. L. Mammel, and S. J. Jang, Ultrabroadband single-mode fibers, MF 4, OFC '83 (February 1983), pp. 10–11.

130. V. A. Bhagavatula and P. E. B.aszyk, Single-mode fiber with segmented core, MF5, OFC '83 (February 1983), pp. 10–11.

3
Optical Fiber Cable

3.1 INTRODUCTION

Unlike conventional copper conductor communication cables, optical fiber cables require particular attention to the following design points.

The loss of the fiber is increased by very small bends. To reduce this microbending loss increase, the fiber must be designed to receive no stress. For graded index (GI) fiber, the microbending loss increase is (refer to Sec. 3.2.1)

$$\alpha_m = k \frac{1}{\Delta^3} \frac{a^4}{b^4} \frac{1}{d^2} \frac{E_p^2}{E_f^2}$$

and for single-mode (SM) fiber,

$$\alpha_m = K\Delta^{-(S+1)} \lambda_c^S W^{-(S-2)}$$

The elongation of the fiber is now generally 5% on the average (minimum about 1%). The breaking strength of fiber with a diameter of 125 μm averages approximately 5 kg (minimum 1 kg). The mechanical design of the cable must be made in full consideration of these values.

When the fiber is coated with plastics, in consideration of the microbending loss increase and the breaking strength and strain, it

179

is desirable to apply first a soft plastic with a low Young's modulus and then a hard plastic with a high Young's modulus.

For reduction in loss increase due to bending, the fiber must not be bent in a diameter of less than 6 cm. It is desirable that the pitch of fiber stranding be not less than 50 mm and preferably 100 mm or over.

Deformation of the plastic sheath is an important factor in avoiding microbending loss increase. The deformation δ of plastic tube is (refer to Sec. 3.2.4)

$$\delta = K \left(\frac{R^{1+2n}}{t^{2+n}} \; \frac{1}{\sigma^*} \; \frac{P}{L} \right)^{1/n}$$

A strength member is indispensable to the fiber cable because the absolute values of elongation and the breaking strength of the fiber are not large. The strength of the strength member must be so determined that when the fiber cable is installed, the elongation of the fiber becomes no more than 0.2%.

The coefficients of thermal expansion per °C of fiber and plastics are about 10^{-7} and 10^{-4}, respectively—a large difference. When the fiber cable is exposed to low temperature, microbends are liable to develop in the fiber owing to shrinkage of plastics, increasing the microbending loss of the fiber.

To prevent such a microbending loss increase at low temperature, we have, for example, a method in which plastic-coated fibers are stranded on a strength member, such as iron wire or FRP wire, with a small coefficient of thermal expansion. The elongation or shrinkage of a composite sheath is (refer to Sec. 3.2.6)

$$\Delta \varepsilon = \frac{E_2(T)A_2}{E_1(T)A_1 + E_2(T)A_2} (\alpha_2 - \alpha_1) \Delta T$$

Optical fiber cables are roughly classified into the following four types (See Table 3.14 in Sec. 3.3.3).

1. Stranding (thick double-coating): suitable for cable with a small or moderate number of fibers; applied mainly in Japan
2. Loose tube high-density: for general use; low microbending loss increase; applied mainly in the United States and Europe
3. Ribbon: suitable for a cable with a large number of fibers; applied mainly in the United States
4. V-groove: for general use; low microbending loss increase; applied mainly in Europe and Canada

3.2 BASIC CONDITIONS OF OPTICAL FIBER CABLE DESIGN

The basic concept of development and design of optical cables is as follows. Optical cable (1) can be handled and installed in the same way as ordinary telecommunications cable; (2) permits field splicing; (3) has electrical and mechanical properties conforming to the conditions under which it is used; (4) has a high reliability and a long service life; and (5) is economical.

3.2.1 Microbending Loss Increase

3.2.1.1 General

Microbending loss is a transmission loss peculiar to the optical axis of the fiber if it is not straight and has a minute bend, and if the angle at which light propagating in the fiber core, which is incident upon the cladding layer, changes, thereby causing the radiation of light energy from the core to the cladding layer. This results in a transmission loss of light, which is called the microbending loss (Fig. 3.1).

Microbending loss is caused in each step of the production of fiber cable, and when improper manufacturing techniques are used, loss may reach 0.1 to 10 dB/km. Reduction of this loss may be regarded as crucial to the technique and know-how of cable design

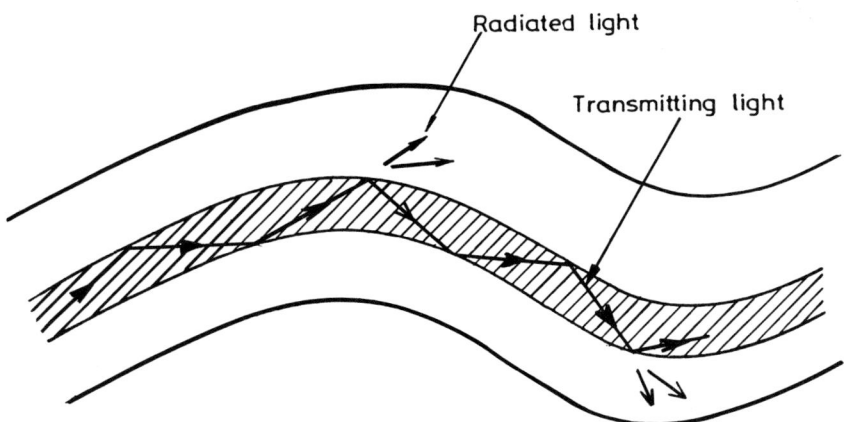

Figure 3.1 Microbending loss of fiber.

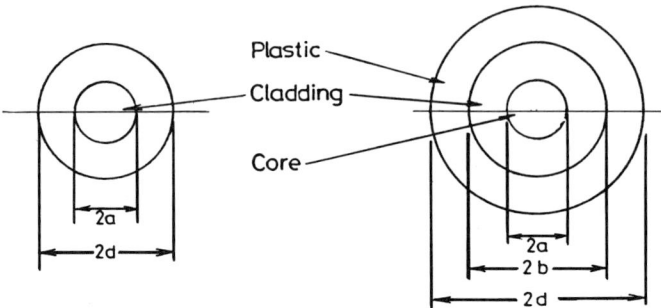

Figure 3.2 Plastic-covered fiber.

and production. To prevent microbending loss, the fiber must be kept free of any minute bend due to external stress during production and after installation.

When in practical use the fiber is generally covered with plastics to retain its strength. The idea of covering the fiber with a soft plastic cover (called the buffer layer) has been worked out to reduce the microbending loss increase α_m.

The loss increase due to microbending of bare optical fiber (α_{m1}) is expressed by Eq. (3.1)[1]:

$$\alpha_{m1} = \frac{K_{m1}}{\Delta^3} \frac{a^4}{b^6} \tag{3.1}$$

where:

Δ = relative refractive index difference = $(n_1 - n_2)/n_1$

a = radius of fiber core

b = radius of fiber cladding

K_{m1} = proportional constant

When plastic-covered fiber receives an external stress, however, the stress is alleviated by the plastic covering; as a result, the loss increase α_{m2} due to microbending of the plastic-covered fiber becomes smaller than α_{m1} and is expressed as follows (Fig. 3.2) [2-4].

$$\alpha_{m2} = \frac{K_{m2}}{\Delta^3} \frac{a^4}{b^4} \frac{1}{d^2} \frac{E_p^2}{E_f^2} \tag{3.2}$$

Basic Conditions of Design

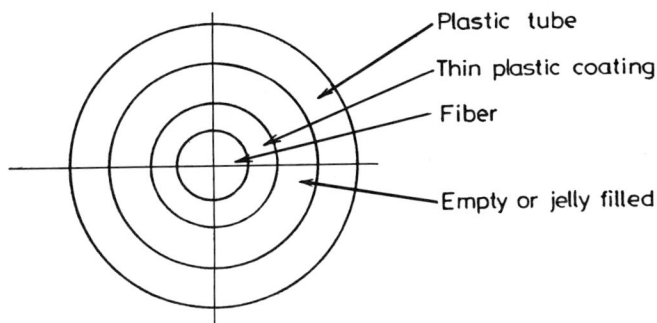

Figure 3.3 Loose-tube-covered fiber.

where:

    a = radius of fiber core

    b = radius of fiber cladding

    d = radius of covered plastic

    E_p = Young's modulus of covered plastic

    E_f = Young's modulus of fiber

    K_{m2} = proportional constant

The microbending loss (dB/km) of bare fiber is compared with that of plastic-covered fiber as follows:

Bare fiber	Plastic-covered fiber
$K_{m1} \dfrac{1}{\Delta^3} \dfrac{a^4}{b^6}$	$K_{m2} \dfrac{1}{\Delta^3} \dfrac{a^4}{b^4} \dfrac{1}{d^2} \dfrac{E_p^2}{E_f^2}$

From the Eqs. (3.1) and (3.2), it is learned that microbending loss increase can be prevented by covering the fiber as thickly as is practical with soft plastics (the so-called buffer layer).

In the Eq. (3.1), if E_p is zero, α_{m2} is zero. For this reason, the construction shown in Fig. 3.3 is sometimes used, in which the fiber is covered with a loose plastic tube.

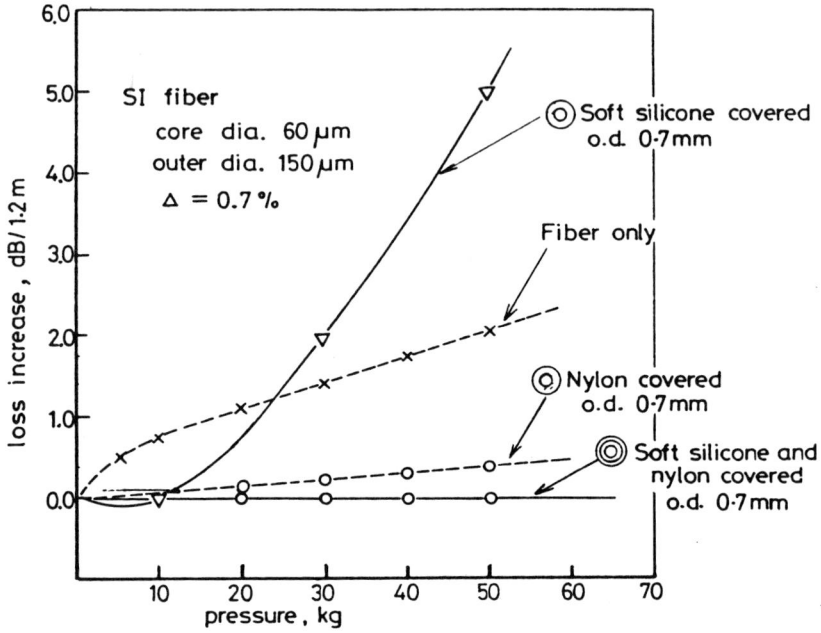

Figure 3.4   Loss increase by lateral pressure. (From Ref. 5.)

Figure 3.4 shows the results of a test made of an increase in the microbending loss of fibers covered with plastics of varied hardness. It indicates a loss increase in the 1.2 m fiber held between boards to which lateral pressure is applied [5].

When the fiber is covered only with soft plastic, stress that directly works on the fiber is small because of the presence of the plastic. Therefore, the microbending loss increase is small. This result is evident from Eq. (3.2). When this stress becomes large, the soft plastic collapses completely and cannot serve as a buffer layer. Thus, the fiber covered only with soft plastic suddenly increases in microbending loss when a stress of a certain degree is applied. This defect is eliminated in a fiber covered with a layer of hard plastic above the soft plastic. In such a hard plastic and buffer-covered fiber, the microbending loss does not increase much even when a substantial stress works on it. It is thus evident that the soft buffer layer on the fiber by itself is not sufficiently effective in reducing the microbending loss increase and that a hard plastic cover must be applied over it to form a crust.

Basic Conditions of Design

Table 3.1 Values for x and y

$\lambda/\lambda c$	1.0	1.1	1.2	1.3	1.4	1.5	1.7	2.0
x	4300	3700	3300	3200	3200	3400	4000	6200
y	2.47	1.61	1.06	0.687	0.444	0.284	0.113	0.0249

3.2.1.2 Microbending Loss Increase of Single-mode Fiber [6]

The microbending loss increase is generally smaller in SM fiber cable than in GI fiber cable because SM fiber is much smaller in core diameter than GI fiber. When SM fiber cable is made with GI fiber cable-manufacturing techniques, its microbending loss increase is about 0 to 0.02 dB/km. There are some papers dealing with theoretical calculation of this loss increase. Here the following formula is used [6]:

$$L_s = xN \left(\frac{1}{R^2}\right) \overline{W}^2 \frac{1}{\Delta} \exp\left[-y\left(\frac{\overline{W}n_1}{\lambda c}\right)^2 \Delta^2\right] \text{ dB/km} \quad (3.3)$$

where:
- N = average number of bends per meter
- $(1/R)^2$ = mean square of the curvature of fiber axis
- W = correlation length
- λc = cutoff wavelength
- n_1 = index of the core
- Δ = relative refractive index difference
- x, y = function of $\lambda/\lambda c$ (Table 3.1 and Figure 3.5)

Approximately,

$$L_s \propto \Delta^{-(S+1)} \lambda_c^S \overline{W}^{-(S-2)} \quad (3.4)$$

$$S = 2\left[y\left(\frac{\overline{w}n_1}{\lambda c}\Delta\right)\right]^2 \quad (3.5)$$

Generally, W = 1 to 1.5 mm. The value of S depends largely on λ, which is approximately 2 in the range from 10 to 0.5. A sample

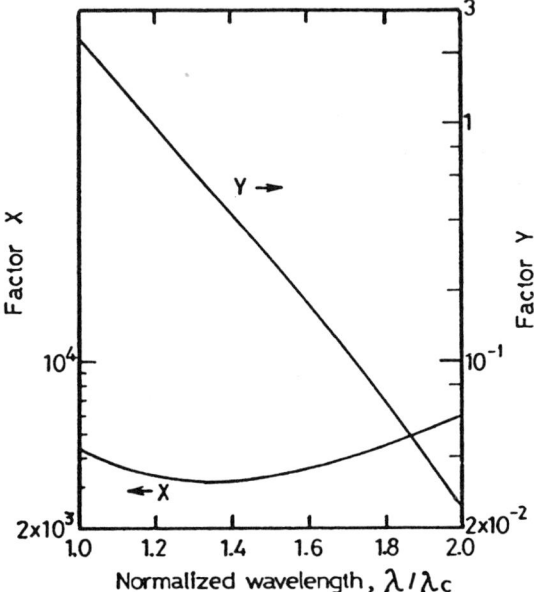

Figure 3.5 Factors x and y. (From Ref. 6.)

calculation is given in Fig. 3.6. When $\Delta = 0.3\%$, the microbending loss increase is less than 0.001 dB/km at 1.3 μm and 0.02 dB/km at 1.55 μm. It must be noted that this value increases sharply as the wavelength is increased.

3.2.2 Mechanical Design of Optical Fiber Cable

The average elongation of silica fiber is about 5%, far less than that of the copper conductor, which is about 25%. The minimum bending diameter of the fiber is 2 to 3 mm. Also in this respect, the fiber greatly differs from the copper conductor, which can be bent on its own diameter (1 mm or less). These characteristics must be noted in the mechanical design of fiber cables.

The optical fiber is usually covered by plastic to prevent corrosion due to scoring and moisture on the surface.

The plastic-covered fiber is subject to various types of mechanical stress during the production process, during and after installation. The type of plastic to be used, its characteristics, and the coat thickness are therefore specified in consideration of resistance to mechanical stress. Designing the thickness of the plastic to be coated on a fiber is described on the next page [7-9].

Basic Conditions of Design

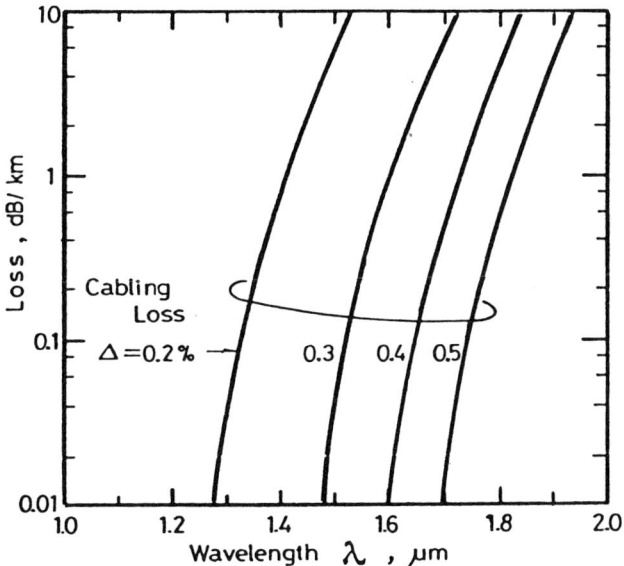

Figure 3.6 Microbending loss increase versus wavelength: $\lambda_c = 1$ μm, $W = 1.2$ mm, $N(1/R_1)^2 = 92$ m^{-3}, and $n_1 = 1.46$. (From Ref. 6.)

3.2.2.1 Tension

When a tensile load W is applied to a plastic-covered fiber, the tensile stress W appearing in the fiber is expressed as

$$\sigma_W = \frac{1}{1 + E_p/E_f[(d_p/d_f)^2 - 1]} \frac{W}{\pi d_f^2} \qquad (3.6)$$

where:

E_p = Young's modulus of plastic cover
E_f = Young's modulus of fiber
d_p = outer diameter of plastic cover
d_f = outer diameter of fiber

3.2.2.2 Bending

When a fiber is bent, the bending stress σ_b appearing in the fiber is expressed as

$$\sigma_b = \frac{E_f d_f}{2R} \tag{3.7}$$

where R is the bending radius.

3.2.2.3 Torsion

When torsion is applied to a fiber, the shearing stress reaches a maximum on the fiber surface. This is expressed as

$$\tau = \frac{G_f d_f}{2} \frac{\theta}{l} \tag{3.8}$$

where:

τ = shearing stress on fiber surface

θ = angle of torsion

l = length of fiber

G_f = rigidity of fiber

3.2.2.4 Tension, Bending, and Torsion

When tension, bending, and torsion are simultaneously applied to a fiber, the maximum combined stress σ_{max} is expressed as

$$\begin{aligned}\sigma_{max} &= \frac{1}{2}(\sigma_w + \sigma_b) + \frac{1}{2}\sqrt{(\sigma_w + \sigma_b)^2 + 4\tau^2} \\ &= \frac{1}{2}\left\{ \frac{1}{1 + \frac{E_p}{E_f}\left[\left(\frac{d_p}{d_f}\right)^2 - 1\right]} \frac{4W}{\pi d_f^2} + \frac{E_f d_f}{2R} \right\} \\ &\quad + \frac{1}{2}\sqrt{\left\{ \frac{1}{1 + \frac{E_p}{E_f}\left[\left(\frac{d_p}{d_f}\right)^2 - 1\right]} \frac{4W}{\pi d_f^2} + \frac{E_f d_f}{2R} \right\}^2 + 4\left(\frac{G_f d_f}{2}\frac{\theta}{l}\right)^2} \end{aligned} \tag{3.9}$$

3.2.2.5 Sample Calculation

A coating material and the thickness of the coat should be selected to satisfy Eq. (3.10) when the rupture strength is

Table 3.2 Properties of Plastics

Plastics	Tensile strength (kg/mm^2)	Elongation (%)	Young's modulus (kg/mm^2 × 10^2)	Thermal expansion (10^{-5}/°C)
Nylon	5.6–6.5	300	1.3–2.4	20
Polyethylene (PE)	—	—	—	—
High density	2.1–3.8	15–100	0.4–0.7	11–13
Low density	0.7–1.4	90–650	0.1–0.24	10–22
Polypropylene	3.3–4.2	200–700	1.1–1.4	8–9.5
Poly (vinyl chloride) (PVC) (soft)	0.7–2.4	200–400	0.1	7–21
Fluoroethylenepropylene (FEP)	2–3.2	250–330	0.35	8.3–10.5

Table 3.3 Properties of Silica

Silica fiber	Tensile strength (kg/mm^2)	Elongation (%)	Young's modulus (kg/mm^2 × 10^2)	Thermal expansion (10^{-5}/°C)
Optical fiber	500	5	71	0.051
Ordinary silica fiber	100	—	—	—

Basic Conditions of Design

$$\sigma_{max} < \frac{\sigma_0}{f} \tag{3.10}$$

where f is the safety coefficient.

The names of plastic materials to be used in cable and their respective properties are listed in Table 3.2. Silica fiber properties are listed in Table 3.3. It is most important to reduce σ_{max} so that Young's modulus of the plastic is large. Plastic materials with a large Young's modulus are nylon, polypropylene, ultraviolet (UV)-cured plastics, and others. Nylon is used as a covering material, especially for fiber, all over the world.

Assuming these properties, examples of plastic materials and covering thickness are given in Figs. 3.7 and 3.8 and Table 3.4 (including safety factors 1, 2, and 3). The value of the outer diameter

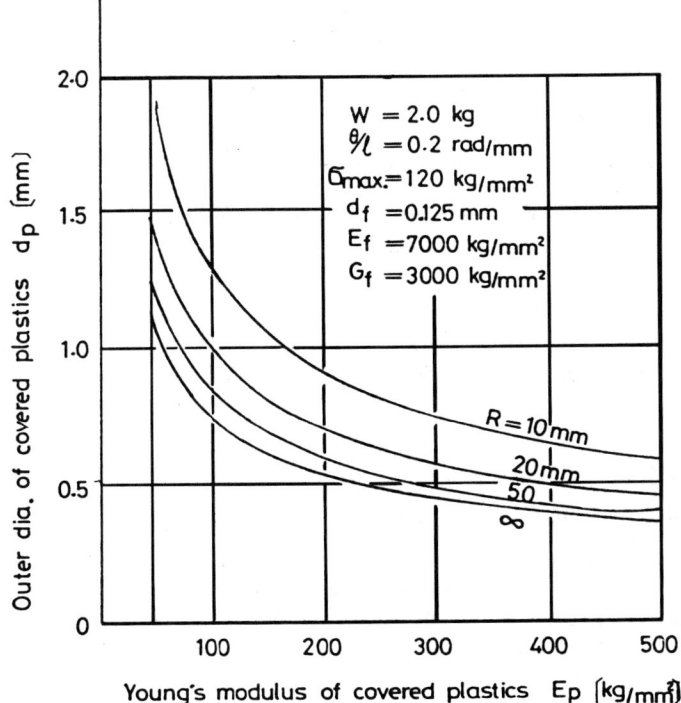

Figure 3.7 Plastic-covered fiber under tension, bending, and torsion. (From Refs. 7 and 8.)

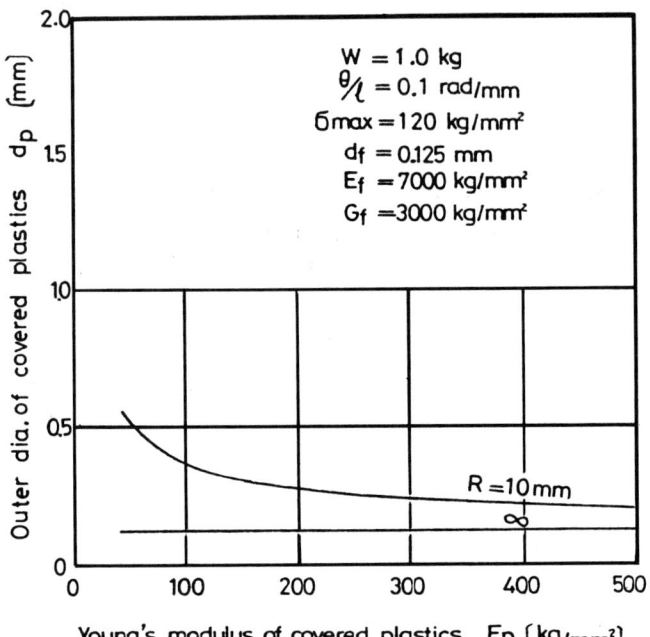

Figure 3.8 Plastic-covered fiber under tension, bending, and torsion. (From Refs. 7 and 8.)

of the plastic-covered fiber d = 0.8 to 1 mm, when the plastic material is nylon, is accepted world wide. In Japan, d = 0.9 mm is now widely used.

3.2.3 Stranded Fibers in the Cable

3.2.3.1 Loss of Uniformly Bent Fibers

Fibers are always stranded and bent when made into a cable core. I therefore relate first the transmission loss of uniformly bent fibers. The loss coefficients α_s and α_g of uniformly bent fibers of the step index and graded index types are expressed by the following equations [10, 11]:

$$\alpha_s = 2n_1 k(\theta_c^2 - \theta^2) \exp\left[-\frac{2}{3} n_1 kR \left(\theta_c^2 - \theta^2 - \frac{2a}{R}\right)^{3/2}\right] \quad (3.11)$$

$$\alpha_g = 2n_1 k(\theta_c^2 - \theta\theta c) \exp\left[-\frac{2}{3} n_1 kR \left(\theta_c^2 - \theta^2 - \frac{2a}{R}\right)^{3/2}\right] \quad (3.12)$$

Table 3.4 Outer Diameter of Plastic Cover[a]

Condition		Outer diameter of covered plastics (mm)		
		Safety factor 1	Safety factor 2	Safety factor 3
I	$W \leq 1$ kg $R = \infty$ $\theta/\ell = 0$	0.125	0.43	0.61
II	$W \leq 1$ kg $R \geq 60$ mm $\theta/\ell = 0$	0.125	0.56	0.85
III	$W \leq 1$ kg $R = \infty$ $\theta/\ell \leq 0.1$ rad/mm	0.125	0.51	0.88
IV	$W \leq 1$ kg $R \geq 60$ mm $\theta/\ell \leq 0.1$ rad/mm	0.125	0.62	1.10

[a]Constants for calculation: $d_f = 0.125$ mm; $E_f = 7000$ kg/mm^2; $G_f = 3000$ kg/mm^2; $E_p = 230$ kg/mm^2; $\sigma_0 = 120$ kg/mm^2.
Source: From Refs. 7 and 8.

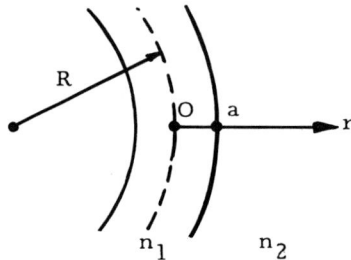

Figure 3.9 Bent fiber.

where:

    θ = transmission angle corresponding to mode

    θ_c = critical angle

    $k = \omega\sqrt{\mu_0 \varepsilon_0} = 2\pi/\lambda$

The bending loss of single-mode fiber of step index type is [12, 13]

$$\alpha = \frac{\sqrt{\pi} U^2}{2W^{3/2} V^2 (Ra)^{1/2} K_1^2(W)} \exp^{-4\Delta W^3 R/3aV^2} \tag{3.13}$$

where:

    $U = a(n_1^2 k^2 - \beta^2)^{1/2}$

    $V = ka(n_1^2 - n_2^2)^{1/2}$

    $W = a(\beta^2 - k^2 n_2^2)^{1/2}$

    K_1 = modified Bessel function

Figure 3.10 shows the radius of curvature R at which the value of the loss increase α obtained from Eqs. (3.2) and (3.11) becomes 0.1 dB/km [14].

When Δ = 1% and α = 1.3 μm, the bending radius against a bend-induced loss increase of 0.1 dB/km is 3.0 cm (graded index type).

The relative refractive index differences Δ against the same loss increase 0.1 dB/km with same R are as follows [14]

Basic Conditions of Design 195

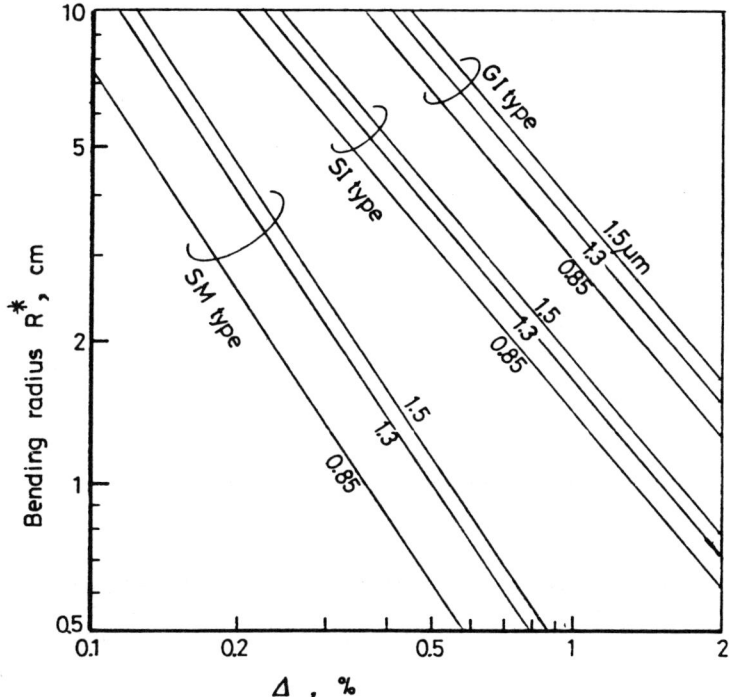

Figure 3.10 Relation between Δ and bending radius R of 1 dB loss increase. (From Ref. 14.)

Single mode	0.25%
Step multimode	0.7%
Graded multimode	1.2%

In an experiment on fiber bending, the loss increase of GI fiber bent at a bending radius of R was as follows (Fig. 3.11) [15, 16]:

$$\alpha_{dB} \simeq 80R^{-1.9} \quad R \text{ in mm} \tag{3.14}$$

where fiber length $\ell = 5$ m).

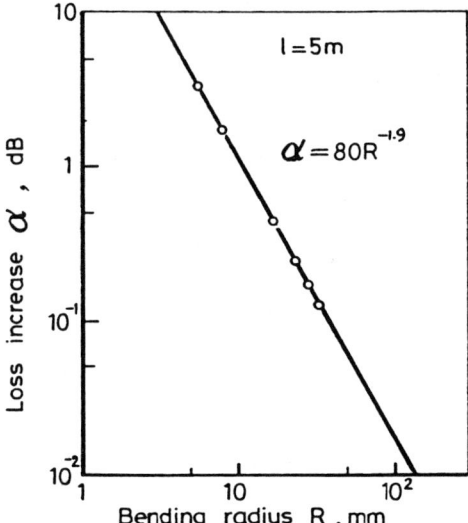

Figure 3.11 Relation between bending radius and loss increase (0.85 μm). Fiber: GI core, 50 μm; OD 125 μm; Δ 1%. Fiber is covered with soft plastic (OD 0.4 mm) and nylon (OD 0.9 mm). (From Refs. 15 and 16.)

Figure 3.12 shows the loss increase of GI fiber wound with a pitch p and a pitch winding diameter r. The equivalent bending radius Re of the fiber is

$$Re = \frac{p^2}{4\pi^2 r} + r \qquad (3.15)$$

The number of turns of fiber N is expressed by the equation

$$N = \frac{1}{\sqrt{(2\pi r)^2 + p^2}} \qquad (3.16)$$

where ℓ is the fiber length.

The solid line in Fig. 3.12 indicates the calculated value from Eq. (3.14), with R replaced by Re. Figure 3.12 demonstrates that the fiber stranding pitch must be no less than 50 mm to keep the loss increase at 0.1 dB/km or less.

Figure 3.11 shows the values obtained by measurement when the transmission mode in the fiber became stationary. These data,

Basic Conditions of Design

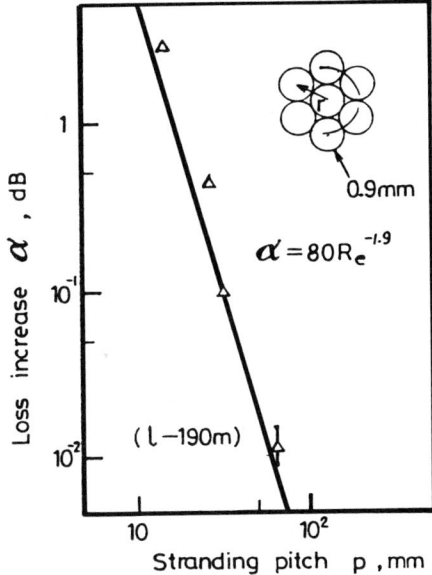

Figure 3.12 Relation between stranding pitch and loss increase (fiber characteristics as in Fig. 3.11). (From Refs. 15 and 16.)

however, substantially differ in absolute value from those given in Fig. 3.10 and Eqs. (3.11) and (3.12). The data in Fig. 3.9 were obtained from a theoretical calculation of radiation loss of a fiber that was bent uniformly. In contrast, Fig. 3.11 shows the losses of the bent fiber and includes microbending loss and others. This is considered a reason for the difference in value between the two figures.

Shown below are data obtained from testing the loss increase of SM fiber owing to bending. The end of SM fiber approximately 5 km long was wound in 10 turns, each in a specified bending diameter, and the loss increase was measured. The results are shown in Fig. 3.13. The fiber used for this measurement was as follows:

Fiber	$\lambda c (\mu m)$	Spot size (μm)
1	1.23	5.41
2	1.44	5.54

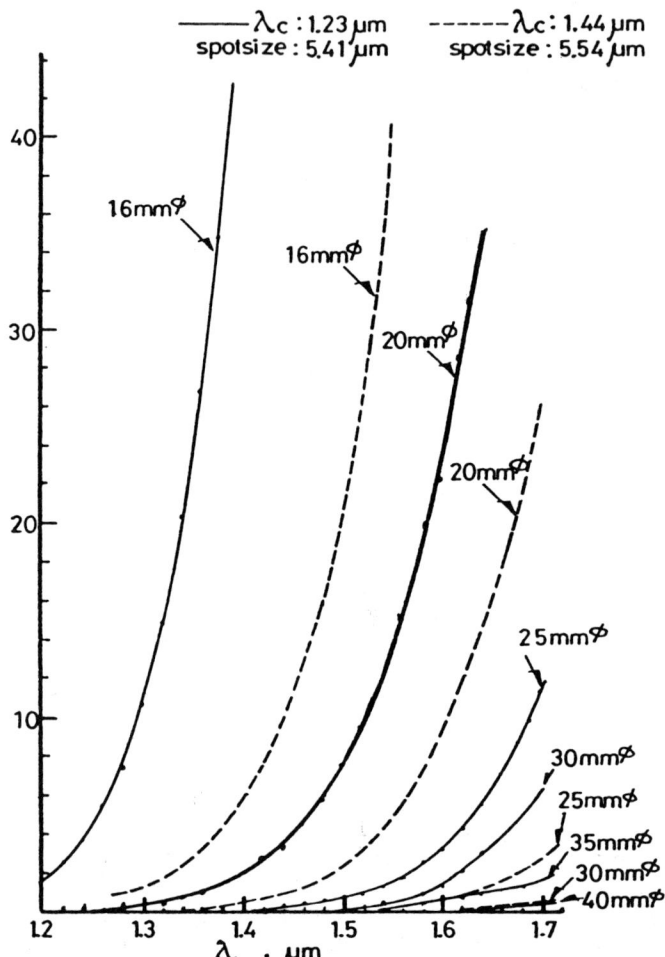

Figure 3.13 Bending loss increase of SM fiber.

Basic Conditions of Design

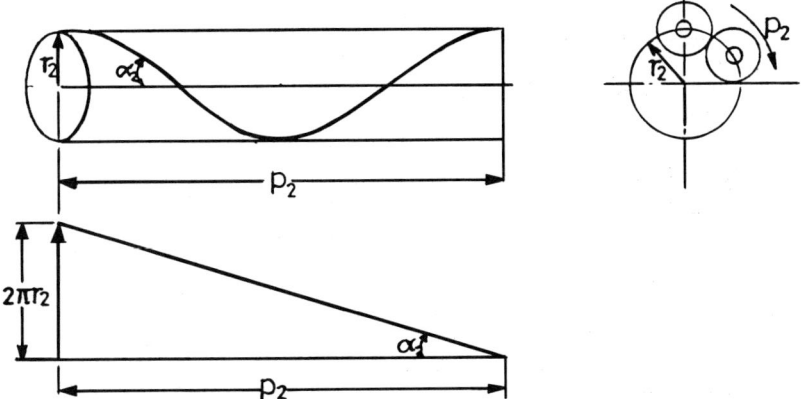

Figure 3.14 Stranding of fiber.

The fiber may be considered practically free from loss increase owing to bending at wavelengths up to 1.55 μm when bent in a diameter of 40 mm or more.

3.2.3.2 Fiber Bend in Stranded Cable

Single-layer Stranded Cable

The radius of curvature ρ_u and bending radius r_u of a fiber wound with a pitch P_2 on a cylinder with radius r_2 (Fig. 3.14) are expressed by the following formulas.

$$r_u = \frac{1}{\rho_u} = \frac{r_2}{\sin^2 \alpha_2} \qquad (3.17)$$

In these equations, α_2 represents the pitch angle and is indicated by

$$\sin \alpha_2 = \frac{2\pi r_2}{\sqrt{(2\pi r_2)^2 + p^2}} \qquad (3.18)$$

Therefore,

$$r_u = r_2 \left[1 + \left(\frac{P_2}{2\pi r_2} \right)^2 \right] \qquad (3.19)$$

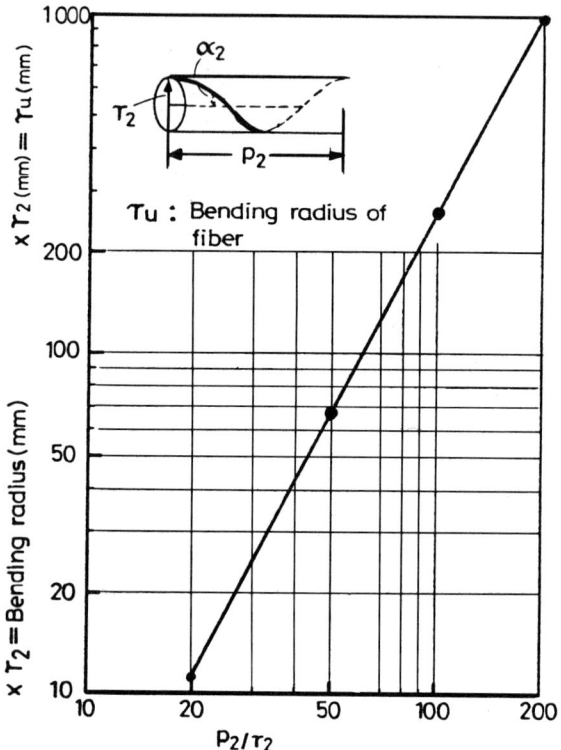

Figure 3.15 Bending radius τ_u and pitch-pitch diameter (for layered cable).

Figure 3.15 shows the relation between p_2/r_2 and r_u.

When the bending radius r_u of a fiber is 30 mm or more, its loss increase caused by bending is in practice very small. The relation between p_2 and r_2 when r_u = 30 mm is as shown in the table below.

Fiber strands	r_2 (mm)	p_2 (mm)
6	1	35
12	2	50

Cables with a small number of fibers are generally those with up to 12 fibers, stranded with a pitch of 50 mm or more, normally 100 mm or more.

Basic Conditions of Design

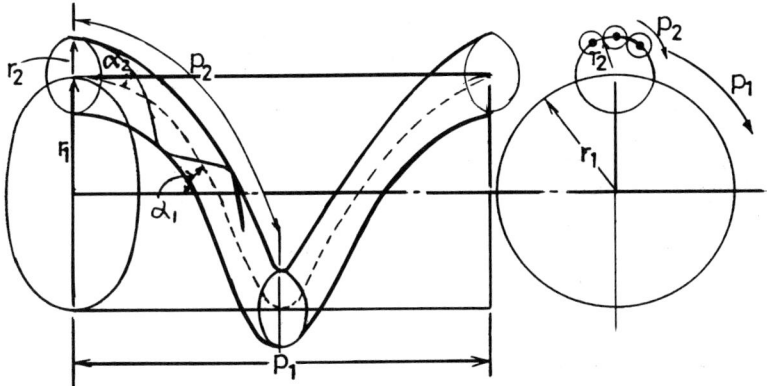

Figure 3.16 Stranding of units.

Unit Cable

For unit cable, 4-12 fibers (generally 6 fibers) are stranded into a unit, and such units are further stranded to form a cable core (Fig. 3.16). The bending radius of fibers of this cable may be calculated.

When the above-mentioned fiber wound with a fiber pitch p_2 on the cylinder, radius r_2, is further wound with a unit pitch p_1 on a cylinder of radius r_1, its radius of curvature ρ_c and bending radius r_c are expressed by [17]

$$r_c = \frac{1}{\rho_c} = \frac{r_1}{\sin^2 \alpha_1} \left[\frac{1}{\cos^2 \alpha_2 + (\sin^2 \alpha^2/r_2)(r_1/\sin^2 \alpha_1)} \right]$$

$$\simeq r_1 \left[1 + \left(\frac{p_1}{2\pi r_1} \right)^2 \right] \left[\frac{1}{1 + r_2/r_1(p_1/p_2)^2} \right] \quad (3.20)$$

Figure 3.17 shows the bending radius of fibers assuming $p_1/r_1 = p_2/r_2$, that is, when the value of the pitch/pitch-diameter of fibers being stranded into a unit is equal to that of pitch/pitch-diameter of units stranded into a cable core. The parameter is r_1/r_2.

For a city trunk cable or a long-haul trunk cable in which 24-60 fibers are contained, $r_1/r_2 \simeq 1$ mm. When the bending radius of the fiber is 30 mm, p_1/r_1 must be more than 35, according to Figure 3.16. $p_1/r_1 \simeq p_2/r_2 = 50-100$ is commonly used.

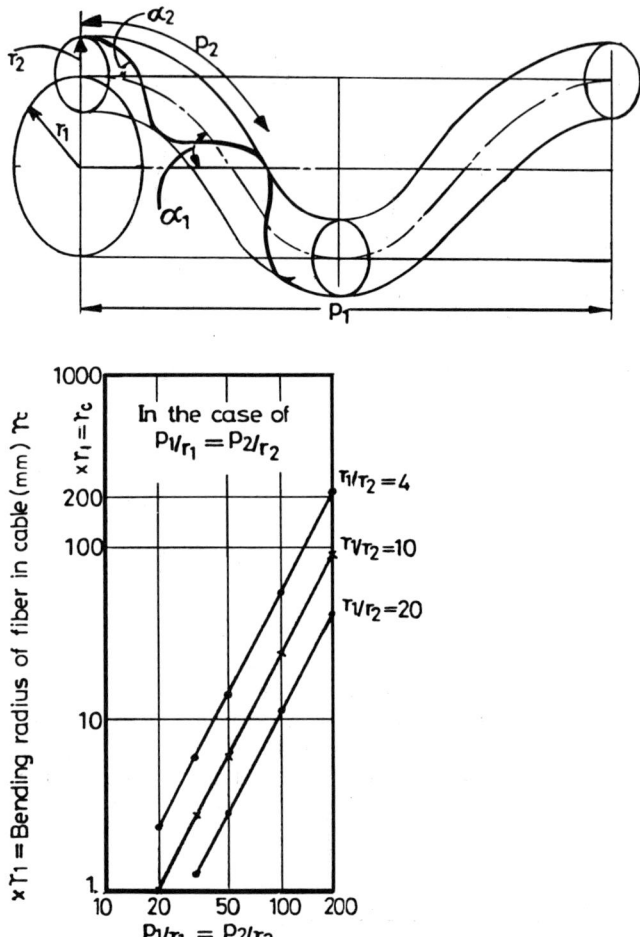

Figure 3.17 Bending radius τ_c and pitch-pitch diameter (for unit cable).

Basic Conditions of Design

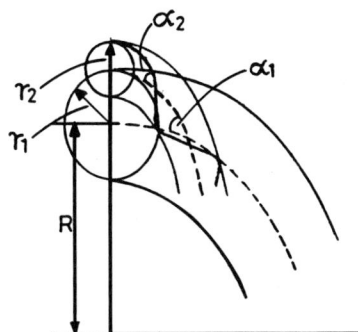

Figure 3.18 Bending of unit cable.

A city subscriber cable is presumed to have 100-600 fibers. In this case, r_1/r_2 is 10-20 and r_2 is about 1 mm. When the bending radius of the fiber is 30 mm, p_1/r_1 must be more than 30. In practice, $p_1/r_1 \simeq p_2/r_2 = 100-200$, generally. The unit stranding pitch of 36-fiber cable is approximately 300-600 mm.

Fibers in a Bent Cable

The bending radius of fibers in a bent single-layer stranded or unit cable is calculated as follows below.

When the cable is bent at radius R (Fig. 3.18), the maximum radius of curvature ρ_{max} and the minimum bending radius R_{min} of the fibers contained in the cable is expressed by the following formula, assuming there is no slippage between fibers [17]:

$$R_{min} = \frac{1}{\rho_{max}} \frac{1}{\cos^2 \alpha_2 [(\cos^2 \alpha_1/R) + (\sin^2 \alpha_1/r_1) + (\sin^2 \alpha_2/r_2)]} \quad (3.21)$$

In this cable construction, the maximum stress ε_{max}, maximum tension F_{max}, and maximum side pressure σ_{max} in the longitudinal direction of the fiber are expressed by

$$\varepsilon_{max} = \frac{rR}{R^2 + k^2 r^2}$$

$$F_{max} = EA\varepsilon_{max}$$

$$\sigma_{max} = \rho_{max} F_{max}$$

$$k = \frac{2\pi R}{p} \tag{3.22}$$

where:

E = Young's modulus of fiber

A = cross-sectional area of fiber

In optical fiber cables of 36-fiber construction six fibers × six units), which is very commonly used,

$$\frac{p_1}{r_1} \simeq \frac{p_2}{r_2} \simeq 50 \sim 100$$

The following table lists the bending radii of fibers in such cables when bent at radii of 50, 100, and 300 mm.

Cable bending radius (mm)	50		100		300	
$p_1/r_1 = p_2/r_2$	50	100	50	100	50	100
Fiber bending radius (mm)	25.9	40.5	34.6	67.5	44.6	121.9

This table shows that in order to prevent fibers from being bent at a radius of 30 mm or less, the cable must be bent at a radius of 100 mm or more.

The maxium stress ε_{max}, maximum tenstion F_{max}, and maximum side pressure σ_{max} calculated on the basis of the previous table are as follows:

Cable bending radius	100 mm	300 mm
ε_{max}	0.04 kg/mm^2	0.013 kg/mm^2
F_{max}	3.43 kg	1.17 kg
σ_{max}	117 g/mm	39 g/mm

Basic Conditions of Design

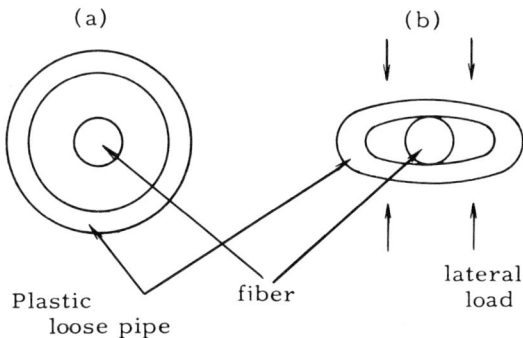

Figure 3.19 Deformation of plastic tube.

The 36-fiber cable has a core diameter of approximately 12 mm. When it is bent at a radius of 100 mm, ε_{max} is 4% and F_{max} 3.4 kg, which are normally least conceivable. These are maximum values for a fiber. The part of the fiber where the stress is greatest moves to a part under less stress. Likewise, the part at maximum tension moves to a part at lower tension. Moreover, as there is inevitable slippage between fibers, these values are reduced. According to our test results, the tension that works on fibers when the cable is bent at a radius of 300 mm is no more than 100 g. In any case, in order to make fibers bent at a radius of no less than 30 mm, it is desirable that cable of this type be bent at a radius of at least 100 mm.

3.2.4 Deformation of Plastic Tube Under Lateral Load*

When fiber is inserted into a loose tube, deformation of the loose tube under a lateral load must be considered. When the plastic tube in state a in Fig. 3.19 is deformed by lateral pressure into state b, there will always be a microbending loss in the fiber (Fig. 3.19). This means that state b is the maximum allowable deformation of the plastic tube. Plastic tube deformation under lateral pressure is discussed below [18].

Let us suppose that, in Fig. 3.20, the distance Q_1Q_2 between points Q_1 and Q_2 of a tube of length L is reduced by δ on the y axis when the tube receives a lateral pressure P. Here δ represents the degree of tube deformation. δ and ε_{max} (maximum strain) are calculated by the following formulas [18].

---

*This section is based on Ref. 18.

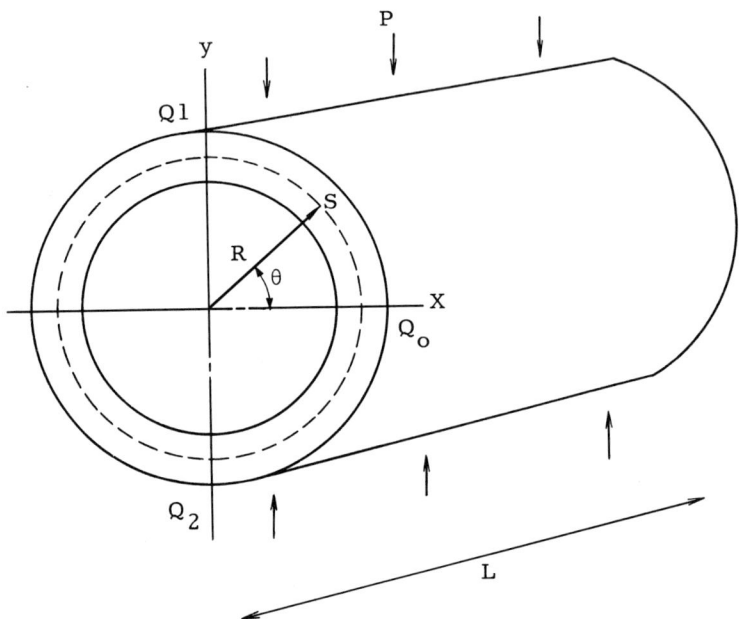

Figure 3.20 Deformation of tube. (From Ref. 18.)

When the pipe has perfect elasticity [18],

$$\delta = \left(\frac{\pi}{4} - \frac{2}{\pi}\right) \frac{1 - \nu^2}{EI} PR^3$$

$$= 12 \left(\frac{\pi}{4} - \frac{2}{\pi}\right) \frac{1 - \nu^2}{E} \left(\frac{R}{t}\right)^3 \frac{P}{L}$$

$$= 1.8 \frac{1 - \nu^2}{E} \left(\frac{R}{t}\right)^3 \frac{P}{L} \qquad (3.23)$$

$$\varepsilon_{max} = \left(3 - \frac{6}{\pi}\right) \frac{RP}{Et^2}$$

$$\doteq 1.1 \frac{RP}{Et^2} \qquad (3.24)$$

where:

δ = deformatlion of tube

E = Young's modulus

Basic Conditions of Design

Table 3.5 Properties of Materials

Materials	E (kg/mm^2)	σ^* (kg/mm^2)	n	ν
Nylon 12 (copolymer)	46	3.7	0.14	0.3
Nylon 12 (homopolymer)	109	6.4	0.14	0.3
PE (black)	17	1.5	0.24	0.45
PVC	1.8	0.83	0.51	—
Al	6300	7.5	0.10	0.35

Source: From Ref. 18.

γ = Poisson's ratio

I = secondary moment of section

L = length of tube

t = thickness of tube

P = lateral pressure

When the tube is made of a plastic material [1]: the strain ε of plastics is approximately expressed as

$$\varepsilon = \frac{\sigma}{E} + \frac{\sigma}{\sigma^*}^{1/n} \qquad (3.25)$$

The second term on the right side of Eq. (3.25) indicates the hardening of deformed plastic (for example by pulling). The values of σ^* and n can be determined by experiment. They are shown in Table 3.5.

Where the strain is large, Eq. (3.25) is approximately modified to

$$\sigma = \sigma^* \varepsilon^n \qquad (3.26)$$

In Fig. 3.21, a comparison is made between the experimental and calculated results of the stress-strain relation of Nylon 12.

Deformation δ of the tube is calculated by using Eq. (3.26):

$$\delta = K \left(\frac{P^*}{\sigma^*}\right)^{1/n}$$

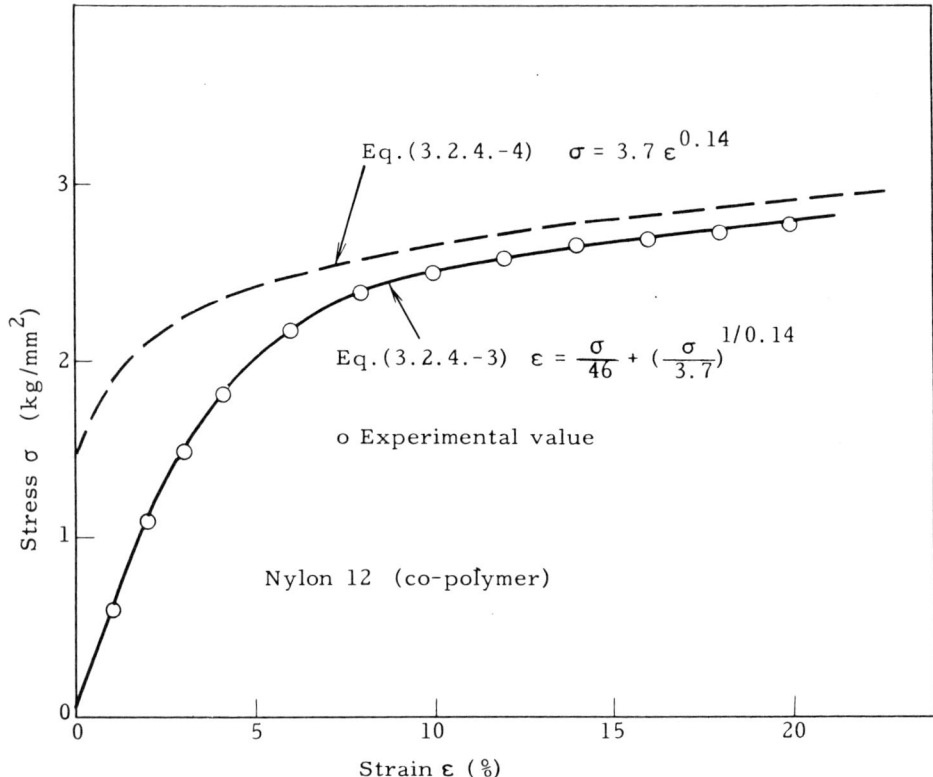

Figure 3.21 Comparison of experimental and calculated results of stress-strain relation. (From Ref. 18.)

$$= K\left(\frac{R^{1+2n}}{t^{2+n}} \frac{1}{\sigma^*} \frac{P}{L}\right)^{1/n} \quad (3.27)$$

where

$$P^* = \frac{R^{1+2n}}{t^{2+n}} \frac{P}{L} \quad (3.28)$$

and where K and n are material constants determined experimentally.

For deformation of plastic tube on the fiber [18], the relation between the lateral load the the deformation δ of a plastic cover fiber (shown in Fig. 3.22) was measured. The results of the measurement are given in Figs. 3.23 and 3.24.

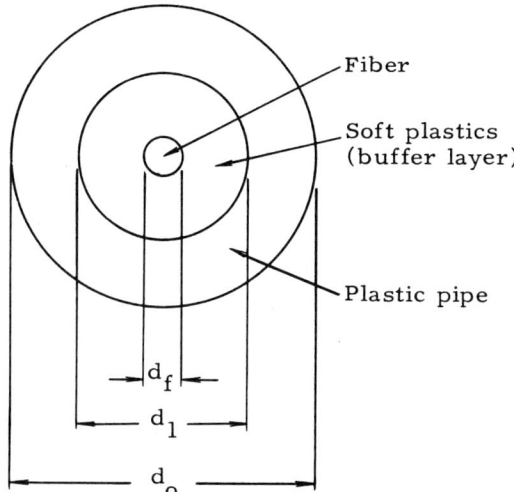

Figure 3.22 Plastic-covered fiber: d_0 = 0.7, 0.9, and 1.1 mm; d_1 = 0.35, 0.4, 0.45, and 0.5 mm; d_f = 0.125 mm. (From Ref. 18.)

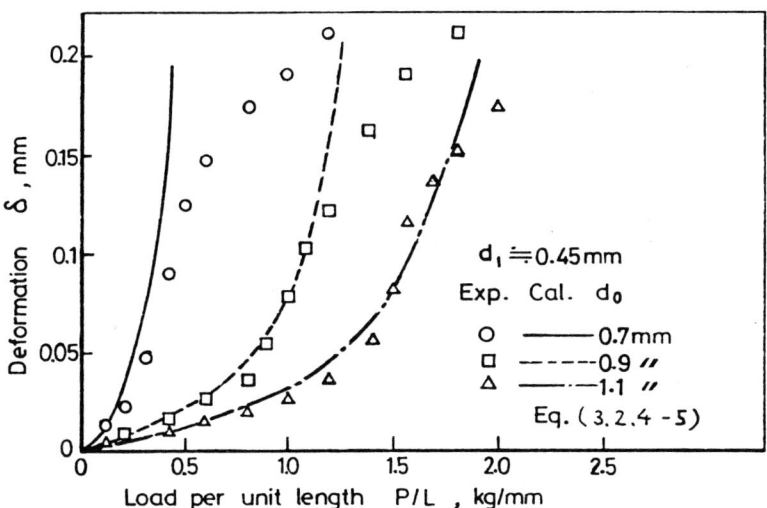

Figure 3.23 Deformation of coated fiber owing to lateral load. (From Ref. 18.)

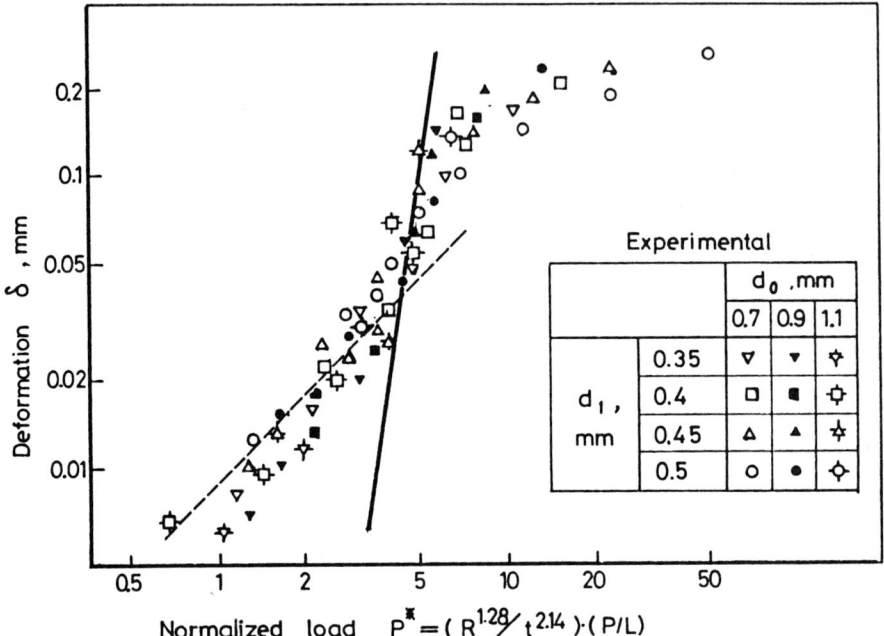

Figure 3.24 Relation between deformation and normalized load. (From Ref. 18.)

In the experiments shown in Figs. 3.23 and 3.24, the plastic-covered fiber shown in Fig. 3.22 was used. The fiber was covered with soft plastic and then with a nylon tube. Figures 3.23 and 3.24 also show the theoretical values determined by Eqs. (3.23) and (3.27). The Young's modulus of soft plastic is disregarded in the calculation because it is very much smaller than that of nylon. Therefore, these experiments and calculations can also be used as they are for the fiber covered with a loose nylon tube.

Figure 3.24 shows the deformation of elastic and plastic tubes, with the abscissa representing the normalized lateral pressure P^*. It has been learned that within the range of these experiments, the relation of log δ and log P^* can be nearly approximated by two straight lines, irrespective of the diameter of the fiber and the dimensions of the plastic pipe.

In these experiments, it seems Eq. (3.23) was used in a range in which δ is small and Eq. (3.27) in a range in which δ is large. From the test data were calculated K and n by Eq. (3.27). From these calculations and experiments,

Basic Conditions of Design

$$\delta = 0.51 \left(\frac{P*}{\sigma*}\right)^{1/0.14} \tag{3.29}$$

where

$$P* = \frac{R^{1.28}}{t^{2.14}} \frac{P}{L} \tag{3.30}$$

The results of calculation by Eq. (3.29) are shown in Fig. 3.24.

The value of δ against the lateral pressure can be calculated by using Fig. 3.24 and Eqs. (3.23) and (3.27). Generally, plastic deformation increases sharply with increasing load and remains even after removal of the load. Therefore, the limit of the plastic tube over the fiber is the intersection of the straight lines of elastic deformation and plastic deformation in Fig. 3.24.

Assuming that δ in Eq. (3.23) is equal to that in Fig. 3.23,

$$\frac{P}{L} = \left[\left(\frac{\pi}{4} - \frac{2}{\pi}\right)\frac{12(1-\nu)}{KE}\right]^{n/(1-n)} \sigma*^{1(1-n)} \frac{t^2}{R}$$

$$= K' \frac{t^2}{R} \tag{3.31}$$

$$p** = K' = \frac{R}{t^2} \frac{P}{L}$$

With the dimensions of the fiber-covering plastic tube obtained from these formulas, the maximum values of side pressure load P/L and deformation can be determined. In Figs. 3.23 and 3.24, $\delta \doteq 0.035$ mm, P/L = 0.6 kg/mm (at d_0 = 0.9 mm), and p** $\doteq$ 7.6. After additional experiments, generally p** $\doteq$ 4-8. The gap between the plastic tube and the fiber is approximately 0.13 mm. The allowable value of deformation of the gap between the tube and fiber is much smaller.

Figures 3.25, 3.26, and 3.27 show the results of tests made on the deformation of the laminated Al polyethylene (LAP) sheath. The deformation of this sheath is also expressed approximately by

$$\delta = 7.53 E^{-2.12} \left(\frac{R^{1.75}}{t^{2.25}} \frac{P}{L}\right)^3 \tag{3.32}$$

where:

R = dc/2

t = thickness of polyethylene

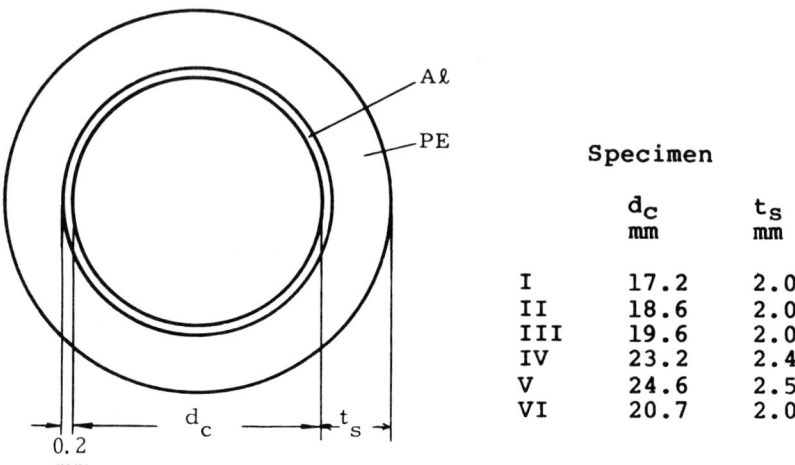

Specimen	d_c mm	t_s mm
I	17.2	2.0
II	18.6	2.0
III	19.6	2.0
IV	23.2	2.4
V	24.6	2.5
VI	20.7	2.0

Figure 3.25 Cross section of LAP sheath. (From Ref. 18.)

Figure 3.27 shows the result of calculation (based on E = 17 kg/mm^2) with Eq. (3.32). The test value and the calculated value agree well in the plastic zone.

3.2.5 Design of Strength Members in Optical Fiber Cable [19, 20]

The fiber is made of silica and therefore has an average elongation of 5% and a minimum elongation of 0.2-0.5%. That is, the breakage strength of the fiber averages about 5 kg, with a minimum of about 1 kg. The breakage strength of fiber guaranteed for a long time is about 0.02 (about 0.2% in terms of elongation). The cable must therefore be designed so that the strain of the fiber in the cable does not exceed about 0.2%.

In order to reduce the elongation of the fiber, a material with a large Young's modulus must be selected for the strength member. If a strength member is provided in the cable core, it must be as light as possible, and where it should be applied must be carefully determined. The requirements of the strength member are as follows:

1. High Young's modulus
2. Small specific gravity
3. A required degree of flexibility
4. Small longitudinal elongation in the low-strain region, with slackening of the strength member in the cable taken into account.

Basic Conditions of Design 213

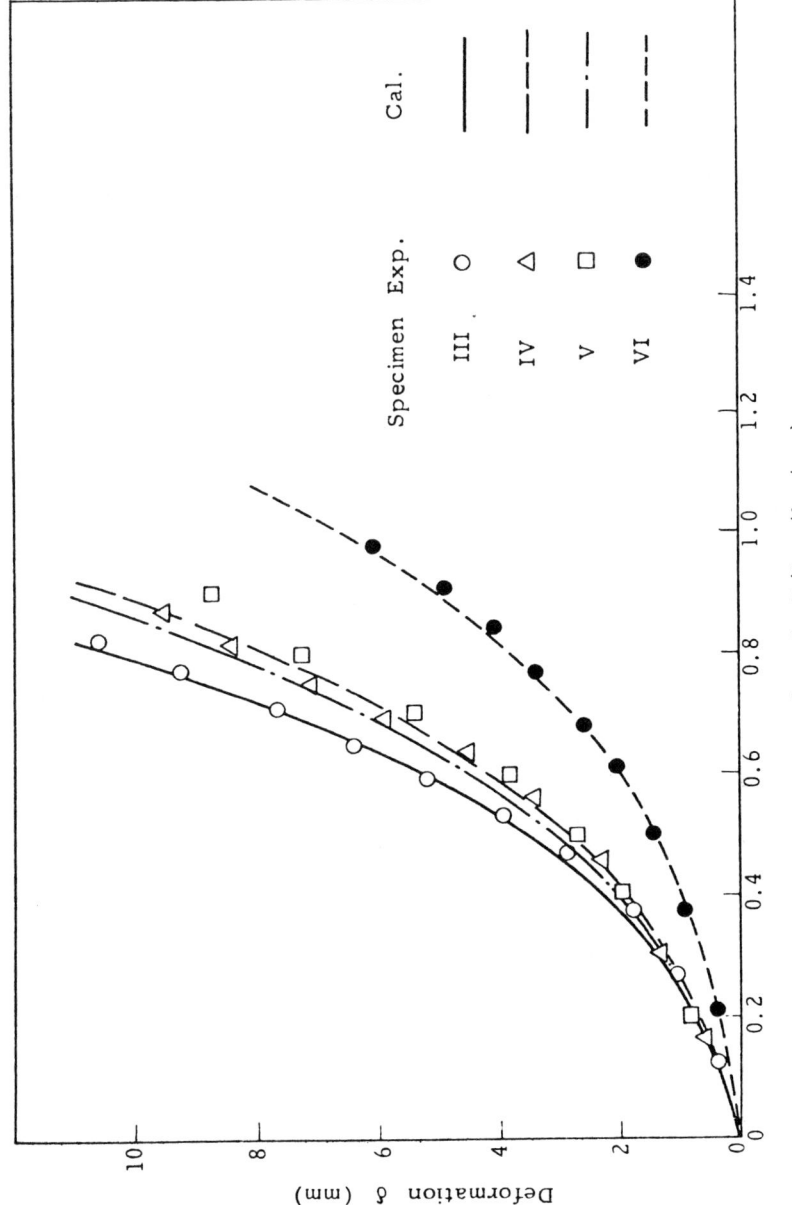

Figure 3.26 Deformation of LAP sheath owing to lateral load. (From Ref. 18.)

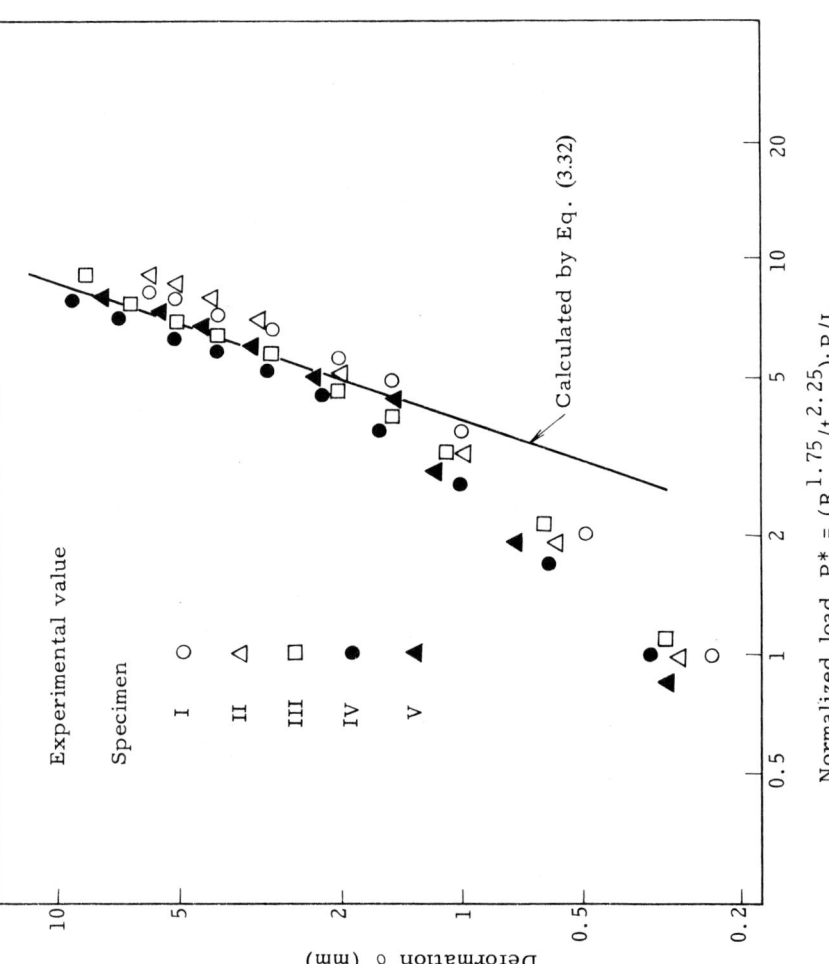

Figure 3.27 Relation between deformation and normalized load for LAP sheath. (From Ref. 18.)

Table 3.6 Materials for Strength Members

Material	Specific gravity	Young's modulus (kg/mm^2)	Yield point stress (kg/mm^2)	Yield point elongation (%)	Stress at breakage (kg/mm^2)	Elongation at breakage (%)
Steel wire	7.86	20,000	40–150	0.2–1	50–300	20–25
G-FRP	2.04	5,100	120	2.4	120	2.4
Nylon yarn	1.14	600–1,300	>80	>6	100–150	15–20
Kevlar 49	1.44	13,000	300	2	300	2
Kevlar 29	1.44	6,000	70	1.2	300	4
Glass yarn	2.48	9,000	300	3	300	3
Carbon yarn	1.5	10,000–20,000	150–200	1.0–1.5	150–200	1.5

With respect to the structure of the cable, the cable must be designed so that if tension works in the longitudinal direction of the cable, the fiber can be kept free from this tension. Table 3.6 lists materials that meet the requirements listed above. Note that when the yield point elongation of the strength member is smaller than the elongation at breakage of the fiber, calculation of the design of the strength member must be made using the yield point elongation of the strength member. When the yield point elongation of the strength member is larger than the elongation at breakage of the fiber, calculation of the design of the strength member must be made using the stress at breakage of the fiber.

When the strength member is a strand of flexible fibrous material, tension working on it loosens the strand, making it incapable of exhibiting its tension-resisting function.

When a single strength member is provided in the center of the cable core, its properties alone are exhibited. On the other hand, when separate strength members are provided in the cable core or when they are inserted in the cable sheath, they are stranded and, when tension works on the cable, sometimes become loose in strand and therefore incapable of fulfilling their function. For this reason, care must be used in the selection of a material for the strength member.

Let us study the cable model shown in Fig. 3.28 [19]. The weight of the cable is

$$W = P_1 A_1 + P_2 A_2 + P_3 A_3 \tag{3.33}$$

The tension F at the allowable elongation of the cable is

$$F = \alpha(E_1 A_1 + E_2 A_2 + E_3 A_3) \tag{3.34}$$

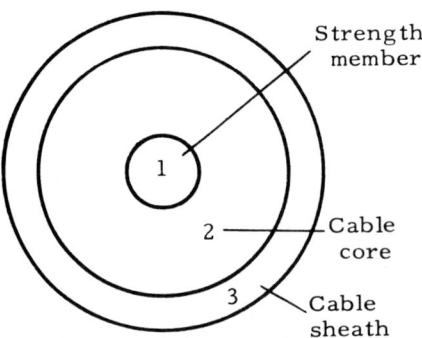

Figure 3.28   Cable section.

Basic Conditions of Design

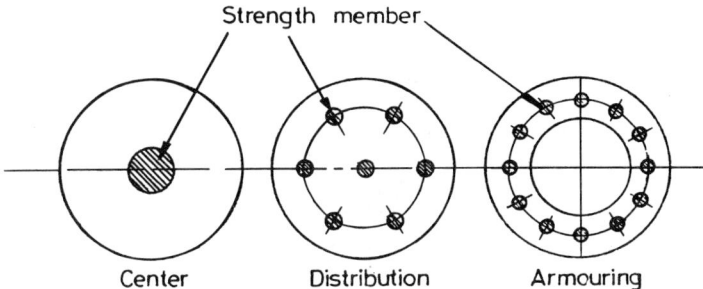

Figure 3.29 Arrangement of strength member.

When the cable is installed with of $F \geq W$ (in this case, the friction coefficient between the cable sheath and the ground or duct is 1, and in general this value is 0.3–0.5),

$$\alpha(E_1 A_1 + E_2 A_2 + E_3 A_3) \geq \rho_1 A_1 + \rho_2 A_2 + \rho_3 A_3$$

$$A_1(\alpha E_1 - \rho_1) \geq A_2(\rho_2 - \alpha E_2) + A_3(\rho_3 - \alpha E_3) \quad (3.35)$$

The Young's modulus and cross-sectional area of the strength member should be selected that meet these conditions. Here, a value of 0.2% is generally taken for

$$A'_1(0.002 E_1 - \rho_1) \geq A_2(\rho_2 - 0.002 E_2) + A_3(\rho_3 - 0.002 E_3)$$

$$(3.36)$$

where:

    A = cross-sectional area of each part
    E = Young's modulus at each part
    α = elongation
    ρ = density at each part
    1, 2, 3 = strength member, cable core, and cable sheath, respectively

The strength member is arranged as follows (Fig. 3.29):

1. Placed in the center of the cable (called the center type).
2. Dispersed in the cable core (called the distribution type).

3. Provided in the cable sheath or on the sheath in a stranded or armored form (called the armored type).

The center type is used widely in optical fiber cable and the armored type for a cable with a large number of fibers. For a single-fiber cable (e.g., office cord or connecting cord), fibrous strength members (e.g., glass yarn) are very often stranded on the plastic-coated fiber. This is one kind of armored type.

It is easy to increase the tensile strength of the center type. For instance, when the cable laying tension reaches 500 kg or more, the diameter of the strength members (e.g., steel wires or FRP wire fiber-reinforced plastics) is usually 2.0 mm or more. It is generally the case that such a strength member is made flexible in a stranded form. In this case, if tension works on the cable, the tension-resistant member becomes loose in strand and longer, with a resultant reduction in apparent tension. It is practical to give the stranded strength member a design tension equal to 0.8 times the theoretical tension.

Table 3.7 is a qualitative comparison of the merits and disadvantages of the different arrangements of the strength member. In the table, the o means that a particular type of member is advantageous with respect to the feature or characteristic indicated; X means it is not advantageous.

For a stranded strength member, tension working on the cable loosens the strand and elongates the stranding pitch, thereby giving a turning force to the cable. In a serious case, the cable may be kinked (twisted); with resultant breakage of the fiber within it. To prevent the cable from turning, either a single strength member is provided along the axis of the cable, or when a stranded type is used, strength members are stranded in two or more layers, their stranding direction being reversed in the successive layers.

Now we will study a cable turning under tension [20]. When a cable is pulled, the relation between the strain $\varepsilon_o = \delta \ell_o / \ell_o$ in the axial direction of the cable and the strain $\varepsilon = \delta \ell_n / \ell_n$ in the direction of each component wire of the strand is approximated as follows:

$$\varepsilon_n = \varepsilon_o \cos^2 \alpha - (\ell \sin^2 \alpha) \phi \qquad (3.37)$$

where:

α = pitch angle

ℓ = cable length

ϕ = angle of cable turn

If the cable does not turn,

Basic Conditions of Design

Table 3.7 Comparison of the Different Arrangements of Strength Members

Item	Center	Distribution	Armored
Resistance to tension	o	X	o
Resistance to compression	X	Δ	o
Loss increase			
Side pressure	X	Δ	o
Bending	Δ	Δ	o
Rigidity	Δ	o	X
Ease of production	o	Δ	Δ
Splicing			
Cable core	o	Δ	o
Sheath	o	Δ	X
Cable outer diameter	o	Δ	Δ

$$\varepsilon_n = \varepsilon_o \cos^2 \alpha$$

$$\sigma_n \doteqdot \frac{E_n}{E_o} \sigma_o \cos^2 \alpha \qquad (3.38)$$

where:

E_o, σ_o = Young's modulus and stress in the axial direction of the cable

E_n, σ_n = Young's modulus and stress of each component wire

The turning force T caused by the stranded member is expressed as follows:

$$T = \sum a_n \sigma_n r_n \sin \alpha_n$$

$$= \sum \frac{\sigma_o}{E_o} E_n a_n r_n \cos^2 \alpha_n \sin \alpha_n \qquad (3.39)$$

where:

a_n = cross-sectional area of each component

α_n = pitch angle of each component

r_n = stranding radius of the strand

$$T = 0 \rightarrow \sum E_n a_n r_n \cos^2 \alpha_n = 0 \qquad (3.40)$$

The cable can be practically prevented from turning if strength members are stranded in two or more layers and their material, dimensions, and stranding pitch are selected to conform with Eq. (3.40).

3.2.6 Optical Fiber Cable Sheath

The sheath of the optical fiber cable may be regarded as equal in basic construction to the sheath of a conventional telecommunications cable. Points that require particular attention about the sheath of the fiber cable are as follows.

The fiber must be kept free from microbend loss increase. Plastics are extruded at about 200°C for sheathing. The plastic sheath naturally shrinks when its temperature drops to the normal level. This shrinkage is thought to cause microbending of the fiber and to increase fiber loss. It is therefore important to use sheath construction and material that cause little shrinkage even when the ambient temperature is low at the site of cable installation. Near the Arctic and Antarctic regions and on high mountains, temperatures drop to −40 to −60°C. Cables to be installed at such sites must have a sheath carefully designed to prevent shrinkage.

The following formula is used for calculating the overall elongation and shrinkage of a sheath composed of plastics and a metal, FRP, or the like that elongates and shrinks less than plastics.

$$\Delta \varepsilon = \frac{E_2(T)A_2}{E_1(T)A_1 + E_2(T)A_2} (\alpha_2 - \alpha_1) \Delta T$$

$$\varepsilon = (\alpha_2 - \alpha_1) \int_{T_o}^{T} \frac{E_2(T)A_2}{E_1(T)A_1 + E_2(T)A_2} dT$$

where:

$E_1(T)$, $E_2(T)$ = Young's modulus of metal (or FRP) and plastics, respectively

Basic Conditions of Design

A_1, A_2 = cross-sectional area of metal (or FRP) and plastics, respectively

α_1, α_2 = thermal elongation coefficient of metal (or FRP) and plastics, respectively

T_o = initial temperature

ε = strain

The equation indicates that in order to minimize ε, E_2 and A_2 must be made as small as possible.

A loss increase of the fiber is feared when H_2 is generated from the sheath or H_2 in the soil permeates through the sheath and H_2 enters the cable core. When a metal is used in the sheath, therefore, it must be covered with plastic to prevent H_2 from being produced by chemical reaction. The sheath must also be made to check the infiltration of H_2 into the cable core even in the presence of H_2 in the soil, for example.

The sheath must use construction and material to minimize the overall elongation of the cable even under tension. (Sheath construction must be studied in conformity with the overall construction of the cable core.)

The sheath must be so built to withstand compressive force, side pressure, and so on, from outside and to sustain little deformation.

Examples of commonly used sheath construction for optical fiber cables are shown in Table 3.8.

3.2.7 Problems of Jelly Filling in the Cable Core

Fiber cables are now very often filled with jelly, for the following reasons.

Jelly prevents the infiltration of H_2 in the fiber cable. It is, however, important that the jelly used is chemically stable and produces no H_2 gas.

In an empty (not jelly-filled) fiber cable, moisture infiltrates, accumulates, and, when temperature drops, freezes, causing a microbend loss increase in the fiber. The jelly-filled cable prevents moisture infiltration and is therefore free from a microbend loss increase even at low temperatures. Figure 3.30 shows how fiber loss increased when water was put in an empty (not jelly-filled) cable and its temperature was reduced to below 0°C.

Contaminants brought into the cable core by infiltrating water may deteriorate the materials that make up the cable. The jelly-filled cable is in no danger of such deterioration.

Table 3.8 Examples of Sheath Construction for Optical Fiber Cable

Al-laminated PE sheath	Double sheath	direct buried	Non metallic sheath	
(Al laminated tape, PE) — commonly used jelly filled core is recommended.	(Al laminated tape, PE, plastic yarns)		(PE, FRP) / (PE, FRP twin)	
Corrugated steel sheath	Al-sheath	aerial and buried		no electro-magnetic induction
(Al laminated tape, PE, corrugated steel tape) — direct buried	(Al, PE)		(FRP, PE)	
Wire armoured sheath	PE-sheath	cord		
(wires, PE) — direct buried	(plastic yarns, PE)		(FRP, PE)	

Basic Conditions of Design

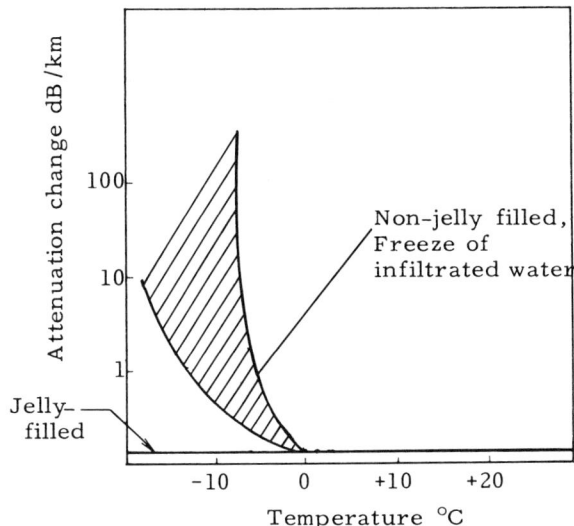

Figure 3.30 Loss increase of fiber in cable with water infiltration.

3.2.8 Low-Temperature Problems of Fiber Cable

The thermal expansion coefficient of a silica fiber is of the order of 10^{-7}; that of plastics is of the order of 10^{-4}. For this reason, plastics shrink far more than does silica fiber when the temperature is lowered, causing microbending of the silica fiber, which in turn increases the fiber loss. This section studies mainly the low-temperature problems of fiber covered with a buffer coating and nylon. The construction of this (graded index) fiber is as follows: Core diameter, 50 μm; outer diameter, 125 μm; buffer layer (soft plastic), 0.4 mm; nylon covering, 0.9 mm.

3.2.8.1 Low-Temperature Properties of Nylon-Covered Fiber [25, 26]

The linear expansion coefficient of the buffer-coated fiber (without nylon cover) is described. It is known that the linear expansion coefficient of a silica fiber itself is $3.4 \times 10^{-7}/°C$. Compared with those of metals (of the order of 10^{-5}) and of plastics (of the order of 10^{-4}), this value for silica is extremely small. The temperature coefficient was measured of the loss of a fiber only with buffer coating without a nylon cover. The outer diameter of the optical fiber was 125 μm and that of the outer coating, 0.35 mm. No loss variations were noticed on the fiber between -60 and +20°C. Therefore, it can be said that the loss temperature coefficient of the buffer-coated

Table 3.9 Construction of Fibers for Low Temperature

Fiber	Ratio of diameter to core diameter	Ratio of Young's modulus of plastic in the outermost layer[a]
1	125:50	1
2	150:50	1
3	170:50	1
4	125:50	0.7
5	125:50	0.5

[a]Based on nylon 12. Fibers 4 and 5 used a material smaller in Young's modulus than nylon 12.
Source: From Ref. 25.

fiber in this range is 1. A G1 fiber, 1% in relative refractive index difference, covered with a buffer layer (outer diameter 0.35 mm) and a nylon layer (outer diameter 0.9 mm) was used in the study. Table 3.9 shows the construction of the fibers used for this experiment [25].

The length of each fiber was 500 m. It was coiled in a diameter of 30 cm, and its loss was measured (λ = 0.84 μm). The loss at 20°C was used as the standard, and loss increments were measured (Figs. 3.31 and 3.32). Figure 3.31 shows how loss changed as the outer diameter of the fiber was changed. According to Fig. 3.31, there was not much loss increase (about 0.6 dB/km or less) when

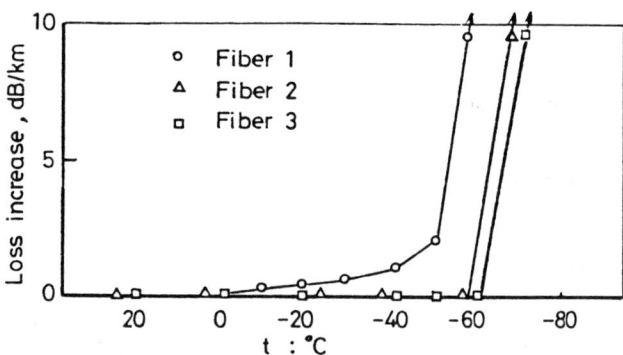

Figure 3.31 Loss increase with falling temperature. (From Ref. 25.)

Basic Conditions of Design

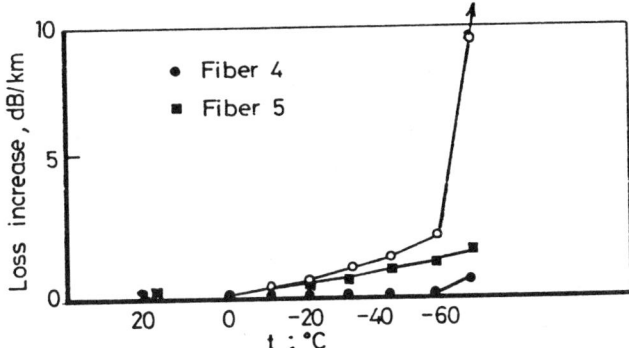

Figure 3.32 Loss increase with falling temperature. (From Ref. 25.)

the temperature was about −40°C. However, the loss sharply increased at −40 to −60°C. The larger the fiber diameter, the lower was the temperature at which the loss increased.

Shown in Fig. 3.32 is the low-temperature characteristic of loss of the fiber determined when the plastic of its outermost layer was given varied Young's moduli. The fiber with a smaller Young's modulus showed little change in a temperature range of +20 to −60°C, but the fiber with a larger Young's modulus indicated a loss increase beginning at about −30°C.

3.2.8.2 Study of Low-Temperature Properties of Plastic-Covered Fiber [25–27]

In Figs. 3.31 and 3.32, the loss increase of a nylon-extruded coiled optical fiber suddenly occurs at a certain low temperature (−50 to −60°C in the figures). Compared with loss increases at previous temperatures, these variations are very large. The thermal expansion coefficients of silica and nylon are 3.4×10^{-7} and 1×10^{-4}, respectively, and the difference between them is considerable. This means that the longitudinal shrinkage of nylon at low temperature is very large compared with that of silica fiber. For this reason, when the temperature reaches a certain low temperature, the silica fiber itself buckles owing to the longitudinal shrinkage of nylon (see Fig. 3.33). The fiber undulates and bends in the soft buffer layer, causing a microbending loss.

Table 3.10 shows the physical constants of the materials used. Nylon shrinks in the longitudinal direction much more than the fiber. Soft UV-cured resin has a small Young's modulus and is responsible for little of the shrinkage. When the nylon-covered fiber is cooled,

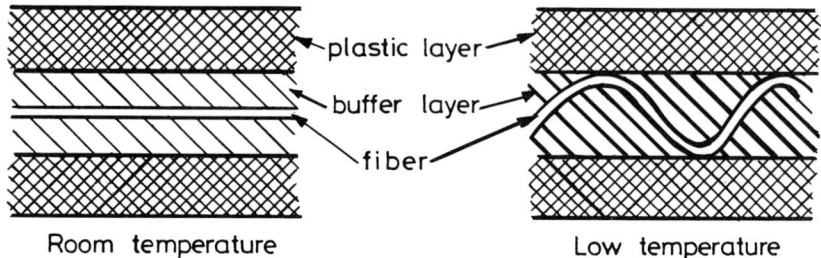

Figure 3.33   Microbending of fiber at low temperature.

the force of contraction P that works on the fiber is approximately expressed by the formula

$$P = E_2(T) A_2 \alpha \, \Delta T$$

where:

P = contractile force that works on the fiber
$E_2(T)$ = Young's modulus of nylon at temperature T
A_2 = cross-sectional area of nylon layer
α = expansion coefficient of nylon
ΔT = temperature difference

In this formula, the contractile force of the buffer layer is neglected because of its small Young's modulus.

Now we consider a case in which a straight fiber elastically supported in the soft buffer layer develops buckling and bends under

Table 3.10   Physical Constants of Materials

Constant	Silica fiber	Soft UV-cured resin (buffer layer)	Nylon
Young's modulus, kg/mm^2	7200	0.1	120
Coefficient of linear expansion, 1/°C	3.4×10^{-7}	1×10^{-4}	1×10^{-4}

Basic Conditions of Design

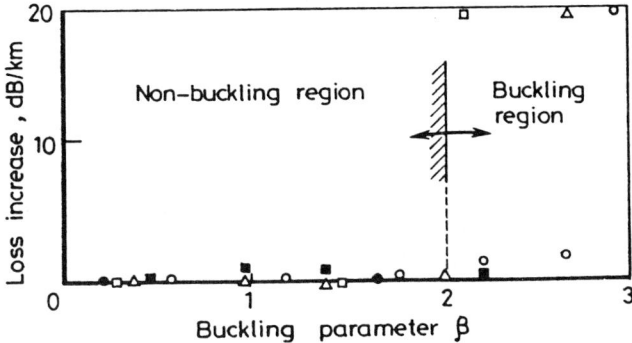

Figure 3.34 Loss increase and buckling parameter. (From Ref. 25.)

a contractile force applied from outside. The minimum compressive force P_{min} that causes the fiber to bend is [27]

$$P_{min} = 2\sqrt{E \frac{\pi}{64} d^4 E_1(T)}$$

where:

E = Young's modulus of fiber

d = diameter of fiber

$E_1(T)$ = Young's modulus of buffer layer at temperature T

Buckling of the fiber occurs when P is equal to or greater than P_{min}. In practice, however, it is impossible to accurately grasp the constants of the materials at low temperature, the fiber is not straight and is not necessarily in the center of the nylon layer; and the temperature T_0 at which the residual stress of the nylon layer becomes zero cannot be estimated. For these reasons we introduce here the parameter β, as follows [25]:

$$\beta = \frac{P}{P_{min}}$$

This β is the structural parameter that indicates how easily a fiber develops buckling. With β, Figs. 3.31 and 3.32 are transformed into Fig. 3.34 [25]. The constants used are $E = 7200$ kg/mm^2; $E_1(T) = 0.1$ kg/mm^2; and $E_2 = 120$ kg/mm^2.

The temperature T_0 at which the residual stress of the nylon layer becomes zero was set at 20°C. From Fig. 3.34 [25], the loss of the fiber sharply increases in the region $\beta \geq 2$. Therefore, the use of the parameter $\beta = P/P_{min}$ makes it possible to calculate the buckling of the plastic-covered fiber and the sharp loss increase.

As is learned from Fig. 3.31 and 3.32, a minor loss increase is observed before a sharp increase. Owing to a dynamic imbalance of the plastic-covered fiber, a minor undulation develops in part of the fiber and is expanded by contraction of the plastic covering. This is presumed to cause a microbending loss increase [28].

3.2.8.3 Linear Expansion Coefficient of Optical Fiber [29, 30]

The loss increase of a plastic-covered fiber at low temperature is primarily caused by the difference in the axial linear expansion coefficients of the materials. Therefore, the linear expansion coefficient of the plastic-covered fiber is described in this section.

As is well known, the linear expansion coefficient of a plastic-covered fiber can be expressed by

$$\alpha = \frac{\Sigma A_i E_i \alpha_i}{\Sigma A_i E_i}$$

where:

    α = linear expansion coefficient

    A_i = cross-sectional area of composite materials

    E_i = Young's modulus of composite materials

    α_i = linear expansion coefficients of composite materials

The characteristics of the materials actually used are shown in Table 3.10. In plastic-covered optical fibers, in most instances fibers are slack inside the plastic covers. For this reason, the shrinkage amount of the plastic-covered fibers is slightly larger than that calculated by the equation above. Conversely, the amount of shrinkage of the optical fibers is slightly smaller.

The linear expansion coefficient of these plastic-covered fibers can be calculated by measuring the temperature coefficient of the pulse delay time τ. In other words, the linear expansion coefficient of a buffer-coated and nylon-covered fiber can be shown by [29, 30]

$$\alpha = 1.28 \left(\frac{1}{\tau} \frac{d\tau}{dT} - 8 \times 10^{-6} \right)$$

Basic Conditions of Design

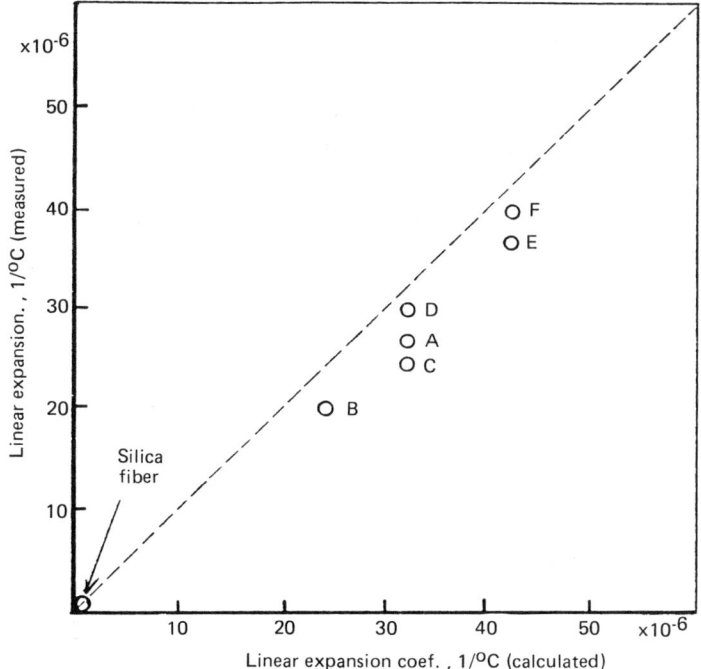

Figure 3.35 Linear expansion coefficient of plastic-covered fibers; A through F are samples of different construction. (From Ref. 29.)

where:

α = linear expansion coefficient of buffer-coated and nylon-covered optical fiber

τ = pulse delay time

T = temperature

Figure 3.35 [29, 30] shows measurement results of linear expansion coefficients of buffer-coated and nylon-covered optical fibers fabricated within the following ranges [29]: fiber diameter, 125–150 μm; buffer diameter, 250–450 μm; and nylon diameter, 0.6–0.9 mm. A through F in Fig. 3.35 are optical fibers fabricated and measured; the dashed line shows calculated values.

The linear expansion coefficients of these plastic-covered optical fibers are approximately $2-5 \times 10^{-5}$ per °C. That the measured values are slightly smaller than calculated values can be attributed to fiber slackness, error in constant values of the materials at low temperature, and other factors.

3.2.8.4 Low-Temperature Properties of Fiber Cable [29, 30]

The results up to the preceding section show that axial shrinkage of covered plastics must be suppressed in order to improve the microbending loss increases of plastic-covered fibers at low temperature. The following solution methods can be considered for this purpose.

1. Use only plastic-covered fiber:

    Make the plastic cover as thin as possible.
    Lower the Young's modulus and thermal expansion coefficient of the plastic cover as much as possible.
    Cover the plastic concentrically on the fiber. Fibers shall not slacken in the plastic cover and shall be as straight as possible.
    Plastic shall be covered on the fibers so as not to have stress remain on the plastic.
    The cross-sectional area of the plastic sheath shall be as small as possible.

2. Suppress microbending loss increases by combining with other materials:

    Combine with a material (e.g., strength member) whose thermal expansion coefficient is the same or slightly smaller than that of plastic-covered fibers.
    Young's modulus and cross-sectional area of the material to be combined shall be as large as possible.

The cable core is formed by combining a plastic-covered fiber with a material (e.g., strength member) with a small coefficient of expansion and a large (Young's modulus) X (cross-sectional area).

In order for a fiber cable to have uniform loss properties over its entire working temperature range, the fiber must have not only good low-temperature properties but also a high resistance to side pressure, bends, and so on, during cable manufacture and during and after installation. Therefore, it is not necessarily advisable to reduce the cross-sectional area of the outermost plastic layer or to use a material with a low Young's modulus in consideration of low-temperature properties only. The cable construction and materials must be determined after a well-balanced study of the following factors:

Basic Conditions of Design

Table 3.11 Expansion Coefficient of Material

Material	Expansion coefficient (per °C)	Young's modulus
Silica	3.4×10^{-7}	7,200 (kg/mm^2)
Steel	1.1×10^{-5}	18,000
Stainless steel	1.6×10^{-5}	18,000
Aluminum	2.3×10^{-5}	7,000
FRP	2×10^{-5}	—
Nylon-covered fiber	$2-5 \times 10^{-5}$	—

1. Manufacture and handling of the cable (chiefly from the viewpoint of dynamics)
2. Transmission property of the fiber
3. Low-temperature properties

Owing to the efforts made to produce a buffer-coated, nylon-covered fiber, it is now easy to obtain a fiber with a loss increase of 0.1 dB/km (at 0.85 µm) at -40°C and 0.5 dB/km at -60°C (at 0.85 µm). However, further efforts must be made to reduce these values when a cable core is formed with this fiber.

The thermal expansion coefficient of plastic-covered fibers, as mentioned in Sec. 3.2.8.3, is $2-5 \times 10^{-5}$ per °C. Table 3.11 presents the thermal expansion coefficients and Young's moduli of materials that can be inserted in the cable core as strength members. The expansion coefficient of steel or stainless steel is one-half to one-third that of nylon-covered fiber. Therefore, for example, the use of steel wire or steel tape is conceivable to limit the longitudinal contraction of the nylon-covered fiber.

Nylon-covered fiber was wound in an orderly fashion on a silica bobbin and on an iron bobbin, and its low-temperature properties were examined. The coiled fiber (not wound on the bobbin) had a loss increase of about 0.5 dB/km (0.85 µm) at -60°C, but the fiber wound on the silica or iron bobbin had no loss increase. These results led us to expect that steel is good enough for use as a contraction-restricting material. On the basis of this study, a six-fiber unit of the construction shown in Fig. 3.36 was investigated. The construction of the unit and material constants are presented in Table 3.12. The thermal expansion coefficient formula used in Sec. 3.2.8.3 is used as the calculation formula. The calculation results of Table 3.12

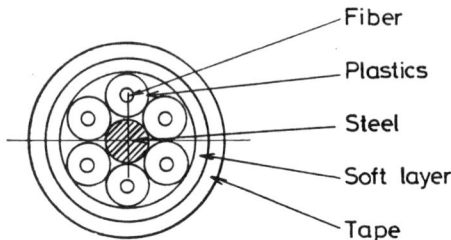

Figure 3.36 Nylon-extruded fiber stranded with steel.

show that the unit thermal expansion coefficient 1.3×10^{-5} is nearly the same as that of a buffer layer-coated nylon-covered fiber ($2-5 \times 10^{-5}$) when the entire unit expands and shrinks as one unit.

Using this construction, the construction of the nylon-covered fiber is restricted by the steel wire in the center. The change in loss before and after assembling the unit was no more than ±0.1 dB/km. There was no change within the measuring accuracy. This unit was coiled in a diameter of about 400 mm, and its loss change at low temperature was measured. The results are shown in Fig. 3.37 (below, left). The loss increase of this unit was 0-0.1 dB/km at -60°C and almost nil at -40°C.

Considering the low-temperature properties determined by these studies, a construction is used in which a strength member with a low expansion coefficient is inserted in the center of the unit and nylon-covered fibers are stranded in close contact with the strength member.

The production engineering data now available are as follows: loss increase at -40°C; 0-0.5 dB/km (at 0.85 μm); and, at -60°C; 0-0.1 dB/km (at 0.85 μm).

3.2.8.5 Cable Sheath at Low Temperature

Let us assume that plastic is used as the sheath for a fiber cable. The extrusion method is normally used to cover the plastic sheath on the cable core. When PE or PVC is used as the sheath material, the extrusion temperature is about 200°C. When the sheath temperature is lowered to room temperature, the sheath shrinks and a microbending loss increase may be caused.

Therefore, sheath construction combining a plastic sheath and a metallic material, or FRP, is considered appropriate for fiber cables. The following are some examples. Combinations using a metal tape, metal wire, or FRP wire are primarily used (Fig. 3.38).

Basic Conditions of Design

Table 3.12 Thermal Expansion Coefficient of Six-fiber Unit

	Outer diameter (mm)	Material	Young's modulus (kg/mm^2)	Thermal expansion coefficient (per °C)
Center strength member	0.95	Steel	18,000	1.1×10^{-5}
Fiber (X6)	0.125	Silica	7,200	3.4×10^{-7}
Buffer layer	0.35	Soft plastics	0.1	1×10^{-4}
Nylon cover	0.9	Nylon	120	1×10^{-4}
Unit	—	—	—	1.3×10^{-5}

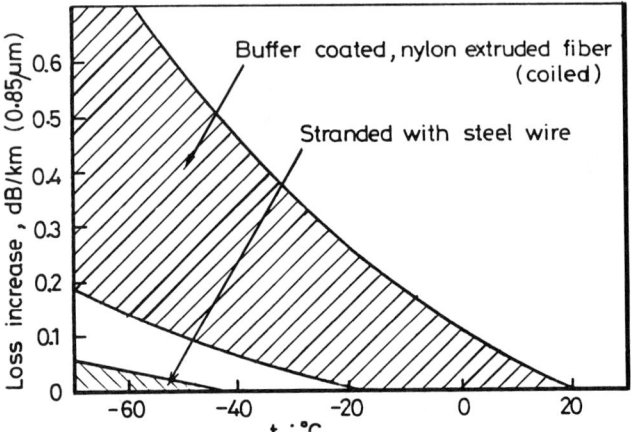

Figure 3.37 Loss increase of plastic-covered fiber at low temperature. (From Refs. 29 and 30.)

In particular, examples a and c are used in many instances. Example c is often used with nonmetallic cables.

3.2.9 Additonal Items for Design of Fiber Cables

3.2.9.1 Design of Plastic Covering on the Fiber from the Viewpoint of Handling by Workers

During manufacturing and installing the cable, the outer diameter of the plastic coating is about 0.3–1.0 mm. In order to achieve higher density in the fiber in the cable, it is desirable to have a smaller diameter for the plastic-covered fiber. From the standpoint of handling at the actual site (e.g., a manhole or electrical pole), however, it is considered that there is a lower limit for the value of this diameter. The diameter of the plastic-covered fiber, the time required for splicing (relative value), and the rate of correct selection of fiber to be spliced (relative value) are shown in Fig. 3.39 [31].

From this figure, it is found that about 0.25–0.9 mm is required for the outer diameter for ease of handling. For ease of handling, mechanical strength, and the problem of microbending, at present soft plastic is used for fiber coating and hard plastic is used for secondary coating, and the outer diameter is larger than 0.25 mm.

Basic Conditions of Design

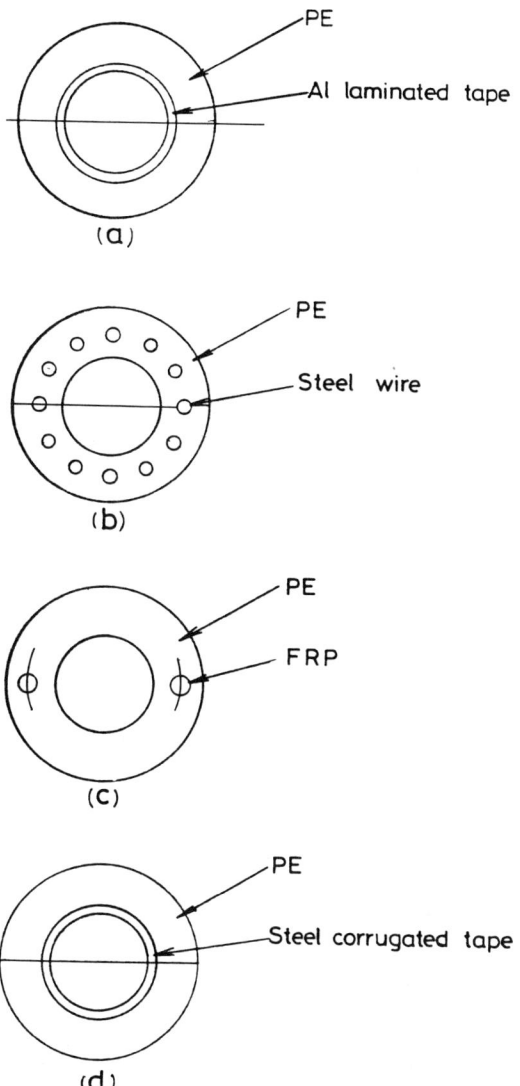

Figure 3.38 Sheath construction of fiber cable.

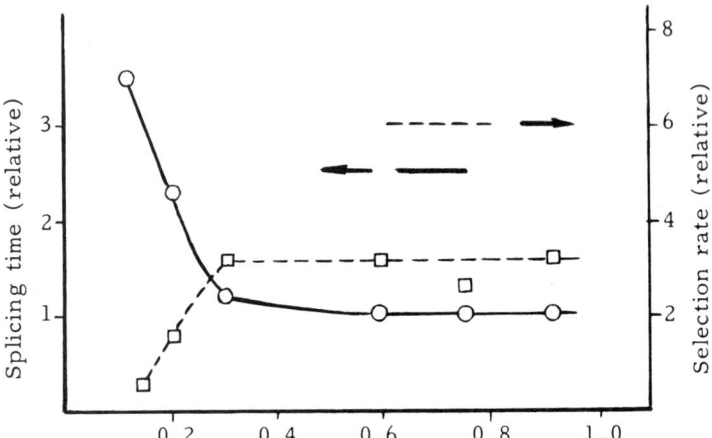

Figure 3.39   Outer diameter of plastic-covered fiber. (From Ref. 31.)

3.2.9.2 Copper Conductors in the Cable Core

Under present conditions, it is difficult to transmit electrical power by fiber. For the transmission of electrical power to the repeater, for monitoring, or for emergency use, the supply of an electrical source is required:

1. Copper conductors are inserted into the core of the fiber cable in a composite structure.
2. A separate copper conductor cable is installed along the fiber cable.
3. Local electrical power is applied.
4. A battery in the repeater is applied.

In a composite cable structure, the copper conductor makes the composite fiber cable much heavier than a cable containing only fibers. The strength member must therefore be made stronger, which in turn increases its weight and the size of the cable. Also, copper conductors in the cable core receive electromagnetic induction from outside and cause electromagnetic interference.

3.2.9.3 Problems of Unit Lengths of Fiber Cables

The unit lengths of communication cables are usually 150 to 500 m. The determining factors of these lengths are the weight of the cable,

Design, Construction, and Properties

the dimensions of the drum, the distance between manholes, and the desire to reduce the number of splicing points. It is considered that unit length will become longer compared with that of the conventional communication cable. At present, the unit length of fiber cable seems to be 1000-2000 m.

3.2.9.4 Caution During Installation in the Duct

When there is no gas maintenance for optical fiber, water may infiltrate it and freeze. Freezing of water in the duct must also be considered. If water enters the cable and freezes, the microbending loss increases, causing the fiber loss to increase by more than 10 dB/km at temperatures below 0°C. The only conceivable way to prevent this is to provide gas maintenance or to use a jelly-filled cable.

It is also possible that water infiltrates into the duct and freezes, crushing the cable. This can be prevented by laying an easily collapsible plastic pipe in the duct, together with the cable, as in coaxial cable installation, to make it absorb the volumetric expansion of ice during freezing.

3.3 DESIGN, CONSTRUCTION, AND PROPERTIES OF OPTICAL FIBER CABLE

In this section, the design and materials of plastic covering for the fiber are first discussed, and then the design of the fiber cable core is described.

3.3.1 Construction of Plastic-Covered Fiber Cable

Table 3.13 shows the representative construction of plastic-covered fiber for the cable core. Table 3.14 shows the representative construction of plastic-covered fiber cables.

3.3.2 Plastic-Covered Fiber

The fiber is covered with plastics to prevent damage and to reduce its microbending loss increase. The most important requirement for covering material is that there be no generation of hydrogen from the material even at high temperature (up to 200°C). Plastic-covered fibers are classified as in Table 3.13. Plastic-covered fibers are compared in the same table.

3.3.2.1 Thin Plastic Coating on Fiber

The fiber is given a thin coating of plastic (primary coating), generally in a diameter of 0.25-0.3 mm. The following are the kinds of plastic and their coating constructions.

Table 3.13 Plastic-Covered Fiber

1) Thin coating		2) Thick double coating	3) Loose tube covering
Hard	Double		
0.25 mm, Fiber, Hard UV cured resin	0.25 mm, Fiber, Soft / Hard) UV cured resin	0.4mm / 0.9mm, Fiber, UV cured soft resin, Nylon or UV cured hard resin	0.25mm, 1.4∿2.0mm, Fiber, UV cured resin, Empty or jelly filled, Loose plastic tube

Size	small	small	middle	large
Microbending loss increase	large	middle	small	very small
Manufacturing	easy	average	slightly troublesome	slightly troublesome
Stranding	special* construction	easy*	easy	very easy
Splicing and connecting	easy	easy	easy	somewhat difficult
Low temperature characteristic	good	good	average	not so good**
Fiber handling	care must be used when the fiber is handled	care must be used when the fiber is used	easy	care must be used when the fiber is handled with the loose tube taken off

[a] Applied for V-grove or loose tube stranding cable core.

[b] The loose-tube-covered fiber has a microbending loss increase caused by shrinkage of the plastic tube in a low-temperature region. To prevent this, full care must be used in designing the stranding for the cable core.

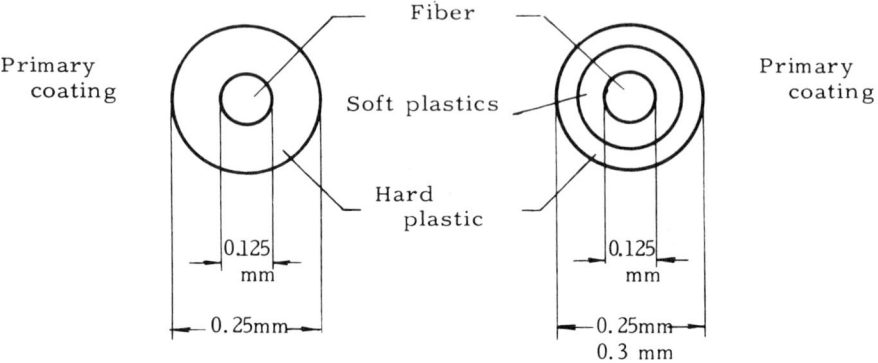

Figure 3.40 Thin coating of fiber: (left) hard coating; (right) double coating.

Material	Kind	Young's modulus, kg/mm^2 (25°C)
Hard coating, hard plastic	UV-cured hard polyurethane acrylate or epoxy acrylate	50–100
Double coating, soft plastic	UV-cured soft polyurethane acrylate or epoxy acrylate	0.1–0.3
Hard plastic	UV-cured hard polyurethane acrylate or epoxy acrylate	50–100

The uniformity (no variation in thickness and stress distribution of plastic; no bubbles in the plastic) of the coated plastics is important to avoid the microbending loss increase of fiber. Recently, double-coating fiber has been generally used (see Fig. 3.40).

3.3.2.2 Thick Double Coating on Fiber

The following conditions are necessary for covering the fiber tightly with plastics.

1. There must be no microbending loss increase.
2. The plastic-covered fiber can withstand general handling and has sufficient mechanical strength.

In order to meet these two requirements, the fiber must be covered first with soft plastic (primary coating) and then with hard plastic

Design, Construction, and Properties

(secondary covering). The optimum thickness of these plastics is considerably greater than the thickness mentioned in the preceding section (see Sec. 3.3.5.1). This thick double-covered fiber can be stranded directed in the same way as conventional communication cables. Following are its construction and materials (see Fig. 3.41).

If UV-curable resins are used for both the soft and hard layers, these resins are coated during the fiber drawing process in a single operation. In this case, the extrusion process after fiber darwing is omitted.

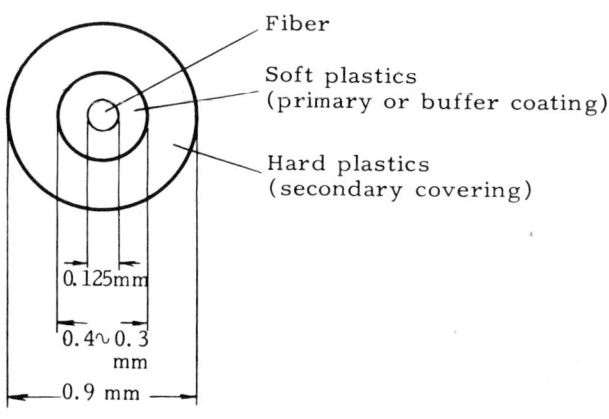

Fiber	Plastic	OD (mm)	Material	Young's modulus kg/mm^2 (25°C)
125 mm OD	Soft (primary or buffer coating)	0.3–0.4	UV-cured soft polyurethane acrylate, epoxy acrylate	0.1–0.3
	Hard	0.85–1.0	UV-cured hard polyurethane acrylate, epoxy acrylate	50–100
			Nylon 6, 12	120

Figure 3.41 Thick double coating on fiber.

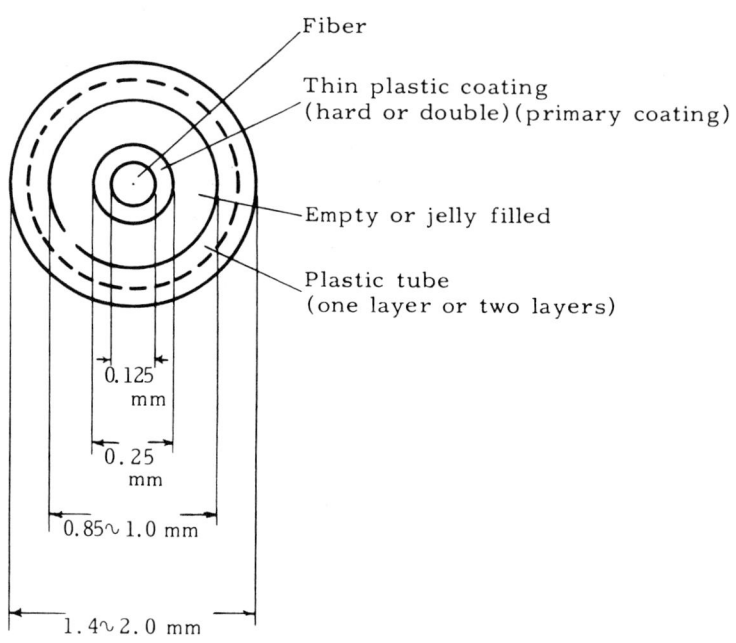

Construction	Material
Thin plastics on the fiber	Hard: UV-cured hard polyurethane acrylate or epoxy acrylate
	Double: UV-cured polyurethane acrylate or epoxy acrylate
	Inner: soft
	Outer: hard
Loose tube	Polycarbonate, polyethylene, terephthalate, polyamide, etc.
Jelly material	No generation of hydrogen; minor change of viscosity at low and high temperatures

Figure 3.42 Loose tube covering on fiber.

Design, Construction, and Properties

3.3.2.3 Loose-Tube-Covered Fiber

The fiber is given a thin plastic coating and then covered with a plastic tube. The inner diameter of the plastic tube is larger than the outer diameter of the thin plastic coating on the fiber. The space between them is sometimes filled with jelly or a similar material. An example of the construction and materials of loose-tube-covered fibers is shown in Fig. 3.42.

This construction corresponds to $E_p = 0$ in the equation $\alpha_m \propto 1/\Delta^3 a^4/b^4 1/d^2 E_p^2/E_f^2$ for the microbending loss increase discussed in Sec. 3.2.1.

Theoretically, no fiber microbending loss increase occurs unless the tube is deformed by external stress and its short diameter is reduced below the outer diameter of the thin plastic coating on the fiber. When, in the production of this type of plastic-covered fiber, the plastic tube is extruded on the fiber, the length of the fiber must be nearly equal to that of the plastic tube. Also, the material of the tube and its inner diameter must be determined so that the fiber can move smoothly without being caught in the tube.

Since the fiber differs greatly from the plastic tube with respect to the coefficient of thermal expansion, its microbending loss is liable to increase, especially at low temperature. Therefore, attention must be paid to the construction of the fiber cable.

When spliced, the loose tube at first must be cut off. Then the fiber with the thin plastic coating is handled for splicing. Handling of a fiber with a thin plastic coating requires the utmost care.

3.3.3 Representative Methods of Construction of Optical Fiber Core

The representative methods of construction of optical fiber cable core are roughly classified according to the following types.

1. Ribbon
2. Stranding
   Layer
   Unit
3. Loose tube
4. V groove

Table 3.14 compares the construction of fiber cable cores.

Table 3.14 Construction and Comparison of Fiber Cable Cores

Cable	Stranding (Thick double coating) layer or unit	Loose tube stranding, Loose tube high density unit	Ribbon	V-groove
Construction				
Number of fibers	Layer: Suitable for 12 fibers or under Unit: Suitable fibers for multiple fibers max. 1,000 fibers	Loose tube stranding: Suitable 12 fibers or under Loose tube high density unit: Suitable for multiple fibers	Suitable for multi-fibers An example of AT&T 12 fibers x 12 = 144 fibers	Suitable for 10 fibers or more
Fiber density in cable core	Small and medium 24 fibers/10 mmϕ	Medium 60 fibers/10 mmϕ	Large 144 fibers/10 mmϕ	Medium 60 fibers/10 mmϕ
Transmission properties	Suitable properties	Low microbending loss increase	Suitable sheath construction is necessary to require stable properties	Trans. properties is very stable The construction and material of V-groove influence the trans. properties of the fiber

Mechanical properties	Strength member(s) are necessary	Strength member(s) are necessary	Strength member(s) are necessary, but where to insert them must be worked out	Strength member(s) in the V-roove are necessary
Interstitial copper conductor	Easy to insert	Easy to insert	Idea needed on inserting position	Easy to insert
Splicing	Splicing of each fiber is easy, but some means must be worked out for the splicing of a group of fibers	Same as left column	Group splicing is easy The connector can be fitted easily	Same an left column
Manufacturing process and machine	Stranding and unit stranding machine are necessary Cable manufacturing machine are similar to the conventional ones	Same as left column Tube covering on the fiber is slightly troublesome	A ribbon process and machine are necessary	V-groove manufacturing machine is necessary. A process and a machine to insert fibers into the V-groove are needed.

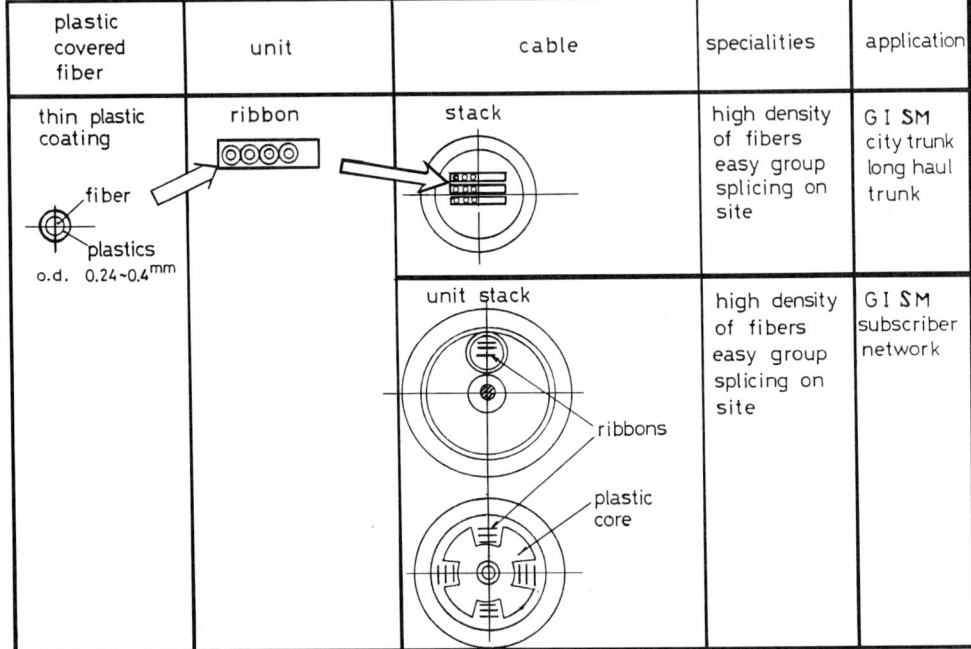

Figure 3.43   Core construction of ribbon cables.

3.3.4   Ribbon Cable

Examples of the core construction of ribbon cables are shown in Fig. 3.43. Fibers, generally 5 to 12 in number, are arranged in parallel in a ribbonlike form and covered. A number of such ribbons are stacked one on top of the other to form a cable core. The density of the fibers in the ribbon cable core is very high, and this ribbon cable is suitable for multifiber cables (about 20 or more fibers per cable). The splicing of fibers as a group is easier, as is connector attachment.

It is somewhat difficult to insert the strength member in the center of this type of cable core. Usually the strength member is provided around the cable core or in or outside the sheath.

When a ribbon of large width is twisted, the stress that works on its center differs from the stress on its edge portions, giving rise to the danger of increased irregularity in microbending loss increase among all fibers.

Other examples of cable core construction to accommodate a large number of fibers are shown in the center of the lower part of Fig. 3.43. That is

Design, Construction, and Properties   247

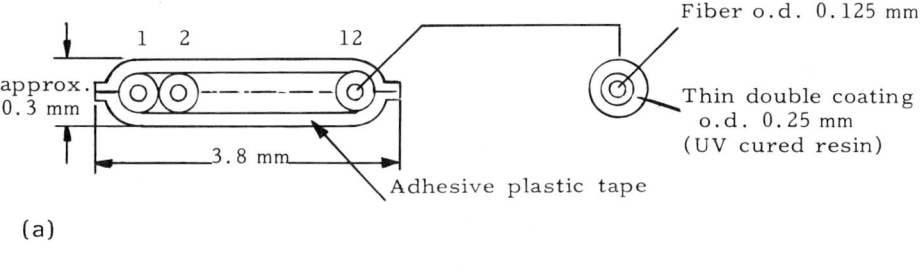

(a)

(b)

Figure 3.44   Construction of ribbons: (a) a 12-fiber ribbon developed and manufactured by AT&T (see Sec. 3.3.4.2) (from Refs. 32-37); (b) a 5-fiber ribbon being developed for a subscriber network in Japan (see Sec. 3.3.4.1) (from Refs. 32-39).

1. Stacked fiber ribbons are covered with plastic tube or Al-laminated PE tube to form a unit, and a number of such units are stranded to form a cable core.
2. Stacked fiber ribbons are inserted into the grooved plastic core.

This ribbon construction is especially suitable for making easy field splicing with connectors. The AT&T Northeast Corridor route is well known for the use of this type of cable. Ribbon cable will be used widely for trunk and subscriber networks. Figure 3.44 shows examples of the ribbon configuration.

3.3.4.1   Design of Ribbon Cable [32-39]

The loss increase at low temperature (-40°C) is roughly shown as Eq. (3.41)[38].

$$\alpha = 3.2 \times 10^{-7} \left(\frac{E_1 E_2}{d_1 - d_0} \right)^2 \quad dB/km \cdot mm \cdot (mm^2/kg)^2 \quad (3.41)$$

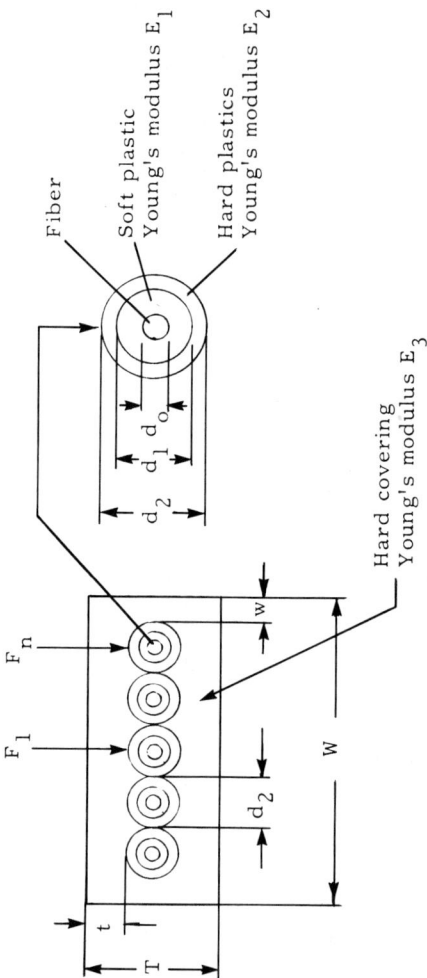

Figure 3.45 Fiber ribbon.

where:

E_1 = Young's modulus of soft plastic on the fiber, kg/mm^2
E_2 = Young's modulus of hard plastic on the soft plastic layer
d_2 = diameter of hard plastic, mm = 0.25 mm constant
d_1 = diameter of soft plastic, mm = 0.15 mm constant
d_0 = diameter of fiber, mm = 0.125 mm constant

The fiber is GI type, Δ = 1%, 50 μm/125 μm.

If t is small (about 0.05-0.2 mm), E_3 has no serious influence on the loss increase at low temperature (see Fig. 3.45). Figure 3.46 shows the loss increase of GI fiber at -40°C.

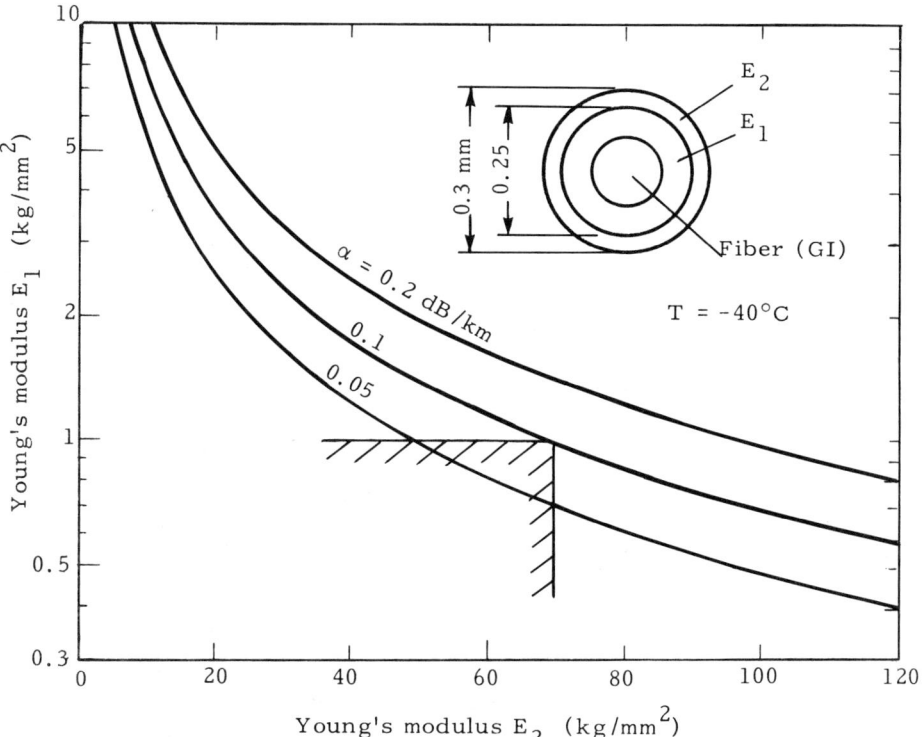

Figure 3.46 Loss increase at -40°C and Young's moduli of plastic materials. (From Ref. 38.)

The side pressure characteristics of ribbon fibers are as follows. Within the range of $d_2 = 0.2$–0.3 mm and $t = 0.05$–0.2 mm, the loss increase of the GI fiber caused by side pressure is approximately within the hatched section in Fig. 3.47. A side pressure applied to the ribbon must be no more than 2 kg/cm.

When the ribbon is twisted, a side pressure given to the twisted part will cause an extremely large loss increase. When the ribbon fiber is cabled with a pitch given to it, the cable configuration must protect the ribbon from exterior strain.

When the fiber ribbon is twisted with pitch p, the strain to the fiber ε is

$$\varepsilon \doteqdot \sqrt{\left(\frac{2\pi r}{p}\right)^2 + 1} - 1 \doteqdot 2\pi^2 \left(\frac{r}{p}\right)^2$$

where p is the distance between the fibers of the center and the edge of the ribbon.

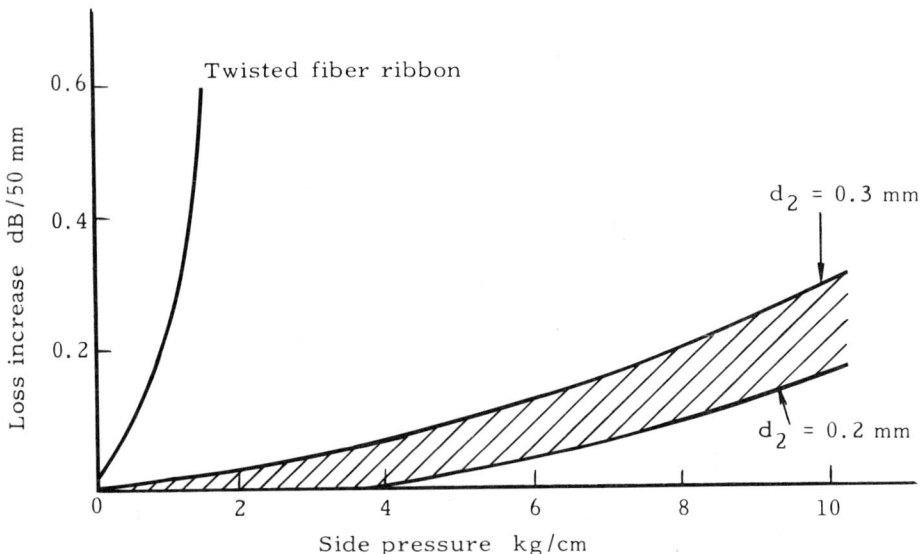

Figure 3.47 Loss increase owing to side pressure. (From Ref. 33.)

Pitch (mm)	r: 1 mm (%)	r: 2 mm (%)
50	0.79	3.16
100	0.20	0.79
200	0.049	0.20
500	0.008	0.03

When the fiber ribbon is inserted in the groove with a back-twist rate of 0% [40], the strain of the fibers (Fig. 3.48) is

$$\varepsilon \doteq \frac{1}{2}\left[\left(\frac{2\pi D}{p}\right)^2 + 2a\left(\frac{2\pi}{p}\right)^2 D \cos \phi\right]$$

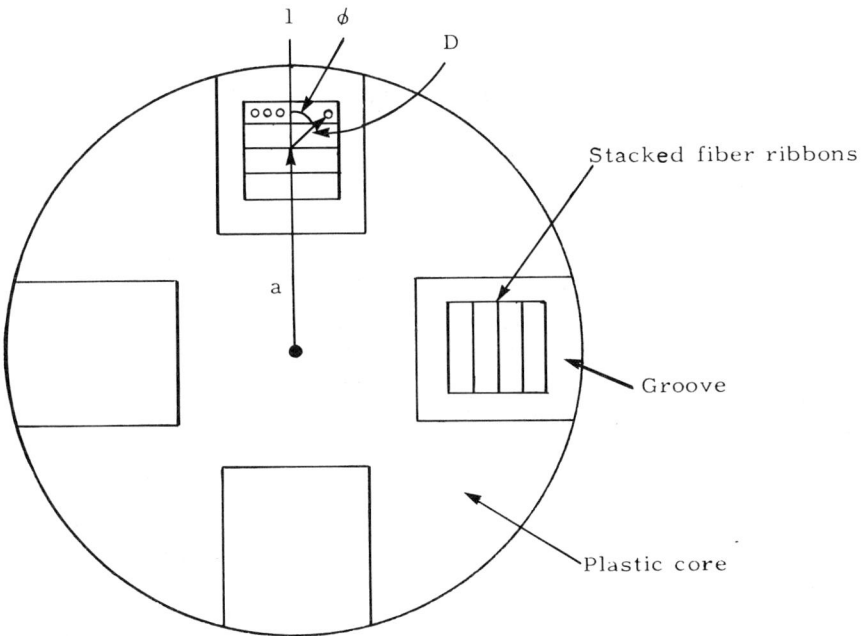

Figure 3.48   Fiber strain for a unit stack configuration. (From Ref. 40.)

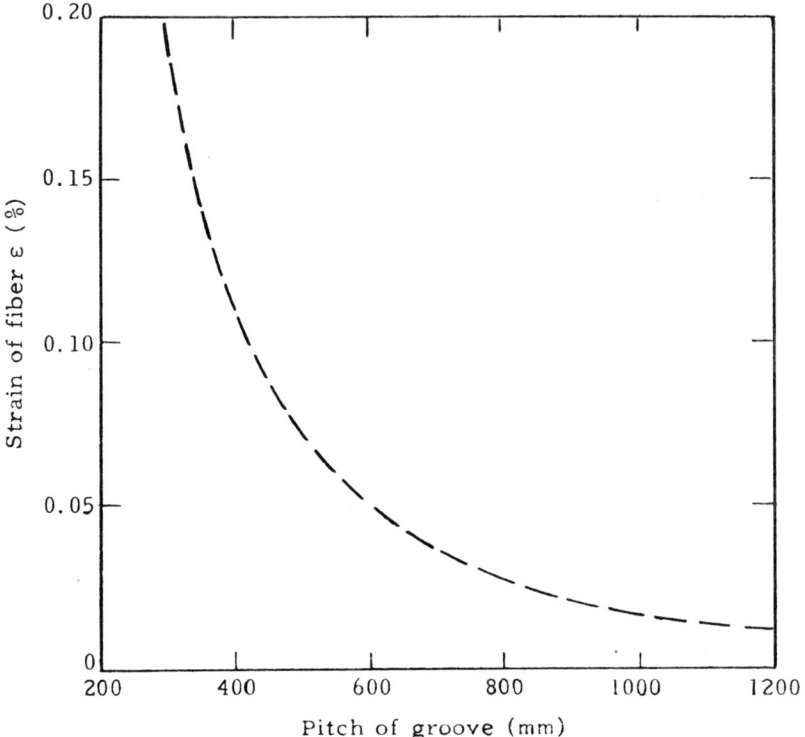

Figure 3.49 Fiber strain: a = 10.7 mm; D = 0.75 mm; φ = 53; ribbon = 0.45 × 1.6 mm; four ribbons in groove. (From Ref. 40.)

where p is the pitch of the groove. In this calculation, it is assumed that there is no slip between fiber ribbons in the stack. Figure 3.49 shows the strain of the fiber in the ribbon.

When the fiber ribbon is inserted in the stranded unit in the cable core with a back-twist rate of 100% [33], the strain ε of the fiber in Fig. 3.50 is expressed as

$$\varepsilon = \frac{2p}{R}$$

$$R = \frac{[1 + (\pi D/P \cos x/p)^2]^{3/2}}{2\pi^2 D/P^2 \sin 2\pi x/P}$$

Design, Construction, and Properties

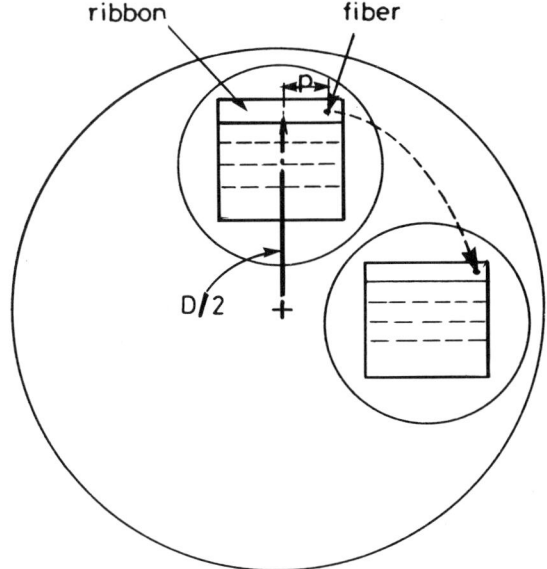

Figure 3.50   Fibers in a ribbon with a back-twist rate of 100%. (From Ref. 33.)

where:

P = pitch of stranding

x = axial position of cable

When D = 15 mm and p = 0.6 mm, the strain ε of the fiber is shown in Fig. 3.51. If $\varepsilon \leqslant 0.1\%$, P is larger than 500 mm.

The deformation of PE and Al-laminated PE sheath on the stacked fiber ribbons are described (Fig. 3.52) [33], as follows. When the sheath receives a lateral pressure in the axial direction of the cable and its deformation (strain) δ is larger than Δ in Fig. 3.52, a stress is given to the fiber ribbon, which causes a loss increase. (See Sec. 3.2.4.)

1. Plastic sheath:

$$\delta = 0.51 \left(\frac{P^*}{\sigma^*}\right)^{7.14}$$

where $p^* = r^{1.28}/t^{2.14}$ R/L.

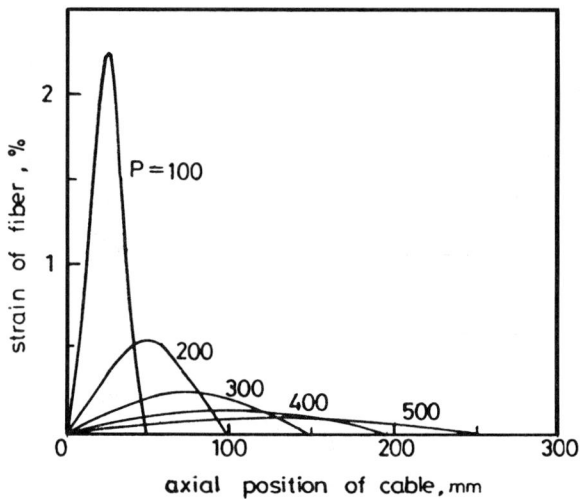

Figure 3.51 Fiber strain in a ribbon with a back-twist rate of 100%. (From Ref. 33.)

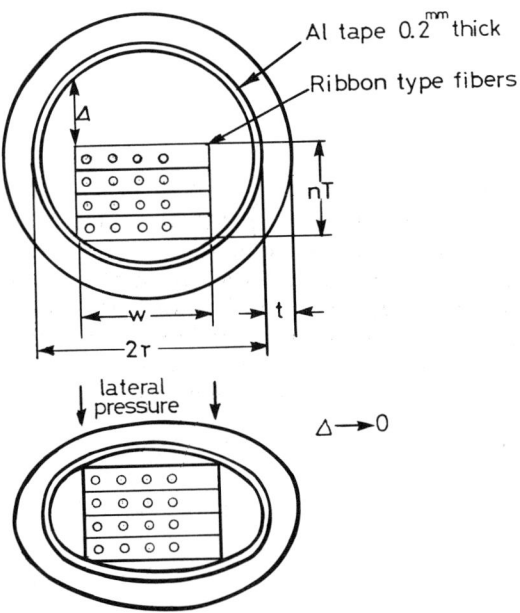

Figure 3.52 Deformation of the plastic sheath. (From Ref. 33.)

2. Al = laminated PE sheath: the thickness of Al tape is fixed at 0.2 mm.

$$\delta = 7.53 E^{-2.12} \left(\frac{r^{1.75}}{t^{2.25}} \frac{P}{L} \right)^3$$

where:

E = Young's modulus of PE

t = thickness of PE

r = inner radius of sheath

P/L = lateral pressure per unit length

3. If $\Delta \geq \delta$, a stress is not given by the deformed sheath on the fiber ribbon.

$$\Delta = \left(\frac{r^2 - w^2}{4} \right)^{\frac{1}{2}} - nT$$

3.3.4.2 Examples of Ribbon Cable [41]

Ribbon Cable Used by AT&T

A cable of this type is widely used by AT&T in the United States. Especially famous is the one used as the Northeast Corridor cable over a distance of about 1000 km between Washington, D.C., New York, and Boston. The following is the design concept of this cable.

1. The cable can be jointed easily in the field.
2. The density of fibers in the cable core must be as high as is practical.

The cable core construction employed to answer these design requirements is the ribbon type shown in Fig. 3.53, where 12 plastic-coated fibers are arranged in parallel rows and held between two layers of polyester tape (thickness 0.025 mm) to form a fiber ribbon. The width of the ribbon is 3.8 mm (0.15 in.). Up to 12 such ribbons are stacked and stranded together and sheathed. GI fibers or SM fibers are used for fiber ribbon:

GI fiber: core, 50 μm, OD of fiber, 125 μm; $\Delta \doteq 0.4\%$
SM fiber: core, 9 μm, OD of fiber, 125 μm; $\Delta \doteq 0.4\%$

The coating on the fiber was a single layer of UV-cured epoxy acrylate during the early field test. It was later changed to a dual coating to prevent microbending loss increase. The fiber is first

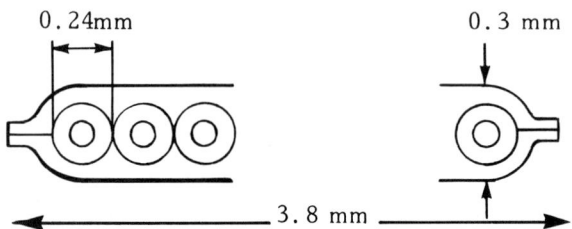

Figure 3.53 Fiber ribbon. (From Refs. 41–46.)

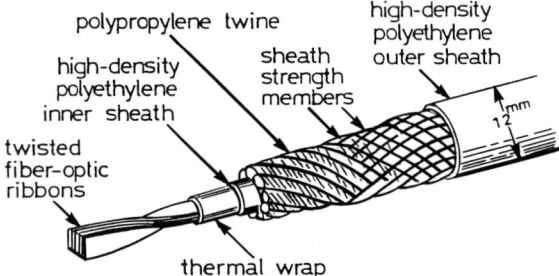

(a) SINGLE-PLY LIGHTGUIDE CABLE (Field test)

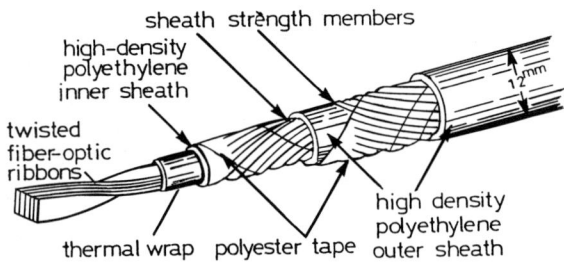

(b) CROSSPLY LIGHTGUIDE CABLE (Commercial use)

Figure 3.54 Comparison of AT&T fiber ribbon cables. (From Refs. 41–46.)

Design, Construction, and Properties 257

given a thermoplastic coating (outside diameter, 190 m) and then a UV-cured epoxy acrylate coating (outside diameter, 240 µm). The cable construction at the time of the early field test differed from that used extensively in commercial application, as seen in Fig. 3.54(a) (field test) and Fig. 3.54(b) (commercial use). Table 3.15 shows the differences between the two. They are interesting as indicative of the progress of optical fiber cables.

As we see in Table 3.15, this cable is characterized by a high fiber density, stable properties, extremely high resistance to mechanical stress (especially impact) from outside, and very easy splicing with connectors. AT&T uses it in large quantities as a standard GI fiber cable and SM fiber cable for systems of medium and short length.

The mechanical properties of cross-ply cable are shown in Table 3.16 [46] and Fig. 3.55 [44].

Examples of Subscriber Cable [47–52]

A cable with a few hundred fibers is necessary for use as a subscriber cable. For this application the cable must have a high fiber density in the cable core. Examples of such cables are shown in Figs. 3.56 through 3.58.

3.3.5 Stranding Cable

In this cable core construction, plastic-covered fibers are stranded. They are of thick double-covered fibers. Such stranding cable cores are classified into the layer and the unit types (Fig. 3.59).

This stranding cable construction calls for attention to

1. Loss increase due to bending in the cable
2. Microbending loss increase at low temperature
3. Loss increase due to side pressure that works on the stranded fibers

3.3.5.1 Design of Buffer Layer [53–58]

From Sec. 3.2.1, the following construction of plastic-covered fiber is thought to prevent microbending loss increase.

1. The fiber is covered with a material with a small Young's modulus, that is, a soft plastic material, such as soft UV-cured polyurethane acrylate or soft UV-cured epoxy acrylate. It is called the buffer or primary coating.
2. The fiber is further covered with a material with a large Young's modulus, that is, a hard plastic material, such as nylon, polypropylene or hard UV-cured polyurethane acrylate. It is called the secondary covering or coating.

Table 3.15 Comparison of Single-ply and Cross-ply Fiber Ribbon Cable

	Single-ply	Cross-ply	Reason for change from column 2 to column 3
Fiber	GI type 50/125 Δ = 1.3%	GI type 50/125 Δ = 1.3%	
Coating on fiber	One layer UV-cured epoxy acrylate, OD = 0.24 mm	Two layers Inner layer: Soft thermoplastic, OD = 0.19 mm Outer layer: UV-cured epoxy acrylate, OD = 0.24 mm	The two-layer construction was used to prevent microbending loss increase in the construction in column 3, loss increase after cabling is < 0.1 dB/km
Cable core	Air spaced	Jelly filled	No water permeation of the construction in column 3
Sheath construction	Plastic tape wrapping HDPE sheath	Plastic tape wrapping HDPE sheath	In column 3 wire armor is applied in two layers, in opposite directions: Therefore,

Polypropylene twine
Steel wires (left-hand lay)

Polyester tape
Steel wires (left-hand lay)

HDPE sheath
Polyester tape

Steel wires (right-hand lay)
HDPE sheath

OD = 12 mm

OD = 12 mm
Weight: 120 kg/km
Tensile road: 180 kg
Tensile stiffness: 550 kg

Laying tension is about twice as large

Tensile creep is almost nil

Cable does not twist when installed; no kink is caused

Fiber property loss

Loss change
< ± 0.1 dB/km
(0.85 μm) at +80 to −20°C

Source: From Refs. 41–46.

Table 3.16 Mechanical Properties of Cross-ply Cable

Property	Remarks
Number of fibers, 12–144	—
OD, 12 mm	—
Weight, 119 kg/km	—
Stress and strain, 820 kg/%	With the safety factor for the fiber of 0.5% screen test
Allowable tension at installation, 270 kg	With the safety factor
Bending radius shock test, 250 mm	Mandrel diameter, 6.3 mm
Once, 30 ft–lb	Mandrel diameter, 12.7 mm
Repeat, 4.75 ft–lb, 400 cycles	
Twist repeat, ±180°C, 2000 cycles	—
Bending repeat, ±90°C, 1400 cycles	Radius, 12.5 cm

Source: From Ref. 46.

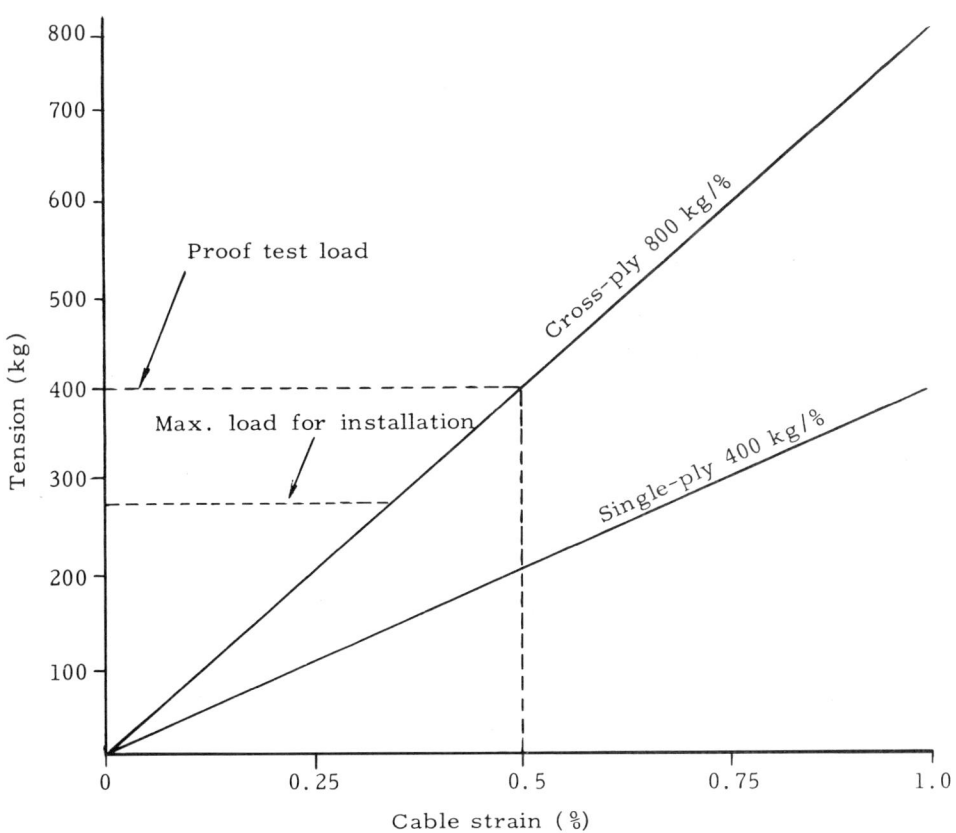

Figure 3.55 Cable tension performance. (From Ref. 44.)

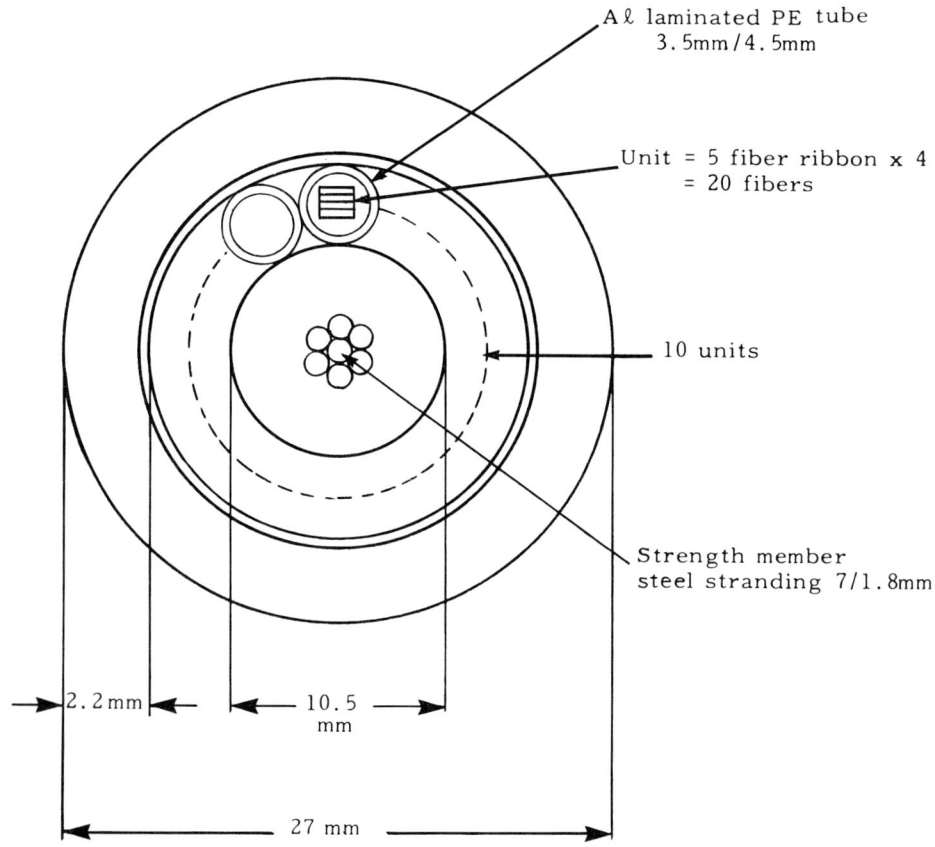

Figure 3.56 Tube unit (200 fibers). (From Refs. 51 and 52.)

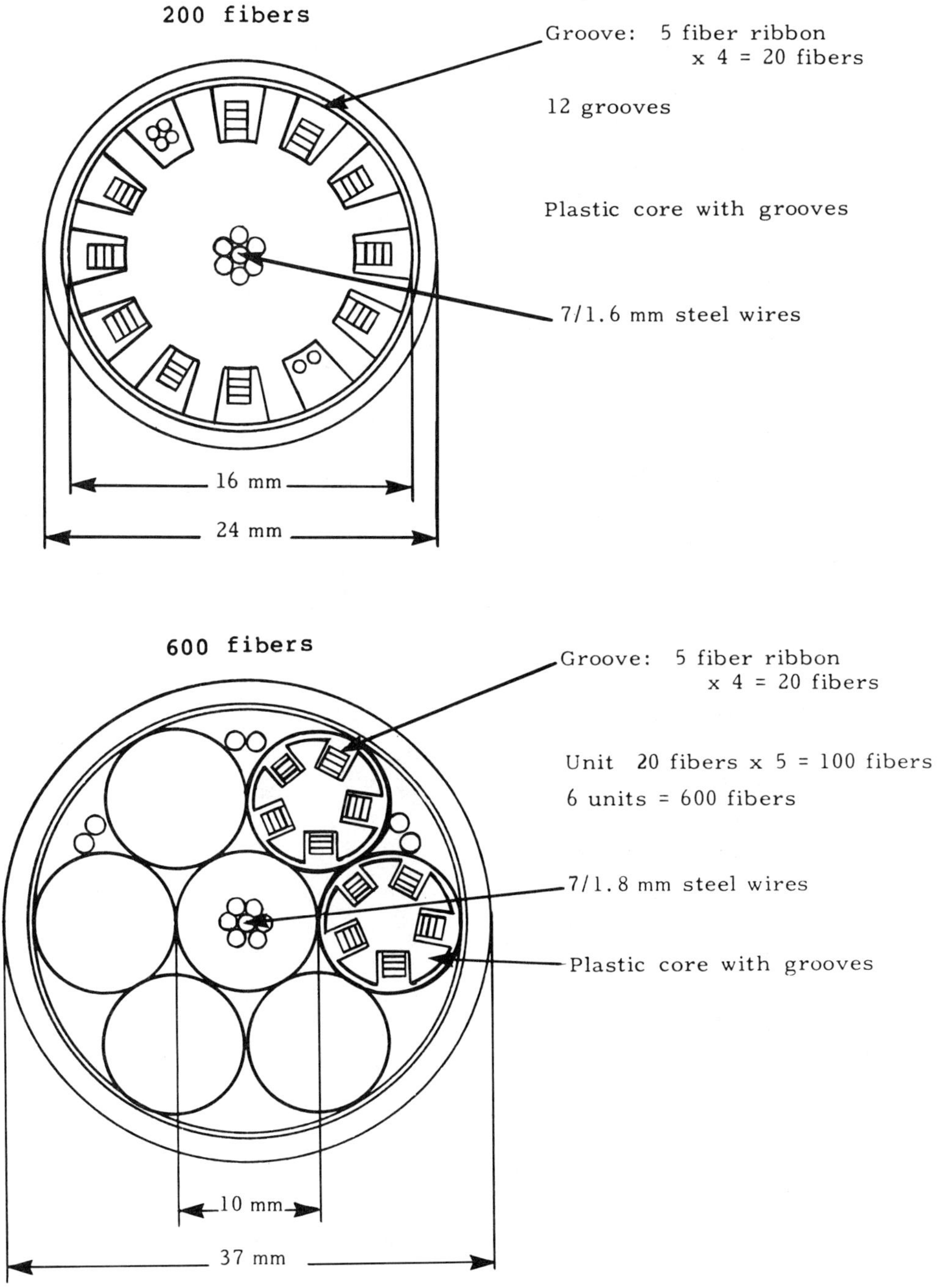

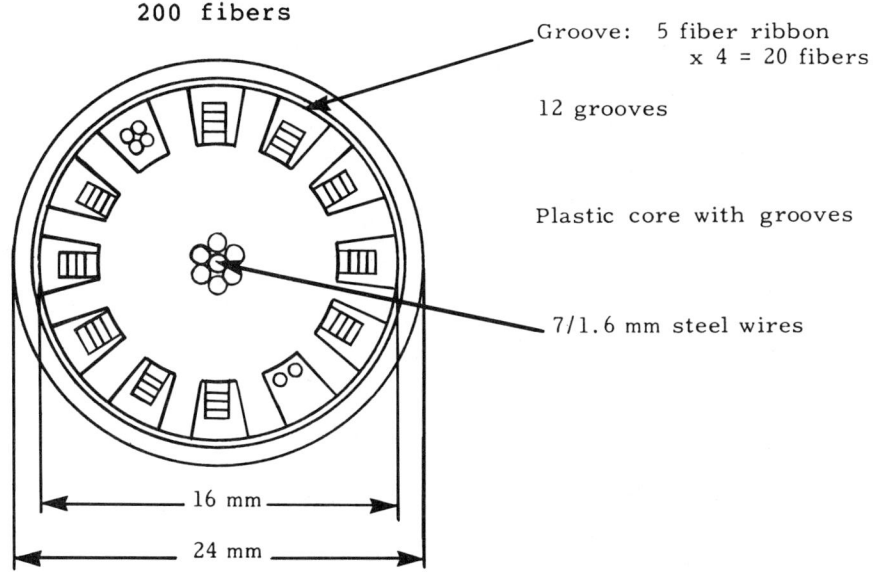

Figure 3.57 Groove unit. (From Refs. 47–50.)

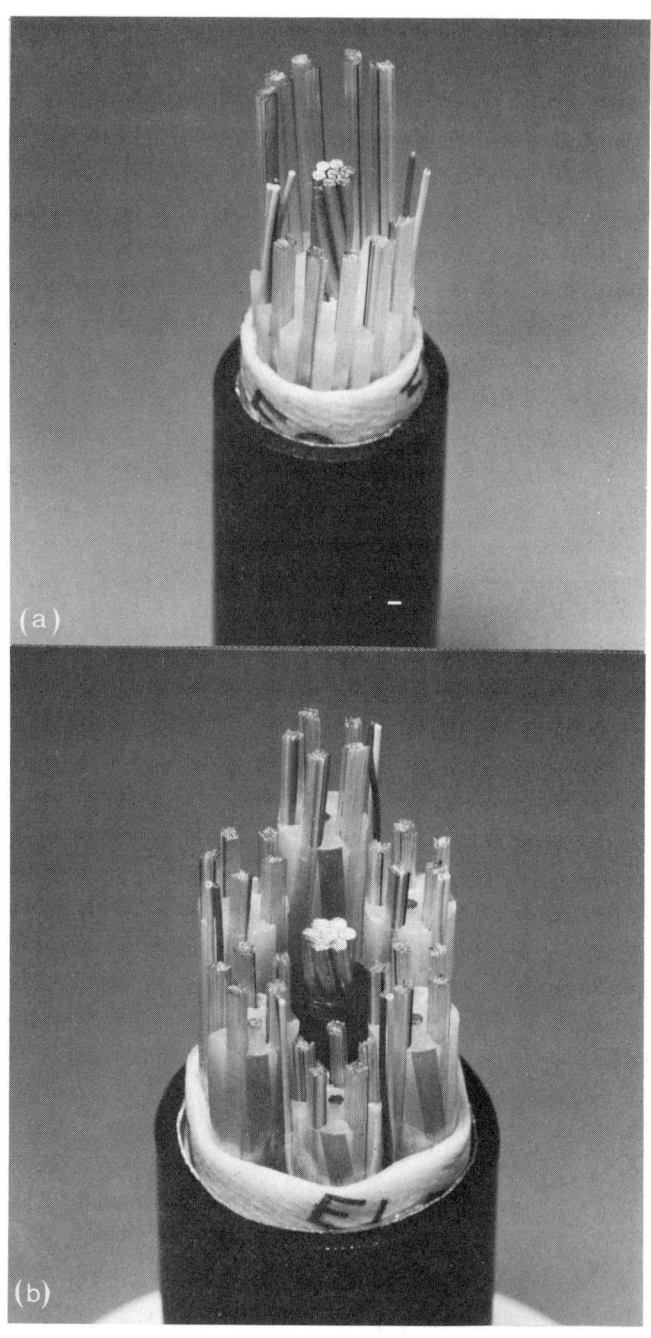

Figure 3.58 Fiber ribbon cable, groove unit: (a) 200 fibers; (b) 600 fibers.

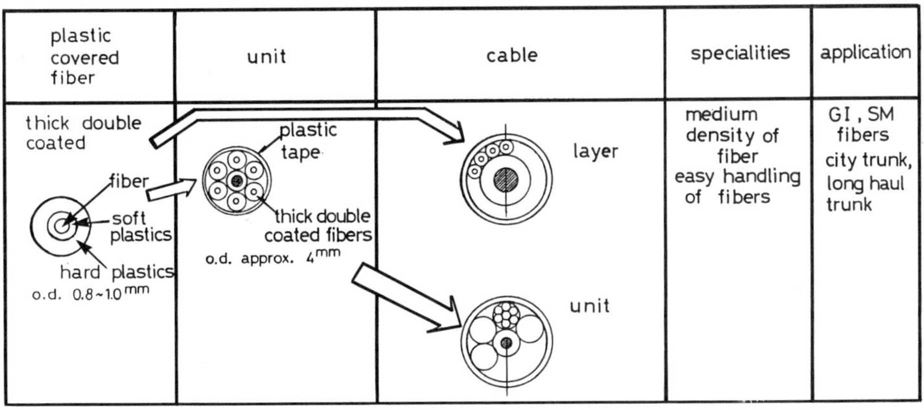

Design, Construction, and Properties

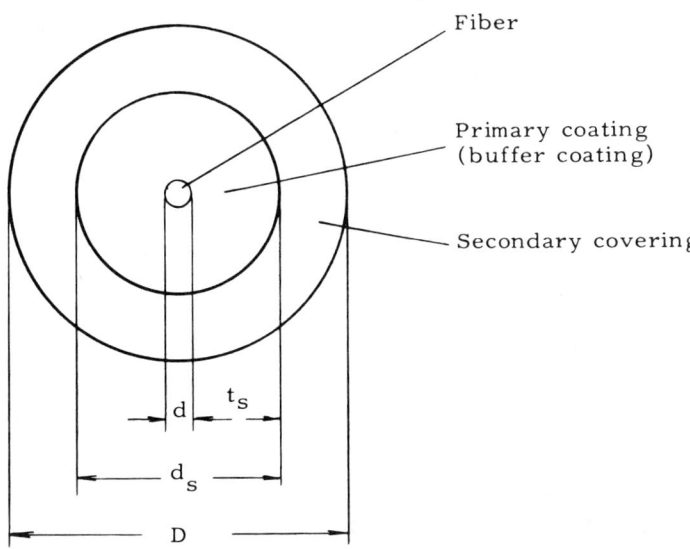

Figure 3.59 Core construction of stranding cables.

With regard to the buffer coating and secondary covering dimensions, there are the following study results (for symbols, see Fig. 3.60). When a compressive force is exerted on the fiber in its radial direction, the stress σ_r exerted on the fiber in its radial direction becomes the minimum under the following conditions [53-57]:

Figure 3.60 Plastic-covered fiber.

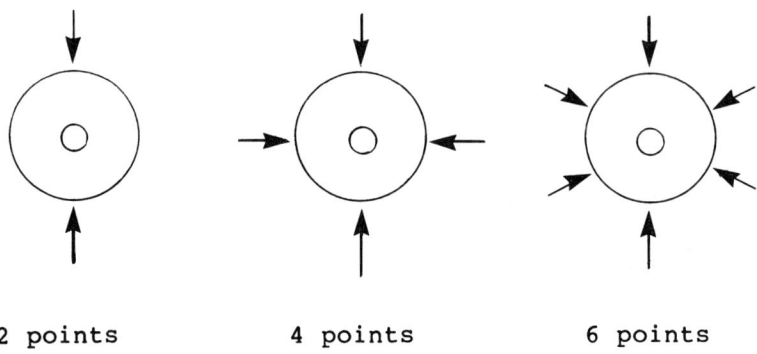

Figure 3.61 Compressive force acting on plastic-covered fibers. (From Refs. 53–56.)

$t_s/D = 0.1$–0.15; $d_s = 0.125 + (0.2$–$0.3)D$ (mm); $D = 0.9$ mm; and $t_s = 0.1$–0.14 mm. This is based on the following calculations [53–57].

Using the finite element method, we calculated the radial stress σ_{r0} and the circumferential stress $\sigma_{\theta 0}$ when compressive forces are exerted at two points, four points, and six points on plastic-covered fibers in their radial direction (Figs. 3.61, 3.62, and 3.63). As a result, it was found that the σ_{r0} in the fiber covered with a buffer

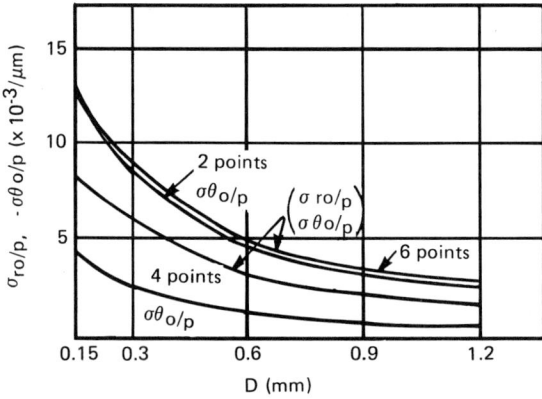

Figure 3.62 Stress acting on fiber and outer diameter of covered plastics (fiber covered with nylon only, without buffer layer). (From Refs. 53–56.)

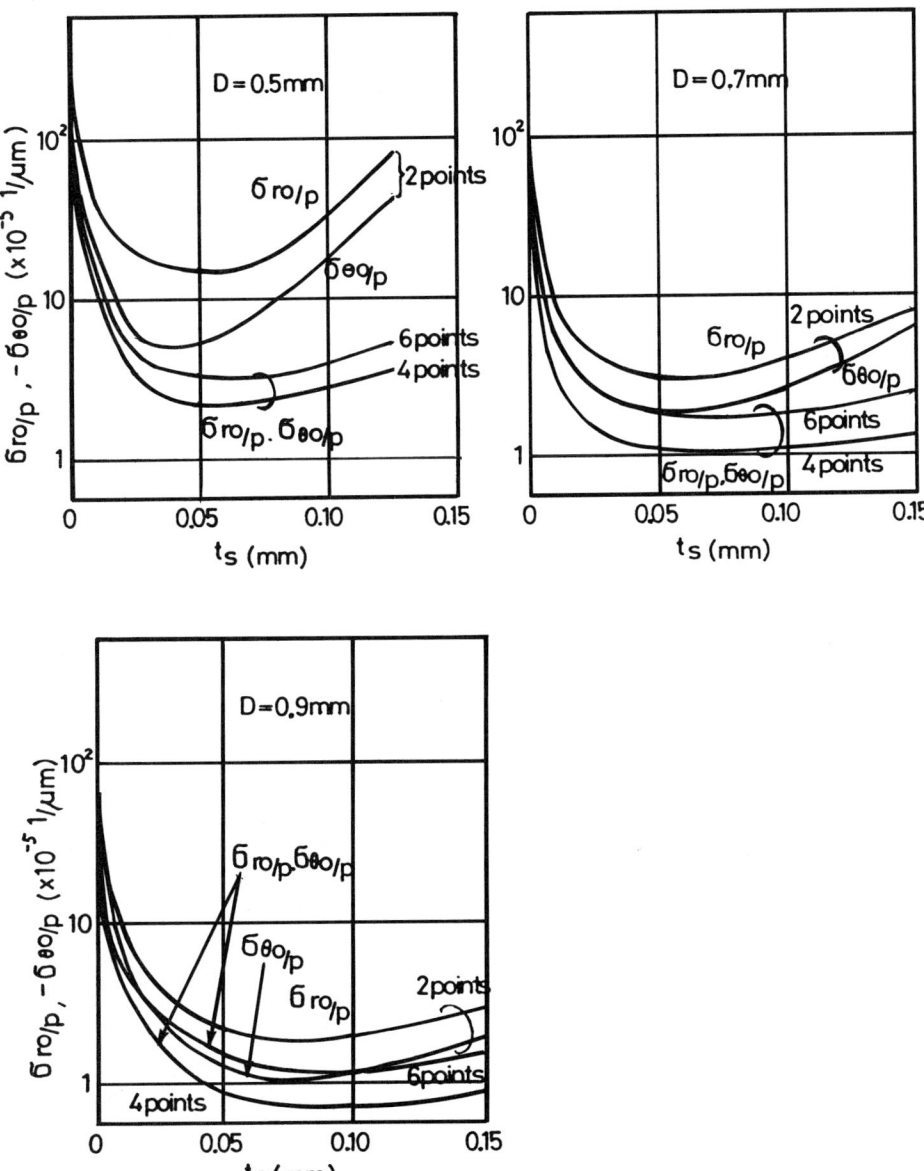

Figure 3.63 Stress acting on fiber and outer diameter of plastic cover (fiber covered with buffer material and nylon). (From Refs. 53–56.)

Table 3.17 Material Constants for Calculations

Constant	Fiber	Secondary covering nylon	Buffer layer	PE
Young's modulus, kg/mm^2	7300	120	0.12	50
Poissons ratio	0.23	0.3	0.3	0.3

coating is about 1/100 that in the fiber without a buffer coating and that there is an optimum value that yields a minimum σ_{r0} [53–57]. The constants of materials used in these calculations are given in Table 3.17.

Further, from the following study on buffer materials with respect to Young's modulus and microbending loss increase, it was considered that there is an optimum value of Young's modulus for the buffer material to reduce the microbending loss increase [58].

The optimum design of the plastic covering on the fiber to minimize the microbending loss increase is as described in Table 3.18.

3.3.5.2 Layer Cable

This is used for relatively small cable with a small number of fibers (generally 2–12 stranded fibers). The thick double-covered fibers are stranded together in a layer as in the conventional layer cable. Because of loss increase due to microbending, a stranded single-layer construction is mainly used. The strength member is provided (1) in the center of the core, (2) distributed in the same layer as for

Table 3.18 Optimum Design of Buffer-Coated, Plastic-Covered Fiber

	Material	Young's modulus (kg/mm^2)	Outer diameter (mm)
Fiber	—	—	0.125
Buffer or primary coating	Soft plastic	0.1–0.2	0.4
Secondary covering	Nylon or hard plastic	100–50	0.9

Design, Construction, and Properties

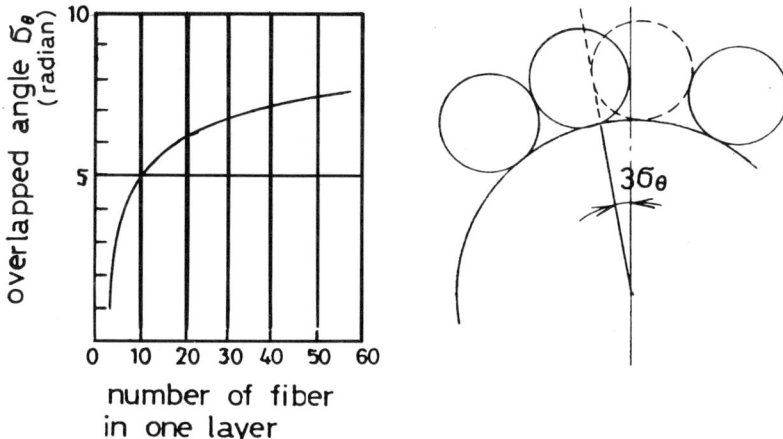

Figure 3.64 Number of fibers in one layer and overlap angle. (From Ref. 59.)

the fibers, or (3) applied outside the core or inside the cable sheath. In some cases, the fibers are stranded with interstitial string or insulated copper conductors. Recently jelly-filled cable has begun to find widespread use. The maintenance of jelly-filled cable is very easy.

The standard stranding design is as follows: fiber bending radius, about 3.0 cm; Fiber stranding pitch, 100–400 mm. For multilayer cable, the microbending loss increase of the fiber is liable to occur even when a soft buffer layer is provided between each layer. This multilayer type is not suitable for fiber cable construction.

Design of One-layer Stranding Cable

The desirable number of fibers in one layer is 10 or less [59]. Even if any more fibers are forced in the layer, 12 fibers are maximum, for the following reason. When plastic-covered fibers are stranded in one layer over the strength member in the center of the cable, it is possible that the plastic layer on the fiber overlaps as a result of change in the diameter of the strength member and plastic-covered fiber, thereby causing side pressure to the fiber. The representative calculated data of this overlap angle are as shown in Fig. 3.64 [59]. From this figure, if the number of fibers in one layer is greater than 12, σ_θ becomes very large.

The stranding pitch, although dependent on the number of fibers, is generally between 100 and 400 mm. When the pitch is too small, a bending strain works on the fiber, and when the pitch is too large,

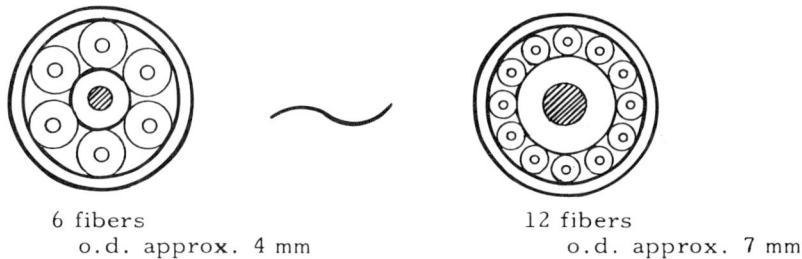

6 fibers
o.d. approx. 4 mm

12 fibers
o.d. approx. 7 mm

Figure 3.65   Layered cable cores: (left) 6 fibers; (right) 12 fibers.

the center strength member and the fiber shrink independently of each other at low temperature, causing a microbending loss increase. All these are taken into consideration in the selection of proper stranding pitch.

The outside diameter of the center strength member must be slightly larger than that obtained theoretically. This is for the purpose of reducing the side pressure that works on the fibers. For a six-fiber cable (outer diameter of plastic-covered fiber, 0.9 mm), the total outside diameter of the strength member must be at least 0.95 mm (theoretical value, 0.9 mm).

Fibers are identified by the colors of the hard plastic, for example, blue, yellow, green, red, purple, and white.

Plastic tape is wound on the stranded fibers in a thickness of 0.3–1 mm. The outside diameter of the cable core is approximately 4 mm (6 fibers) to 7 mm (12 fibers) (Fig. 3.65).

Examples of One-layer Stranding Cable [21]

For one-layer stranding cable, the number of fibers in the cable is generally 12 or less. It is in widespread use in many countries. It

Application	Distance (km)
Long-distance communications	20–3000
City junction lines	1–20
Intracity communications	0.5–10
CATV	1–20
Short-distance communications (e.g., within a factory or building)	0.2–3

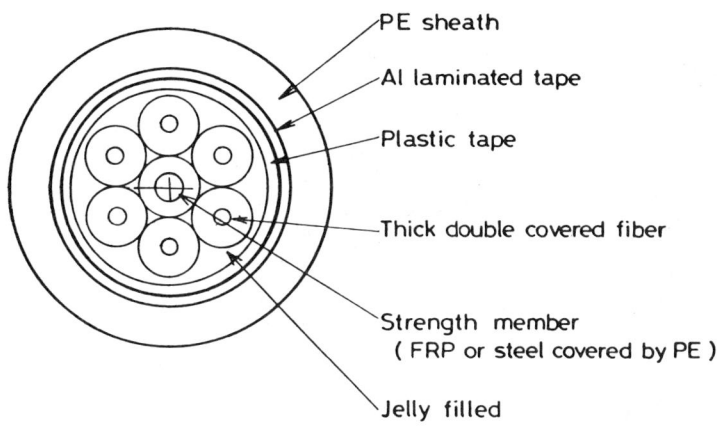

Number of fibers	2–6	7–12
Cable OD, mm	11	13
Weight, kg/km	100	150
Pulling tension, kg	50	150
Minimum bending radius, mm	80	100
Compressive force, kg per 5 cm	70	70
Standard length, m	1000	1000

(From Ref. 61.)

Figure 3.66   Ordinary cable design.

is used for general information transmission, and the following are some examples of its practical application.

Figures 3.66 through 3.69 show some examples of the construction of stranding cable that are used extensively. In these examples of cable design, the following conditions are common.

1. The fiber is given a thick double coating. Fiber: 50 μm/125 μm GI fiber or 8–10 μm/125 μm SM fiber. Covering: soft plastic OD, 0.4 mm; hard plastic OD, 0.9 mm.
2. It is a one-layer stranding cable. The number of fibers in the cable is not very large, 6–12 fibers.

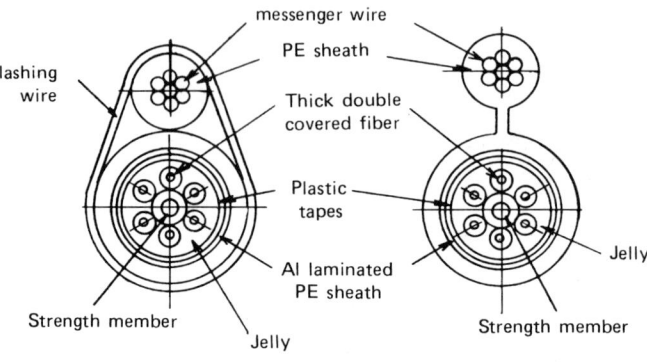

Number of fibers	2–6	7–12
Cable OD, mm	11	13
Messenger wire, mm	7 × 2.0	7 × 2.3
Weight, kg/km	350	450
Pulling tension, kg	900	1150
Standard length, m	1000	1000

(From Ref. 61.)

Figure 3.67 Design of self-supporting cable used for aerial installations. The cable on the left is bound with lashing wire.

3.3.5.3 Unit Cable [60–67]

The unit cable is used for a cable having a relatively large number of fibers, 12 or more in most cases and a maximum of more than 500 fibers. The number of fibers in each unit is four to eight, normally six. Thick double-coated fibers (OD approximately 0.9 mm) are stranded together on the strength member to constitute the unit. The unit is either wound with a plastic tape or covered with a soft plastic tube. Units are stranded together to make a cable core.

Design of Unit Cable

Each unit of six fibers has in the center a 0.95 mm diameter copper-plated steel wire serving as the tension member. This wire is made slightly larger in diameter than the plastic-coated fiber (0.9 mm) to prevent fibers from pushing one another when stranded into a unit. Fibers, with the copper-plated steel wire in the center, are stranded

Design, Construction, and Properties

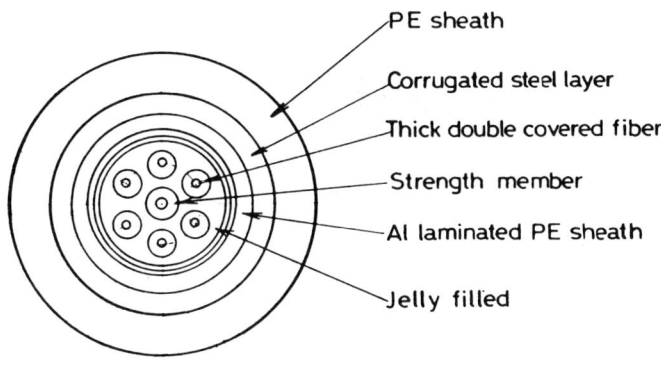

Number of fibers	2–6	7–12
Cable OD, mm	20	22
Weight, kg/km	370	450
Pulling tension, kg	100	200
Minimum bending radius, mm	400	500
Compressive force, kg per 5 cm	200	200
Standard length, m	1000	1000

(From Ref. 61.)

Figure 3.68 Design of corrugated steel LAP cable used under rigorous conditions, such as railroad tracks.

with plastic yarn and wound with overlapped layers of plastic tape. The diameter of this fiber unit is approximately 4 mm.

A quad of 0.9 mm PEF insulated wires is used for power feeding to repeaters, for alarm systems, and for monitoring systems. The diameter of this quad is about 4 mm, nearly equal to that of the six-fiber unit. Therefore, the fiber units and the copper wire quad can be stranded together in the same layer. This makes cable design easy.

For the same reason as in the case of one-layer cable, the stranding pitch of fibers in the unit and the stranding pitch of units in the cable are approximately as follows: stranding pitch of fibers in the unit, 100–400 mm; stranding pitch of units in the cable, 300–1000 mm.

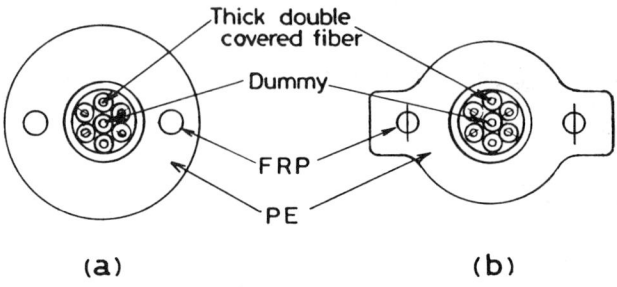

Number of fibers	2–6	7–12
Cable OD, mm	17	21
Weight, kg/km	—	—
Cable a	210	320
Cable b	180	280
Pulling tension, kg	200	250
Minimum bending radius, mm	150	200
Standard length, m	1000	1000

(From Ref. 61.)

Figure 3.69 Design of nonmetallic cable. This type of cable is most suitable for communications, measuring systems, and control systems in high electromagnetic fields.

The most suitable thickness of the covering for six fibers in the unit is 0.6–0.7 mm [60]. When a stress P is applied to the unit, the relation between the stress σ_r that works on the fiber, the thickness of the covering on each unit T_u, and the diameter d of the plastic-covered fiber, determined by the finite element method, is as shown in Fig. 3.70 [60]. (In this case the number of fibers in a unit is six.)

A strength member is provided in the center of the cable [64, 66]. The material and structure of the strength member are selected to keep the elongation of the cable at 0.2% or less when the cable is pulled into a duct for installation under the maximum tension of 300 kg/km.

Considering the safety factor, a 7/1.6 mm steel wire is used for a cable with 20 or more fibers and a 7/1.4 mm steel wire for a cable with 18 or fewer fibers (Fig. 3.71) [64, 66].

Design, Construction, and Properties

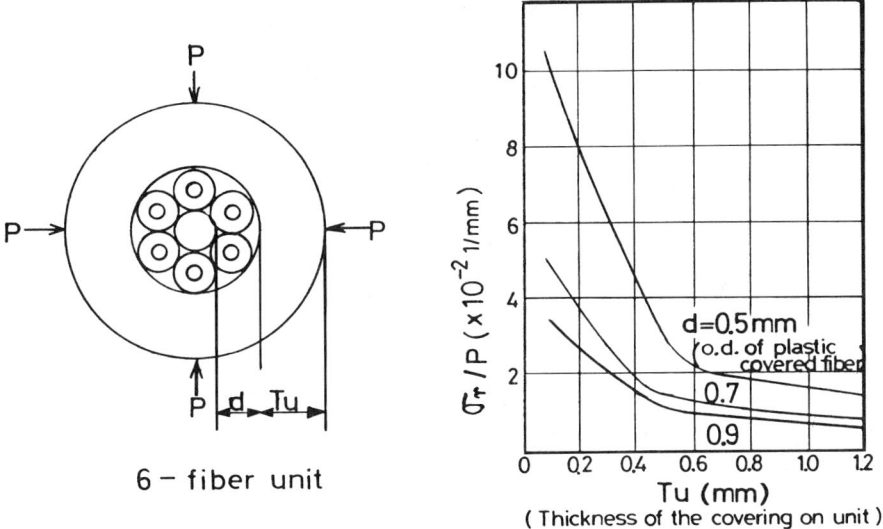

Figure 3.70 Design of thickness for the covering of a unit. (From Ref. 60.)

Examples of Unit Cable

The unit cable is used for a multifiber cable with 12 or more fibers in the following applications:

1. City trunk networks: repeating distance, 5–15 km (12–200 fibers)
2. Long-distance trunk networks: repeating distance, 20–40 km (12–60 fibers); system length, 2500 km
3. City subscriber networks, ∿1000 fibers

Cable of this type is used in areas where a large information-transmitting capacity is required.

In Japan, the first field test (called FR-1) of the application of an optical fiber cable for a city trunk system was made in 1978, and the second test (called FR-2) was carried out in 1980 [61–67]. The 1978 field test FR-1 was for 0.85 μm, 32 Mb/sec and 100 Mb/sec systems with a repeater span of 5 km, using a total of 20 km of the 48 GI fiber unit cable. The test with a 1000 km long fiber was the world's largest in scale at that time. The test of FR-2 in 1980 was for 1.3 μm, 32 and 100 Mb/sec transmission, the largest field test of 1.3 μm transmission in the world at that time. Also in 1980, a field test (called FR-L) of SM fiber cable for a long trunk system was made. The test of FR-L was for 1.3 μm, 400 Mb/sec transmission

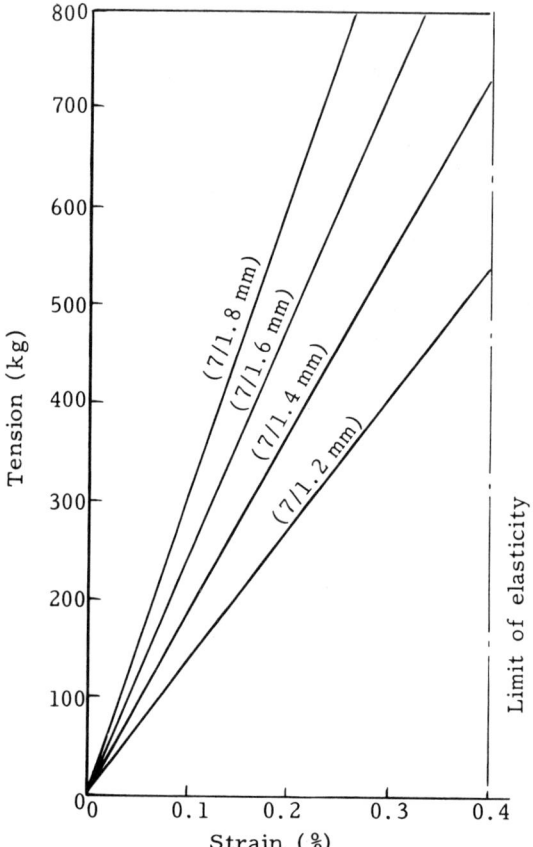

Figure 3.71 Tension and strain of stranded steel wires. (From Ref. 64.)

with a repeater span of 25 km. These three field tests built a firm basis for the design of multifiber city trunk cables and nationwide long trunk cables in Japan.

In Japan, the single-mode fiber cable is now in use in the nationwide trunk communications network and graded index fiber cable is in use in the city trunk network. They are six-fiber unit stranding cables. The single-mode fiber cable was installed from 1983 to 1985 as Japan's main trunk lines, a 400 Mb/sec system with a repeater span of 25-35 km. The total cable length is about 5000 km, and the total length of the single-mode fiber is about 80,000 km. The graded index fiber cable has been installed since 1982 for a city trunk network, 100 and 32 Mb/sec system with a repeater span about 10 km.

Table 3.19 Plastic-Covered Fibers

Fiber	GI fiber	SM fiber
Core diameter, μm	50	—
Spot size diameter, μm	—	10.0 ± 0.10
Refractive index difference	0.015 ± 0.003	—
Relative refractive index difference	1%	$\doteq 0.3\%$
Cutoff wavelength	—	$1.10 \sim 1.28$
Eccentricity GI: w/50 SM: w/62.5 (w in μm)	≤6%	≤3%
Ellipticity $\dfrac{d_1 - d_2}{50} =$ GI $\dfrac{d_1 - d_2}{62.5} =$ SM (d_1, d_2 in μm)	≤6%	≤10%
Plastic-covered fiber		
Soft plastic, mm	0.4	0.4
Nylon covered, mm	0.9	0.9

Source: From Ref. 65.

Examples of the cables now in use in Japan's public communications are discussed as follows. The main dimensions of GI and SM fiber are shown in Table 3.19. The plastic covering on the fiber is composed of a soft plastic (buffer layer covering), 0.4 mm in diameter, and on it a nylon covering, 0.9 mm in diameter, in order to minimize the microbending loss of the fiber and in consideration of its mechanical properties.

Table 3.20 Standard Construction of GI and SM Fiber Unit Cable for Public Communications (Standard Length 1000 m)

Fiber, GI or SM	GI $\Delta = 1\%$	50 μm/125 μm
	SM $\Delta = 0.3\%$	9 μm/125 μm
	Plastic covering	
	Soft plastic	OD 0.4 mm
	Nylon	OD 0.9 mm
Unit	Six fiber unit, center strength member	
	Copper-plated steel	OD 0.95 mm
	Plastic tape overalp	OD 4 mm
Cu wire quad	0.9 mm copper wire, PEF insulation	OD 1.6 mm
	Quadding, plastic tape overlap	OD 4 mm
Plastic pipe with slit (for carrying gas)	PE pipe with longitudinal slit	ID 2.5 mm
		OD 3.9 mm
Center strength member	Stranded steel wires	≤18 Fibers ≤20 Fibers
		OD 7/1.4 mm OD 7/1.6 mm
	Steel wire PE sheath	OD 6 mm OD 7 mm
Sheath	Al-laminated	12 Fibers 24 Fibers
	PE OD	21 mm 22 mm
	Weight	420 kg/km 480 kg/km

Source: From Refs. 61–67.

Design, Construction, and Properties 279

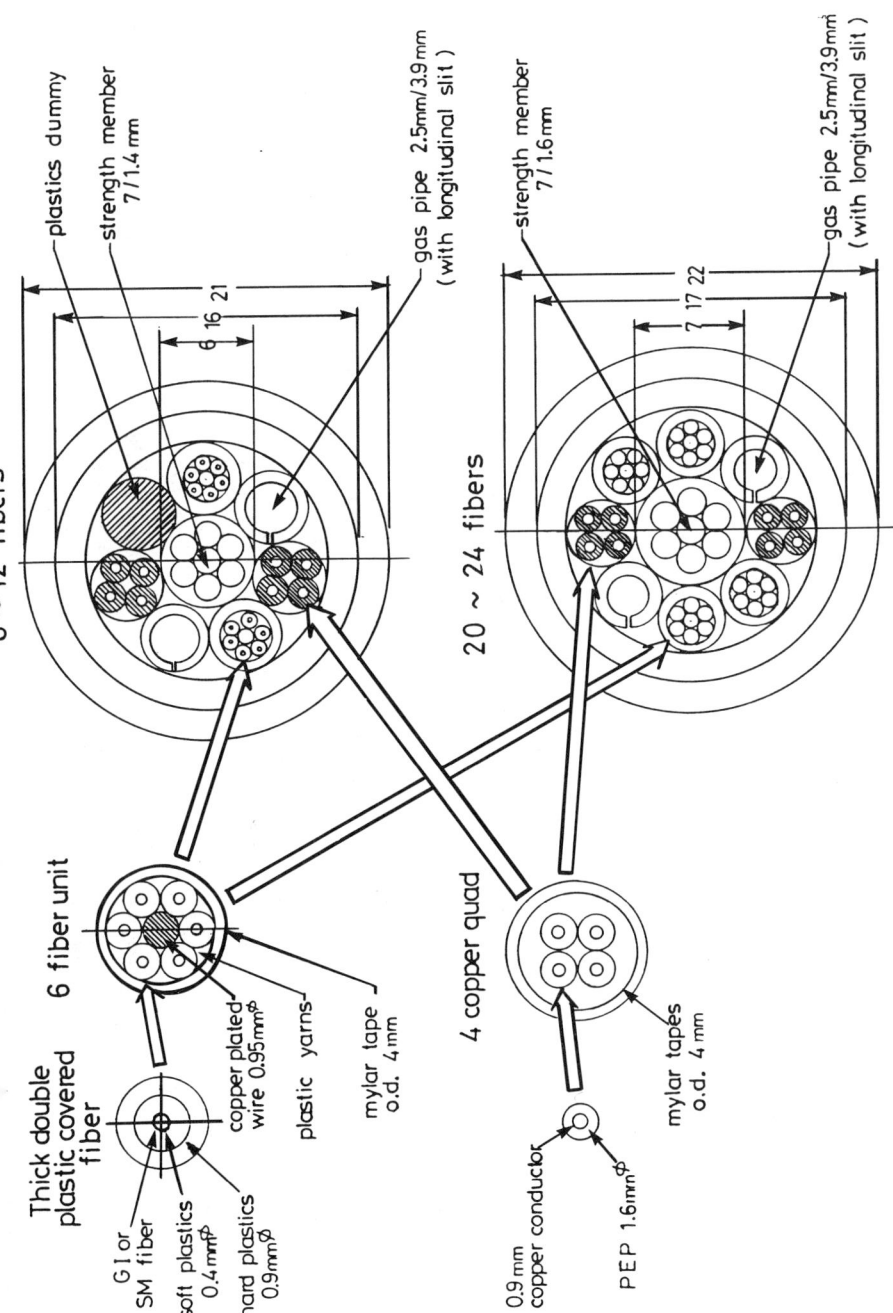

Figure 3.72 Single-mode and graded index unit cables for public communications. (From Ref. 64.)

Table 3.21 Mechanical Properties of SM and GI Fiber Unit Cable

Test	Test condition	Measurement	Result
Pulling	Length, 2 m Tension, 0–2000 kg	Strain Breakage of fiber	See Fig. 3.74 0
Bending	Bending radius, 20 cm Bending angle, 180° 10 times, go and return	Flatness[a] Loss change Breakage of fiber	Maximum 1.8% Maximum ±0.03 dB 0
Lateral pressure	Length, 5 cm Weight, 100 kg	Flatness Loss increase	Maximum 10% 0
Twisting	Length, 1 m Twist, ±180°, twice Weight, 50 and 100 kg	Loss increase Breakage of fiber	Maximum +0.02 dB None

Bending and pulling[b]	Bending radius, 300 and 600 mm Tension, 300–500 kg 5 times, go and return	Loss increase Flatness	0 Maximum 7%
Shock	25 mm ⌀ rod Height, 90 cm Weight, 2.3 kg 5 times	Loss increase Flatness	0 0

[a] Flatness = $(a - a')/a$, where a is the cable diameter before the test and a' is the cable diameter after the test.

[b] Bending and pulling:

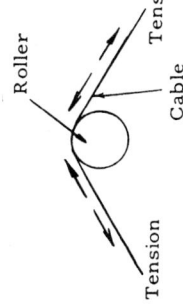

Source: From Refs. 66 and 67.

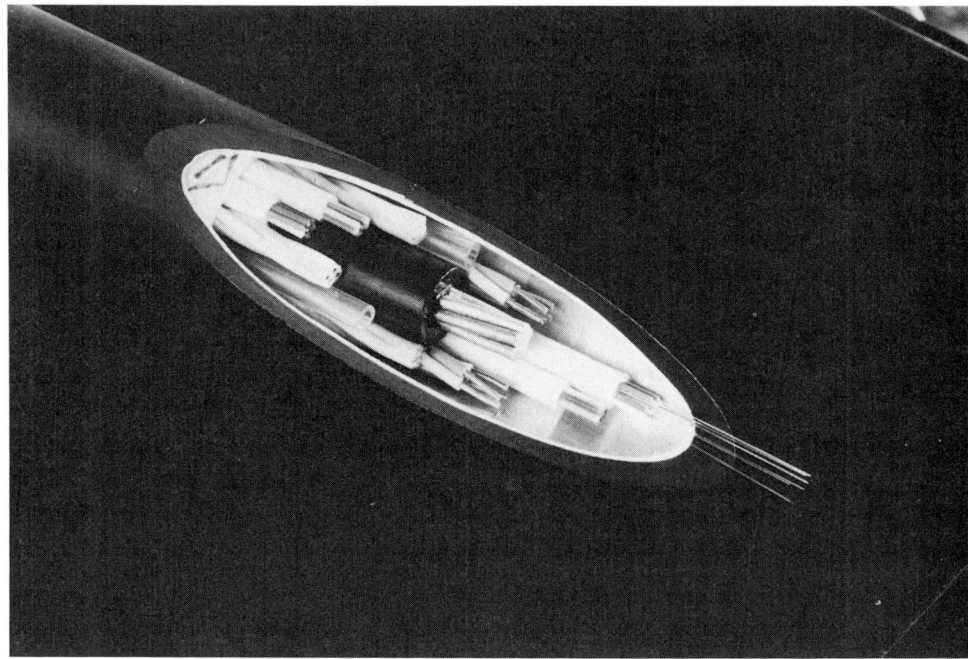

Figure 3.73 A 24-fiber unit cable.

Since the cable is used for city trunk networks or long trunk networks, it needs to have a relatively large number of fibers, that is, 12-48 fibers in a cable. A stable six-fiber unit cable configuration is used. Table 3.20 and Fig. 3.72 show the main constructions of GI and SM fiber unit cable for public communications. Figure 3.73 shows an example of the unit fiber cable.

The mechanical properties of SM and GI fiber unit cable are shown in Table 3.21 (see also Fig. 3.74).

The transmission characteristics of the unit cable are shown in Figs. 3.75 and 3.76.

3.3.6 Loose Tube Cable

The loose tube cable is roughly classified as follows:

A thin plastic-covered fiber is covered with a loose tube. The tube is sometimes filled with jelly. A number of tube-covered fibers are stranded to form a cable core. This type is used for fiber cable with no more than 20 fibers (Fig. 3.77). Let us call this cable configuration loose tube stranding cable.

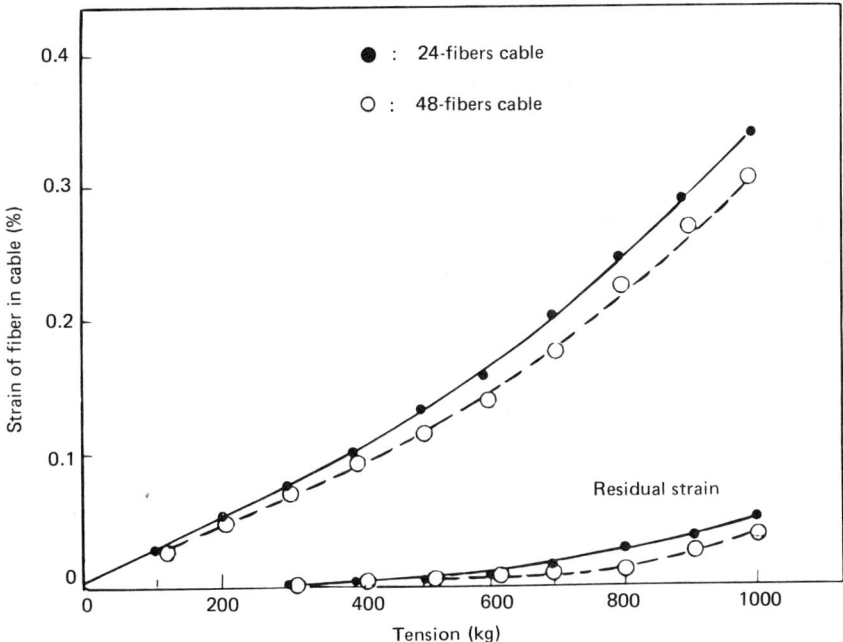

Figure 3.74 Fiber strain in a cable. (From Ref. 66.)

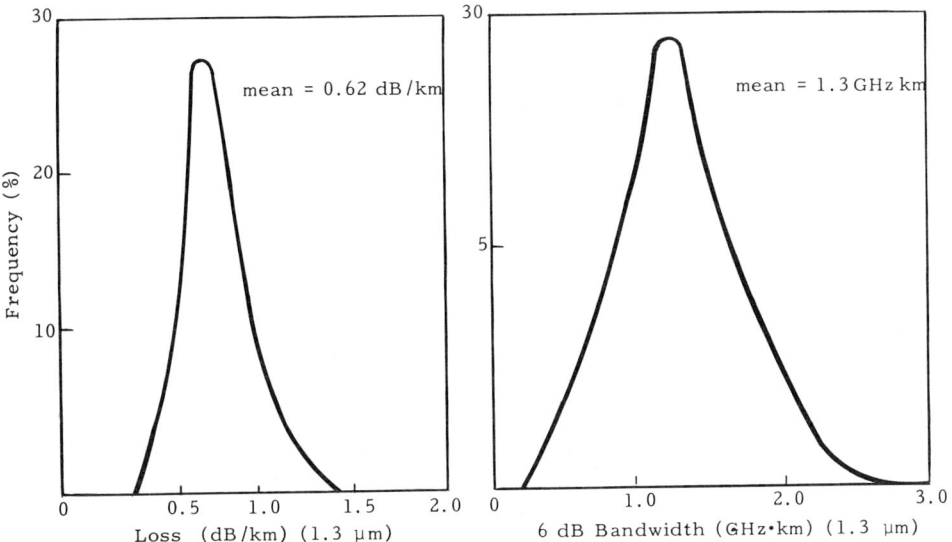

Figure 3.75 Transmission characteristics of graded index fibers in a cable. (From Ref. 65.)

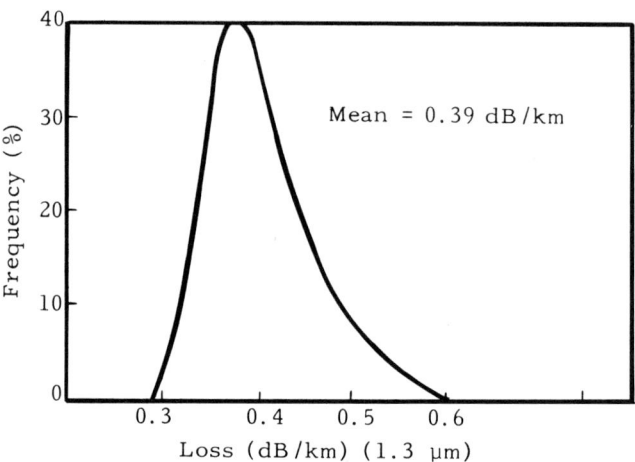
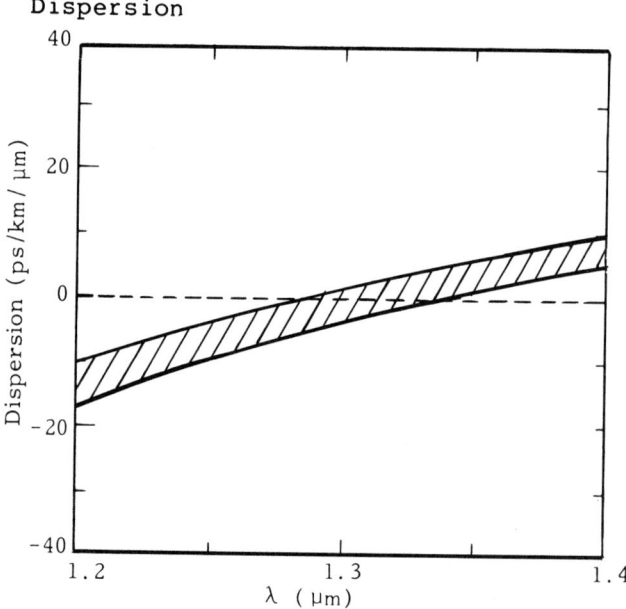

Figure 3.76 Transmission characteristics of single-mode fibers in a cable: (top) loss; (bottom) dispersion. (From Ref. 65.)

Design, Construction, and Properties 285

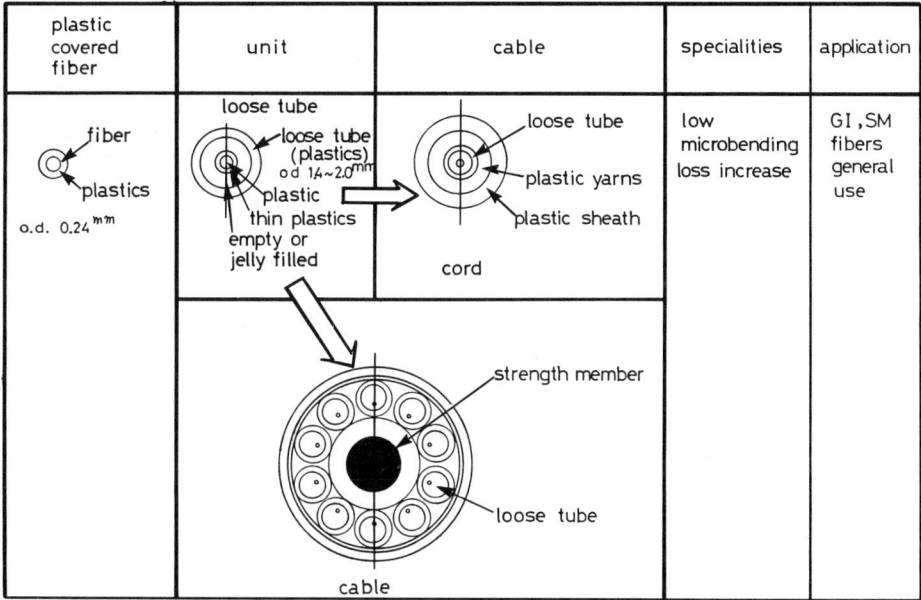

Figure 3.77 Loose tube cable.

From four to eight thin plastic-covered fibers are stranded around a strength member and covered with a loose tube. The tube is sometimes filled with jelly. We call this the loose tube high-density cable. It is widely in use (especially in the United States) for cables with a small number of fibers and those with multiple fibers (Fig. 3.78).

From 4 to 12 fibers are bunched (not stranded) and wound with strings to form a unit. A number of units are bunched (not stranded) for the cable core, and a plastic tube is extruded loosely over the cable core. The tube is filled with a jelly compound (Fig. 3.79). This cable is manufactured and used for the AT&T SM fiber cable for long trunk networks.

The features of this loose tube cable may be summarized as follows.

1. When loose-tube-covered fibers are stranded together, the fibers themselves are kept free of direct lateral pressure and therefore sustain little microbending loss increase.
2. Even when the length of the cable changes under tension or contractive force, the fiber can move in the loose tube in the

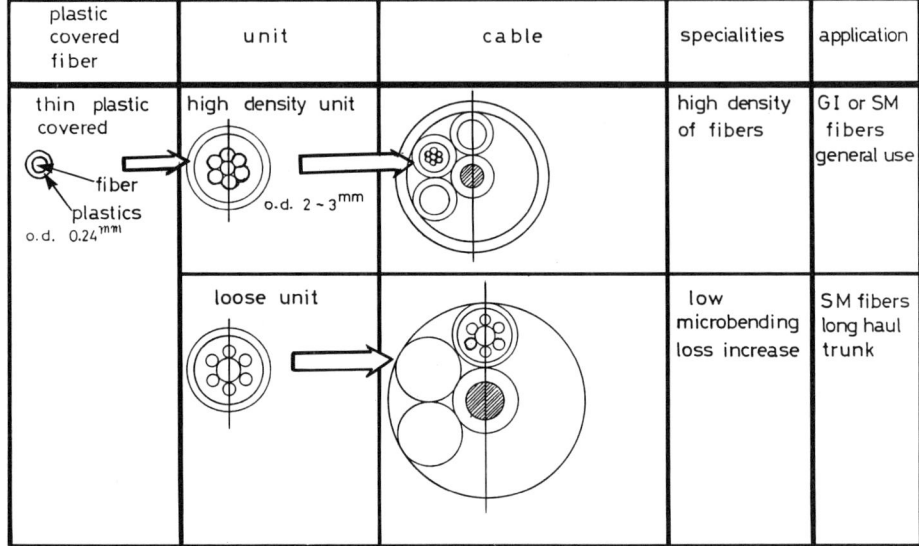

Figure 3.78 Loose tube cable: high-density and loose stranding units.

Figure 3.79 Loose tube cable: bunch unit.

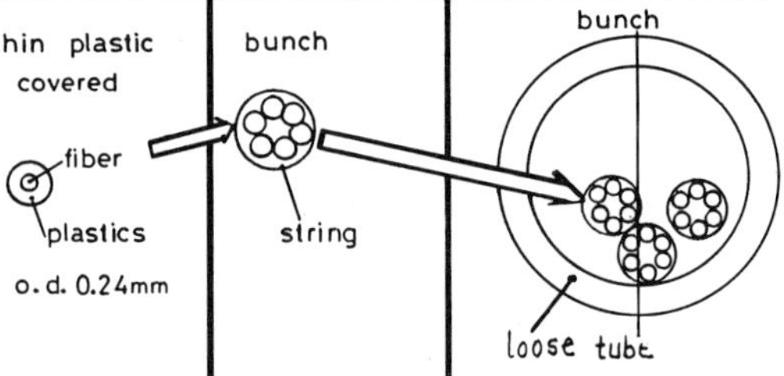

Design, Construction, and Properties

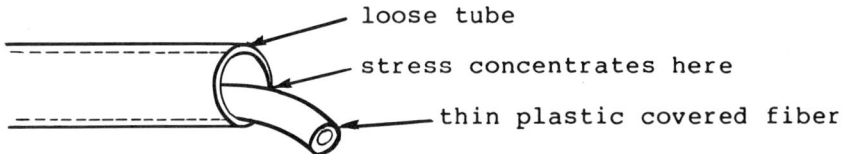

Figure 3.80 Stress-strain behavior of loose tube cable.

radial direction of the cable and therefore receives no strain. This results in little microbending loss increase.
3. The size of the loose tube stranding cable is larger than that of the other types of cable.
4. Stress is liable to concentrate on the part shown in Fig. 3.80 during fiber splicing. The fiber must be handled with care.

3.3.6.1 Stress-Strain Behavior of Loose Tube Cable

Assume a fiber is loosely inserted in a loose tube, as shown in Fig. 3.81 [68]. The fiber excess length η_T can be expressed by the following equation:

$$\eta_T = \frac{\pi^2 W^2}{2P}$$

where:

  W = inner clearance of loose tube

  P = helix pitch of fiber

The suitable value of η_T is normally approximately 0.1%. If η_T is excessively large, the loss increase due to microbending and macrobending of the fiber in a loose tube becomes large (see Fig. 3.82) [68]. If η_T is excessively small, tension is applied to the fiber even if weak tension is applied to the tube, and the fiber loss increases (Fig. 3.83) [68].

A case of placing fibers in loose tubes and stranding them together is considered. The fiber can move in the loose tube. As illustrated in Fig. 3.84, it moves to the outermost side of the tube when the cable receives a contractive force and to the innermost side when the cable receives a stretching force.

When the stranding pitch is p, the pitch diameter of stranding of loose tube D, and the pipe diameter d, the rate of difference between the fiber lengths ε when the fiber moves from the outermost side of tube to the innermost side of the tube (provided that the pitch is constant) is

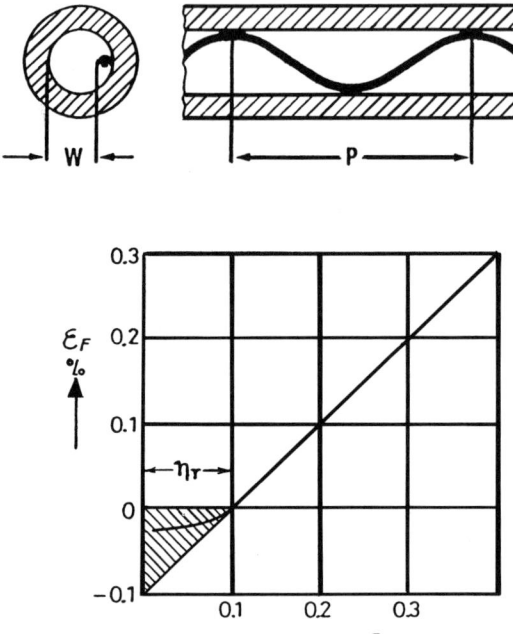

Figure 3.81 Fiber strain ε_F versus cable strain ε_c for a single-fiber cable (loose tube buffer); η_T = fiber excess length (allowed tube strain). (From Ref. 68.)

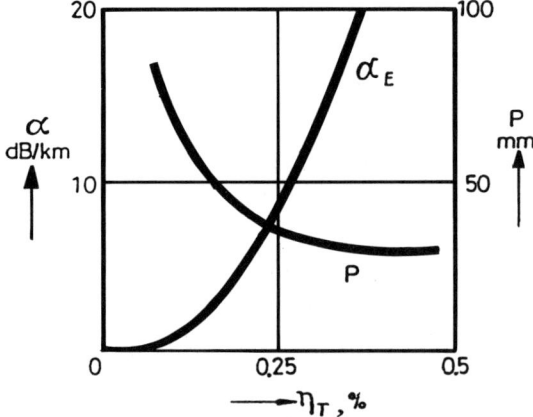

Figure 3.82 Excess attenuation α and helix period P versus fiber length η_T (straight loose tube, W = 0.8 mm). (From Ref. 68.)

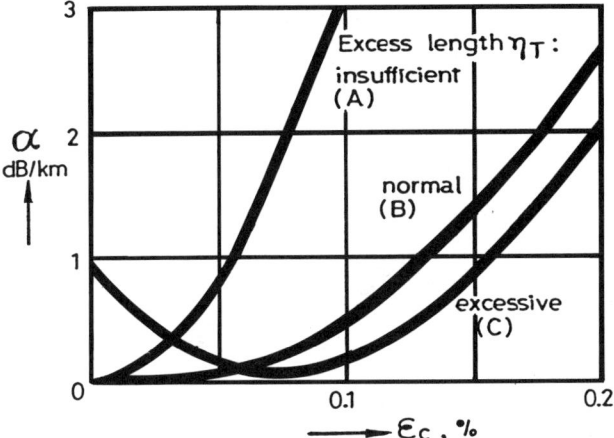

Figure 3.83 Excess attenuation α versus cable strain ε_c for a single-fiber cable (W = 0.7 mm). (From Ref. 68.)

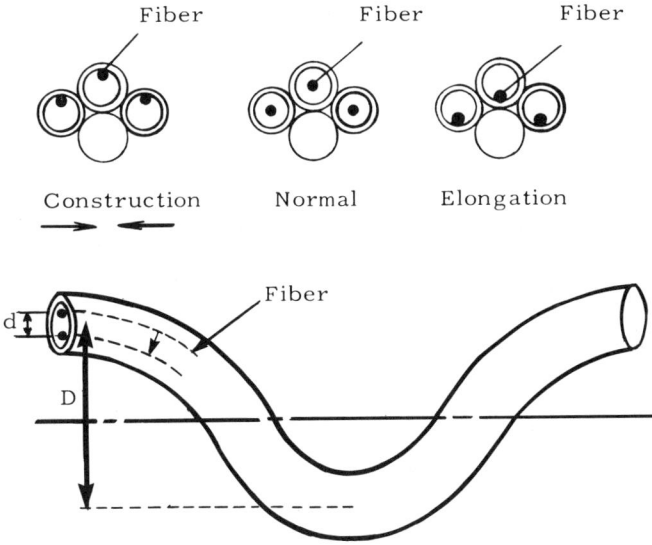

Figure 3.84 Stranding of loose tube cable. (From Ref. 68.)

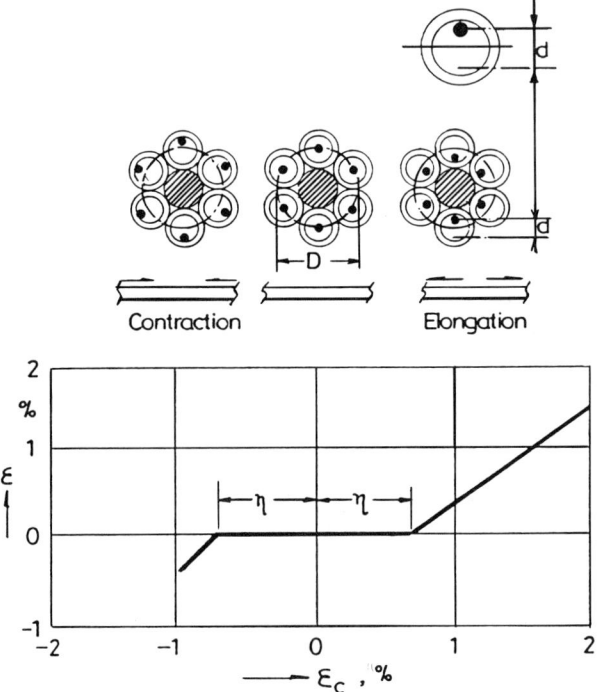

Figure 3.85 Fiber strain ε versus cable strain ε_c for a stranded cable; η = allowed elongation or contraction window as determined by clearance d and pitch diameter D. (From Ref. 68.)

$$\varepsilon = \frac{\sqrt{\pi^2(D+d/2)^2 + p^2}}{p} - \frac{\sqrt{\pi^2(D-d/2)^2 + p^2}}{p}$$

$$\doteq \frac{\pi^2 dD}{p^2} \doteq \frac{10dD}{p^2}$$

The fiber is inserted by at least $5dD/p^2$ longer in the cable. This value is about 1.0–0.3%. For example, with d = 1 mm and D = 3 mm:

p, mm	50	70	100	200
ε_ℓ, %	1.2	0.6	0.3	0.08

Design, Construction, and Properties

As long as the elongation of the cable does not exceed this limit, the fiber is kept free of tension or compressive force, and theoretically speaking, its properties remain unchanged. Therefore the relation between the elongation of the fiber and that of the cable is as in Fig. 3.85 [68]. The value η of the allowable window of ε_c shown in Fig. 3.85 is generally 0.3-0.5% and is normally considerably larger than the η_T mentioned above.

Figure 3.86 [68] shows the relation between the pitch diameter D and inner clearance W for a constant fiber bend radius of 80 mm.

As mentioned, fiber of this type, when stranded, for example, on the FRP wire or a metal wire, elongates and contracts with them and therefore undergoes little loss increase caused by microbending. Figure 3.87 [68], shows an example. The hatched area in Fig. 3.87 indicates the range of the loss change of fibers in cable.

When the cable undergoes tension and elongates beyond a certain limit, from there on tension works on the fiber and causes a microbending loss increase to the fiber. An example is given for a 10-fiber cable in Fig. 3.88 [68]. This example is of a relatively small cable with loose tubes, each 0.7 mm in inside diameter of the tube,

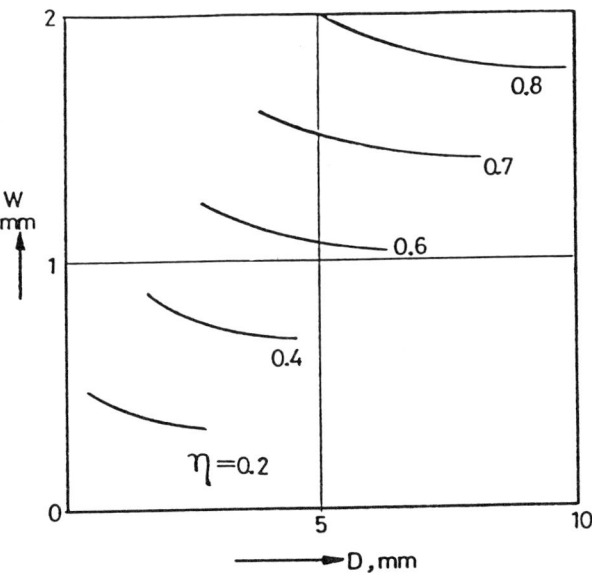

Figure 3.86 Relation of elongation or contraction window η, pitch diameter D, and inner clearance W. Constant fiber bend radius = 80 mm. (From Ref. 68.)

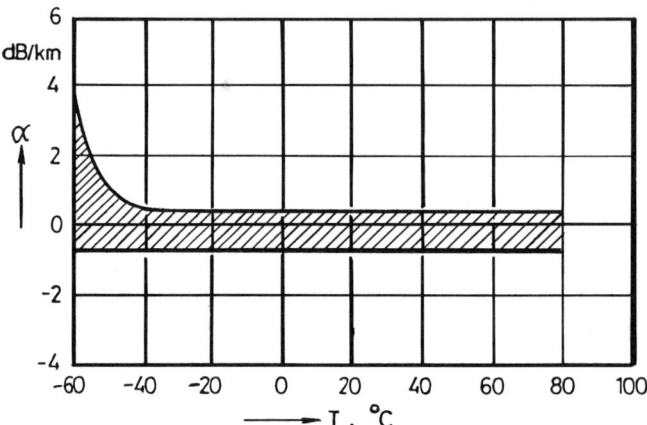

Figure 3.87 Loss change α versus ambient temperature T of a 10-fiber cable (loose tube, 0.7 mm diameter).

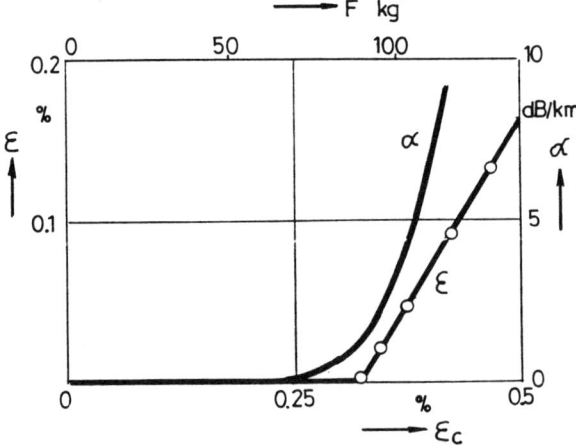

Figure 3.88 Fiber strain ε and loss increase α versus cable tensile force F and cable strain ε_c in a 10-fiber cable (D = 3.5 mm; d = 0.7 mm). (From Ref. 68.)

Design, Construction, and Properties

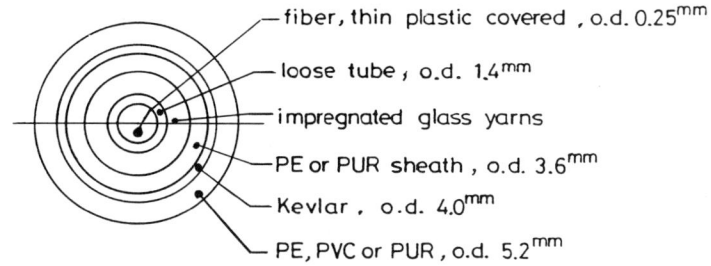

Single fiber general purpose cable

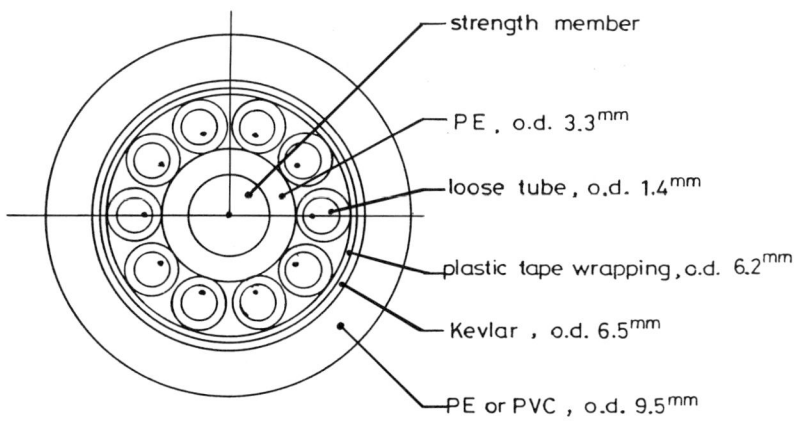

10 fibers general purpose cable

Figure 3.89 Loose tube cables. (From Refs. 68 and 69.)

stranded in a pitch diameter of 3.5 mm. Also in this example, no loss increase occurs to the fiber if the elongation of the cable during installation is 0.2% or less.

3.3.6.2 Examples of Loose Tube Cables [68, 69]

Examples of cable construction of the loose tube cable are shown in Fig. 3.89. Cables of this type are almost replaced by the loose tube high-density cable.

3.3.6.3 Examples of Loose Tube Unit High-Density Cables

As mentioned, the unit of this type consists of stranded thin plastic-coated fibers generally covered with a loose plastic tube. This cable

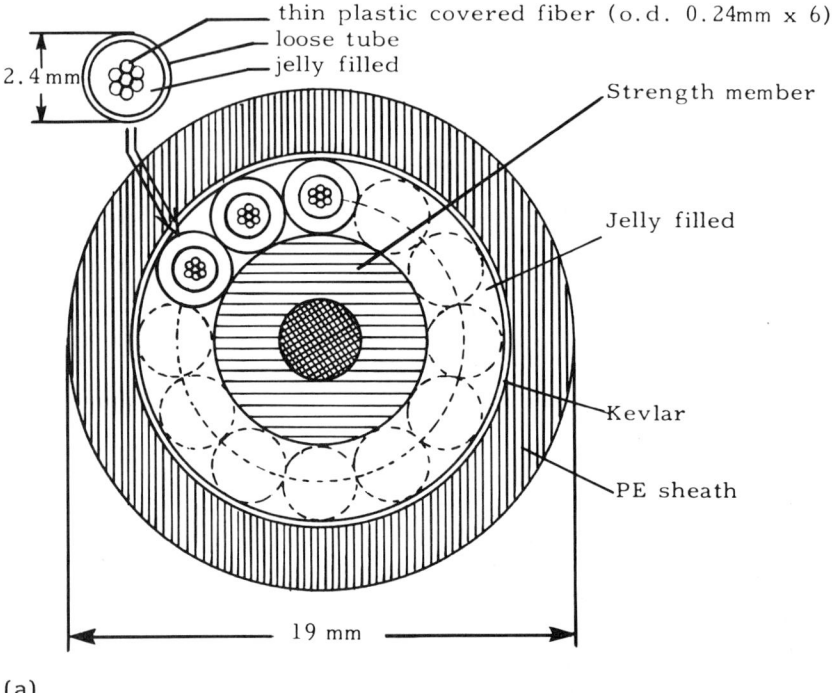

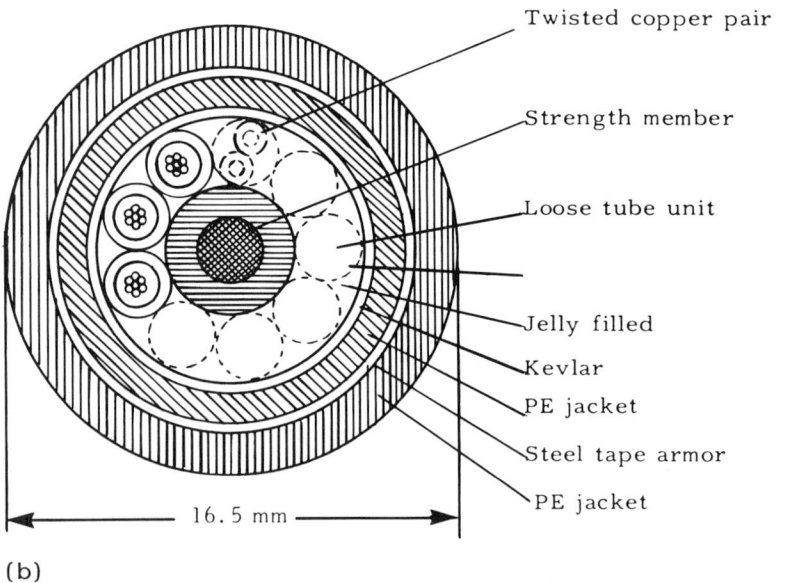

Figure 3.90 Construction of the loose tube unit of a high-density cable: (a) 72 fibers, plain sheath; (b) 48 fibers, tape armored. (From Refs. 70 and 71.)

Table 3.22 Construction and Properties of Loose Tube Unit High-Density Cables (Representative Single-Mode Cable)

Number of fibers	8	16	48	90	144
Nominal weight, kg/km	95	129	145	217	324
Diameter, mm	11.4	12.9	13.6	16.6	20.6
Temperature range, °C Storage on reel Operating installed		−40 to +70 −40 to +70			
Maximum tensile rating, kg During installation Long-term installed			270 60		
Minimum bend radii, mm During installation Free bend installed	225 150	225 150	225 150	250 200	250 230
Crush resistance, long-term installed, kg/cm			5		
Maximum vertical rise, m	324	238	174	125	86

Source: From Ref. 75.

is, needless to say, characterized by a high fiber density in the cable core, 30% to about 50% higher than the cable of unit stranding type. Cable of this construction is used widely in practical applications [70]. The construction and properties of typical cables are shown in Fig. 3.90 and Tables 3.22 through 3.24.

Table 3.23 SM Fiber Parameters

Cutoff wavelength (transmission method) λ_c, 1130–1270 nm

Refractive index difference Δ, 0.3 ± 0.4%

Core concentricity, <1 μm

Cladding diameter, 125 ± 3 μm

Coating diameter, 250 ± 15 μm

Core diameter 2a, 8.7 μm

Spot size $2W_0$, 10 μm

Zero dispersion range λ_0, 1295–1325 nm

Source: From Ref. 75.

Table 3.24 Feeder-Bundle Cable

Number of fibers	12	24	48	96	168	192
Nominal weight, kg/km	122	122	176	238	399	470
Diameter, mm	12.5	12.5	14.8	16.9	22.5	24.5
Temperature range, °C						
Storage on reel			−40 to +70			
Operating installed			−30 to +60 Duct			
			−40 to +70 Aerial			
Maximum tensile rating						
During installation			350			
Long-term installed			80			
Minimum bend diameter D			20D			
During installation			10D			
Crush resistance, long-term installed, kg/km			5			
Maximum vertical rise, m	325	325	225	166	99	84

Source: From Ref. 75.

The transmission and mechanical characteristics of the single-mode fiber in the cable are shown in Table 3.25 [71].

If water enters and freezes inside the cable, the volume of water increases, causing the fiber loss to increase owing to microbending. The space inside a loose tube and between loose tubes is filled with compound to prevent this problem. Table 3.26 [76] presents the characteristics required in the compound. Figure 3.91 [76] shows the low-temperature loss characteristics of a compound-filled loose tube high-density cable and of an unfilled cable. By filling with a compound, the fibers can easily move inside the tube, causing cable characteristics to be very stable.

The following test methods simulated the installation and handling of optical fiber cables at installation sites [70, 77]. A long cable is fixed with two chuck-drums and is looped three times between two shafts that are 20–25 m apart. Fiber loss changes are measured by changing the distance between the shafts and by applying tension to the cable while fixing the cable (Fig. 92) [70, 77].

Figure 3.93 shows the relation between the temperature and loss change measured while a GI fiber cable is fixed. The loss change of the GI fiber at 0.875 μm was −0.1 to +0.3 dB/km at +60 to −30°C.

Table 3.25 Transmission and Mechanical Characteristics of SM Fibers in a Cable

Fiber loss in cable		
1.3 μm dB/km	Average: 0.44	α: 0.06
1.525 μm dB/km	0.28	0.07
Dispersion	3.5 psec/nm·km (1285–1350 nm)	
Tensile test	0.3% cable strain at 300 kg No loss change	
Impact	0.3 kg·m × 100 No fiber break	
Cyclic flex	4X cable OD × 1000 17 kg tension No fiber break	
Crush	25 kg/cm No loss increase	
Temperature	−30 to +60°C No loss change of fiber	

Source: From Ref. 71.

Table 3.26 Requirements for Compound

Viscosity stability, from −40 to +80°C

Nondripping at 60°C

Minimal shrinkage

Compatibility with other cable components

Easy removal

Good processibility

Dermatologically safe

Economical

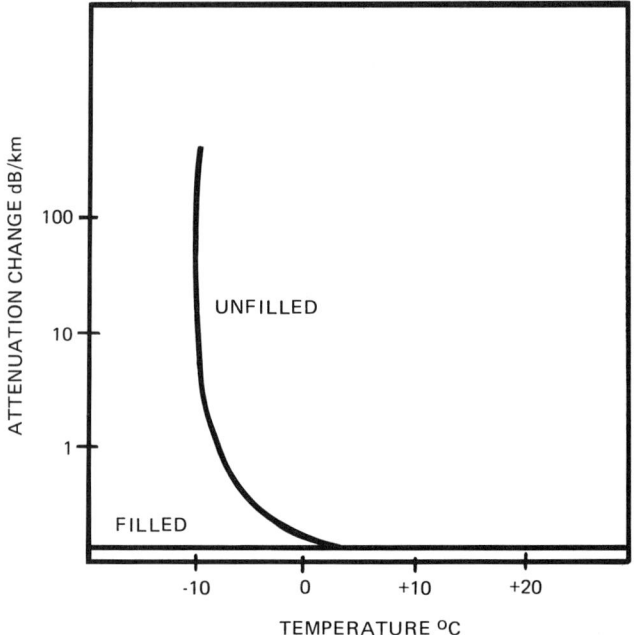

Figure 3.91 Microbending loss increase of loose tube high-density cable. (From Ref. 76.)

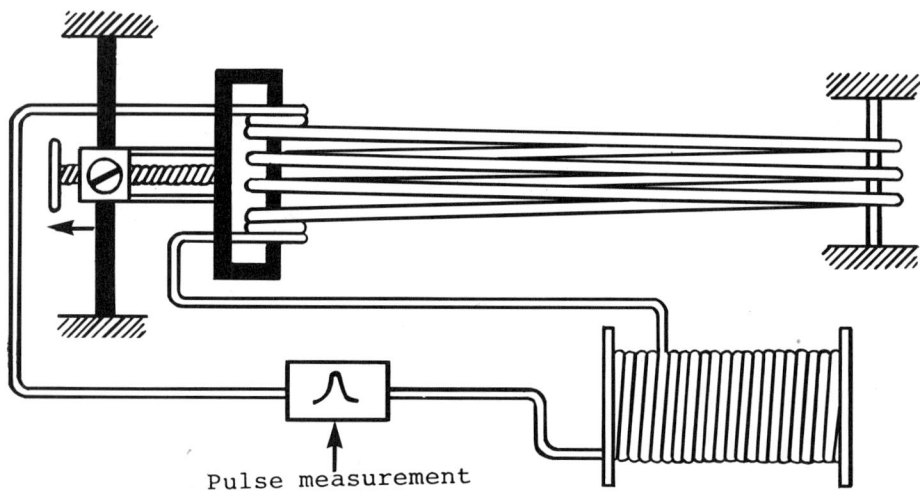

Figure 3.92 Long-length tensile tester. (From Refs. 70 and 77.)

Design, Construction, and Properties

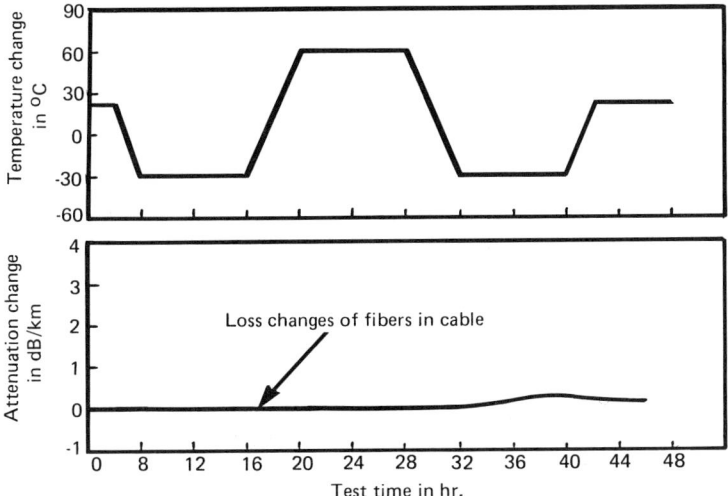

Figure 3.93 Typical temperature results. (From Ref. 77.)

Figure 3.94 shows the test results when tension is applied to a GI fiber cable while changing the distance between shafts. The fiber elongation is <0.3%, and the loss change is 0.2 dB/km at 0.875 μm when tension between 0 and 270 kg is applied. These data show that the loose tube high-density GI fiber cable can be used in commercial applications without problems.

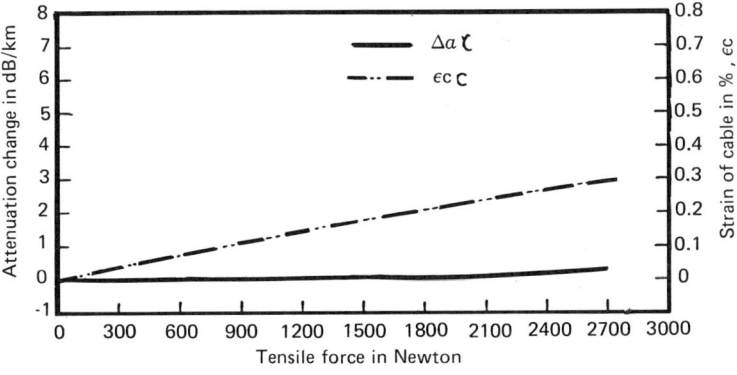

Figure 3.94 Typical tensile results. (From Ref. 77.)

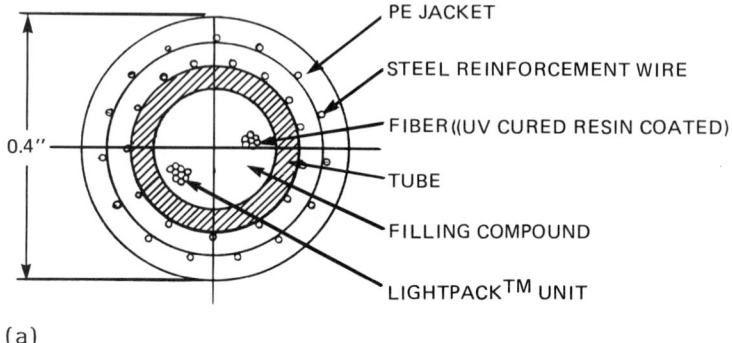

(a)

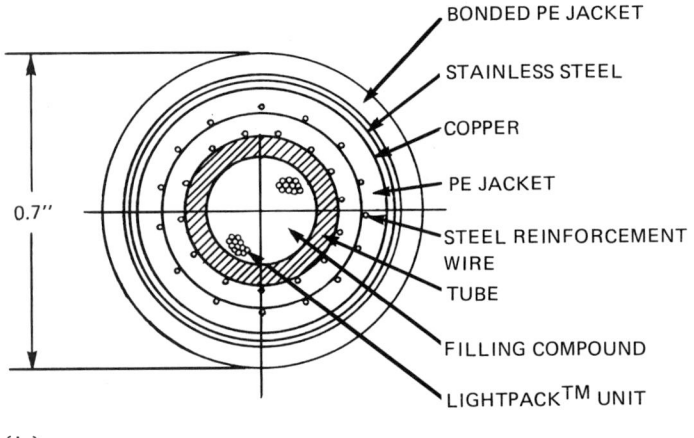

(b)

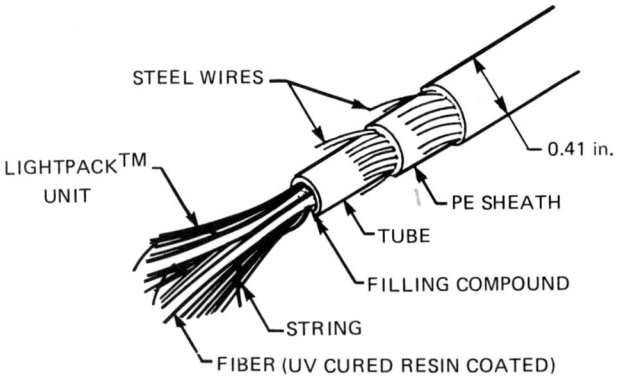

(c)

Figure 3.95 The AT&T Lightpack cable: (a) steel-reinforced cross-ply sheath; (b) cross-ply sheath with rodent and lightning protection; (c) Cross section showing layers in the Lightpack cable.

3.3.6.4 Examples of Single-Mode Fiber Loose Tube Bunch Unit Cable [72-74]

At AT&T Technologies, a single-mode fiber loose tube cable is used in the long-haul optical fiber unit. It is a 1.31 nm, 417 Mb/sec system (in the future, a 1.7 Gb/sec system) with a repeater span of 46 km maximum. The fiber is an 8.3 μm/125 μm depressed cladding single-mode fiber.

This cable was at first a loose tube loose stranding type, as shown in Fig. 3.78 (lower middle). AT&T Technologies changed its design to make it appropriate for quantity production. The company is now making this redesigned cable in a mass production line, calling it the Lightpack cable (Fig. 3.95). It is used mainly in long-haul transmission systems. The single-mode ribbon cable is used for relatively short-haul applications, chiefly subscriber network systems, because it can be spliced in one by a connector.

The basic construction of the Lightpack cable is that the fibers, in a bunched, not stranded form, are covered loosely with a tube. Cable of this type requires no revolving parts in manufacturing equipment, both on the side where fibers are supplied and on the side where the cable core is taken up, and can be made much faster. It is also reduced in diameter and is therefore easy to handle.

The cable configuration is shown in Fig. 3.95a. From 4 to 12 fibers are bunched (not stranded) and wound with color-coded strings to form a unit. A number of units are ganged, and a plastic tube is extruded loosely over the bunched units for a cable core. The tube is filled with a jelly compound. The sheath of this cable is the same as that given the AT&T ordinary fiber cables.

From 4 to 48 fibers can be accommodated in this 10 mm diameter cable. The cable weighs 120 kg/km and withstands a laying tension of up to 270 kg.

The transmission characteristics of the cable are shown in Figs. 3.96 and 3.97. Figure 3.97 shows the low-temperature characteristics of the cable. The loss variation of the fiber is no more than 0.05 dB/km (1310 and 1550 nm) at temperatures between -29 and $+88°C$.

The mechanical characteristics of the cable are shown in Table 3.27 [73].

Figure 3.98 [73] shows the relation between the tension applied to the optical fiber cable during its installation (the fiber is pulled by winding it on a pulley with a discontinuous ramp) (Fig. 3.99) [73] and fiber break during installation of optical fiber cable using a plowing machine. Figure 3.98 shows that fiber break is not caused by an installation tension less than 450 kg when installing the Lightpack cable. The cable weight is approximately 120 kg/km, and the allowable maximum installation tension is 270 kg. The value of 450 kg has a sufficient margin for installation tension.

Figure 3.100 [73] shows the relation between the cable squeeze percentage and broken fiber in a cable squeeze test (bend and tension).

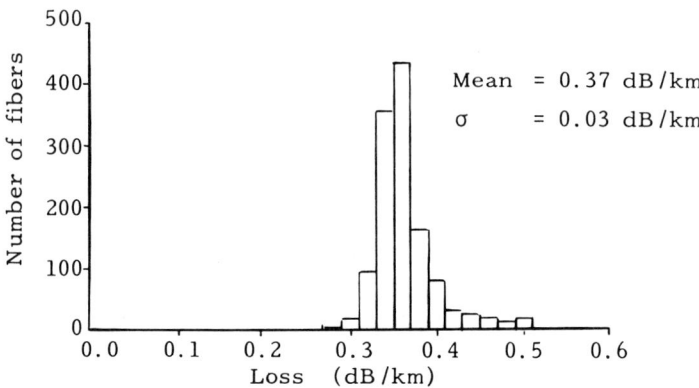

(a) 1310 nm

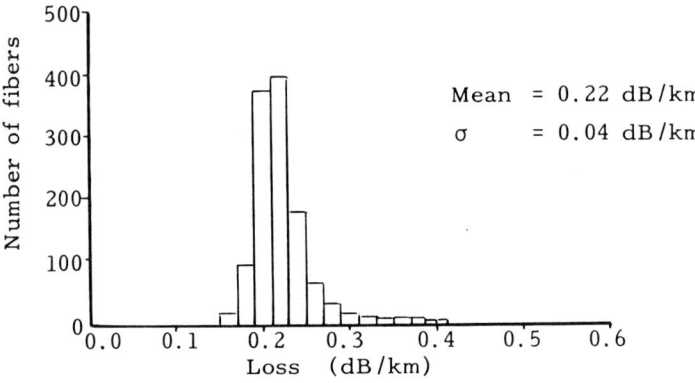

(b) 1550 nm

Figure 3.96 Transmission loss of cable. (From Ref. 74.)

Design, Construction, and Properties

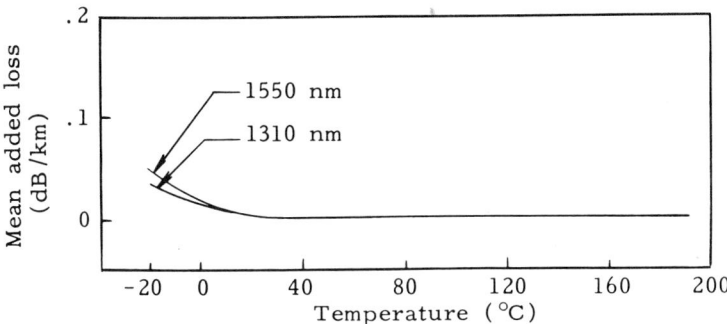

Figure 3.97 Loss change with temperature. (From Ref. 73.)

$$\text{Squeeze \%} = \frac{\text{Diameter of original cable} - \text{short diameter after squeeze test}}{\text{Diameter of original cable}} \times 100$$

The fiber in the Lightpack cable does not break if the squeeze is 45% or less.

Table 3.27 Mechanical Properties of Cable

Property		Loss increase[a] (dB)
Bending	20D 150 m length Tension, 270	<0.03
Bending	10D 25 cycles (rate, 30 cycles/min)	<0.05
Impact	25 impacts (rate, 30 impacts/min)	<0.05
Compression	445 kg per 10 cm, 10 min	<0.06
Twist	Sample 4 m ±180° rotation 10 cycles	<0.06
Bending	10D −29 to +60°C	<0.05

[a] No sheath failure.
Source: From Ref. 73.

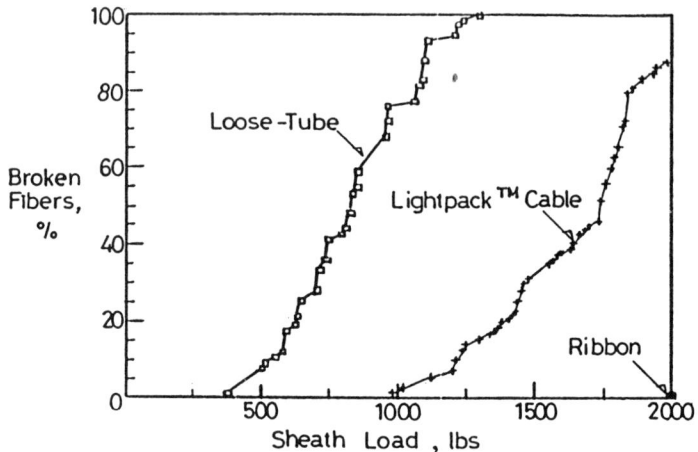

Figure 3.98   Plow simulation results.   (From Ref. 73.)

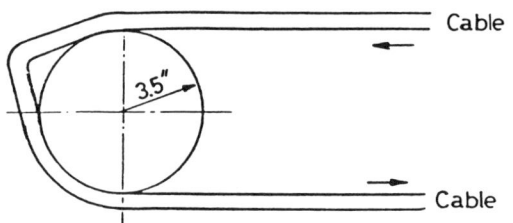

Figure 3.99   Simulation of installation tension.   (From Ref. 73.)

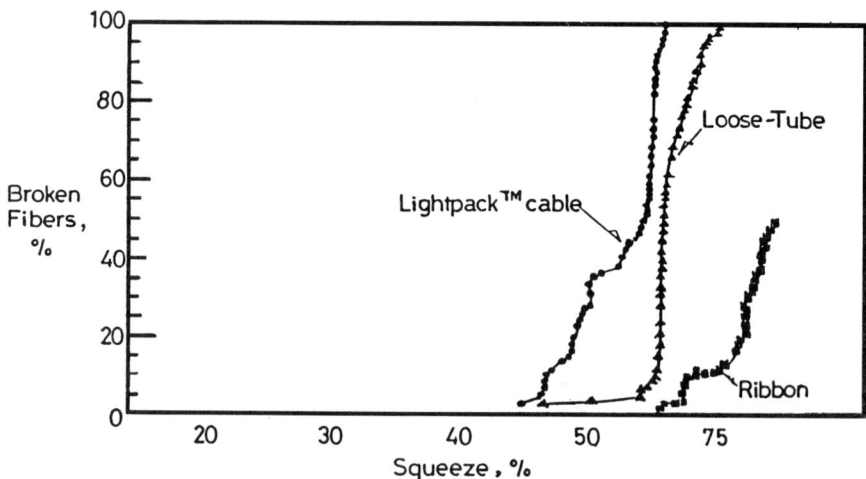

Figure 3.100   Dynamic squeeze results.   (From Ref. 73.)

Design, Construction, and Properties 305

A 24-fiber cable in a length of 1000 m was installed in a duct. (In the test, the cable was bent at an angle of 180° using a 61 cm sheave 500 m away.) The installation tension was 120 kg per 1000 m. The fiber loss, however, did not change.

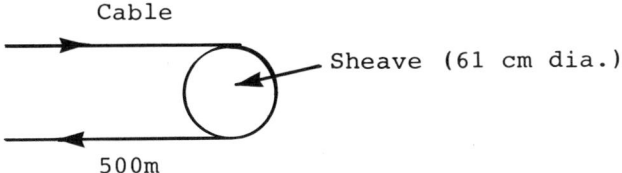

3.3.7 V-groove Cable

As a means to protect fibers from external stress when they are made into a cable or after the fiber cable is installed, fibers are accommodated in a V groove. Such grooves are formed in a flat or round shape, and a single fiber or multiple fibers are placed in each (Fig. 3.101). The flat V-groove type a is being replaced by the ribbon cable and is now out of use. Types b and c are in use.

The characteristics of cable with round grooves may be summarized as follows:

1. Even when a crushing force works on the cable from outside, the round V grooves protect the fibers from stress and prevent their microbending loss increase.
2. By proper selection of the V-groove materials (steel or FRP wires are inserted in PE) and construction, the coefficient of thermal expansion of the groove can be much reduced. This

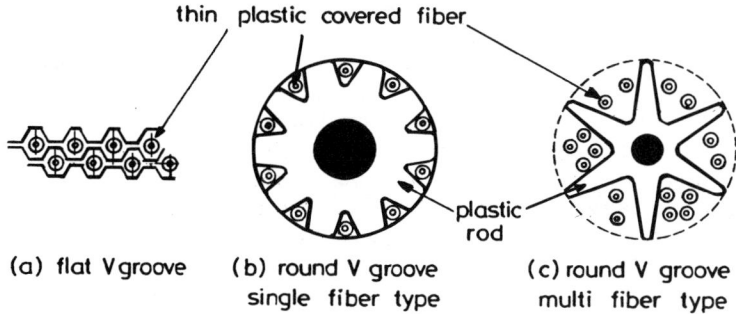

Figure 3.101 V-groove cable.

enables almost no microbending loss increase of the fiber when the temperature changes.

Construction of the V-groove cable is shown in Fig. 3.102.

In designing round V-groove cable, the fiber is inserted loosely in the V-groove [78–82]. The stress-strain behavior of fiber in the V groove is the same as in the loose tube (see Sec. 3.3.6.1).

Coefficient of Thermal Expansion of Round V Groove

The round V groove is generally made of PE, polypropylene, or polyurethane and uses steel wires, FRP wires, or the like in the center to reduce its coefficient of thermal expansion. The thermal expansion coefficient of this composite material is

$$\alpha = \frac{\Sigma \alpha_i E_i S_i}{\Sigma E_i S_i}$$

where:

E_i = Young's modulus of each material

S_i = cross-sectional area of each material

α_i = thermal expansion coefficient of each material

α = thermal expansion coefficient of composite material

In order to reduce the value of α, it is necessary to reduce the cross-sectional area of the plastic part as much as possible and ensure firm adhesion between the plastic and the center material.

V-Groove Core

The material (mainly PE) is extruded on the strength member using the V-groove die (rotating or oscillating), or the material is extruded in a round cross section and then grooved on the surface with a cutter.

The groove can be in one direction or the SZ direction. During the stranding process, it is necessary to control the speed of fiber insertion in the groove to prevent tension from working on the fiber. If the cable must be jelly filled, the fiber is first placed in the groove by the stranding machine and jelly can be applied over it.

Moreover, the length of the grooved rod during the stranding process must be strictly controlled. That is, utmost care must be used to ensure that no stress will work on fibers even when the cable expands or contracts after production or installation. For this reason, the following measures are required when the fiber is placed in the groove.

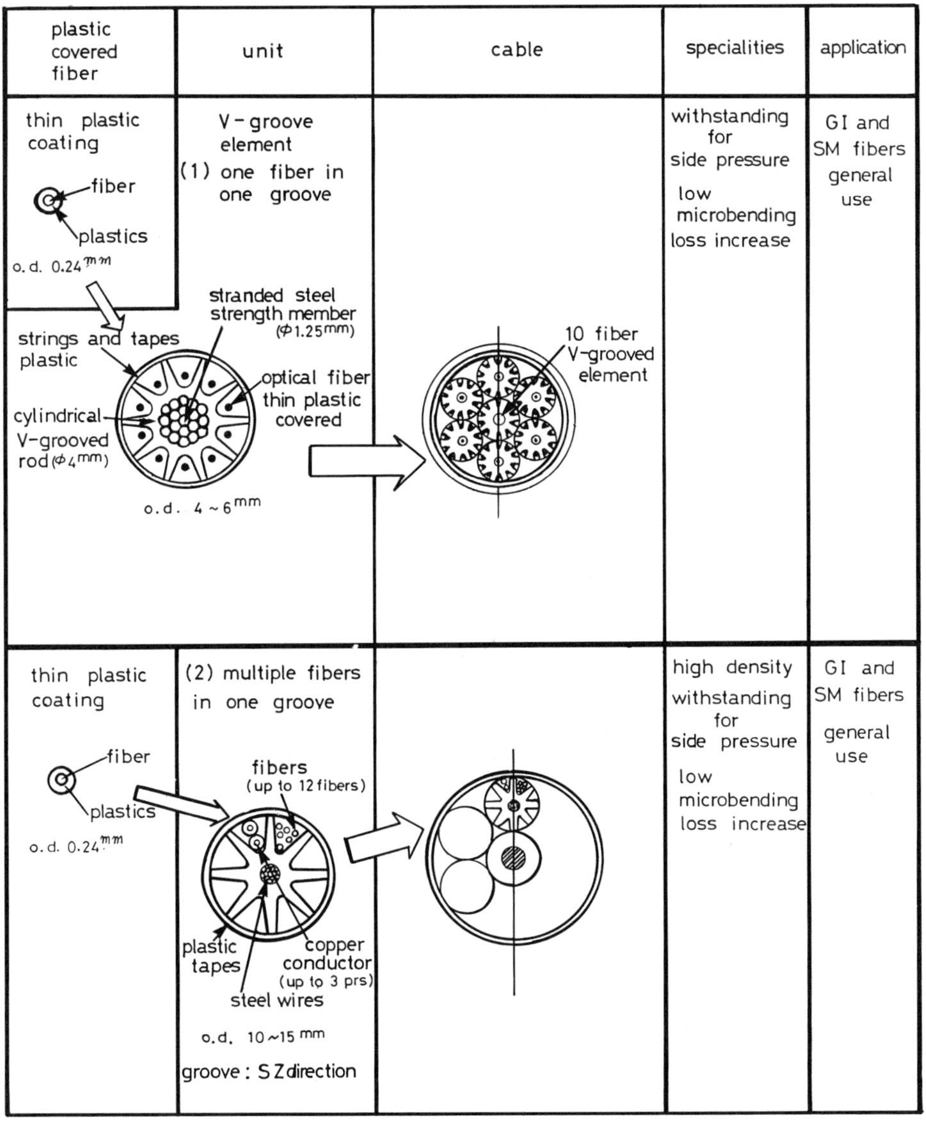

Design, Construction, and Properties

plastic covered fiber	unit	cable	specialities	application
thin plastic coating fiber plastics o.d. 0.24 mm	V-groove element (1) one fiber in one groove stranded steel strength member (φ1.25mm) optical fiber thin plastic covered strings and tapes plastic cylindrical V-grooved rod (φ4mm) o.d. 4~6 mm	10 fiber V-grooved element	withstanding for side pressure low microbending loss increase	GI and SM fibers general use
thin plastic coating fiber plastics o.d. 0.24 mm	(2) multiple fibers in one groove fibers (up to 12 fibers) plastic tapes copper conductor (up to 3 prs) steel wires o.d. 10~15 mm groove : SZ direction		high density withstanding for side pressure low microbending loss increase	GI and SM fibers general use

Figure 3.102 Construction of V-groove cable.

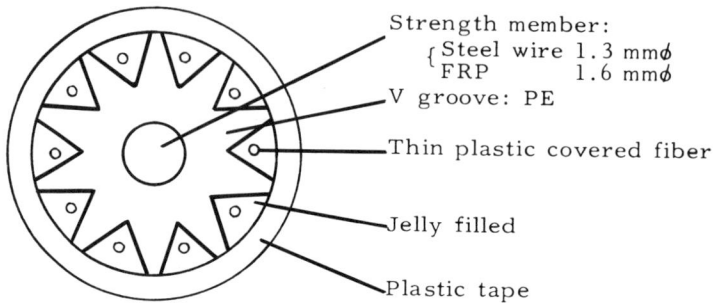

Figure 3.103 V-groove (10 fibers). (From Refs. 78-82.)

1. The grooved rod is kept under fixed tension.
2. The grooved rod is kept at a fixed temperature.

There are methods of fiber identification: coloring of the primary coating on the fiber and coloring of the upper edge of the groove.

Examples of Round V-Groove Single-Fiber Cable [78-82]

This is the standard construction of communication cables in France. As shown in Fig. 3.103, 10 grooves are made in the rod and 10 fibers are inserted in them, one in each groove, to form a unit. A typical grooved rod is made by covering a 1.3 mm diameter steel wire or FRP wire (OD 1.6 mm) with LDPE or polypropylene in a diameter of 4 mm. The diameter of 4 mm is equal to that of the small coaxial core. The groove is made in one direction or the SZ direction about 1 mm depth and width. Each groove contains a thin plastic-covered fiber. The following are sample components of V-groove single-fiber cable design (see Fig. 3.104) [78-82].

Thin plastic-covered fiber, OD 170-240 μm
Unit with V-groove (10 fibers), OD 4.0 mm
 Plastic tape, OD 4.3 mm
Cable: plastic tape and welded-corrugated Al sheath:

No. fibers	OD (mm)	Weight (kg/km)
10	14.5	185
30	19.5	300
70	21.5	390

Loss changes of the GI fiber in the cable (0.85 μm) with temperature are as follows:

Design, Construction, and Properties

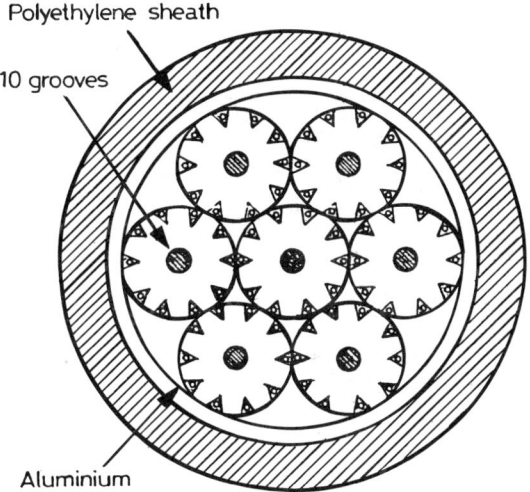

Figure 3.104 Cross section of a cable (70 fibers).

The thermal range of the cable is greater than −40 to +50°C.

Temperature (°C)	Loss change (dB/km)
−40	0.01
20	0
50	0

Construction and Production of Round V-Groove, Multiple-Fiber Cable [83, 84]*

Each groove contains 4−12 fibers, each with a primary coating, arranged in parallel, not stranded. The support rod is about 8−25 mm in diameter, with grooves of the SZ direction. Primary-coated fibers are inserted in the groove without being stranded. Control of fiber-inserting speed is important to prevent tension on the fiber during production. The fibers not stranded in the groove must be identified by color. A fiber cable with about 120 fibers can be made by one stranding process. The density of fibers in the cable is high.

---

*Northern Telecom optical fiber cable.

310   *Optical Fiber Cable*

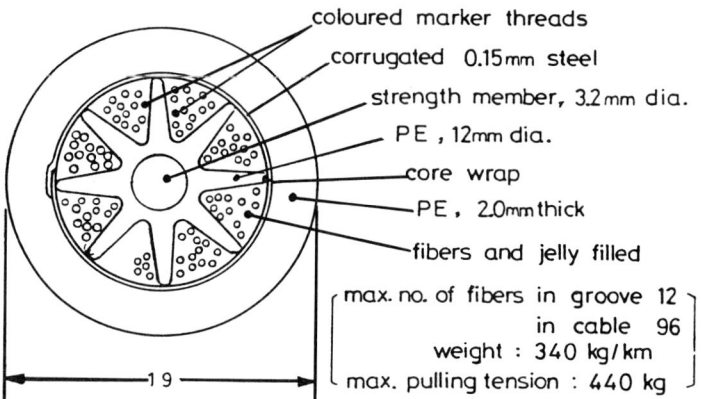

8 grooves, steel peth jacket

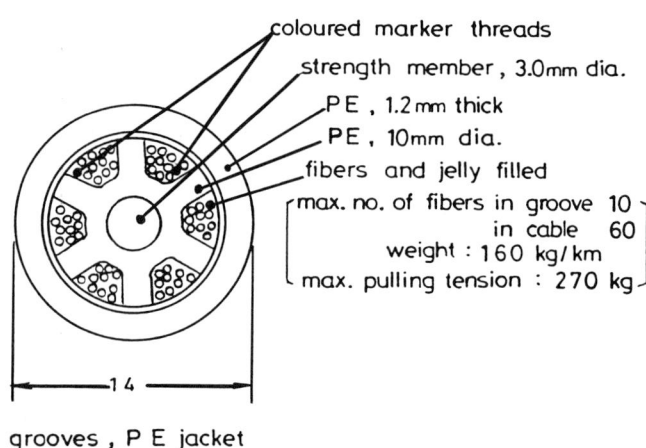

6 grooves, P E jacket

Figure 3.105 Examples of V-groove multifiber cable construction. (Northern Telecom.)

In this V-groove structure, the groove is large and offers a wide range of movement for a fiber inserted in it. Therefore, fiber properties change little under a strain applied outside the cable.

The characteristics and construction of multifiber V-groove cable are shown in Table 3.28 and Figs. 3.105 through 3.109. A test [83] was made using the filled cable filling powder (e.g., a stearate-coated chalk and powdered polyacrylamide) in V grooves of a fiber cable. Figure 3.110 [83] shows the loss change of the fiber

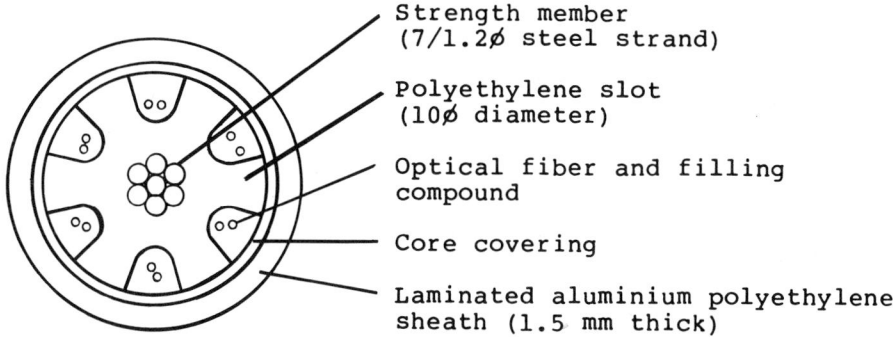

Figure 3.106 V-groove multifiber cable for duct application: maximum number of fibers per slot, 5; maximum number of fibers per cable, 30; maximum number of copper pairs per slot, 1 (0.65 mm conditional diameter); maximum pulling force, 285 kg·ft; cable diameter, 15 mm; approximate cable weight, 200 kg/km; minimum bend radius, static, 150 mm, and dynamic, 240 mm. (From Ref. 85.)

Table 3.28 Characteristics of Multifiber V-groove Cable (GI Fiber, 1.3 μm)

Characteristic	Loss change (dB)
Tension, 550 kg	0
Bending, 12.5 cm radius	0.02
Flexibility, 14 cm radius, 90° bend 25 cycles per sec, 2 min	0
Twist, 2 m, 360° twist, 10 cycles	0
Crush, 75 kg per 25 cm	0

Temperature
  20 to −40°C
  20 to 60°C
	=0
	=0

Source: From Ref. 83.

312 *Optical Fiber Cable*

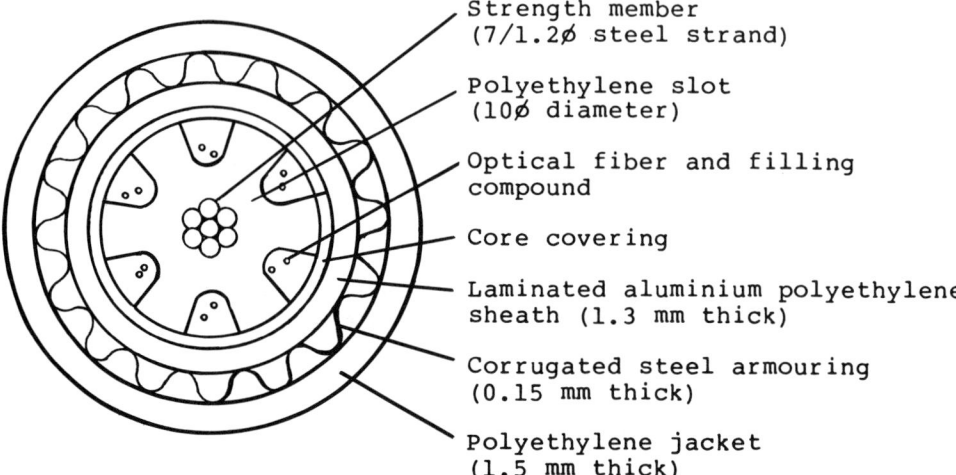

Figure 3.107 V-groove multifiber cable for direct buried application: maximum number of fibers per slot, 5; maximum number of fibers per cable, 30; maximum number of copper pairs per slot, 1; maximum pulling force, 285 kg·ft; cable diameter, 17.5 mm; approximate cable weight, 380 kg/km; minimum bend radius, static, 290 mm, dynamic, 320 mm. (From Ref. 85.)

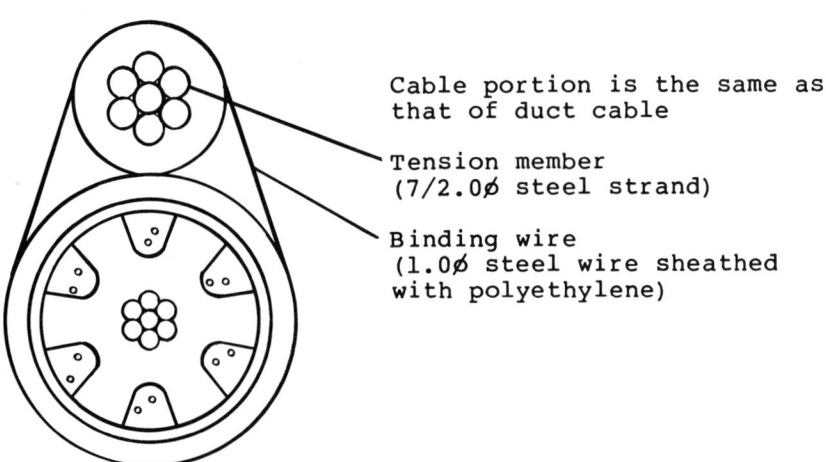

Figure 3.108 V-groove multifiber cable for aerial application: maximum number of fibers per slot, 5; maximum number of fibers per cable, 30; maximum number of copper pairs per slot, 1; maximum pulling force, 285 kg·ft; cable diameter, 15 × 23 mm; approximate cable weight, 430 kg/km; minimum bend radius for side direction, static, 150 mm, dynamic, 240 mm. (From Ref. 85.)

Design, Construction, and Properties 313

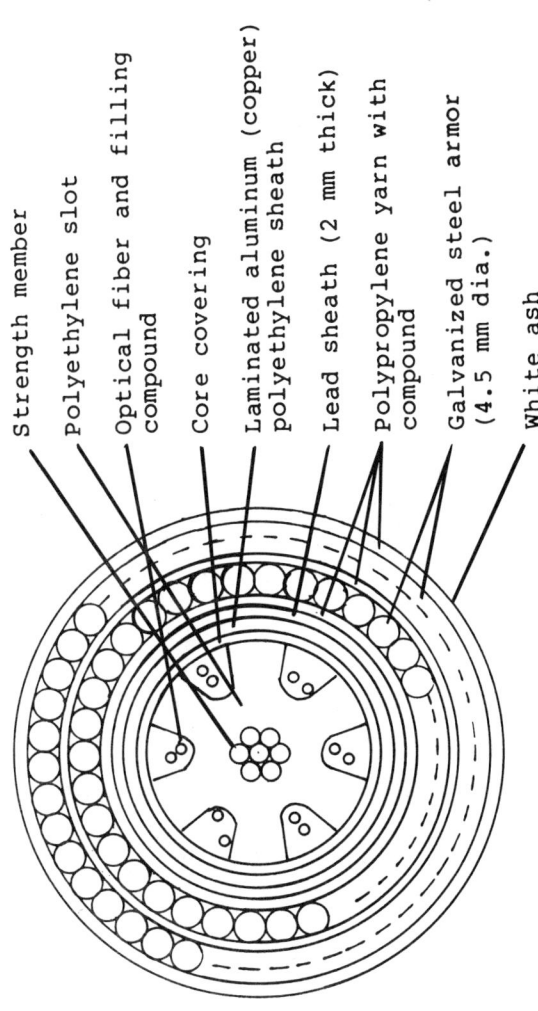

Maximum number of fibers per slot: 5
Maximum number of fibers per cable: 30
Maximum number of copper pairs per slot: 1
Cable diameter: 53 mm
Approximate cable weight: 7000 kg/km
Minimum bend radius static: 1060 mm

Figure 3.109 V-groove multifiber cable for wire armor: maximum number of fibers per slot, 5; maximum number of fiber per cable, 30; maximum number of copper paris per slot, 1; cable diameter, 53 mm; approximate cable weight, 7000 kg/km; minimum bend radius, static, 1060 mm. (From Ref. 85.)

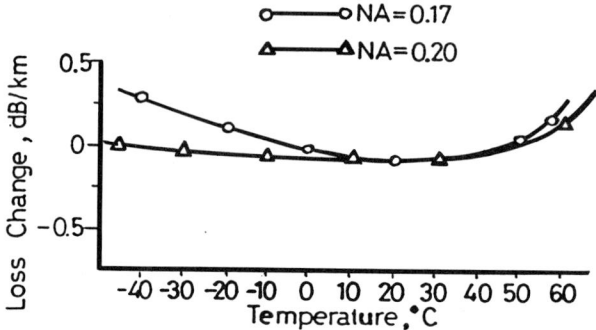

Figure 3.110 Loss change versus temperature for filled cables.

cable at the ambient temperature. The loss change was <0.25 dB/km at −30 to +60°C (at 0.85 µm wavelength, 0.17 NA, GI fiber). Table 3.29 shows the mechanical properties of this filled cable [83]. The data show that the powder does not affect the properties of the fiber.

Table 3.29 Mechanical Properties of Filled Multifiber V-Groove Cable

Test	Condition	Loss change
Tensile	500 m length, 460 kg, 30 min	No
Crush	890 kg–ft, 25 cm, 10 min	No
Impact	750 g 2.5 cm diameter hammer, 1.1 m height, dropped 5 times	No
Twist	2 m, ±360°, 10-day cycles	No

REFERENCES

1. D. Olshansky, Distortion losses in cable optical fibers, *Appl. Opt.*, *14*(1) (January), 20–21 (1975).

2. Y. Matsuda, S. Inao, and K. Ishihara, Study of optical fiber coating, Natl. Conv. IECEJ, 1682, 1682 (March 1978), pp. 7–250.

3. H. Murata, S. Inao, Y. Matsuda, and T. Kuroha, Optimum design for optical fiber used in optical cable system, 4th ECOC (September 1978), pp. 242–248.

4. Y. Matsuda, S. Inao, and H. Tatsuta, Constructional consideration of GI fiber, Natl. Conv. IECEJ, 1673 (March 1978), pp. 7–241.

5. N. Susa and N. Uchida, Covering materials and microbend loss, Natl. Conv. IECEJ, 1683 (March 1978), pp. 7–251.

6. K. Furuya and Y. Suematsu, Random-bend loss in single-mode and parabolic-index multimode optical fiber cables, *Appl. Opt.*, *19*(5) (May), 1493–1500 (1980).

7. Y. Matsuda, private communications, 1973.

8. Y. Matsuda, S. Inao, T. Shibata, H. Murata, and H. Noake, Mechanical properties of fiber cable, Tech. Res. Report IECE J CS74–149 (December 1974), pp. 111–123.

9. H. Murata, Broadband optical fiber cable and connecting, 2nd ECOC (September 1976), pp. 167–174.

10. D. Gloge, Bending loss in multimode fiber with graded and ungraded core index, *Appl. Opt.*, *11*(11) (November) 2506–2513 (1972).

11. S. Ohara and T. Kimura, Optical Communication, Corona (November 1981), pp. 33–36.

12. J. Sakai and T. Kimura, Bending loss of propagation modes in arbitrary-index profile optical fibers, *Appl. Opt.*, *17*(10) (May), 1499–1506 (1978).

13. D. Marcuse, Curvature loss formula for optical fibers, *J. Opt. Soc. Amer.*, *66*(3) (March), 216–220 (1976).

14. K. Noda et al., *Optical Fiber Communication*, 2nd ed., IECE J, (November 1982), pp. 50–53.

15. N. Nakatani, K. Ishihara, S. Mochizuki, and M. Tateda, Optical loss increase due to stranding in optical cable, Trans. IECE '79/10, 62-B, 10 (October 1979), pp. 956–958.

16. T. Yabuta, M. Kawase, and K. Ishihara, Stranding pitch selection of an optical fiber cable, Trans. IECE '79/7, 62B, 7 (July 1979), pp. 704–705.

17. H. Kumamaru, Y. Hattori, S. Yoneji, and N. Ishida; Basic study of fiber cable design, Natl. Conf. IECE J, 1745 (March 1977), pp. 7–329.
18. N. Mitsunaga, U. Katsuyama, and Y. Ishida; Optical cable deformation characteristics under lateral load, Report IEEE J, J64-B No. 2 (February 1981), pp. 142–149.
19. T. Hondo, Private communication, December 1979.
20. T. Isobe, H. Murata, and S. Kohno, Non-twist stranded wires for transoceanic cable, Natl Conv. IECE J, 403 (March 1959).
21. Furukawa Catalogues, 1985.
22. P. F. Gagen and M. R. Santana, Design and performance of a crossply lightguide cable sheath, 28th IWCS (November 1979), pp. 391–395.
23. C. H. Gartside, III, W. T. Anderson, P. F. Glodis, and L. C. Hotchkiss, A single-mode lightguide cable, design for long-haul transmission, ECOC '83 (October 1983), pp. 223–226.
24. M. Ogai, K. Omae, M. Higashimoto, and Y. Ishida, Non-metallic optical fiber cable for use under low temperature, 7ECOC (September 1981), pp. 12.2-1 to 12.2-4.
25. T. Yabuta, K. Yamashita, K. Ueno, and Y. Negishi, Excess loss of jacketed fiber at low temperature, Trans, IECE J, J.62–B, 11 (November 1979), pp. 1061–1063.
26. Y. Yabuta, O. Kawata, and Y. Miyajima, Excess loss increase mechanism of jacketed fibers at low temperature, Trans. IECE J, J.63–B, 4 (April 1980), pp. 392–393.
27. T. Hayashi, Theory and application of light construction (I), Japan Sci. Eng. Ass., 188, 1969.
28. E. G. Hanson, Origin of temperature dependence of attenuation in optical cables, *Opt. Fiber Commun.* (March), *TuE5*: 28–30 (1979).
29. Y. Sugawara, T. Kobayashi, M. Tanaka, A. Mogi, K. Inada, and K. Ishihara, Attenuation increase mechanism of jacketed and cabled fibers at low temperature, Trans, IECE J, J.62–C, 12 (December 1979), pp. 864–871.
30. Y. Sugawara, T. Kobayashi, M. Tanaka, and A. Mogi, Attenuation increase mechanism of jacketed and cabled fibers at low temperature, Tech. Res. Rep. CS78–212 (March 1979), pp. 49–54.
31. K. Masuno and K. Ishihara, Optical fiber cable as a transmission media, Joint Conv. 4 IEEJ (October 1977), pp. 7–29 to 7–32.

References

32. F. Nihei, Y. Oyamada, S. Hatano, A. Otake, H. Horima, and Y. Sugahara, A study on the constructions of optical fiber cable for subscriber, Tech. Res. Rep. CS79-6 (April 1979), pp. 41-48.

33. M. Kawase and T. Fuchigami, A study on the design of the high density optical subscriber cable, Tech. Res. Rep. CS81-151 (January 1982), pp 23-30.

34. M. Kawase, S. Hatano, Y. Katsuyama, and T. Fuchigami, High density optical subscriber cable, ECL Tech. Report, 34(7) (July), 1111-1118 (1985).

35. M. Oda, M. Ogai, O. Otake, S. Tachigami, and K. Ohkubo, Nylon extruded fiber ribbon and its connection, OFC '82, THAA6 (April 1982), pp. 46-47.

36. M. Ogai, F. Takahashi, N. Sato, and M. Nishimura, High-speed dual coating and UV-resin covered fiber ribbon, OFC '86, WI4 (February 1986), pp. 114-115.

37. Y. Katsuyama, S. Hatano, T. Kokubun, and K. Hogari, Design and performance of several-hundred-core high-density optical fiber ribbon cable, IOOC-ECOC '85 (October 1985), pp. 375-378.

38. Y. Katsuyama, S. Hatano, K. Hogai, T. Matsumoto, and E. Maekawa, Single-mode optical fiber ribbon cable for subscriber line, IOOC-ECOC '85 (October 1985), pp. 383-386.

39. N. Nirasawa, Y. Yamazaki, S. Tanaka, S. Suzuki, and I. Ogasawara, Design of fiber tape with improved lateral pressure resistance, IOOC-ECOC '85 (October 1985), pp. 379-383.

40. K. Hogari, S. Hatano, and Y. Katsuyama, Considerations on spacer-type optical fiber cable, Natl. Conv. Commun. IECE J 481 (October 1984), pp. 2-126.

41. M. I. Schwartz, R. A. Kempf, and W. B. Gardner, Design and characterization of an exploratory fiber optic cable 2nd ECOC (September 1976), pp. 311-314.

42. M. I. Schwartz, W. A. Reenstra, and J. H. Mullins, The Chicago lightwave communications project, IOOC '77, C12 (June 1977) p.d., pp. 53-56.

43. M. J. Buckler, M. R. Santana, and M. J. Saunders, Lightguide cable manufacture and performance, BSTJ (July-August 1978), pp. 1745-1757.

44. P. F. Gagen and M. R. Santana, Design and performance of a crossply lightguide cable, 28th IWCS (November 1979), pp. 391-395.

45. M. I. Schwarz, Design and performance of the FT-3 lightguide trunk transmission medium, ICC '81 (June 1981), pp. 5.1.1-6.1.8.

46. B. R. Eichenbaum, M. R. Santana, L. D. Tate, and R. Sabia, Design and performance of a filled, high-fiber-count, multimode optical cable, 31st IWCS (November 1982), pp. 396-400.
47. N. Nirasawa, Y. Yamazaki, S. Tanaka, S. Suzuki, and I. Ogasawara, Design of fiber tape with improved lateral pressure resistance, IOOC-ECOC '85 (October 1985), pp. 379-382.
48. Y. Katsuyama, K. Hogari, S. Hatano, and T. Kokubun, Optical loss characteristics of slotted rod cable composed of single-mode optical fiber ribbons, Natl. Conv. IECE J, 2062 (March 1986), pp. 9-91.
49. F. Takahashi, H. Hiramatsu, A. Takase, H. Fujiwara, and M. Ogai, High density slot type cable, Natl. Conv. IECE J, 2060 (March 1986), pp. 9-89.
50. K. Hogari, T. Kokubun, S. Hatano, and Y. Katsuyama, Residual strain design of optical fiber ribbon cable composed of slot unit, Tech. Res. Rep. IECE J, OQE 85-106 (November 1985), pp. 45-51.
51. Y. Katsuyama, S. Hatano, T. Kokubun, and K. Hogari, Design and performance of several-hundred-core high-density optical fiber ribbon cable, IOOC-ECOC '85 (October 1985), pp. 375-378.
52. M. Kawase, S. Hatano, Y. Katsuyama, and T. Fuchigami, High density optical subscriber cable, *ECL Tech J.* 34(7) (July), 1111-1118 (1985).
53. S. Mochizuki, K. Ishihara, and N. Nakatani, Structure design of optical fiber cable, *ECL Tech J.*, 27(11) (November) 2451-2466 (1978).
54. K. Ishihara, N. Nakatani, S. Mochizuki, and Y. Mitsunaga, A study on the thickness of optical fiber covering, Natl. Conv. IECE J, 1681 (March 1978), pp. 7-249.
55. S. Mochizuki, N. Nakatani, and K. Ishihara, Construction design of optical fiber cable, Natl. Conv. Commun. IECE J, S3-1 (October 1978), 559.
56. N. Nakatani, S. Mochizuki, and K. Ishihara, Lateral pressure properties of plastic covered fiber, Natl. Conv. IECE J, 1872 (march 1979), pp. 7-311.
57. K. Ishihara, S. Mochizuki, N. Nakatani, N. Uchida, and H. Fukutomi, Determination of optimum structure in coated optical fiber and unit, Proc. IECE J, J-63B, 1 (January 1980), pp. 70-77.

58. H. Namikawa, T. Sato, M. Nishimura, and K. Yoshida, A study on the buffer material, Natl. Conv. IECE J, 1878 (March 1979), pp. 7-317.
59. K. Ishihara, S. Seikai, S. Mochizuki, Y. Katsuyama and K. Kitayama, Optical cable in the experimental system—structure design and transmission characteristics, ECL Tech J., 29(2) (February) 217-231 (1980).
60. S. Mochizuki, N. Nakatani, and K. Ishihara, Design of the construction for optical fiber cable, Nat. Conv. Commun., S3-1 (October 1978), pp. 559-560.
61. N. Uesugi Y. Ishida, M. Ohashi, and N. Uchida, Design and transmission characteristics of single-mode optical cables in the 1.3 μm wave length region, ICC '84, 34.4 (May 1984), pp. 1067-1070.
62. K. Ishihara, M. Tokuda, N. Uchida, S. Inao, M. Hosikawa, and I. Inada, Characteristics of optical cables, CS78-173, Tech Res. Rep., IECE J (December 1978), pp. 31-36.
63. M. Tokuda, Y. Ishida, M. Miyauchi, S. Seikai, K. Takahashi, and S. Nakagome, Characteristics of optical transmission lines in field trail, CS80-146, Tech Res. Rep., IECE J (October 1980), pp. 73-78.
64. Y. Ishida, Y. Katsuyama, S. Seikai, K. Okubo, M. Hoshikawa, and K. Inada, Design and characteristics of graded-index multimode optical cables, CS80-183, Tech. Res. Rep., IECE J (January 1981), pp. 37-42.
65. NTT, NTT 2nd International Symposium—Optical fiber transmission technology (April 1984), pp. 1-141.
66. N. Ishida, Y. Katsuyama, S. Seikai, C. Tanaka, and Y. Mitsunaga, Design and characteristics of graded-index optical cables for use in medium/small capacity optical fiber transmission systems, ECL Tech. Rep. 30(9) (September), 2167-2179 (1981).
67. C. Tanaka, K. Kitayama, Y. Mitsunaga, and N. Ishida, Single-mode optical cable design and performances, ECL Tech. Rep. 32(3) (March), 621-631 (1983).
68. P. R. Bark, U. Oestreich, and G. Zeidler, Stress-strain behavior of optical cables. 28th IWCS (November 1979), pp. 385-390.
69. U. Oestreich, Design of fiber optic cables, Telecommun. Rep. 4.4 (December 1981), pp. 225-245.
70. D. O. Lawrence and P. Bark, Recent development in mini-unit cable, 32nd IWCS (November 1983), pp. 301-307.

71. D. O. Lawrence and P. R. Bark, Large scale manufacturing and testing of single-mode cables, ICC '84, 34.2 (May 1984), pp. 1051–1055.

72. C. H. Gartside, III, and R. W. Tarwater, The first installation of single-mode lightguide cable by AT&T, ICC '84, 34-1, (May 1984), pp. 1047–1050.

73. P. D. Patel and C. H. Gartside, III, Compact lightguide cable design, 34th IWCS (November 1985), pp. 21–27.

74. C. H. Gartside, III, and C. F. Cottingham, Production and field experience with AT&T Lightpack cable, OFC '86, WI 2 (February 1986), pp. 112–113.

75. Siecore Catalogue, 1986.

76. P. R. Bark and D. O. Lawrence, Design and performance of filled fiber optic cables.

77. P. R. Bark, U. Oestreich, and G. Zeidler, Fiber optic cable design, testing and installation experience, 27th IWCS (November 1978), pp. 379–384.

78. G. Le Noane, M. de Vecchis, and J. P. Hulin, Experimental result of cylindrical V-grooved structure optical cables laid, in ducts and spliced, 4ECOC (September 1978), pp. 218–223.

79. M. de Vecchis, J. P. Hulin, and J. C. Staath, Ultra low loss cables using the cylindrical V-grooved structure, 30th IWCS (November 1981), pp. 228–235.

80. M. de Vecchis, J. P. Demey, J. P. Hulin, J. Personne, and J. C. Staath, Cylindrical V-grooved non metallic optical fiber cable, 32nd IWCS (November 1983), pp. 215–219.

81. G. Le Noane, C. Audoux, P. Cheron, and B. Missout, Metalfree cylindrical V-grooved optical cable, 32nd IWCS (November 1983), pp. 228–235.

82. D. Boscher, B. Nonclercq, A. Le Boutet, and B. Missout, Manufacture, laying and splicing of mono-mode optical fiber cables with low losses, 32nd IWCS (November 1983), pp. 308–315.

83. T. S. Hope, R. J. Williams, and K. Abe, Developments in slotted core optical fiber cables, 30th IWCS (November 1981), pp. 220–227.

84. T. S. Swiecicki, F. D. King, and F. P. Kapron, Unit core cable structures for optical communications system, 27th IWCS (November 1978), pp. 404–411.

85. Furukawa: Technical explanation on optical fiber cable system (December 1985).

4
Splicing of Fibers

4.1 INTRODUCTION

Offset and tilt are main causes of splicing loss (<0.1 dB):

Fiber	Offset (μm)	Tilt (°)
SM	<0.8	<0.3
GI	<3	<0.7

Representative fusion splicing machines are as follows.

| Machine | Fiber | Splicing loss (dB) | |
		Average	Maximum

Fully automatic
  Automatic
  alignment
  Direct core
  monitor
	SM
	GI
		0.03
		0.02
			0.18
			0.06

Semiautomatic
  Weight: 1.5 kg
  Size: 12 × 10 ×
  11 cm
  Battery operated
	SM (eccentricity
	  < 1%)
	GI
		0.1
		
		0.03
			0.3
			
			0.09

| | | Splicing loss (dB) | |
Machine	Fiber	Average	Maximum
Mass fusion, five fibers in one-arc discharge	SM (eccentricity < 1%)	0.13	0.4
	GI	0.04	0.12

For reinforcement of the fiber splice, polyethylene (PE) shrinkable tube (with steel wire) is used (refer to Sec. 4.4.3).

4.2 GENERAL CONCEPTS

We use the terms "splicing," "joining," and "connecting," defined as follows.

1. Splicing: permanent uniting of two fibers. Spliced fibers cannot be separated from each other except by cutting.
2. Joining: uniting of two optical fiber cables in which the fibers, copper conductors, strength members, and so on in the cable core are spliced and put in a cable joint sleeve or box and then the cable sheaths are joined.
3. Connecting: uniting of two fibers with a connector. The connector permits the fibers to be attached to and detached from each other freely.

Optical fiber splicing requires the following conditions:

1. Field splicing can be done easily in a short time.
2. Splicing loss is small.
3. The length to be spliced is small, and the diameter of each fiber to be splice is small.
4. The splice is reproducible.
5. The splice is sufficiently strong.
6. Splicing is economical.
7. The properties of the splice are stable and reliable for a long time.

There is extensive development of fiber splicing techniques in many countries, and various practical methods, apparatus, and accesories for field splicing have been reported and are in use.

4.3 FIBER SPLICING LOSS [1-6]

Fibers, when spliced, suffer a splicing loss because they differ from each other in refractive index, physical properties, and dimensions and also because they offset, tilt, and undergo end separation during splicing. This phenomenon of splicing loss, not seen in copper conductor cables, must not be forgotten when fiber transmission is considered. Loss resulting from fiber splicing is discussed first.

There are at least six sources of splicing loss of fibers, that is (Fig. 4.1) [1].

1. Reflection loss at the end surface of fiber
2. Offset of fibers
3. Tilt of fibers
4. End separation of fibers
5. Deformation of end surfaces of fibers
6. Differences in fiber parameters

4.3.1 Reflection Loss at the End Surfaces of Fibers [1]

When light travels through media having different refractive indexes, it reflects and is refracted at the boundary of such media. If,

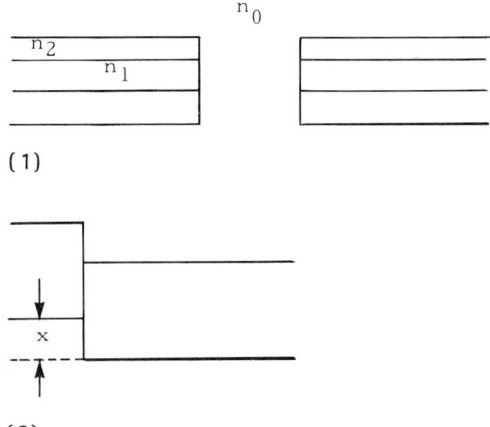

Figure 4.1 Fiber splicing: (1) reflection at the end surface; (2) offset; (3) tilt; (4) end separation; (5) deformation of end surface—end face tilt (left) and end face convex (right); (6) differences in fiber parameters—core diameter (top), NA (middle); profile (bottom).

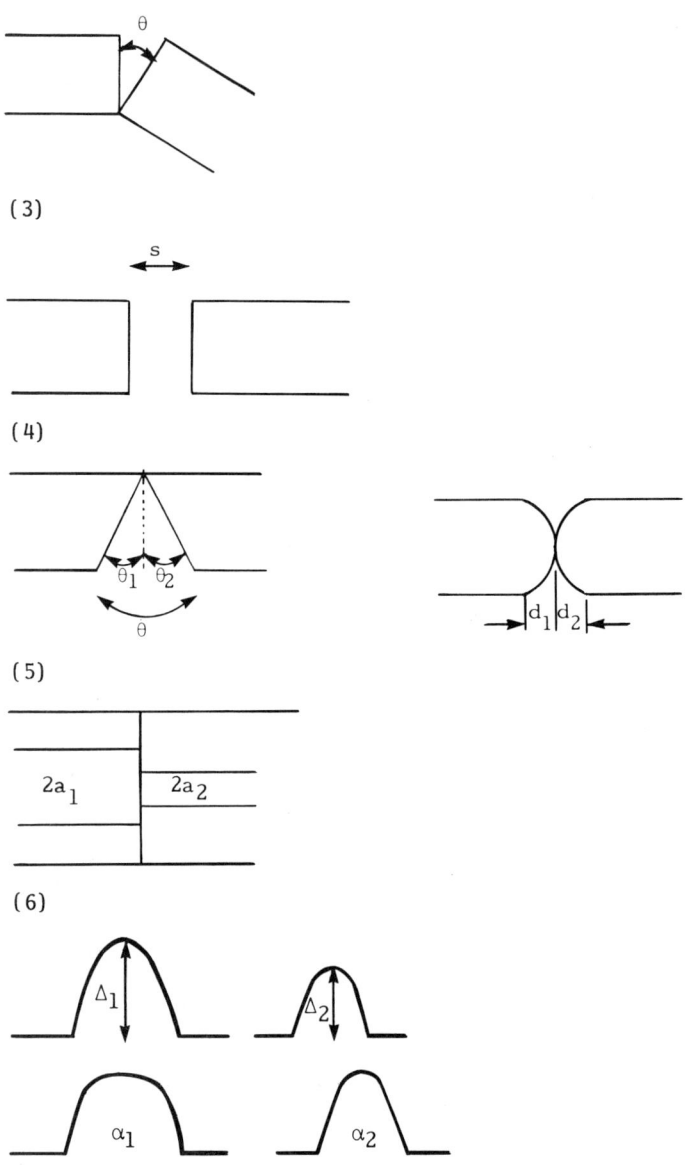

Figure 4.1 (Continued)

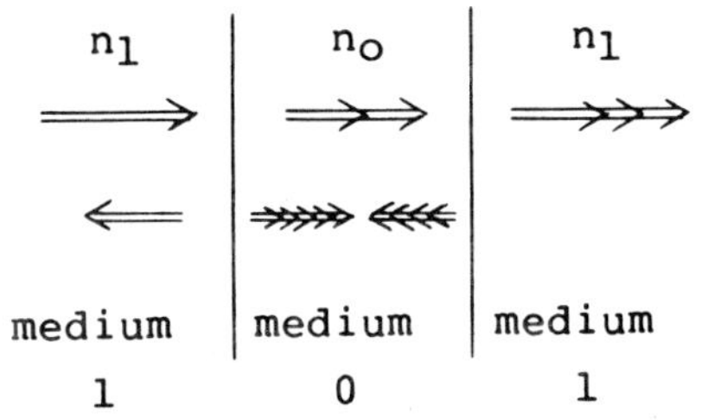

Fiber Splicing Loss

```
   n₁        n₀        n₁
  ──→      ──→→      ──→→→
  ←──     →→→ ←←←

medium    medium    medium
  1         0         1
```

Figure 4.2   Reflection loss.

between two fibers, there is a different type of medium, for example, air, a loss is caused by the reflection between the boundaries of such media (Fig. 4.2). The splicing efficiency between such media is expressed by Eq. (4.1). In this case, the splicing efficiency and transparent efficiency are the same.

$$\eta = \tau = \left[\frac{4n_1 n_0}{(n_1 + n_0)^2}\right]^2 = \frac{16k^2}{(1+k)^4}$$

where:

$k = n_1/n_0$

η = splicing efficiency

τ = transparent efficiency

n_1 = refractive index of medium 1

n_0 = refractive index of medium 0 (intermediate medium)

When n_0 and n_1 are air and silica, respectively, $n_0 = 1$ and $n_1 = 1.46$; therefore, $\eta = \tau = 0.93$. If two fibers are not closely in contact with each other, end to end, and there is no layer of air between them, a reflection loss of about 0.32 dB occurs. To prevent this, either a liquid having nearly the same refractive index as the fibers must be applied between their end surfaces or the fibers must be fused together directly. The liquid used for such purposes is generally called matching oil.

4.3.2   Offset of Fibers [1-4]

Loss caused by the offsetting of fibers in the splice is called offset loss (Fig. 4.3) [1]. The coupling efficiency η of the multimode fiber is expressed by the following formulas [1].

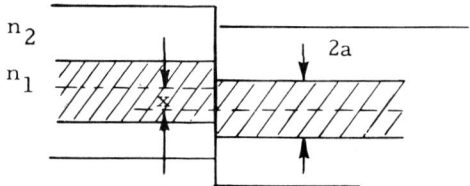

Figure 4.3 Fiber offset. (From Ref. 1.)

$$\eta_{step} = \frac{16k^2}{(1+k)^4} \frac{1}{\pi} \left\{ 2 \cos^{-1} \frac{x}{2a} - \frac{x}{a} \left[1 - \left(\frac{x}{2a}\right)^2 \right]^{\frac{1}{2}} \right\} \quad (4.2)$$

the uniform distribution of modes.

$$\eta_{graded} = \frac{16k^2}{(1+k)^4} \frac{1}{\pi} \left(2 \cos^{-1} \frac{x}{2a} - \frac{x}{a} \sqrt{4 - \left(\frac{x}{a}\right)^2} \right.$$
$$\left. \left\{ 1 - \frac{1}{12} \left[2 + \left(\frac{x}{a}\right)^2 \right] \right\} \right) \quad (4.3)$$

the uniform distribution of modes.

$$\eta_{graded} = \frac{16k^2}{(1+k)^4} \left[1 - 2.35 \left(\frac{x}{a}\right)^2 \right] \quad (4.4)$$

the steady state of modes, where $k = n_1/n_0$.

The coupling efficiency of the single-mode (SM) fiber is as below, if the distribution of propagation mode is Gaussian [2,4]:

$$\eta_{single} = \frac{16k^2}{(1+k)^4} e^{-(x/w)^2} \quad (4.5)$$

where:
$$k = \frac{n_1}{n_0}$$

$$W = 0.65 + \frac{1.619}{V^{3/2}} + \frac{2.879}{V^6}$$

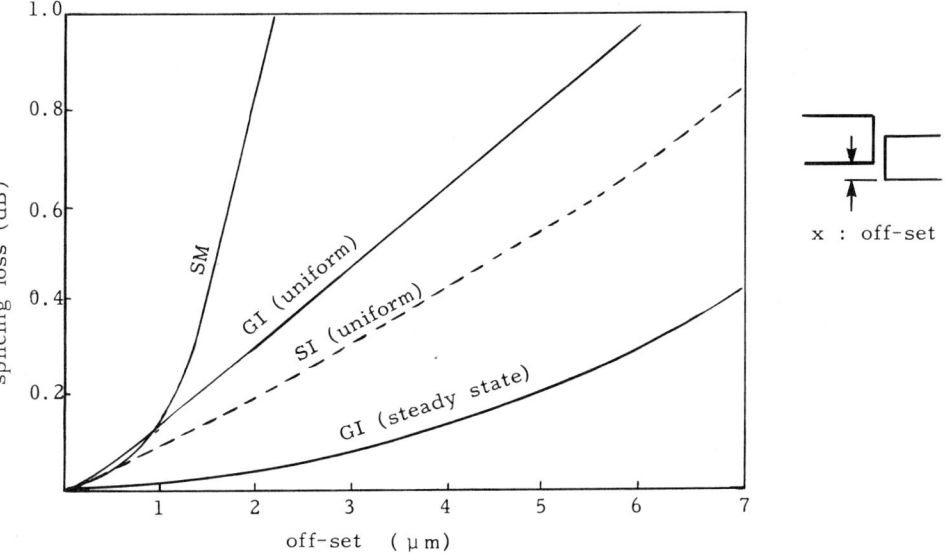

Figure 4.4 Splicing loss from offset. (From Refs. 1, 2, and 4.)

$$V = 2\pi a n_1 \sqrt{\frac{2\Delta}{\lambda}}$$

$$\Delta = \frac{n_1 - n_2}{n_1}$$

The splicing losses $L = -10 \log \eta$ are shown in Fig. 4.4 where, for the graded index (GI) fiber, $2a = 50$ μm and $\Delta = 1\%$ and for the single-mode fiber, $2a = 10$ μm and $\Delta = 0.3\%$.

According to Fig. 4.4, when the splicing loss is less than 0.1 dB, the offsets of spliced fibers are as follows:

Fiber	Offset (μm)
GI	<3.0
SM	<0.8

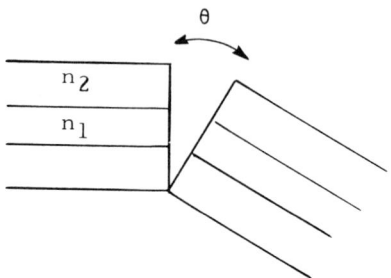

Figure 4.5 Fiber tilt. (From Ref. 1.)

4.3.3 Tilt of Fibers [1]

The coupling efficiency of fibers to be spliced with tilt angle θ is shown in the following formulas (see Fig. 4.5).

$$\eta_{step} = \frac{16k^2}{(1+k)^4} \left(1 - \frac{\theta}{\pi k \sqrt{2\Delta}}\right) \quad (4.6)$$

$$\eta_{graded} \doteq \frac{16k^2}{(1+k)^4} \left(1 - \frac{8\theta}{3\pi k \sqrt{2\Delta}}\right) \quad (4.7)$$

uniform distribution of modes

$$\eta_{graded} = \frac{16k^2}{(1+k)^4} (1 - 1.68\theta^2) \quad \text{steady state} \quad (4.8)$$

$$\eta_{single} = \frac{16k^2}{(1+k)^4} e^{-(\pi n_2 w \theta/\lambda)^2} \quad (4.9)$$

$$\frac{w}{a} = 0.65 + \frac{1.619}{V^{3/2}} + \frac{2.879}{V^6}$$

The splicing loss (<0.1 dB) due to the tilt of the fibers is shown in Fig. 4.6 and is <0.7° for the graded index fiber and <0.3° for the single mode.

4.3.4 End Separation of Fibers [1–3]

When the gap of end separation of fiber is s (Fig. 4.7), the coupling efficiency is as follows [1, 3].

Fiber Splicing Loss

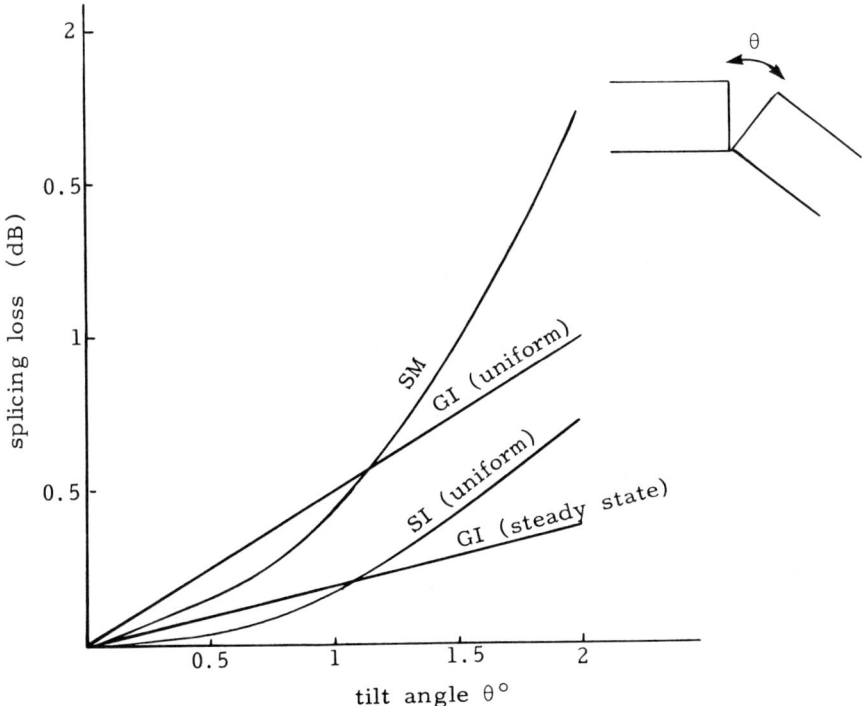

Figure 4.6 Splicing loss from tilt. (From Refs. 1, 2, and 4.)

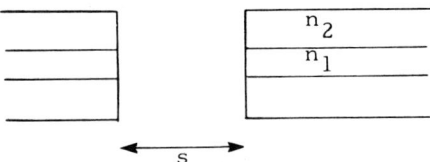

Figure 4.7 End separation of fibers. (From Ref. 1.)

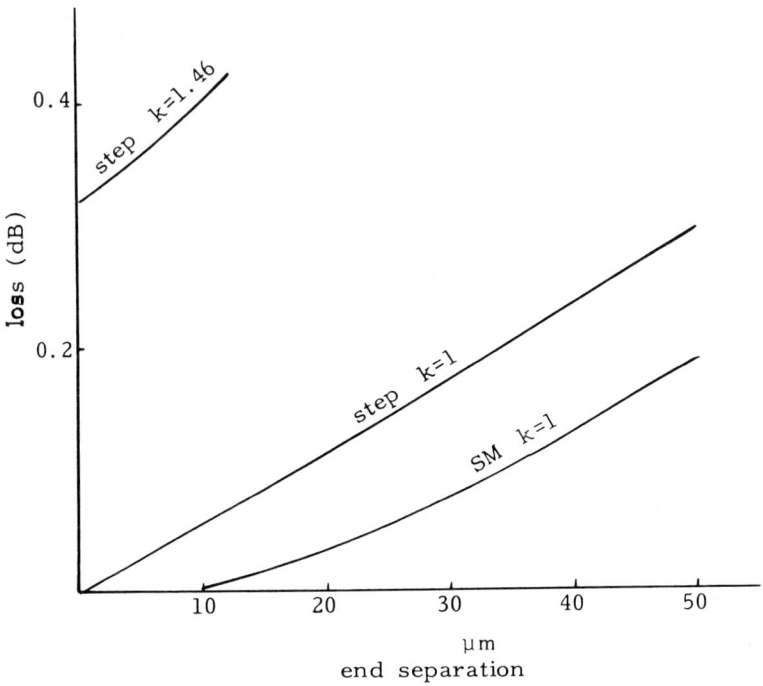

Figure 4.8 Splicing loss from end separation. (From Refs. 1–3.)

$$\eta_{step} = \frac{16k^2}{(1+k)^4}\left[1 - \frac{s}{4a}\,k(2\Delta)^{1/2}\right] \quad \text{uniform distribution} \tag{4.10}$$

$$\eta_{single} = \frac{1}{(1+(\lambda s)^2/(2\pi n_2 w^2)^2} \tag{4.11}$$

The splicing loss by end separation of fibers is shown in Fig. 4.8.

4.3.5 Deformation of End Surfaces of Fibers [1]

The following two types of end surface deformation are most conceivable for fibers.

4.3.5.1 End Face Tilt

The coupling efficiency of fibers whose end surfaces are inclined, not at right angles to their axes, is expressed by Eq. (4.12) (Fig. 4.9) [1]. Their splice loss is as shown in Fig. 4.10.

Fiber Splicing Loss

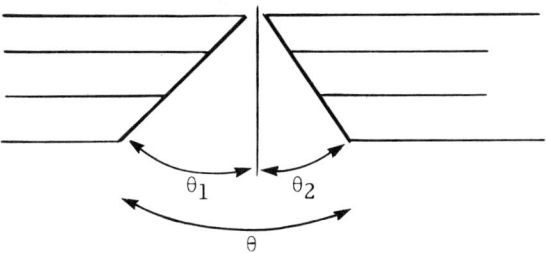

Figure 4.9 End face tilt. (From Ref. 1.)

$$\eta_{step} = \frac{16k^2}{(1+k)^4} \left[1 - \frac{|k-1|}{\pi k\sqrt{2\Delta}} (\theta_1 + \theta_2) \right] \quad \text{uniform distribution}$$

(4.12)

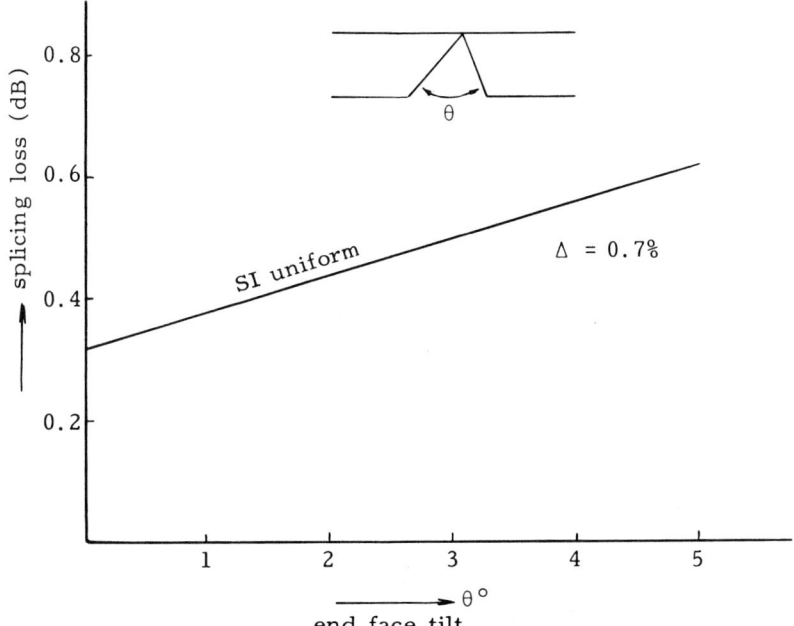

Figure 4.10 Splicing loss from end face tilt. (From Ref. 1.)

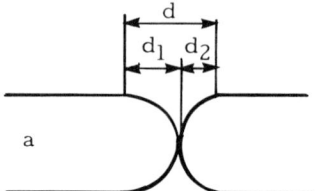

Figure 4.11 End face convex. (From Ref. 1.)

4.3.5.2 End Face Convex

Equation (4.13) expresses the coupling efficiency of fiber with their end surfaces curving convexly (Fig. 4.11). Figure 4.12 shows the splice loss.

$$\eta_{step} = \frac{16k^2}{(1+k)^4} \left[1 - \frac{1}{2\sqrt{2\Delta}} \frac{|k-1|}{k} \frac{(d_1 + d_2)}{a} \right] \quad \text{uniform distribution} \quad (4.13)$$

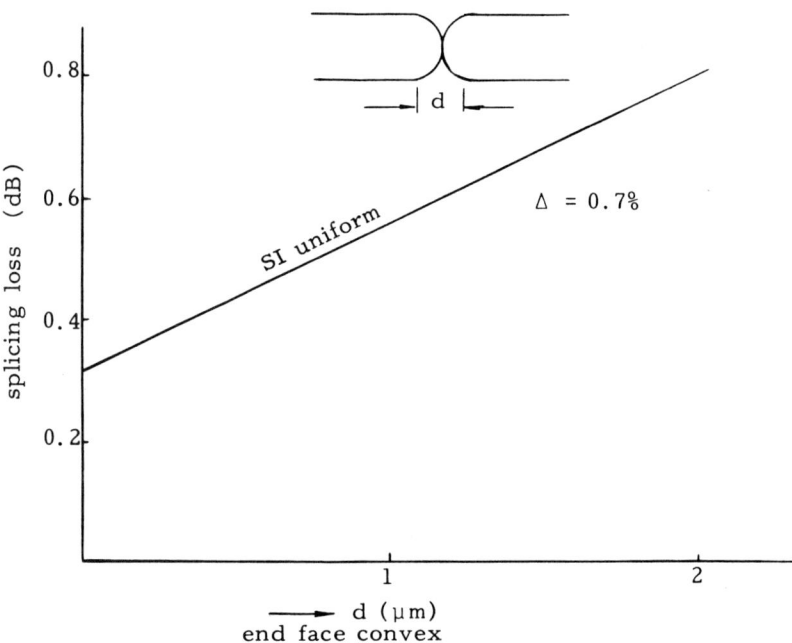

Figure 4.12 Splicing loss with end face convex. (From Ref. 1.)

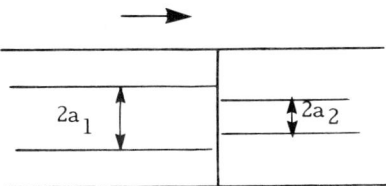

Figure 4.13 Difference in core diameters. (From Ref. 1.)

4.3.6 Differences in Fiber Parameters [1]

Splicing loss due to difference in fiber parameters is possible chiefly in the following four ways.

1. Difference in core diameter (SI and GI) (Figs. 4.13 and 4.14) (uniform distribution) [1].

$$\eta_{step} = \eta_{graded} = \frac{16k^2}{(1+k)^4} \left(\frac{a_2}{a_1}\right)^2 \qquad a_1 \geqslant a_2 \qquad (4.14)$$

$$= \frac{16k^2}{(1+k)^4} \qquad a_1 < a_2$$

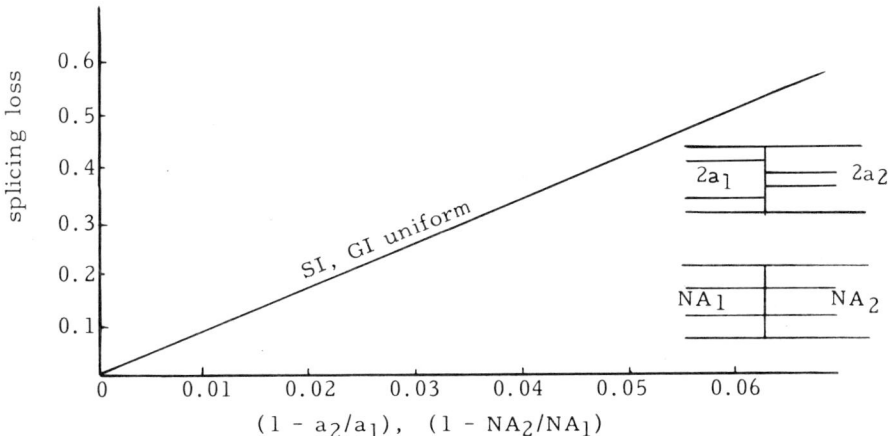

Figure 4.14 Splicing loss from difference in core diameters and NA. (From Ref. 1.)

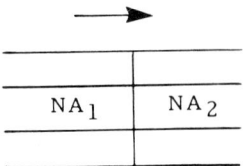

Figure 4.15 Difference in NA.

2. Difference in NA (SI and GI) (Figs. 4.15 and 4.16)(uniform distribution) [1].

$$\eta_{step} = \eta_{graded} = \frac{16k^2}{(1+k)^4}\left(\frac{NA_2}{NA_1}\right)^2 = \frac{16k^2}{(1+k)^4}\frac{\Delta_2}{\Delta_1}$$

$$NA_1 \geq NA_2 \quad (4.15)$$

$$= \frac{16k^2}{(1+k)^4}$$

$$NA_1 < NA_2$$

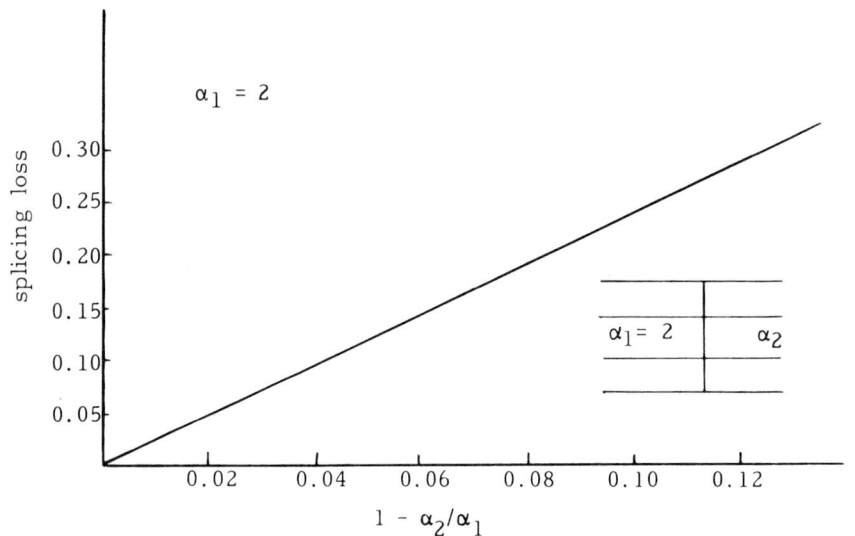

Figure 4.16 Splicing loss from difference in NA. (From Ref. 1.)

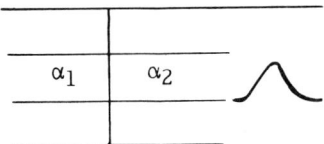

Figure 4.17 Differences in profiles. (From Ref. 1.)

3. Difference in profile (GI) (Fig. 4.17) (uniform distribution) [2].

$$\eta_{graded} = \frac{16k^2}{(1+k)^4} \frac{\alpha_2(\alpha_1+2)}{\alpha_1(\alpha_2+2)} \qquad \alpha_1 \geq \alpha_2 \qquad (4.16)$$

$$= \frac{16k^2}{(1+k)^4} \qquad \alpha_1 < \alpha_2$$

4. Difference in core diameter and NA of single-mode fibers (Fig. 4.18) [5]:

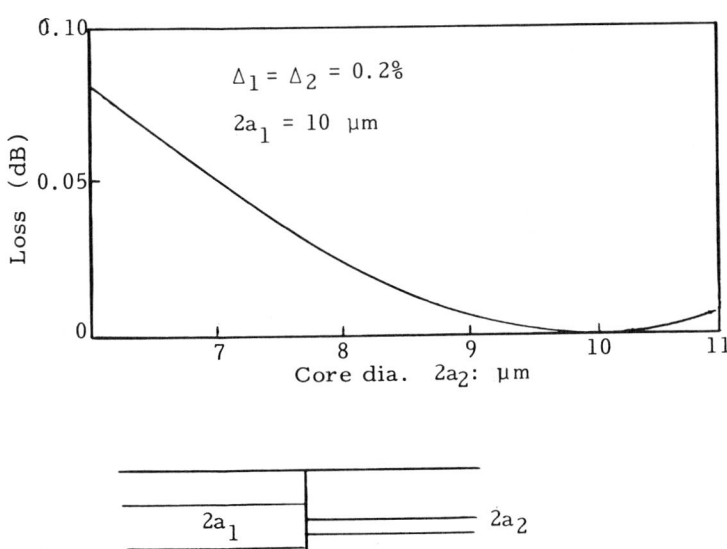

Figure 4.18 Splicing loss of SM fibers and difference in core diameters. (From Ref. 5.)

Table 4.1 Splicing Loss of GI and SM Fibers

Causes of splicing loss	Splicing	Example of calculation	
		SM	GI
Off-set		$x = 2\ \mu m$	$x = 2\ \mu m$
		0.74 dB	0.06 dB
Tilt		$\theta = 1°$	$\theta = 1°$
		0.46 dB	0.15 dB
End face tilt		$\theta = 1°$	$\theta = 1°$
		0.21 dB	0.03 dB
Difference of cores		$2a_1 = 10\ \mu m$ $2a_2 = 8\ \mu m$	$2a_1 = 50\ \mu m$ $2a_2 = 48\ \mu m$
		0.02 dB	0.15 dB
Difference of Δs		$\Delta_1 = 0.2\%$ $\Delta_2 = 0.25\%$	$\Delta_1 = 1.0\%$ $\Delta_2 = 0.8\%$
		0.03 dB	0.32 dB

Source: From Ref. 12.

Fiber Splicing

$$\eta_{single} = \frac{1}{4}\left(\frac{w_1}{w_2} + \frac{w_2}{w_1}\right)^2 \qquad (4.16)$$

$$w = a\left(0.65 + \frac{1.619}{V^{1.5}} + \frac{2.879}{V^6}\right)$$

4.3.7 Calculated Examples of Splicing Loss [6]

Table 4.1 shows the main causes of splicing loss and examples of its calculation.

1. Splicing of single-mode fibers: the offset and tilt of cores should be made as small as possible. For splicing loss < 0.1, offset is <0.8 μm and tilt is <0.3. These values are far less than those for GI fiber.
2. Splicing of GI fibers (50 μm per 125 μm) in the case of equal cross-sectional construction, for splicing loss < 0.1 dB, offset is <3 μm and tilt is <0.7°. The differences in core diameter Δ, offset, and tilt should be minimized.

4.4 FIBER SPLICING

Methods of fiber splicing are classified into the sleeve method, the V-groove or rod method, and the fusion method (Table 4.2). The merits and disadvantages of the three methods are also shown in Table 4.2.

4.4.1 Fusion Splice

Fusion splice is now very popular world wide and because of the automatic splicing machine is easily manufactured and applied.

"Fusion splice" is a method of splicing fibers by heating their end surfaces and fusing them together. Theoretically, the splicing loss of the fibers is likely to become very small because their end surfaces melt and stick to each other. The means of heating and fusion are shown below.

1. Electric heating using nichrome wire or the like. This means of heating cannot produce the high temperatures sufficient for fiber fusion and is therefore no longer in use.
2. CO_2 laser heating. Used experimentally, the CO_2 laser permits heating in a very clean state and offers the possibility of making a high-strength splice. It requires a large, expensive splicing apparatus, however.

Table 4.2 Fiber Splicing Method

Method	Sleeve	V groove or Rods	Fusion
(a)	T4.2-a	T4.2-b	T4.2-c
(b)	fiber	fiber	
Splicing process	Adhesive material required	Adhesive material required	Electric discharge; flame; laser

Fiber Splicing

Particulates			
	Least affected by dust	1. Parts to be spliced can be held in the V groove easily without deviation during splicing 2. Easy multifiber splicing	1. Easy automatic splicing process
Dimensions of apliced part	Midele	Middle	Same as outer diameter of fiber
Splicing tool and machine	Simple but handwork	Simple but handwork	Automatic machine or handwork
Work ability and operation	Some skill required; splicing time slightly long		By automatic machine, process simple and splicing time short
Splicing loss	0.15 dB	0.15 dB	0.1 dB

3. H_2 flame heating. Automatic flame control is difficult. The use of H_2 and Cl_2 gases produces a very strong splice. This method is usable for special applications, such as fiber splicing for submarine cables.
4. Heating by electrical arc discharge. Local high temperatures are easy to obtain by this heating method. The automatic control of electrical arc discharge is relatively easy. It is most generally and widely used for fiber splicing. An apparatus for this method is called an arc fusion splicing machine.

Now I shall further explain about the arc fusion splicing apparatus and fusion splice using H_2 flame heating.

4.4.2 Arc Fusion Splicing Machine [7-14]

Arc fusion splicing is now most commonly used for fiber splicing. The arc fusion splicing machine now available is sufficiently practical because (1) the arc fusion process and the machine as a whole can be easily made automatic, (2) it is easy to design the machine in a small size and light weight, and (3) the machine can be so designed as to be easy to use and to make a highly reproducible and stable splice. The arc fusion splicing machines now in practical use are chiefly of the following three types:

1. Automatic (no core alignment), for GI and SM (with small eccentricity) fibers
2. Automatic with core alignment, mainly for SM fiber
3. Direct core monitoring, for SM fiber

The arc fusion splicing machine must have the following mechanisms

1. Accurate axial alignment of fibers: for GI fiber, fitted in the outer diameter of the fibers; for SM fiber, fitted in the center of fiber cores
2. Fine movement of fiber
3. Stable arc discharge and its control

4.4.2.1 Axial Alignment of Fibers [7]

The offset and tilt of fibers to be spliced are the main causes of splice loss. To eliminate these causes, highly accurate axial alignment of the fibers is important. In splicing, the fibers must be moved in the axial direction toward the splicing point. To do so, the fibers need to be fixed on the bottom of the V groove made with a high dimensional accuracy. The fibers are fixed in two ways, as follows (Fig. 4.19).

Fiber Splicing

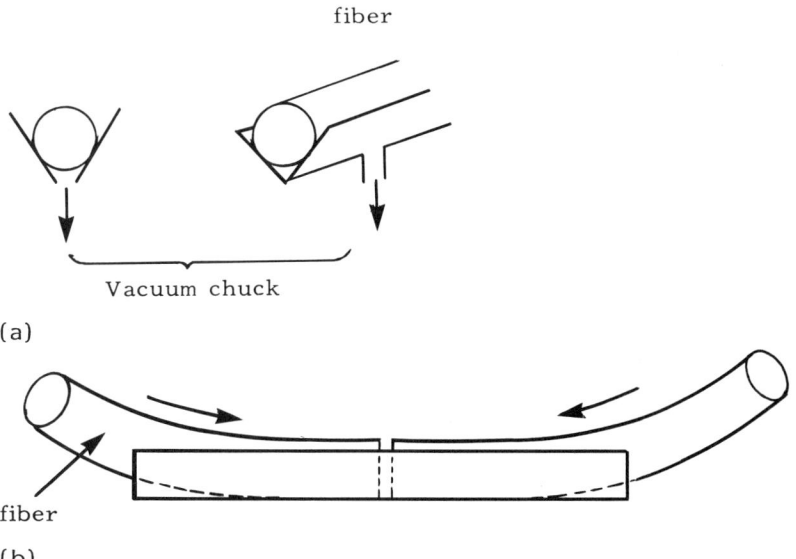

Figure 4.19   V groove for fiber splicing.

1. A vacuum chuck is provided on the bottom of the V groove, as shown in Fig. 4.19a to draw the fibers to the bottom.
2. As shown in Fig. 4.19b, the fibers are inserted into the V groove from the upper inclined position and bent along the bottom of the groove to rest there. This alignment method is now generally used.

4.4.2.2   Electrical Arc Discharging [7-11]

Fibers are inserted between electrodes (spacing of electrodes, 1-2 mm) pointed 30-40° at their ends, and AC voltage is applied to them. AC discharge causes a spark discharge at a 2000-4000 V, which in turn generates ions between the electrodes. The ions reduce the spark voltage about 300-600 V. The alternating current is about 15-20 mA, and the required power for splicing is about 5-10 W.

In the arc fusion process, if fiber ends are fused in a butted position, bubbles develop in the fused part and the state of the end surfaces greatly affects splicing loss. Therefore, the end surfaces of the fibers are spaced slightly apart from each other, then melted and spliced. This is called a prefusion method. The splicing process is as follows (Table 4.3) [7, 11].

Table 4.3 Prefusion Splicing Method by the Electric Arc

GI fibers	SM fibers	
	with core eccentricity > 1 μm	core eccentricity ≤ 1 μm
1)[a] — core, electrod, 15∼20 μm, spacing plate	1) — core	1)
	1)' alignment of cores	
2) Pre-fusion — discharge	2) Pre-fusion	2) Pre-fusion

[a] These numbers refer to steps listed in the text.

Fiber Splicing

Table 4.3 (Continued)

GI fibers	SM fibers	
	with core eccentricity > 1 μm	core eccentricity ≤ 1 μm
3)	3)	3)
4)-6)	4)-6) 7)	4)-6)
	X	

Source: From Refs. 7 and 11.

1. The two fibers to be spliced are aligned along the end surfaces and kept about 15-20 μm apart from each other by a spacing plate.
2. The spacing plate is moved downward, and the electric discharge is started and melts the surfaces of the fiber ends.
3. The fibers are moved in the axial direction.
4. The two fiber ends are brought into contact and pushed against each other in a specified length (see Table 4.4).
5. The movement of the fibers is stopped. Discharge is continued for regular heating.
6. Discharge is stopped to complete the fusion.

In the prefusion splicing of GI fibers, the two fibers to be spliced are aligned diameter to diameter and their end surfaces are melted and then brought into contact with each other to form a splice. The cores of the two fibers are automatically linked by the surface tension of the melted part. When cores have an offset, they are connected in a bent state, as shown in Table 4.3 (far left column).

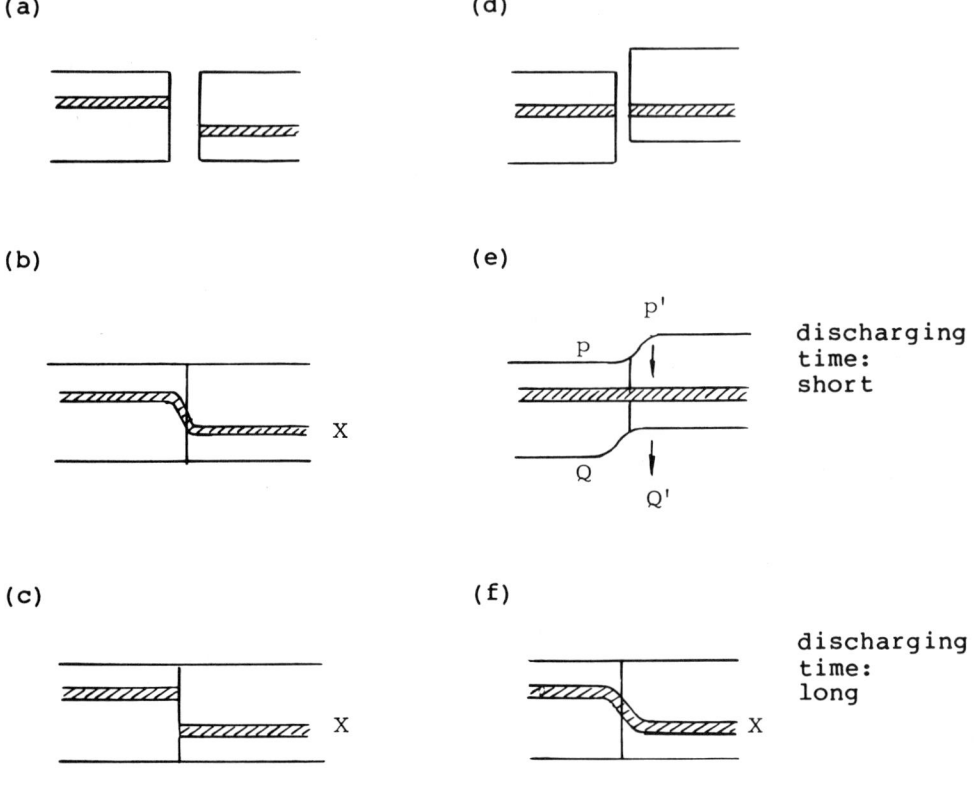

Figure 4.20 Splicing of SM fibers by electric arc discharge.

The splicing of SM fibers is the same as the splicing of GI fiber where there is eccentricity ≤ 1 μm (Table 4.3, far right column).

If, however, the cores have eccentricity >1 μm, the following points apply.

1. If the fibers are matched with each other in periphery and given arc fusion, the cores are connected in a sharp bent stage or not spliced, as shown in Fig. 4.20b and c.
2. If the fibers are spliced with the cores in alignment with each other and if the arc discharging time is short (normally about 1 sec), the splice becomes as shown in Fig. 4.20e and Table 4.3, center [10-12], making it possible to expect a low splicing loss. If the arc discharging time is increased, however, a force caused by the surface tension of the molten fibers to fit the fibers on the periphery works on the molten parts PP' and QQ' (Fig. 4.20e).

Fiber Splicing

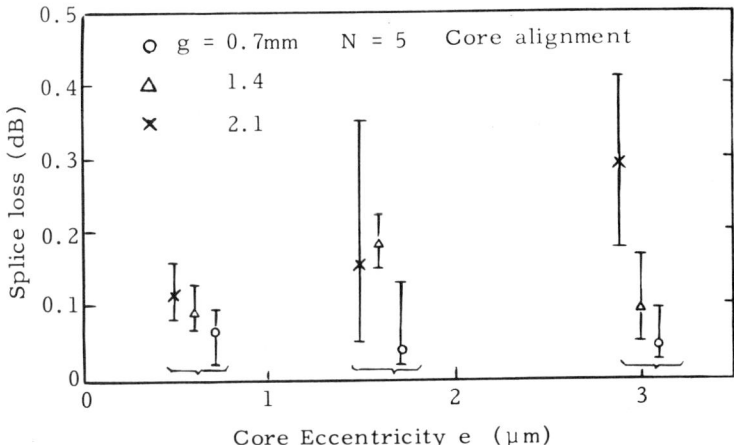

Figure 4.21 Relationship between electrode gap g and splice loss for fibers with various core eccentricities. N is the number of data points. (From Ref. 11.)

As a result, the fiber cores are bent as shown in Fig. 4.20f, thereby increasing the splicing loss.

Figures 4.21 and 4.22 show examples of splicing conditions and the splicing loss of SM fibers [11]. Figure 4.21 shows the relationship between electrode gap and splice for SM fibers with various core eccentricities. The splicing loss increases with an increase in core eccentricity. From Fig. 4.22, the splicing loss increases when the discharging time exceeds 2 sec. (On the other hand, to increase the strength of the splice to some extent, an excessively short arc discharge time is a problem.) From these figures, SM fibers with core eccentricity >1 μm must be spliced with core alignment.

All these considered, the most suitable conditions for the splicing of fibers are shown in Table 4.4.

4.4.2.3 Automatic Alignment of SM Fibers [12, 15]

When single-mode fibers are spliced, an offset of 0.8 μm is equivalent to a splicing loss of 0.1 dB. Therefore, the precise alignment of fibers is required. Figure 4.24 shows the fundamental principles of the precise alignment mechanism for fibers [13]. The alignment of fibers can be made automatic if a motor is used to control the position of the fibers.

In the alignment method of Fig. 4.24, the alignment range is ±10 μm, and its step 0.1 μm. These fibers can be set with an accuracy of 0.5 μm.

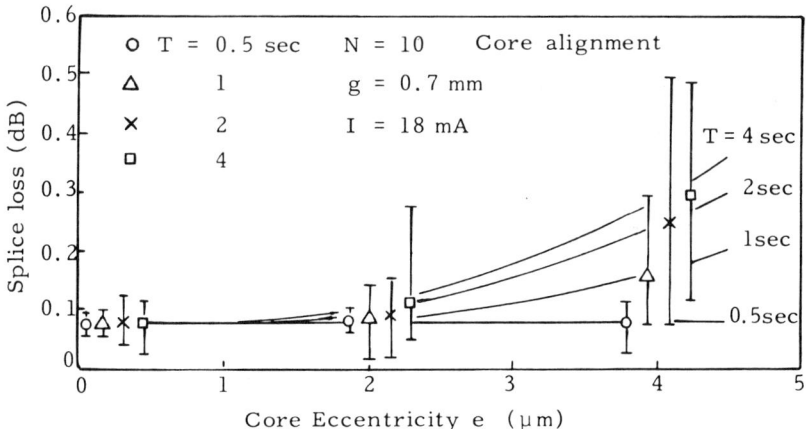

Figure 4.22 Dependence of splice loss on electric discharge duration in splicing fibers with various core eccentricities. N is the number of data points. (From Ref. 11.)

Figure 4.25 [12, 15] shows the principle of automatic core alignment.

1. The optical energy is launched to the fiber core from the far end of the fibers (Fig. 4.25a) (e.g., at the repeater station) or at the bent part of the fiber near the splicing point (Fig. 4.25b) (so-called local launching).
2. The optical energy that passes through the splicing point is detected at the far end of the spliced fiber Fig. 4.25 or by local

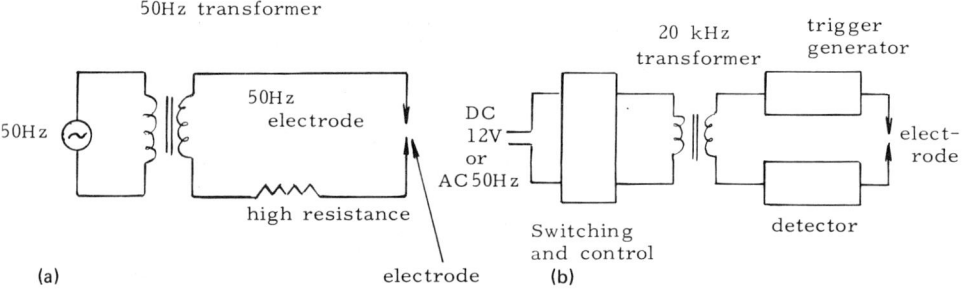

Figure 4.23 Discharge circuits for fusion splice: (a) ordinary discharge circuit (50 Hz); (b) 20 kHz discharge circuit with trigger generator. (From Ref. 13.)

Fiber Splicing

Table 4.4 Examples of Suitable Conditions for the Arc Fusion Splice

	GI SM (core eccentricity ≤ 1 μm)	SM (core eccentricity >1 μm) with core alignment
Frequency, kHz[a]	20	20
Distance between electrodes, mm	1.5	0.8
Diameter of electrode, mm	1	1
Spark voltage, kV	3.5	2.5
Wattage of discharge, W	10	10
Spacing between fiber ends, μm	20	10
Preheating time, sec	0.12	0.12
Heating time, sec	3	1
Pressing speed, μm/sec	160	50
Pressing length, μm	20	10

[a]When the frequency of the power source is increased, the transformer becomes lighter in roughly inverse proportion to the frequency. Also, the electrical input power for discharge and the weight of the transformer can be saved by the use of a trigger discharge circuit (Fig. 4.23). When the frequency is 50 Hz, the weight of the transformer required for the splicing machine is about 2 kg. The weight of the transformer using 20 Hz with a trigger generator is only 40 g, and its size compared with 50 Hz is less than half [13].

detecting in which the fiber is bent at a point immediately after the splice point and the optical energy radiated from there is detected (Fig. 4.25d). The local launching and local detecting methods require the use of only the entry port or pole where field splicing is made. Detected power is fed back to the splice point. The fibers are moved automatically in such a manner that the value of the detecting power becomes maximum.

4.4.2.4 Fiber Core Alignment by Direct Core Monitoring [16, 17]

For fiber core alignment of SM fiber splicing, a direct core monitoring system is also used.

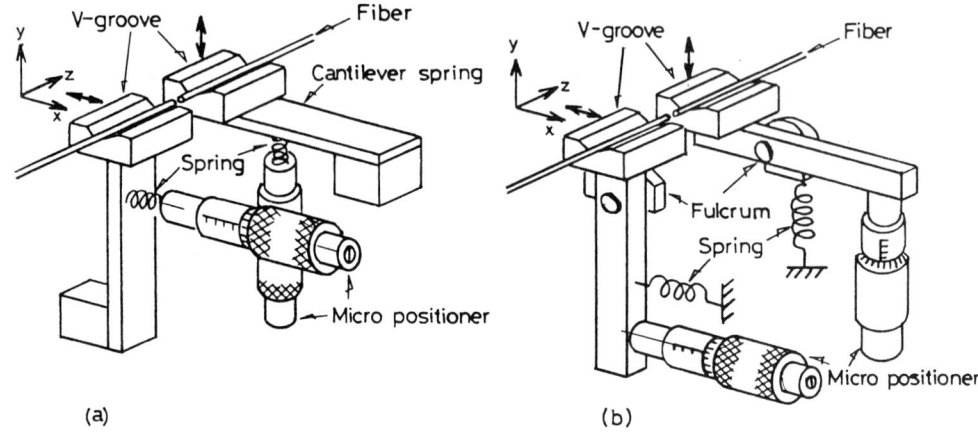

Figure 4.24 Fundamental principles of precise alignment mechanism: (a) cantilever spring type; (b) leverage type. (From Ref. 13.)

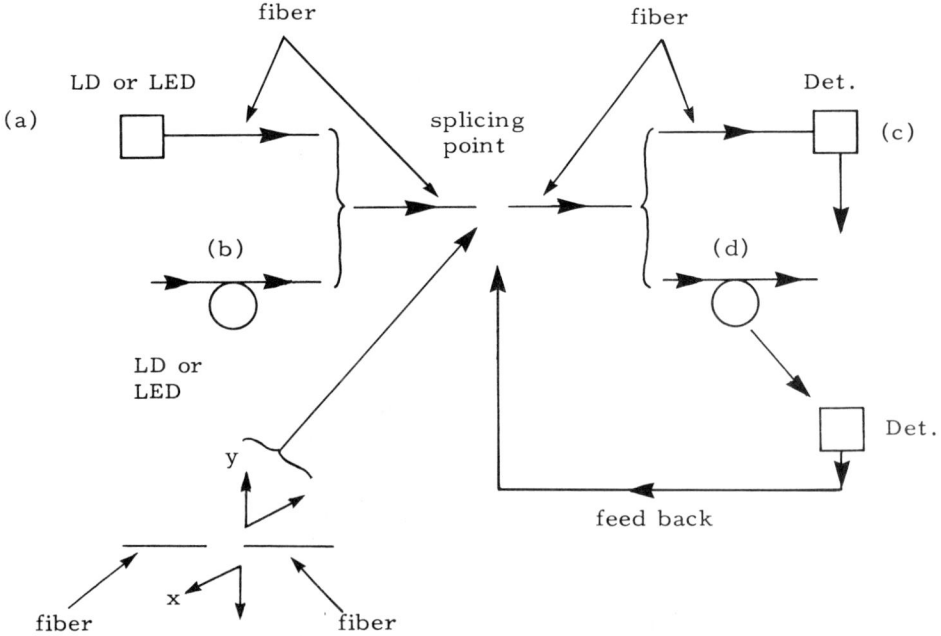

Figure 4.25 Core alignment method. (From Refs. 12 and 15.)

Fiber Splicing

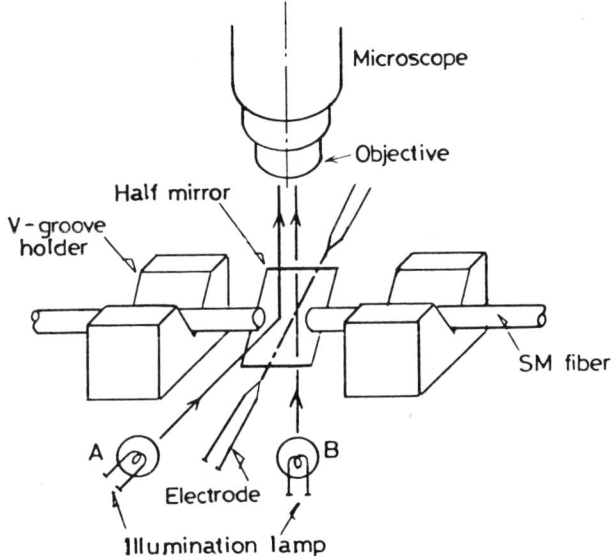

Figure 4.26 Direct core monitoring machine for SM fiber splice. (From Ref. 16.)

The direct core monitoring mechanism is shown in Fig. 4.26 [16]. Lights A and B, at right angles, are launched to the fiber ends. Offsets in the horizontal and vertical directions are monitored with the microscope. The automatic alignment process is applied as shown in Fig. 4.27 [18]. A resolving power of this process is

$$d = \frac{\lambda}{NAn}$$

where,

  d = resolving power

  λ = wavelength

  NA = NA of objective lens

  n = magnification of microscope

4.4.2.5 Fusion Mass Splice of Fibers [19-21]

A cable with a large number of optical fibers can be joined very easily in a short time if some fibers can be spliced in a group. This is especially helpful if fiber splicing can be done ribbon by ribbon

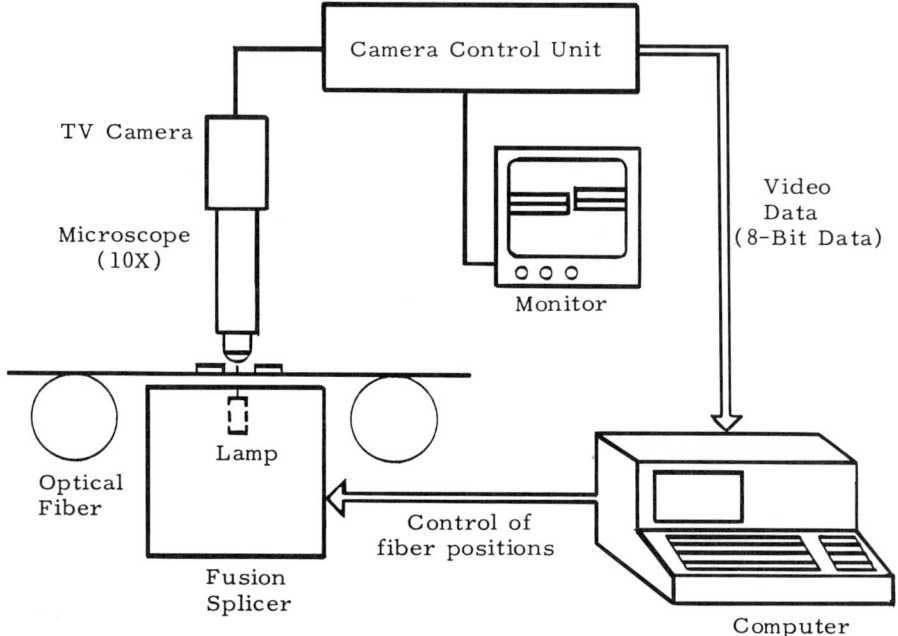

Figure 4.27 Automatic alignment of fibers by direct core monitoring. (From Refs. 17 and 18.)

for fiber ribbon cables and unit by unit for fiber unit cables. The following introduces a mass splice fusion machine capable of splicing five-fiber ribbons or five fibers arranged in parallel by the arc discharge at one time.

The five fibers can be cut by a simple fiber cutter similar to that used for a single fiber to get a smooth mirror surface. The ends of the five fibers are uneven, however. The process of alignment of the fibers is shown in Fig. 4.28 [19].

The distribution of electic current intensity by arc discharge is shown in Fig. 4.29 [21]. To achieve heating uniformity, fibers to be spliced are positioned on the same electric current intensity, as shown in Fig. 4.29. An offset from the electrode axis is 0.2 mm in this figure.

Schematic diagrams of the mass splicing machine are shown in Fig. 4.30 [19]. This splicing machine is used for five fibers. The five fibers are 0.3 mm apart from each other. A pair of electrodes is used with a 2.5 mm space between them. Power is supplied by a trigger generator. Its frequency is 25 kHz. As shown in Fig. 4.30, the five fibers are 0.3 apart from each other with comblike teeth

Fiber Splicing 351

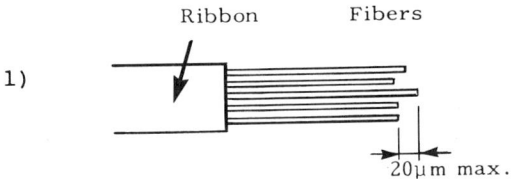

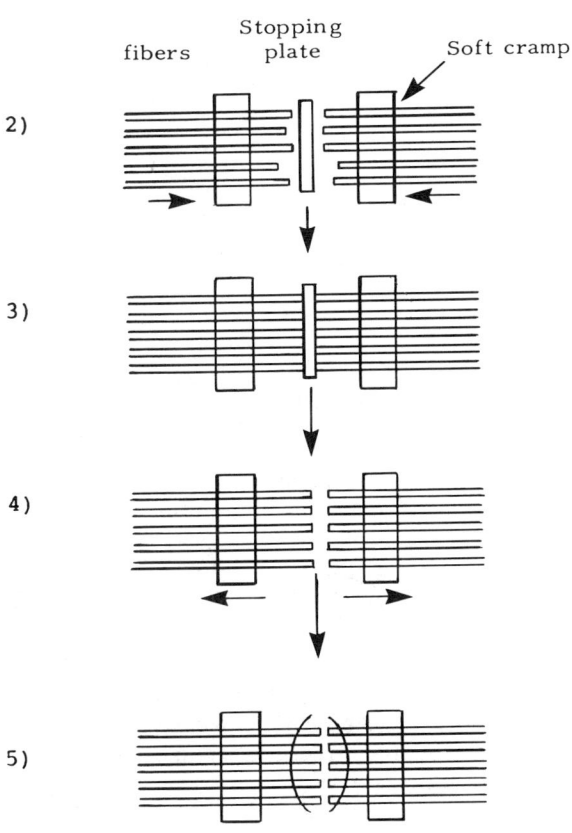

Figure 4.28 Alignment of fibers in a ribbon: (1) cutting ends of fibers in ribbon; (2) before alignment (uneven end-to-end spacing); (3) fiber ends in contact with the stopping plate (adjustment of fiber end preparation); (4) removal of the stopping plate (fibers move by soft clamping action); (5) arc discharging (preheating and regular heating). (From Ref. 19.)

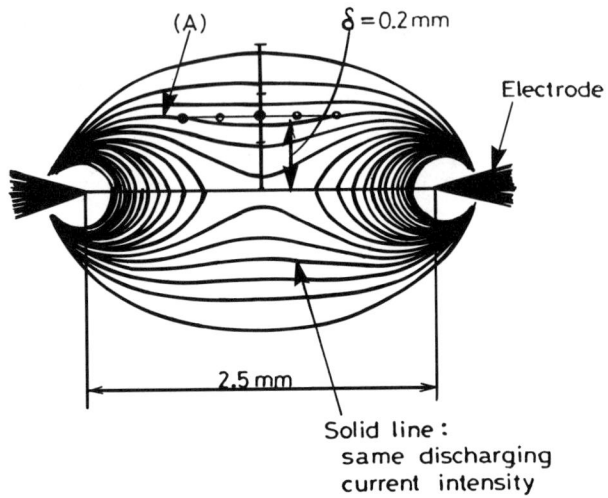

Figure 4.29 Distribution of electric currents by arc discharge. (From Ref. 21.)

and are held by a soft clamp. The fibers then slip into V grooves for axial alignment and hit a stopping plate. A soft clamp provided near the stopping fibers can be cut by a simple fiber cutting tool similar to that used for a single fiber to obtain a smooth mirror surface. The ends of the five fibers are uneven. When they hit the stopping plate, their deflection is absorbed by the soft clamp. Uneven fiber positions of up to about 100 µm are absorbed. Ordinarily, the uneven fiber position is less than 20 µm.

4.4.2.6   Flame Fusion Splicing [22]

If a mechanical stripper is used in arc fusion splicing to remove plastic over the fiber, the breaking strength of the spliced fiber is reduced below one-tenth of the breaking strength (approximately 0.4-1 kg) of the original fiber (approximately 6-8 kg). This is due to a flaw given the fiber by the mechanical stripper or a minute flaw caused to the fiber surface by the arc.

The AT&T laboratory is experimenting with a high-strength splicing method using flame [22]. I am introducing this method here because, although it is not yet available for practical use, it will be used for splicing of submarine cables in the future in an attempt to make very strong spliced fibers. It uses H_2Cl_2 flame for fusion splicing in place of the ordinary H_2O_2 flame because the presence of H_2O in the splicing reduces the breaking strength of the fiber.

Fiber Splicing

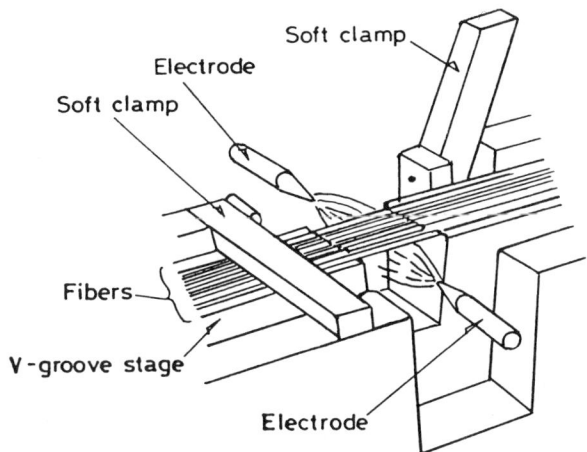

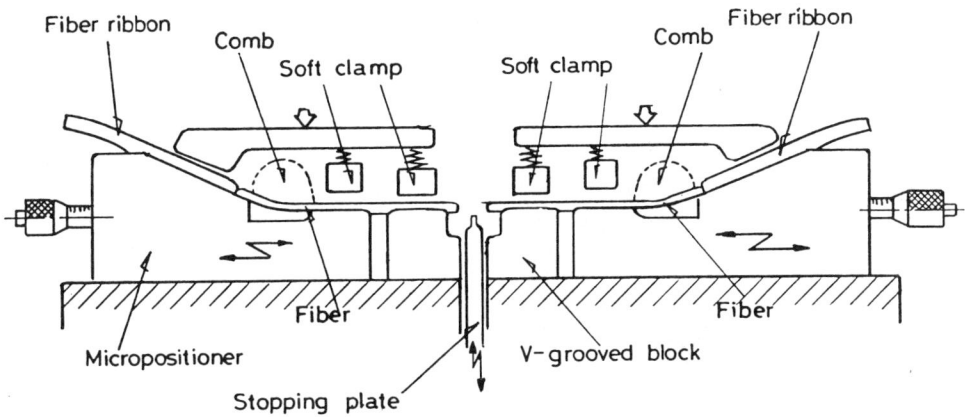

Figure 4.30   Mechanisms of the mass-splicing machine.   (From Ref. 21.)

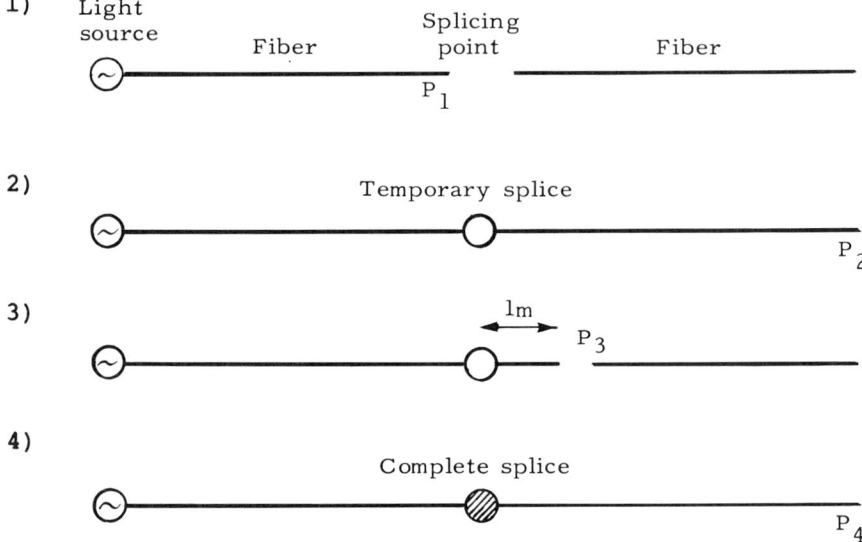

Figure 4.31   Process of splice loss measurement. (From Ref. 23.)

In experiments, this method proved extremely effective, giving spliced fibers an average breaking strength of 5.9 kg/mm^2 and a minimum of 3.4 kg/mm^2. The conditions of making high-strength spliced fibers are as follows [22].

1. Fibers must be spliced in clean dust-free atmosphere.
2. Fibers must have no mechanical flaws; therefore, the coating material on the fiber must not be removed with a mechanical stripper. The splicing loss of single-mode fibers spliced by this method is as follows.

Splicing	Eccentricity (μm)	Splice loss, median (dB/splice)
Same fibers	<0.3	0.09
Different fibers	0.3–1	0.17

No power monitor was used in either case.

Fiber Splicing 355

4.4.2.7 Measurement of Splicing Loss: The Temporary Splicing Method [23]

The splicing loss of fibers has been measured by the temporary splicing method shown in Fig. 4.31. The procedure is as follows:

1. Measure output power P_1.
2. Measure output power P_2 after temporary splicing at the splicing point.
3. Measure output power P_3. The fiber, temporarily spliced in step 2, is cut through at a point about 1 m to the right from the splice, and the output P_3 is measured there.
4. The fibers are then spliced completely, and the output power P_4 is measured.
5. Splice loss α_s is calculated by

$$10 \log \frac{P_1}{P_3} \frac{P_2}{P_4} \text{ dB} = \alpha_s$$

This method is used when the splice loss is about 0.2 dB maximum and 0.1 dB average. It takes about 10 min and requires much labor.

4.4.2.8 A Wet Fusion Splice Method and a Convenient Measurement of Splicing Loss [24]

A wet fusion splice method using a matching oil has been developed to save measurement time and the labor of splicing (Fig. 4.32) [23].

1. Fibers are placed in V grooves and moved to butt against the stopper.
2. The matching oil is pushed up to the top of the stopper by surface tension and adheres to the end surfaces of the fibers.
3. The fibers are brought close to each other (spaced at least 10-20 µm), and fiber cores are aligned. After core alignment the end surfaces of fibers are brought together, and the optical energy P_1 that has passed through the splicing point is measured. From test results, the splicing loss with matching oil in this process may be assumed to be zero.
4. The fibers are spaced 10 µm apart and spliced by electric arc discharge. The matching oil evaporates during the arc discharge.
5. The optical energy P_2 that has passed through the splice is measured.

$$\text{Splicing loss } \Delta P = 10 \log \frac{P_1}{P_2}$$

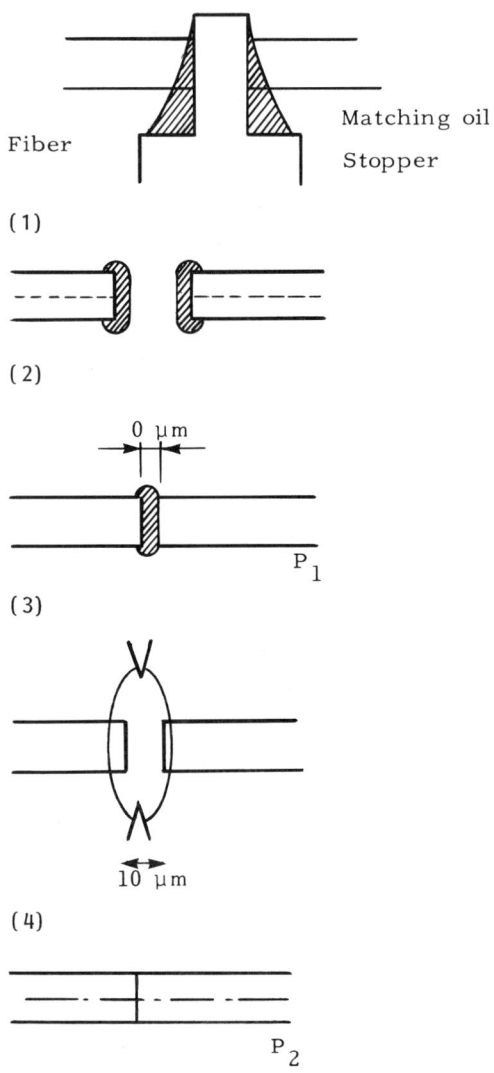

Figure 4.32 Wet fusion splice method: (1) initial setting, butting at the stopper; (2) stopper released, matching oil adheres; (3) core axis alignment; (4) discharge; (5) completed splice. (From Ref. 24.)

Fiber Splicing

According to the results of experiments, the relationship between ΔP and α_s, splicing loss, is as follows.

$$\alpha_s = (\Delta P + 0.02) \pm 0.01 \text{ dB}$$

The accuracy of ΔP is ± 0.01 dB, and there is no practical problem even when a splicing loss of ΔP is used.

The time of splice measurement by this method is 2 min or less, which is a substantial reduction from the 10 min required by conventional measuring methods (Sec. 4.4.2.7).

4.4.3 Reinforcement of the Fiber Splice

Fibers, when spliced, are stripped of their plastic coatings with a plastic stripper and cut off at the end. Therefore, stripped fibers often receive accidental touch by hand and sustain very small flaws or cracks. As a result, the breaking strength of a fiber splice made under normal conditions is reduced to about 0.4–1 kg on the average, nearly one-tenth of the fiber's strength. This makes it necessary to reinforce the splice. The reinforcing parts shown in Fig. 4.33 have been studied.

Parts a and b in Fig. 4.33 need an adhesive to fix the spliced fibers in position, and this adhesive takes much time to harden. It is difficult to incorporate this reinforcing step in the automatic splicing machine.

The reinforcing tube in Fig. 4.33c, although slightly larger in size, requires no adhesive and can be incorporated in the automatic splicing process relatively easily. This method is widely in use in Japan and is described below.

The fiber splice is inserted in the ethylene vinyl acetate (EVA) tube and heated from outside. The EVA tube softens, and the shrinkage is about 2.5 mm. Figure 4.34 [27] shows the breakage strength and low-temperature property of the spliced fibers before and after this reinforcement is given.

4.4.4 The Other Splicing Methods

4.4.4.1 Glass Terminus Method [28]

The AT&T Bell Laboratories use this method for splicing SM fibers. They do not use discharge splicing for SM fibers because discharge heating deforms fiber cores, because fiber alignment becomes inaccurate if a matching oil is not used before splicing, and because the fiber position is deviated by the surface tension of the fused part. (These problems have been all but solved with the arc fusion splicing method.) The following method was developed by Bell Laboratories to eliminate such problems and is now in practical use.

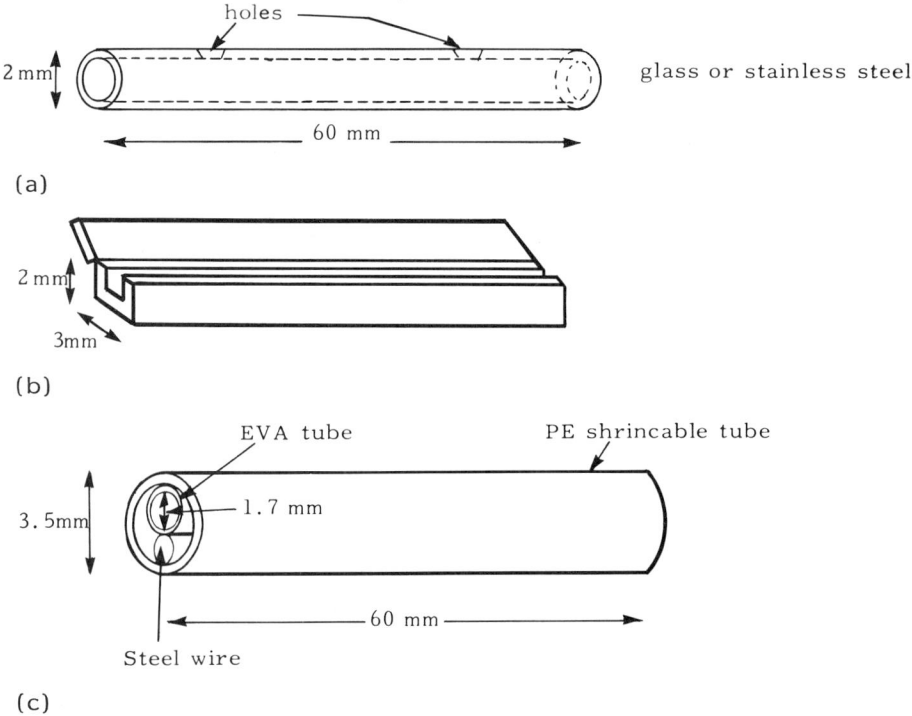

Figure 4.33 Reinforcement of fiber splice.

SM fibers to be spliced are inserted in a precision-made glass terminus and bonded together with an ultraviolet (UV)-curable adhesive. The fiber ends are polished, and the termini are fitted to the splice supports and pressed against each other by a spring in the compression assembly. A UV-curable cement, which serves as a matching oil, is applied to the tips of the fibers. The fibers are fitted end to end and so moved as to maximize the energy of light passing through the splice. The cement is cured with a flash polymerization lamp to form a fiber splice. The fibers are aligned automatically by the local launching and local detecting method.

The construction of the fiber splice is shown in Fig. 4.35 [28]. The SM splicing loss in the field is, for example, an average of 0.022 dB and a maximum of 0.186 dB. The variation of loss by temperature is at −40 to 77°C, with a loss change < ±0.02 dB.

4.4.4.2 Splicing on a V groove [29]

A V groove is cut accurately into an FRP sleeve (Fig. 4.36). Fibers are placed on the V groove, fitted end to end with an adhesive, and

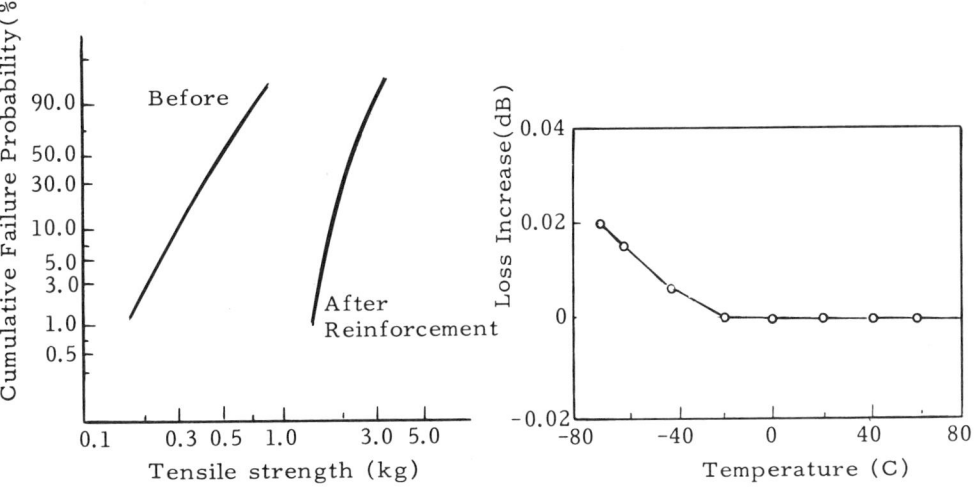

Figure 4.34 Characteristics of reinforced spliced fibers. (From Ref. 27.)

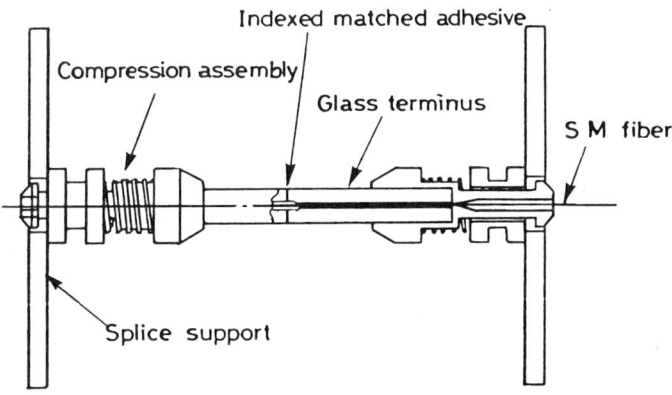

Figure 4.35 Glass terminus method. (From Ref. 28.)

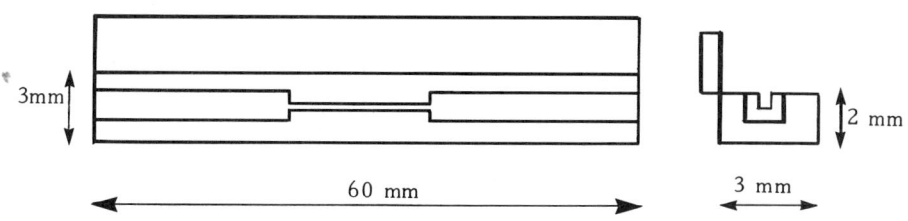

Figure 4.36 FRP V groove. (From Ref. 29.)

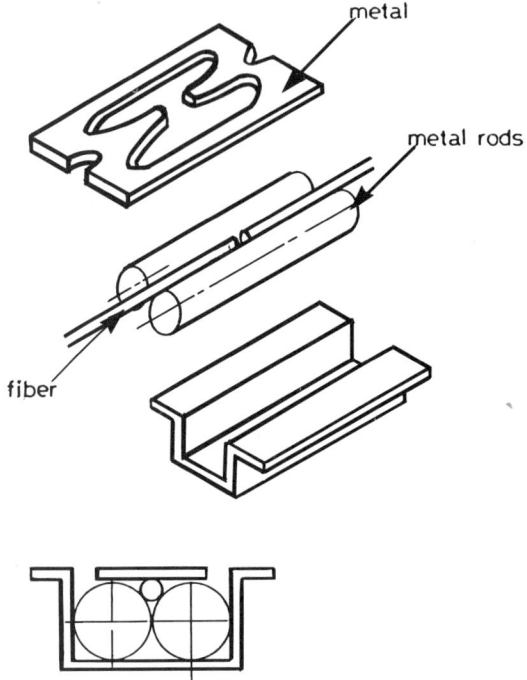

Figure 4.37 Splicing using round rod "Springroove." (From Ref. 30.)

held by a cover plate from above. This method is used in emergency fiber repair or simple laboratory splicing because, although producing a somewhat large splicing loss, it can be done easily by hand.

An example of splicing loss by this method is an average of about 0.07 dB and a maximum of 0.10 dB in the case of GI fibers (50 μm per 125 μm).

4.4.4.3 Splicing Using Round Rods [30, 31]

Round rods are used as a fiber splicing base. This method is in practical use in Italy. The groove is called the "Springroove" (Fig. 4.37) [30]. Fibers to be spliced are held between two cylinders, which are easy to make with high precision. The size of the cylinders is so determined as to make the upper part of the fibers held between them protrude a little above the upper edge of the sleeve. The cover serves as a spring and holds the two fibers in position. The fibers are fixed with an adhesive. The splicing loss of GI fibers spliced by this method is an average of 0.05 dB and a maximum of 0.14 dB.

Fusion Splicing Machines

4.5 EXAMPLES OF FUSION SPLICING MACHINES [31]

4.5.1 Fusion Splicing Machine for GI Fibers and SM Fibers with Small Eccentricity

Figure 4.38 [31] shows the small fusion splicing machine for GI fibers and SM fibers with small eccentricity.

I. Features: Suitable for field splicing, the smallest in the world, light, battery operated, heater for reinforcement built in
   A. Applicable fiber
      1. Silica fiber, 125 m outer diameter
      2. Plastic coating diameter 0.25-0.9 mm GI
      3. SM eccentricity < 1%
   B. Splicing loss (example)
      1. GI: average 0.03 dB, maximum 0.09 dB
      2. SM (eccentricity <1%) average 0.1 dB, maximum 0.3 dB
   C. Splicing time, 2 min
II. Machine
   A. Dimensions, 120 mm high × 96 mm wide × 117 mm diameter
   B. Weight, 1.5 kg
   C. Heater built in (for reinforcement of spliced fibers)
   D. Battery and charger attached: 12 V, 5 A (50 splices per charge)
III. Reliability tests
   A. Temperature test: splice loss of the fiber after 1 hr in an atmosphere of -10 and $+40°C$: $-10°C$, $\overline{X} = 0.02$ dB; $40°C$, $\overline{X} = 0.03$ dB (n = 20)
   Vibration test: splice loss of the fiber after 20 min of vibrations in each of the X, Y, and Z directions with a frequency of 23 Hz and an amplitude of ± 1 mm: $\overline{X}$ = splicing loss average, for example, $\overline{X} = 0.05$ dB (n = 50)

4.5.2 Fusion Splicing Machine for SM and GI Fibers with an LID (Local Injection, Local Detection) System [31]

Figure 4.39 [31] shows the splicing machine with full automatic alignment of SM fiber cores by the local injection local detection system.

I. Features
   A. Splicing by the LID system needs only one operator.
   B. The built-in microcomputer enables automatic core alignment. The splicing time of single-mode fibers is about 3 min.
   C. Flowcharts of each working step are displayed on the liquid crystal display.
   D. Splicing loss is displayed automatically on the liquid crystal display immediately after finishing the splice. (A wet fusion process is applied.)

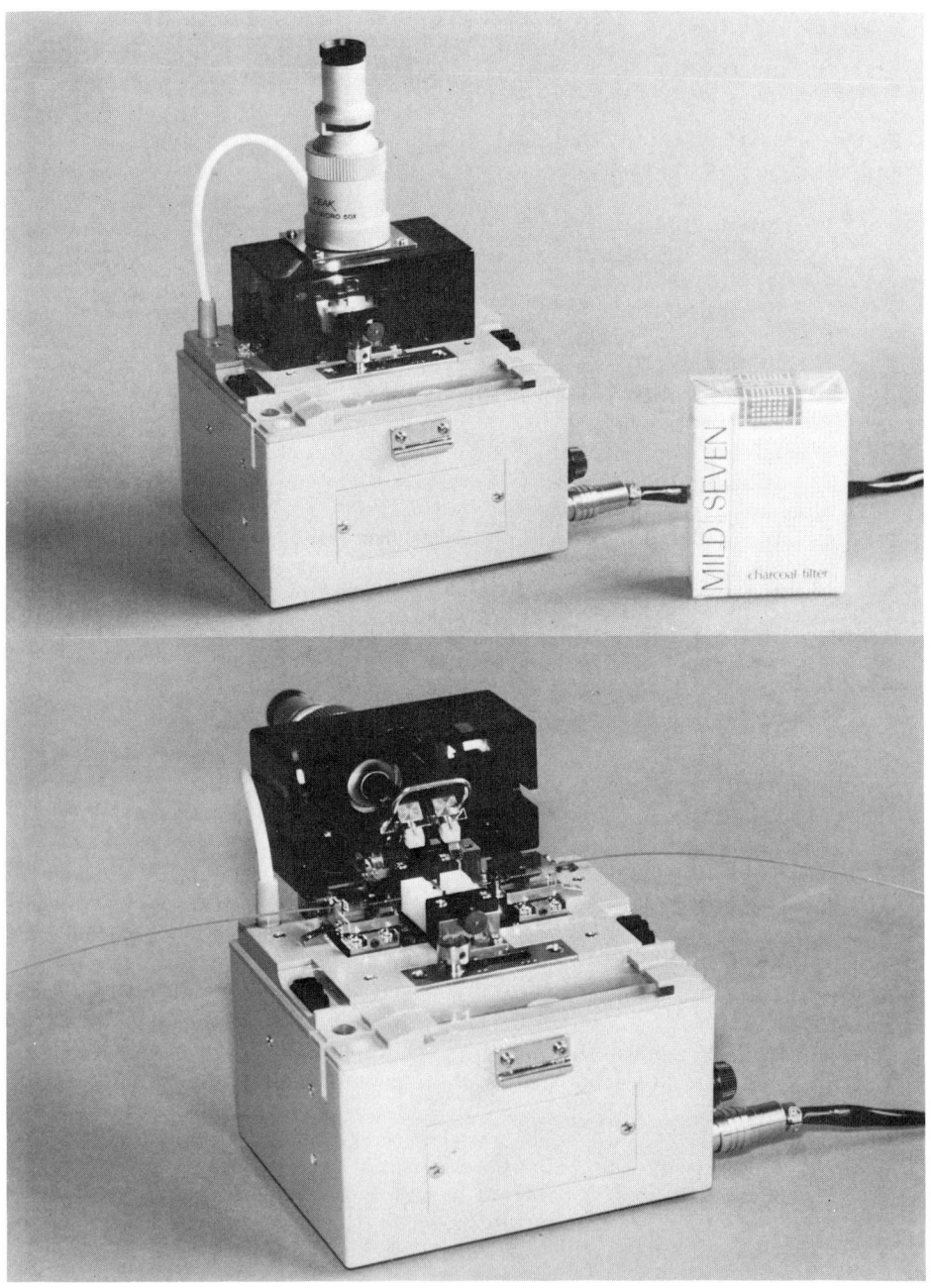

Figure 4.38 Fusion splicing machine (S-145 Microsplicer) for GI fibers and SM fibers with small eccentricity. (From Ref. 31.)

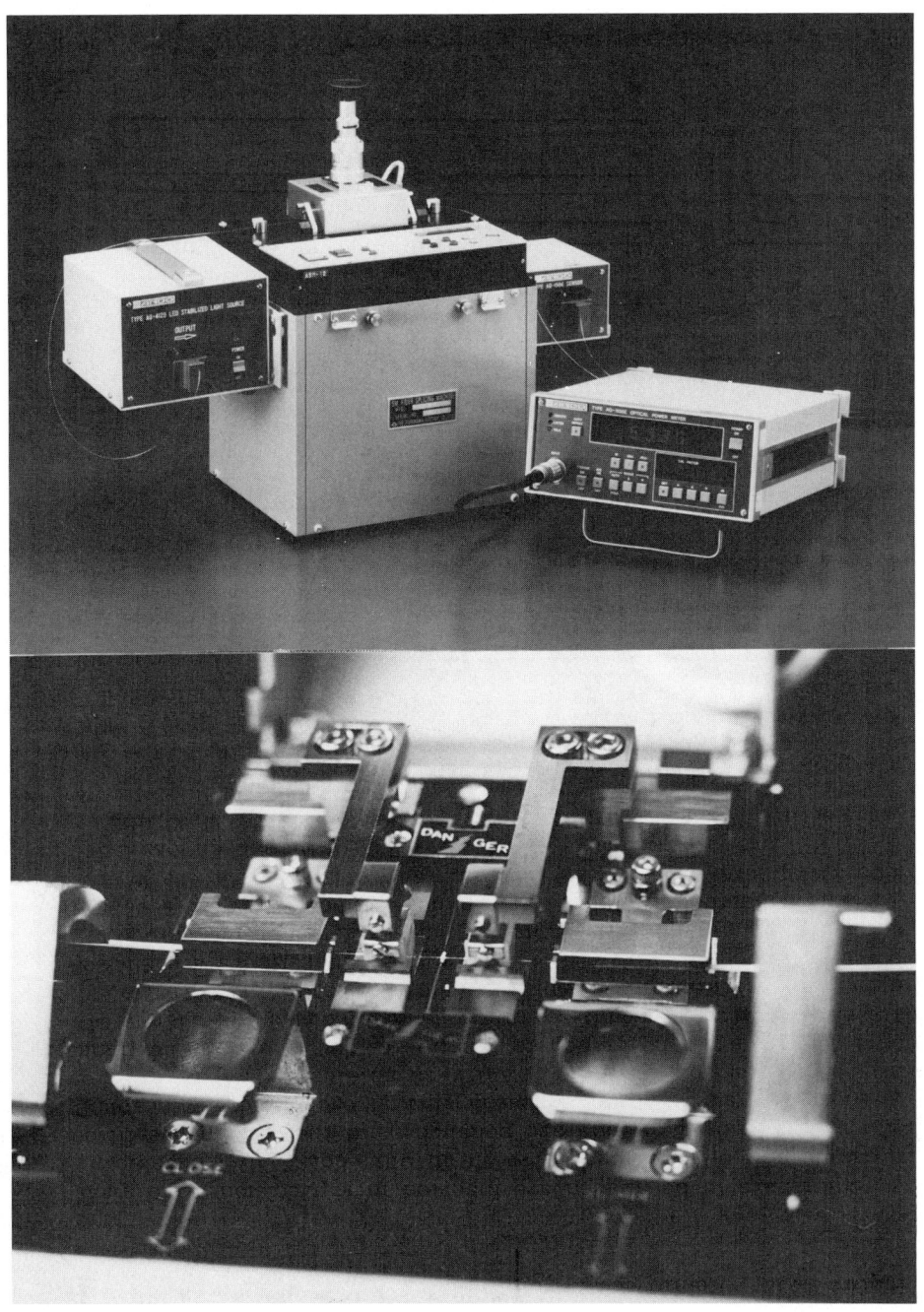

Figure 4.39 SM fiber splicing machine with automatic alignment system by LID. (From Ref. 31.)

E. The machine can be used for the splicing of GI fibers.
II. Splicing machine
   A. Power source: 100-240 V AC, 50/60 Hz
   B. Fusion splicer (including fiber alignment mechanism and microcomputer), <100 VA
   C. Light source for local injection, <5 VA
   D. Power meter, <20 VA
   E. Physical dimensions

	Size height × width × diameter (mm)	Weight (kg)
Fusion machine	285 × 240 × 210	10.0
Light source	155 × 160 × 165	2.5
Detector	60 × 70 × 65	0.3
Power meter	100 × 280 × 200	3.5

   F. Applicable fibers
      1. SM, 8-10 µm per 125 µm: coating diameter, 250 µm (for clear coating material)
      2. GI, 50 µm per 125 µm: coating diameter, 250 µm
III. Splicing loss
   A. SM: 0.03 dB average, 0.18 dB maximum
   B. GI: 0.02 dB average, 0.06 dB maximum
IV. Splicing time, 3 min per fiber

4.5.3 Fusion Splicing Machine by Direct Core Monitoring [31]

Figure 4.40 [31] shows the fusion splicing machine by direct core monitoring for SM fibers.

   I. Features: By predischarging, dusts and plastic residuals on the surface of fiber ends were burned and removed. Consequently, the splicing of fiber was carried out with high accuracy. Fibers (SM and GI) are spliced with fully automatic alignment.
   II. Machine:
      A. Size (mm)
         1. Main machine, 250 wide × 220 diameter × 320 high, 14 kg
         2. Controller unit, 390 wide × 320 diameter × 240 high, 16 kg
      B. AC, 100-220 V

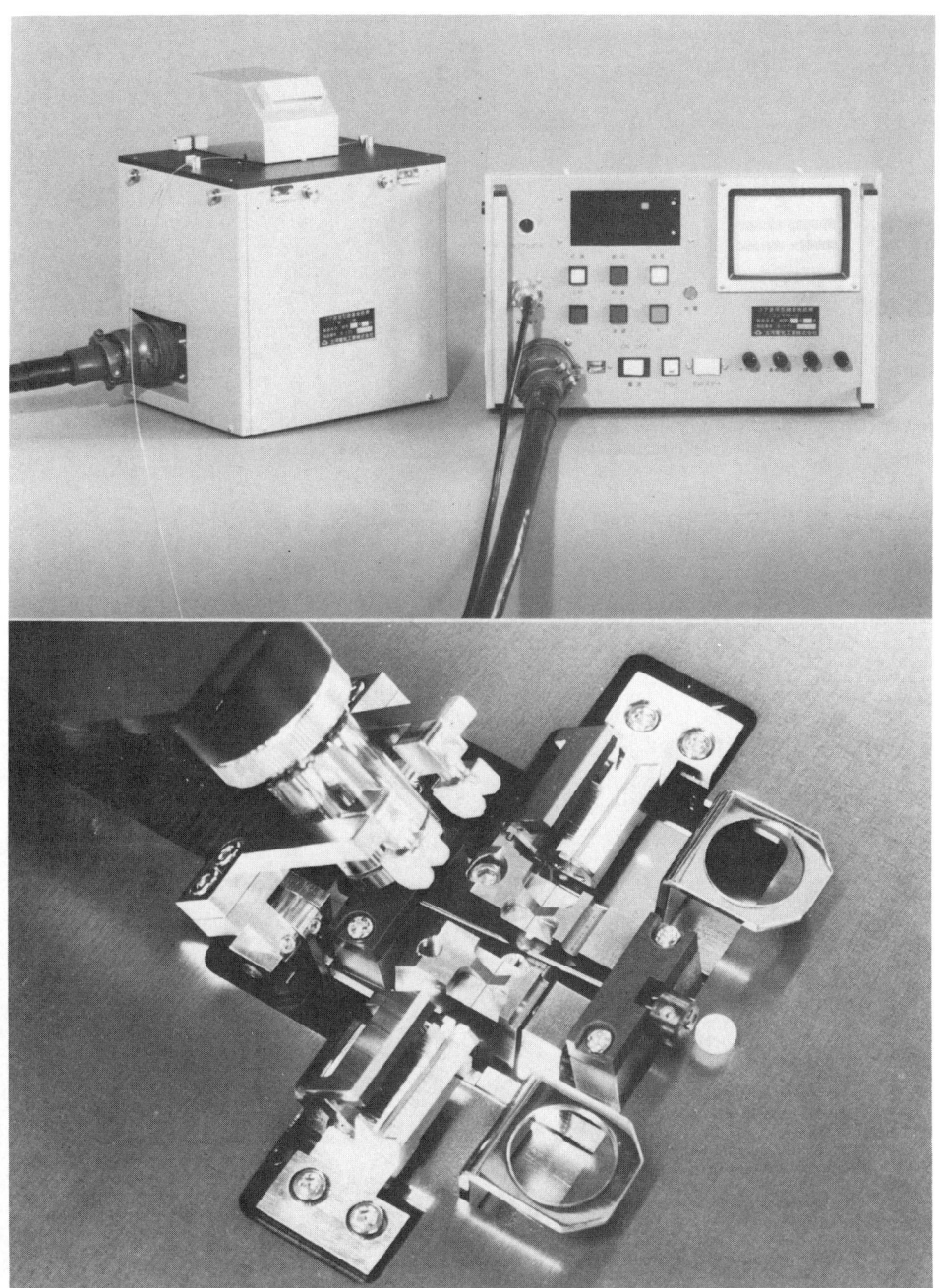

Figure 4.40 Mass fusion splicing machine for five-fiber core monitoring. (From Ref. 31.)

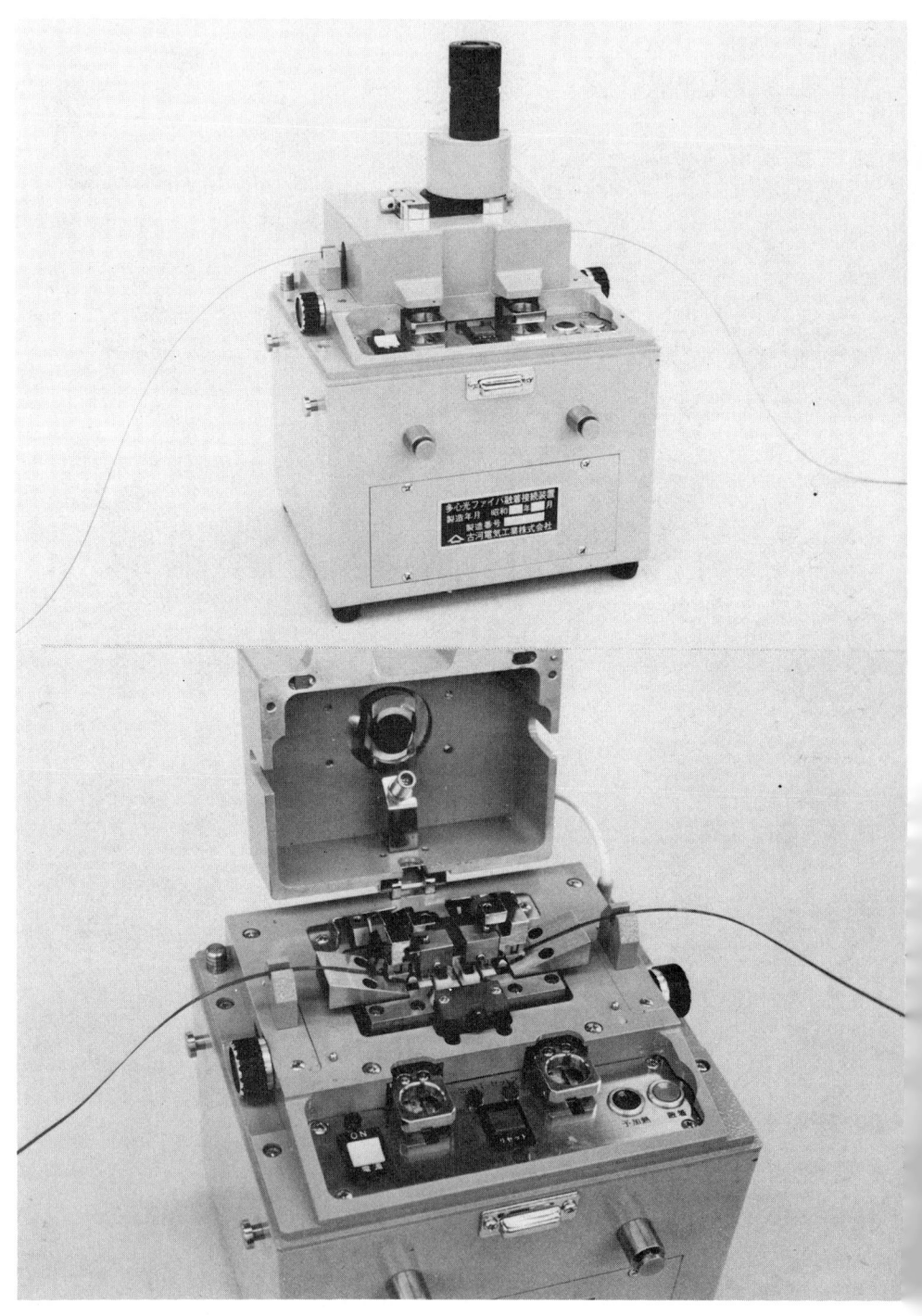

Figure 4.41 Mass fusion splicing machine for five-fiber ribbon. (From Ref. 31.)

Figure 4.41 (Continued)

III. Splicing loss
   A. SM: 0.07 dB average, 0.18 dB maximum
   B. GI: 0.03 dB average, 0.08 dB maximum

4.5.4 Mass Fusion Splicing Machine [31]

Figure 4.41 shows the mass fusion splicing machine for a five-fiber ribbon.

I. Features: The five fibers are spliced with a one-time discharge. An average of 5 min is required for the splicing of five fibers (from the start of cutting the fibers to the end of their fusion). This is far shorter than the time required for five single-fiber splicings (about 15 min for five single-fiber splicings).
II. Splicing loss
   A. GI: 0.04 dB average, 0.12 dB maximum
   B. SM (eccentricity 1%): 0.13 dB average, 0.4 dB maximum

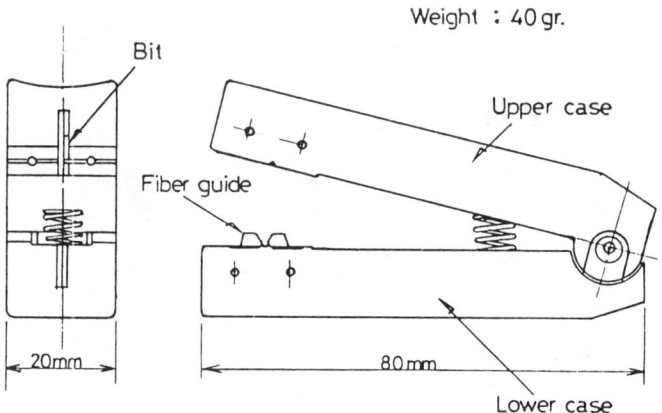

Figure 4.42   Plastic stripper.   (From Ref. 31.)

4.6   FIBER SPLICING ACCESSORIES

4.6.1   Plastic Stripper [31]

When plastic-covered fibers are spliced, their plastic coverings are removed with a stripper. The plastic stripping tool must satisfy the following requirements.

1. It must be small, light weight, and easy to handle.
2. It must contribute no flaws to the fiber.

The basic function of this stripper is to grip, cut off, and remove plastics. The knife blade has a semicircular recess to prevent the fiber from sustaining flaws (Figs. 4.42 and 4.43).

A method is also being studied in which plastics are dissolved by a chemical without the use of a tool. This chemical means keeps the fiber surface unharmed and therefore makes the fiber splice stronger than one made with the stripper. Full consideration must be given to the possibility of using the chemical at the place of work, work time, and temperature, and other factors.

4.6.2   Fiber Breaker

When a fiber is cut off for splicing, to keep the cutting length constant its section must be

1. Smooth as a mirror and free from lip, mist, and hackle
2. At right angles to the fiber axis

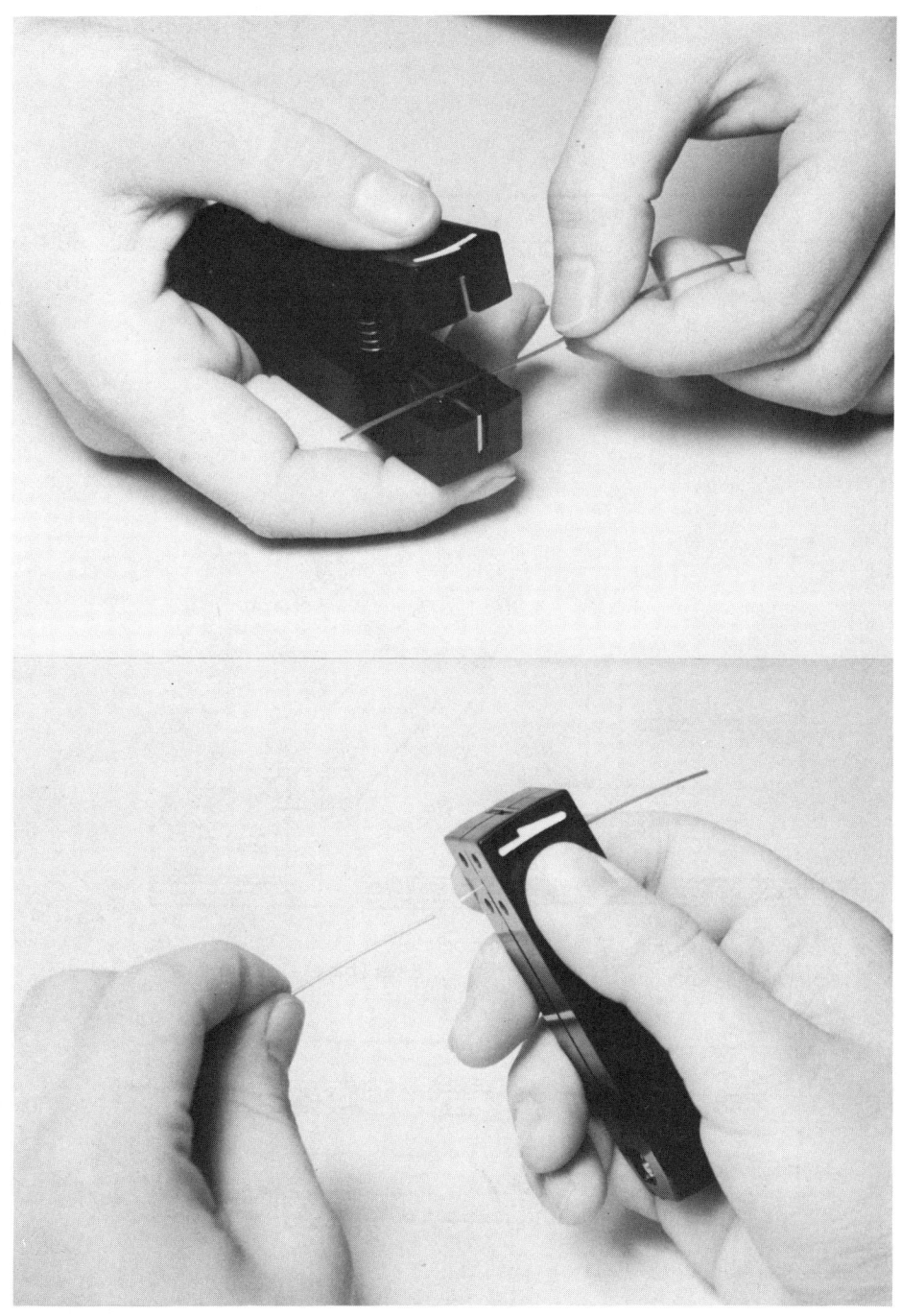

Figure 4.43 Plastic stripper. (From Ref. 31.)

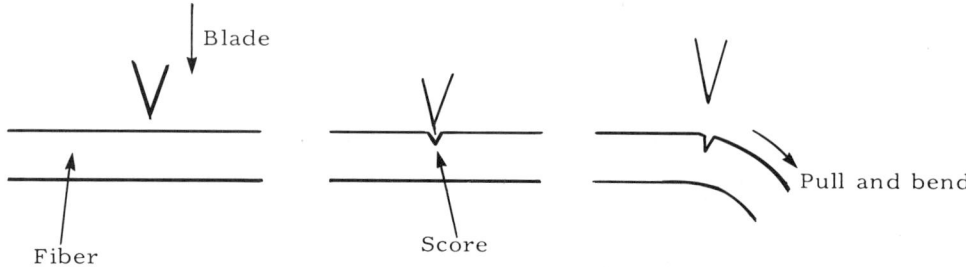

Figure 4.44 Fiber breaking.

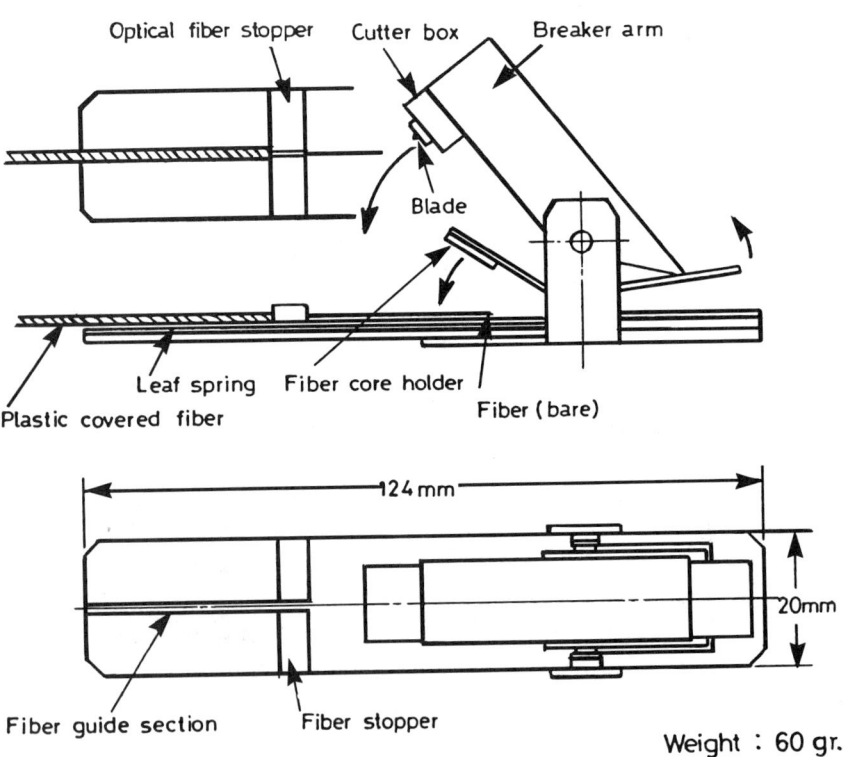

Figure 4.45 Fiber breaker. (From Ref. 31.)

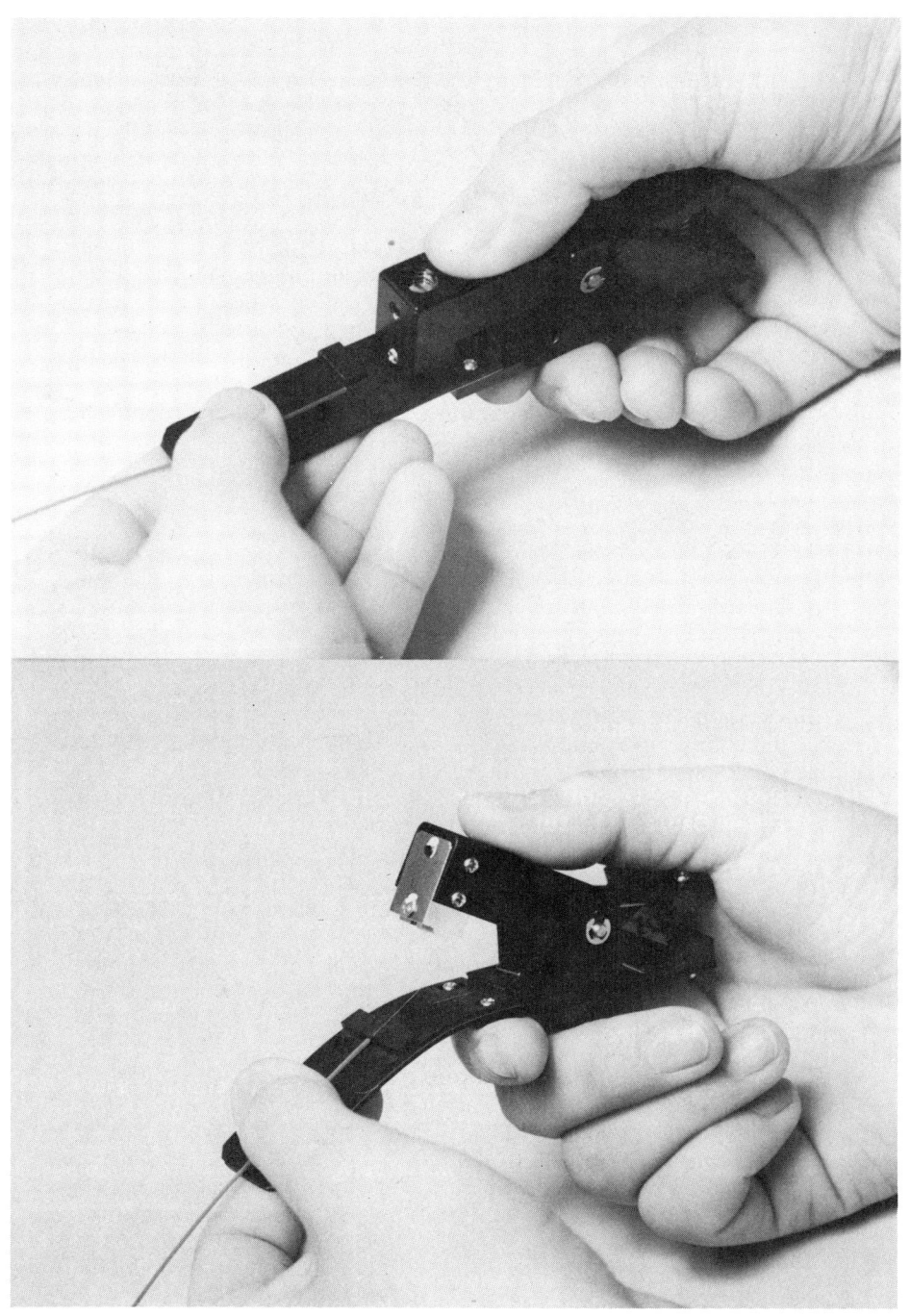

Figure 4.46   Fiber breaker. (From Ref. 31.)

The fiber is cut off basically in the same way as is sheet glass, as follows:

1. The fiber is scored on the surface.
2. It is then bent at the score under tension (Fig. 4.44).

Proper tension and bend cause the fiber to crack at right angles to its axis at a proper speed and make a mirror surface at the broken end.

An example of the construction of a fiber breaker is shown in Fig. 4.45. The breaker arm is brought down and pressed from above the fiber. The fiber is scored on the surface. The breaker arm is brought back to its original position. The fiber is bent along the leaf spring to break at the scored part (Fig. 4.46). An example of fiber breakage angle is 0.6° average and 2° maximum.

REFERENCES

1. H. Tsuchiya, H. Nakagome, and N. Shimizu, Loss of double eccentric connectors for optical fibers, Tech. Res. Rep., *IECE J.*, OQE 75-52: 81-90 (May 1975).
2. H. Yanai, Optical communication handbook, Asakura 440-445 (September 1982).
3. D. Marcuse, Loss analysis of single mode fiber splices, *BSTJ*, 56(5): 703-718 (May, June 1977).
4. D. Gloge, Off-set and tilt loss in optical fiber splices, *BSTJ*, 55(7): 905-916 (September 1976).
5. T. Arai, O. Watanabe, K. Inada, and Y. Katsuyama, 5ECOC, 6.2-1-6.2-4 (September 1979).
6. K. Inada, Cabling and splicing of single mode fiber, 23-3, 4 Joint Natl. Conv. IEE, *IECE J.*, 4-35-4-36 (October 1981).
7. M. Hirai, S. Seikai, N. Kashima, M. Shimoda, and N. Uchida, Arc-fusion splice and splice machine for multi-mode fibers—prefusion method, *ECL Tech. J.* ECL, NTT, 27(11): 2467-2479 (November 1978).
8. M. Hirai, S. Seikai, Y. Kamikura, and M. Ogai, Optical fiber splicing tools for field application, *Furukawa Elec. Rev.*, 68: 123-129 (March 1980).
9. I. Hatakeyama and H. Tsuchiya, Fusion splices for optical fibers, OQE 75-92, Res. Tech. Rep. *IECE J.*, 25-32 (December 1975).
10. I. Hatakeyama and H. Tsuchiya, Fusion splices for single-mode optical fiber, *ECL Tech. J.*, 28(6): 981-997 (June 1979).
11. Y. Kato, S. Seikai, and M. Tatoda, Arc fusion splicing of single-mode fibers, 1. Optimum splice conditions, *Appl. Opt.*, 21(7): 1232-1336 (April 1982).

12. N. Kashima and F. Nihei, Design and performance of a small sized optical fiber fusion splicing machine with very small power consumption, *ECL Tech. J.*, ECL, NTT, *31*(9): 1719–1730 (September 1982).
13. N. Kashima and F. Nihei, Optical fiber fusion splice using high frequency discharge with high voltage trigger, *Trans. IECE J.*, (E), *64*(8): 529–537 (August 1981).
14. Y. Kato, S. Seikai, N. Shibata, S. Tachigami, Y. Toda, and O. Watanabe, Arc-fusion splicing of single-mode fibers, 2. A practical splice machine, *Appl. Opt.*, *21*(11): 1916–1921 (June 1982).
15. H. Murata, Splicing method of fibers, Patent open laid, Tokukai 54–151455, Filing date, May 19, 1978.
16. T. Yamada, Y. Osato, M. Suzuki, and O. Watanabe, Single-mode fiber splicer by core axis observation, Natl Conv. *IECE J.*, *2202*: 9–171 (March 1984).
17. O. Kawata, K. Hoshino, and Y. Miyajima, Automated low-loss single-mode fiber splicing using core direct monitoring, Natl. Conv. *IECE J.*, *2200*: 9–170 (March 1984).
18. O. Kawata, Y. Miyajima, M. Ohnishi, and K. Hoshino, Single-mode splicing technique using core monitoring, Res. Tech. Rep., *IECE J.*, CS83–52 85–92 (June 1983).
19. M. Tachikura and F. Nihei, Fusion mass-splicing of optical fibers by high-frequency discharge, Res. Tech. Rep. *IECE J.*, CS92–15 pp. 41–48 (May 1982).
20. I. Sankawa, S. Nagasawa, H. Murata, and T. Yoshizawa, Multiple extrusion ribbon fiber mass-splice-technique in optical cables with very large number of fibers, Res. Tech. Rep. *IECE J.*, CS 81–152 31–38 (January 1982).
21. M. Tachikura and I. Sankawa, Fusion mass-splicing of optical fibers by discharge heating, Res. Tech. Rep. *IECE J.*, CS 80–189, pp. 73–78 (January 1981).
22. J. T. Krause and C. R. Kurkjian, Improved high strength flame fusion single-mode splices, IOOC '83 29A4–6 pp. 96–97 (June 1983).
23. M. Tokuda, Optical fiber splicing technology, NTT 2nd Int. Symp. pp. 124–141 (April 1984).
24. Y. Kato, T. Tanifuji, N. Kashima, and R. Arioka, Arc-fusion splicing of single-mode fibers. 3: A highly efficient splicing technique, *Appl. Opt.*, *23*(15): 2654–2659 (August 1984).
25. H. Murata, S. Inao, and Y. Matsuda, Connection of optical fiber cable, Top. Meet, O.F. Trans. WA5, pp. WA5–1–4 (Januray, 1975).
26. M. Hirai, S. Seikai, N. Kashima, and N. Uchida, Arc-fusion splice and splice machine for multi-mode fibers—pre-fusion method, *ECL Tech. J.*, ECL, NTT, *27*(11): 2467–2479 (November 1978).

27. M. Miyauchi, M. Matsumoto, and T. Haibara, Arc-fusion splice of optical fiber at its reliability in field, 31st IWCS pp. 169–176 (November 1982).
28. M. P. Reynolds and P. F. Gagen, Field splicing of single-mode lightguide cable, ICC '84, 34.7, pp. 1071–1074 (May 1984).
29. K. Mochida, K. Inada, and K. Watanabe, Splicing of SM fibers by V-groove connector, Natl. Conv. 905, *IECE J.*, pp. 4–209 (March 1977).
30. CSELT, Optical fiber communication, CSELT, pp. 558–559 (1980).
31. Furukawa Catalogues (1985).

5
Connectors

A connector to be fitted to the ends of optical fibers must meet the following requirments.

1. It permits two fibers to be connected and disconnected easily.
2. It minimizes connection loss and keeps it stable.
3. It can be attached easily to fiber ends, if possible, at the site of fiber cable installation.
4. It is available at a low cost.

Requirement 3 is met by a simple connector.
 As described previously, when fibers are connected to each other, a splice loss is caused by offset and tilt. Especially in the case of single-mode (SM) fiber, a slight offset (about 1 m) or tilt (1°) causes a splice loss of 0.1 dB or more. The value of splice loss of SM fibers and graded index (GI) fibers are shown in Fig. 5.1. The Fresnel reflection loss (0.32 dB) between the fiber end and the air layer is excluded.
 It is important to reduce the connecting loss of the connector, as is evident from the above figure, to minimize the offset and tilt between the fibers to be spliced, polish their end surfaces in parallel with each other, and bring them to a tight end-to-end contact with each other (no air layer between the end surfaces of fibers). A more detailed treatment of connectors may be found in Calvin Miller's *Optical Fiber Splices and Connectors* (Marcel Dekker, 1986).

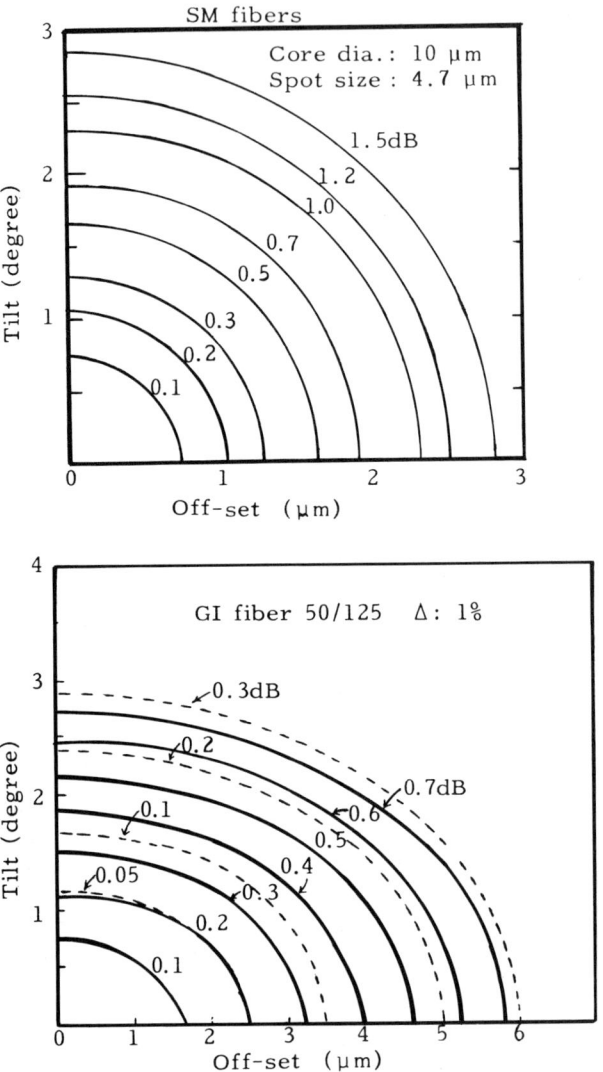

Figure 5.1 Splicing loss: uniform distribution (solid line); stationary distribution (dashed line). (From Ref. 1.)

Precision Ferrule Connectors

5.1 SINGLE-FIBER CONNECTORS

Connectors of various designs have been proposed in many countries; those shown in Table 5.1 are now in practical or experimental use.

5.2 PRECISION FERRULE CONNECTORS [2]

Plugs and an adapter are used for the connector (Figs. 5.2 and 5.3). As shown in the following figure, the adapter is composed of a housing and, provided within it, a split sleeve. The outside diameter of the split sleeve is very slightly smaller than the inside diameter of the housing. The sleeve is therefore provided somewhat loosely in the housing. It is made of phosphor bronze and the housing is made of stainless steel.

As shown in Fig. 5.4, the ferrule is a ceramic cylinder with a hole in the center that is a little larger than the fiber diameter set in the center of a stainless steel housing. This ceramic cylinder made possible more accuracy and stability than the metallic ferrule.

The fiber is inserted in the center hole of the ceramic ferrule and fixed in position with an adhesive, and the ferrule is inserted and fixed in the stainless steel housing. Then the end surface of the fiber is polished. The ferrule in the stainless steel housing is inserted in the split sleeve as if to expand it, and two ferrules so inserted hold each other elastically.

The connecting loss characteristics of the connector are as follows [1].

GI fiber (50 μm per 125 μm, Δ = 1%: fitted at the factory, 0.1 dB average, 0.4 dB maximum; at the site, 0.2 dB average, 0.7 dB maximum; no matching oil used.

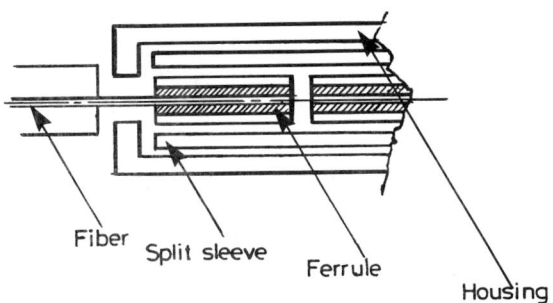

Figure 5.2   Precision ferrule connector.

Table 5.1 Single-fiber Connector

Connector	Rough Construction	Applicable fiber	Connecting loss	Fiber setting	Remarks
Precision ferrule type	(High precision ferrule, Fiber)	GI SM	0.1 dB 0.3 dB	at site	A precision-made ferrule is used in the center of plug, and fibers are inserted in the center hole and bonded.
Lens type	(Lens, Fiber)	GI	0.8 dB	at factory	A ball lens is applied to the end surface of the fiber. The allowance of the off-set of fiber is increased.
Biconic type	(Molded plastic cone, Fiber)	GI SM	0.2 dB 0.3 dB	at site	The fiber is inserted in the center of a core-shaped molded plug, bonded, and inserted in a biconical sleeve.

Single-Fiber 379

Ball type	(figure: Fiber, Ball)	GI	0.7 dB	at site	Ceramic balls are put in a mold, and fibers are inserted in their center, made firm with plastics, and used as a ferrule.
Plastic type	(figure: Plastic ferrule, Fiber)	GI SM	0.1 dB 0.3 dB	at site	Fiber is transfer-molded with high precision for ferrule.

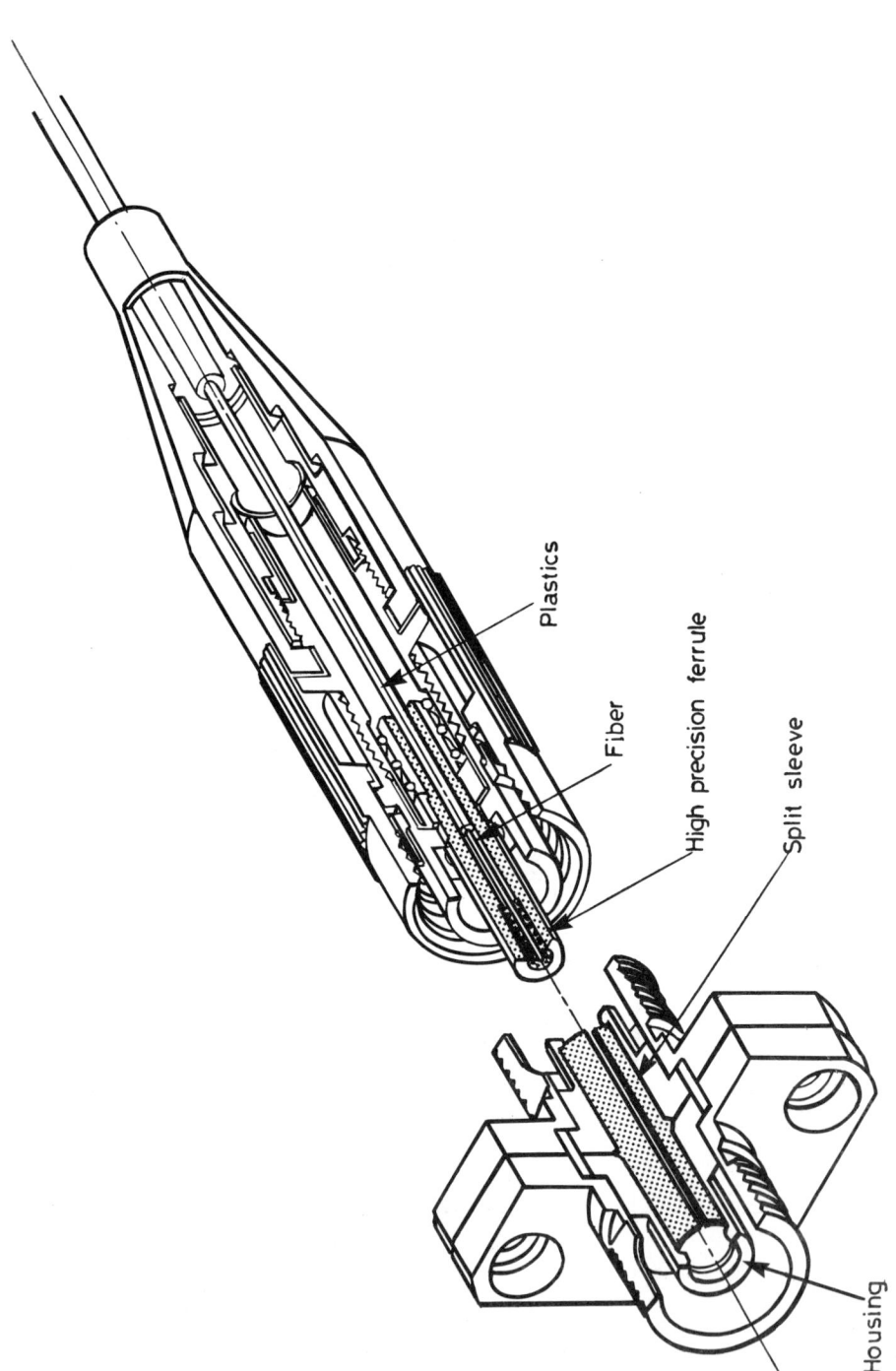

Figure 5.3 Precision ferrule connector. (From Ref. 2.)

Precision Ferrule

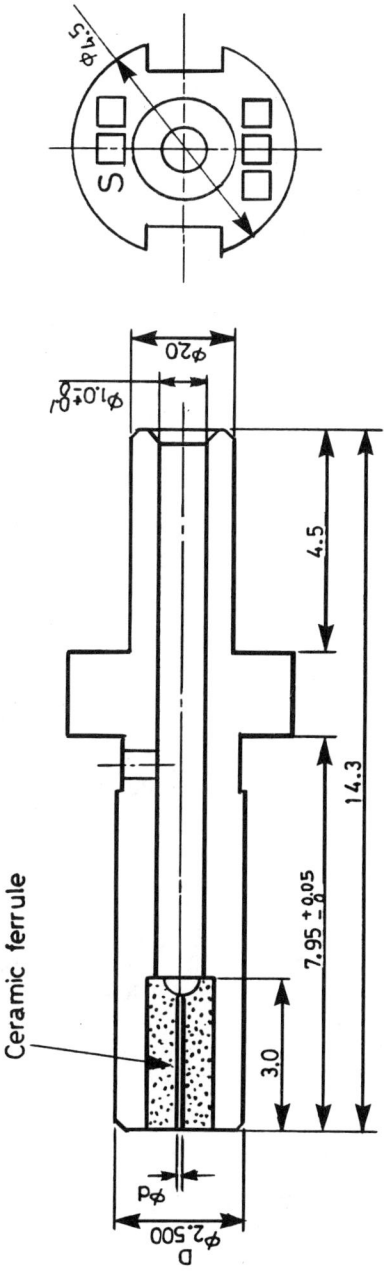

Figure 5.4 Ferrule (units are millimeters). (From Ref. 2.)

Table 5.2 Environmental Test Result

Test items	Test condition	Connecting loss change (dB)
Heat cycles	−25 to +80°C 8 hr/cycle × 10 cycles	0.08
High temperature	80°C	0.03
Low temperature	−20°C	0.03
Vibration	55 cycles/sec ±1.5 mm 4 hr two directions	0.02
Shock	100 g, 10 cycles, two directions	0.02
Durability	1000 cycles	0.08
Twist	±180°	0.05
Tension	10 kg	0.1

Source: From Ref. 2.

SM fiber (9 μm per 125 μm, Δ = 0.3%): 0.3 dB average, 0.9 dB maximum; no matching oil used

Environmental test results are shown in Table 5.2 [2].

5.3 LENS CONNECTOR

When a lens is applied between two fibers to be spliced, the optical energy transmitted can be expanded (Fig. 5.5), which, in turn, makes it possible to enlarge the allowable offset. In ordinary connection, fibers are brought in close contact with each other end to end. If this is repeated, the end portions of the fibers are damaged or coated with dust, causing an increase in connection loss. The lens reduces

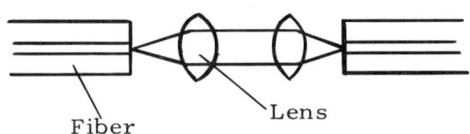

Figure 5.5 Connection by lens.

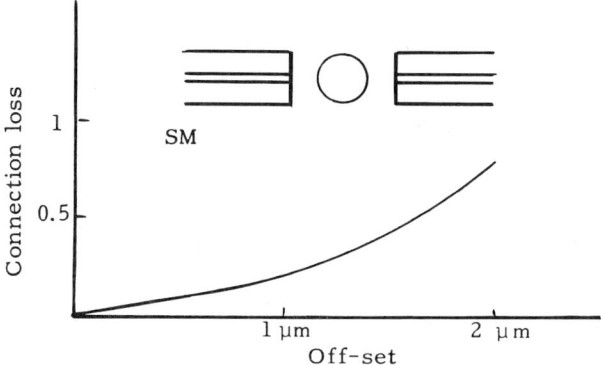

Figure 5.6 Connection by a ball lens (Fresnel reflection excluded).

the problem of such fiber end damage and contamination. The use of the lens, however, makes the construction of the connector that much more complicated and its on-site assemblage difficult. At any time the loss of the Fresnel reflection of 0.32 dB exists at the connection point of a lens connector.

As mentioned above, this connector can take a larger offset than those of other types but causes a connection loss by tilt.

Figure 5.6 shows an example of the relationship between the offset and the connection loss of SM fibers connected by the use of a ball lens.

5.4 BICONIC CONNECTOR [3, 4]

A well-known connector of this type is that developed by Bell Laboratories. It is extensively in use in the AT&T FT-3 system (for GI fibers) and SM fiber systems.

As shown in Fig. 5.7, this connector consists of two transfer-molded plugs and a biconic plastic sleeve. The plugs are aligned on the sleeve. The fiber is molded with plastic. In molding, molten plastic is made to flow in the axial direction of the fiber to eliminate macro- and microbend loss increase and to form isotropic alignment of the fiber with the plug.

The ferrule must be made in a highly precise absolute diameter. On the other hand, the absolute diameter of the biconic connector need not be so precise. All that is necessary is to align fibers concentrically in the center of the tapered plug. The length of this tapered plug is strictly controlled with a special gauge. Needless to say, the fiber end is polished.

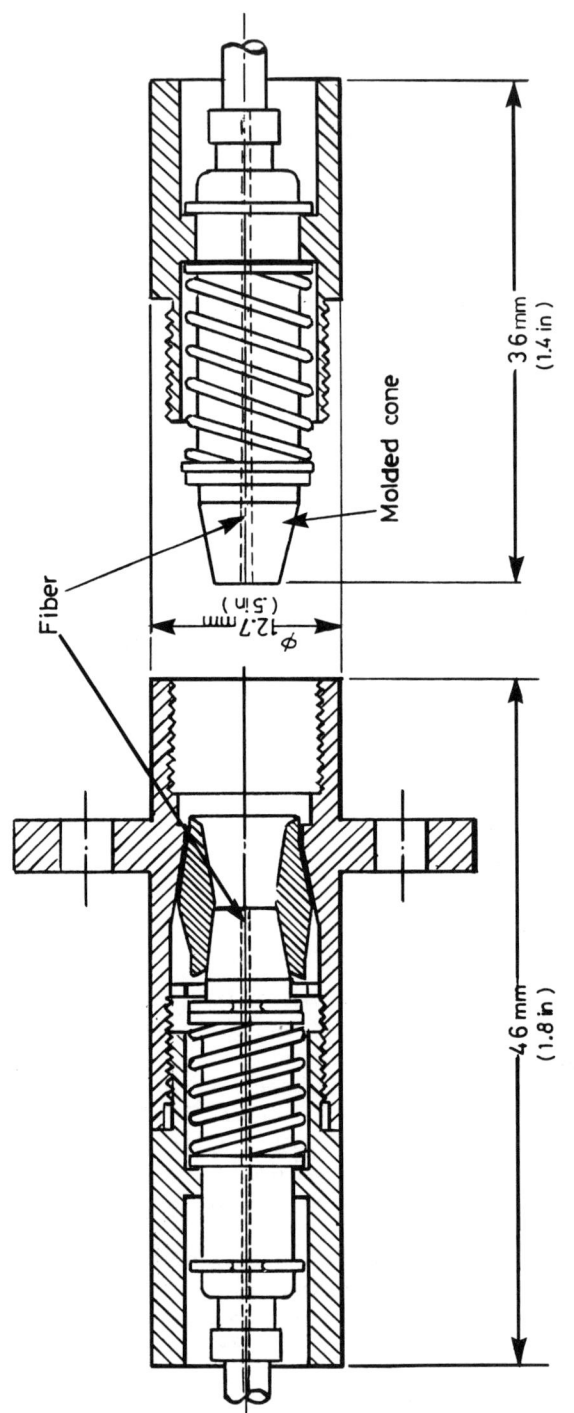

Figure 5.7 Biconic connector. (From Refs. 4 and 5.)

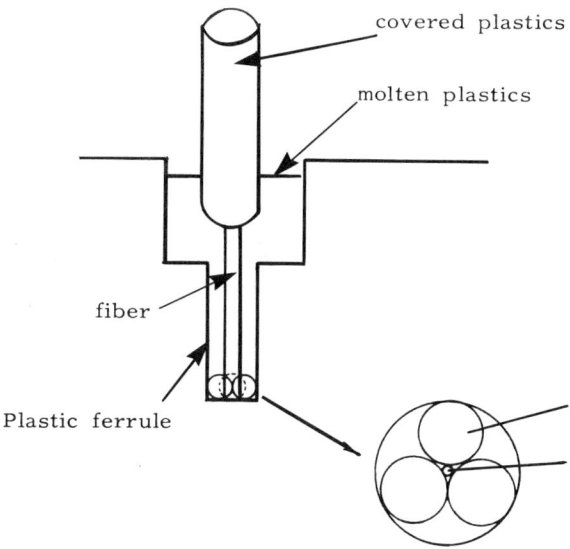

Figure 5.8 Ball connector.

This connector was first developed and used for GI fibers. It is now used also for SM fibers by reducing the eccentricity of the tapered cone and fiber core eccentricity (0.33 μm or less) and the tilt angle of fibers (0.35 degrees or less). The connecting loss averages 0.28 dB and is a maximum of 0.65 dB for GI fibers, 50 μm per 125 μm, NA 0.23, and an average of 0.28 dB and a maximum of 0.7 dB for SM fibers.

5.5 BALL CONNECTOR

Precision-made ceramic or metal balls are placed in a mold and fibers are placed between the balls. Then an adhesive or plastic is poured in the mold. A connector plug so formed is taken out of the mold (Fig. 5.8).

This connector features easy fiber fitting on the field. The ball ferrule is, of course, used in metal connectors. The ferrule is made of plastic, and the recent trend is toward all-plastic connectors. Now an all-plastic connector equal in all outer dimensions to the ferrule connector shown in Fig. 5.2 is made and used. The connecting loss of GI fibers by this ball plastic connector is an average of 0.7 dB and a maximum of 1.5 dB.

5.6 MULTIFIBER CONNECTOR

Fiber-by-fiber splicing inevitably takes a long time in joining multifiber cables. A multifiber connector is therefore required to reduce the splicing time. Compared with the single-fiber connector, it must be made with extremely high precision.

Basically, the multifiber connector is composed of a plug in which multiple fibers are fitted and an adapter in which the plug is inserted. It is important that the cores of the fibers are fitted with a high degree of accuracy in the specified position in the plug.

The multifiber connector is the ultimate connector. Because of difficulties in its design and production, however, it is available only in the following three main types:

1. V-groove connector: used mainly for round V-groove fiber cable; round type and flat type; connecting loss: 0.3 dB (GI fiber) with matching oil
2. Silicon V-groove flat connector: metal silicon given precision V grooves by etching; fibers laid in parallel in the groove and inserted in the adapter; used widely for ribbon cable; connecting loss: 0.2 dB (GI fiber), 0.4 dB (SM fiber) with matching oil
3. Plastic multifiber connector: can be fitted at the site; easy to use for subscriber cable, fiber cable for Local Area Networks (LAN), and other systems; connecting loss: 0.3 dB (GI fiber) with matching oil

5.7 V-GROOVE ROUND CONNECTOR [6]

The following is an example of connecting a V-groove round cable. A rod or plate with V grooves (Fig. 5.9) is cut through in the middle. Fibers to be connected are inserted in the grooves of the right and left pieces of the rod and bonded together. The ends of the fibers protrude a little from the ends of the rod or plate. The protruding end portions of the rod or plate are sawn off. The cut surfaces of the fibers are connected to each other by a guide.

A rough connecting structure is shown in Figs. 5.10 and 5.11. Connecting loss averages 0.3 dB (GI fiber). Connecting time is 1 hr per 10 fibers.

The end surface of the stack is finished by polishing. The stack is inserted in the guide for connection. A matching oil is used.

The dimensional deviation of the silicon chip is no more than an average of 2.5 μm from the specified values. Splicing loss averages 0.2 dB with a maximum of 0.4 dB for GI fibers and averages 0.4 dB or less for SM fibers.

In summary, this silicon connector

V-Groove Round Connector

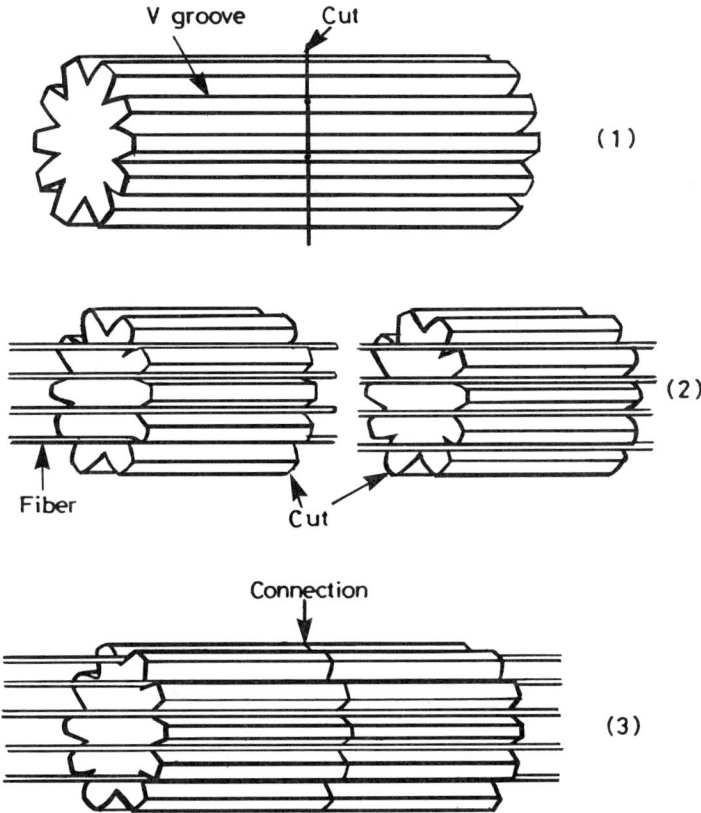

Figure 5.9 V-groove connection. (From Ref. 5.)

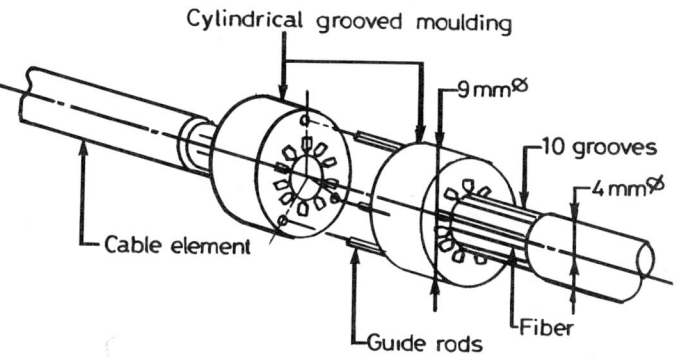

Figure 5.10 Round V-groove connection. (From Ref. 5.)

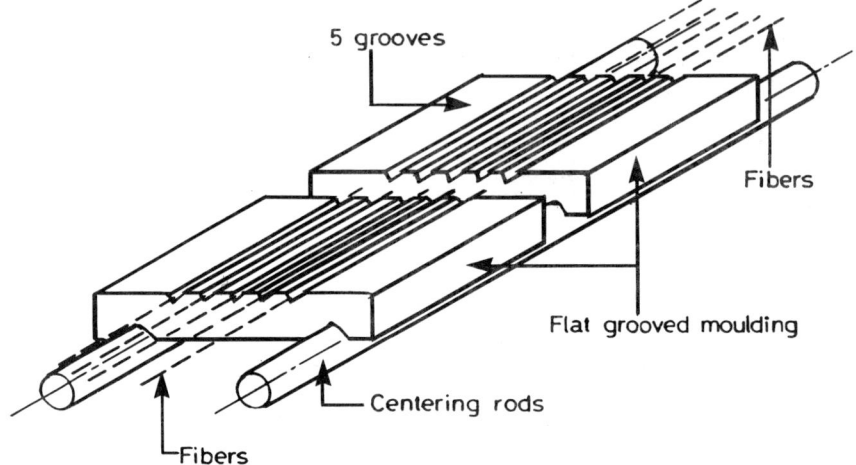

Figure 5.11 Flat V-groove connection. (From Ref. 5.)

1. Is small and light and permits easy connection of fiber ribbons (144 fibers, 12 fibers × 12 ribbons, can be spliced in about 10 min)
2. Is fitted at the factory (fitting at the site is somewhat difficult)
3. Normally uses a matching oil for fiber connection

As mentioned above, the silicon connector was developed at first for the connection of GI fiber ribbon cables. SM fiber cables are now increasingly in demand. The first SM fiber cable of AT&T Technologies was of the stranded unit type. The fibers of this cable were spliced one by one. Recently, an SM fiber ribbon cable has been developed and put in use. It is identical in construction to the GI fiber ribbon cable. Therefore, the silicon chip connector has come to be used for the connection of the SM fiber ribbon [6]. This is made possible by the fact that the eccentricity and diametric deviation of the SM fiber core have been reduced.

5.8 FIBER RIBBON CONNECTOR [7–9]

For the splicing of the fiber ribbon, an etched silicon chip was developed [7–9]. As shown in Fig. 5.12, the silicon chip is etched by the photolithographic method to make V grooves [8]. Fibers are held in the grooves and bonded. The silicon chips are stacked and bonded to one another to form a block (Fig. 5.13) [7–9].

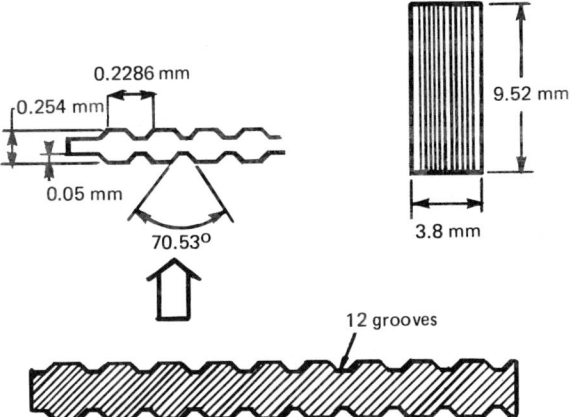

Figure 5.12 Cross section of a typical alignment chip with dimensions. (From Ref. 9.)

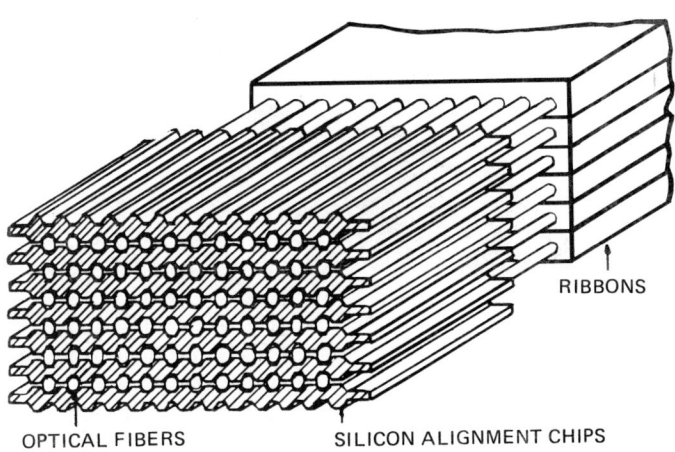

Figure 5.13 Schematic diagram of a multifiber silicon chip. (From Refs. 7–9.)

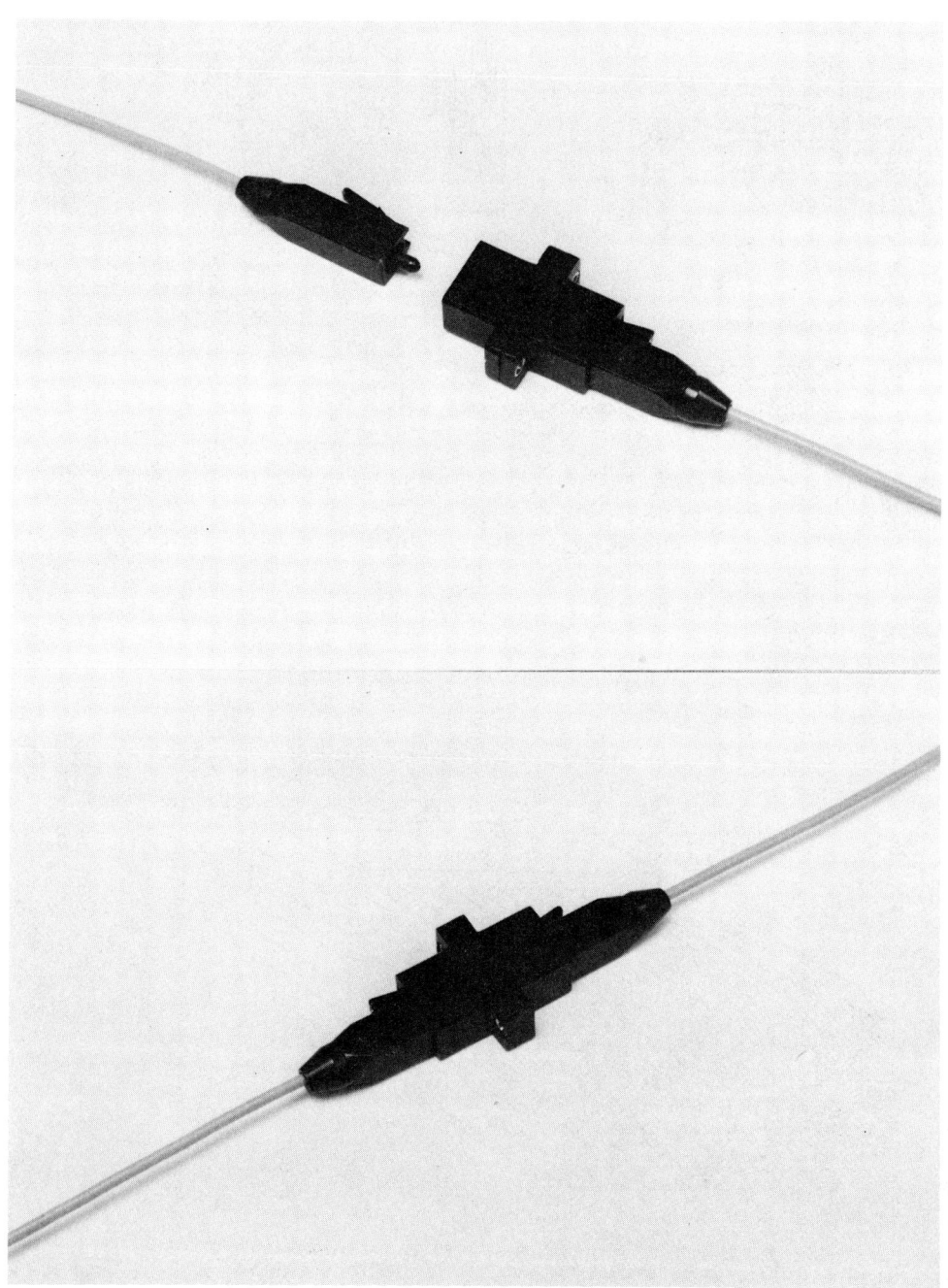

Figure 5.14 Plastic connector (single fiber).

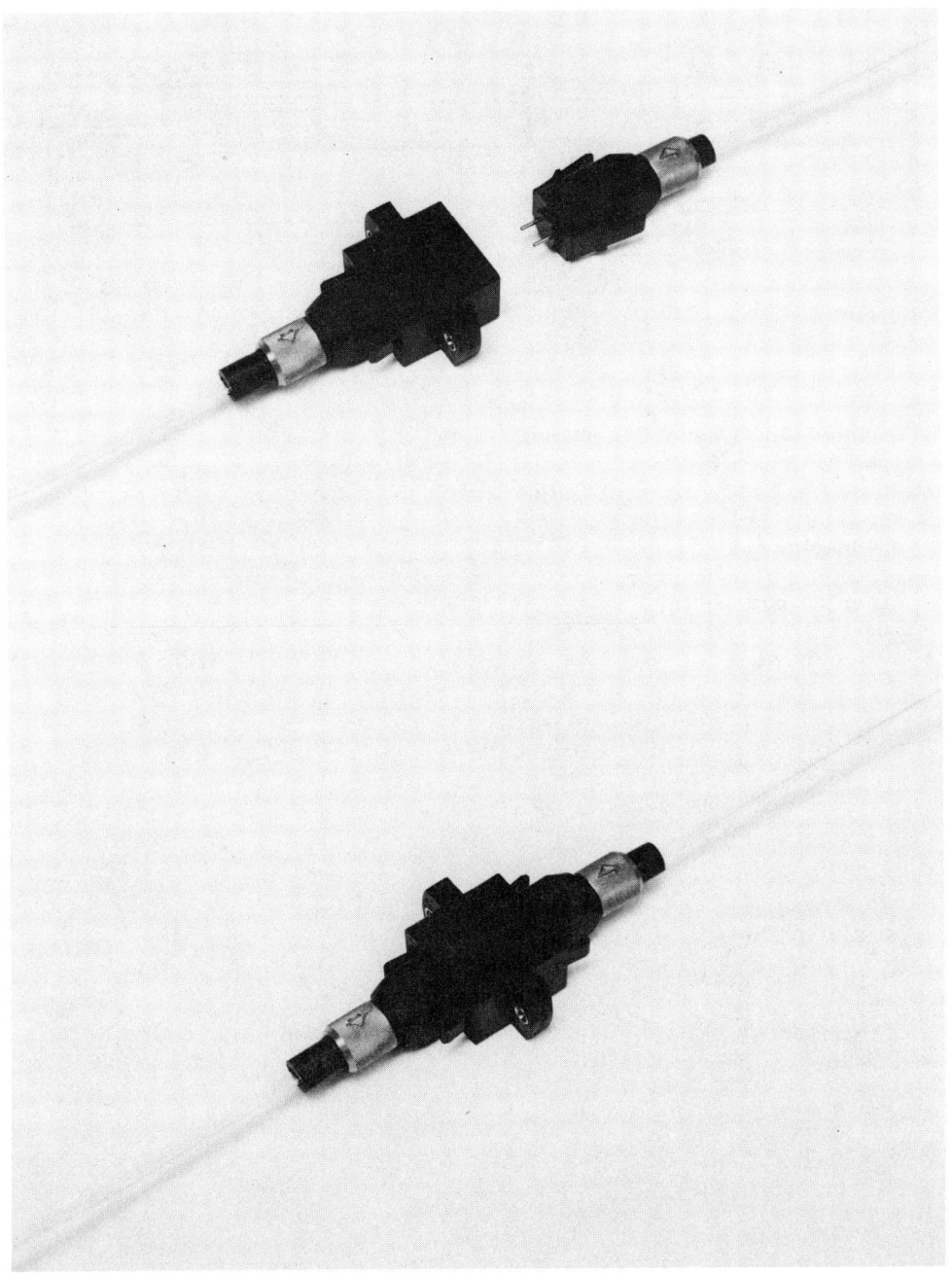

Figure 5.15　Plastic connector (five fibers).

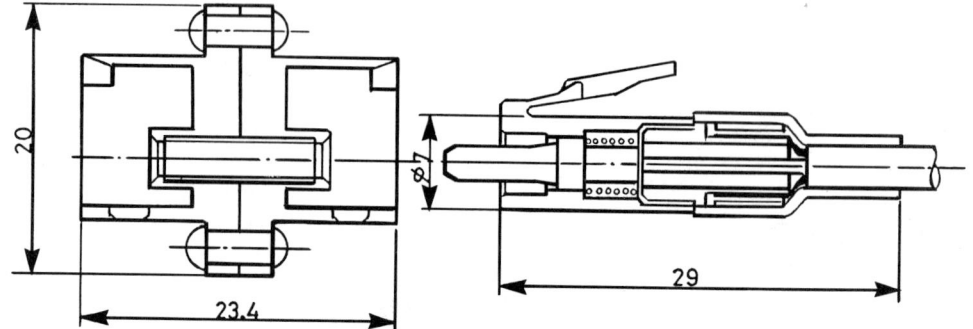

Figure 5.16 Push-on connector (single fiber). (From Refs. 10 and 11.)

Table 5.3 Plastic Connectors

Connector	Single fiber		Multi-fiber (5 fibers)	
	GI	SM	GI	SM
Average connecting loss (dB)	0.1	0.3	0.2	0.5
Matching oil	No	No	With	With
Connection loss change (dB)				
Heat cycle −30 to +70°C, 100 cycles	<0.2	<0.2	<0.2	<0.2
Low temperature, −40°C, 100 hr	<0.2	<0.2	<0.1	<0.1
High temperature, 80°C, 100 hr	<0.1	<0.1	<0.1	<0.1
High temperature, high humidity, 60°C, 95% RH, 100 hr	<0.1	<0.1	<0.1	<0.1
Vibration, 10−55 Hz/sec, 10^6 cycles, 1.5 mm amplitude	<0.1	<0.1	<0.1	<0.1
Tension, kg	>10	>10	>10	>10

Plastic Connectors

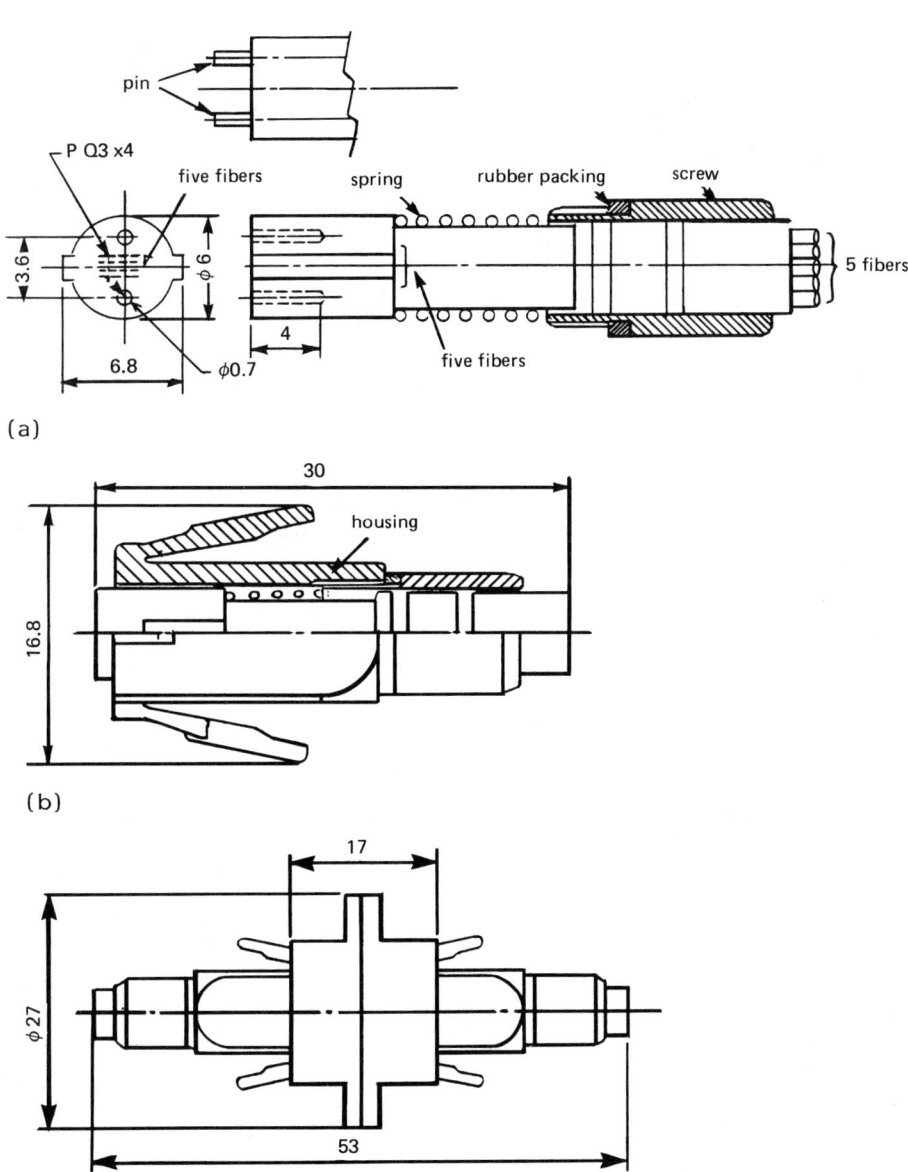

Figure 5.17 Push-on connector (five fibers): (a) plug for five fibers; (b) housing; (c) connector. (From Refs. 10 and 11.)

5.9 PLASTIC CONNECTORS (SINGLE AND MULTIFIBER CONNECTORS [10, 11]

High-precision plastic connectors are manufactured by the transfer-mold process Figs. 5.14 and 5.15. Figure 5.16 shows the construction of a plastic connector (push-on type). In Fig. 5.17, parallel fibers are covered with plastics by high-precision transfer molding to form a plug, and two guide pins to fix the fiber positions are provided on the plug. Plugs are fixed in the adapter only by the push-on action (no screwing).

Field arrangement of the fiber ribbon to the connector is done on site in the following way. Fibers stripped of plastic covering are inserted into the center chip for the plug with the fiber guide and fixed in position with an adhesive. The fibers are polished and finished smooth on their end surfaces. The guide pins are also put in the holes and fixed with the adhesive. The center chip is then inserted in the plug (which serves as the covering of the chip).

The connecting loss and properties of connectors are shown in Table 5.3.

REFERENCES

1. K. Nawata, Multi-mode and single-mode fiber connectors technology, *IEEE Quant. Electron*, QE-16, 6: 61 (June 1980).

2. Seiko Instr. & Electron Catalogue (1984).

3. W. C. Young, L. Curtis, T. L. Williford, and P. Kaiser, Design and performance of the biconic connector used in the FT 3 lightwave system, 30th IWCS, pp. 411-418 (November 1981).

4. W. C. Young, L Curtis, and P. Kaiser, Biconic single-mode connectors with insertion losses below 0.3 dB, OFC '82 P.D. paper, pp. P.D. 5-1-5-2 (April 1982).

5. G. Le Noane, Experimental results on mass splicing techniques applied on optical fiber cables in the field, 30th IWCS pp. 419-422 (November 1981).

6. C. H. Gartside, III, M. R. Santana, and R. W. Tarwater, High performance single-mode lightguide media, GLOBECOM 84, 42.1 pp. 1382-1385 (November 1984).

7. C. M. Miller, A fiber-optic-cable connector, *BSTJ*, 54(9): 1547-1550 (November 1975).

8. C. M. Miller, Fiber-optic array splicing with etched silicon chips, *BSTJ* 57(1): 75-90 (January 1978).

References

9. C. M. Schroeder, Accurate silicon spacer chips for an optical fiber cable connector, *BSTJ* 57(1): 91–97 (January 1978).
10. S. Tachigami, Private communication.
11. Furukawa Catalogue (1986).

6
Joining of Optical Fiber Cables

6.1 GENERAL CONCEPTS

Telecommunication plastic cables were mainly joined by combining soft and hard adhesive tapes and lead or plastic sleeves. Rubber packings were not used very much. Generally, the range of applicable cable diameters for rubber packings was approximagely ±1 mm of the prearranged value. The outside diameters of telecommunication plastic cables ranged between 10 and 60 mm, depending on the number of pairs. If rubber packings were to be used, packings of approximately 30 different sizes had to be kept in stock. Therefore, it was difficult to use rubber packings with cable joining of telecommunication plastic cables.

However, the range of the outside diameters of optical fiber cables is not large. Therefore, rubber packings are frequently used in joining optical fibers.

6.2 BASIC CONDITIONS

The basic conditions for the joining of optical fiber cables are as follows:

1. Joining is possible in the field in a short period of time.
2. The work of joining is simple and easy.
3. The weight of the joining parts should not be heavy.
4. The cost is low.

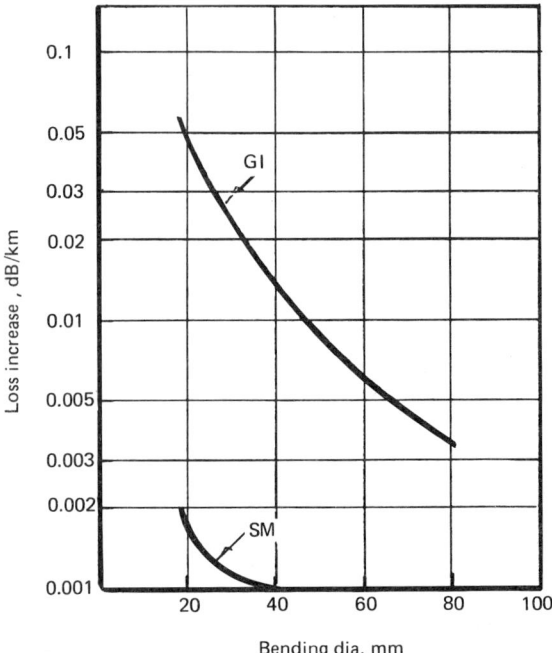

Figure 6.1   Bending loss increase (1.3 μm).

Spare lengths of optical fibers are needed for the cable joining part, and these spare lengths of fibers are bent in a loop in the closure of a cable joint. Figure 6.1 shows the relationship between the optical fiber bending diameter and the loss increase. The diagram shows that a bending diameter of more than 6 cm is needed. Therefore, the inside diameter of the sleeve of the joint should be approximately 8 cm.

Either or both of the following items are used in the border between the cable and the joining: (1) soft and hard plastic tapes and (2) rubber packings.

As shown in Fig. 6.2, each optical fiber is bent and placed on a plastic or metal sheet for fiber splicing. These plastic or metal sheets are stacked to form a joining part.

6.3 OPTICAL FIBER CABLE JOINING [1, 2]

Cable joining methods are divided roughly into the following two types. (1) Soft adhesive tapes and plastic sleeve are

Optical Fiber Cable Joining

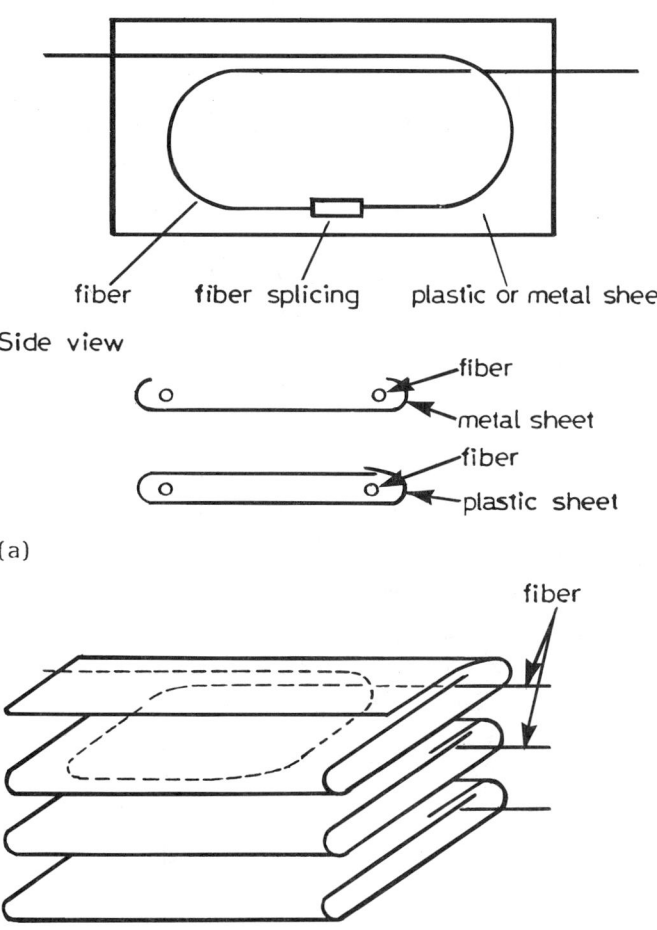

Figure 6.2 Plastic (or metal) sheet for fiber splicing in the joint sleeve: (a) cross section (top) and side view (bottom); (b) stack.

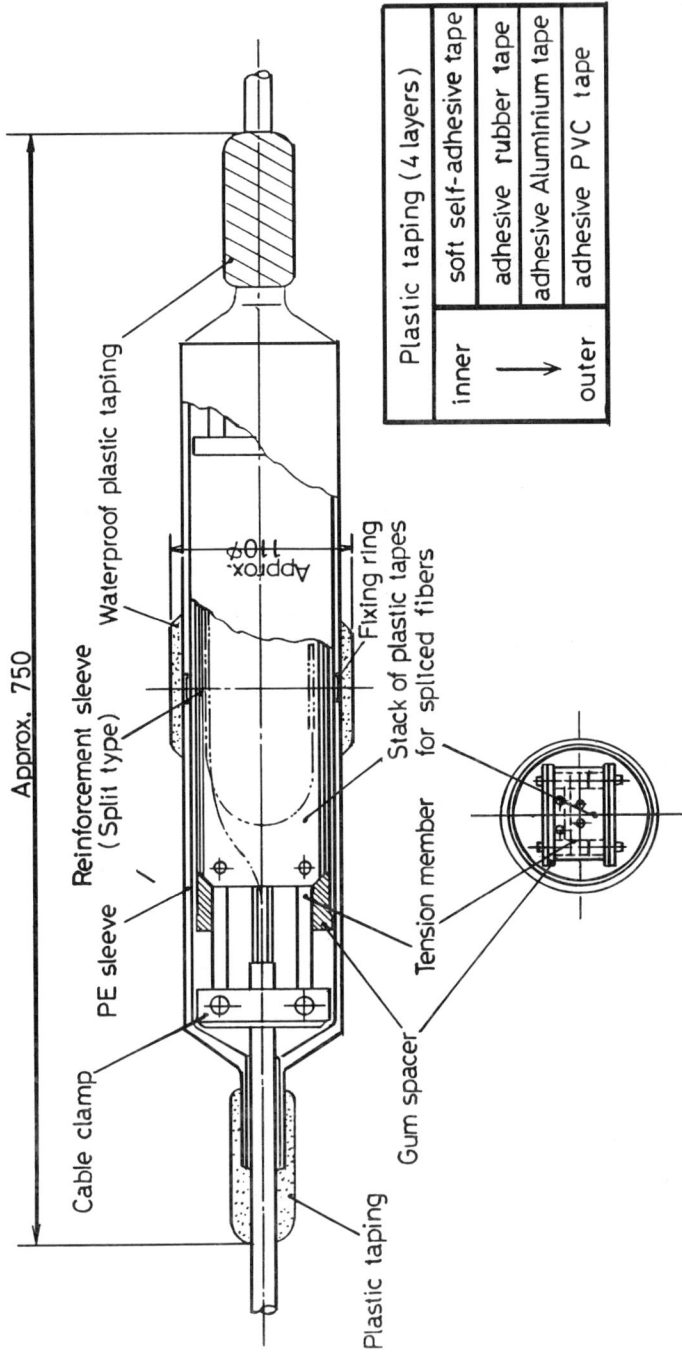

Figure 6.3 Cable joint (adhesive tape and polyethylene sleeve). (From Ref. 2.)

Optical Fiber Cable Joining

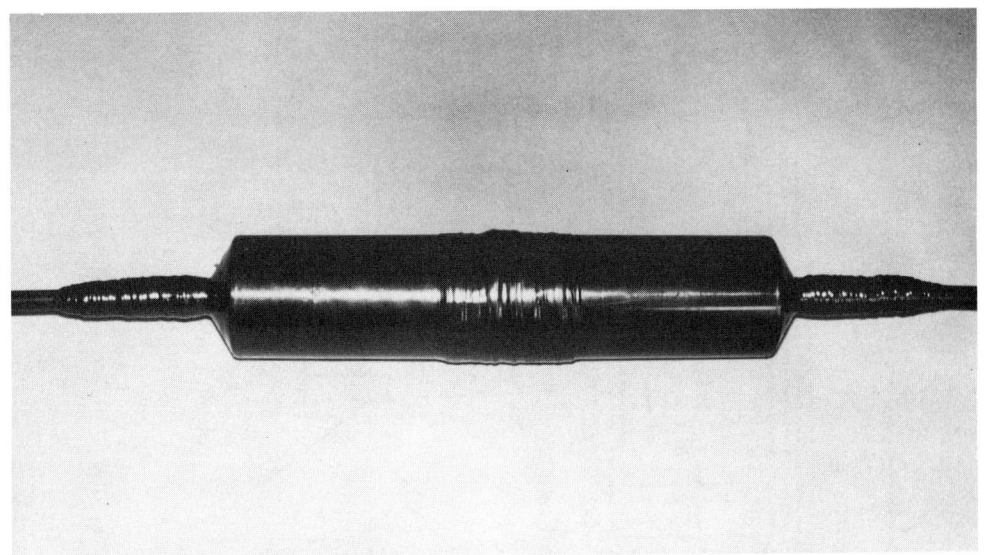

Figure 6.4   Soft adhesive tape and plastic sleeve joint.

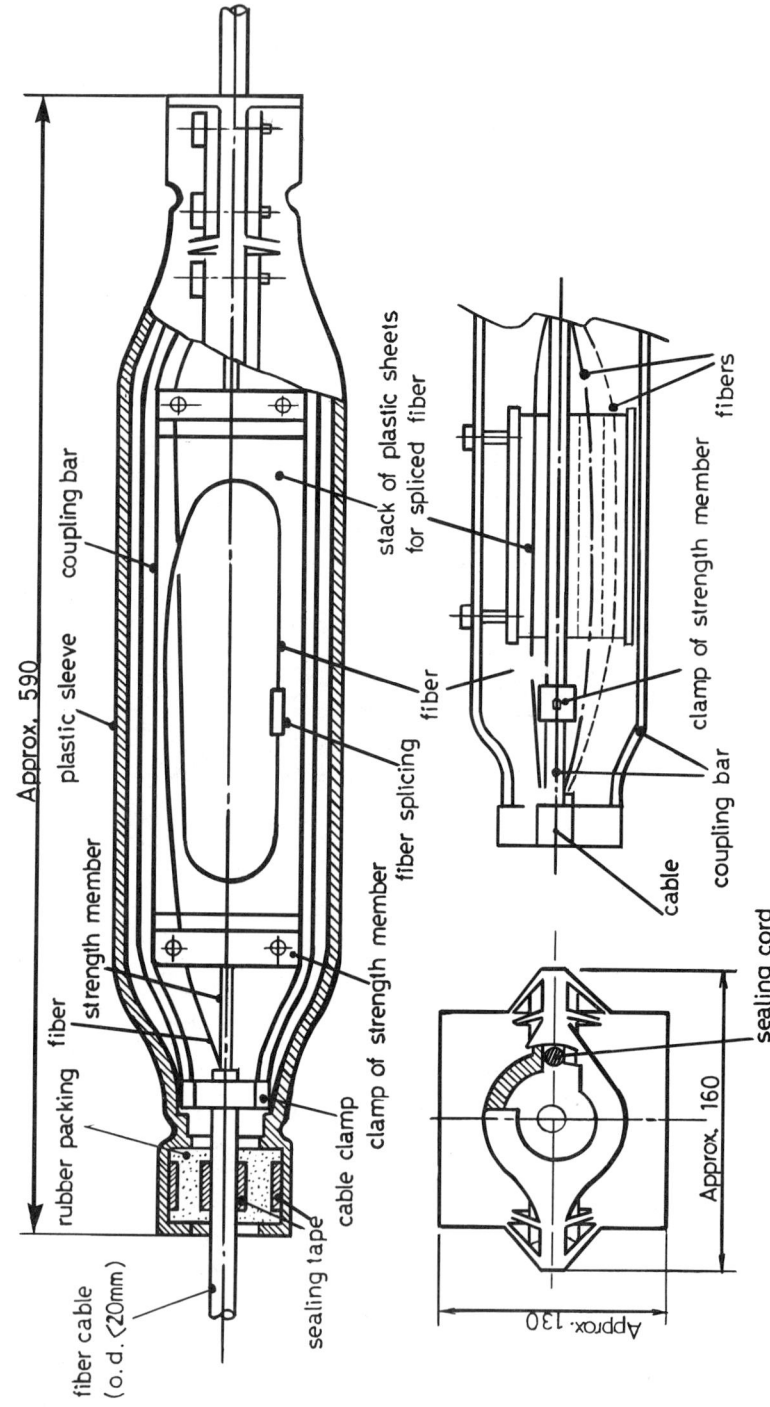

Figure 6.5 Cable joint for general use (rubber packing and plastic sleeve). (From Ref. 2.)

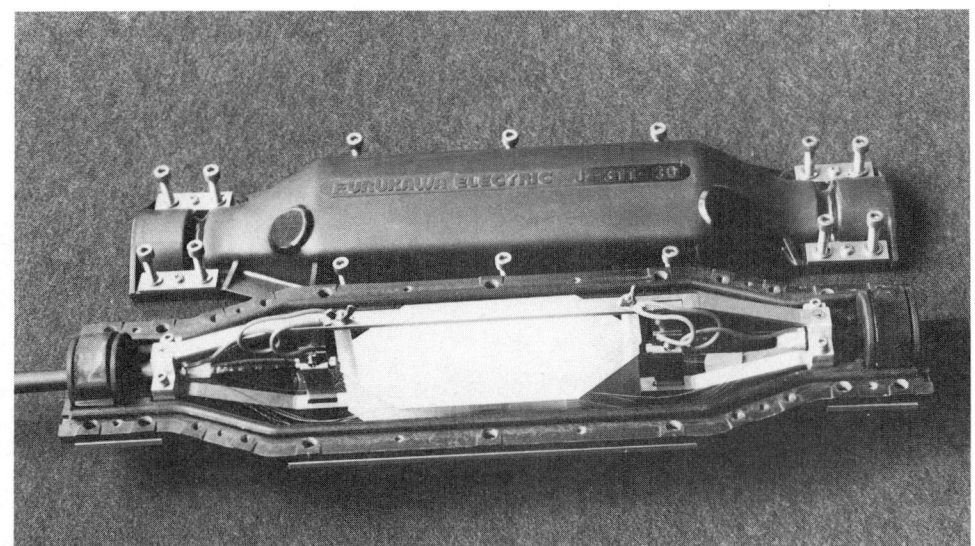

(a)

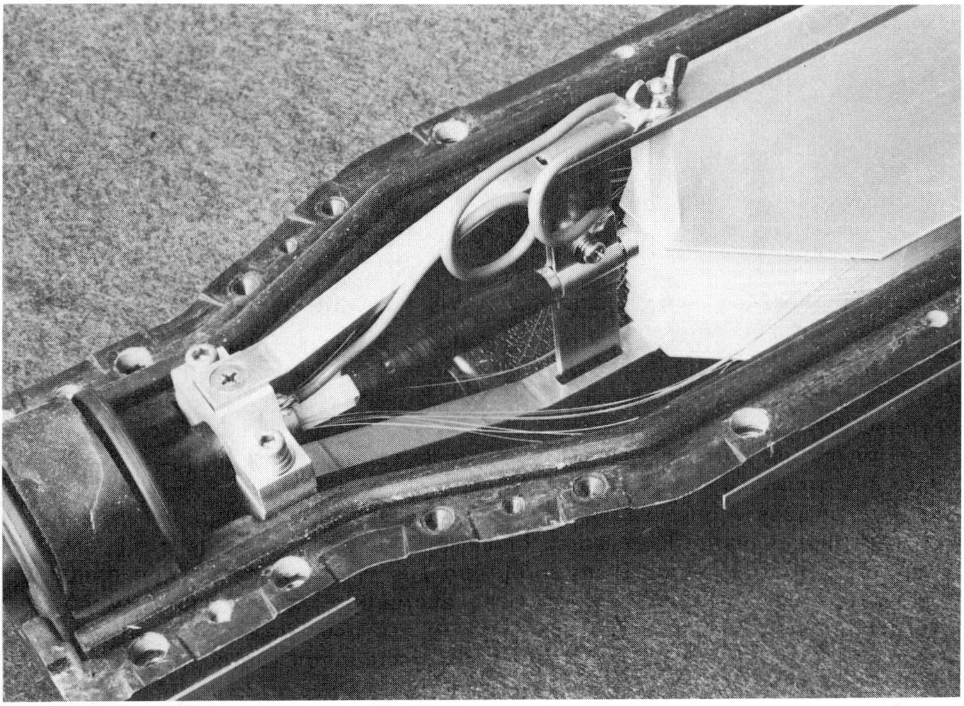

(b)

Figure 6.6 Rubber packing and FRP sleeve joint: (a) general view; (b) cable clamp and rubber packing; (c) spliced fiber stack.

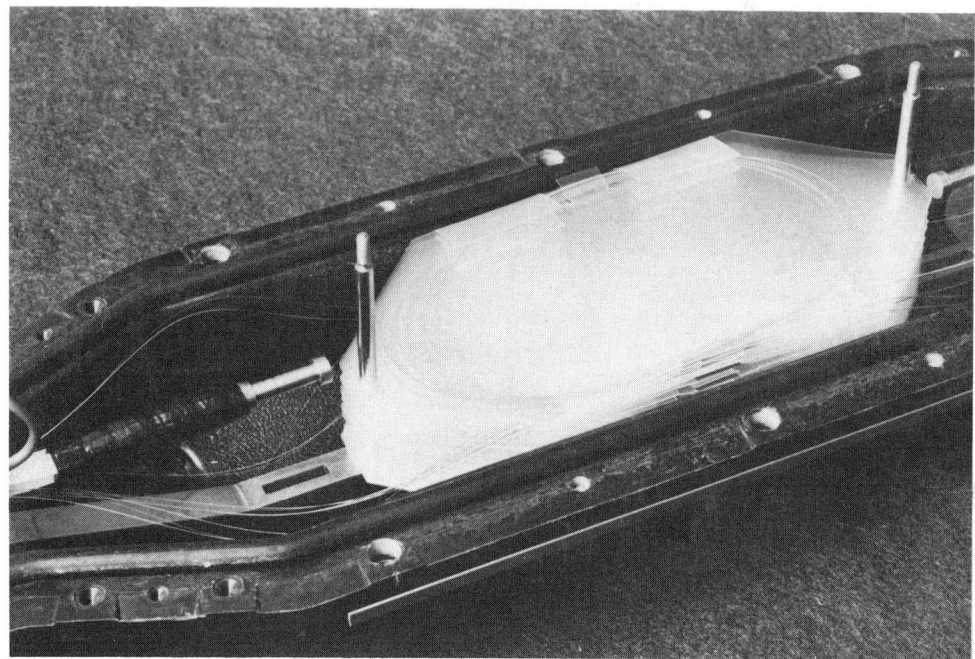

(c)

Figure 6.6 (Continued)

Used with cables containing a relatively small number of optical fibers
Cannot be used with gas-filled cables
The reliability of these joints relates to quality of taping work
The joint construction is relatively simple and is relatively economical

Figures 6.3 and 6.4 show construction examples of this method.
  (2) Rubber packing and FRP sleeve are

Used with many types of optical fiber cables
Can be used with gas-filled cables
The workability of this joint type is good, and the joint can be
  assembled relatively easily
This method is higher in cost than with method 1.

Figures 6.5 and 6.6 show construction examples of this method.

Table 6.1 Test Conditions for the Cable Joint

Item	Test condition	Result
Air tightness		
Room temperature	Inner pressure, 1 kg/cm^2, 20°C 24 hr No leak	No leak
Heat cycle	Inner pressure, 1 kg/cm^2 $-20 \gtrless +60°C$, 50 cycles (two to three cycles per day)	No leak
	$0 \gtrless +80°C$, 50 cycles (two to three cycles per day)	No leak
Cable bending air tightness		No leak
	Inner pressure, 1 kg/cm^2 Bending radius = 6 × outer diameter of cable three times, go and return	
Vibration		No leak
	Inner pressure, 1 kg/cm^2 Vibration: amplitude ±5 mm 10 Hz/sec, 10^6 cycles	
Water tightness	Inner pressure, 1 kg/cm^2 Outer water pressure, 3 kg/cm^2	No leak
	Inner pressure, 0 kg/cm^2 Outer water pressure, 2 kg/cm^2	No leak

Table 6.1 (Continued)

Item	Test condition	Result
Breakage	10 mm/min, R = 160 mm, Joint closure, 250 mm	No leak
	Weight speed, 10 mm/min, 150 kg	No break
Grip strength of cable	(Strength of cable sheath) × 0.7	No breakage
Grip strength of strength member	50 kg	No breakage

6.4 TEST CONDITIONS FOR THE CABLE JOINT [3]

Table 6.1 [3] presents cable joint test conditions.

REFERENCES

1. S. Tachigami, H. Miyazawa, and S. Ohta, private communication, 1986.
2. Furukawa catalogues (1986).
3. Furukawa, Standard specifications for test conditions of cable joint (1985).

7
Measurement of Optical Fibers

Optical fibers and optical fiber cables are generally measured for the following purposes. First, measurements are made to provide the data needed to design optical fiber communications systems. Loss and bandwidth particularly are characteristics that are needed for system design. Optical fiber constructions (refractive index distribution and dimensions) are needed to estimate splicing losses and coupling efficiencies with the light source. The second purpose is control of quality and manufacturing processes. It is important to make clear the relationship between the manufacturing conditions of optical fibers or optical fiber cables and product quality in manufacturing qualified products. The third purpose is optical fiber cable installation and maintenance. The fourth purpose is clarification of optical fiber design and properties. It is important to analyze the relationship between optical fiber construction, construction deviation from design values, operative light wavelength, incidental mode distribution, and so on, and transmission characteristics (loss and bandwidth) in comparison with theory and to establish design processes for optical fibers and optical fiber cables.

This chapter introduces typical measuring techniques employed when optical fiber cables are offered based on the first viewpoint. Measuring techniques on the following principal specification items of optical fibers shown below are outlined.

---
*This chapter was mainly written by Dr. Yashikazu Matsuda, my young colleague in the Furukawa Electric Co., Ltd.

1. Structural parameters: geometric structure, and refractive index distribution and NA
2. Transmission characteristics: loss and bandwidth

7.1 MEASUREMENT OF STRUCTURAL PARAMETERS OF THE FIBER [1]

7.1.1 Structural Parameters of GI Fiber

Table 7.1 shows the items that specify the multimode fiber structures. Specification values of these items are decided after taking into consideration the factors required, such as transmission bandwidth, attenuation, splicing loss, and microbending loss.

However, the characteristics that receive an emphasis for optical fiber transmission lines differ depending on optical fiber application fields, and numeric values and their tolerances of structural parameters differ depending on the optical fiber application areas. Table 7.1 shows the values of graded index (GI) fibers for short-haul transmission systems.

7.1.1.1 Definition of Structural Parameters

The structural parameters of GI fibers are defined entirely based on the refractive index distribution.

Core Diameter (Fig. 7.1)

The locus of a refractive index distribution n_3 for the core area given by the following equation can be obtained based on the refractive index distribution $n(r)$ measured. The cross-sectional area inside this locus is called the core area.

$$n_3 = n_2 + k(n_1 - n_2) \qquad (7.1)$$

where

n_1 = maximum refractive index difference of core

n_2 = refractive index of the region with uniform cladding

k = constant

As a k value, the GI fiber shown in Table 7.1 uses $k = 0.05$.

The diameter of the circle best fitting the n_3 locus by the least-squares method is defined as the core diameter, and its center, the core center.

Structural Parameters

Table 7.1 Example of Structural Parameters of Multimode Graded Index Fibers

---

Core diameter 2a, 50 ± 3 μm

Reference surface diameter 2b, 125 ± 3 μm

Core/reference surface concentricity error c, <6%

Core noncircularity, <6%

Reference surface noncircularity, <2%

Index profile n(r), near parabolic

Maximum theoretical NA NAth, 0.18 to 0.23 (λ = 0.8 to 0.9 μm); 0.15 to 0.30 (λ = 1.3 μm)

Cladding Diameter (Fig. 7.1)

The region surrounding the core is called the cladding. The external cylindrical surface of the cladding is used as a reference surface for optical fiber axial alignment when fibers are spliced and is called the reference surface. In the cross section of a fiber, the diameter of a circle best fitting the closed curve that defines this reference surface by the least-squares method is called the cladding surface diameter, and the center of this circle, the cladding surface center.

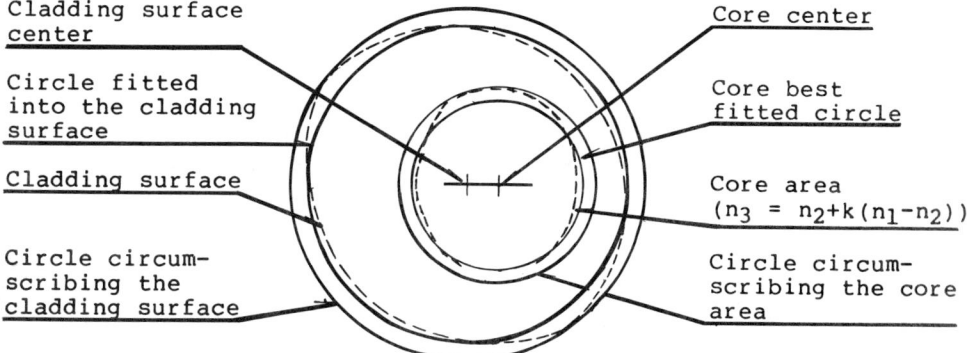

Figure 7.1 Geometric parameters of multimode fibers. (From Ref. 1.)

Core Noncircularity

A circle that has the same center as that best fitted in the core area and circumscribed in the core area can be defined. A core noncircularity is defined by the difference between the diameter of this circumscribed circle and the core diameter divided by the core diameter.

Cladding Surface Noncircularity

A circle that has the same center as that best fitted on the cladding surface and circumscribed on the cladding surface can be defined. The difference between the diameter of this circumscribed circle and the cladding surface diameter divided by the cladding surface diameter is defined as a cladding surface non-circularity.

Core-Cladding Surface Concentricity Error

The distance between the core center and the cladding surface center divided by the core diameter is defined as the core-cladding surface concentricity error.

Maximum Theoretical NA

The maximum theoretical NA is defined by the following equation:

$$NA = (n_1^2 - n_2^2)^{\frac{1}{2}} \qquad (7.2)$$

where

n_1 = core maximum refractive index difference

n_2 = refractive index of cladding region in which the refractive index becomes uniform

7.1.1.2 Measurement of Fiber Dimensions

A microscope is used generally for the measurement of fiber dimensions. Sometimes, video devices are coupled to the microscope. The end surface of the fiber is cut perpendicularly to the fiber axis and is polished smooth. The fiber surface is sometimes etched to distinguish clearly the boundary between the core and the cladding.

7.1.1.3 NFP Method (Measurement of Refractive Index Profile)

The NFP (near field pattern) is an optical intensity distribution at a fiber output end surface. The NFP method is a typical method to

Structural Parameters

measure refractive index profiles. This method is based on the principle that the optical intensity distribution at the optical fiber output end, that is, NFP, approximates the refractive index profile. Compared with the RNF method described in the next section, adjustment of the measuring system and measuring procedure of this method are simple. For this reason, this method is widely used.

The local NA of an optical fiber is defined by the following equations:

$$NA(r) = n(r) \sin \theta(r)$$
$$= [n^2(r) - n_2^2]^{\frac{1}{2}} \qquad (7.3)$$

where

$n(r)$ = refractive index profile
r = radial distance
n_2 = refractive index of cladding region
$\theta_c(r)$ = local acceptance angle

The optical power $P(r)$ transmitted in an optical fiber at a radial distance by r from the core axis can be given by the following equation when the fiber launched end is illuminated by an incoherent light source, such as a Lambertian light source, and when the entire mode is uniformly excited in the optical fiber [2].

$$P(r) = P(0) \frac{NA^2(r)}{NA^2(0)} = P(0) \frac{n^2(r) - n^2(a)}{n^2(0) - n^2(a)} \qquad (7.4)$$

Here, a = core radius.

If the refractive index distribution is expressed as

$$n^2(r) = \begin{cases} n_1^2 \left[1 - 2\Delta f\left(\frac{r}{a}\right) \right] & (r \leqslant a) \\ n_2^2 = n_1^2 [1 - 2\Delta] & (r > a) \end{cases} \qquad (7.5)$$

The next equation is obtained:

$$\frac{P(r)}{P(0)} = 1 - f\left(\frac{r}{a}\right) \qquad (7.6)$$

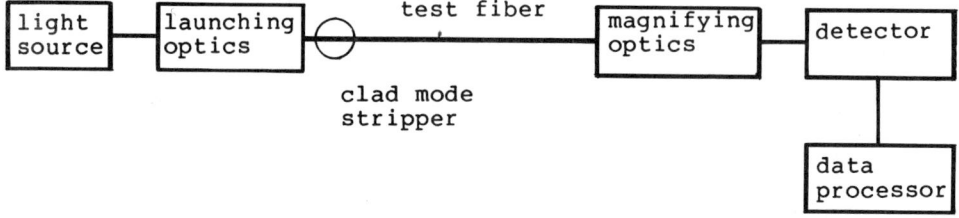

Figure 7.2 Basic arrangement of NFP measurment. (From Refs. 1 and 5.)

The profile f(r/a) of the refractive index distribution can be obtained by measuring NFP, namely, P(r), if each mode equally attenuates and there is no mode coupling.

Figure 7.2 shows the basic configuration of the NFP method. A tungsten halide lamp, light-emitting diode (LED), or other incoherent light source is used. To achieve the uniform excitation of all modes in the optical fiber to be measured, a launching optics system is set so that the intensity distribution of the incident light at the optical fiber launched end becomes uniform and the incident NA becomes larger than the optical fiber NA. The use of an incident beam with a spot diameter of 70 μm or more and incident NA of 0.3 or more is one example with optical fibers shown in Table 7.1. Incident optics systems are as follows (Fig. 7.3):

1. A lens and pinhole are combined [3].
2. An optical fiber is directly joined with an LED.
3. A step index optical fiber with a large core diameter and high NA is spliced with the optical fiber to be measured.

Shorten the optical fibers as much as possible so that the individual modes equally attenuate to satisfy the condition that does not produce modal coupling. A cladding mode stripper in the incident section is set to remove unwanted modes that propagate in the cladding.

The optical intensity distribution (NFP) on the optical fiber output end surface is enlarged by the magnification optics system and is measured by the detector after obtaining a necessary spatial resolution. The two methods shown in Fig. 7.4 are frequently used to detect expanded NFP.

1. A detector with a pinhole is scanned on the NFP image focusing surface.
2. TV camera and image processing equipment are used.

Structural Parameters

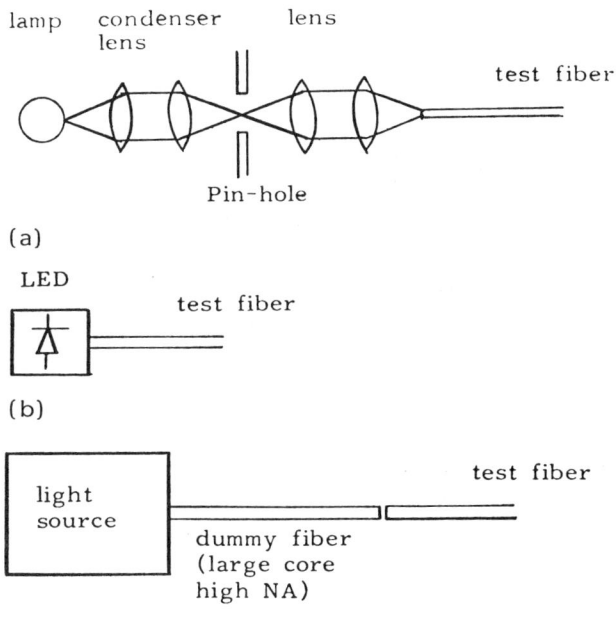

Figure 7.3 Launching optics in NFP measurment: (a) pinhole and lens system; (b) butt joint; (c) dummy fiber. (From Refs. 1, 3, and 5.)

Optical fiber construction parameters are calculated in accordance with the definition described in Sec. 7.1.1.2.

7.1.1.4 RNF Method (Measurement of Refractive Index Profile) [4]

The RNF (refractive near field) method measures the refractive index profile by detecting the light that is not trapped in the core. (The NFP method measures the profile by detecting the light that is trapped and is transmitted in the core.) For this reason, no correction is needed for the leaky mode, and the refractive indices of not only the core, but also of the cladding can be measured.

As shown in Fig. 7.5, an optical fiber is immersed in a liquid of which refractive index is slightly higher than that of its cladding. A light is launched at the input end face of the optical fiber using a lens of which the NA is larger than that of the optical fiber. Part of the light is transmitted through the optical fiber. However, the remaining light is radiated outside the optical fiber. Of the light

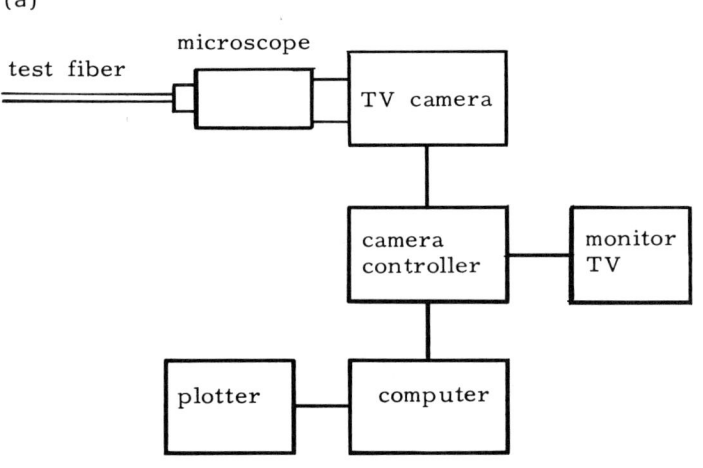

Figure 7.4 Detecting system for NFP measurement: (a) scanning detector with pinhole; (b) television camera with a microscope. (From Refs. 1 and 5.)

Structural Parameters

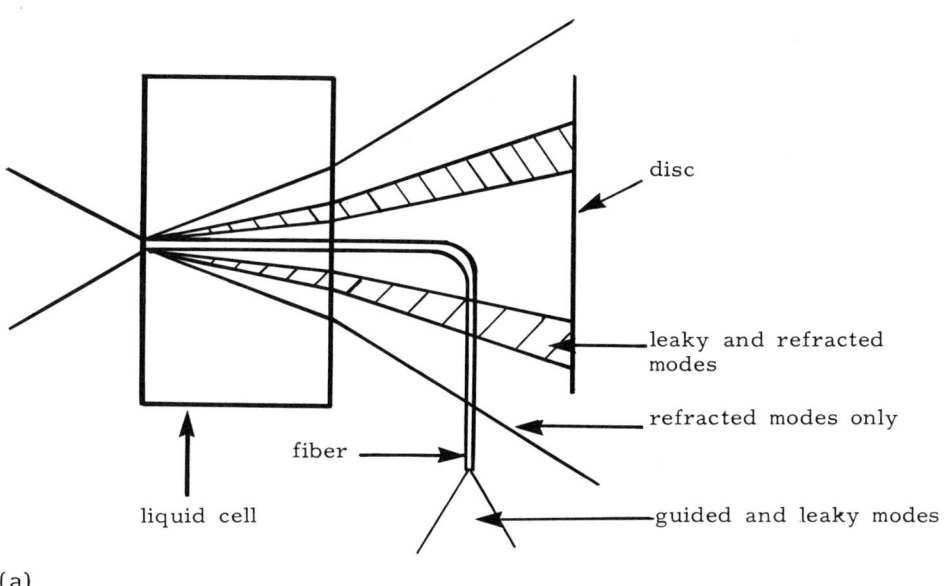

(a)

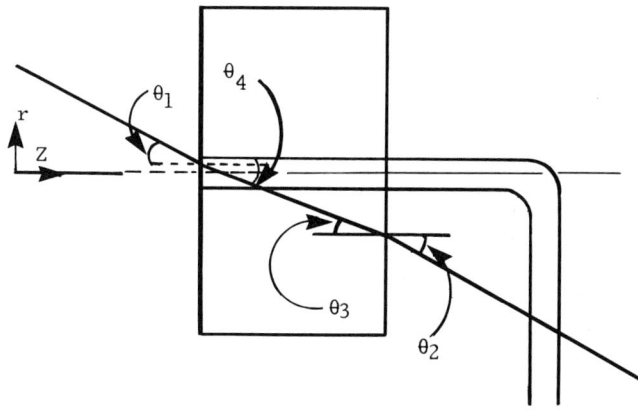

(b)

Figure 7.5 Refractive near-field technique: (a) schematic diagram; (b) propagation of light. (From Refs. 1, 4, and 5.)

radiated outside the optical fiber in the shape of a hollow cone, a leaky mode is contained in the light whose radiation angle is small. However, a light with a large radiation angle contains only refracted light. The magnitude of the optical power carried by a leaky mode cannot be evaluated accurately. As shown in Fig. 7.5a a disk is used to block the part having a small radiation angle to remove the leaky mode and the refracted lights only are detected. For this reason, this method has the following two advantages compared with the NFP method mentioned above. First, the effect of the leaky mode can be removed and the refractive index distribution can be measured accurately. Second, the resolution can be high by increasing the NA of the incident lens and reducing the incident beam spot.

As shown in Fig. 7.5b, variations of the refractive index exist in the r direction only. The Z components of the wavenumber vector in the fiber, β, and refractive index of liquid are constant. This means that

$$\frac{\beta}{k_0} = n(r) \cos \theta_4 = n_L \cos \theta_3 \qquad (7.7)$$

where

$k_0 = 2\pi/\lambda$

λ = wavelength

θ_3, θ_4 = angles toward optical axes

n_L = refractive index of liquid

$n(r)$ = refractive index of the optical fiber at a radial distant by r from the axis

The following equation can be obtained when Snell's law is applied to the incident and output planes of a liquid cell and when Eq. (7.7) is taken into consideration.

$$n^2(r) = \sin^2 \theta_1 + n_L^2 - \sin^2 \theta_2 \qquad (7.8)$$

A light with an angle larger than θ_2, which is defined by the disk edge, is detected. θ_2 can be regarded constant independent of the light incident position r when the distance to the disk is made sufficiently large compared with the optical fiber diameter. As n_L is constant, the refractive index $n(r)$ can be calculated by measuring $\sin^2 \theta_1$.

θ_1 is measured as optical power contained in an angle larger than angle θ_1. When launching a uniform parallel light after focusing by lens, $P_1(\theta_1)$ can be obtained as follows:

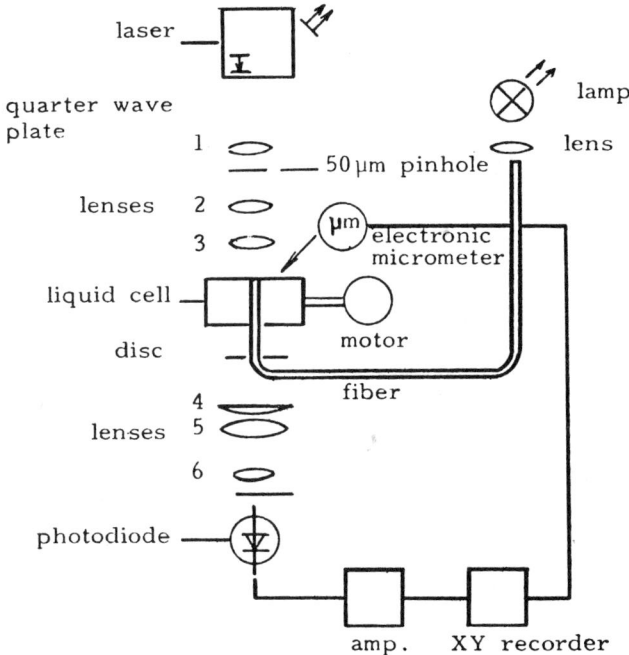

Figure 7.6 Typical arrangement of the refracted near-field test setup. (From Refs. 1, 4, and 5.)

$$P_1(\theta) = P(0)\left(1 - \frac{\tan^2 \theta_1}{\tan^2 \theta_{max}}\right) \quad (7.9)$$

In this equation, θ_{max} is an angle that can be defined by NA of the lens.

In an actual system, $\theta_1 \ll 1$ is generally considered, and the approximation $\tan^2 \theta_1 \doteq \sin^2 \theta_1$ is possible. Therefore, $P_1(\theta)$ varies in proportion to $\sin^2 \theta_1$. Therefore, $n^2(r)$ is measured as an amount that varies in proportion to $P_1(\theta)$.

Figures 7.6 and 7.7 show the measuring system of the RNF method and a measurement example, respectively. Normally, a HeNe laser at 0.633 μm is used as a light source. A quarter-wavelength plate converts linear polarization light into circular polarization light and eliminates the polarization dependence of the reflection ratio on the interface between the air and the glass. A laser beam is changed to a parallel light flux with a uniform intensity distribution using a ×3

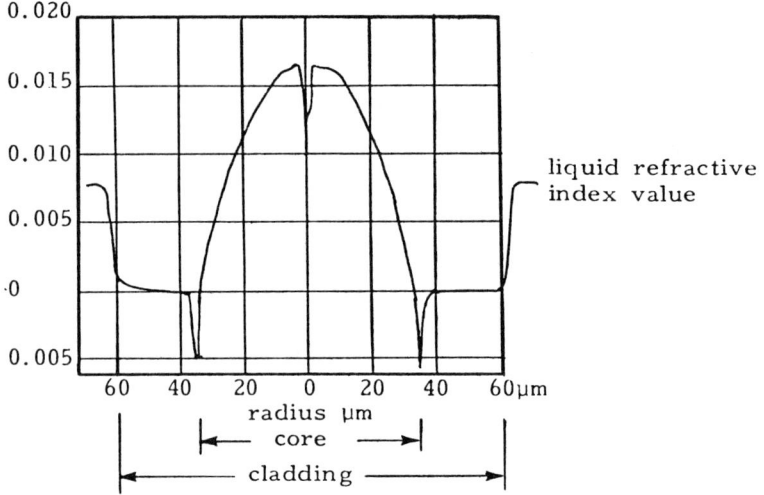

Figure 7.7 Profile obtained by the RNF method. (From Refs. 1, 2, and 5.)

lens, a 50 μm pinhole, and a ×5 lens. This parallel light flux is focused using a ×20 lens to form a very small light spot on the optical fiber launching end surface. The measurement resolution is determined by this spot size, and a spot as small as possible is required. This light spot is radially scanned on the launching end surface of the fiber, and output is detected as a function of the spot position. The refractive light passing the outer side of the disk that blocks the leaky mode becomes the output light to be detected and is focused on the photodiode by a 10 cm planoconvex lens, a 10 cm biconvex lens, and a 20 cm biconvex lens to avoid a reflection loss by injecting into the photodiode at a large angle.

7.1.1.5 FFP Method (Measurement of NA)

The FFP (far field pattern) is the distribution of optical energy at a part somewhat away from the output end surface of the fiber. It is used in the measurement of NA.

When the optical energy radiated from the output end surface of the fiber is assumed to be uniform in the range of critical angle $\theta_c(r)$ [refer to Eq. (7.3), $NA(r) = n(r) \sin \theta_c(r)$], the optical power detected in the direction of θ is expressed by the following equation.

$$\frac{P(Q)}{P(O)} = \left(1 - \frac{\sin^2 \theta}{2\Delta n^2(O)}\right)^{2/\alpha}$$

$$= \left(1 - \frac{\sin^2 \theta}{NA^2}\right)^{2/\alpha}$$

$$\doteqdot 1 - \frac{\sin^2 \theta}{NA^2} \qquad (7.10)$$

P(O) is measured by a system such as that shown in Fig. 7.8a. An example of this measurement is shown in Fig. 7.8b. In this figure, NA is defined for the sake of convenience by the following formula according to θ_m, the value of θ in $P(\theta)/P(O) = 0.05$.

$NA = \sin \theta_m$

NA is measured accurately by the RNF method mentioned previously. The FFP method is, however, used widely for the measurement of NA, because it is far easier than the RNF method.

For the FFP measurement, the light source, the launching condition, and the elimination of cladding modes are the same as the measurement of NFP. The length of the fiber measured is ordinary 2 to 3 m. The distance from the output end surface of the fiber to the detector is about 20 to 40 cm.

7.1.2 Structural Parameters of Single-Mode Fiber [5]

The items that specify the structure of a single-mode (SM) fiber are shown in Table 7.2. The mode field diameter and cutoff wavelength are the items that differ from those for GI fibers. These items correspond with the core diameter, NA, and the refractive index distribution in the GI fiber.

7.1.2.1 Mode Field Diameter

The mode field diameter characterizes the field distribution of the fundamental mode LP_{01} by one parameter. The mode field diameter is an important parameter that is closely related to fiber splicing losses and coupling efficiencies with the light source and has the same physical meanings as the core diameter in the GI fiber. The definition of the mode field diameter and two principal methods regarding its measurement are described.

Offset Method [1,5,6]

Figure 7.9 shows a measuring method called the offset technique. When the optical power passing a splice is measured as a function of offset, the output optical power becomes largest when the offset is

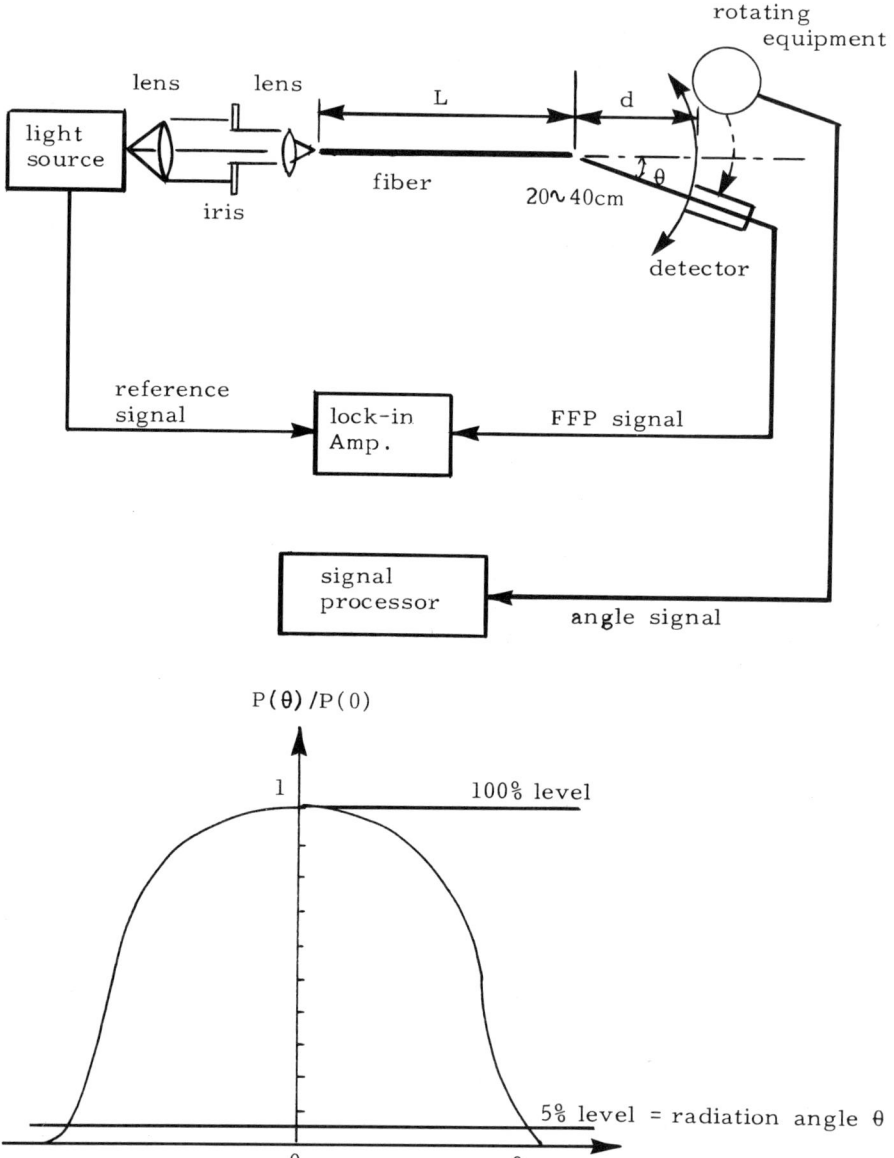

Figure 7.8 Measurement of FFP. (From Refs. 1 and 5.)

Table 7.2 Example of Structural Parameters of SM Fibers

Mode field diameter, 9–10 μm ($\lambda = 1.3$ μm)

Cladding diameter 2b, 125 ± 3 μm

Mode field concentricity error, 0.5–3 μm

Cladding noncircularity <2%

Cutoff wavelength λ_c, 1100–1280 nm

---

zero, and the output optical power decreases as the offset increases. The relationship between output optical power and offset reflects the field spreading, and the mode field is defined utilizing this relationship. The optical energy passing the splice point of fibers can be expressed as the following equation:

$$T = \left| \int_0^\infty \int_0^{2\pi} E(r, \theta) E(r'\theta') \, r \, d\theta \, dr \right|^2 \tag{7.11}$$

where

$E(r, \theta)$ = transverse field distribution

$E(r', \theta')$ = transverse field distribution by offset

for r, θ, r', θ', and see Fig. 7.9a.

By the use of this measuring system, the output T of the spliced fiber, its offset changed, is measured by the detector. The output at the time of no axial deviation (d = 0) is normalized "1" and the axial deviation d_e at an output T of 1/e is determined. This d_e is the spot size, and $2d_e$ is the mode field diameter w.

The measurement method of w is as follows (Fig. 7.9). A light source with a wavelength having a narrow spectrum width (10 μm or less) and a stable light emitting intensity is used. The launching optics system is set to excite a fundamental mode into the SM fiber using one of the following methods:

1. Butt joint with other exciting fiber
2. Application of an appropriate lens system

To remove the higher order and cladding modes that have unnecessarily been excited or generated, a mode filter and cladding mode

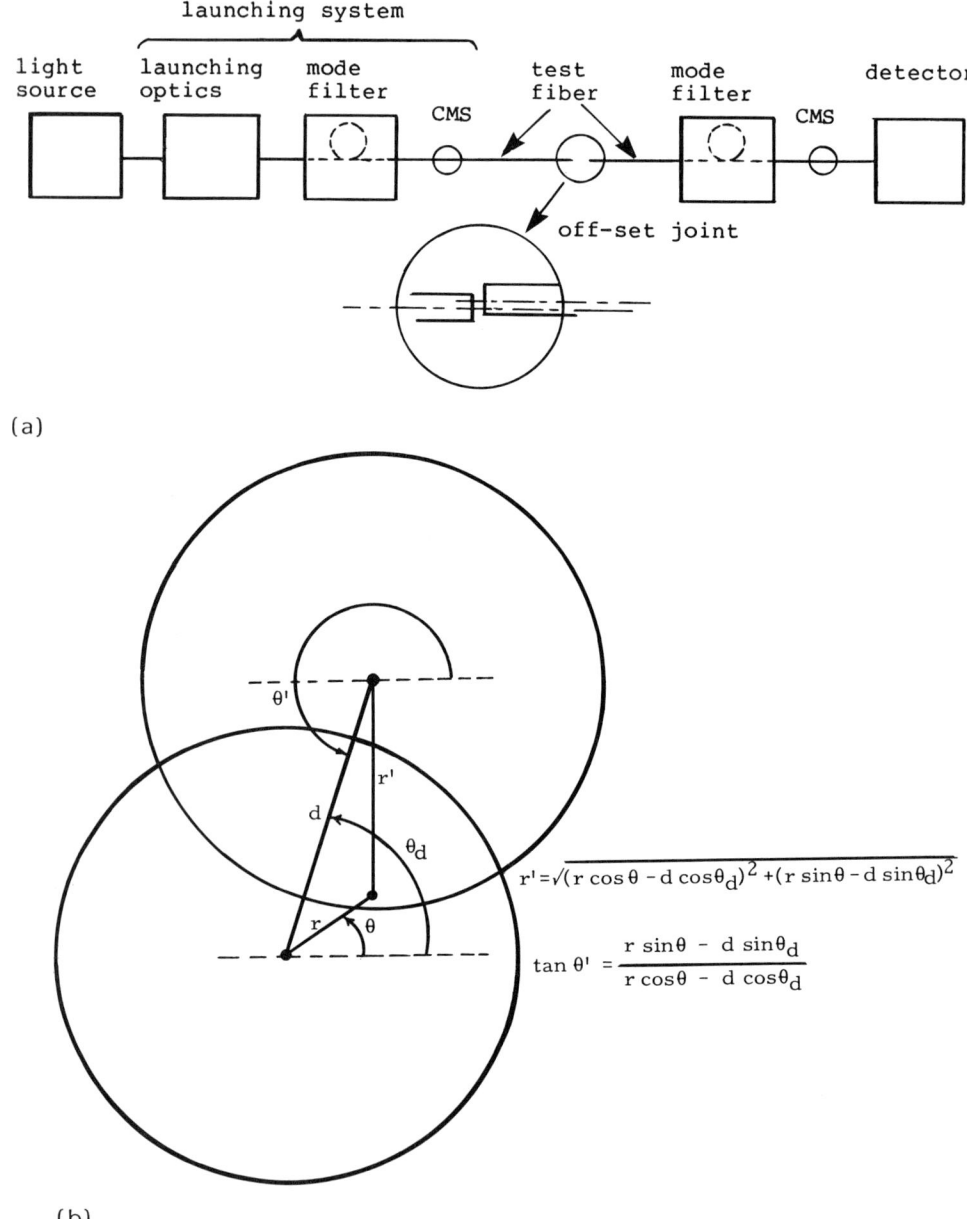

Figure 7.9 Offset technique for mode field diameter measurement: (a) block diagram; CMS = cladding mode stripper; (b) parameters of the power transmission function. (From Refs. 1, 5, and 6.)

Structural Parameters

stripper are installed at the locations shown in the figure. A looped fiber is frequently used as a mode filter.

This measurement uses a 2 m SM fiber, which is cut nearly at the center and is spliced. The spliced gap is less than 5 m, and a matching oil may be filled in the splicing part.

The optical power is detected as an offset function in the spliced part, and the mode field diameter is calculated in accordance with the definition.

Transmitted Field Pattern Method [1,7,8]

The TFP method is available for the measurement of the mode field diameter. In this method, the mode field diameter is determined directly from the measurement of the near field pattern or the far field pattern.

The offset method produces the mode field diameter indirectly from the measurement of the splice coupling. In contrast, the TFP method gives the mode field diameter directly and also makes it easy to determine the noncircularity, cladding diameter, eccentricity of mode field, and so on.

The mode that propagates in the fiber is characterized by the near and the far field patterns. The mode field diameter is defined by these transmitted field patterns. The near field pattern $f(r)$ or far field pattern $F(q)$ are measured, where $q = \sin\theta/\lambda$, where θ is the cone angle of the far field.

These field distributions are fitted to the following Gaussian fields:

$$g(r) = \frac{2}{w} e^{(-r^2/w^2)}$$

$$G(r) = \frac{2}{W} e^{(-q^2/W^2)}$$

where $W = 1/\pi w$.

The spot size w is determined to maximize the overlapping integral of the following equation.

$$\frac{\left[\int_0^\infty rf(r)g(r)\,dr\right]^2}{\int_0^\infty rf^2(r)\,dr \int_0^\infty rg^2(r)\,dr} = \frac{\left[\int_0^\infty qF(q)G(q)\,dq\right]^2}{\int_0^\infty qF^2(q)\,dq \int_0^\infty qG^2(q)\,dq}$$

where $w = 2W$

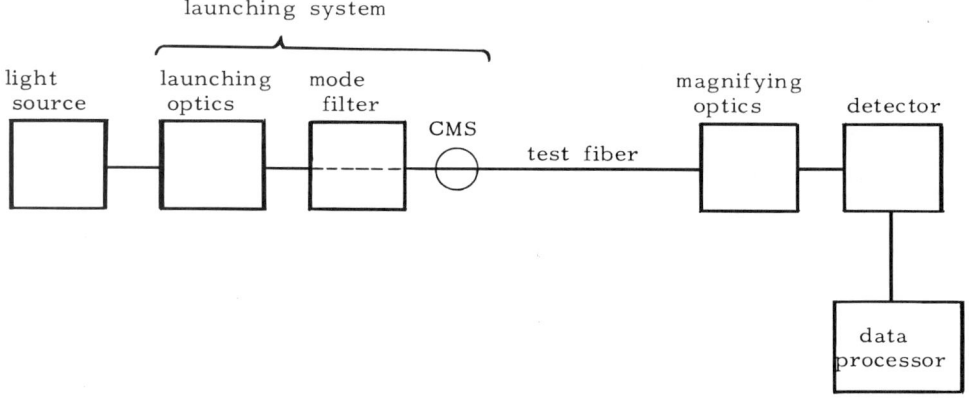

Figure 7.10 TFP technique for mode field diameter; CMS = cladding mode stripper. (From Refs. 1, 5, 7, and 8.)

where

W = mode field diameter

w = spot size

This definition of w has a physical meaning of the coupling efficiency, becoming maximum when an optical fiber is launched by a Gaussian beam with a spot size w, determined as mentioned above.

Figure 7.10 shows the measuring system. Basically, the measuring system does not differ from that of the NFP method. The enlarging optics system is used for the NFP method and is not used for the FFP method. The launching system, mode filter, and cladding mode stripper are used as described for the offset method.

7.1.3 Cutoff Wavelength λ_c [5, 9]

A single-mode fiber operates in the so-called single mode at a wavelength longer than the cutoff wavelength λ_c. This cutoff wavelength has two characteristics, one is called a theoretical cutoff wavelength, calculated based on the core diameter and refractive index distribution, having a character purely as a construction parameter. The theoretical cutoff wavelength can be calculated as follows with step index fibers:

$$\frac{2\pi a}{\lambda} \sqrt{n_1^2 - n_2^2} = 2.405$$

where

    a = core radius

    λ = wavelength

    n_1 = refractive index of core

    n_2 = refractive index of cladding

The other has the character of a transmission characteristic. The propagation mode field spreads not only in the core but also to the cladding. The spreading of this field becomes prominent with wavelengths near the cutoff wavelength, becoming more susceptible to a microbending loss or an absorption loss of the cladding materials. Theoretically, the second higher order mode can propagate in an optical fiber even at a wavelength that is slightly shorter than the cutoff wavelength. For the foregoing reasons, it cannot actually propagate a long distance. The wavelength at which the higher order mode cannot practically propagate is called an effective cutoff wavelength. Therefore, the effective cutoff wavelength sensibly depends not only on the fiber length but also on the condition in which the optical fiber is placed, such as the bending.

Generally, a cutoff wavelength is measured by using a fiber of 2 m length.

The transmitted power method is generally used in measuring the cutoff wavelength. Figure 7.11 shows the measuring system. The measuring system shown in Fig. 7.11 basically does not differ from that for the loss spectra mentioned later except for the incident optics system. As in the fundamental mode LP_{01}, the second higher mode LP_{11} is also excited, and the following launching systems are used.

1. A GI fiber is butt joined.
2. An appropriate optics system is applied using lenses, for example.

The measurement process of the cutoff wavelength is as follows. First, the output power $P(\lambda)$ of the test fiber is measured as a function of wavelength (Fig. 7.11a). Next, the reference optical power $Pr(\lambda)$ is measured. For the measurement of the reference optical power, two methods are used. One is to measure the optical power, bending one loop of the test fiber to a radius of 30 mm on the output side of the test fiber, as shown in Fig. 7.11b. The other method is the substitution method (Fig. 7.11c).

GI fiber (1 to 2 m) is spliced to the launching system and the output power $Pr(\lambda)$ is measured.

The ratio between $P(\lambda)$ and $Pr(\lambda)$,

$$R(\lambda) = \left| 10 \log \frac{P(\lambda)}{Pr(\lambda)} \right| \qquad (7.12)$$

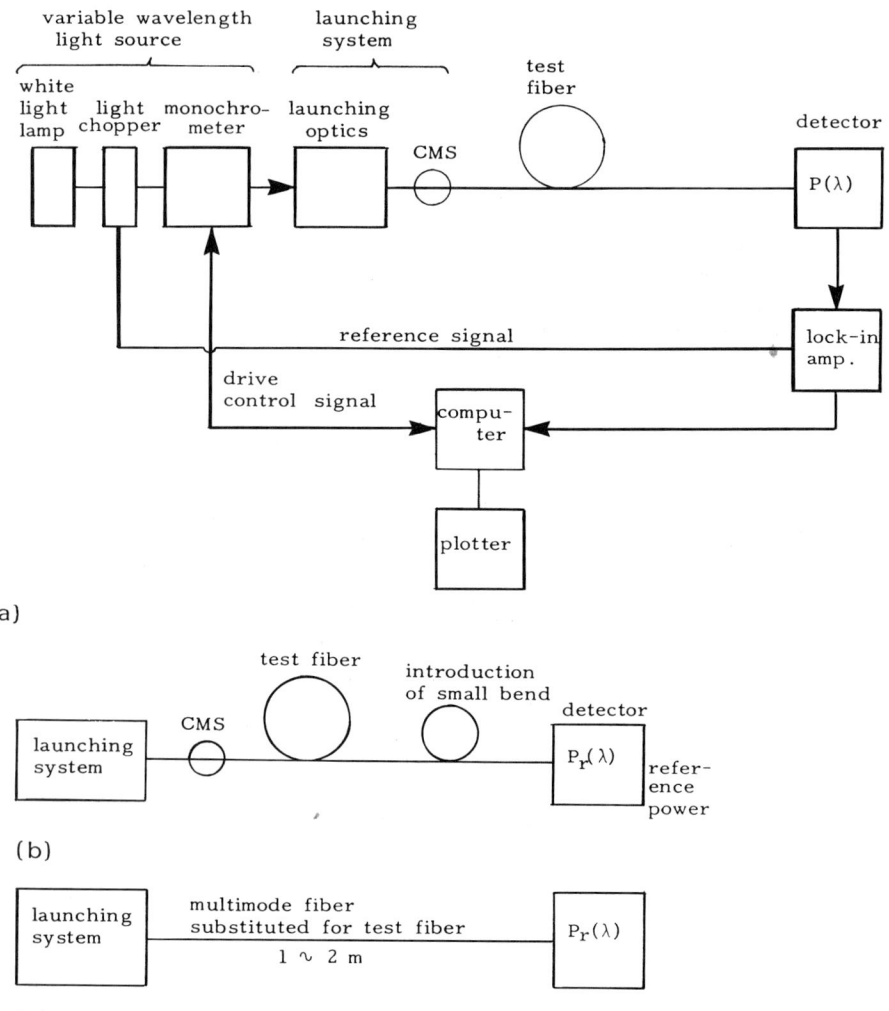

Figure 7.11 Typical setup of cutoff wavelength measurement: (a) setup; CMS = cladding mode stripper; (b) bending; (c) substitution. (From Refs. 1, 5, and 9.)

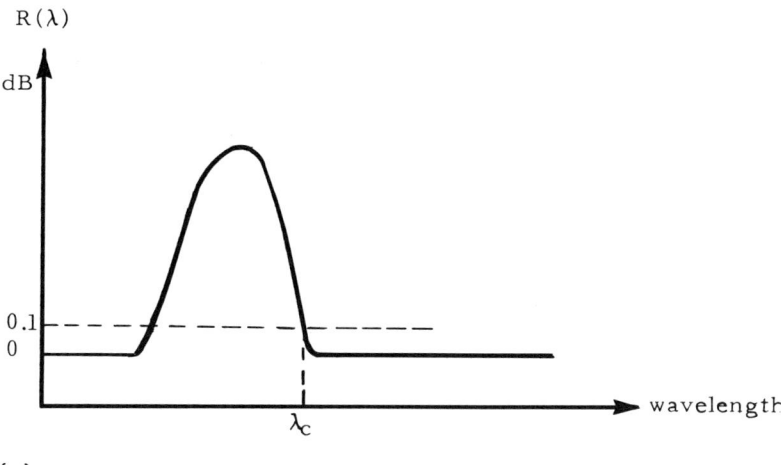

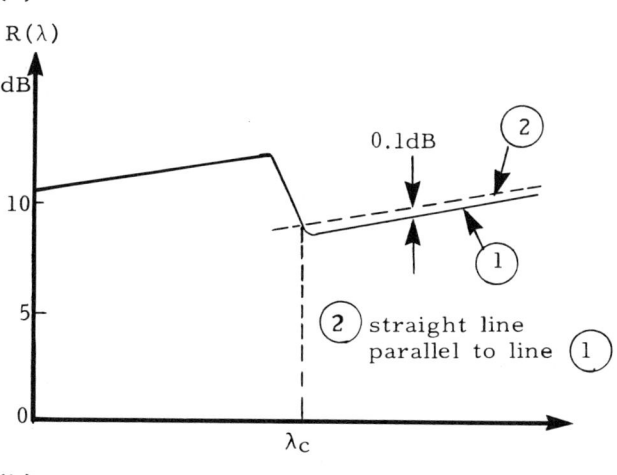

Figure 7.12 Typical measurement graphs of the cutoff wavelengths: (a) single-mode reference (bending method); (b) multimode reference (substitution method). (From Refs. 1, 5, and 9.)

is plotted as a function of wavelength as in Fig. 7.12. The cutoff wavelength is defined as the wavelength at the points shown in the figure.

7.2 MEASUREMENT OF TRANSMISSION CHARACTERISTICS

7.2.1 Loss

The loss (λ) at the wavelength λ between points (or attenuation coefficients) z_1 and z_2 is defined by the following equation.

$$(\lambda) = 10 \log \frac{P_1}{P_2} \text{ (dB)} \tag{7.13}$$

P_1 and P_2 is optical power that passes the optical fiber cross section at z_1 and z_2, respectively.

Based on the loss between points (distance between points L), the loss per unit distance can be calculated by the following equation:

$$\alpha(\lambda) = \frac{10}{Z_2 - Z_1} \log \frac{P_1}{P_2} \text{ (dB/km)}$$

$$= \frac{10}{L} \log \frac{P_1}{P_2} \text{ (dB/km)} \tag{7.14}$$

The measuring system for loss is shown in Figs. 7.13 and 7.14.

The attenuation coefficient is a useful parameter in designing fiber communications systems and is one of the important parameters to characterize fiber performance. However, the following problems have to be taken into consideration when using this value. One is the lengthwise uniformity of the optical fiber construction or material, even though this is not a measurement problem. Large variations in uniformity increase loss variations of optical fibers in the length direction, no longer allowing accurate calculations of a loss of a certain length using that attenuation coefficient. The meaning of losses per unit length is lost.

Another problem concerns launching conditions in measurement and the modal distribution propagating in a fiber. This is not a major problem with SM fibers. However, with multimode fibers, the attenuation coefficient is dependent on the optical fiber length unless a light propagates in the so-called steady-state mode distribution. Therefore, excitation in a steady-state modal distribution is used in loss measurements of multimode optical fibers.

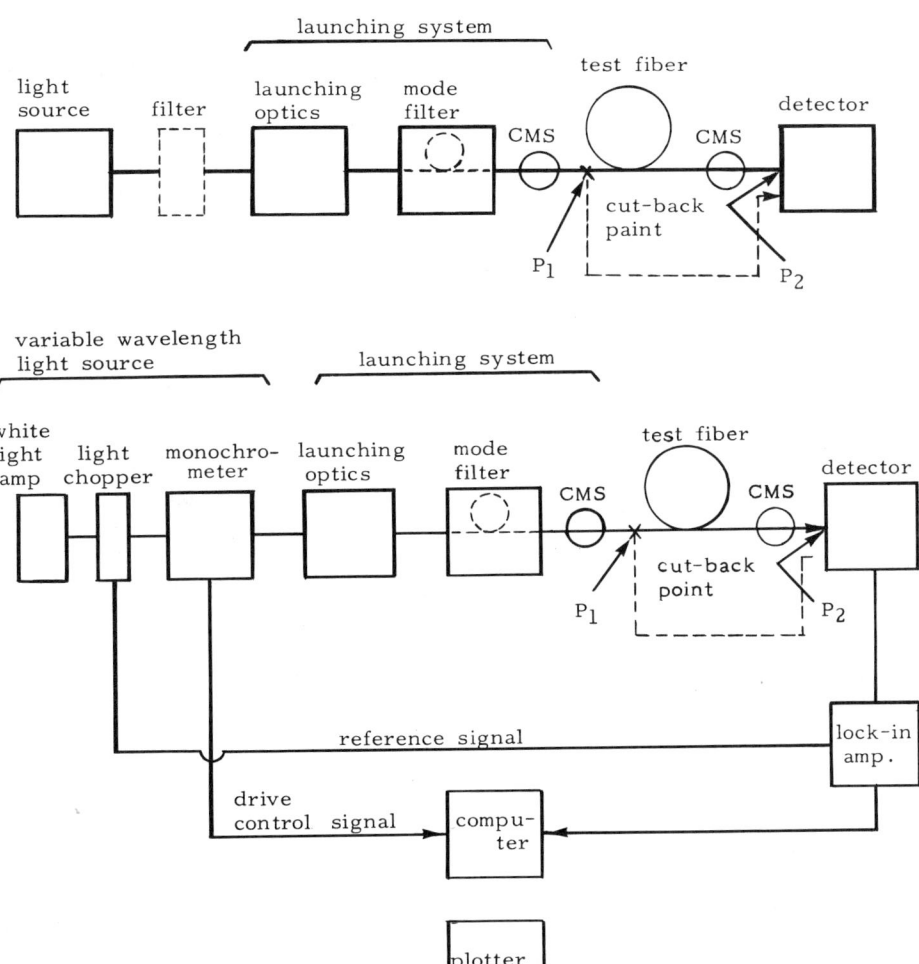

Figure 7.13 Typical setup of attenuation measurement (cutback method); CMS = cladding mode stripper. (From Refs. 1 and 5.)

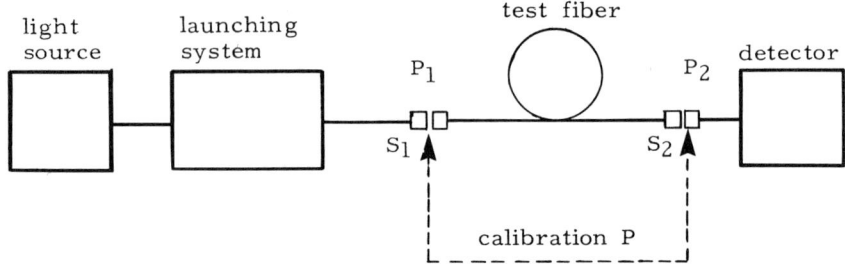

Figure 7.14 Typical setup of attenuation measurement (insertion method); S_1 and S_2 represent a fiber coupling device, such as a connector or a splice using a V groove. (From Refs. 1 and 5.)

Steady-state mode distribution is considered obtainable after optical power propagates a sufficiently long distance in the fiber and is substantially independent of the launching mode distribution. It is empirically found as a mode distribution when a sufficiently long optical fiber is used or when several optical fibers are spliced.

Examples of an approximate steady-state mode distribution are shown by the following field parameters for multimode fibers in Table 7.1:

1. The half-value width of an optical spot calculated form a near field: 26 μm
2. The NA value calculated as a half-value width of a far field: 0.11

An optics system that realizes such a mode distribution normally has three functions: mode scrambler, mode filter, and cladding mode stripper. The mode scrambler prevents the mode distribution from depending on the light source characteristics. The mode filter makes the mode distribution approximately a steady-state mode distribution. The cladding mode stripper removes unwanted cladding modes. The following are the launching optics systems that have these functions in combination.

1. Optical fiber exciter of a graded-step-graded sequence (GI fiber 2-3 m + SI fiber 2-3 m + GI fiber 2-3 m, in series splicing)
2. Dummy fiber

The steady-state mode distribution differs depending on the optical fiber construction or manufacturing lots. A steady-state mode distribution has to be determined in accordance with the circumstances.

Transmission Characteristics 431

In the case of single-mode optical fibers, only the fundamental mode is excited, and the following methods are used.

1. An appropriate SM fiber (normally, an optical fiber of the same construction) is butt joined.
2. An optics system using lenses is applied.

A mode filter obtained by small looping of the SM fiber to remove the higher order mode and a cladding mode stripper to remove unwanted cladding mode are used.

For the measurement of loss, three methods are applied:

1. Cutback method (commonly used)
2. Insertion method
3. Backscatter method (applied especially on site)

7.2.1.1 Cutback Method

This method is commonly and widely used for the measurement of the loss of fibers. Figure 7.13 shows a measuring system. An optical power level P_2 at the optical fiber output end at a distance z_2 is measured. Then, the optical fiber is cut at a distance z_1 (normally 2 m) and the optical power level P_1 on that point is measured. Optical fiber loss can be calculated using Eq. (7.14).

Figure 7.13a shows a loss measuring system at a wavelength λ. An LED or LD is used as the light source. A filter is used when necessary to narrow the spectrum width. An optical power meter is normally used as a detector.

Figure 7.13b shows a loss spectrum measuring system. A variable-wavelength light source is built using a white light source (tungsten halide lamp) and monochrometer.

7.2.1.2 Insertion Method

Figure 7.14 shows such a measuring system. First, the optical output level P_1 at the light source is measured. This value is considered the optical fiber incident power. Next, the optical fiber to be measured is set in the measuring system. The splicing between the light source and fiber, S_1 in Fig. 7.14, is adjusted so that the optical output level of the optical fiber becomes maximum, and the optical output level P_2 is measured. The loss can be calculated using Eq. (7.14).

Basically, the insertion method is the same as the cutback method. However, the light source output power is used as the incident power of the optical fiber to be measured, and the splicing loss between the light source and the fiber is added to the fiber loss. The splicing loss has to be corrected by some method to accurately obtain the fiber loss.

7.2.1.3 Backscattering Method [11]

The optical pulse launched into an optical fiber is absorbed and scattered as it propagates in the optical fiber and is attenuated. Part of the scattered light returns to the launched end. The optical fiber loss can be calculated by analyzing the intensity of this backscattering light and the time at which the scattered light returns at the incident end.

Let us assume that an optical pulse with a width of T and power P(O) is launched. This optical pulse propagates in the optical fiber at a group velocity v_g, and the optical power transported by the optical pulse varies in accordance with the following equation.

$$P(Z) = P(O) \, e^{(-\alpha(Z))} \tag{7.15}$$

A scattering light power generated in a very small section z to z + dz of an optical fiber can be calculated using the following equation.

$$dP_s(Z) = \alpha_R P(Z) \, dz \tag{7.16}$$

where

dP_s = scattering light power

α_R = scattering loss coefficient

Assuming that part of this scattering light returns to the incident end at a rate S, the scattering light power at Z, $dP_{bs}(Z)$, can be calculated by the following equation.

$$dP_{bs}(Z) = S\alpha_R P(Z) \, dz \tag{7.17}$$

Considering the loss when returning from z to the incident end, a scattering light power is detected at the launched end as the following equation.

$$dP_d(Z) = dP_{bs}(Z) \, e^{(-2\alpha(Z))} \tag{7.18}$$

where

$dP_d(Z)$ = the scattering light power returned to the launched end.

Substituting Eq. (7.17), the following equation can be obtained.

$$dP_d(Z) = S\alpha_R P(O) \, e^{(-2\alpha(Z))} \tag{7.19}$$

Transmission Characteristics

Time $t = 2Z/v_g$ is required before the optical pulse reaches the point z and returns to the launched end, and the optical power detected at the launched end at time t, P(t), will be calculated by the following equation.

$$P(t) = \frac{1}{2} S \alpha_R P(0) v_g T \, e^{[-2\alpha(v_g t/2)]} \tag{7.20}$$

The optical fiber loss can be calculated by analyzing this formula.

Figure 7.15 shows the measuring system. A light is launched into the optical fiber by the light source through the optical coupler (e.g., a half-mirror) and launching system. The light, which backscatters in the optical fiber, is detected in the detector through the optical coupler after passing through a reverse path. The output electric power to the detector is output after being amplified or averaged to improve the S/N ratio. Figure 7.15b shows an example of this output signal.

The light source, optical coupler, and so on, are arranged as shown in the figure. Unlike in the initial period when research of the backscattering method was started, recently, they are combined in one unit and are sold on the market as a measuring unit called an optical reflectometer, for example.

7.2.2 Bandwidth

In optical fiber communications, information is generally transmitted by modulating the intensity of a light at a certain wavelength. The optical fiber response to the modulation signal is called baseband response and is an important characteristic to determine the optical fiber transmission capacity. The baseband response can be expressed by either a time domain or a frequency domain.

The impulse response h(t) in a time domain can be calculated as one that couples the waveform x(t) and output pulse waveform y(t), which is the response of x(t), when an optical pulse x(t) is launched to the optical fiber, as shown by the following equation.

$$y(t) = \int_0^\infty h(t - \tau) x(\tau) \, d\tau \tag{7.21}$$

Assuming Fourier transformation of the impulse response h(t), input signal x(t), and output signal y(t) to be H(w), X(w), and Y(w), the following relationship can be obtained based on Eq. (7.21).

$$Y(w) = H(w) X(w) \tag{7.22}$$

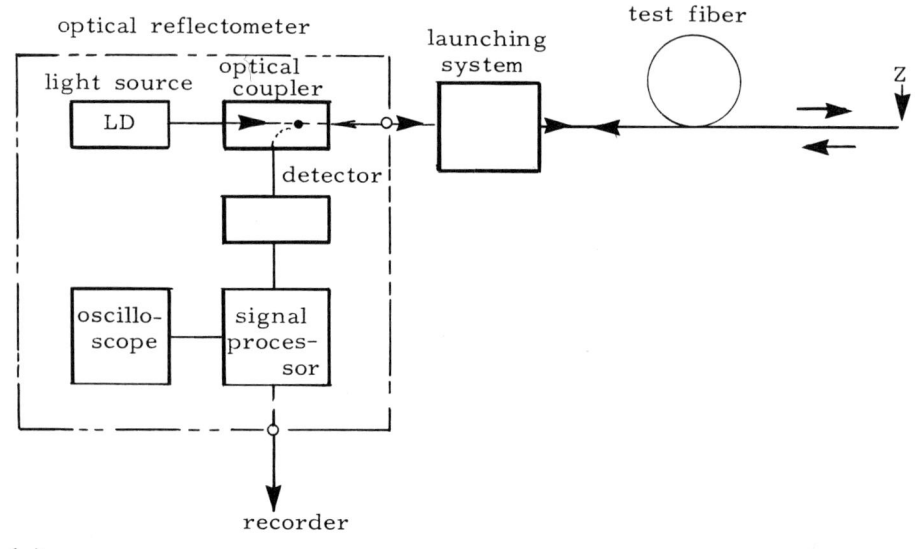

(a)

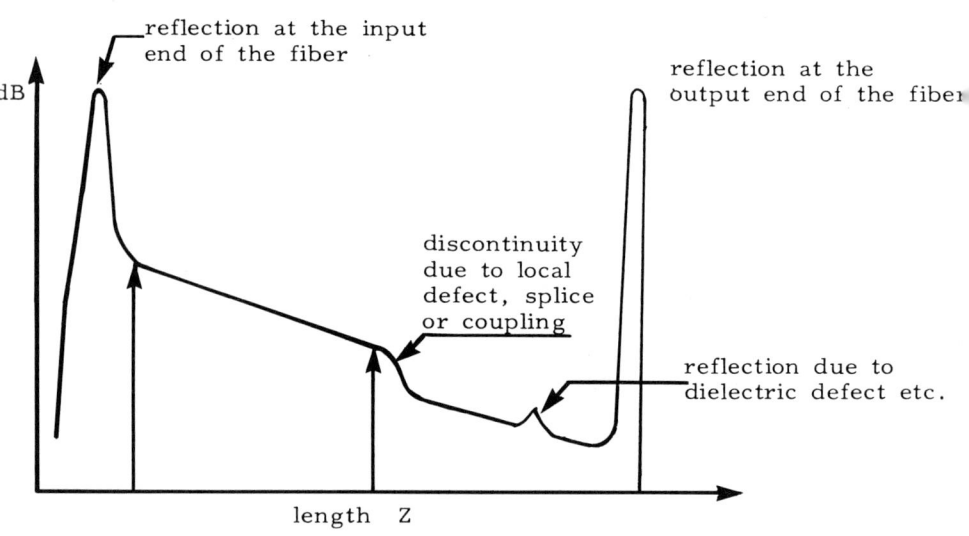

(b)

Figure 7.15 Measurement of backscattering: (a) setup; (b) typical curve. (From Refs. 1, 5, and 11.)

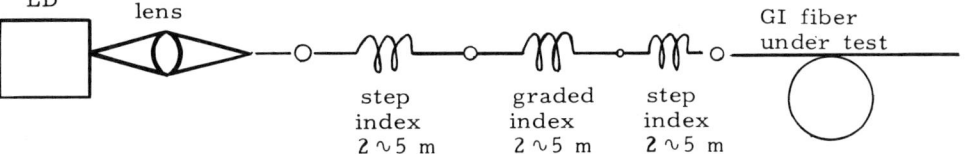

Figure 7.16 Launching for bandwidth measurement. (From Refs. 1 and 5.)

The baseband response in a frequency domain H(w) is the relationship of the input and output of the signal modulated by a sine wave, expressing such a relationship by a function of the modulation frequency w.

The absolute value and phase of the baseband frequency response are called the baseband amplitude response and the baseband phase response, respectively. In many cases, the baseband response means the baseband amplitude response.

For the measurement of bandwidth, two methods are used:

1. Measurement in the time domain
2. Measurement in the frequency domain

In measurement in the time domain, the amplitude and phase response can be obtained. In measurement in the frequency domain, the amplitude response can be obtained.

The bandwidth at the modulation frequency w is defined by the following equation.

$$20 \log H(w) = -6 \text{ dB} \tag{7.23}$$

Mode dispersion of an SM fiber is zero, and the bandwidth of an SM fiber is very wide. Therefore, the baseband response is not used ordinarily for the SM fiber. Dispersion is used for the SM fiber to characterize the bandwidth.

The group velocity of each propagation mode differs with multimode optical fibers, and the bandwidth of the multimode fiber differs depending on the mode distribution in the fiber.

For this reason, the launching condition to the multimode fiber and the reproducibility of the measurement results are very important for the bandwidth measurement of the multimode fiber.

For good reproducibility of the measurement results, an exciter with a uniform mode distribution is ordinarily used (Fig. 7.16).

Figure 7.17 shows a measuring system of baseband frequency response. A laser diode is used as the light source for direct

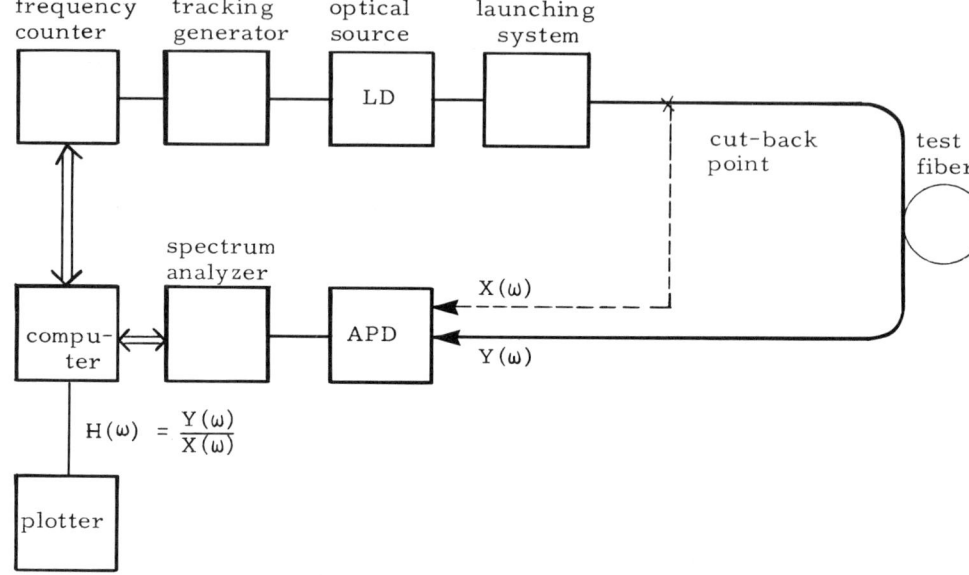

Figure 7.17 Typical setup of baseband frequency response measurement. (From Refs. 1 and 5.)

modulation. In the light emitting spectrum width, $\Delta\lambda$ is less than 5 nm in the $\lambda = 0.8$ to 0.9 μm band and is less than 10 nm in the $\lambda = 1.2$ to 1.3 and 1.5 to 1.6 μm band.

As the launching system, the uniform mode exciter of step-graded-step, is used.

After measuring the frequency response Y(w) transmitted in the optical fiber, the optical fiber is cut at a point 2 m from the launched system to measure the frequency response X(w), which becomes a reference. Then the computer outputs the baseband response $Y(w)/X(w) = H(w)$.

Figure 7.18 shows a system for measuring the time domain response. It is basically the same as Fig. 7.17, but the laser is modulated by pulse. As shown in the figure, the waveform received is a function of time, Y(t) and X(t). This is converted into $Y(w) = Y_1(w) + jY_2(w)$ and $X(w) = X_1(w) + jX_2(w)$ to obtain the baseband response $Y(w)/X(w)$.

7.2.3 Chromatic Dispersion

The chromatic dispersion of an SM fiber is defined as the group delay difference per spectral broadening of wavelength and is calculated by the following equation:

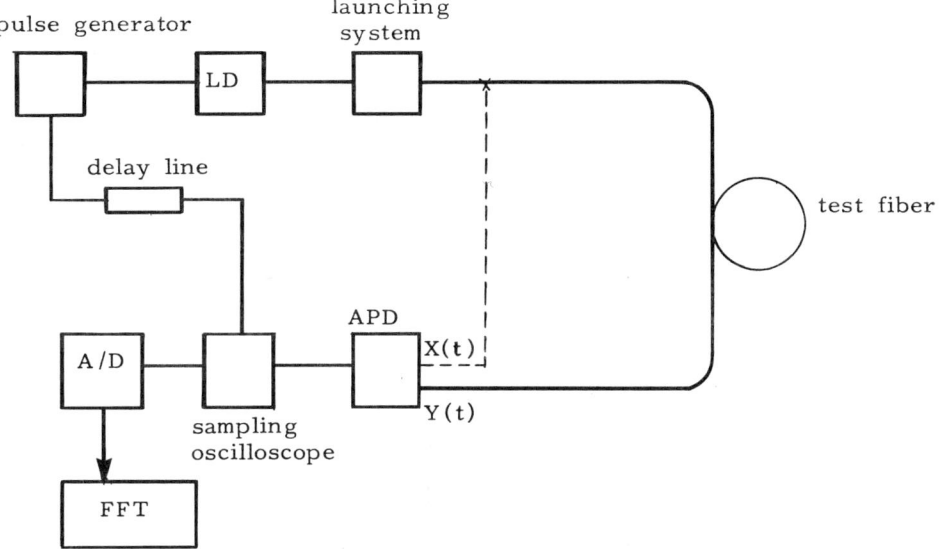

Figure 7.18 Typical setup of time domain measurement; FFT is fast Fourier transform. (From Refs. 1 and 5.)

$$S = \frac{dt}{d\lambda}$$

In accordance with this definition, dispersion is measured as follows. Assuming group delay time is t_0 at a wavelength λ_0, and at a wavelength λ group delay is t, the delay time difference of the following equation is measured:

$$\Delta t = t - t_0$$

This difference is approximated to a power series of a wavelength by the least-squares method and is differentiated regarding wavelength to calculate chromatic dispersion as follows:

$$S = \frac{t - t_0}{\Delta \lambda} = \frac{dt}{d\lambda}$$

where S = chromatic dispersion.

Group delay time is mainly measured by the following two methods. The first method measures the propagation time of a pulse wavelength with a narrow width (Fig. 7.19). A light source whose light emission

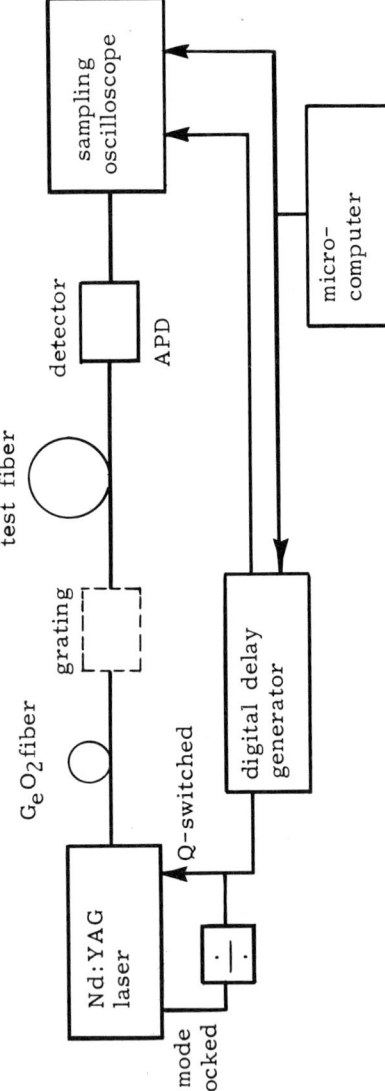

Figure 7.19 Arrangement for measuring chromatic dispersion (measurement of delay time). (From Refs. 1, 5, 12, and 13.)

Transmission Characteristics

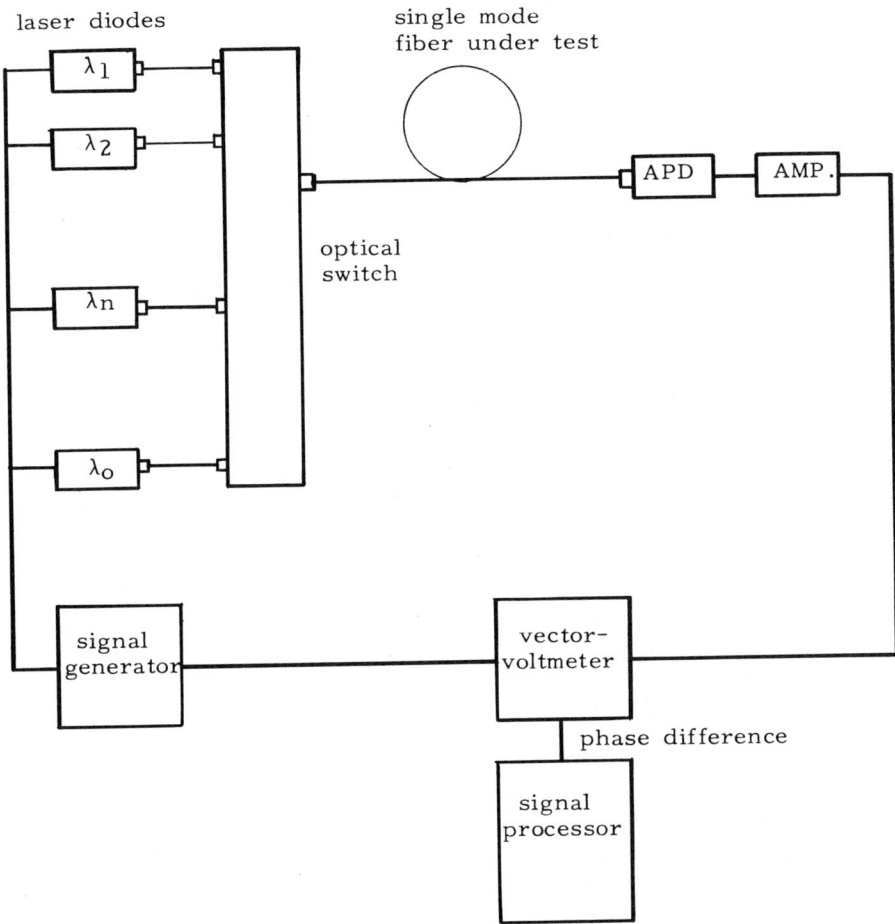

Figure 7.20 Arrangement for measuring chromatic dispersion (measurement of phase difference). (From Refs. 1, 5, 12, and 13.)

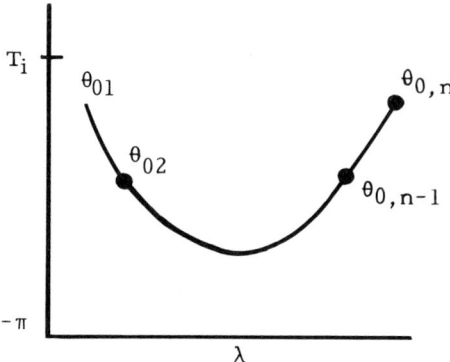

Figure 7.21 Measurement of chromatic dispersion. (From Refs. 1, 5, 12, and 13.)

wavelength and intensity are stable and whose spectrum width is sufficiently small is required. Raman fibers using a laser diode or an Nd-YAF laser as an excitation light source are frequently used.

Figure 7.19 shows a system for measuring dispersion by Raman scattering. Raman fiber (e.g., GeO_2 core fiber) is excited by the Nd-YAG laser. As a result of Raman scattering, many pulse trains with different wavelengths are generated in the Raman fiber at the 1-1.6 μm range. The time of propagation of these pulses is measured, and the curve of measurement is differentiated with respect to λ (wavelength) to determine dispersion.

The second method measures the phase difference of fiber input and output signals using a beam that is sine wave modulated in order to calculate the propagation time.

Figure 7.20 shows a dispersion measuring system using the measurement of phases. Laser diodes with wavelength $\lambda_i (i = 1-n)$ are modulated by sine wave and launched to the fiber to be measured. Its phase is measured at the output of the fiber. This phase is denoted by $\theta_i + wT_i$, where θ_i = initial angle of transmission signal, w = measuring angular frequency, and T_i = delay time.

Next, the light source and APD are connected to each other with a very short fiber in place of the fiber to be measured, and its phase is measured. This value may be assumed to be constant irrespective of the light source, because the fiber is short. This phase is expressed as follows.

$$\theta_i + wT_0$$

Therefore, the phase differences θ_{0i} are shown as follows (Fig. 7.21).

$$\theta_{0i} = w(T_i - T_0)$$

The dispersion $dT_i/d\lambda$ can be obtained from $d\theta_{0i}/d\lambda$.

7.3 PROFILE MEASUREMENT OF THE PREFORM [14-16]

By measuring the refractive index distribution of the preform, the bandwidth characteristics of the fiber can be estimated. Therefore, this is an important measuring method indispensable to process inspection in fiber production.

Figure 7.22 shows the principle of the profile measurement of a preform. The preform is immersed in a matching oil whose refractive index nearly equals that of the cladding layer of the preform. Parallel beams are launched in the side surface of the preform perpendicular to the preform axis (Fig. 7.22). The path of the beam launched in point A of coordinate y is bent as shown in Fig. 7.22 in

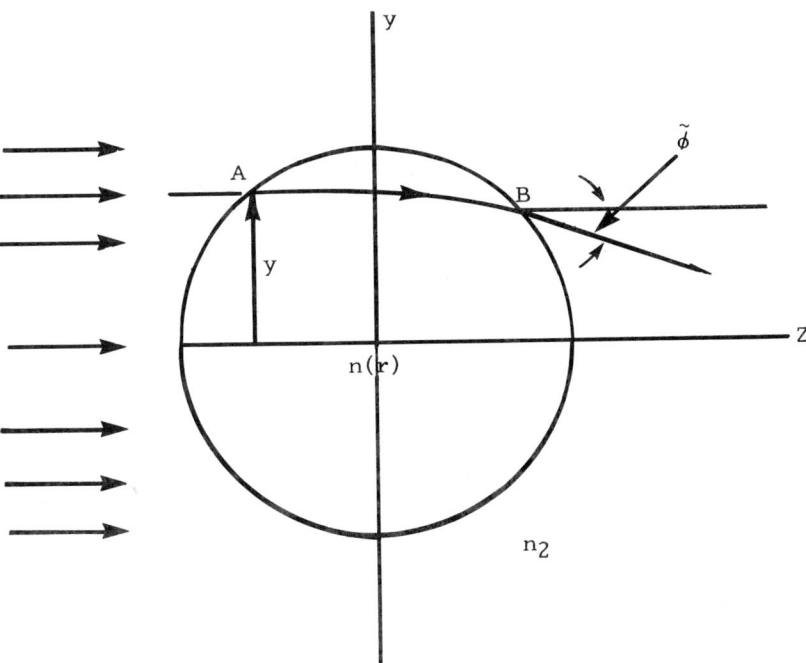

Figure 7.22 Light beam launching in the preform. (From Refs. 14-16.)

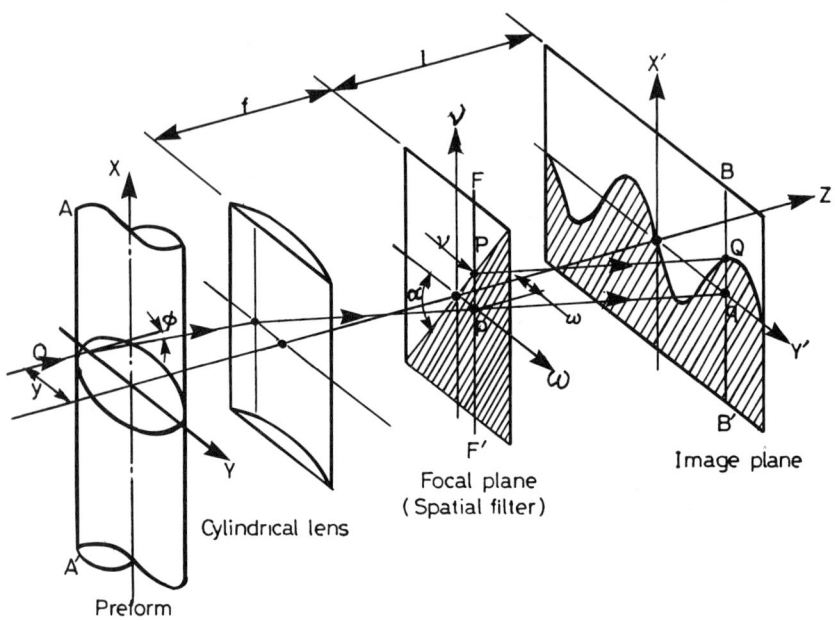

Figure 7.23 Principle for the measurement of the refractive index of the preform. (From Refs. 15 and 16.)

accordance with the core refractive index profile and emerges from point B at angle $\tilde{\phi}$. Assuming that the refractive index $n(r) \doteq n_2$ (n_2 = refractive index of cladding of the preform), that is, the launching and emerging position of ordinates are also equal, the core refractive index can be expressed by the following equation:

$$n(r) = n_2 \left(1 - \frac{1}{\pi} \int_r^a \tilde{\phi}(y) \frac{dy}{\sqrt{y^2 - r^2}} \right) \qquad (7.24)$$

where a = core radius in the preform. Therefore, by measuring the emergent angle as a function of the launching position, the core refractive index can be calculated by simple calculations using this equation.

Using Fig. 7.23, the method to measure the emergent angle is explained [2]. The image of the x − y plane of the preform focuses into an image on the image plane x' − y' using a cylindrical lens. The beam launched at position 0, whose distance from the z − x plane is y, is emerged from the preform at angle $\tilde{\phi}$ and emerges at the interface between the matching oil container and the air with

Profile Measurement of the Preform

angle $\tilde{\phi}$ and passes through the beam path as shown in Fig. 7.23. The positions of the beam on the focusing plane (v-w plane) and image plane (x'-y' plane) are assumed to be points p and q, respectively. The positions of p and q, namely, w and y', respectively, can be related to the emergent angle $\tilde{\phi}$ and launching position y by the following equations:

$$w = f \tan \phi \tag{7.25}$$

$$y' = \frac{l}{f} y \tag{7.26}$$

The beam launched into the preform at positions AA', whose distance from the x-z plane is y, passes the focal plane on position FF' and focuses into an image on the image plane in position BB'. If a spatial filter is inserted, disabling half of the focal plane to pass beams on a boundary angle α, QB' becomes dark and QB becomes light on the image plane. Since the beam paths p-q and P-Q are parallel, the coordinate x' of the boundary Q of light and shade can be expressed as follows:

$$x' = \nu = w \tan \alpha = (f \tan \alpha) \tan \phi \tag{7.27}$$

Coordinate y' can be calculated using Eq. (7.26).

Thus, by measuring the boundary x'-y' of light and shade on the image plane, the relationship between the launching position y and emergent angle $\tilde{\phi}$ of a beam launched to the preform with the parallel axis can be calculated. The refractive index profile can be calculated using Eq. (7.24). The following relationship exists on the interface between the matching oil container and the air because of Snell's law:

$$\sin \tilde{\phi} = n_2 \sin \phi \tag{7.28}$$

A boundary between light and shade is measured by scanning a photodiode array in an x' direction and by feeding the data to a computer.

Figure 7.24 shows an improvement of the foregoing method [3]. An ordinary convex lens is used, and the detector is fixed on a light axis (axis z) on the image plane. By sliding the preform by y from the light axis z, the beam launched in the light axis is launched in the preform from position Y, as shown in Fig. 7.22. Therefore, as shown in Fig. 7.24, the emergent beam from the preform passes through position P on the focal plane (νw plane) and focuses into an image at origin Q on the image plane (x'-y' plane). The launching position y can be measured directly from the sliding amount of the preform, and the emergent angle φ is measured as a

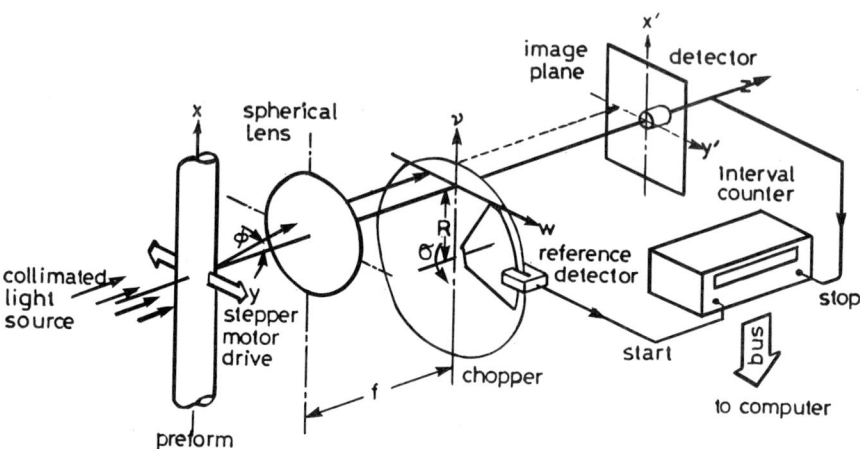

Figure 7.24 Equipment for measuring the refractive index of the preform. (From Refs. 15 and 16.)

time amount after detecting the position w on which a beam passes the focusing plane, using a rotating spatial filter. The beam passing position on the focal plane is calculated based on the time after the chopper generated a reference signal and before it passes a beam. The emergent angle is measured by sliding the preform using a step motor, and data are processed by a computer. Compared with the method shown in Fig. 7.22, one advantage of this method is that longitudinal refractive index profile variations can be determined easily by the same method by moving the preform in an X-axis direction.

REFERENCES

1. CCITT, Red Book Vol. III, Fascicle III. 2-Rec. G651, Characteristics of 50/125 m multimode graded index optical fibre cable, pp. 241–272 (1985).

2. D. Gloge and E. A. J. Marcatilli, Multimode theory of graded-core fibers, *BSTJ*, 52(9): 1563–1578 (1973).

3. F. M. Sladen, D. N. Payne, and M. J. Adams, Determination of optical fiber refractive index profiles by a near-field scanning technique, *Appl. Phys. Lett.*, 28(5): 255–258 (1976).

4. K. I. White, Practical application of the refractive near-field technique for the measurement of optical fiber refractive index profiles, *Opt. Quantum Electron.*, *11*(2): 185–196 (1979).

5. CCITT, Red Book Vol. III, Fascicle III. 2-Rec. G652, Characteristics of a single-mode optical fiber cable, pp. 272–291 (1985).

6. J. Sreckert, New method for measuring the spot size of single-mode fibers, *Opt. Lett.*, *5*(12): 505–506 (1980).

7. W. T. Anderson and D. L. Philen, Spot size measurement for single-mode fibers—A comparison of four techniques, *J. Lightwave Technol.*, *LT-1*(1): 20–26 (1983).

8. W. T. Anderson, Consistency of measurement methods for the mode field radius in a single-mode fiber, *J. Lightwave Technol.*, *LT-2*(2): 191–197 (1984).

9. K. Kitayama, M. Ohahi, and Y. Ishida, Length dependence of effective cutoff wavelength in single-mode fibers, *J. Lightwave Technol.*, *LT-2*(5): 629–634 (1984).

10. D. L. Frazen, Determining the effective cutoff wavelength of single-mode fibers: An interlaboratory comparison, *J. Lightwave Technol.*, *LT-3*(1): 128–134 (1985).

11. M. K. Barnoski, M. D. Bourke, S. M. Jensen, and R. T. Melville, Optical time domain reflectometer, *Appl. Opt.*, *16*(9): 2375–2379 (1977).

12. K. Kitayama, Y. Kato, S. Seikai, and M. Tateda, Broadband (0.6–1.6 m) subnanosecond pulse emission using an ultra-low-loss single-mode fibers, *Appl. Opt.*, *20*(14): 2428–2432 (1981).

13. P. J. Vella, P. M. Garel-Jones, and R. S. Lowe, Measurement of chromatic dispersion of long spans of single-mode fiber: A factory and field test method, *Electron Lett.*, *20*(4): 167–168 (1984).

14. D. Marcuse, Refractive index determination by the focusing method, *Appl. Opt.*, *18*(1): 9–13 (1979).

15. I. Sasaki, D. N. Payne, and M. J. Adams, Measurement of refractive-index profiles in optical-fiber preforms by special filtering technique, *Electron Lett.*, *16*: 219–221 (1980).

16. I. Sasaki, D. N. Payne, R. J. Mansfield, and M. J. Adams, Variation of refractive-index profiles in single-mode fiber preforms measured using an improved high-resolution spatial-filtering technique, 6th ECOC, pp. 140–143 (September 1980).

8
Installation of Optical Fiber Cable

Needless to say, the development of the optical fiber and optical fiber cable required parallel studies of optical fiber splicing and optical fiber cable joining, as well as of their installation. In the development history of the millimeter-wave circular waveguide, the development of waveguide installation was not sufficient. In the final analysis, this was the reason that millimeter-wave circular waveguides failed to be commercialized.

The standard length of one optical fiber cable length is 1 to 2 km, compared with 150 to 500 m with copper conductor cable because the optical fiber cables are light and small in mechanical dimensions and because the total loss of fiber splices must be minimized by increasing the cable length.

The following considerations require particular attention in the installation of fiber cable.

1. The elongation of the fiber itself is approximately 5% on average, the minimum being approximately 1%. The elongation of the copper wire is more than 25%, and this elongation value greatly differs. As mentioned in Chap. 2 (Secs. 2.4 and 2.5), to prevent the optical fiber from breaking for a long period of time, the elongation distortion applied to the fiber must be kept to less than 0.5%. Taking these values into consideration, the safety value of the optical fiber elongation during optical fiber cable installation should preferably be kept to less than 0.2%.
2. As the fiber cable lengths are long, 1 to 2 km, fiber cables are sometimes passed through manholes and bent during installation. Necessary precautions should be taken to prevent applying unnecessary tension to the cable. Calculation formulas of the tension during optical fiber cables installation are given below.

$T = \mu WL$

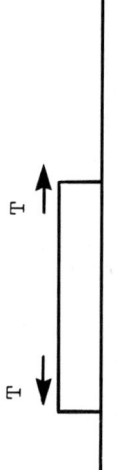

Horizontal

Pulling upward: $T' = WL(\mu \cos \theta + \sin \theta)$

Pulling downward: $T'' = WL(\mu \cos \theta - \sin \theta)$

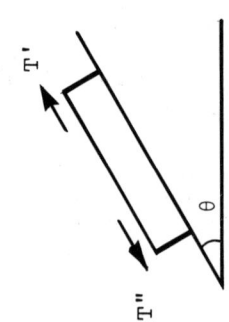

$T = WR \sinh \left(\mu \theta + \sinh^{-1} \dfrac{T_1}{WR} \right)$

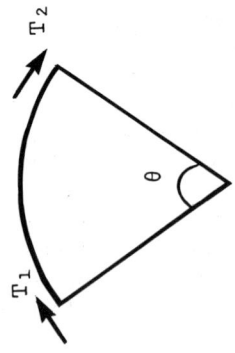

Horizontally curved

Pulling upward: $T_2 = \dfrac{WR}{1+\mu^2}[(1-\mu^2)\sin\theta + 2\mu(e^{\mu\theta} - \cos\theta)]$

  $+ T_1 e^{\mu\theta}$

When $\theta = \pi/2$,

$T_2 = \dfrac{WR}{1+\mu^2}[(1-\mu^2) + 2\mu e^{\mu\pi/2}] + T_1 e^{\mu\pi/2}$

Pulling downward: $T_2 = \dfrac{WR}{1+\mu^2}[2\mu\sin\theta - (1-\mu^2)(e^{\mu\theta} - \cos\theta)]$

  $+ T_1 e^{\mu\theta}$

When $\theta = \pi/2$,

$T_2 = \dfrac{WR}{1+\mu^2}[2\mu - (1-\mu^2)e^{\mu\pi/2}] + T_1 e^{\mu\pi/2}$

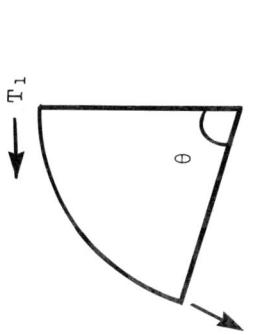

Vertically curved

Pulling downward: $T_2 = T_1 e^{\mu\theta} - \dfrac{WR}{1+\mu^2} (1-\mu^2) \sin\theta$

$\qquad\qquad\qquad + 2\mu (e^{\mu\theta} - \cos\theta)$

When $\theta = \pi/2$,

$T_2 = T_1 e^{\mu\pi/2} - \dfrac{WR}{1+\mu^2} [(1-\mu^2) + 2\mu e^{\mu\pi/2}]$

Pulling upward: $T_2 = T_1 e^{\mu\theta} - \dfrac{WR}{1+\mu^2} [2\mu\cos\theta - (1-\mu^2)e^{\mu\theta}$

$\qquad\qquad\qquad - \cos\theta)]$

When $\theta = \pi/2$,

$T_2 = T_1 e^{\mu\pi/2} - \dfrac{WR}{1+\mu^2} [2\mu - (1-\mu^2)e^{\mu\pi/2}]$

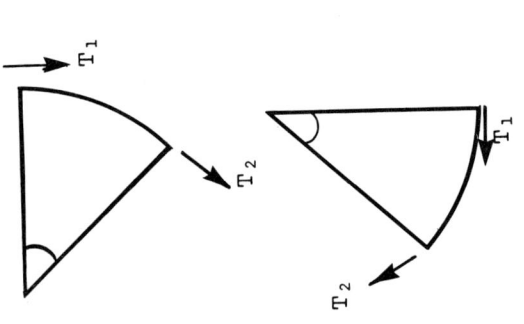

Vertically curved (continued)

Installation of Cable

where

T, T', T'' = tension applied to the cable

T_1 = tension to the cable before the curved section

T_2 = tension to the cable after the curved section

μ = friction coefficient

W = cable weight per unit length

θ = angle

L = cable length

The values of μ for various duct materials are approximately as follows.

PVC, 0.4 μ
Cast iron, 0.5 to 0.6 μ
Concrete, 0.7 μ

Strength members are inserted inside the cable during cable design so that the tension corresponding to a cable elongation of 0.2% nearly equals the weight of a 1 km cable. Because the friction coefficient of the polyvinyl chloride (PVC) duct is 0.4, this cable design equals a safety factor of 2.5. The tension to the fiber cable correspondingly increases when the cable passes a curved section during its installation.

The tension applied to the optical fiber cable in a horizontally curved section, as mentioned above, can be expressed as follows:

$$T_2 = WR \sinh \left(\mu\theta \sinh^{-1} \frac{T_1}{WR} \right)$$

If $WR \gg T_1$

$$\frac{T_2}{T_1} = \frac{WR}{T_1} \sinh \mu\theta + \cosh \mu\theta \qquad (8.1)$$

If $WR \ll T_1$,

$$\frac{T_2}{T_1} = e^{\mu\theta} \qquad (8.2)$$

If Eq. (8.2) is used and when $\mu = 0.4$ and $\theta = \pi/2$,

$$\frac{T_2}{T_1} = 1.87 \doteqdot 2$$

The tension applied to the fiber cable at each 90° curved section is approximately double.

Figure 8.1 shows the relationship between curved angle θ and T_2/T_1. If T_1 is small, the absolute value of T_2 should also be small. A frequently used method to make T_1 as near as possible to 0 in the curved section is to pull the fiber cable in the intermediate point of cable installation using a cable sender (Fig. 8.2). An installation example of an optical fiber cable with curved sections is shown in Fig. 8.3. Examples of the cable tension at the installation intermediate points using cable senders and of pulling only the cable end are shown in Fig. 8.4.

Pulling wire is installed in the duct beforehand. The tension T_1 when the cable is pulled by the cable sender before the curved

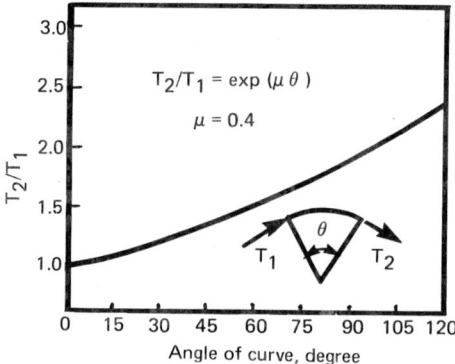

Figure 8.1 Relationship between curve angle and cable-pulling tension. (From Ref. 1.)

Installation of Cable

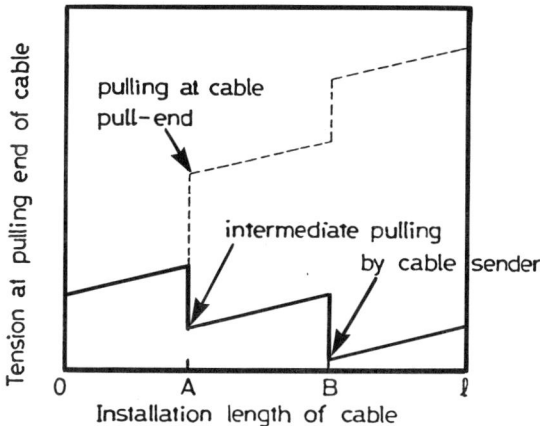

Figure 8.2 Pulling tension during installation of cable. (From Ref. 1.)

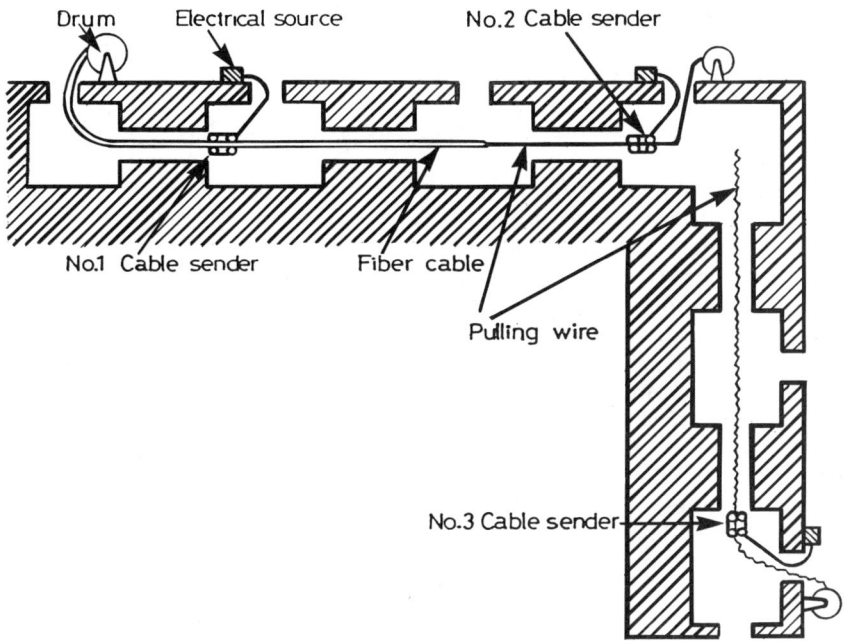

Figure 8.3 Cable installation through the curved section. (From Ref. 1.)

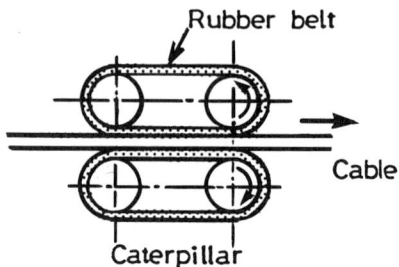

Figure 8.4 Cable sender.

section and passes the curved section is nearly 0. In this case, T_2 will become very small. Generally, rubber belt caterpillars (Fig. 8.3) are used for the cable sender (Fig. 8.2).

The cable sender requires the following conditions:

1. The pull strength of the cable sender is less than the allowable cable tension and is stable.
2. The lateral pressure applied to the cable during cable pulling is a value that does not make the cable flat.
3. The cable should be compact and light and should be able to be assembled easily even in the manhole.

Cable senders weighing approximately 50 kg are sold on the market at present.

The fiber cable is pulled by cable senders before curved sections, and the pulling wire is wound on the small drums as shown in Fig. 8.3. The fiber cable is reconnected to the pulling wire and is pulled through the curved section and enters the next duct. If pulling speeds of the cable senders do not match, or if on-and-off operation of the cable sender are not appropriate when more than two cable senders are used simultaneously (see Fig. 8.3), a surging phenomenon of the tension applied to the cable may be caused. Figure 8.5 shows an example of this. The maximum tension by surging is roughly twice the forecast value. As mentioned earlier, the safety factor of 2 versus the tension can be recognized to be appropriate.

Flexible pipes, for example, should preferably be used to reduce the friction coefficient when installing a cable in the curved section or in ducts of different levels. Figure 8.6 shows an example using flexible pipe.

The figure-8 method as described below is used if cable senders cannot be used halfway in the ducts (Fig. 8.7)[3]. When a long fiber cable is being installed and it is impossible to pull the cable from end to end, the drum should be set up at an intermediate

Installation of Cable

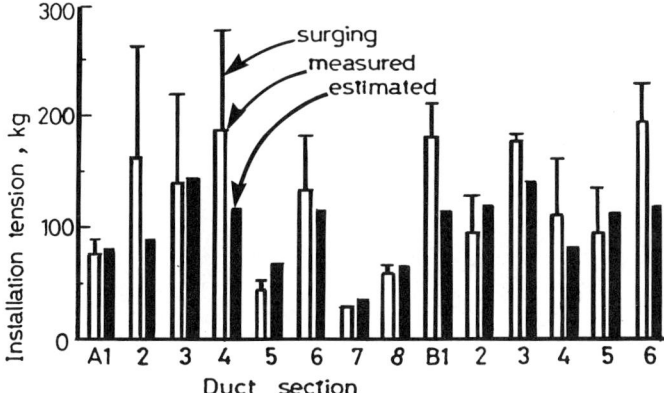

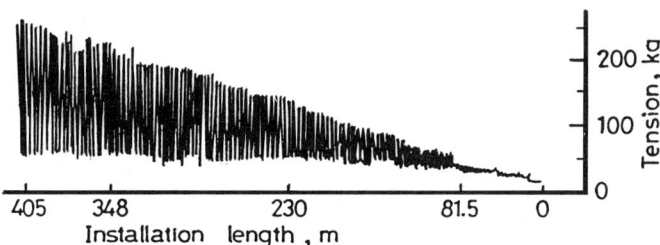

Figure 8.5 Installation tension on the fiber cable. (From Refs. 1 and 2.)

manhole and the longer cable (first part of the cable, Fig. 8.7) should first be pulled into the duct. Then the remaining cable (second part of the cable, Fig. 8.7) on the drum should be removed and piled on the ground, layer upon layer, in a figure-8 formation having dimensions of about 2 × 5 m. The end of the cable should then be pulled in a direction opposite to the first pulling (to duct #2).

When passing the cable down into the manhole, the utmost care should be taken to ensure that the cable is not twisted and that any natural twist is not concentrated on the cable in the manhole.

A pulling eye is provided at the pulling end of the fiber cable to pull it as shown in Fig. 8.8. The fiber cable end should be processed so that the pulling tension mainly applies to the strength members inside the cable. The outside diameter of the pulling eye should be nearly the same as that of the cable. A pressed sleeve is provided with the strength member, and a pulling eye is mounted on it.

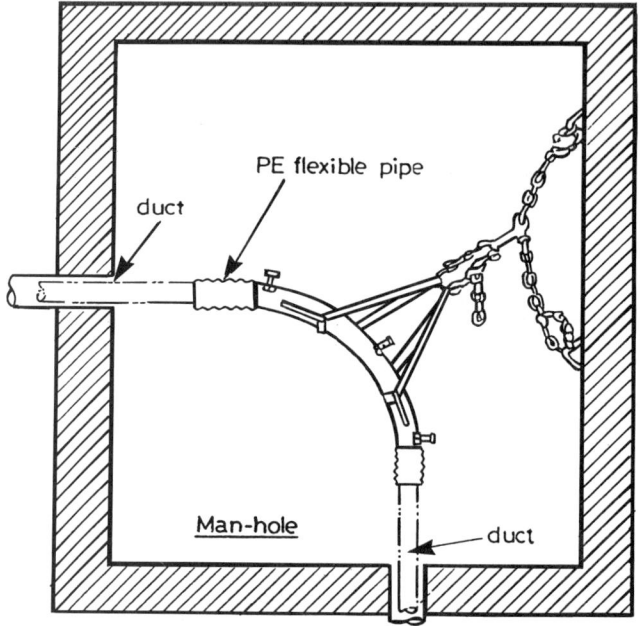

(a)

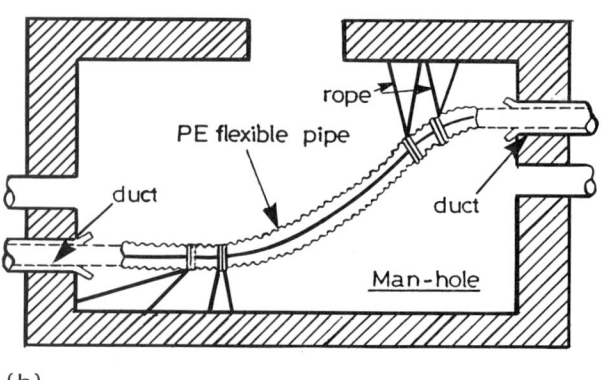

(b)

Figure 8.6 Installation through a manhole: (a) curved section; (b) different levels. (From Refs. 1 and 2.)

Installation of Cable 457

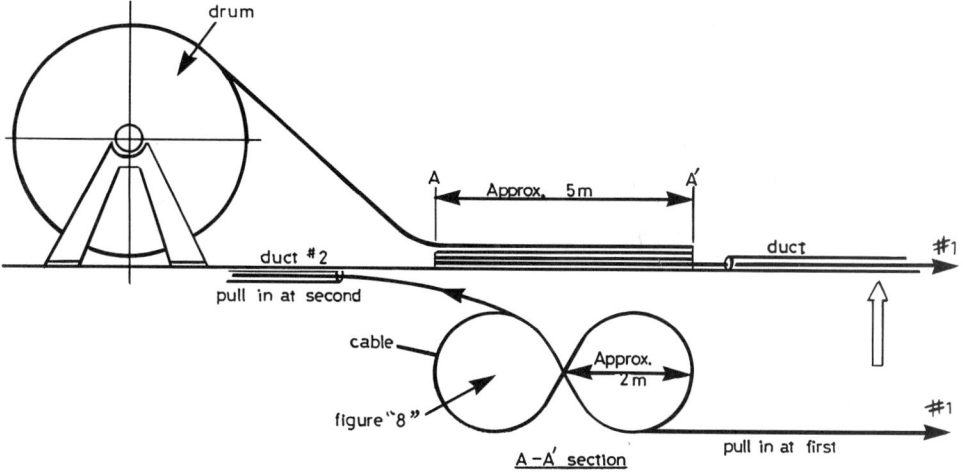

Figure 8.7 Method for winding back cables in a figure 8. (From Ref. 3.)

The outside diameter of the fiber cable is generally small compared with that of copper wire cables and is less than 35 mm for practical uses. The duct dimensions are 3 to 4 in., and several fiber cables can be pulled in one duct.

However, in this case, the cables themselves tangle as the cables rotate. If installers try to pull out a cable, as where there is a fiber or cable fault, a large tension is applied to the cable, and this cable sometimes cannot be pulled out. To avoid such a phenomenon,

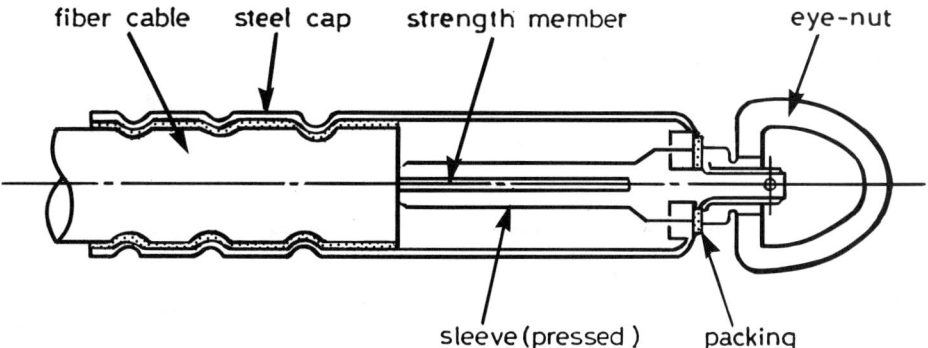

Figure 8.8 Pulling eye. (From Refs. 1 and 2.)

458   Installation of Cable

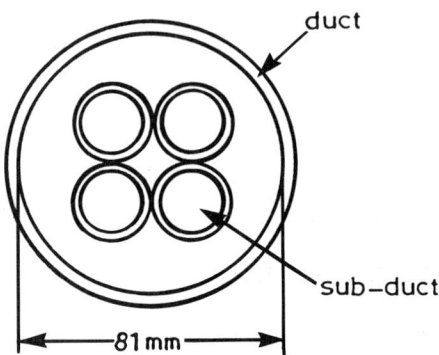

Figure 8.9   Subduct. (From Ref. 1.)

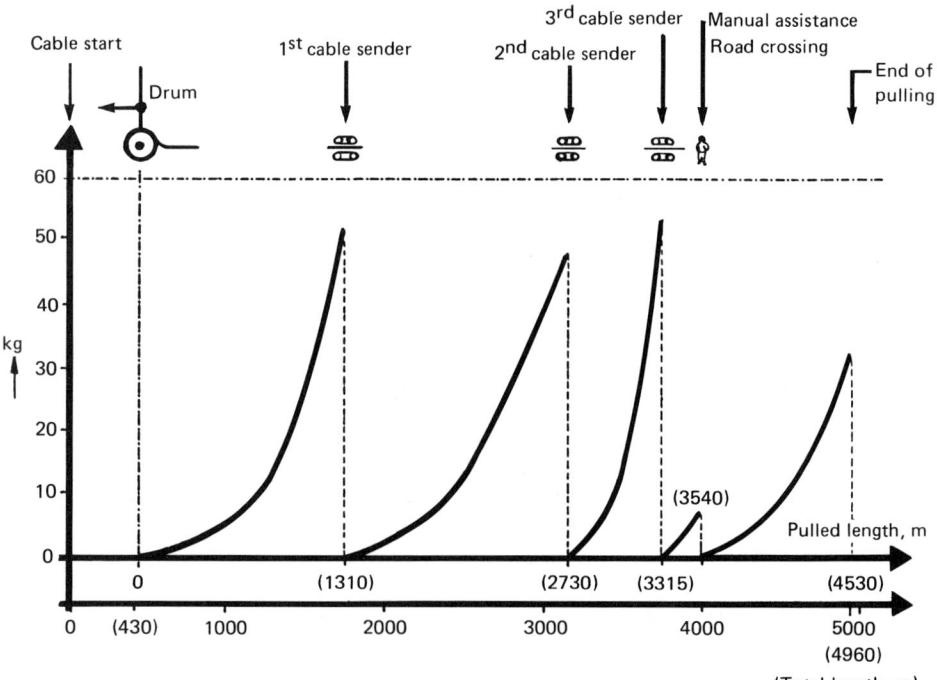

Figure 8.10   Pulling load applied to a 5000 m cable (with microball). (From Ref. 4.)

several subducts of small diameter are pulled in the duct beforehand and one fiber cable for each such subduct is pulled in during installation.

Figure 8.9 shows one example. Four plastic pipes, which are called subducts, are bundled and are inserted inside a 3 in. duct. The outside and inside diameters of the plastic pipe bundle are approximately 27 and 24 mm. By this method, fiber cables approximately 15 mm in outside diameter maximum can be pulled in the subduct.

The microball technique [4] has been studied as a means to reduce the friction coefficient of the cable when pulling a long fiber cable into a duct during the cable installation. Nylon balls 0.2 to 0.4 mm in diameter are blown into the duct. These nylon balls adhere on the cable surface to make pulling of the cable into the duct easier. The nylon balls reduce the friction coefficient between the cable and duct to less than 0.1. Figure 8.10 shows the friction data of 10-fiber V-groove cable 10.4 mm in outside diameter and 5000 m in length being installed in a duct using this technique. The cable was pulled using cable senders at three locations in manholes. The installation speed was 100 m/min.

REFERENCES

1. N. Unchida, Installation system for the optical fiber cable of 2km length, Nikkei Electron, pp. 126–151 (May 1980).

2. T. Saito, S. Nakagome, H. Kawakami, K. Takayama, M. Kitagawa, and S. Yoshitake, Installation of optical cable, *ECL Tech. J.*, 28(9): 1907–1919 (September 1979).

3. Furukawa Report, Installation of optical fiber cable, TD-84071 pp. 1–27 (August 1984).

4. D. Boscher, B. Nonclercq, A. Le Boutet, and B. Missout, Manufacture, laying and splicing of mono-mode optical fiber cables with low losses, 32nd IWCS pp. 308–315 (November 1983).

Index

Applications of optical fibers and cables, 13–14
Arc fusion splicing machine, 340–357

Ball connector, 379, 385
Bandwidth, transmission:
 of GI fiber, 38–49
 measurement of, 433–436
 of spliced fibers, 51–54
Biconic connector, 378, 383–385
Breaking of silica fiber, 62–66
Brillouin scattering loss, 30

Carbon dioxide (CO_2) laser beam fiber drawing machine, 109–110, 111
Chemical relaibility of fiber, 71–87
 long-term relaibility of plastic-covered fiber, 87
Chemical vapor deposition (CVD) production method, 88

Chromatic dispersion, measurement of, 436–441
Circular waveguide, properties of, 10–11
Cladding diameter, 409
Cladding surface noncircularity, 410
Coaxial cable, properties of, 10–11
Connectors, 375–395
 ball connector, 379, 385
 biconic connector, 378, 383–385
 fiber ribbon connector, 388–389
 lens connector, 378, 382–383
 multifiber connector, 386
 plastic connectors, 379, 390, 391, 392, 393, 394
 precision ferrule connectors, 377–382
 requirements for, 375
 single-fiber connectors, 377, 378–379
 V-groove round connector, 386–388
Connecting, definition of, 322
Construction methods of fiber cable, 243–314

[Construction methods of fiber cable]
 loose tube cable, 243, 244–245, 282–305
 ribbon cable, 243, 244–245, 246–257, 258–259
 stranding cable, 243, 244–245, 257–282
  layer, 243, 268–271
  unit, 243, 272–282
 V-groove cable, 243, 244–245, 305–314
Copper conductors in the cable core, 236
Core-caldding surface concentricity error, 410
Core diameter, 408–409
Core noncircularity, 410
Cutoff wavelength (λ_c), 54–57
 measurment of, 424–428

Deformation of plastic tube under lateral load, 205–212
Design of fiber cables, basic conditions for, 181–237
 cable sheath, 220–221, 222
 caution during installation in the duct, 237
 copper conductors in the cable core, 236
 deformation of plastic tube under lateral load, 205–212
 design of plastic covering on the fiber, 234
 design of strength members in the cable, 212–220
 low-temperature problems, 223–234
 mechanical design, 186–192
 microbending loss increase, 181–186
 problems of jelly filling in the cable core, 221
 problems of unit lengths of cable, 236–237

[Design of fiber cables, basic conditions for]
 stranded fibers in the cable, 192–205
Dielectric fiber surface waveguides, 4
Dielectric waveguides, 3, 4
Dopants:
 material requirements for, 88
 properties of, 21
 recommended combination of, 18
 refractive index of, 21
 for silica fiber, 19–20

Features of fiber, 8–14
FFP (far field pattern) method for measurement of NA, 418–419
Fiber breaker, 368–372
Fiber drawing, 104–112
 furnaces for
  CO_2 laser beam drawing machine, 109–110, 111
  comparison of, 111
  graphite resistance furnace, 104, 105–109, 111
  zirconia furnace, 104, 109, 111
Fiber ribbon connector, 388–389
Flame fusion splicing, 352–354
Flares, 1
Flaring towers, 1
Furnaces for fiber drawing:
 CO_2 laser beam drawing machine, 109–110, 111
 comparison of, 111
 graphite resistance furnace, 104, 105–109, 111
 zirconia furnace, 104, 109, 111
Fusion splice, 337–340
Fusion splicing machines, 361–367
 arc fusion splicing machine, 361–367

Index

[Fusion splicing machines]
  for GI fibers, 361–364
  for SM fibers, 361–364, 364–367

Gas lens, 3
Glass terminus splicing method, 357–358
Goals of optical fiber development, 15
Graded index (GI) fiber, 3, 4
  fusion splicing machine for, 361–364
  measurement of structural parameters of, 408–419
  transmission bandwith of, 38–49
Graphite resistance furnace, 104, 105–109, 111

High-precision plastic connectors, 390, 391, 394
History of optical communications, 1–14
  chronology or research and development of optical transmission, 3–5
  features of fiber and comparison with other transmission media, 8–14
  optical fiber cables, 6–8
  optical fibers, 2–6
Hydrogen problems with fiber, 71–87

Image transmission, applications of fiber and cables in, 13
Information transmission, applications of fiber and cables in, 13

Infrared absorption, loss of fiber by, 29–30
Installation of fiber cables, 447–459
  conditions required by cable sender, 454–459
  considerations requiring particular attention, 447–454

Jelly filling in the cable core, 221
Joining of fiber cables, 322, 397–406
  basic conditions for, 397–398
  methods of, 398–404
  test conditions for cable joint, 405–406

Laser, 2
Laser beam fiber drawing machine, 109–110, 111
Layer stranding cable, construction of, 243, 268–271
Lens array waveguides, 3
Lens connector, 378, 382–383
Light transmission, applications of fiber and cables in, 13
Loose tube cable:
  construction of, 243, 244–245, 282–305
  deformation under lateral load of, 205–212
Loss:
  from fiber splicing, 323–337
  calculated examples of, 337
  deformation of end surfaces of fibers, 330–332

[Loss]
    differences in fiber parameters, 333–336
    end separation of fibers, 328–330
    measurement of, 354, 355
    offset of fibers, 325–328
    reflection loss at the end surfaces, 323–325
    transmission loss, measurement of, 20–23, 428–433
Low-loss silica fiber, 2, 4, 5
Low-temperature problems of fiber cable, 223–234

Manufacturing of fiber, 18, 88–139
    comparison of manufacturing processes, 112, 114
    fiber drawing, 104–112
        CO_2 laser beam drawing machine for, 109–110, 111
        comparison of furnaces for, 111
        graphite resistance furnace for, 104, 105–109, 111
    MCVD (modified CVD) method, 18, 92–97
        development of, 4
        merits and disadvantages of, 95–96
        process data for, 113–127
    OVD (outside vapor deposition) method, 18, 92, 99–101
    PCVD (plasma CVD) method, 18, 92, 97–98
    PMCVD (plasma-enhanced CVD) method, 18, 92, 98–99
    VAD (vapor-phase axial deposition) method, 5, 18, 92, 101–103
        process data for, 127–139

Mass fusion splicing machine, 365, 366, 367
Materials for fiber, 19–37
    fiber materials and dopants for silica fiber, 19–20
    graphs for expressing fiber loss, 33
    intrinsic loss in material, 27–33
    loss of fiber caused by extrinsic factors, 23–27
    transmission loss of fiber, 20–23
    ultimate low loss of silica fiber, 33–37
Maximum theoretical NA, 410
Measurement of fiber, 407–445
    profile measurement of the preform, 441–444
    structural parameters of the fiber, 408–428
        cutoff wavelength (λ_c), 424–428
        GI fiber, 408–419
        single-mode (SM) fiber, 419–424
    transmission characteristics, 428–441
        bandwidth, 433–436
        chromatic dispersion, 436–441
        loss, 20–23, 428–433
Mechanical design of fiber cables, 186–192
Mechanical properties of fiber, 18, 59–66
    breaking of silica fiber, 62–66
Mechanical reliability of fiber, 67–71
Metal impurities, loss of fibers caused by, 23–25
Microbending loss increase, 181–186
Mie scattering loss, 30
Millimeter wave communications, 2

Index 465

Mode field diameter (spot size), 57–58
Modified chemical vapor deposition (MCVD) production method, 18, 92–97
  comparision of other fiber manufacturing processes with, 114
  development of, 4
  merits and disadvantages of, 95–96
  process data for, 113–127
Multifiber connector, 386

NA:
  FFP method for measurement of, 418–419
  maximum theoretical, 410
NFP (near field pattern) method for measurement of refractive index profile, 410–413

Optical transmission:
  applications of fibers and cables in, 13–14
  chronology or research and development of, 3–5
Outside vapor deposition (OVD) production method, 18, 92, 99–101
  comparison of other manufacturing processes with, 114

Plasma CVD (PCVD) production method, 18, 92, 97–98
  comparison of other manufacturing processes with, 114

[Plasma CVD (PCVD) production method]
Plasma-enhanced CVD (PMCVD) production method, 18, 92, 98–99
  comparison of other manufacturing processes with, 114
Plastic connectors, 379, 390, 391, 392, 393, 394
Plastic-covered fiber, 237–243
  design of covering, 234
  long-term reliability of, 87
Plastic-covered fiber cable, construction of, 237, 238–239, 244–245
Plastic stripper, 368, 369
Precision ferrule connectors, 377–392
Preform, profile measurement of, 441–444
Properties of fiber cable, 10–11
Push-on type plastic connector, 392, 394

Raman scattering loss, 30
Rayleigh scattering loss, 30–31
Refractive index profile, measurement of, 410–418
Reliability of fibers, 67–87
  chemical reliability (hydrogen problem), 71–87
  long-term relaibility of plastic-covered fiber, 87
  mechanical reliability, 67–71
Ribbon cable, 180
  construction of, 243, 244–245 246–257, 258–259
RNF (refractive near field) measurement method of refractive index profile, 413–418

Index

Rod splice, 337, 338–339, 360
Round rods, splicing using, 337, 338–339, 360
Rubber packing and FRP sleeve for cable joining, 402, 403–404

Scattering loss for fibers, 30–33
Semaphore signaling system, 1
Sheath construction for cable, 220–221, 222
Single-fiber connectors, 377, 378–379
Single-mode (SM) fibers, 139–151
  fiber design, 140–147
  fusion splicing machine for, 361–364, 364–367
  measurement of structural parameters of, 419–424
  1.55 µm zero dispersion SM fibers, 151–169
    fiber 1, 159–161
    fiber 2, 161–165
    fiber 3, 165–169
  precautions in manufacturing fibers for 1.3 µm wavelength, 147–151
  technical terms used in design of, 54–58
Soft adhesive tape and plastic sleeve joint for cable joining, 398–404
Splicing of fibers, 321–374
  definition of, 322
  fusion splicing machines, 361–367
  general concepts, 322
  splicing accessories, 368–372
  splicing loss, 323–337
    calculated examples of, 337
    deformation of end surfaces, 330–332

[Splicing of fibers]
    differences in fiber parameters, 333–336
    end separation of fibers, 328–330
    measurement of, 354, 355
    offset of fibers, 325–328
    reflection loss at the end surfaces, 323–325
  splicing methods, 337–360
    arc fusion splicing machine, 340–357
    fusion splice, 337–340
    glass terminus method, 357–358
    reinforcement of the splice, 357
    rod splice, 337, 338–339, 360
    V-groove splice, 337, 338–339, 358–360
  transmission bandwidth of spliced fibers, 51–54
Spot size (mode field diameter), 57–58
Stranded fibers in the cable, 192–205
Stranding (thick double-coating) cable, 180
  construction of, 243, 244–245, 257–282
  layer, 243, 268–271
  unit, 243, 272–282
Strength members in the cable, design of, 212–220
Structural parameters of the fiber, measurement of, 408–428
  cutoff wavelength (λ_c), 424–428
  GI fiber, 408–419
  single-mode (SM) fiber, 419–424

Telegraphy, 1
Telescopes, 1

Temporary splicing method, 354, 355
Test conditions for cable joints, 405–406
Thin-film optical waveguide, 3
Transmission bandwidth of fiber, 15, 37–58
 of GI fiber, 38–49
 measurement of, 433–436
 of spliced fibers, 51–54
Transmission characteristics, measurement of, 428–441
 bandwidth, 433–436
 chromatic dispersion, 436–441
 loss, 20–23, 428–433
Transmission media, comparison of properties of, 8–14
Trially made graded index fiber, 4

Ultra-low-loss fiber, 5
Ultraviolet absorption, loss of fiber by, 27–29
Unit cable, construction of, 243, 272–282

Vapor-phase axial depostion (VAD) production method, 5, 18, 92, 101–103
 comparison of other manufacturing processes with, 114
 process data for, 127–139
V-groove cable, 180
 construction of, 243, 244–245, 305–314
V-groove round connector, 368–388
V-groove splicing method, 337, 338–339, 358–360

Waveguide imperfection, loss of fiber by, 27
Waveguides, 3, 4, 10–11
Wet fusion splicing method, 355–357
Wireless telegraphy, 1

Zero dispersion of SM fibers (1.55 μm), 151–169
 fiber 1, 155–161
 fiber 2, 161–165
 fiber 3, 165–169
Zirconia furnace, 104, 109, 111